Introduction to Politics of the Developing World

Contributors

Ervand Abrahamian
BARUCH COLLEGE

Amrita Basu
AMHERST COLLEGE

Merilee S. Grindle
HARVARD UNIVERSITY

William A. Joseph
WELLESLEY COLLEGE

Mark Kesselman
COLUMBIA UNIVERSITY

Darren Kew
UNIVERSITY OF MASSACHUSETTS,
BOSTON

Atul Kohli
PRINCETON UNIVERSITY

Joel Krieger
WELLESLEY COLLEGE

Peter Lewis
AMERICAN UNIVERSITY

Alfred P. Montero
CARLETON COLLEGE

Introduction to Politics of the Developing World

Political Challenges and Changing Agendas

Fourth Edition

General Editors

William A. Joseph
Wellesley College

Joel Krieger
Wellesley College

Mark Kesselman
Columbia University

Houghton Mifflin Company
Boston   New York

To our children, who are growing up in a complex and ever more challenging world;
MK—for Ishan and Javed
JK—for Nathan and Megan
WAJ—for Abigail, Hannah, and Rebecca

Sponsoring Editor: Katherine Meisenheimer
Development Editor: Leslie Kauffman
Project Editor: Andrea Dodge
Editorial Assistant: Kristen Truncellito
Production/Design Coordinator: Jill Haber
Marketing Manager: Nicola Poser
Cover Image: © Peter Adams/Digital Vision/Getty Images

Printed in the U.S.A.

Library of Congress Control Number: 2005937098

Instructor's Exam Copy:
ISBN 13: 978-0-618-73199-2
ISBN 10: 0-618-73199-7

For orders, use student text ISBNs:
ISBN 13: 978-0-618-60448-7
ISBN 10: 0-618-60448-0

1 2 3 4 5 6 7 8 9-CRS-09 08 07 06 05

BRIEF CONTENTS

1 Introducing Politics of the Developing World   1

2 China   35

3 India   93

4 Mexico   143

5 Brazil   191

6 Nigeria   247

7 Iran   305

CONTENTS

Preface   xv

1 Introducing Politics of the Developing World   1

❶ The Global Challenge of Comparative Politics   2
An Uncertain World Order   2
Globalization and Politics of the Developing World   3
Making Sense of Turbulent Times   5

❷ What—and How—Comparative Politics Compare   6
Levels of Analysis   7
Causal Theories   8

❸ Developing Nations in a World of Transition   11
Third World or Developing World?   11
The Development Gap   12
Third World States   15

❹ Themes for Comparative Analysis   17
Theme 1: The Democratic Idea   17
Theme 2: A World of States   21
Theme 3: Governing the Economy   23
Theme 4: The Politics of Collective Identity   25

❺ Organization of the Text   27
1: The Making of the Modern State   27
2: Political Economy and Development   27
3: Governance and Policy-Making   29
4: Representation and Participation   30
5: Politics in Transition   30

2 China   35

William A. Joseph

❶ The Making of the Modern Chinese State   37
Politics in Action   37
Geographic Setting   38
Critical Junctures   39
From Empire to Republic (221 B.C.–1911 A.D.)   39
Warlords, Nationalists, and Communists (1912–1949)   40
Mao in Power (1949–1976)   42
Deng Xiaoping and the Transformation of Chinese Communism (1977–1997)   45
From Revolutionary Leaders to Technocrats (1997 to the Present)   45

Themes and Implications   47
    Historical Junctures and Political Themes   47
        The World of States   47
        Governing the Economy   48
        The Democratic Idea   49
        The Politics of Collective Identity   49
    Implications for Comparative Politics   49

❷ Political Economy and Development   50
    State and Economy   50
        The Maoist Economy   50
        China Goes to Market   51
        Remaking the Chinese Countryside   53
        The Political Impact of Economic Reform   55
    Society and Economy   55
    China in the Global Economy   58

❸ Governance and Policy-Making   61
    Organization of the State   61
    The Executive   63
        The Chinese Communist Party   63
        The Government of the PRC   66
        The Bureaucracy   67
    Other State Institutions   69
        The Military and the Police   69
        The Judiciary   71
        Subnational Government   71
    The Policy-Making Process   72

❹ Representation and Participation   73
    The Legislature   73
    Political Parties and the Party System   74
        The Chinese Communist Party   74
        China's Noncommunist Parties   75
    Elections   75
    Political Culture, Citizenship, and Identity   76
        From Communism to Consumerism   76
        Citizenship and National Identity   78
        China's Non-Chinese Citizens   79
    Interests, Social Movements, and Protest   81
        Mechanisms of Social Control   82
        Protest and the Party-State   82

❺ Chinese Politics in Transition   84
    Political Challenges and Changing Agendas   84
        Scenes from the Chinese Countryside   84
            Huaxi, Jiangsu Province   84
            Naliang, Shaanxi Province   84
            Beihe, Shandong Province   84
            Daolin, Hunan Province   84
            Beiwang, Hebei Province   85

Economic Management, Social Tension, and Political Legitimacy   85
China and the Democratic Idea   87
Chinese Politics in Comparative Perspective   88
China as a Communist Party-State   88
China as a Third World State   89

3 India   93

Atul Kohli and Amrita Basu

❶ **The Making of the Modern Indian State   95**
Politics in Action   95
Geographic Setting   96
Critical Junctures   97
The Colonial Legacy (1757–1947)   97
The Nationalist Movement (1885–1947)   98
The Nehru Era (1947–1964)   101
The Indira Gandhi Era (1966–1984)   102
Coalition Governments (1989 to the Present)   104
India after September 11   105
Themes and Implications   105
Historical Junctures and Political Themes   105
India in a World of States   105
Governing the Economy   105
The Democratic Idea   106
The Politics of Collective Identity   106
Implications for Comparative Politics   106

❷ **Political Economy and Development   107**
State and Economy   107
The Economy Under British Rule   107
The Economy After Independence   108
Economic Liberalization   109
Reforms in Agriculture   110
Social Welfare Policy   111
Society and Economy   112
India in the Global Economy   114

❸ **Governance and Policy-Making   116**
Organization of the State   116
The Executive   116
The President and the Prime Minister   116
The Cabinet   117
The Bureaucracy   118
Other State Institutions   118
The Military and the Police   118
The Judiciary   119
Subnational Government   121
The Policy-Making Process   123

❹ Representation and Participation   124
  The Legislature   124
  Political Parties and the Party System   126
    The Congress Party   126
    The Janata Party   128
    The Bharatiya Janata Party (BJP)   128
    The Communist Party of India (CPM)   130
  Elections   131
  Political Culture, Citizenship, and Identity   131
  Interests, Social Movements, and Protest   133

❺ Indian Politics in Transition   136
  Political Challenges and Changing Agendas   136
    Kashmir Within a World of States   136
    Nuclear Power Status   138
    The Challenge of Ethnic Diversity   138
    Economic Performance   139
  Indian Politics in Comparative Perspective   139

4 Mexico   143

Merilee S. Grindle

❶ The Making of the Modern Mexican State   145
  Politics in Action   145
  Geographic Setting   146
  Critical Junctures   146
    Independence and Instability (1810–1876)   147
    The *Porfiriato* (1876–1911)   148
    The Revolution of 1910 and the Sonoran Dynasty (1910–1934)   149
    Lázaro Cárdenas, Agrarian Reform, and the Workers (1934–1940)   151
    The Politics of Rapid Development (1940–1982)   152
    Crisis and Reform (1982–2001)   152
    The Fox Presidency and Post-September 11 Mexico (2001 to the Present)   154
  Themes and Implications   155
    Historical Junctures and Political Themes   155
    Implications for Comparative Politics   156

❷ Political Economy and Development   156
  State and Economy   156
    Import Substitution and Its Consequences   157
    Sowing the Oil and Reaping a Crisis   160
    New Strategies: Structural Reforms and NAFTA   161
  Society and Economy   162
  Mexico in the Global Economy   163

❸ Governance and Policy-Making   164
  Organization of the State   165
  The Executive   165
    The President and the Cabinet   165

The Bureaucracy   167
The Para-Statal Sector   167
Other State Institutions   167
The Military   167
The Judiciary   168
Subnational Government   169
The Policy-Making Process   169

❹ **Representation and Participation   170**
The Legislature   170
Political Parties and the Party System   171
The PRI   172
The PAN   174
The PRD   176
Other Parties   177
Elections   178
Political Culture, Citizenship, and Identity   178
Interests, Social Movements, and Protest   180

❺ **Mexican Politics in Transition   183**
Political Challenges and Changing Agendas   183
Mexican Politics in Comparative Perspective   187

5 Brazil   191

Alfred P. Montero

❶ **The Making of the Modern Brazilian State   193**
Politics in Action   193
Geographic Setting   194
Critical Junctures   194
The Brazilian Empire (1822–1889)   194
The Old Republic (1889–1930)   196
The 1930 Revolution   197
The Populist Republic (1945–1964)   199
The Rise of Bureaucratic Authoritarianism (1964–1985)   199
The Transition to Democracy and the First Civilian Governments (1974–2001)   201
After September 11, 2001   202
Themes and Implications   203
Historical Junctures and Political Themes   203
Implications for Comparative Politics   204

❷ **Political Economy and Development   205**
State and Economy   205
The Environmental Costs of State-Led Growth   207
The Fiscal System   208
The Problem of Inflation   209
Society and Economy   210
The Welfare System   211
Agarian Reform   212
Brazil in the Global Economy   213

❸ Governance and Policy-Making   216
   Organization of the State   216
   The Executive   217
      The Bureaucracy: State and Semipublic Firms   218
      The Military and the Police   220
   Other State Institutions   221
      The Judiciary   221
      Subnational Government   222
   The Policy-Making Process   223
❹ Representation and Participation   224
   The Legislature   225
   Political Parties and the Party System   226
   Elections   231
   Political Culture, Citizenship, and Identity   232
   Interests, Social Movements, and Protest   235
❺ Brazilian Politics in Transition   237
   Political Challenges and Changing Agendas   237
   Brazilian Politics in Comparative Perspective   240

6 Nigeria   247

Darren Kew and Peter Lewis

❶ The Making of the Modern Nigerian State   249
   Politics in Action   249
   Geographic Setting   250
   Critical Junctures   251
      The Precolonial Period (800–1900)   253
      Colonial Rule and Its Impact (1860–1945)   254
      Divisive Identities: Ethnic Politics Under Colonialism (1945–1960)   255
      The First Republic (1960–1966)   255
      Civil War and Military Rule (1966–1979)   256
      The Second and Third Republics, and Predatory Military Rule (1979–1999)   257
      The Fourth Republic (1999 to the Present)   259
   Themes and Implications   260
      Historical Junctures and Political Themes   260
         Nigeria in the World of States: Oil Dependence and Decline   260
         Governing Nigeria's Economy   260
         Democratic Ideas Amid Colonialism and Military Rule   261
         Nigeria's Fragile Collective Identity   261
      Implications for Comparative Politics   262
❷ Political Economy and Development   262
   State and Economy   263
      Origins of Economic Decline   263
      From 1985 to the Present: Deepening Economic Crisis and the Search for Solutions   264
         Structural Adjustment   264
         Economic Planning   267
         Social Welfare   269

Society and Economy 270
  Ethnic and Religious Cleavages 270
  Gender Differences 272
Nigeria in the Global Economy 273
  Nigeria and the Regional Political Economy 273
Nigeria and the Political Economy of the West 273

❸ Governance and Policy-Making 275
Organization of the State 275
  The National Question and Constitutional Governance 275
  Federalism and State Structure 276
The Executive 276
  Evolution of the Executive Function 276
  The Executive Under Military Rule 278
  The Obasanjo Administration 278
  The Bureaucracy 280
  Para-statals 281
Other State Institutions 281
  The Judiciary 281
    State and Local Judiciaries 282
  State and Local Government 282
The Policy-Making Process 286

❹ Representation and Participation 287
The Legislature 287
The Party System and Elections 289
  Old Roots and New Alignments: The PDP and the Other Parties of the Fourth Republic 291
Political Culture, Citizenship, and Identity 293
  Modernity Versus Traditionalism 294
  Religion 294
  The Press 294
Interests, Social Movements, and Protest 295
  Labor 295
  The Business Community 296
  Other Social Groups 296

❺ Nigerian Politics in Transition 297
Political Challenges and Changing Agendas 297
Nigerian Politics in Comparative Perspective 299
  A World of States 299
  Governing the Economy 300
  The Democratic Idea 300
  Collective Identities 301

7 Iran **305**

Ervand Abrahamian

❶ The Making of the Modern Iranian State 307
Politics in Action 307
Geographic Setting 308

Critical Junctures   309
   The Safavids (1501–1722)   309
   The Qajars (1794–1925)   311
   The Pahlavis (1925–1979)   313
   The Islamic Revolution (1979)   315
   The Islamic Republic (1979–2001)   318
   Iran after September 11th (2001 to the Present)   319
Themes and Implications   320
   Historical Junctures and Political Themes   320
   Implications for Comparative Politics   321

❷ Political Economy and Development   322
State and Economy   322
   The Economy in the Nineteenth Century   323
   The Oil Economy   323
Society and Economy   324
Iran in the Global Economy   327
   Under the Shah   327
   Iran's Economy Under The Islamic Republic   328

❸ Governance and Policy-Making   330
Organization of the State   330
   The Leader   330
The Executive   333
   The President and the Cabinet   333
   The Bureaucracy   333
   Semipublic Institutions   334
Other State Institutions   335
   The Military   335
   The Judiciary   335
   Subnational Government   335
The Policy-Making Process   336

❹ Representation and Participation   338
The Legislature   339
Political Parties and the Party System   339
Elections   340
   The First Majles (1980)   340
   The Second Majles (1984)   341
   The Third (1988), Fourth (1992), and Fifth (1996) Majleses   341
   The Sixth Majles (2000)   344
   The 2005 Presidential Election   345
Political Culture, Citizenship, and Identity   346
Interests, Social Movements, and Protest   347

❺ Iranian Politics in Transition   348
Political Challenges and Changing Agendas   348
Iranian Politics in Comparative Perspective   349

Glossary   353
About the Authors and Contributors   361
Index   363

PREFACE

The preface to the third edition of *Introduction to Politics of the Developing World* (IPDW) observed: "We hope that book will help students analyze new (and old) political challenges and changing (and persistent) agendas." The same hope animates this thoroughly revised and updated edition of IPDW.

The fact that the headings in the table of contents of the country chapters in this edition of *Introduction to Politics of the Developing World: Political Challenges and Changing Agendas* (IPDW) are quite similar to those in the previous edition might appear to support Francis Fukuyama's prediction concerning the end of history.[i] Yet such an appearance is misleading: even a cursory review of the turbulent events of the few years since the publication of the previous edition of ICP in 2004 suggests both that it is difficult to discern a clear-cut trend to world history and that the profound changes since 2004 provide sufficient material to occupy historians—and students of comparative politics—for years to come.

Consider: since the third edition of this book was published, the "wave" of democratization that began to sweep much of the world beginning in the 1980s has reached Georgia, Ukraine, and Kyrgyzstan, former Soviet republics that many observers thought were locked into authoritarian regimes. In the Middle East, another part of the world often said to be inhospitable to democratic values, there have been important developments that suggest change may be coming

to the region. There was a massive outpouring of "people power" in Lebanon in early 2005 that led to the withdrawal of Syrian troops from the country; in May 2005, the parliament in Kuwait voted to give women equal political rights with men; and Egypt's first multi-candidate presidential elections were held in September 2005.

However, any notion of an inexorable historical movement toward democracy and capitalism is belied by a host of other changes. In Russia, the state's manipulation of the courts and the media, as well as its suppression of political autonomy and dissent, suggest that the pendulum has swung away from democracy. Latin America's democratic transition has experienced several bumps in the road, most notably in Venezuela, Bolivia, and Ecuador. More than two years after the United States-led coalition toppled the regime of Saddam Hussein in Iraq in 2003, the prospect of stable democracy continues to appear remote. The ability of authoritarian rulers in China, Iran, Togo, Uzbekistan, and Zimbabwe to retain or gain power challenges confident claims about the march of liberal democracy in the world. In a more theoretical vein, recent scholarship persuasively analyzes why one should not expect an orderly progression from democratic transitions to democratic consolidation.[ii] Also, *New York Times* commentator Thomas Friedman may celebrate globalization as the *deus ex machina* that is flattening the world in a way

---

[i] Francis Fukuyama, "The End of History?" *The National Interest* 16 (Summer 1989); reprinted in Mark Kesselman and Joel Krieger, eds., *Readings in Comparative Politics: Political Challenges and Changing Agendas* (Boston: Houghton Mifflin, 2006). The outline of this anthology is parallel to that of *Introduction to Comparative Politics* and provides a range of readings that engage in comparative analysis of issues surveyed in ICP.

[ii] See, inter alia, Guillermo O'Donnell, "Illusions About Consolidation," *Journal of Democracy* 7, no. 2 (April 1996): 34–51; Thomas Carothers, "The End of the Transition Paradigm," *Journal of Democracy* 13, no. 1 (January 2002); and Steven Levitsky and Lucan A. Way, "The Rise of Competitive Authoritarianism," *Journal of Democracy* 13, no. 2 (April 2002): 51–65. These articles are reprinted in Kesselman and Krieger, *Readings in Comparative Politics*. From a different perspective, Fareed Zakaria, *The Future of Freedom: Illiberal Democracy at Home and Abroad* (New York: W. W. Norton, 2003) questions whether liberal democracy is the norm even in those countries considered to be its birthplace.

that promotes meritocracy on a global scale, but "altermondist" (other-world) activists passionately proclaim, on the contrary, that globalization and U.S.-style neo-imperialism are accentuating the peaks and valleys of global inequality.[iii] As this text will amply demonstrate, neither history nor interpretive debates have ended.

This edition of *Introduction to Politics of the Developing World* reflects several significant developments:

• We address the consequences of globalization on domestic politics in each country in a more focused and comprehensive manner than in the third edition.
• We analyze the consequences of the terrorist attacks on the United States on September 11, 2001, and the subsequent global war on terrorism for political institutions, processes, party competition, and potential regime change in each country case study.
• We consider the political repercussions of these developments—as well as the war in Iraq and its aftermath—for relations with the United States and for the changing contours of the world-of-states theme in its global dimensions.
• We underscore the significance of immigration for shaping—and for understanding the political challenges of—multi-ethnic and multi-religious societies.

Structure of the Book

Although we highlight certain key developments of the past few years, especially the reverberations of September 11 for countries throughout the world, the core elements of *Introduction to Politics of the Developing World* have not changed. In this edition, we have retained the basic framework and approach of past editions. We believe that the four constituent elements that comprise our analytical framework help students both to highlight the particular features of the country case studies in IPDW and to engage in rigorous cross-national comparisons.

We are pleased that instructors and students have generously praised the analytical framework, lively writing, and high level of scholarship in *Introduction to Politics of the Developing World*. Although we are committed to probing the complexity of developments when appropriate, we aim to make the book accessible to students with little or no background in political science. We value readable, direct prose that is free of jargon, and we have maximized symmetry in the topical outline of country chapters to facilitate cross-national comparison. We use vignettes to open the country chapters and elsewhere to engage students and highlight particular features of each country's political patterns, and provide an array of ancillary visual materials to complement the written text.

Introduction to Politics of the Developing World emphasizes patterns of state formation, political economy, domestic political institutions and processes, and the politics of collective identities within the context of globalization. A distinctive feature of the book is the use of four comparative themes to frame the presentation of each country's politics. We explain the themes in Chapter 1 and present an intriguing "puzzle" for each to stimulate student thinking. These themes—described in the first section of each country study and analyzed throughout the chapter—focus attention on the continuities and contrasts among the country studies:

• The Democratic Idea explores the challenges posed by citizens' demands for greater control and participation in both democracies and authoritarian regimes.
• A World of States highlights the importance of state formation, the internal organization of the state, and the inter-state system for political development. In this edition, we highlight how the events of September 11 have influenced political institutions and policies.
• Governing the Economy analyzes state strategies for promoting economic development and competitiveness and stresses the effects of economic globalization on domestic politics.
• The Politics of Collective Identities considers the political consequences of race, ethnicity, gender, religion, and nationality and their complex interplay with class-based politics.

Through our four themes, the methods of comparative analysis come alive as students examine similarities and differences among countries and within and between political systems. The thematic approach facilitates dis-

---

[iii] For spirited arguments on both sides, see Thomas L. Friedman, *The World is Flat: A Brief History of the Twenty-First Century* (New York: Farrar, Straus and Giroux, 2005); for opposing views, see John Cavanagh and Jerry Mander, eds., *Alternatives to Economic Globalization: A Better World is Possible,* 2nd ed. (San Francisco: Berrett-Koehler, 2004) and Leo Panitch and Colin Leys, eds., *The New Imperial Challenge: Socialist Register 2004* (New York: Monthly Review Press, 2003).

ciplined analysis of political challenges and changing agendas within countries.

Introduction to Politics of the Developing World uses a country-by-country approach and strikes a balance between the richness of each country's national political development and cross-national comparative analysis. Chapter 1 explains the comparative method, analyzes the four key themes of the book, gives an overview of what is meant by the "developing world," and describes core features of political institutions and processes. Each country chapter that follows consists of five sections. Section 1 treats the historic formation of the modern state, its geographic setting, critical junctures in its political development, and the country's significance for the study of comparative politics. Section 2 describes the political economy of past and current national development. Section 3 outlines the major institutions of governance and policy-making. Section 4 explains the widely varying processes of representation, participation, and contestation. Finally, Section 5 reflects on the major issues that confront the country and are likely to shape its future.

Several special features assist in the teaching and learning process.

• At the beginning of each chapter, students will find a data box providing basic demographic, social, economic, and political information to aid in comparing countries. We have expanded the data presented for this edition and have redesigned their presentation.
• Throughout the chapters a wide array of maps, tables, charts, photographs, and political cartoons enliven the text and present key information in clear and graphic ways.
• Each country study includes several boxes that highlight interesting and provocative aspects of politics. These include Leaders, biographies of important political leaders; Institutional Intricacies, important features of a political system that warrant careful discussion; Citizen Action, unconventional forms of participation; Global Connection, examples of connections between domestic and international politics; and Current Challenges, issues of today and the future that help shape important dimensions of national politics.
• Key terms are set in boldface when first introduced and are defined in the Glossary at the end of the book. Students will find that the Glossary defines many key concepts that are used broadly in comparative politics.
• Each chapter concludes with a list of suggested readings and links to websites that enable students to explore in greater depth issues relating to the country.

New to This Edition

Chapter 1 has been expanded to provide a more ample survey of the diversity of approaches to studying comparative politics as well as a richer discussion of democratic transitions. We share the concerns of scholars who have identified the prevalence of "hybrid" regimes in which the trappings and some elements of democracy stably co-exist with authoritarian practices. We warn students against assuming that there is a linear movement from authoritarian regimes to transitional democracies to stable, consolidated democracies. We want them to understand that democratization is often a protracted process with ambiguous results, rather than a clearly delineated path toward completion.

Each of the country chapters has been slightly shortened to produce a leaner book, but we also provide a thoroughly updated description of current political developments to take account of major events and regime changes. Particular attention is paid in this edition of *Introduction to Politics of the Developing World* to the challenges to the developing world posed by globalization and the aftermath of the events of September 11.

As in the last edition of IPDW, this edition provides instructors with much greater flexibility and choice regarding the countries that they may include in their course. For those who prefer the convenience of a pre-selected set of countries, the fourth edition contains the same countries covered in the previous two editions. However, instructors who would prefer to cover fewer countries or a different selection of countries can now easily and inexpensively arrange for a customized edition of *Introduction to Politics of the Developing World* to be produced for their course. All the chapters of the regular edition are posted in an online database. Also in the database are additional country choices, available only in a customized edition. The number of countries in the database has been expanded, and now includes the following:

• South Africa, by Tom Lodge
• Indonesia, by Annette Clear
• Turkey, by Ersin Kalaycioglu
• Cuba, by Marifeli Pérez-Stable

In addition, a chapter on the Republic of Korea will be available in 2007 in the database of countries that instructors can select for their course. To learn more about the database, or to create a custom edition, visit the Houghton Mifflin online catalog at *http://www.college.hmco.com* or contact your Houghton Mifflin representative.

Acknowledgments

We thank research assistants for their assistance in preparing some of the country chapters for this edition: Halbert Jones for Mexico; and Stephen Frenkel, Ifeoma Malo, and Victor Brobbey for Nigeria. We are also grateful to colleagues who have reviewed and critiqued the previous editions of this book: Michael Bratton, Michigan State University; Rachel Califf, PA Homeschoolers; Liv Coleman, University of Wisconsin-Madison; William Crowther, University of North Carolina; Louise K. Davidson-Schmich, University of Miami; Chris Hamilton, Washburn University; Kenji Hayao, Boston College; Maria Perez Laubhan, College of Lake County; Richard Leich, Gustavus Adolphus College; Sherry L. Martin, Cornell University; Mahmood Monshipouri, Quinnipiac University; Vladimir Povov, Carleton University; Len Schoppa, University of Virginia; Peter M. Siavelis, Wake Forest University; Toshiyuki Yuasa, University of Houston.

Finally, our thanks to the talented and professional staff who helped edit and publish ICP4: at Houghton Mifflin, Katherine Meisenheimer, sponsoring editor; Jeff Greene, senior development editor; Andrea Dodge, project editor; and Nicola Poser, executive marketing manager; at LEAP Publishing Services, Leslie Kauffman, senior development editor, Shay Carpenter, assistant project manager; and Jay Boggis, copyeditor.

W. A. J.
J. K.
M. K.

Introduction to Politics of the Developing World

CHAPTER 1

Introducing Politics of the Developing World

William A. Joseph, Mark Kesselman, and Joel Krieger

Section ❶   The Global Challenge of Comparative Politics

When did our current era begin? Although a precise moment might be hard to identify, a frequently cited date is 1989, which marked the crumbling of the Berlin Wall. Until then, the wall separated communist-controlled East Berlin from West Berlin. More broadly, it separated the two Germanies: the German Democratic Republic, allied with the Soviet Union, and the Federal Republic of Germany, part of the **North Atlantic Treaty Organization (NATO)** alliance. At the most general level, the wall served as a powerful symbol of the division of the world into a communist bloc of countries, under the control of the Soviet Union, and the "Western" world, led by the United States. The collapse of the Berlin Wall swiftly ushered in a series of peaceful revolutions against the **communist party-states** of East Central Europe and the Soviet Union. The implosion of these **regimes,** and their replacement by governments proclaiming a commitment to democratic rule, marked the end of the grim and sometimes deadly **cold war** that had pitted the Soviet and American alliances against one another in many parts of the world.

Recent decades have also witnessed a flood of history-making events in the developing, or **Third World**, nations of Asia, Africa, and Latin America. (The use of the terms *developing* and *Third World* is discussed in Section 3 below.) China, for example, long one of the world's poorest countries, has become the world's most dynamic economy. The brutally racist apartheid regime in South Africa has been replaced, largely through the process of a nonviolent political revolution, by a multiracial democracy. Latin America has been transformed from a region dominated by harsh military regimes to one in which nearly every country is either a democracy or can be said to be moving toward democratization.

We have also seen increased instability and conflict in the developing world. It has become clear that freedom, peace, and a reasonable standard of living cannot be built on hopes alone. In many developing countries, economic scarcity, widespread poverty, and extreme inequality make it especially hard to turn such dreams into reality. Toppling dictatorial regimes often proves less difficult than building new democracies.

In some Third World nations, the rush to democracy awakens new and restless constituencies with demands that cannot easily be met by the government. Even in a relatively long-established Third World democracy like India, religious divisions periodically explode into communal violence that not only threatens the social order but also shakes the very foundations of the country's democratic political system.

An Uncertain World Order

Political changes since the cold war have also produced new forms of international cooperation and competition, as well as new sources of international tension and violence. The grim, but predictable, bipolar world of superpower rivalry between the United States and the Soviet Union has been replaced by the uncertainties of a more fragmented map of power. Increasing economic, religious, and ethnic divisions create tensions in every corner of the globe. There has been a surge of brutal clashes between and within countries. Even among close allies, there has been a less violent dynamic of fierce economic competition and trade disputes, as well as diplomatic conflict (note, for example, the strong opposition of most of America's European allies to the invasion of Iraq).

These international changes have had a far-reaching effect on developing countries. During the cold war, the rivalry between the Soviet Union and the United States was often fought out and contained in the Third World—at a safe distance from the superpowers, as in the Vietnam War and the conflicts in Angola and Nicaragua. This situation caused much political instability and human suffering in the Third World, but the superpower standoff also gave the developing nations some bargaining power when it came to securing economic or military aid as the Americans and Soviets wooed allies among Third World leaders.

The end of the cold war has meant an end to such strategic leverage for the Third World. Indeed, the collapse of communism diverted economic resources away from the Third World as the developed nations and international organizations channeled more funds to help the struggling democracies and market economies of Russia and East Central Europe. Yet one reason that democracy has been able to spread throughout much of the Third World in the last twenty years or so is that dictators can no longer rely on their superpower patrons to keep them in power for strategic reasons.

In short, both the national and international contexts of politics in the developing world changed profoundly in the last decades of the twentieth century, and they remain very much in flux into the new century. Yet (as we will discuss in more detail later) there are still very important continuities in the domestic and global situations of the developing nations of Asia, Africa, and Latin America that continue to distinguish them in significant ways from the world's economically richer and politically more powerful countries.

At about the time when the Berlin Wall came tumbling down, an important and controversial analysis of world events was published with an audacious title, "The End of History?"[1] For its author, Francis Fukuyama, the failure of communism was of historic significance not only in itself, but also because it signified the end of any feasible alternative to Western-style regimes: that is, regimes that combine capitalist organization of the economy with a democratic political system. There was, he claimed, only one model of political and economic development for the world. He also claimed that history had ended, in the sense that never again would there be the kind of global struggle between competing ideologies that had marked previous eras and that in the twentieth century alone, had led to two world wars and the cold war.

Fukuyama's hypothesis had particularly dramatic implications for the Third World countries, which had often been pulled between the socialist and liberal models of development. Now, the argument went, there was no choice: the "Western" way—the way that the United States, Canada, Western Europe, Japan, and other industrialized capitalist democracies had gone— was the only way for the Third World to develop economically and politically. He did recognize that the way would not be easy for many developing countries. He predicted that because of deeply entrenched nationalist and ethnic cleavages much of the Third World

could not easily escape history and would "be a terrain of conflict for many years to come."

Was Fukuyama correct? Proving that "history" has ended is a long-term proposition. But in the short run, his analysis, despite its underlying ethnocentric triumphalism *(We won!)*, does point to several crucial issues that present the Third World with both promise and peril in the uncertain international order following the cold war. Nearly every developing country (only a few isolated nations like North Korea and Burma are exceptions) faces the challenges of adjusting to a global economic system totally dominated by developed capitalist countries and international organizations committed to promoting free market capitalism. Many are also struggling, often under intense pressure, to build democratic governments in very difficult economic and social circumstances and after decades of **authoritarian** rule. And Fukuyama was certainly right—as the ethnic cleansing and genocide in Rwanda and the Sudan painfully remind us—that historically rooted antagonisms continue to exact a terrible toll in some countries and still fester just below the surface in many others. These issues are discussed in more detail in this chapter and are central concerns in the country chapters that follow.

Globalization and Politics of the Developing World

By the year 2000, a new and distinctive lens for analyzing politics within and among countries seemed to be gaining great attention. This lens was **globalization.** The key new question that promised to dominate the political agenda of the early twenty-first century was whether the processes of globalization—the global diffusion of investment, trade, production, and electronic communication technologies—would promote a worldwide diffusion of opportunity and enhance human development or whether it would reinforce the comparative advantages of the more prosperous and powerful nations and peoples, undermine local cultures, and intensify regional conflicts.

These issues are very much with us today and frame the country studies in this book. Yet the terrorist attacks of September 11, 2001, on the United States and their aftermath have forced us to rethink, at least in part, the meaning of globalization. (The attacks have also led many people to conclude that

Fukuyama was premature and naive to predict that the history of global ideological conflict had ended!) Before September 11th, the economic aspects of globalization claimed major attention. Since 9/11, political and military concerns have been at the forefront, involving issues such as how U.S. power will recast global alliances and affect both national politics and people's lives throughout the world. We have also learned that international terror networks (another and especially sinister example of globalization) can strike anywhere—from the World Trade Center in New York and the Pentagon in Washington to a nightclub in Bali, Indonesia; and from a train station in Madrid, Spain, to an elementary school in Beslan, Russia, or in the subway and on a bus in London. But these post-9/11 issues do not replace concerns about economic globalization. Instead, we are challenged to develop a more complex understanding of globalization and how it structures both politics throughout the world and the study of world politics.

The terms *globalization* and *global era* are everywhere applied as general catch phrases to identify the growing depth, extent, and diversity of cross-border connections that are a key characteristic of the contemporary world. Discussion of globalization begins with accounts of economic activities, including the reorganization of production and the global redistribution of the work force (the "global factory"), as well as the increased extent and intensity of international trade, finance, and foreign direct investment. Globalization also involves the movement of peoples due to migration, employment, business, and educational opportunities.[2]

Globalization includes other profound changes that are less visible but equally significant. For example, new applications of information technology (such as the Internet and CNN) blur the traditional distinction between what is around the block and what is around the world—instantly transforming cultures and eroding the boundaries between the local and global. These technologies make instantaneous communication possible and link producers and contractors, headquarters, branch plants, and suppliers—in real time, anywhere in the world. Employees may be rooted in time and place, but employers can take advantage of the ebb and flow of a global labor market. A secure job today may

be gone tomorrow. Globalization fosters insecurity in everyday life and presents extraordinary challenges to government, especially in developing nations, which are often in a disadvantaged and vulnerable position in the international system.

The dilemma that globalization represents for the Third World can be illustrated by the theme "Global Inequalities" chosen by the American Political Science Association (the official organization of U.S.-based political scientists) for its 2004 Annual Meeting. The program announcement for the Meeting declared, "While inequalities are hardly new, their relevance has become newly visible as the fading memory of the Cold War is replaced by the omnipresence of various North-South clashes. This invites systematic reflection. The enormous concentration of wealth and power in some parts of the world coexists with the marginalization of other countries and people."[3] The major source of international tensions has shifted from the East-West ideological conflict (between communist powers and capitalist democracies) to a North-South split between the "have" nations, often called the "North" because most developed countries are located in the northern hemisphere, against the "have not" nations, many of which are clustered in the southern half of the globe.

Globalization has forged new forms of international governance, from the **European Union (EU)** to the **World Trade Organization (WTO),** in an attempt to regulate and stabilize the myriad flows of globalization. An alphabet soup of other organizations and agreements—such as UNDP, IMF, IBRD, OECD, NAFTA, and APEC,[4] to name but a few—have also been enlisted in this attempt.

Globalization has also provoked challenges from grassroots movements in every region of the world that are concerned with its negative impact on, for example, poor people, the environment, and labor rights. The first such challenge occurred when the World Trade Organization sponsored a meeting of government ministers in Seattle in 1999 that was disrupted by fifty thousand protesters. Ever since then, conferences called to develop rules for global commerce have been the site of demonstrations by coalitions of environmental, labor-based, and community activists from around the world. Thus, to Seattle, one can add the names of cities on many continents—Washington, D.C., Prague, Genoa, Miami, and Cancun—where activists have assembled to protest the activity of international financial institutions. One can also identify sites, notably, Mumbai, India, and Porto Alegre, Brazil, where activists from around the world have assembled annually to exchange ideas and develop alternatives to the current form of economic globalization.[5]

All of these globalization processes complicate politics, just as they erode the ability of even the strongest countries to control their destinies. No state can secure the economic security and general well-being of its citizens in isolation from the rest of the world. None can preserve pristine national models of economic governance or distinctly national cultures, values, understandings of the world, or narratives that define a people and forge their unity. Many of the most important problems confronting governments are related to globalization, including pandemics like AIDS, global climate change, financial panics, and international terrorism. Although these problems may be global in scope, a government's popularity with its own people depends in considerable measure on how successfully it addresses them at home.

It is clear that countries face a host of challenges simultaneously from above and below. The capacities of states to control domestic outcomes and assert sovereignty are compromised by regional and global technological and market forces, as well as by growing security concerns. The very stability and viability of many countries are simultaneously assaulted by ethnic, nationalist, and religious divisions that often involve both internal and external components. The bright line separating domestic and international politics has been rubbed out by the complex set of cross-border economic, cultural, technological, governance, and security processes, institutions, and relations that constitute the contemporary global order. And nowhere else are the challenges of globalization more monumental or its impacts more momentous than in the developing world.

Making Sense of Turbulent Times

The flash of newspaper headlines and television sound bites, the upheavals, rush of events, and sheer range and complexity of the cross-border phenomena of globalization tend to make politics look overwhelming and chaotic beyond comprehension. Although the study of comparative politics can help us understand current events in a rapidly changing world, it involves much more than snapshot analysis or Monday-morning quarterbacking. This book describes and analyzes in detail the governments and politics of several developing countries and identifies common themes that explain longer-term causes of both political changes and continuities. It also provides cross-national comparisons and explanations based on four themes that we believe are central for understanding politics in the developing world:

- The spread of democracy and the challenges of democratization
- The historical formation, internal organization, and interaction of states within the international order
- The role of the state in economic management
- The sources and political impact of diverse **collective identities,** including class, gender, ethnicity, and religion

We also expect that these four themes will be useful for analyzing where the countries discussed in this book may be heading politically in the twenty-first century. Moreover, the themes illustrate how comparative politics can serve as a valuable tool for making political sense of even the most tumultuous times. The contemporary period presents an extraordinary challenge to those who study comparative politics, but the study of comparative politics also provides a unique opportunity for understanding the developing world in this uncertain era.

In order to appreciate the complexity of politics and political transitions in developing countries around the world, we must look beyond any single national perspective. Today, business and trade, information technology, mass communications and culture, immigration and travel, as well as politics, forge deep connections—as well as deep divisions—among people worldwide. It is particularly urgent to develop a truly global perspective as we explore the politics of different countries and their growing interdependence on one another.

The contemporary world provides a fascinating laboratory for the study of comparative politics and gives unusual significance to the subject. We hope that you share our sense of excitement in the challenging effort to understand the complex and ever-shifting terrain of politics in the developing world. We begin by exploring what comparative politics actually compares and how comparative study enhances our understanding of politics generally.

Section ❷ What—and How—Comparative Politics Compares

To "compare and contrast" is one of the most common human mental exercises, whether in the classroom study of literature or politics or animal behavior—or in selecting dorm rooms or listing your favorite movies. In the observation of politics, the use of comparisons is very old, dating in the Western world at least from Aristotle, the ancient Greek philosopher. Aristotle categorized Greek city-states in the fifth century B.C. according to their form of political rule: rule by a single individual, rule by a few, or rule by all citizens. He also added a normative dimension (a claim about how societies *should* be ruled) by distinguishing ("contrasting") good from corrupt versions of each type, according to whether those with power ruled in the interest of the common welfare of all citizens or only in their own interest. The modern study of comparative politics refines and systematizes the age-old practice of evaluating some feature of X by comparing it to the same feature of Y in order to learn more about it than isolated study would permit.

Comparative politics is a subfield within the academic discipline of political science, as well as a method or approach to the study of politics.[6] The subject matter of comparative politics is the domestic politics of countries or peoples. This book focuses on the comparative study of several developing nations, whereas other comparative politics books might focus, for example, on the industrial democracies of Western Europe. Within the discipline of political science, comparative politics is one of four areas of specialization. In addition to comparative politics, most political science (or government) departments in U.S. colleges and universities include courses and academic experts in three other fields: political theory, international relations, and American politics.

Special mention should be made of the distinction between comparative politics and international relations. Comparative politics involves comparing domestic political institutions, processes, policies, conflicts, and attitudes in different countries; international relations involves the study of foreign policy and interactions among countries, the role of international organizations such as the United Nations, and the growing influence of a wide range of global actors from multinational corporations to terrorist networks. In a globalized world, the distinction sometimes becomes questionable, and there is a large gray zone where the two fields overlap. In 2005, the U.S. government announced that it would phase out subsidies for domestic cotton farmers in order to comply with a ruling by the World Trade Organization (WTO), an organization to which the United States belongs that is designed to facilitate cross-border trade and investment. Did this decision fall within the field of comparative politics or the field of international relations? The answer is both.[7]

However, it makes sense to maintain the distinction between comparative politics and international relations. Much of the world's political activity continues to occur within state borders, and comparisons of domestic politics, institutions, and processes enable us to understand critical features that distinguish one country's politics from another. Furthermore, we believe that, despite increased international economic integration (a key aspect of globalization), national states are the fundamental building blocks in structuring political activity. Therefore, this book is built around in-depth case studies of a cross-section of important developing countries around the world.

The comparative approach principally analyzes similarities and differences among countries by focusing on selected institutions and processes. As students of comparative politics (we call ourselves **comparativists**), we believe that we cannot make reliable statements about most political situations by looking at only one case. We often hear statements such as "The United States has the best health care system in the world." Comparativists immediately wonder what kinds of health care systems exist in other countries, what they cost and how they are financed, who is covered by health insurance, and so on. Besides, what does "best" mean when it comes to health care systems? Is it the one that provides the widest access? The one that is the most technologically advanced? The one that is the most cost-effective? The one that produces the healthiest population? None of us would announce the best movie or the best car without considering other alternatives or deciding what specific factors enter into our judgment.

Comparativists often analyze political institutions or processes by looking at two or more cases that are selected to isolate their common and contrasting features. For example, a comparativist might ask what explains the vastly different political roles of the military in India and in Nigeria (both former British colonies).[8] One of the strengths of democracy in India is that the military has never intervened in politics, whereas the Nigerian military has done so frequently and with disastrous political and economic consequences for the country. Other comparative political studies take a thematic approach and analyze broad issues, such as the causes and consequences of revolutions in different countries.[9] Comparative studies may also involve comparisons of an institution, policy, or process through time, in one or several countries. For example, some studies have analyzed a shift in the orientation of economic policy that occurred in many advanced capitalist countries in the 1980s from Keynesianism, an approach that gives priority to government regulation of certain aspects of the economy, to neoliberalism, which emphasizes the importance of market-friendly policies.[10]

Levels of Analysis

Comparisons can be useful for political analysis at several different levels. Political scientists often compare developments in different cities, regions, provinces, or states. Comparative analysis can also focus on specific institutions in different countries, such as the legislature, executive, political parties,

social movements, or court systems, as well as specific processes and policies. The organization of *Introduction to Politics of the Developing World* reflects our belief that the best way to begin the study of comparative politics is with **countries.** Countries comprise distinct, politically defined territories that encompass political institutions, cultures, economies, and ethnic and other social identities. Although often highly divided by internal conflicts, countries have historically been the most important source of a people's collective political identity, and they are the major arena for organized political action in the modern world.

Within a given country, the **state** is almost always the most powerful cluster of institutions. But just what is the state? The way the term is used in comparative politics is probably unfamiliar to many students. In the United States, it usually refers to the states in the federal system—Texas, California, and so on. But in comparative politics, the state refers to the key political institutions responsible for making, implementing, enforcing, and adjudicating important policies in a country.[11] Thus, we use phrases such as the "Mexican state" and the "Iranian state." In many ways, the state is synonymous with what is often called the "government."

The most important state institutions are the national **executive**—usually, the president and/or prime minister and the **cabinet**—but in some cases, the executive includes the Communist Party leader (such as in China), the head of a military government (as in Nigeria until 1999), or the supreme religious leader (as in the Islamic Republic of Iran). Other key state institutions include the military, police, administrative **bureaucracy,** the legislature, and courts.

States claim, usually with considerable success, the right to issue rules—notably, laws, administrative **regulations,** and court decisions—that are binding for people within the country. Even democratic states—in which top officials are chosen by procedures that authorize all citizens to participate—can survive only if they can preserve enforcement (or coercive) powers both internally and with regard to other states and external groups that may threaten them. A number of countries have highly repressive states whose political survival depends largely on military and police powers. But even in such states, long-term stability requires that the ruling regime have some measure of political **legitimacy;** that is, a significant segment of the citizenry (in particular, more influential citizens and groups) must believe that the state is entitled to command compliance from those who live under its rule. Political legitimacy is greatly affected by the state's ability to deliver the goods through satisfactory economic performance and an acceptable distribution of economic resources. Moreover, in the contemporary period, legitimacy seems to require that states represent themselves as democratic in some fashion, whether or not they are in fact. Thus, *Introduction to Politics of the Developing World* looks closely at both the state's role in governing the economy and the pressures exerted on states to develop and extend democratic participation.

The fact that states are the fundamental objects of analysis in comparative politics does not mean that all states are the same. Indeed, the organization of state institutions varies widely, and these differences have a powerful impact on political, economic, and social life. Hence, the country studies in this book devote considerable attention to variations in institutions of governance, participation, and representation—along with their political implications. Each country study begins with an analysis of how the institutional organization and political procedures of the state have evolved historically. The process of **state formation** fundamentally influences how and why states differ politically.

One critical difference among states that will be explored in our country studies involves the extent to which citizens in a country share a common sense of nationhood, that is, a belief that the state's geographic boundaries coincides with citizens' collective identity. When state boundaries and national identity coincide, the resulting formation is called a **nation-state.** A major source of political instability is that they often do not coincide. China, Brazil, Mexico, and Iran are examples of developing countries that have a fairly strong sense of national identity based on existing state boundaries.

In many countries, however, nationalist movements within a state's borders challenge existing boundaries and seek to secede to form their own state, sometimes in alliance with movements from neighboring countries with whom they claim to share a common heritage. Such is the case with the Kurds,

who have large populations in Turkey and Iraq, and have long sought and fought to establish an independent nation-state of Kurdistan. When a nationalist movement has distinctive ethnic, religious, and/or linguistic ties opposed to those of other groups in the country, conflicts are likely to be especially intense. Nationalist movements may pursue their separatist goal peacefully within established political institutions. Or they may act outside established institutions and engage in illegal activity, including violence against political authorities and civilians. One of the major sources of political instability throughout the world involves nationalist movements challenging established states. India and Nigeria have, for example, experienced particularly violent episodes of ethnonationalist conflict.

Causal Theories

Because countries are the basic building blocks in politics and because states are the most significant political organizations and actors, these are the two critical units for comparative analysis. The comparativist seeks to measure and hopefully explain similarities and differences among countries or states. One influential approach in comparative politics involves developing causal theories—hypotheses that can be expressed formally in a causal mode: "If X happens, then Y will be the result." Such theories include factors (the independent variables, symbolized by X) that are believed to influence some outcome (the dependent variable, symbolized by Y) to be explained.

For example, it is commonly argued that if a country's economic pie shrinks, conflict among groups for resources will intensify. This hypothesis suggests what is called an inverse correlation between variables: as X varies in one direction, Y varies in the opposite direction. As the total national economic product (X) decreases, then political and social conflict over economic shares (Y) increases. This relationship might be tested by statistical analysis of a very large number of cases, a project facilitated in recent years by the creation of data banks that include extensive historical and contemporary data. Another way to study this issue would be to focus on one or several country cases and analyze how the relevant relationships have varied historically. Even when explanation does not involve the explicit testing of hypotheses (and often it does not), comparativists try to identify similarities and differences among countries and to discover significant patterns.

It is important to recognize the limits on just how "scientific" political science, and thus comparative politics, can be. Two important differences exist between the "hard" (or natural) sciences like physics and chemistry and the social sciences. First, social scientists study people who exercise free will. Because people have a margin for free choice, even if one assumes that they choose in a rational manner, their choices, attitudes, and behavior cannot be fully explained. This does not mean that people choose in a totally arbitrary fashion. We choose within the context of material constraint, institutional dictates, and cultural prescriptions. Comparative politics analyzes how such factors shape political preferences and choices in systematic ways; indeed, a recent study by three political scientists concluded that political beliefs are, to a certain degree, genetically determined.[12] But there will probably always be a wide gulf between the natural and social sciences because of their different objects of study.

A second difference between the natural and social sciences is that in the natural sciences, experimental techniques can be applied to isolate the contribution of distinct factors to a particular outcome. It is possible to change the value or magnitude of a factor—for example, the force applied to an object—and measure how the outcome has consequently changed. However, like other social scientists, political scientists and comparativists rarely have the opportunity to apply such experimental techniques.

Some political scientists have conducted experiments with volunteers in controlled settings. But laboratories provide crude approximations of natural settings, since only one or several variables can be manipulated. The real world of politics, by contrast, consists of an endless number of variables, and they cannot easily be isolated or manipulated. Another attempt to deal with this problem is by statistical techniques that seek to identify the specific causal weight of different variables in explaining variations in political outcomes. But it is difficult to measure precisely how, for example, a person's ethnicity, gender, or income influences her or his choice when casting a ballot. Nor can we ever know for sure what exact mix of factors—conflicts among elites, popular ideological appeals, the weakness of the state, the organizational capacity of rebel leaders, or the discontent of the masses—precipitates a successful revolution. Indeed, different revolutions may result from different configurations of factors, such that one cannot develop a single theory to explain the origins of all revolutions.

There is a lively debate about whether the social sciences should seek scientific explanations comparable to what prevails in the natural sciences, such as physics. Some scholars claim that political scientists should aim to develop what have been called covering laws to explain political outcomes: that is, political phenomena should be explained by universal laws in a similar way to how physicists develop universally applicable laws to explain specific features of the physical world. Critics of this view claim that the social world is essentially different from the natural world. Some contend that the social sciences should seek to identify particular recurring patterns and structures that fulfill similar functions in different settings, but they recognize that this is a more modest goal than fully explaining outcomes.

Another group of scholars claims that social science should focus on identifying unique configurations of factors that coexist in a particular case. Proponents of this approach do not seek a definitive explanation or the development of covering laws.[13] And yet a fourth approach advocates what the anthropologist, Clifford Geertz, has designated "thick description," which seeks to convey the rich and subtle texture of any given historical situation, including the subjective and symbolic meaning of that situation for its participants.[14] Comparativists who favor this approach highlight the importance of understanding each country's distinctive **political culture,** which can be defined as the attitudes, beliefs, values, and symbols that influence political behavior.

An approach largely borrowed from economics, called **rational choice theory,** has been especially influential—and highly controversial—in political science, as well as in comparative politics, in recent years.[15] Rational choice theory focuses on how individuals act strategically (that is, rationally) in an attempt to achieve certain goals or maximize their interests when it comes to things like voting for a particular candidate or rebelling against the government. Proponents of rational choice generally use highly quantitative methods to construct models and general theories of political behavior that they believe can be applied across all types of political systems and cultures. This approach has been criticized for claiming to explain large-scale and complex social phenomena by reference to individual choices. It has also been criticized for dismissing the importance of variations in historical experience, political culture, identities, institutions, and other factors that are key aspects of most explanations of the political world.

Issues involving the appropriate choice of theory, methodology, research approaches, and strategies are a vital aspect of comparative politics. However, students may be relieved to learn that we do not deal with such issues in depth in *Introduction to Politics of the Developing World.* We believe that students will be in a much better position to consider these questions after gaining a solid grasp of political continuities and contrasts in diverse countries around the world. It is this goal that we put front and center in this book.

Returning to our earlier discussion of the level of analysis, most comparativists probably agree on the value of steering a middle course that avoids both focusing exclusively on one country and combining all countries indiscriminately. If we study only individual countries without any comparative framework, comparative politics would become merely the study of a series of isolated cases. It would be impossible to recognize what is most significant in the collage of political characteristics that we find in the world's many countries. As a result, the understanding of patterns of similarity and difference among countries would be lost, along with an important tool for evaluating what is and what is not unique about a country's political life.

If we go to the other extreme and try to make universal claims, we would either have to stretch the truth or ignore significant national differences and patterns of variation. The political world is incredibly complex, shaped by an extraordinary array of factors and an almost endless interplay of variables. Indeed, after a brief period in the 1950s and 1960s, when many comparativists tried—and failed—to develop a grand theory that would apply to all countries, most comparativists now agree on the value of **middle-level theory,** that is, theories focusing on specific features of the political world, such as institutions, policies, or classes of similar events, such as revolutions or elections.

For example, comparativists have analyzed the process in which many countries with authoritarian forms of government, such as military **dictatorships** and one-party states, have gone on to develop more participatory and democratic regimes. In studying this process, termed *democratic transitions,* comparativists do not treat each national case as unique or try to construct a universal pattern that ignores all differences. Applying middle-level theory, we identify the influence on the new regime's political stability of specific variables such as institutional legacies, political culture, levels of economic development, the nature of the regime before the transition, and the degree of ethnic conflict or homogeneity. Comparativists have been able to identify patterns in the emergence and consolidation of democratic regimes in southern Europe in the 1970s (Greece, Portugal, and Spain) and have compared them to developments in Latin America, Asia, and Africa since the 1980s and in Eastern and Central Europe since the revolutions of 1989.[16] We can study, for example, the transition from military rule to democracy in Brazil and Nigeria, progress toward deeper democratization in Mexico, and the prospects for democratic change in China and Iran, knowing that these cases fit within a broader comparative framework.

The study of comparative politics has many challenges, including the complexity of the subject matter, the fast pace of change in the contemporary world, and the impossibility of manipulating variables or replicating conditions. What can we expect when the whole political world is our laboratory? When we put the method of comparative politics to the test and develop a set of themes derived from middle-level theory (see Section 4), we discover that it is possible to discern patterns that make sense of a vast range of political events and link the experiences of states and citizens in countries around the globe. We believe that the comparative approach can be a very powerful tool for analyzing politics in the developing world.

Section ③   Developing Nations in a World of Transition

Most textbooks and courses in comparative politics were traditionally organized according to categories that distinguished among industrial (primarily Western) democracies, which were referred to as the "First World"; communist party-states in the "Second World"; and the less developed countries of Asia, Africa, and Latin America of the "Third World." This categorization was based, in part, on distinctive economic features that helped characterize different political systems. Economic organization and performance both affected and reflected the realities of politics in these different political systems: the capitalist (or market) economies and high standard of living in North America, Western Europe, Japan, and a few other countries; the socialist (or planned) economies of countries ruled by a communist party, such as the Soviet Union and China; and the low level of economic development and extensive poverty characteristic of the Third World.

Democracy was another dividing line in this way of looking at the nations of the world. The capitalist industrialized countries were not only wealthy but also stable and democratic; communist systems were unquestionably authoritarian; and most Third World nations had personal despots, one-party rule, military regimes, or—at best—democracies marred by high levels of social conflict and political violence.

One of the consequences of the many profound political and economic changes in the world in recent decades is that the old categories of First, Second, and Third World have lost or changed meaning. For example, following the collapse of the Soviet bloc, there are only a handful of communist party-states—China, Cuba, Vietnam, Laos, and North Korea. Even some of these (particularly China and Vietnam) are adopting market-based economic policies and forging close ties with capitalist nations. Obviously, "Second World" is no longer a useful term with which to classify countries.

Furthermore, sharp differences in growth rates among developing countries in recent decades make it difficult to generalize with confidence about the Third World in terms of economic characteristics. For example, from 1975–2002, China's economy grew at an annual average per capita rate of 8.2 percent, whereas India's growth rate was less than half that (3.3 percent per year), and Nigeria experienced negative growth during that period (–0.6 percent per year). The Third World has changed a lot politically, too. In 1975, most Third World countries had some kind of authoritarian government; by the early twenty-first century, scores of developing nations from Argentina to Zambia, have become democratic, or moved in that direction. The view that what Third World countries have in common is poverty and dictatorship is certainly not valid today, if it ever was.

So should the term "Third World" be jettisoned altogether as a category for scholarly analysis? Recent trends have profoundly challenged and complicated the way that comparativists classify the world's countries. But we believe that despite major political and economic differences, the countries included in this book continue to share many distinct characteristics that allow us to group and study them together as part of the developing world and, indeed, that a good case can be made for the validity of the Third World as an analytical category.

Third World or Developing World?

The term *Third World* was coined by French authors in the 1950s to draw attention to the plight of the world's poorer nations, which they believed to be as important as the headline-grabbing cold war and its superpower adversaries. To make their point, these authors adapted terminology from the French Revolution of the eighteenth century to dramatize the global inequalities of the mid-twentieth century: a long-neglected and oppressed *Third* World, they noted, was struggling against the *First* World (the industrial democracies) and the *Second* World (the Soviet Union and other Communist countries) for recognition and power just as the *Third* Estate of the common people in France had struggled against the privileged and powerful clergy (the *First* Estate) and the nobility (the *Second* Estate) in the 1790s.

Some people criticize the label as suggesting a numerical order in which the Third World ranks behind the First World and the Second World in a cultural sense. But its creators intended the term *Third World* to embody the struggle of poor nations for empowerment in the international system and a fairer share of global wealth. For many, the term *Third World* remains a powerful symbol of common purpose and determination and is still widely used by academics, government officials, diplomats, and others to describe the developing countries of Asia, Africa, and Latin America.[17]

This book uses the terms *developing world* and *Third World* interchangeably to refer to the economically poorer ("less developed") nations. Many people also use the term *South* as a way of referring collectively to developing nations in contrast to the developed nations of the "North."[18] Like *Third World, South* has achieved a certain symbolic importance by conveying the fact that there are enormous differences between the richer and poorer nations of the world. Granted, *South* is geographically somewhat misleading since there are developed nations in the Southern Hemisphere (like Australia) and less developed nations in the northern part of the globe (like Afghanistan).

But, whatever term you prefer, it is very important to recognize that the developing countries (which contain about 85 percent of the world's population) are very diverse geographically, economically, politically, and culturally. Some observers have asserted that there is such enormous diversity among developing nations that it is questionable whether it is still valid to use such a catchall category as *Third World* because it implies too much similarity in the challenges facing the developing nations and too much unity in their international policies. Such observers point to the huge differences in levels of economic development among countries usually considered part of the Third World. They question whether a country like Ethiopia with its extreme poverty ($90 average annual income) and overwhelmingly rural population (84 percent) has much in common with Mexico, which is much more prosperous ($6,230 average annual income) and highly urbanized (75 percent). Others argue not for abandoning such categories as developing countries or Third World, but for taking account of the differences among developing countries by adding more nuanced distinctions such as "low income," "least developed," or even "Fourth World" to refer to the poorest countries.

This book acknowledges the rich diversity of the developing world. In fact, the countries examined here were chosen, in part, to reflect this variety, as well as to illustrate important issues in the study of comparative politics. Table 1 indicates some of the important differences that mark developing nations.

The Development Gap

If there are such extensive differences among developing nations, what gives coherence to the concept of the Third World? Simply put, Third World nations are poorer, their peoples have a lower standard of living, and their economies are not as modernized as the industrialized countries: in other words, they are less developed. A few examples should make the realities of this development gap between the Third World and the industrialized countries clearer.[19]

The **World Bank,** a major international organization that provides financial assistance to the Third World, divides developing countries according to their annual **gross national income (GNI)** per capita (a broad measure of the total output of an economy divided by the total population) into three groups: low income ($765 or less), lower middle income ($766–$3,035), and upper middle income ($3,036–$9,385). The industrialized (high-income) countries are those with a GNI per capita above $9,386, but these countries have an average GNI per capita of about $29,000 per year. (For more about the meaning of these statistics and alternative approaches, see "Global Connection: How Is Development Measured?")

Generally, a country's GNI per capita reflects its level of economic development and modernization. But it also tells us a lot about the capacity of a government or an economy to meet the material needs of the people of a country. Thus, low GNI per capita figures reflect the low average standard of living and greater poverty that distinguish less developed from more developed nations.

The stark contrasts among countries in statistics used to measure some of the important noneconomic aspects of development can give you a sense of just

Table 1

Diversity in the Developing World

Country	Location	Political System	Economy
Brazil	South America	Transitional democracy	Upper-middle income, low to moderate growth
China	East Asia	Communist party-state	Low-middle income, high growth
India	South Asia	Established democracy	Low income, moderate growth
Iran	Middle East	Islamic Republic; theocracy	Lower-middle income, moderate growth, heavily dependent on oil exports
Mexico	Northern Central America	Recent transition from one-party dominant to competitive democracy	Upper-middle income, low to moderate growth
Nigeria	West Africa	Early stages of transition from military rule to democracy	Low income, volatile growth, heavily dependent on oil exports

what low GNI per capita means in terms of people's lives:

- **Illiteracy** (people over age fifteen who cannot read or write) averages 39 percent in the low-income countries (and up to 70 to 80 percent in some) and about 10 percent in the middle-income countries. In the developed countries, almost all adults can read, although there is some debate about how functionally literate a sizable part of the population of these countries really is.
- **Life expectancy** in the 61 countries the World Bank classifies as low-income averages only fifty-eight years; in the 93 middle-income developing countries, it is about seventy years; and in the 78 high-income developed countries, a person can expect to live seventy-eight years on average. In the poorest countries, such as Afghanistan, life expectancy is only about forty-two; in Sierra Leone, it is thirty-seven.
- The **child mortality rate** (which measures how many children die between birth and age five) in low-income countries is 148.5 per 1,000 live births, and in the very poorest countries it reaches well over 250 per 1,000; in the middle-income countries, the average child mortality rate is 41.7 per 1,000; in

the world's richest countries, the child mortality rate drops to 6.6 per 1,000 live births.

One of the leading causes of death for the approximately 10 million children under five who die annually in developing countries is diarrhea, a disease that people in developed countries consider to be at most an uncomfortable nuisance usually associated with foreign travel and easily dealt with by popping a couple of Imodium or Pepto Bismol tablets. For nearly 2 million children in Third World countries each year, diarrhea contracted from unsafe water means death from severe dehydration. The solution to this killer of children is simple and cheap: oral rehydration therapy (ORT), which involves giving the stricken child a solution of sugar and salt that allows the body to retain fluids. The solution can be easily mixed at home, *if* there is access to the ingredients; premixed packets cost about $0.20 each—that's twenty *cents*.

It is very important to recognize that there are vast differences in the noneconomic quality of life statistics even among Third World countries that have roughly similar levels of GNI per capita. For example, China, India, and Nigeria are all in the World Bank's lowest two income-defined categories of countries. Yet China's life expectancy of seventy-one years is

Global Connection: How Is Development Measured?

This book makes frequent reference to three commonly used measures of the overall strength or power of a country's economy:

- **Gross Domestic Product** (GDP), which is a calculation of the total goods and services produced by the country during a given year.
- **Gross National Product** (GNP), which is GDP plus income earned abroad by the country's residents.
- **Gross National Income** (GNI), which is a new name for GNP that has been adopted by the World Bank.

The numbers generated by GDP or GNI/GNP are, of course, different, but not hugely so. As conventionally measured by GDP or GNI/GNP—in other words, in terms of total output—the United States has, by far, the world's largest economy, followed by Japan, Germany, Britain, France, Italy, and China.

A better way to measure the level of development and the standard of living in different countries is to look at GDP/GNI per capita, which is the total economic output divided by total population. From the perspective of GNI per capita, Luxembourg ranks first ($45,740), while the United States is fourth ($38,870), Japan is seventh ($34,180), and China is number 134 ($1,100) out of 208 countries measured.

But these figures use a calculation based on the American dollar and **official international currency exchange rates,** which would, for example, tell you how many Mexican pesos or Russian rubles you could get for US$1. Many economists believe this approach does not give a very accurate sense of the real standards of living in different countries because it does not tell what goods and services (such as housing, food, and transportation) people can actually buy with their local currencies.

An alternative and increasingly popular means of comparing levels of economic development across countries is called **purchasing power parity** (PPP). PPP takes into account the actual cost of living in a particular country by figuring what the purchasing price of the same basket of goods is in different countries. For example, how many dollars in the United States, pesos in Mexico, or

rubles in Russia does it take to buy a certain amount of food or to pay for housing? Many analysts think that PPP provides a more reliable (and revealing) tool for comparing standards of living among countries.

The data boxes at the beginning of each country chapter in this text give both total and per capita GNI at official exchange rates and using PPP. As you will see, the differences between the two calculations can be quite dramatic, especially for developing countries. When PPP is used, China jumps from the seventh largest economy in the world to second place behind the United States. And, as noted above, China's exchange-rate GNP per capita is $1,100 (ranked 134th); using the PPP calculation it is $4,980, which places it at 119th out of 208 nations in 2003. Simply put, PPP takes into account that the cost of living in China is less than in the United States, so smaller incomes go farther when it comes to purchasing things.

The data boxes also give information about other ways to measure a country's development. The most important of these is the **Human Development Index** (HDI), which the United Nations introduced as a way to evaluate a country's level of development that considers more than just economic factors. The formula used to calculate a country's HDI takes into account *longevity* (life expectancy at birth), *knowledge* (literacy and average years of schooling), as well as *income* (according to PPP). Based on this formula, each country of the world, for which there are enough data, is assigned an HDI decimal number between 0 and 1; the closer a country is to 1, the better is its level of human development.

Out of 177 countries ranked according to HDI by the United Nations Development Programme on data collected in 2002, Norway (.956) was at the top and Sierra Leone (.273) was last. Countries such as the United States (8), Japan (9), Britain (12), France (16), Germany (19), the Republic of Korea (28), Poland (37), Cuba (52), and Mexico (53) were classified as having "high human development"; Russia (57), Brazil (72), China (94), Iran (101), South Africa (119), and India (127) were in the "medium human development" category; and Pakistan (142) and Nigeria (151) were scored as having "low human development."

considerably higher than India's (sixty-three years) and Nigeria's (forty-five years). China also has much lower levels of child mortality and illiteracy than do India and Nigeria. The case studies in this book analyze how such differences reveal important contrasts in the historical experiences and government policies of various developing nations.

We also need to be aware that national averages tend to mask class, gender, racial, and regional inequalities *within* countries. Although this is true in all countries, developing or developed, the disparities are particularly acute in the Third World. A couple of examples: Pakistan has an overall adult literacy rate of 41.5 percent, but among women it is only 28.5 percent (for males, it is 53.4 percent). Some people have even suggested that poor women in the least developed "Fourth World" countries should be called the "Fifth World" because they are, indeed, the poorest of the poor.

Now consider the jaw-dropping statistics that tell the story of China's spectacular economic growth since the early 1980s: a quadrupling of GDP, a twenty-fold increase in per capita income, from near zero foreign investment to over $500 billion (half a trillion!) in capital from abroad injected into the Chinese economy, from thirty-second place to sixth among the world's trading nations. But these numbers only tell us part of the story of the China miracle; they don't tell us that the benefits of the country's rapid development have been spread *very* unequally, with the coastal areas doing much better than the interior and urban living standards rising much faster than those in the countryside. In fact, China has gone, over the last few decades, from being one of the world's most egalitarian (if poor) countries to being one of the most unequal in terms of the distribution of income and wealth.

Many developing nations have achieved significant progress over the past few decades. A few have experienced impressive economic growth, and in the developing world as a whole the mortality rates for children under five have dropped by 60 percent in the last forty years, due largely to a reduction in diarrhea-related deaths through ORT. Similar positive trends are apparent in some of the other figures that are used to measure poverty in the less developed countries. In what was seen as a hopeful sign by many, in mid-2005, the **G-8** (the Group of 8, a coalition of the most industrialized nations) announced a plan that would erase the nearly $40 billion that the poorest countries owe to international lenders and significantly increase the amount of aid to Africa. The "Live 8" rock concerts that were held in multiple cities and broadcast worldwide on the Internet just prior to the opening of the July 2005 G-8 summit in Gleneagles, Scotland, were meant both to increase public awareness of human suffering in the Third World and put pressure on the leaders.

Nevertheless, most Third World countries still have very low and sometimes even negative economic growth rates, and for many of their citizens, the physical quality of life is hardly improving and may even be deteriorating. Life expectancy in sub-Saharan Africa dropped from an already low 50 years in 1990 to 46 in 2003. Some countries may be experiencing increases in production, but their swelling populations are swallowing up the gains of increased output, making real economic expansion impossible. The economy of Guatemala, for example, grew by an average of 3.6 percent per year in the period 1993–2003, but its population grew 2.6 percent per year during the same period. The result? Per capita income in Guatemala hardly grew at all. Thus, the enormous development gap that separates most of the Third World and the industrialized nations (which have *very* low population growth rates) is at best closing very slowly—and, in some ways, is even widening—and remains one of the most important ways of categorizing the world's countries (see Figure 1).

Third World States

There are many types of political systems in the Third World. Table 1 gives a sampling of the political diversity of countries in the developing world. India is an established, highly competitive democracy. Mexico had been a single-party-dominant democracy (meaning that one party always won the elections) for decades but has recently moved toward multiparty competition. Two of the countries listed can be categorized as transitional democracies, but one (Brazil) is fairly far along in the transition from a military dictatorship, while the other (Nigeria) started its rocky democratic transition less than a decade ago. And two are authoritarian regimes, but China's Communist party-state and Iran's theocracy (where supreme political power is held by the religious elite) have very little else in common. Analyzing the differences

Figure 1

The Development Gap

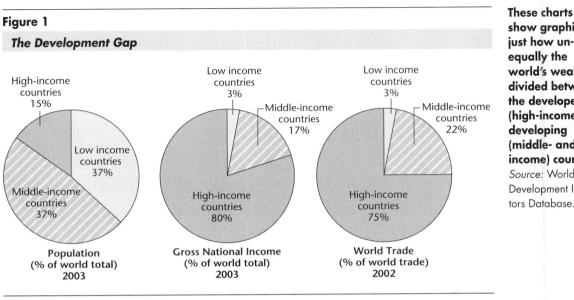

Population
(% of world total)
2003

Gross National Income
(% of world total)
2003

World Trade
(% of world trade)
2002

These charts show graphically just how un-equally the world's wealth is divided between the developed (high-income) and developing (middle- and low-income) countries.
Source: World Development Indicators Database.

among such varied types of political systems is one of the most central and interesting tasks in the study of comparative politics. But it is also important to note some of the political characteristics shared by Third World states in general that distinguish them politically from the developed nations.

First, politics and government in most developing countries are shaped by the basic facts of scarce economic resources, extensive poverty and inequality, and a relatively weak position in the international system. Government leaders in less developed countries simply have fewer options available in resolving problems or in responding to demands from various groups for a bigger piece of the national economic pie. Economic conflicts therefore are more likely to lead to violence or repression in Third World states; for example, peasants may rebel in their quest for more land, or the government may actively suppress labor unions striking for higher wages. Corruption is a very serious problem in much of the Third World because public officials personally profit from the state's control over various kinds of economic transactions and from the weakness of mechanisms for holding those with political power accountable to the law. Resistance to democratization in the Third World has often come—as it also did during earlier stages in the political development of Europe and North America—from elites who fear that greater popular control

of the government will jeopardize their economic privileges as well as their political power.

Second, the political legitimacy of many Third World states is very weak. Citizens often lack faith in their political leaders and perhaps even in the entire political system of their country. They may obey the law, and they may even vote. But they do not see the government as being very relevant to their lives or as being able to do anything about their most serious concerns; they may even regard the national government as having an adverse impact on their lives if their only contact with the authorities comes through experiences like tax collection, official corruption, or police brutality. Membership in a religious or ethnic group is often a much more important source of collective identity in the Third World than formal citizenship in a particular country. For example, many Tibetans feel only loosely (and perhaps negatively) connected to the Chinese government, even though Tibet is formally part of the People's Republic of China.

There are various causes of weak state legitimacy in the Third World. The government may be seen as favoring one ethnic, religious, or economic group—or even actively discriminating against some groups. Economic failure, political repression, extreme corruption, and military defeat may cause people to lose faith in the government. New democracies, which are quite common in the developing world, simply have not had enough time to establish legitimacy in the eyes of their citizens. Whatever the cause, states with weak legitimacy are prone to political violence, radical and sudden changes (such as a military **coup d'état**), and government paralysis. Such chronic instability only further erodes the legitimacy of governments.

Third, the effective power of governments in the less developed countries is often very limited. The state may have little ability to exert its authority much beyond the capital city and a few large urban centers. In the rural areas and small towns, where much or most of the population lives, political life is frequently based more on the relationship between powerful and usually wealthy individuals ("patrons") and those they

control ("clients") by dispensing favors or instilling fear, a use of power that comparativists call **patron-client politics.** In much of the Third World, the formal aspects of government such as laws, parties, and elections are less important to most people than informal politics based on personal relationships.

There are significant variations in how governments in the developing countries face the political struggle over scarce resources, weak legitimacy, and the influence of patron-client politics. But to one degree or another, they all experience these problems in ways that make the Third World state a distinctive and important entity in the study of comparative politics.

Section ❹   Themes for Comparative Analysis

This section describes the four themes we use in *Introduction to Politics of the Developing World* to organize the information on institutions and processes in the country chapters. These themes help explain continuities and contrasts among countries and demonstrate what patterns apply to a group of countries and why, and what patterns are specific to a particular country. We also suggest a way that each theme highlights a particular puzzle in contemporary Third World politics.

Before we introduce the themes, a couple of warnings are necessary. First, our four themes cannot possibly capture the infinitely varied experience of politics throughout the developing world. Our framework, built on these core themes, provides a guide to understanding many political features of Third World states. But we urge students (and rely on instructors!) to challenge and expand on our interpretations. Second, we want to note that a textbook builds from existing theory but does not construct or test new hypotheses. That task is the goal of original scholarly studies. The themes are intended to provide a framework to organize some of the most significant developments in the field of contemporary comparative politics as they apply to developing countries.

Theme 1: The Democratic Idea

One of the most important and astounding political developments in recent years has been the rapid

spread of democracy throughout much of the world. There is overwhelming evidence of the strong appeal of the democratic idea, by which we mean the claim by citizens that they should, in some way, exercise substantial control over the decisions made by their states and governments. According to Freedom House (a research organization based in the United States), in 1973, there were 43 countries that could be considered "free" (or democratic), 38 that were "partly free," and 69 that they classified as "not free." By 2004, their count was 89 free, 54 partly free, and 49 not free. In terms of population, in 1973, 35 percent of the world's people lived in "free" countries, 18 percent in "partly free," and 47 percent were citizens of countries ranked as "not free." In 2004, the percentages were 44 percent free, 21 percent partly free, and 35 percent not free.[20] Many of these new democracies are in Asia, Africa, and Latin America, a fact that has fundamentally transformed politics in the developing world. As Nobel Prize–winning economist and comparative public policy analyst Amartya Sen puts it, "While democracy is not yet uniformly practiced, nor indeed uniformly accepted, in the general climate of world opinion, democratic governance has now achieved the status of being taken to be generally right."[21] What do we mean by democracy? As with many other important concepts, debate over the meaning of democracy is contentious. The wide popularity of the term conceals some important ambiguities.

Should democracy be defined solely on the basis of the procedures used to select top governmental office-holders? That is, for a political system to qualify as democratic, is it sufficient that occupants of the highest offices of the state be selected on the basis of free and fair elections in which opposing parties are allowed to organize to present candidates and all citizens are entitled to cast a vote for a contending party? Or must there be respect for citizens' civil liberties (including rights of free expression, dissent, and privacy), regardless of what a democratically elected government might desire? What is the relationship between religious practice and the exercise of political power? To what extent must all citizens be guaranteed certain minimum economic and social rights and resources in a democratic regime, as distinct from political and civil rights (such as the right to vote and criticize the government)? Otherwise put, what is the relationship between democracy defined in purely procedural terms and democracy defined as a system that provides an adequate level of resources and promotes substantive equalities?

Despite intense debates about the meaning(s) of democracy, a rough consensus has emerged among practitioners and scholars about the minimum political features required for a regime to qualify as democratic. It is generally agreed that the following conditions must be present:

- Selection to the highest public offices is on the basis of free and fair elections. For an election to qualify as fair, votes must be counted accurately, with the winning candidate(s) selected according to preexisting rules that determine the kind of plurality or majority required to gain electoral victory.
- Political parties are free to organize, present candidates for public office, and compete in elections. The opposition party or parties—those not in power—enjoy adequate rights of contestation, that is, the right to organize and to criticize the incumbent government.
- The elected government develops policy according to specified procedures that provide for due process, transparency in decision-making, and accountability of elected executives (at the next election, through judicial action, and, in parliamentary systems, to the legislature).

- All citizens possess civil and political rights—the right to participate and vote in elections periodically held to select key state officeholders—and civil liberties—the rights of free assembly, conscience, privacy, and expression, including the right to criticize the government.
- The political system contains a judiciary with powers independent of the executive and legislature, charged with protecting citizens' political rights and civil liberties from violation by government and other citizens, as well as with ensuring that governmental officials respect constitutionally specified procedures.

In contrast to democracies, authoritarian states lack some or all of the above characteristics. The term *authoritarianism* refers to political systems in which power (or authority) is highly concentrated in a single individual, a small group of people, a single political party, or institution. Furthermore, those with power claim an exclusive right to govern and use various means, including force, to impose their will and policies on all who live under their authority.

What explains the recent trend from authoritarianism to democracy in the developing world? Comparativists have devoted enormous energy to studying this question. One scholar notes, "For the past two decades, the main topic of research in comparative politics has been democratization."[22] Yet, for all the attention it has received, there is no scholarly consensus on how and why democratization occurs. Or, rather, what we have learned is that there is no one path to democracy. The country studies in *Introduction to Politics of the Developing World* analyze the diverse causes and sources of support for (or resistance to) democracy.

In certain historical settings, democracy may result from a standoff or compromise among political contenders for power, in which no one group can gain sufficient strength to control outcomes by itself.[23] Democracy may appeal to citizens in authoritarian nations because democratic regimes often rank among the world's most stable, affluent, and cohesive countries. In some cases, a regional demonstration effect occurs, in which a democratic transition in one country provokes democratic change in neighboring countries. (This occurred in southern Europe in the 1970s, Latin America and parts of East Asia in the 1980s, and

Eastern and Central Europe in the 1990s.) Another important pressure for democracy is born of the human desire for dignity and equality. Even when dictatorial regimes appear to benefit their countries—for example, by promoting economic development or nationalist goals—citizens are likely to demand democracy. Although authoritarian governments can suppress demands for democratic participation, the domestic and (in recent years) international costs of doing so are high. However, not all authoritarian regimes have crumbled. Indeed, China, the world's most populous country and most dynamic economy remains resolutely undemocratic.

Authoritarian states frequently claim that they embody a form of democracy, particularly in the contemporary era when the democratic idea seems so persuasive and powerful. For example, according to the Chinese Communist Party, the political system of the People's Republic of China is based on "socialist democracy," which it argues is superior to the "bourgeois democracy" of capitalist countries that, in the end, benefits only wealthier citizens. But most political scientists would conclude that there is little substance to such claims and that in these states dictatorship far outweighs democracy.

However, we should not overlook certain features of authoritarian states that reflect democratic values and practices. In Iran, which is basically a theocratic authoritarian regime, there are vigorously contested multiparty elections, although the extent of contestation is defined and limited by the Islamic clergy who ultimately exercise sovereign power. And in China, for the last decade or so, a form of grassroots democracy has been implemented in the 700,000 rural villages, where a majority of the country's population lives. Even though the Communist Party still oversees the process to keep dissent from getting out of hand, China's rural dwellers now have a real choice when they elect their local leaders, and there have been many instances when exercising that choice has resulted in the ouster of corrupt and unpopular officials. Such democratic elements in Iranian and Chinese politics certainly make a difference in important ways to the citizens of those countries and they may well be seeds of future democratization, but they do not alter the essential authoritarian character of the state.

Is it possible to identify conditions that are necessary or sufficient for democracy to flourish? Comparativists have proposed, among the factors, secure national boundaries, a stable state, at least a minimum level of economic development, the widespread acceptance of democratic values, agreement on the rules of the democratic game among those who contend for power—one might extend the list, but the point should be clear! But democracy can and has flourished in unlikely settings—for example, in India, a country with a vast population whose per capita income is among the lowest in the world—and has failed where it might be expected to flourish—for example, in Germany in the 1930s. Democracies vary widely in terms of how they came into existence and in their concrete historical, institutional, and cultural dimensions.

Displacing authoritarian regimes and then holding elections does not mean that democracy will prevail or endure. A wide gulf exists between what comparativists have termed a *transition* to democracy and the *consolidation* of democracy. A transition involves toppling an authoritarian regime and adopting the rudiments of democracy; consolidation requires fuller adherence to democratic procedures and making democratic institutions more sturdy and durable.

Consolidated democracies are regimes in which there is relatively consistent adherence over several decades to the five democratic principles that we specified above. We do not claim that consolidated democracies never violate democratic norms—they do, and sometimes in shocking ways, but they generally practice the democracy they preach. There are very few consolidated democracies in the developing world. India, which has been a democracy for over fifty years, is certainly one—but take note: in 2005, Freedom House placed India in its lowest category of "Free" countries (2.5) and just a notch above its first "Partly Free" category (3.0) largely because of what it judged to be shortcoming in protecting the civil liberties of all its citizens. The worst examples of the nondemocratic aspect of the Indian state are the all too frequent occurrence of horrific communal violence in India, in which Muslim, Sikh, and Christian minorities have been massacred, sometimes with the active complicity of government officials.

Most Third World democracies, such as Brazil, Mexico, Nigeria, and Indonesia, are transitional. In many transitional democracies, a façade of democratic institutions conceals informal practices that violate the checklist of bedrock features of democracy.[24] As a general matter, there is greater legal protection of citizens' rights and liberties in transitional democracies than in authoritarian regimes (like China, Iran, and Cuba)—but considerably less than in consolidated democracies. Transitional democracies are usually "hybrid regimes" in which democratic forms of governance coexist with a disturbing persistence of authoritarian elements.[25] In such systems, as compared to consolidated democracies, political authorities are much more likely to engage in corruption, control of the media, intimidation, and violence against opponents in order to limit criticism of the government, undermine opposition parties, and ensure that the ruling party is reelected. Vote rigging and other abuses may be used if all else fails. Despite what the constitution may specify, the judiciary is often packed with ruling party faithful, and top military officers often exercise extraordinary political power.

We want to emphasize that the study of comparative politics does not support a philosophy of history or theory of political development that identifies a single (democratic) end point toward which all countries will eventually converge. One important work, published at the beginning of the most recent democratic wave, which began in Latin America in the 1970s, captured the tenuous process of democratization in its title: *Transitions from Authoritarian Rule: Tentative Conclusions About Uncertain Democracies.*[26]

Scholars have suggested that it is far easier for a country to hold its first democratic election than its second or third. As noted above, powerful groups have often opposed democratization because they fear that democracy will threaten their social and economic privileges. But disadvantaged groups may also oppose the democratic process because they see it as unresponsive to their deeply felt grievances. As a result, reversals of democratic regimes and restorations of authoritarian rule have occurred in the past and will doubtlessly occur in the future. In brief, the fact that the democratic idea is so powerful does not mean that all countries will adopt or preserve democratic institutions.

Finally, the theme of the democratic idea requires us to examine the incompleteness of democratic agendas, even in countries with the longest experiences of representative democracy. In recent years, many citizens in virtually every democracy have lost confidence in or turned against the state when their living standards were threatened by high unemployment and economic stagnation.

At the same time, **social movements** have targeted the state because of its actions or inactions in such varied spheres as environmental regulation, reproductive rights, and race or ethnic relations. Comparative studies confirm that the democratic idea fuels political conflicts in even the most durable democracies because a large gap usually separates democratic ideals and the actual functioning of democratic political institutions. Moreover, social movements often organize because citizens perceive political parties—presumably one of the important established vehicles for representing citizen demands in democracies—as ossified and out of touch with the people. Even in countries with impressive histories of democratic institutions, citizens may invoke the democratic idea to demand that their government be more responsive and accountable.

A puzzle: Is there a relationship between democracy and political stability? Comparativists have debated whether democratic institutions contribute to political stability or, on the contrary, to political disorder. On the one hand, democracy by its very nature permits political opposition: one of its defining characteristics is competition among those who aspire to gain political office. Political life in democracies is turbulent and unpredictable. On the other hand, and perhaps paradoxically, the very fact that political opposition and competition are legitimate in democracies appears to deepen support for the state, even among opponents of a particular government. The democratic rules of the game may promote political stability by encouraging today's losers to remain in the game, rejecting the use of violence to press their claim to power, because they may win peacefully in future competition. Although there is a troubling tendency for deep flaws to mar democratic governance in countries that have toppled authoritarian regimes, the odds are that, once a country adopts a democratic regime, that regime will endure.[27] As you learn about different developing countries, look for the stabilizing and destabilizing consequences of recent democratic transitions, the pressures (or lack of pressure) for democratization in authoritarian states, and the persistence of undemocratic elements even in established democracies.

Theme 2: A World of States

The theme we call a world of states reflects the fact that for about 500 years, states have been the primary actors on the world stage. Although international organizations and private actors like transnational corporations—and ordinary citizens organized in political parties and social movements—may play a crucial role, for the most part it is the rulers of states who send armies against other states and territories. It is the legal codes of states that make it possible for businesses to operate within their borders and beyond. States provide more or less well for the social protection of citizens through the provision—in one way or another—of health care, old age pensions, aid to dependent children, and assistance to the unemployed. It is states that regulate the movement of people across borders through immigration law. And the policies of even the most influential international organizations reflect to a considerable extent the balance of power among member states. That said, and as we noted above when discussing globalization, there is increasing overlap between the study of international relations and the study of comparative politics. Therefore we emphasize the interactive effects of domestic and international forces in shaping politics in the developing world.

We distinguish two important components of the world of states theme, one that focuses on a state's relationship to the international arena, the other focusing on its internal development. The external element highlights the impact on a state's domestic political institutions and processes of its relative success or failure in competing economically and politically with other states. What sphere of maneuver is left to states by imperious global economic and geopolitical forces? How do CNN, the Internet, McDonald's, television, and films (whether produced in Hollywood or in Bollywood, that is, Bombay, the city that has been renamed Mumbai and that is the site of India's thriving film industry) shape local cultures and values, influence citizen perceptions of government, and affect political outcomes?

A state's international geopolitical situation has a powerful impact on its domestic politics. When George Washington warned the United States, in his farewell address as president, not to "entangle our peace and prosperity" in alliances with other nations, he meant that the United States would be more successful if it could remain detached from the global power politics of the time (centered in Europe). That kind of disengagement might have been possible in the eighteenth century, but not in today's globalized world.

When President George W. Bush assumed office in 2001, he advocated a modest role for the United States in the world and opposed U.S. involvement in nation-building projects abroad. Months later, with the attacks of September 11, that policy orientation changed. Since then, the United States has toppled the Taliban regime in Afghanistan and sought to shape regimes in Iraq and elsewhere in the Middle East, as well as in other regions of the developing world, on the grounds that stable democratic regimes are in the interests of their own citizenry and are in the interests of the United States as well because terrorism is less likely to flourish in democratic countries. Even a president who proclaimed the value of unilateralism— going it alone—has spent considerable time trying to assemble international coalitions to achieve his goals.

But no state, even the most powerful, such as the United States, can shape the world to suit its own designs. Nor is any state unaffected by influences originating outside its borders. A wide array of international organizations and treaties, including the United Nations, the European Union, the World Trade Organization, the World Bank, the **International Monetary Fund (IMF),** and the North American Free Trade Agreement (NAFTA), challenge the sovereign control of national governments. Transnational corporations, international banks, and currency traders in New York, London, Hong Kong, and Tokyo affect countries and people throughout the world. A country's political borders do not protect its citizens from global warming, environmental pollution, or infectious diseases that come from abroad. More broadly, developments linked to technology transfer, the growth of an international information society, immigration, and cultural diffusion challenge state supremacy and have a varying but significant impact on the domestic politics of virtually all countries.[28]

Thanks to the global spread of radio, television, and the Internet, people nearly everywhere can become remarkably well informed about international developments. This knowledge may fuel popular local demands that governments intervene to stop atrocities in, for example, faraway Kosovo or Rwanda, or rush to aid the victims of natural disasters as happened after the great tsunami struck South and Southeast Asia in late 2004. And heightened global awareness may encourage citizens to hold their own government to internationally recognized standards of human rights and democracy. In the recent past, dictatorial rulers in Peru, Ukraine, and Kyrgyzstan have yielded power after popular movements took to the streets to challenge rigged election results. In mid-2005, hundreds of Iranian women demonstrated to protest sex discrimination in the Islamic Republic and to demand that candidates for the presidency discuss how they would address the issue.

States may collapse altogether when challenged by powerful rivals for power. And a similar outcome may occur when leaders of the state violate the rule of law and become predators, preying on the population. Political scientist Robert Rotberg suggested the term "failed states" to describe this extreme situation, and cited as cases Sierra Leone, Somalia, and Afghanistan before and under the Taliban.[29] The political situation in such countries has approached the anarchical state of nature described by the seventeenth-century English philosopher Thomas Hobbes. In a state of nature, he warned in the *Leviathan,* the absence of effective state authority produces a war of every man against every man, in which life involves "continual fear, and danger of violent death; and the life of man [is] solitary, poor, nasty, brutish, and short."

Although few states decline to the point of complete failure, all states in this new century are experiencing intense pressures from an expanding and increasingly complex mix of external influences. But international political and economic influences do not have the same impact in all countries, and a few privileged states have the capacity to shape the institutional structure and policy of international organizations in which they participate. It is likely that the more advantages a state possesses, as measured by its level of economic development, military power, and resource base, the more global influence it will have. Conversely, the policies of countries with fewer advantages are more extensively molded by other states, international organizations, and broader international constraints.

The theme we identify as a world of states includes a second important component that recognizes the fact that individual states (countries) are still the basic building block in world politics. Our case studies emphasize the importance of understanding similarities and contrasts in state formation and design across countries. Here we study the ways that states have developed historically, diverse patterns of political institutions, the processes and limits of democratization, the ability of the state to control social groups and sustain power, and the state's economic management strategies and capacities.

In the country chapters that follow, we highlight what we call critical junctures in state formation: that is, key events like colonial conquest, defeat in war, economic crises, or revolutions that had a durable impact on the character of the state. It is particularly important to note how the experiences of colonialism and imperialism shaped the formation of contemporary Third World states. In India, for instance, the British established a professional civil service staffed by Indians to help run the country, a legacy that greatly influenced the shape of independent India's government and has contributed to the durability of Indian democracy. By contrast, in Iran, Britain and the United States supported a despotic monarchy because it protected Western oil interests; the end result was the revolution that produced that country's current Islamic Republic.

The world-of-states theme is also intended to draw attention to the importance of regime variations among states, in other words, the overall mix of their political institutions that distinguishes, for example, democratic from authoritarian regimes. This theme is also intended to highlight the importance of variations in the configuration of institutions within a given regime type, such as the contrast between presidential and parliamentary forms in democratic states.

A puzzle: How do states in the developing world deal with the many challenges to their authority that they face from both internal and external forces? Increasingly, the politics and policies of such states are shaped by diverse external factors, often lumped together under the category of globalization. At the same time, many Third World states face increasingly restive constituencies who challenge the power and legitimacy of central governments. In reading the country case studies, try to assess what impact pressures from both above and below—outside and inside—have had on the role of the state in carrying out its basic functions and sustaining the political attachment of its citizens. How can weaker states (in terms of economic and military power) pursue and defend their interests in a world where a few great powers, particularly the United States, are trying to define the global agenda in terms of their own perceived national security needs? More broadly, is a significant degree of national autonomy and policy innovation for the states of the developing world compatible with globalization? For the countries in this book, try to assess their relative position in the international system, particularly their relationship with the developed nations. How do you account for the similarities and differences in how various developing countries fit into the world of states in the early twenty-first century?

Theme 3: Governing the Economy

The success of states in maintaining sovereign authority and control over their people is greatly affected by their ability to ensure that an adequate volume of goods and services is produced to satisfy the needs of their populations. Certainly, inadequate economic performance was an important reason for the rejection of communism and the disintegration of the Soviet Union. In contrast, the economic achievements of China's Communist Party are a major factor in explaining why communist rule has survived in that country.

Effective economic performance is near the top of every state's political agenda, and how a state "governs the economy"[30]—how it organizes production and the extent and character of its intervention in the economy—is a key element in its overall pattern of governance. It is important to analyze, for example, how countries differ in the balance between agricultural and industrial production in their economies, how successful they are in competing with other countries that offer similar products in international markets, and the

relative importance of private market forces versus government direction of the economy.

The term **political economy** refers to how governments affect economic performance and how economic performance in turn affects a country's political processes. We accord great importance to political economy in *Introduction to Politics of the Developing World* because we believe that politics in all countries is deeply influenced by the relationship between government and the economy in both domestic and international dimensions. However, the term *economic performance* may convey the misleading impressions that there is one right way to promote successful economic performance and one single standard by which to measure performance. In fact, both issues are far more complex.

There are many wrong ways to manage an economy; there are multiple right ways as well. Economic historian Alexander Gerschenkron pointed out long ago that the major European powers were forced to develop distinctive ways to promote industrialism because of the different places they occupied in the sequence of industrializing powers.[31] Britain had the good fortune to be the first country in the world to industrialize. Britain enjoyed a head start in economic competition; hence, it was possible for the state to adopt a relatively hands-off posture and for a market system of production to develop slowly—an approach involving relatively little state involvement in the market, an arrangement that came to be known by the French term **laissez-faire,** which literally means "let do," and more broadly refers to a free enterprise economy. All later developers, both those located in Europe in the nineteenth century and those located elsewhere in the world in the twentieth and twenty-first centuries, have had to catch up to an industrial leader. As a result, they did not have the luxury of adopting the British state's style of low-profile management but were forced to develop varieties of crash programs of economic development.

What formulas of state management have made for success in this later period? On the one hand, both economic winners and losers display a pattern of extensive state intervention in the economy; thus, it is not the degree of state intervention that distinguishes the economic success stories from those that have fared less well. On the other hand, the winners do not share a single formula that enabled them to excel. For example, a study directed by Peter A. Hall and David Soskice of the world's affluent capitalist economies identifies quite different patterns of political economy.[32] Studies seeking to explain the Asian "economic miracles"—Japan, South Korea, and more recently China—as well as the variable economic performance of other countries, highlight the diversity of approaches that have been pursued.[33]

There is agreement on a list of practices that *hinder* economic development (although it borders on the commonsensical): such states tolerate dishonesty and corruption, set tax rates so high as to discourage productive economic activity, and fail to provide public goods like education and transportation facilities that promote a productive economy. However, there is less agreement on the economic policies that states *should* adopt.

The matter becomes even more complex when one considers the appropriate yardstick to measure economic success. Should economic performance be measured solely by how rapidly a country's economy grows? By how equitably it distributes the fruits of economic growth? By the quality of life of its citizenry, as measured by such criteria as life expectancy, level of education, and unemployment rate? What about the environmental impact of economic growth? There is now much greater attention than just a few decades ago to this question, and more countries are emphasizing **sustainable development,** which promotes ecologically sound ways to modernize the economy and raise the standard of living. We invite you to consider these questions as you study the political economies of the developing countries analyzed in this book.

Most developing countries are taking steps to reduce the state's role in regulating the economy and are increasing the nation's involvement in the international economy by expanding exports and seeking foreign investment. The collapse of communism and the discrediting of the socialist model of extensive government control of the economy have vastly increased the global economic influence of the world's great capitalist powers, including the United States, Japan, and Germany. Furthermore, the World Bank and the International Monetary Fund are taking the lead—sometimes quite forcefully—in steering developing countries toward **economic liberalization.**

Some observers see the emphasis on free markets and international competition that are at the heart of economic liberalization as a blueprint for development and modernization. Others see the pressures on developing countries to liberalize their economies as an example of **neo-imperialism,** in which the powerful countries are once again dictating policies to the Third World. In either case, the trend toward economic liberalization—which, in one way or another, affects nearly every developing country—demonstrates how a state's approach to governing its economy is strongly shaped by its position in the world of states.

A puzzle: What is the relationship between democracy and successful national economic performance? This is a question that students of political economy have long pondered—and to which there are no fully satisfactory answers. There are several aspects of this puzzle that you should ponder while reading the country case studies that follow.

First, are democratic states more or less able to pursue effective developmental strategies? Although all economies, even the most powerful, experience ups and downs, the United States, Canada, and the longer-standing members of the European Union (in particular, the fifteen member-states prior to the 2004 enlargement to twenty-five members)—all durable democracies—have been notable economic success stories. On the other hand, several East Asian countries with authoritarian regimes also achieved remarkable records of development. The Republic of Korea (South Korea), Taiwan, and Singapore surged economically in the 1960s and 1970s, and Malaysia and Thailand followed suit in the 1980s and 1990s. (Korea, Taiwan, and Thailand subsequently adopted democratic institutions.) China, a repressive communist party-state that enjoyed one of the highest growth rate in the world since the early 1990s, provides a vivid case of development without democracy. And how can you explain that a democratic India for decades pursued economic policies that hampered economic growth, but more recently adopted measures that have led to impressive economic performance? In new democracies, the poor may gain a voice in government, but the economic elite can also use their political power to block needed changes (such as land reform or poverty alleviation). In light of such contradictory evidence,

Amartya Sen has argued, "There is no clear relation between economic growth and democracy in *either* direction."[34] As you read the country studies, try to identify why some states have been more successful than others in "governing the economy," that is, in fostering successful economic performance. Are there any consistent patterns that apply across countries?

Second, what special burdens do the difficult economic conditions typical of the developing world impose on a country that is trying to establish or sustain democracy? As noted above, many social scientists have argued that democracy requires a certain level of economic development—one characterized, for example, by a decent average standard of living, extensive urbanization, a large middle class, and high literacy rates. Yet democratization has recently spread to some of the world's poorest countries which do not meet any of these socioeconomic prerequisites. What chance does democracy have to flourish in such circumstances?

Nigeria is a good case of a poor developing country in the early stages of the transition from authoritarianism to democracy. Its struggle to establish democracy must be understood within the context of the economic challenges it faces as a low-income developing nation. Do these challenges make it harder for Nigeria to build the kind of basic national consensus and spirit of compromise on which a healthy democracy depends? Economic failure was one of the principal causes of the collapse of many dictatorial regimes in recent decades. The political fate of the new democracies of the Third World will also depend largely on their economic records.

Third, in what ways, and with what effects, do economic development and modernization create pressures for further democratization in the Third World? Social scientists have observed that as an economy and society become more modern and complex, as incomes and educational levels rise, and as a country becomes more connected economically and in other ways to the outside world, the pressures on a state to democratize tend to grow. These pressures may come from within the government itself, from the society below, or from abroad. In what ways has economic development influenced the process of democratization in countries such as Brazil and Mexico? How has successful economic development in China generated powerful pressures for political change that confront an authoritarian government with fundamental challenges?

Theme 4: The Politics of Collective Identity

How do individuals understand who they are in political terms? On what basis do groups of people form to advance common political aims? In other words, what are the sources of collective political identities? At one time, social scientists thought they knew. Observers argued that the age-old loyalties of ethnicity, religious affiliation, race, gender, and locality were being dissolved and displaced by economic, political, and cultural modernization. Comparativists thought that **social class**—solidarities based on the shared experience of work or, more broadly, economic position—had become the most important source of collective identity. They believed that most of the time, groups would pragmatically pursue their interests in ways that were not politically destabilizing. We now know that the formation of group attachments and the interplay of politically relevant collective identities are far more complex and uncertain.

In many long-established democracies, the importance of identities based on class membership has declined, although class and material sources of collective political identity remain significant in political competition and economic organization. But in much of the Third World, class remains a very potent source of identity and political conflict because of the extreme socioeconomic inequalities and barriers to social mobility that are found in these countries. Furthermore, contrary to earlier predictions, in many countries nonclass identities have assumed growing, not diminishing, significance. Such affiliations are based on a sense of belonging to particular groups sharing a common language, region, religion, ethnicity, race, nationality, or gender.

The politics of collective political identity involves struggles to form politically influential groups and to define which ones are influential participants in the political process and which are marginalized or even excluded. This struggle involves a constant tug of war among groups over relative power and influence, both symbolic and substantive. Issues of inclusion, political recognition, and priority remain pivotal in many countries, and they may never be fully settled.

In addition, questions of representation are hard to resolve: Who is included in a racial or ethnic minority community, for example? How is it determined who speaks for the community or negotiates with a governmental authority on its behalf? One reason that conflict around these questions can be so intense is that political leaders in the state and in opposition movements often seek to mobilize support by exploiting ethnic, religious, racial, or regional rivalries and by manipulating issues of identity and representation. Another reason is that considerable material and nonmaterial stakes derive from the outcome of these struggles.

Identity-based conflicts appear in every multiethnic country, developed or developing. In Britain, France, and Germany, issues of nationality, citizenship, and immigration—often with ethnic or racial overtones—have been hot-button issues and have often spilled over into electoral politics. These conflicts have been particularly intense in postcolonial developing countries, such as Nigeria, where colonial powers forced ethnic groups together in order to carve out a country whose borders were drawn with little regard to preexisting collective identities. This process of state formation sowed seeds for future conflict in Nigeria and elsewhere and threatens the survival of democracy and perhaps the state itself in many postcolonial nations.

Even nations with a high degree of ethnic homogeneity may experience political tensions based on ethnicity. China, for example, continues to be challenged by identity-based conflict both in Tibet and in the Muslim regions of the country. Many states are also challenged (sometimes violently) by nationalist movements that seek to secede to form their own country. This was the root cause of the civil war in 1971 that led to the creation of Bangladesh, which was once part of Pakistan. The crisis in Northern Ireland, the separatist movement in Quebec, and the war in Chechnya show that developed countries like the United Kingdom, Canada, and Russia are not immune from high-stakes identity clashes.

Religion is another source of collective identity—as well as of severe political conflict, both within and among religious communities. Violent struggles among religious groups have recently occurred in many countries, including India, Sri Lanka, Nigeria, and the United Kingdom (again, in Northern Ireland). Such conflicts may spill over national boundaries and involve an especially ugly form of globalization. For example, Al Qaeda, the network responsible for the September 11, 2001, attacks in the United States, identified the presence of non-Muslim Western forces in what they regarded as the sacred Islamic territory of Saudi Arabia as a principal reason for its actions. At the same time, the political orientation of a particular religious community is not predetermined but is rather a product of what has been called "political entrepreneurship," that is, the efforts of leaders seeking power by mobilizing support within the community. The political posture associated with Christian, Jewish, Muslim, or Hindu beliefs cannot simply be read from the sacred texts, as is evidenced by the intense conflict *within* most religious communities today that pits more liberal, secular elements against those who defend what they claim is a more orthodox, traditional interpretation.

A puzzle: How does collective identity affect a country's **distributional politics,** that is, the process of deciding who gets what and how resources are distributed? Once identity demands are placed on the national agenda, can governments resolve them by distributing political, economic, and other resources in ways that redress the grievances of the minority or politically weaker identity groups? Collective identities operate at the level of symbols, attitudes, values, and beliefs as well as at the level of material resources. However, the contrast between material- and nonmaterial-based identities and demands should not be exaggerated. In practice, most groups are animated by both feelings of attachment and solidarity and by the desire to obtain material benefits and political influence for their members. Nonetheless, the analytical distinction between material and nonmaterial demands remains useful. Further, it is worth considering whether the nonmaterial aspects of collective identities make political disputes over ethnicity or religion or language or nationality especially divisive and difficult to resolve.

In a situation of extreme scarcity, as is found in much of the developing world, it may prove nearly impossible to reach any compromise among groups with conflicting material demands. But if an adequate level of material resources is available, such conflicts may be easier to resolve through distributional politics because groups can negotiate at least a minimally satisfying share of resources.

However, the nonmaterial demands of ethnic, religious, and nationalist movements can be very difficult to satisfy. Distributional politics may be quite ineffective, as when a religious group demands that the government require all citizens to conform to its values and practices or when a dominant linguistic group insists that a single language be used in education and government throughout the country. In such cases, political conflict tends to move from the distributive realm to the cultural realm, where compromises cannot be achieved by simply dividing the pie of material resources. Our country studies examine a wide range of conflicts involving collective identities. It is worth pondering whether, and under what conditions, they can be resolved by the normal give and take of political bargaining—and when, instead, they lead to the fury and blood of political violence.

These four themes provide our analytic scaffold. With an understanding of the method of comparative politics and the four themes in mind, we can now discuss how the text is organized for comparative analysis of politics in the developing world.

Section ⑤   Organization of the Text

The core of this book consists of case studies selected for their significance in terms of our comparative themes and their ability to provide a reasonable sample of types of political regimes and geographic regions. Although each of the country studies makes important comparative references, the studies are primarily intended to provide detailed descriptions and analyses of the politics of individual countries. At the same time, the country studies have common section and subsection headings to help you make comparisons and explore similar themes across the various cases. The following are brief summaries of the main issues and questions covered in the country studies.

1: The Making of the Modern State

Section 1 in each chapter provides an overview of the forces that have shaped the particular character of the state. We believe that understanding the contemporary politics of any country requires some familiarity with the historical process through which its current political system took shape. "Politics in Action" uses a specific event to illustrate an important political moment in the country's recent history and to highlight some of the critical political issues it faces. "Geographic Setting" locates the country in its regional context and discusses the political implications of this setting. "Critical Junctures" looks at some of the major stages and decisive turning points in the state's development. This discussion should give you an idea of how the country assumed its current political order and a sense of how relations between state and society have developed over time.

"Themes and Implications" shows how the past pattern of state development continues to shape the country's current political agenda. "Historical Junctures and Political Themes" applies the text's core themes to the making of the modern state: How has the country's political development been affected by its place in the world of states? What are the political implications of the state's approach to economic management? What has been the country's experience with the democratic idea? What are the important bases of collective identity in the country, and how do these relate to the people's image of themselves as citizens of the state? "Implications for Comparative Politics" discusses the broader significance of the country for the study of comparative politics.

2: Political Economy and Development

Section 2 in each chapter traces the country's recent and contemporary economic development. It explores the issues raised by the core theme of governing the economy and analyzes how economic development has affected political change. The placement of this section near the beginning of the country study reflects our belief that understanding a country's economic situation is essential for analyzing its politics. "State and Economy" discusses the basic organization of the country's economy, with emphasis on the role of the state in managing economic life and on the relationship between the government and other economic actors. How do the dynamics and historical timing of

the country's insertion into the world economy—and its current position and competitiveness within the globalized economy—affect domestic political arrangements and shape contemporary challenges? This section also analyzes the state's social welfare policies, such as health care, housing, and pension programs. "Society and Economy" examines the social and political implications of the country's economic situation. It asks who benefits from economic change and looks at how economic development creates or reinforces class, ethnic, gender, regional, or ideological

---

What's in the Data Boxes?

At the beginning of each of the following chapters is a data box that presents important factual and statistical information. We hope most of this information is self-explanatory, but a few points of clarification may be helpful.

- The social and economic data largely comes from the CIA *World Factbook*, the World Bank *World Development Indicators*, and the United Nations *Human Development Report*, all of which are issued annually.*
    The data presented is as up to date as possible. Unless otherwise indicated, it is from 2002–2005.
- Several important terms used in the data boxes are explained in the Glossary, including Gross Domestic Product (GDP), Gross National Product/Index (GNP/GNI), Purchasing Power Parity (PPP), and Gini Index.
- At the end of each data box are six broad categories that rate and rank countries on the basis of statistically derived measurements of various aspects of their political or economic development. We think these provide an interesting, if sometimes controversial approach to comparative analysis. The categories include the following:†

- **The Human Development Index (HDI):** A summary composite index used by the United Nations "that measures a country's average achievements in three basic aspects of human development: longevity, knowledge, and a decent standard of living. Longevity is measured by life expectancy at birth; knowledge is measured by a combination of the adult literacy rate and the combined primary, secondary, and tertiary gross enrollment ratio; and standard of living by GDP per capita (PPP US$)." The higher the score, the better the HDI.

- **The Gender-Related Development Index (GDI):** HDI "adjusted to account for inequalities between men and women" by comparing, for example, gender differentials in life expectancy, literacy, and income. The higher the score, the better the GDI.

- **The Gender Empowerment Measure (GEM):** Also developed by the UN "to measure gender inequality in three basic dimensions of empowerment—economic participation and decision making, political participation and decision making and power over economic resources." The higher the score, the better the GEM.

(continued)

What's in the Data Boxes? *(cont.)*

- **The Corruption Perceptions Index (CPI):** A measure developed by Transparency International that "ranks countries in terms of the degree to which corruption is perceived to exist among public officials and politicians. It is a composite index, drawing on corruption-related data in expert surveys carried out by a variety of reputable institutions. It reflects the views of businesspeople and analysts from around the world, including experts who are locals in the countries evaluated." Range: 10 (highly clean) to 0 (highly corrupt).
- **The Environmental Sustainability Index (ESI):** "A composite index developed at Yale and Columbia universities tracking a diverse set of socioeconomic, environmental, and institutional indicators that characterize and influence environmental sustainability at the national scale." The current range is from 29.2 (worst) to 75.1 (best).
- **Freedom in the World Rating:** An annual evaluation by Freedom House of the state of freedom in countries around the world measured according to political rights and civil liberties through "a multi-

layered process of analysis and evaluation by a team of regional experts and scholars." Countries are ranked in .5 gradations between 1.0 and 7.0, with 1.0–2.5 being "Free;" 3.0–5.0, "Partly Free;" and 5.5–7.0, "Not Free."

---

*These reports and other statistics can be found at www.cia.gov/cia/publications/factbook/index.html, www.worldbank.org/data/, and http://hdr.undp.org/.
†The explanatory quotations for the composite categories are taken from:

- The Human Development Index: http://hdr.undp.org/statistics/indices/about_hdi.cfm
- The Gender-Related Development Index: http://hdr.undp.org/statistics/data/indic/indic_282_1_1.html
- The Gender Empowerment Measure: http://hdr.undp.org/statistics/data/indic/indic_283_1_1.html
- The Corruption Perceptions Index: http://www.transparency.org/cpi/2004/cpi2004_faq.en.html
- The Environmental Sustainability Index: http://www.yale.edu/esi/
- Freedom in the World Rating: http://www.freedomhouse.org/research/freeworld/2004/methodology.htm.

---

cleavages in society. "The Global Economy" considers the country's global role: How have patterns of trade and foreign investment changed over time? What is the country's relationship to regional and international organizations? To what degree has the country been able to influence multilateral policies? How have international economic issues affected the domestic political agenda?

3: Governance and Policy-Making

In Section 3, we describe the state's major policy-making institutions and procedures. "Organization of the State" lays out the fundamental principles—as reflected in the country's constitution, its official ideology, and its historical experience—on which the political system and the distribution of political power are based. It also sketches the basic structure of the state, including the relationship among different levels and branches of government. "The Executive" encompasses the key offices (for example, presidents, prime ministers, communist party leaders) that are at the top of the political system, focusing on those with the most power, how they are selected, and how they use their power to make policy. This section looks at the national bureaucracy and its relationship to the chief executive and the governing party and its role in policy-making. "Other State Institutions" looks at the military, the judiciary and the legal system, semipublic agencies, and subnational government. "The Policy-making Process" summarizes how public policy gets made and implemented. It describes the roles of formal institutions and procedures, as well as informal aspects of policy-making, such as patron-client relations and interest group activity.

4: Representation and Participation

The relationship between a country's state and society is the topic of Section 4. How do different groups in society organize to further their political interests, how do they participate and get represented in the political system, and how do they influence policy-making? Given the importance of the U.S. Congress in policymaking, American readers might expect to find the principal discussion of "The Legislature" in Section 3 ("Governance and Policy-making") rather than Section 4. But the United States is quite exceptional in having a legislature that in much of the policy process is a coequal branch of government with the executive. In most other political systems, the executive dominates the policy process, even when it is ultimately responsible to the legislature, as in a parliamentary system. In most countries other than the United States, the legislature functions primarily to represent and provide a forum for the political expression of various interests in government; it is only secondarily (and in some cases, such as China, only marginally) a policymaking body. Therefore, although this section does describe and assess the legislature's role in policymaking, its primary focus is on how the legislature represents or fails to represent different interests in society.

"Political Parties and the Party System" describes the overall organization of the party system and reviews the major parties. "Elections" discusses the election process and recent trends in electoral behavior. It also considers the significance of elections (or lack thereof) as a vehicle for citizen participation in politics and in bringing about changes in the government. "Political Culture, Citizenship, and Identity" examines how people perceive themselves as members of the political community: the nature and source of political values and attitudes, who is considered a citizen of the state, and how different groups in society understand their relationship to the state. The topics covered may include political aspects of the educational system, the media, religion, and ethnicity. How have globalization and events relating to September 11, 2001, shaped collective identities and collective action? "Interests, Social Movements, and Protests" discusses how various groups pursue their political interests outside the party system: When do they use formal organizations (such as unions) or launch movements (such as Green environmental, antiglobalization, or peace movements)? What is the relationship between the state and such organizations and movements? When and how do citizens engage in acts of protest? And how does the state respond to such protests?

5: Politics in Transition

In Section 5, each country study returns to the book's focus on the major challenges that are reshaping our world and the study of comparative politics. "Political Challenges and Changing Agendas" lays out the major unresolved issues facing the country and assesses which are most likely to dominate in the near future. Many of the country studies address issues that have generated intense conflicts around the world in the recent period—conflicts involving globalization, collective identities, human rights and civil liberties, the war in Iraq, and the consequences of America's exercise of global hegemony. "Politics in Comparative Perspective" returns to the book's four core themes and highlights the implications of the country case for the study of comparative politics. How does the history—and how will the fate—of the country influence developments in a regional and global context? What does this case study tell us about politics in other countries that have similar political systems or that face similar kinds of political challenges?

We realize that it is quite a challenge to set out on a journey with the goal of trying to understand contemporary politics around the globe. We hope that the timely information and thematic focus of this book will prepare and inspire you to explore further the often troubling, sometimes inspiring, but endlessly fascinating and increasingly important subject of politics in the developing world.

Key Terms

North Atlantic Treaty Organization (NATO)

communist party-state

regime

cold war

Third World

authoritarian

globalization

European Union (EU)

World Trade Organization (WTO)

collective identities

comparative politics

comparativists

countries

state

executive

cabinet

bureaucracy

regulations

legitimacy

state formation

nation-state

political culture

rational choice theory

middle-level theory

dictatorships

democratic transitions

World Bank

gross domestic product (GDP)

gross national product (GNP)

gross national income (GNI)

official international currency exchange rates

purchasing power parity (PPP)

Human Development Index (HDI)

illiteracy

life expectancy

child mortality rate

Group of 8 (G-8)

coup d'état

patron-client politics

social movements

International Monetary Fund (IMF)

political economy

laissez-faire

sustainable development

economic liberalization

neo-imperialism

social class

distributional politics

Suggested Readings

Anderson, Benedict. *Imagined Communities: Reflections on the Origins and Spread of Nationalism.* Rev. ed. London: Verso, 1991.

Bates, Robert. *Prosperity and Violence: The Political Economy of Development.* New York: W.W. Norton & Company, 2001.

Bhagwati, Jagdish. *In Defense of Globalization.* New York: Oxford University Press, 2004.

Black, Maggie. *The No-Nonsense Guide to International Development.* New York: Verso, 2002.

Cammack, Paul, Pool, David, and Tordoff, William. *Third World Politics: A Comparative Introduction.* 3rd ed. Baltimore: Johns Hopkins University Press, 2006.

The Developing World. Annual Editions, Guilford, CT: Duskin, published annually.

Enloe, Cynthia. *The Curious Feminist: Searching for Women in a New Age Of Empire.* Berkeley: University of California Press, 2004.

Grindle, Merilee S. *Despite the Odds: The Contentious Politics of Education Reform.* Princeton, N.J.: Princeton University Press, 2004.

Handelman, Howard S. *The Challenge of Third World Development,* 3rd ed. New York: Prentice Hall, 2003.

Isbister, John. *Promises Not Kept: The Betrayal of Social Change in the Third World.* 6th ed. West Hartford, Conn.: Kumarian Press, 2003.

Klitgaard, Robert. *Tropical Gangsters: One Man's Experience with Development and Decadence in Deepest Africa.* New York: Basic Books, 1991.

Kohli, Atul. *State-Directed Development: Political Power and Industrialization in the Global Periphery.* New York: Cambridge University Press, 2004.

Landes, David S. *The Wealth and Poverty of Nations: Why Some Are So Rich and Some So Poor.* New York: W. W. Norton, 1999.

Mittelman, James. *The Globalization Syndrome: Transformation and Resistance.* Princeton: Princeton University Press, 2001.

Nordquist, Joan. *Third World Women And Development: Bibliography.* Santa Cruz, CA: Reference and Research Services, 2001.

Nussbaum, Martha C. *Women and Human Development: The Capabilities Approach.* Cambridge and New York: Cambridge University Press, 2000.

Rapley, John. *Understanding Development: Theory and Practice in the Third World,* 3rd ed. Boulder, Colo.: Lynn Rienner, 2002.

Sachs, Jeffrey, *The End of Poverty: Economic Possibilities for Our Time.* New York: Penguin, 2005.

Scott, James. *Weapons of the Weak: Every Day Forms of Peasant Resistance.* New Haven, Conn.: Yale University Press, 1987.

Seabrook, Jeremy. *The No-Nonsense Guide to World Poverty.* New York: Verso, 2004.

Seligson Mitchell A., and Passé-Smith, John T., eds. *Development and Underdevelopment: The Political Economy of Global Inequality.* 3rd ed. Boulder, Colo.: Lynn Reinner, 2003.

Sen, Amartya. *Development as Freedom.* New York: Random House, 1999.

Smith, B. C. *Understanding Third World Politics: Theories of Political Change and Development.* 2nd ed. Bloomington: Indiana University Press, 2003.

Toft, Monica Duffy. *The Geography of Ethnic Violence: Identity, Interests, and the Indivisibility of Territory.* Princeton, N.J.: Princeton University Press, 2003.

Whitehead, Laurence. *Democratization.* Oxford: Oxford University Press, 2002.

Wolf, Martin. *Why Globalization Works.* New Haven, Conn.: Yale University Press, 2004.

Wolfensohn, James D. *Voice for the World's Poor: Selected Speeches and Writings of World Bank President James D. Wolfensohn, 1995–2005.* Washington: World Bank Publications, 2005.

Wrong, Michela. *I Didn't Do It for You: How the World Betrayed a Small African Nation.* New York: Harper Collins, 2005.

Suggested Websites

CIA World Factbook
www.cia.gov/cia/publications/factbook
Development Gateway
home.developmentgateway.org
Freedom House
www.freedomhouse.org
NationMaster
www.nationmaster.com
United Nations Development Programme
www.undp.org
World Audit
www.worldaudit.org
World Bank
www.worldbank.org

Endnotes

[1]Francis Fukuyama, "The End of History?" *The National Interest* 16 (Summer 1989) 3-18. The article is reprinted in Mark Kesselman and Joel Krieger, eds., *Readings in Comparative Politics: Political Challenges and Changing Agendas* (Boston: Houghton Mifflin, 2006).

[2]For collections of articles on globalization, see Mark Kesselman, ed., *Readings in Globalization* (Boston: Houghton Mifflin, 2006); and Joel Krieger, ed., *Globalization and State Power: A Reader* (New York: Pearson/Longman, 2006). For a lively account of changes involved in the current phase of globalization, see Thomas L. Friedman, *The World Is Flat: A Brief History of the Twenty-First Century* (New York: Farrar, Straus and Giroux, 2005).

[3]*PS: Political Science and Politics* 37, no. 6 (July 2004): 566. This issue also has the full program from the 2004 APSA annual meeting.

[4]United Nations Development Programme (UNDP), International Monetary Fund (IMF), International Bank for Reconstruction and Development (IBRD), Organization for Economic Cooperation and Development (OECD), North American Free Trade Agreement (NAFTA), and Asia Pacific Economic Cooperation (APEC) Forum.

[5]For descriptions by sympathetic participant-observers, see John Cavanagh and Jerry Mander, eds., *Alternatives to Economic Globalization: A Better World Is Possible,* 2nd ed. (San Francisco: Berrett-Koehler, 2004); and Robin Broad, ed., *Global Backlash: Citizen Initiatives for a Just World Economy* (Lanham, Md.: Rowman & Littlefield, 2002). For spirited defenses of globalization, see Jagdish Bhagwati, *In Defense of Globalization* (New York: Oxford University Press, 2004); and Martin Wolf, *Why Globalization Works* (New Haven, Conn.: Yale University Press, 2004).

[6]See Philippe Schmitter, "Comparative Politics," in Joel Krieger, ed., *The Oxford Companion to Politics of the World,* 2nd ed. (New York: Oxford University Press, 2001), 160–165. For a more extended discussion and different approach, see David D. Laitin, "Comparative Politics: The State of the Subdiscipline," in Ira Katznelson and Helen V. Milner, eds., *Political Science: The State of the Discipline* (New York: Norton, 2002), pp. 630–659. For a collection of articles in the field of comparative politics, see Kesselman and Krieger, eds., *Readings in Comparative Politics.*

[7]For a landmark article that analyzed how political decisions often reflect pressures from both the domestic and international arena, see Robert Putnam, "Diplomacy and Domestic Politics: The Logic of Two-Level Games," *International Organization* 42 (Summer 1988): 427–460.

[8]Although not specifically on the Indian and Nigerian militaries, see David Schwam-Baird, "Ideologies and Military Institutions in Third World Politics: Five Models," *Journal of Third World Studies* 17, no. 1 (Spring 2000): 105–132.

[9]See, for example, Theda Skocpol, *Social Revolutions in the Modern World* (Cambridge: Cambridge University Press, 1994).

[10]Peter A. Hall, *Governing the Economy: The Politics of State Intervention in Britain and France* (New York: Oxford University Press, 1986); and Mark Blyth, *Great Transformations: Economic Ideas and Institutional Change in the Twentieth Century* (Cambridge: Cambridge University Press, 2002).

[11]For reviews of recent literature on the state, see Margaret Levi, "The State of the Study of the State," Miles Kahler, "The State of the State in World Politics," and Atul Kohli, "State, Society, and Development," in Katznelson and Milner, eds., *Political Science: State of the Discipline,* 84–117.

[12]John R. Alford, Carolyn L. Funk, and John R. Hibbin, "Are Political Orientations Genetically Transmitted?", in *American Political Science Review,* vol. 99, no. 2, May 2005, 153–167.

[13]For diverse views, see Gary King, Robert O. Keohane, and Sidney Verba, *Designing Social Inquiry: Scientific Inference in Qualitative Research (*Princeton, N.J.: Princeton University Press, 1994); Mark Irving Lichbach and Alan S. Zuckerman, eds., *Comparative Politics: Rationality, Culture, and Structure* (Cambridge: Cambridge University Press, 1997); Katznelson and Milner, eds., *Political Science;* Henry E. Brady and David Collier, eds., *Rethinking Social Inquiry: Diverse Tools, Shared Standards* (Lanham, Md.: Rowman and Littlefield, 2004).

[14]Clifford Geertz, *The Interpretation of Cultures: Selected Essays* (New York, Basic Books, 1973).

[15]For discussion of rational choice theory in the popular press, see "Political Scientists Debate Theory of 'Rational Choice'," in the *New York Times,* February 26, 2000, p. B11; and Jonathan Cohn, "Irrational Exuberance: When Did Political Science Forget About Politics?" *New Republic,* October 25, 1999, 25–31. For an application of rational choice theory in comparative politics, see Robert H. Bates, Avner Greif, Margaret Levi, Jean-Laurent Rosenthal, and Barry R. Weingast, *Analytic Narratives* (Princeton, N.J.: Princeton University Press, 1998). For a lively exchange about the value of applying this approach to explaining large-scale historical change, see a critical review of *Analytic Narratives* by Jon Elster, "Rational Choice History: A Case of Excessive Ambition," and a reply by the authors of the book: Elster, "Rational Choice History: A Case of Excessive Ambition," and Robert H. Bates et al., "The Analytic Narrative Project," *American Political Science Review* 94, no. 3 (September 2000): 685–702.

[16]For the most influential example, see Juan J. Linz and Alfred Stepan, *Problems of Democratic Transition and Consolidation: Southern Europe, South America, and Post-Communist Europe* (Baltimore: Johns Hopkins University Press, 1996). However, for a warning that generalizations of this kind may neglect important differences among countries, for example, between formerly authoritarian and communist countries, see Valerie Bunce, "Rethinking Democratization: Lessons from the Postcommunist Experience," *World Politics* 55, no. 2 (Jan. 2003): 170–189. Selections of both are included in Kesselman and Krieger, eds., *Readings in Comparative Politics.*

[17]See, for example, the academic journal *Third World Quarterly: Journal of the Emerging Areas* and the following recently published books: John Parratt, ed., *An Introduction to Third World Theologies* (New York: Cambridge University Press, 2004); Rajagopal Balakrishnan, *International Law from Below: Development, Social Movements and Third World Resistance* (Cambridge: Cambridge University Press, 2003); Mike Davis, *Late Victorian Holocausts: El Niño Famines and the Making of the Third World* (London: Verso, 2002); and Lee Kuan Yew, *From Third World to First: The Singapore Story, 1965–2000* (New York: HarperCollins, 2000).

[18]See, for example, Focus on the Global South, at www.focusweb.org, and South-North Development Monitor, at www.sunsonline.org.

[19]Among the best sources for development statistics are the annual publications of the United Nations Development Program (*The Human Development Report*) and the World Bank (*The World Development Report*).

[20]Assorted Comparative Charts and Graphs, Freedom in World Reports, 2003, available at www.freedomhouse.org/research/freeworld/2003/tables.htm, and 2005, available at www.freedomhouse.org/research/survey2005.htm.

[21]Amartya Sen, "Democracy as a Universal Value," *Journal of Democracy* 10, no. 3 (July 1999): 3–17, available at http://muse.jhu.edu/demo/jod/10.3sen.html. This article is included in Kesselman and Krieger, *Readings in Comparative Politics.*

[22]Andrew Roberts, "Review Article: The Quality of Democracy," *Comparative Politics* 37, no. 3 (April 2005): 357.

[23]This view was first developed by Dankwart Rustow. His original article and commentaries are the focus of Lisa Anderson, ed., *Transitions to Democracy* (New York: Columbia University Press, 1999). This approach has been further developed by Adam Przeworski, *Democracy and the Market: Political and Economic Reforms in Eastern Europe and Latin America* (Cambridge: Cambridge University Press, 1991).

[24]See, for example, Guillermo O'Donnell, "Illusions About Consolidation," *Journal of Democracy* 7, no. 2 (April 1996): 34–51; Thomas Carothers, "The End of the Transition Paradigm," *Journal of Democracy* 13, no. 1 (January 2002): 5–21; and Steven Levitsky and Lucan A. Way, "The Rise of Competitive Authoritarianism," *Journal of Democracy* 13, no. 2 (April 2002): 51–65. All are reprinted in Kesselman and Krieger, *Readings in Comparative Politics.*

[25]Larry Diamond, "Thinking about Hybrid Regimes," in *Journal of Democracy,* 13.2 (2002), 21–35.

[26]Guillermo O'Donnell and Philippe Schmitter, *Transitions from Authoritarian Rule: Tentative Conclusions About Uncertain Democracies* (Baltimore: Johns Hopkins University Press, 1986). The concept of waves of democratization is taken from Samuel Huntington, *The Third Wave: Democratization in the Late Twentieth Century.* (Norman, Ok.: University of Oklahoma Press, 1991).

[27]Przeworski et al., *Democracy and Development.*

[28]One statement of the case that globalization has decisively weakened state supremacy is Martin van Creveld, "The Fate of the State," *Parameters* (Spring 1996): 4–17, reprinted in Kesselman and Krieger, *Readings in Comparative Politics.* Other articles in this collection develop the case that states retain a commanding position. See also Joel Krieger, *Globalization and State Power: Who Wins When America Rules?* (New York: Pearson/Longman, 2005).

[29]Robert I. Rotberg, "Failed States in a World of Terror," *Foreign Affairs* 81, no. 4 (July–August 2002). The article is reprinted in Kesselman and Krieger, *Readings in Comparative Politics.*

[30]This term is borrowed from Peter A. Hall, *Governing the Economy* (New York: Oxford University Press, 1986).

[31]Alexander Gerschenkron, *Economic Backwardness in Historical Perspective* (Cambridge: Cambridge University Press, 1966).

[32]Peter A. Hall and David Soskice, eds. *Varieties of Capitalism: The Institutional Foundations of Comparative Advantage* (New York: Oxford University Press, 2001). Also see Herbert Kitschelt, Peter Lange, Gary Marks, and John Stephens, eds., *Continuity and Change in Advanced Capitalist Democracies* (New York: Cambridge University Press, 1998); and David

Coates, ed., *Varieties of Capitalism, Varieties of Approaches* (Basingstoke, UK: Palgrave/Macmillan, 2005).

[33]For a sample of an enormous and diverse literature, see Chalmers Johnson, *MITI and the Japanese Miracle: The Growth of Industrial Policy* (Stanford: Stanford University Press, 1982); Stephan Haggard, *Pathways from the Periphery: The Politics of Growth in the Newly Industrializing Countries* (Ithaca, N.Y.: Cornell University Press, 1990); Mancur J. Olson, *The Rise and Decline of Nations: Economic Growth, Stagflation, and Social Rigidities* (New Haven, Conn.: Yale University Press, 1982); Peter Evans, *Embedded Autonomy: States and Industrial Transformation* (Princeton, N.J.: Princeton University Press, 1995); Linda Weiss and John M. Hobson, *States and Economic Development: A Comparative Historical Analysis* (Cambridge: Polity Press, 1995); and Meredith Woo-Cummings, ed., *The Developmental State* (Ithaca, N.Y.: Cornell University Press, 1999). For a review article questioning many commonly offered explanations,

see Robert Wade, "East Asia's Economic Success: Conflicting Perspectives, Partial Insights, Shaky Evidence," *World Politics* 44, no. 2 (1992): 270–320. Recent important contributions are Atul Kohli, *State-Directed Development: Political Power and Industrialization in the Global Periphery* (Cambridge: Cambridge University Press, 2005), and Jeffrey D. Sachs, *The End of Poverty: Economic Possibilities for Our Time* (New York: The Penguin Press, 2005).

[34]Sen, p. 3 (Internet text version). For an influential study of this question, on which Sen draws, reaches a similar conclusion, see Adam Przeworski et al., *Democracy and Development: Political Institutions and Well-Being in the World, 1950–1990* (Cambridge: Cambridge University Press, 2000). For a study that reaches a different conclusion—that there is a correlation between democracy and economic growth—see Yi Feng, *Democracy, Governance, and Economic Performance: Theory and Evidence* (Cambridge, MA: MIT Press, 2005).

CHAPTER 2

China

William A. Joseph

People's Republic of China

Land and People

Capital	Beijing
Total area	3,705,286 sq mi/ 9,596,960 sq km (slightly smaller than the United States)
Population	1.306 billion

Annual population growth rate (%)		
	1975–2000	1.2
	2002–2015 (projected)	0.6

Urban population (%)	39	
Ethnic composition (%)	Chinese (Han)	91.9
	Others (Hui, Uygur, Tibetan, Zhuang)	8.1
Major language(s)	Standard Chinese or Mandarin (based on the Beijing district); plus many other dialects such as Cantonese and Shanghaiese, and minority languages	
Religious affiliation (%)	Officially atheist.	
	Daoist (Taoist), Buddhist, Muslim	1–2
	Christian	3–4

Economy

Domestic currency	Yuan (CNY) (Note: also referred to as the *renminbi* (RMB) US$1: 83 CNY (2004)	
Total GNI (US$)	1.4 trillion	
GNI per capita (US$)	1,100	
GNI at purchasing power parity (US$)	6.4 trillion	
GNI per capita at purchasing power parity (US$)	4,980	
GDP annual growth rate (%)	1983–1993	9.5
	1993–2003	8.6
	2002	8.3
	2003	9.1
GDP per capita average annual growth rate (%)	1983–1993	7.9
	1993–2003	7.6
Inequality in income or consumption (2001) (%)	Share of poorest 10%	2
	Share of poorest 20%	5
	Share of richest 20%	50
	Share of richest 10%	33
	Gini Index (2001)	44.7
Structure of production (% of GDP)	Agriculture	13.8
	Industry	52.9
	Services	33.3
Labor force distribution (% of total)	Agriculture	49
	Industry	22
	Services	29
Exports as % of GDP		34.3
Imports as % of GDP		31.8

Society

Life expectancy at birth	72.27	
Infant mortality per 1,000 live births	24.18	
Adult illiteracy (% of population of age 15+)	9	
Access to information and communications (per 1,000 population)	Telephone lines	137
	Mobile phones	110
	Radios	339
	Televisions	312
	Personal computers	19

Women in Government and the Economy

Women in the national legislature		
Lower house or single house (%)		20.2
Women at ministerial level (%)		5.1
Female economic activity rate (age 15 and above) (%)		72.5
Estimated earned income (PPP US$)	Female	3,571
	Male	5,435

Composite Ratings and Rankings

Human Development Index (HDI) ranking (value) out of 177 countries	94 (.745)
Gender-related Development Index (GDI) ranking (value) out of 78 countries	71 (.741)
Gender Empowerment Measure (GEM) ranking (value) (out of 78 countries)	N/A
Corruption Perception Index (CPI) ranking (value) out of 146 countries	71 (3.4)
Environmental Sustainability Index (ESI) ranking (value) out of 146 countries	133 (38.6)
Freedom in World Rating	Not Free (6.5)

| **Political Organization** | |

Political System   Communist party-state; officially, a socialist state under the people's democratic dictatorship.

Regime History   Established in 1949 after the victory of the Chinese Communist Party (CCP) in the Chinese civil war.

Administrative Structure   Unitary system with twenty-two provinces, five autonomous regions, four centrally administered municipalities, and two Special Administrative Regions (Hong Kong and Macao).

Executive   Premier (head of government) and president (head of state) formally elected by legislature, but only with approval of CCP leadership; the head of the CCP, the general secretary, is in effect the country's chief executive, and usually serves concurrently as president of the PRC.

Legislature   Unicameral National People's Congress; 2,985 delegates elected indirectly from lower-level people's Congresses for five-year terms. Largely a rubber-stamp body for Communist Party policies, although in recent years has become somewhat more assertive.

Judiciary   A nationwide system of people's courts, which is constitutionally independent but, in fact, largely under the control of the CCP; a Supreme People's Court supervises the country's judicial system and is formally responsible to the National People's Congress, which also elects the court's presidents.

Party System   A one-party system, although in addition to the ruling Chinese Communist Party, there are eight politically insignificant "democratic" parties.

Section ❶   The Making of the Modern Chinese State

Politics in Action

When the International Olympics Committee announced in July 2001 that Beijing had been chosen as the site of the 2008 summer games, an estimated 200,000 Chinese citizens poured into Tiananmen ("Gate of Heavenly Peace") Square in the heart of China's capital to celebrate the honor that had been bestowed on their country. They saw the awarding of the games to Beijing as overdue recognition of the remarkable modernization of the Chinese economy, the stunning successes of Chinese athletes in international sports competitions, and the emergence of the People's Republic of China (PRC) as a major global power.

But there were also many voices that were extremely critical of the IOC's decision. Human rights organizations such as Amnesty International argued that the decision rewarded one of the world's most oppressive governments. Some compared the Beijing Games to those held in Berlin, Germany, in 1936, shortly after Hitler had come to power, games that the Nazis used to gain international legitimacy. The Dalai Lama, the exiled spiritual leader of Tibet, which has been occupied by China since 1950, strongly objected to awarding the games to Beijing. As his spokesman noted, "This will put the stamp of international approval on Beijing's

human rights abuses and will encourage China to escalate its repression."[1] Critics of the Beijing games also pointed out the irony that the Olympics celebrations in Tiananmen Square were held very near the place where, in 1989, China's Communist leaders ordered troops to crush a prodemocracy movement and killed hundreds of civilians, many of them college students.

Others argued that hosting the Olympics could be a force for positive change in China. PRC leaders would not want to risk an international boycott of the Beijing Games by engaging in highly visible repression. This, in turn, could embolden China's democracy activists, who have been largely silent since the Tiananmen massacre. In this way, the 2008 Beijing Olympics might spur much-needed political reform, as did the 1988 Olympics in Seoul, an important impetus to South Korea's transition from a military dictatorship to a democracy.

The controversy over the Beijing Olympics reflects the fundamental contradiction that defines contemporary Chinese politics. The People's Republic of China is one of only a few countries in the world that is still a **communist-party state** in which the ruling party claims an exclusive monopoly on political power and proclaims allegiance (at least officially) to the ideology of **Marxism-Leninism.** At the same time, the country has experienced dramatic economic and social liberalization—and even considerable political relaxation since the bloodshed in Tiananmen—and is more fully integrated into the world than at any other time in its history. But the Chinese Communist Party (CCP) rejects any meaningful movement toward democracy, and the rift between a tyrannical political system and an increasingly modern and globalized society remains deep and ominous.

Geographic Setting

The PRC is located in the eastern part of mainland Asia at the heart of one of the world's most strategically important and regions. It shares land borders with more than a dozen countries, including Russia, India, Pakistan, Vietnam, and the Democratic People's Republic of Korea (North Korea) and is a relatively short distance by sea from Japan, the Philippines, and Indonesia. China, which had largely assumed its present geographic identity by the eighteenth century, is slightly smaller than the United States in land area, and is the fourth largest country in the world, after Russia, Canada, and the United States.

The PRC is bounded on all sides by imposing physical barriers: the sea to the east; mountains to the north, south, and west (including the world's highest, Mount Everest); deserts, vast grasslands, and dense forests in various parts of the north; and tropical rain forests to the south. In traditional times, these barriers isolated China from extensive contact with other peoples and contributed to the country's sense of itself as the "Middle Kingdom" (which is the literal translation of the Chinese term for China, *zhongguo*) that lay not only at the physical, but also at the political and cultural center of the world.

Administratively, the PRC is made up of twenty-two provinces, five **autonomous regions,** four centrally administered cities (including the capital, Beijing), and two Special Administrative Regions (Hong Kong and Macao). The sparsely populated but territorially vast western part of the country is mostly mountains, deserts, and high plateaus. The northeast, which is much like the U.S. plains states in terms of weather and topography, is both a wheat-growing area and China's industrial heartland. Southern China has a much warmer, and in places even semitropical, climate, which allows year-round agriculture and intensive rice cultivation. The country is very rich in natural resources, particularly coal and petroleum (including significant, but untapped onshore and offshore reserves), and is considered to have the world's greatest potential for hydroelectric power. Still, China's astounding economic growth in recent decades has created an almost insatiable demand for energy resources, which has, in turn, led the PRC to look abroad for critical raw materials.

Although China and the United States are roughly equal in geographic size, China's population of about 1.3 billion—the world's largest—is five times greater. But only a relatively small part of China's land is usable for agriculture. China has a little over 20 percent of the world's population but only 10 percent of the world's arable land. The precarious balance between people and the land needed to feed them has been a dilemma for China for centuries and remains one of the government's major concerns.

China has more than 140 cities with a population of a million or more, the three largest being Shanghai (17.1 million), Beijing (14.5 million), and Tianjin (10.1 million). In 1997, the former British colony of Hong Kong, one of the world's great commercial centers (population 6.9 million), became part of the PRC. Nevertheless, about 60 percent of China's people still live and work in rural areas. The countryside has played—and continues to play—a very important role in China's political development.

China's population is highly concentrated along the eastern seaboard and in the most agriculturally fertile areas around three great rivers: the Yellow River in north China, the Yangtze (Yangzi) in the central part of the country, and the Pearl River in the south. The vast majority (92 percent) of China's citizens are ethnically Chinese (referred to as the Han, after one of China's earliest dynasties). The remaining 8 percent is made up of more than fifty ethnic minorities, who differ from the Han in at least one of several major ways, including race, language, culture, and religion. Most of these minority peoples live in the country's geopolitically sensitive border regions, including Tibet. This makes the often uneasy and sometimes hostile relationship between China's minority peoples and the central government in Beijing a crucial and volatile issue in Chinese politics today.

Critical Junctures

The People's Republic of China was founded in 1949. But understanding the critical junctures in the making of the modern Chinese state requires that we go back much further into China's political history. Broadly considered, that history can be divided into three periods: the imperial period (221 B.C.–1911 A.D.), during which China was ruled by a series of dynasties and emperors; the relatively brief republican period (1912–1949), when the country was plagued by civil war and foreign invasion; and the communist period, from the founding of the PRC in 1949 to the present.

From Empire to Republic (221 B.C. –1911 A.D.)

Modern China is heir to one of the world's oldest cultural and political traditions. The roots of Chinese culture date back more than 4,000 years, and the Chinese empire first took political shape in 221 B.C., when a number of small kingdoms were unified under China's first emperor, who laid the foundation of an imperial system that lasted for more than twenty centuries until its overthrow in 1911. During those many centuries, China was ruled by more than a dozen different family-based dynasties and experienced extensive geographic expansion and far-reaching political, economic, social, and cultural changes. Nevertheless, many of the core features of the imperial system remained remarkably consistent over time.

There are several reasons that the Chinese empire survived for such a long time. First, imperial China developed an effective national government with a merit-based bureaucracy chosen through competitive examinations long before the strong monarchical states of Europe took form in the seventeenth century. Second, the traditional Chinese economy was a source of great strength to the empire. Urbanization expanded in China much sooner than it did in Europe, and Westerners, like Marco Polo, who journeyed to China as early as the thirteenth century, were amazed by the grandeur of the Middle Kingdom's cities.

Third, the structure of traditional Chinese society, especially in the million or more small villages that were its foundation, gave imperial China great staying power. The vast majority of the village population was made up of poor and relatively poor peasants. But life was dominated by landlords and other local elites who worked with the national government to maintain and sustain the system.

Fourth, the traditional order was supported by the enduring influence in Chinese society of Confucianism. This philosophy, based on the teachings of Confucius (c. 551–479 B.C.), stresses the importance of the group over the individual, deference to one's elders and superiors, and the need to maintain social harmony. Confucianism did contain a teaching, the "Mandate of Heaven," that said the people had the right to overthrow an unjust ruler. Nevertheless, Confucianism was, in essence, a conservative philosophy that justified an autocratic state, a patriarchal culture, and a highly stratified society. Finally, the Chinese imperial system endured because, throughout most of its history, China was by far the dominant political, military, and cultural force in its known world. Even when it was conquered from the outside, as it was in 1214 A.D. by the Mongols and in 1644 A.D. by the Manchus, the invaders wound up establishing a new dynasty much on the pattern of the old and adapting many aspects of Chinese civilization.

Imperial China experienced many internal rebellions, often quite in large scale, during its lengthy history. Some even led to the overthrow of the ruling dynasty, but the result was always the establishment of a new dynasty built on traditional foundations. However, in the late eighteenth and nineteenth centuries, the Chinese empire was confronted with an unprecedented combination of internal crises and external challenges. A population explosion (the result of a long spell of peace and prosperity under the Qing dynasty) contributed to the onset of economic stagnation, which along with a significant rise in official corruption and exploitation of the peasants by both landlords and the government fomented widespread social unrest. The internal disorder culminated in the Taiping Rebellion (1850–1864), a massive revolt that took 20 million lives and nearly toppled the Qing.

In the meantime, the West, which had surged far ahead of China in industrial and military development, was pressing the country to open its markets to foreign trade. China showed little interest in such overtures and tried to limit the activities of Westerners in China. But Europe, most notably Britain, in the midst of its era of mercantile and colonial expansion, used its military supremacy to compel China to engage in "free" trade with the West. China's efforts to stop Britain from selling opium in China led to military conflict between the two countries. After suffering a humiliating defeat in the Opium War (1839–1842), China was literally forced to sign a series of unequal treaties that opened its borders to foreign merchants, missionaries, and diplomats on terms dictated by Britain and other Western powers. China also lost control of significant pieces of its territory to foreigners (including Hong Kong), and important sectors of the Chinese economy fell into foreign hands.

There were many efforts to revive or reform the Qing dynasty in the late nineteenth and early twentieth centuries, but political power in China remained largely in the hands of staunch conservatives who resisted change. As a result, when change came, it was in the form of a revolution in 1911 that both toppled the ruling dynasty and brought an end to the 2,000-year-old imperial system.

Warlords, Nationalists, and Communists (1912–1949)

The Republic of China was established on January 1, 1912, with Dr. Sun Yat-sen,[*] then China's best-known revolutionary, as president. However, the

---

[*]In China, family names come first. For example, Sun Yat-sen's family name was "Sun," and his given name was Yat-sen, and he is referred to as Dr. Sun.

Critical Junctures in Modern China's Political Development

1911   Revolution led by Sun Yat-sen overthrows 2,000-year-old imperial system and establishes the Republic of China.

1912   Sun Yat-sen founds the Nationalist (*Guomindang*) Party to oppose warlords who have seized power in the new republic.

1921   Chinese Communist Party (CCP) is founded.

1927   Civil war between Nationalists (now led by Chiang Kai-shek) and Communists begins.

1934   Mao Zedong becomes leader of the CCP.

1937   Japan invades China, marking the start of World War II in Asia.

1949   Chinese Communists win the civil war and establish the People's Republic of China.

1958–1960   Great Leap Forward.

1966–1976   Great Proletarian Cultural Revolution.

1976   Mao Zedong dies.

1978   Deng Xiaoping becomes China's paramount leader.

1989   Tiananmen massacre.

1997   Deng Xiaoping dies; Jiang Zemin becomes China's most powerful leader.

2002–2003   Hu Jintao succeeds Jiang as head of the CCP and president of the People's Republic of China.

Western-educated Sun was not able to hold onto power, and China soon fell into a lengthy period of conflict and disintegration, with parts of the country run by rival military leaders known as warlords. Sun set about organizing another revolution to reunify the country under his Nationalist Party (the *Guomindang*).

In 1921, the Chinese Communist Party (CCP) was established by a few intellectuals who had been inspired by the Russian revolution in 1917 and by the anti-imperialism of the newly founded Soviet Union to look for more radical solutions to China's problems. In 1924, the small Communist Party, acting on Soviet advice, joined with Sun Yat-sen's Nationalists to fight the warlords. After some initial successes, this alliance came to a tragic end in 1927 when Chiang Kai-shek, a military leader who had become the head of the Nationalist Party after Sun's death in 1925, turned against his coalition partners and ordered a bloody suppression that nearly wiped out the communists. Chiang then proceeded to unify the Republic of China under his personal rule, largely by striking an accommodation with some of the country's most powerful remaining warlords who supported him in suppressing the communists.

In order to survive, the Communist Party had to relocate its headquarters deep into the Chinese countryside. Ironically, this retreat created the conditions for the eventual rise to power of the man who would lead the CCP to nationwide victory, Mao Zedong. Mao, who had been one of the junior founders of the Communist Party, strongly advocated paying more attention to China's suffering peasants as a potential source of support. "In a very short time," he wrote in 1927, "several hundred million peasants will rise like a mighty storm, like a hurricane, a force so swift and violent that no power, however great, will be able to hold it back."[2] It was while the CCP was based in the rural areas that Mao began his climb to the top of the party leadership.

In 1934–1935, the Chinese communists undertook their mythologized Long March, an epic journey of 6,000 miles through some of China's roughest terrain, to escape attack by Chiang's forces. At the end of the Long March, the CCP established a base in Yanan, which was located in a remote and impoverished area of northwestern China. In Yanan, Mao consolidated his political and ideological control of the CCP, sometimes through ruthless means, and was elected party chairman in 1943, a position he held until his death in 1976.

Japan's invasion of China in 1937 started World War II in Asia and pushed the Nationalist government to the far southwestern part of the country, effectively eliminating it as an active combatant against Japanese aggression. In contrast, the CCP base in Yanan was on the front line against Japan's troops in northern China, and Mao and the Communists successfully mobilized the peasants to use **guerrilla warfare** to fight the invaders. By the end of World War II in 1945, the CCP had vastly expanded its membership and controlled much of the countryside in north China. The Nationalists, on the other hand, were isolated and unpopular with many Chinese because of the corruption, political repression, and economic mismanagement of Chiang Kai-shek's regime.

After the Japanese surrender, the Chinese civil war quickly resumed. The Communists won a decisive victory over the U.S.-backed Nationalists, who were forced to retreat to the island of Taiwan, 90 miles off the Chinese coast. (See "Global Connection: The Republic of China on Taiwan.") On October 1, 1949, Mao Zedong stood on a rostrum in Tiananmen near the entrance to the former imperial palace in Beijing and declared the founding of the People's Republic of China.

Mao in Power (1949–1976)

The CCP came to power on the crest of an enormous wave of popular support because of its reputation as a party of social reformers and patriotic fighters. Chairman Mao and the CCP quickly turned their attention to some of the country's most glaring problems. For instance, a massive land reform campaign redistributed property from the rich to the poor and increased productivity in the countryside. Highly successful drives eliminated opium addiction and prostitution from the cities, and a national law greatly enhanced the legal status of women in the family and allowed many women to free themselves from unhappy arranged marriages. Although the CCP did not hesitate to use violence to achieve its objectives and silence opponents, the party gained considerable legitimacy because of its successful policies during these years.

Between 1953 and 1957, the PRC implemented a Soviet-style five-year economic plan. The complete nationalization of industry and **collectivization** of agriculture carried out as part of this plan were decisive steps away from the mixed state-private economy of the early 1950s and toward **socialism.** Although the plan achieved good economic results for the country, Mao was troubled by the growth of the government bureaucracy and the persistence of inequalities, especially those caused by the emphasis on industrial and urban development and the relative neglect of the countryside.

In 1956, Mao used the media to issue a call to the Chinese people to "let a hundred flowers bloom, let a hundred schools of thought contend"; that is, they should come forward to offer their frank opinions about how the Communist Party was governing China. His goals for this **Hundred Flowers Movement** were to shake up the bureaucrats and encourage broader participation in making public policy, especially among the country's intellectuals. But the outpouring of public criticism and a wave of large-scale industrial strikes revealed the fact that many people were harboring deep resentments about Communist policies and about the growing political dictatorship.

Mao's reaction to the unexpectedly severe Hundred Flowers criticism was to order a vicious crackdown—the **Anti-Rightist Campaign** of 1957—in which hundreds of thousands of people were accused of being enemies of the revolution ("Rightists") and punished by being demoted, fired, or sent to labor camps. This campaign completely stifled political debate in China and "destroyed the hope that China's 'transition to socialism' might proceed on the basis of some form of popular democracy and with some real measure of intellectual freedom. It reinforced . . . that the exercise of state power was a monopoly of the Communist Party."[3]

Mao's discontent with the direction in which he perceived the PRC was heading continued to build, even after his critics had been silenced. In response, he launched the **Great Leap Forward** (1958–1960), a utopian effort to accelerate the country's economic development by relying on the labor power and revolutionary enthusiasm of the masses while also propelling China into a radically egalitarian era of true **communism.**

The Great Leap was a great flop and turned into "one of the most extreme, bizarre, and eventually catastrophic episodes in twentieth-century political history."[4] In the rural areas, irrational policies, wasted resources, poor management, and the lack of labor incentives combined with bad weather to produce a famine that claimed between 20 and 30 million lives. An industrial depression soon followed the collapse of agriculture, causing a terrible setback to China's economic development.

In the early 1960s, Mao took a less active role in day-to-day decision making. Two of China's other top leaders at the time, Liu Shaoqi and Deng Xiaoping,

Global Connection: *The Republic of China on Taiwan*

Despite the victory of the Chinese Communist Party in the civil war and the founding of the People's Republic of China on the Chinese mainland in October 1949, the Republic of China (ROC) under Chiang Kai-shek and the Nationalist Party continued to function on the island of Taiwan, just 90 miles off the coast. The Chinese Communists would likely have taken over Taiwan at the end of the civil war if the United States had not intervened to protect the island. The U.S. government, alarmed by the outbreak of the Korean War in 1950, saw the defense of the Nationalist government on Taiwan as part of the effort to stop the further expansion of communism in Asia.

When Chiang Kai-shek and his supporters fled across the Taiwan Strait in 1949, the island was already firmly under the control of Nationalists, who had killed or arrested many of their opponents on Taiwan in the aftermath of a popular uprising in February 1947. The harsh dictatorship imposed by Chiang's Nationalists deepened the sharp divide between the mainlanders, who had come over to escape the communists, and the native Taiwanese majority, whose ancestors had settled on the island centuries before and who spoke a distinctive Chinese dialect.

Economically, Taiwan prospered under Chiang Kai-shek's rule. With large amounts of U.S. aid and advice, the Nationalist government sponsored a successful and peaceful program of land reform and rural development, attracted extensive foreign investment, and encouraged an export-led strategy of economic growth that made Taiwan a model newly industrializing country (NIC) by the 1970s. The government also invested heavily in the modernization of Taiwan's roads and ports, and it promoted policies that have given the island health and education levels that are among the best in the world and a standard of living that is one of the highest in Asia.

Political change, however, came more slowly to Taiwan. After his death in 1975, Chiang Kai-shek was succeeded as president by his son, Chiang Ching-kuo, whom most people expected to continue the authoritarian rule of his father. Instead, the younger Chiang permitted some opposition and dissent, and he gave important government and party positions, previously dominated by mainlanders, to Taiwanese. When he died in 1988, the presidency of the republic passed to the Taiwanese vice president, Lee Teng-hui, who also became head of the Nationalist Party.

Under President Lee, Taiwan made big strides toward democratization. Laws used to imprison dissidents were revoked, the media were freed of all censorship, and open multiparty elections were held for all local and island-wide positions. In presidential elections in 1996, Lee Teng-hui won 54 percent of the vote in a hotly contested four-way race, reflecting both the new openness of the political system and the credit that Taiwan's voters gave the Nationalist Party for the island's progress.

But in 2000, an opposition party candidate, Chen Shui-bian of the Democratic Progressive Party (DPP), won the presidency, which many observers saw as reflecting a further maturing of Taiwan's democracy. Chen's victory was due in part to a combination of the desire for change, especially in light of a serious downturn in the island's economic growth and a split within the Nationalist Party.

The most contentious political issue in Taiwan, which is still formally called the Republic of China, is whether the island should continue to work, however slowly, toward reunification with the mainland, as was the Nationalists' policy under Lee Teng-hui, or declare formal independence. A big factor in Chen's election was the growing popularity of the DPP's position that Taiwan should seriously consider the independence option. Public opinion is sharply divided, with most people seeming to prefer the status quo in which Taiwan is, for all intents and purposes (including its own strong military), a separate political entity from China, but not an internationally recognized independent country. Chen was re-elected in 2004 in a close and contentious election, but he and the DPP have toned down

(continued)

their independence rhetoric. The political status of Taiwan is also a very sensitive matter in relations between the United States and the People's Republic of China. The U.S. is committed to a "peaceful solution" of the situation in the Taiwan Strait and continues to sell military technology to Taiwan. Beijing regards Taiwan as an inalienable part of China and has refused to renounce the use of force if the island moves toward formal separation. The PRC government often criticizes American policy toward Taiwan as interference in China's internal affairs.

Taiwan and China have developed extensive economic relations with each other, and millions of people from Taiwan have gone to the mainland to do business, visit relatives, or just sightsee. The PRC and ROC have engaged in some negotiations about further reconciliation and possible reunification, and in 2005 the current head of the Nationalist Party went to the mainland and held talks with CCP leader (and PRC president) Hu Jintao, in the first direct contact between the two political parties since the end of the civil war. Nevertheless, the governments that rule mainland China and Taiwan remain far apart because of their vastly differing political, economic, and social systems.

Taiwan

Land area	13,895 sq mi/ 35,980 sq km (slightly smaller than Maryland and Delaware combined)
Population	22.9 million
Ethnic composition	Taiwanese 84%, mainland Chinese 14%, aborigine 2%
GDP at purchasing power parity (US$)	$576 billion
GDP per capita at purchasing power parity (US$)	$25,300
GDP growth rate (2004)	6.0%
Life expectancy	77.3
Infant mortality (per 1,000 live births)	6.4
Literacy	96%

were put in charge of efforts to revive the economy and used a combination of careful government planning and market-oriented policies to stimulate production, particularly in agriculture.

This strategy did help the Chinese economy, but once again Mao found himself profoundly unhappy with the consequences of China's development. By the mid-1960s, the chairman had concluded that the policies of Liu and Deng had led to a resurgence of elitism and inequality that were threatening his revolutionary goals for China by setting the country on the road to capitalism.

The result of Mao's disquiet was the **Great Proletarian Cultural Revolution** (1966–1976), an ideological crusade designed to jolt China back toward his vision of socialism. Like the Great Leap Forward, the Cultural Revolution was a campaign of mass mobilization and utopian idealism, but its methods were much more violent, and its main objective was the political purification of the party and the nation through struggle against so-called class enemies, not accelerated economic development. Using his unmatched political clout and charisma, Mao put together a potent coalition of radical party leaders, loyal military officers, and student rebels (called Red Guards) to purge anyone thought to be guilty of **revisionism,** that is, betrayal of his version of communist ideology known as Mao Zedong Thought.

In the Cultural Revolution's first phase (1966–1969), 20 million or so Red Guards went on a rampage across the country, harassing, torturing, and killing people accused of being class enemies, particularly intellectuals and discredited party leaders. During the next phase (1969–1971), Mao used the People's Liberation Army (PLA) to restore political order, while the final phase (1972–1976) involved intense factional conflict over who would succeed the aging Mao as party chairman. Mao died in September 1976 at age eighty-two. A month later, the power struggle was settled when a coalition of relatively moderate leaders masterminded the arrest of their radical rivals, the so-called Gang of Four, who were led by Mao's wife, Jiang Qing. The arrest of the Gang (who were sentenced to long prison terms) marked the end of the Cultural Revolution, which had claimed at least a million lives and brought the nation to the brink of civil war.

Deng Xiaoping and the Transformation of Chinese Communism (1977–1997)

In order to help them repair the damage caused by the Cultural Revolution, China's new leaders restored to office many of the veteran officials who had been purged by Mao and the radicals, including Deng Xiaoping. By 1978, Deng had clearly become the most powerful member of the CCP leadership—although he preferred to install a loyal lieutenant in the formal position of party leader rather than take it for himself. He lost little time in putting China on a path of reform that dramatically transformed the nation.

Deng's policies were a profound break with the Maoist past. State control of the economy was significantly reduced, and market forces were allowed to play an increasingly important role in all aspects of production. Private enterprise was encouraged, and the economy was opened to unprecedented levels of foreign investment. On the cultural front, Chinese artists and writers saw the shackles of party dogma that had bound them for decades greatly loosened. Deng took major steps to revitalize China's government by bringing in younger, better-educated officials. The results of Deng's initiatives were, by any measure, extraordinary. After decades of stagnation, the Chinese economy experienced spectacular growth throughout the 1980s and beyond (see Section 2).

Then came June 1989 and the massacre near Tiananmen Square. Discontent over inflation and official corruption, as well as a desire, especially among students and intellectuals, for more political freedom, inspired large-scale demonstrations in Beijing and several other Chinese cities that spring. The demonstrations in Beijing grew through April and May, and at one point more than a million people from all walks of life gathered in and around Tiananmen. For several months, the CCP, constrained by internal divisions about how to handle the protests and intensive international media coverage, did little other than engage in some threatening rhetoric to dissuade the demonstrators. But China's leaders ran out of patience, and the army was ordered to clear the square during the very early morning hours of June 4. By the time dawn broke in Beijing, Tiananmen Square had indeed been cleared, but with a death toll that still has not been revealed.

Following the Tiananmen massacre, China went through a few years of intensified political repression and economic retrenchment. Then in early 1992, Deng Xiaoping took some bold steps to accelerate reform of the economy. He did so in large part because he hoped reform would help the PRC avoid a collapse of the Communist system such as had occurred just the year before in the Soviet Union.

From Revolutionary Leaders to Technocrats (1997 to the Present)

Another important consequence of the 1989 Tiananmen crisis was the replacement as formal head of the CCP of one Deng protégé, Zhao Ziyang, by another, Jiang Zemin. Zhao was ousted by Deng because he was considered too sympathetic to the student demonstrators, and Jiang was promoted from his previous posts as mayor and CCP chief of Shanghai because of his firm but relatively bloodless handling of similar protests in that city. Although Deng remained the power behind the throne for several years, he gradually turned over greater authority to Jiang, who, in addition to his positions as head (general secretary) of the CCP and chair of the powerful Central Military Commission, became president of the PRC in 1993. When Deng Xiaoping died in February 1997, Jiang was secure in his position as China's top leader.

Under Jiang's leadership, China continued the process of economic reform and its record of remarkable

This cartoon captures the contradiction between economic reform and political repression that characterized China under the leadership of Deng Xiaoping. *Source:* © 1992, *The Boston Globe.* Distributed by Los Angeles Times Syndicate. Reprinted with permission.

economic growth. The PRC became even more fully integrated into the global economy, as exemplified by its admission to the World Trade Organization (WTO) in 2001, and enhanced both its regional and international stature as a rising power. Overall, the country was politically stable during the Jiang era. But the CCP still repressed any individual or group perceived as challenging its authority, and the country faced serious problems, including mounting unemployment, pervasive corruption, and widening gaps between the rich and the poor.

Upon his retirement, Jiang was succeeded as CCP general secretary in November 2002 and PRC president in March 2003 by Hu Jintao, who had previously served as China's vice president. At age sixty when he took these offices, Hu Jintao was considerably younger than most of China's recent leaders. But both Jiang and Hu represented a new kind of leader for the PRC. Mao Zedong and Deng Xiaoping were career revolutionaries who had participated in the CCP's long struggle for power and were among the founders of the Communist regime when it was established in 1949. In contrast, Jiang and Hu were technocrats, officials with academic training (in their cases, as engineers) who worked their way up the party ladder by a combination of professional competence and political loyalty.

Another significant aspect of the transfer of power from Jiang to Hu was how predictable and orderly it

was. In fact, some observed that it was the first relatively tranquil top-level political succession in China in more than 200 years. Jiang had retired after two terms in office, as required by both party rules and the state constitution, and Hu had, for several years, been expected to succeed Jiang.

This smooth leadership transition, however, masked much that echoed the secretive and highly personalistic methods that have long characterized Chinese politics. First, Hu Jintao had been designated years before by Deng Xiaoping to be Jiang's successor. So Hu's "election" to the posts of CCP general secretary and PRC president was less the result of an institutionalized process than of personal and factional machinations.

Second, despite retiring from all party and government positions, Jiang Zemin retained considerable political power and influence. He was, in various ways, able to orchestrate his enshrinement as the successor to Mao and Deng as one of the great luminaries in party history. He also kept at least an ear in the inner sanctum of decision making through the placement of numerous close associates in the party's most powerful organizations Nevertheless, the coming to power of Jiang Zemin and then Hu Jintao did mark a critical juncture in China's political history, in that it reflected the passing of power from the revolutionary to the technocratic generation of Chinese Communist leaders.

In early 2005, Hu further consolidated his hold on power when he took over from Jiang as chair of the Central Military Commission (which controls the armed forces). He has also started to stake out a distinctive program and approach to leadership. On the one hand, he has tried to project himself as something of a populist by placing more emphasis on dealing with the country's most serious socioeconomic problems, such as enormous inequalities between regions, that have resulted from China's rapid economic growth over the last two decades. On the other hand, Hu appeared to be more hardline than Jiang in limiting dissent in society and even disagreement within the party leadership. In any case, there is little reason to expect that Chinese politics at the top will change much under Hu Jintao or that he will deviate significantly from the combination of economic reform and political repression that has been the CCP's formula for retaining power since the days of Deng Xiaoping.

Themes and Implications

Historical Junctures and Political Themes

The World of States.   When the People's Republic was founded in 1949, China was in a weak position in the international system. For more than a century, its destiny had been shaped by incursions and influences from abroad that it could do little to control. Mao made many tragic and terrible blunders, but one of his great achievements was to build a strong state able to affirm and defend its sovereignty. China's international stature has increased as its economic and military strength have grown in recent decades. Although still a relatively poor country by many per capita measures, the sheer size of its economy makes the PRC an economic powerhouse whose import and export policies have an important impact on many other countries. China is a nuclear power with the world's largest conventional military force, and it is an active and influential member of nearly all international organizations, including the United Nations, where it sits as one of the five permanent members of the Security Council. Clearly, China has become a major player in the world of states.

The making of the modern Chinese state has also been profoundly influenced at several critical points by

Student demonstrators erected a statue called the "Goddess of Democracy" in Beijing's Tiananmen Square in late May 1989 to symbolize their demands for greater political freedom in China. In the background is an official portrait of former Chinese Communist Party leader, Mao Zedong. Chinese troops toppled and destroyed the statue after they occupied the square on June 4, 1989, a process that also resulted in the death of many protestors.   Source: AP/ Wide World Photos.

China's encounters with other countries. The end of the Middle Kingdom's relative isolation from the non-Asian world and the conflict with the militarily superior West in the nineteenth century was a major factor in the collapse of the imperial system in 1911. Anger over European and U.S. treatment of China, admiration for the Russian Revolution, and the invasion of

China by Japan in the 1930s all played a role in propelling the CCP to power in 1949.

American hostility to the new Communist regime in Beijing helped push the PRC into an alliance with the Soviet Union and follow the Soviet model of development in the early 1950s. But Mao's disapproval of the direction in which Soviet Communist leaders were taking their country greatly influenced his decisions to launch both the Great Leap Forward in 1958 and the Cultural Revolution in 1966. The former communist allies became embroiled in an ideological dispute that eventually spilled over into global diplomatic rivalry, serious border tensions, and even small-scale military conflict that could have escalated into all out war. In the early 1970s, Mao supported the beginnings of détente with the United States in response to what he saw as a growing and more immediate threat to China from the Soviet Union. The relationship between China and the United States deepened throughout the 1970s and helped pave the way for the marketization and globalization of the Chinese economy under Deng Xiaoping.

Sino-American interaction (*sino* means "China," as derived from the Latin) is, arguably, the most important bilateral diplomatic relationship in the post–cold war world. There have been numerous ups and downs in that relationship ever since the two countries resumed ties in the 1970s. U.S. presidential administrations (and even presidential advisors within a single administration) have differed about whether China's rise as a great power should be seen as an opportunity for the United States, particularly in terms of trade and investment, or a threat to American interests. A particularly low point came after the 1989 Tiananmen massacre, when the United States cut back contacts with the Beijing regime. But shared economic and geopolitical interests have brought the United States and China closer since then., However, disagreements over issues like human rights and the political status of Taiwan and incidents such as the accidental bombing of the PRC embassy in Belgrade, Yugoslavia, by U.S. aircraft during the Kosovo war in July 1999 and the collision of an American spy plane with a Chinese jet fighter off the coast of China in April 2001 have, at times, caused serious friction.

The terrorist attacks of September 11, 2001, had a significant impact on Sino-American relations. The PRC became a key ally in the U.S.-led war on terrorism, which put almost all of the disputes between Beijing and Washington on the diplomatic backburner. China's leaders were quite happy to have tensions with the United States off their already overly burdened agenda. Indeed, one observer concluded, "the country that has benefited most from 9/11 is China."[5] The United States also needs the PRC's help to resolve the conflict with North Korea (China's neighbor and one-time close communist ally) over that country's nuclear weapons program.

Nevertheless, U.S-China relations are, at best, in a rather uncertain stage. On the one hand, in late 2004, then secretary of state, Colin Powell, declared that Sino-American relations were "the best" they had been "in over 30 years," and, a few months later, his successor, Condoleezza Rice, affirmed "the constructive, growing, and deepening relationship with China."[6] But, in mid-2005, secretary of defense Donald Rumsfeld and an official Pentagon report injected a note of caution in the Bush administration's assessment of U.S. ties with the PRC when they emphasized the threat posed to Asian security and American interests by China's military buildup.[7]

Governing the Economy.   Economic issues were central to the revolutionary process that resulted in the founding of the People's Republic. The Western powers were primarily motivated by the lure of the China market in their aggressive policies toward the Chinese empire in the nineteenth century. Chiang Kai-shek's Nationalist government lost popular support partly because of its mismanagement of the economy and its inability to control corruption. Mass poverty and extreme economic inequality fueled the Chinese revolution and led millions of peasants and workers to back the Communist Party in the civil war.

The history of the PRC is largely the story of experimentation with a series of very different economic systems: a Soviet-style planning system in the early 1950s, the radical egalitarianism of the Maoist model, and market-oriented policies implemented by Deng Xiaoping and his successors. Ideological disputes within the CCP over which of these development strategies China should follow were the main cause of the ferocious political struggles, such as the Cultural Revolution, that have so often wracked the country.

Deng's bold reforms were, in large measure, motivated by his hope that improved living standards would restore the legitimacy of the CCP, which had been badly tarnished by the economic failings of the Maoist era. The remarkable successes of those reforms have helped sustain the CCP in power at a time when most other Communist regimes have disappeared. Continuing China's economic progress will be one of the most important challenges facing Hu Jintao and China's other leaders.

The Democratic Idea.   The CCP also faces major political challenges, especially the challenge of the democratic idea, which has had a troubled history in modern China. The revolution of 1911 that overthrew the imperial system and established the Republic of China under Sun Yat-sen was the culmination of the first effort to establish a Chinese government in which citizens would have a voice. But the combination of warlordism, civil war, world war, and Chiang Kaishek's sharp turn toward dictatorship undermined any real progress toward democracy. Any hope that the democratic idea might take root in the early years of Communist rule in China was violently dispelled by the building of a one-party Communist state and Mao's unrelenting campaigns against alleged enemies of his revolution. The Deng Xiaoping era brought much greater economic, social, and cultural freedom for the Chinese people, but time and again the CCP acted to strangle the stirrings of the democratic idea, most brutally in Tiananmen Square in 1989. Jiang Zemin and Hu Jintao have been faithful disciples of Deng; they have not only vigorously championed economic reform in China, but also made sure that the CCP retains its firm grip on power.

The Politics of Collective Identity.   Because of its long history and high degree of cultural homogeneity, China has a very strong sense of national identity. Memories of past humiliations and suffering at the hands of foreigners still influence the international relations of the PRC. For example, Beijing's insistence that Britain return Hong Kong to Chinese control in 1997, largely on its terms, was shaped by the desire to redress what it saw as one of the most blatant injustices of China's defeat in the Opium War of the mid-nineteenth century. China also believes that Japan should apologize more fully for atrocities committed by the Japanese army during World War II before the two Asian powers can have completely cordial diplomatic relations. And as faith in communist ideology has weakened, party leaders have increasingly turned to nationalism as a means to rally the Chinese people behind their government, as reflected in the large-scale public celebrations that greeted Beijing's selection as the site for the 2008 Summer Olympics.

China's cultural homogeneity has also spared it the kind of widespread ethnic or religious violence that has plagued so many other countries in the modern world. The exception has been in the border regions of the country, where there is a large concentration of minority peoples, particularly in Tibet and the Muslim areas of China's northwest (see Section 4).

But China did experience a particularly vicious and destructive kind of identity politics during the Maoist era. Although landlords and capitalists had lost their private property and economic power by the mid-1950s, Mao continued to promote violent class struggle that pitted workers, peasants, and loyal party activists against "capitalist roaders" and other alleged counterrevolutionaries. When he took over in the late 1970s, Deng Xiaoping called for an end to such divisive class struggles and proclaimed an era of social harmony in which the whole nation could concentrate its energies on the overarching goal of economic development, a trend that was continued and deepened by his successors. But economic reform has led to new (or renewed) cleavages in Chinese society, including glaring inequalities between those who have profited handsomely from the marketization of the economy and those who have done less well or even been disadvantaged by the changes. These inequalities could become the basis of class, regional, or other kinds of identity-based conflicts that severely test the economic and political management skills of China's leaders.

Implications for Comparative Politics

China is a particularly important case for the study of comparative politics. First, the PRC can be compared with other communist party-states with which it shares or has shared many political and ideological features. From this perspective, China raises intriguing questions: Why has China's communist party-state so far proved more durable than that of the Soviet Union and nearly all other similar regimes? By what combination of reform and repression has the CCP held onto power? What signs are there that it is likely to continue to be able to do so for the foreseeable future? What signs suggest that Communist rule in China may be weakening? Studying Chinese politics is important for understanding the past, present, and future of a type of political system, the communist party-state, that has had a major impact on the modern world.

China can also be fruitfully compared with other developing nations that face similar economic and political challenges. Although the PRC is part of the Third World as measured by the average standard of living of its population, its record of growth in the past several decades has been far better than almost all other developing countries. Furthermore, the educational and health levels of the Chinese people are quite good when compared with many other countries at a similar level of development, for example, India

and Nigeria. How has China achieved such relative success in its quest for economic and social development? On the other hand, while much of the Third World has gone through a wave of democratization in recent decades, China remains a one-party dictatorship. How and why has China resisted this wave of democracy? What does the experience of other developing countries say about how economic modernization might influence the prospects for democracy in China?

Napoleon Bonaparte, emperor of France in the early nineteenth century, is said to have remarked, "Let China sleep. For when China wakes, it will shake the world."[8] There is no doubt China has awakened. Given the country's geographic size, vast resources, huge population, surging economy, and formidable military might, the PRC is certain to be among the world's great powers in the near future and surely deserves the attention of all students of comparative politics.

Section ❷   Political Economy and Development

The growth of China's economy since the late 1970s has been called "one of the century's greatest economic miracles," which has led to "one of the biggest improvements in human welfare anywhere at any time."[9] Such superlatives seem justified in describing overall economic growth rates that have averaged around 9 percent per year for more than two decades, while most of the world's other economies have been growing much more slowly. Measured in terms of purchasing power parity (which adjusts for price differences between countries), China now has the second largest economy in the world after the United States, and per capita incomes in the rural areas (where most people still live) have increased twenty-fold, while urban incomes are up about fifteen times. Although there are still many very poor people in China, more than 300 million have been lifted from absolute poverty to a level where they have a minimally adequate supply of food, clothing, and shelter. China's economic miracle has involved much more than growth in GDP and personal income. There has also been a profound transformation of the basic

nature of economic life in the PRC from what it had been during the Maoist era.

State and Economy

The Maoist Economy

When the CCP came to power in 1949, the Chinese economy was suffering from the devastating effects of more than a hundred years of rebellion, invasion, civil war, and bad government. The first urgent task of China's new communist rulers was the stabilization and revival of the economy. Although a lot of property was seized from wealthy landowners, rich industrialists, and foreign companies, much private ownership and many aspects of capitalism were allowed to continue in order to gain support for the government and get the economy going again.

Once production had been restored, the party turned its attention to economic development by following the Soviet model of state socialism. The essence of this model was a **command economy,** in which the state owns or controls most economic resources, and economic activity is driven by government planning and commands rather than by market forces.

The command economy in China was at its height during the First Five-Year Plan of 1953–1957, when the government took control of the production and distribution of nearly all goods and services. The Plan yielded impressive economic results, but it also created huge bureaucracies and new inequalities, especially between the heavily favored industrial cities and the investment-starved rural areas. Both the Great Leap Forward (1958–1961) and the Cultural Revolution (1966–1976) embodied the Maoist approach to economic development that was intended to be less bureaucratic and more egalitarian than the Soviet model.

For example, in the Great Leap, more than a million backyard furnaces were set up throughout the country to prove that steel could be produced by peasants in every village, not just in a few huge modern factories in the cities. In the Cultural Revolution, revolutionary committees, controlled by workers and communist activists, replaced the Soviet-style system of letting managers run industrial enterprises. Both of these Maoist experiments were less than successful. The backyard furnaces yielded great quantities of useless steel and squandered precious resources, while the revolutionary committees led many factories to pay more attention to politics than production.

The economic legacy of Maoism was mixed. Under Mao, the PRC "did accomplish, in however flawed a fashion, the initial phase of industrialization of the Chinese economy, creating a substantial industrial and technological base that simply had not existed before."[10] In addition, by the end of the Maoist era, the people of China were much healthier and more literate than they had been in the early 1950s. But for all of its radical rhetoric, the Maoist strategy of development never broke decisively with the basic precepts of the command system. Political interference, poor management, and ill-conceived projects led to wasted resources of truly staggering proportions. Overall, China's economic growth rates, especially in agriculture, barely kept pace with population increases, and the average standard of living changed little between the 1950s and Mao's death in 1976.

China Goes to Market

After he consolidated power in 1978, Deng Xiaoping took China in an economic direction far different from Mao's, or from that which had ever been followed by a communist party-state anywhere. His pragmatic views on how to promote development were captured in his famous 1962 statement, "It doesn't matter whether a cat is white or black, as long as it catches mice."[11] Deng meant that China should not be overly concerned about whether a particular policy was socialist or capitalist if it in fact helped the economy. It was just such sentiment that got him in trouble with Mao and made Deng one of the principal victims of the Cultural Revolution.

Once he was in charge, Deng spearheaded a program of sweeping reforms that remade the Chinese economy, touched nearly every aspect of life in the PRC, and redefined the role of the communist party and the meaning of socialism in China. These reforms greatly reduced the role of government control while allowing market mechanisms, such as the profit motive, to operate in increasingly large areas of the economy. They also involved a significant degree of decentralization in the economy. Authority for making economic decisions passed from bureaucrats to individual families, factory managers, and private entrepreneurs, all of them presumably motivated by the desire to make more money.

Almost all prices are now set according to supply and demand, as in a capitalist economy, rather than by administrative decree, and in most sectors of the economy decisions about what to produce and how to produce it are no longer dictated by the state. Many government monopolies have given way to fierce competition between state-owned and non-state-owned firms. For example, the government-run national airline, which was the country's only airline until 1985, now competes with dozens of foreign and domestic carriers. Reflecting a new awareness of the importance of consumer appeal, the name of the state-owned airline was also changed from the bureaucratic-sounding "Civil Aviation Administration of China" (CAAC) to the more market-friendly "Air China."

A decade ago there were over 100,000 state-owned enterprises (SOEs) in China; now there are about a quarter of that number. In 1978, SOEs generated about 80 percent of China's gross domestic product; by 2003 that figure had dropped to 17 percent. These economic dinosaurs still employ nearly 70 millions workers. They also dominate critical parts of the economy such as the production of steel and petroleum.

But even SOEs must now be responsive to market forces. Those that are unable to turn a profit are forced to restructure or even threatened with bankruptcy. Some have been semiprivatized, but many of those that remain are vastly overstaffed and have outdated facilities and machinery that make them unattractive to potential foreign or domestic buyers. SOEs also hinder modernization of key sectors of the Chinese economy and remain a huge drain on the country's banks (mostly government-controlled), which are still required to bail out many failing state-owned enterprises with large loans that are rarely, if ever, paid back. More drastic SOE reform has been stymied because the country's leaders are understandably concerned about the political and social consequences that would result from an even more massive layoff of industrial workers.

Overall, the role of the state sector in China's economy continues to shrink as private and collective enterprises (which are usually run by combinations of local governments and private entrepreneurs) are expanding at a much faster rate. The Chinese government encourages private ownership, and the private sector now accounts for more than a third of China's total GDP. In Beijing, about 90 percent of retail and service businesses are privately owned, and these employ over 70 percent of the city's workers.

The economic results of China's move to the market have been phenomenal (see Figure 1). The PRC has been the fastest-growing major economy in the world for more than two decades and even weathered, relatively unscathed, the severe financial crisis that struck the rest of East Asia in the late 1990s. China's GDP per capita (that is, the total output of the economy divided by the total population) grew at an average rate of 7.6 percent per year from 1993–2003. By way of comparison, the per capita GDP of the United States grew at

Figure 1

The Economic Transformation of China

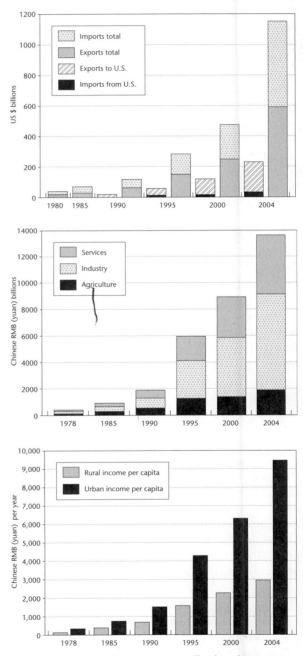

These charts show how dramatically the Chinese economy has been transformed since the market reforms introduced by Deng Xiaoping in 1978.
Sources: U.S.-China Business Council; United States Census Bureau; Xinhua; Chinability.com.

3.4 percent per year during the same period, Japan's at 1.2 percent, and India's at 4.1 percent.

A booming economy and rapidly rising incomes have unleashed a consumer revolution in the PRC. In the late 1970s, the only places people in the cities could shop for most consumer goods were at state-run stores that carried a very limited range of products, many of which were of shoddy quality. Today most of China's urban areas are becoming shopping paradises, with domestic and foreign stores of every kind, huge malls, fast food outlets, and a myriad of entertainment options. Whereas just a few decades ago, hardly anyone owned a television; now nearly every urban household has a color TV, and a large proportion of rural families have at least a black-and-white set. And cell phones are everywhere.

The PRC says that it currently has a **socialist market economy.** Although this terminology may seem to be mere ideological window dressing to allow the introduction of capitalism into a country still ruled by a communist party, the phrase conveys the fact that China's economy now combines elements of both socialism and capitalism. In theory, the market remains subordinate to government planning and CCP leadership, which is supposed to prevent too much capitalist-like exploitation and inequality.

Despite these comprehensive changes, the Chinese economy is not fully marketized. Central planning, although greatly refined and reduced, has not been eliminated altogether, and national and local bureaucrats still exercise a great deal of control over the production and distribution of goods, resources, and services. The extent of private property is still restricted, and unproductive state enterprises continue to exert a considerable drag on major economic sectors. Although the market reforms have gained substantial momentum that would be nearly impossible to reverse, the CCP still wields the power to decide the future direction of China's economy.

Remaking the Chinese Countryside

The economic transformation of China has been particularly striking in the countryside, where over 700 million people live and work.

One of the first revolutionary programs launched by the CCP after it came to power in 1949 was a land reform campaign that confiscated the property of landlords and redistributed it as private holdings to the poorer peasants. But in the mid-1950s, as part of the transition to socialism, China's peasants were reorganized into collective farms made up of about 250 families each. The land then belonged to the collective, and local officials working in coordination with the state plan directed production and labor. Individuals were paid according to how much they worked on the collective land, while most crops and other farm products had to be sold to the state at low fixed prices. During the Great Leap Forward, the collective farms were merged into gigantic **people's communes,** each made up of several thousand families. Although the size of the communes was scaled back following failure of the Leap, the commune system remained the foundation of the rural economy throughout the rest of the Maoist period. The system of collectivized agriculture proved to be one of the weakest links in China's command economy. Per capita agricultural production and rural living standards were essentially stagnant from 1957 to 1977.

The first changes in the organization of agriculture in post-Mao China came from the spontaneous actions of local leaders who were looking for ways to boost production. They moved to curtail the powers of the commune and allow peasants more leeway in planting and selling their crops. In the early 1980s, Deng Xiaoping used his newly won political power to support this trend and moved to "bury the Maoist model once and for all" in the countryside.[12] The communes were replaced by a **household responsibility system,** which remains in effect today. Under this system, farmland is contracted out to individual families, who take full charge of the production and marketing of crops. Families can sign contracts for thirty years or more, but there has been no move to privatize agriculture fully by selling the land to individuals. The freeing of the rural economy from the constraints of the communal system led to a sharp increase in agricultural productivity and income for most farm families.

But nothing contributed more to the remaking of the Chinese countryside than the spread of a rural industrial and commercial revolution that, in speed and scope, was unprecedented in the history of the modern world. Although the foundations of rural industrialization were laid during the Maoist period, **township and**

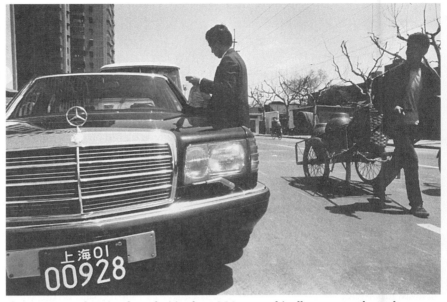

This picture, taken in Shanghai in the 1990s, graphically captures how the modern and the traditional exist side-by-side in China. It also shows how the market-style reforms introduced by Deng Xiaoping greatly increased disparities in wealth, a problem that could lead to growing social and political tensions in the future. *Source:* Dan Habib.

village enterprises (TVEs) expanded enormously under Deng Xiaoping's economic reforms. These rural factories and businesses, which vary greatly in size, from a handful of employees to thousands, are generally owned and run by local governments and private entrepreneurs, and are now attracting a considerable amount of foreign investment. Although they are called collective enterprises, TVEs operate outside the state plan, make their own decisions about all aspects of the business process, and are responsible for their profits and losses.

For much of the 1980s and 1990s, TVEs were the fastest-growing sector of the Chinese economy. But the economic Darwinism of the market caught up with the rapid expansion of TVEs by the turn of the century, and many were forced out of business. Nevertheless, there are over 20 million TVEs in China, employing nearly 130 million people and generating over 34 percent of GDP. They have become increasingly important in producing for the export market, particularly in areas such as textiles and toys.

The transformation of the Chinese countryside has not been without serious problems. Local officials who run TVEs "often behave more like business tycoons than public servants" and pay more attention to making money for themselves than to their civic duties.[13] Peasant protests, which sometimes turn violent, against high taxes, corrupt local officials, environmental desecration, illegal land seizures, and delays in payments for agricultural products purchased by the government have increased significantly in recent years.

The growth of agriculture has slowed considerably since the first burst of reform: from a high of 12.5 percent growth in 1985, it averaged a little over 4 percent per year in the 1990s and dropped to under 3 percent in the early 2000s. Agricultural output appeared to be bouncing back with an increase of 7 percent in 2004 in response to government efforts to stimulate the rural economy. Nevertheless, there is a huge gap between the average incomes of urban residents and those who live in the countryside (see Fig. 1) and farmers in

China's poorer areas have faced years of stagnating or even declining incomes. Furthermore, the social services safety net provided for China's rural dwellers by the communes has all but disappeared with the return to household-based farming and the market economy. Many rural clinics and schools closed once government financial support was eliminated. The availability of health care, educational opportunities, disability pay, and retirement funds now depends on the relative wealth of families and villages. China's controversial one-child population control policy (see "Current Challenges: China's One-Child Policy") has particularly disadvantaged poor rural families who need more household labor.

The Political Impact of Economic Reform

Efforts to transform the economy through market-style policies have had an important impact on China's domestic politics. First, both Deng Xiaoping and then Jiang Zemin faced opposition from other party leaders who believed that China was moving too fast and too far toward a market economy. The critics of reform worried about the spread of capitalist influences, including calls for more democracy, at home and from abroad. Deng was able to accommodate such challenges, and the emergence of Jiang and, more recently, Hu Jintao as Deng's successors has kept power in the hands of leaders strongly committed to continuing economic reform. But a major economic setback or widespread political turmoil could still lead to a resurgence of antireform elements in the party.

Second, the **decentralization** of economic decision making, which has been an important factor in the success of the market reforms, has also greatly increased the autonomy of subnational governments in China. Local governments often defy or ignore the central government by, for example, evading taxes or undertaking massive construction projects without consulting Beijing.

Finally, China's economic transformation has brought far-reaching social change to the country, creating new pressures on the political system and new challenges to the CCP. The party wants the Chinese people to believe that economic growth depends on the political stability that only its firm leadership can provide. CCP leaders hope that growing prosperity will leave most people satisfied with the communist party and reduce demands for political change. But economic reform has created many groups—entrepreneurs, professionals, middle-class consumers, the hundreds of thousands of Chinese students who have studied abroad—who cannot be repressed if the party wants to sustain the country's economic progress. In time, these and other emerging groups are likely to press their claims for a more independent political voice and to confront the regime with some fundamental questions about the nature of Communist power in China.

Society and Economy

Market reform and globalization of the Chinese economy have created a much more diverse and open society. People are vastly freer to choose careers, travel about the country and internationally, practice their religious beliefs, buy private homes, join nonpolitical associations, and engage in a wide range of other activities that were prohibited or severely restricted during the Maoist era. But economic change has also caused grave social problems. There has been a sharp increase in crime, prostitution, and drug use; although such problems are still far less prevalent in China than in many other countries, they are serious enough to be a growing concern for national and local authorities.

Economic reform has also brought significant changes in China's basic system of social welfare. The Maoist economy was characterized by what was called the **iron rice bowl.** As in other state socialist economies such as the Soviet Union, this meant that employment, a certain standard of living (albeit, a low one), and basic cradle-to-grave benefits were guaranteed to most of the urban and rural labor force. In the cities, the workplace was more than just a place to work and earn a salary; it also provided its employees with housing, health care, day care, and other services.

China's economic reformers believe that such guarantees led to poor work motivation and excessive costs for the government and enterprises, and they have implemented policies designed to break the iron rice bowl. Income and employment are no longer guaranteed but are more directly tied to individual effort.

Current Challenges: China's One-Child Policy

While he was in power, Mao Zedong did not see a reduction of China's population growth rate as an important national priority. On the contrary, he viewed vast amounts of human labor and the revolutionary enthusiasm of the masses as precious national assets. As a result, little was done to promote family planning in China during most of the Maoist era.

By the early 1970s, China's population had reached over 800 million, and because of greatly improved health conditions, it was growing at about 2.8 percent per year. This meant that the number of people in China would double in just twenty-five years, which threatened to put a great strain on the country's resources. Cutting the birthrate came to be seen as a major prerequisite to economic development. Since the 1980s, the Chinese government has enforced a stringent population control policy that has, over time, used various means to encourage or even force couples to have only a single child. Intensive media campaigns have lauded the patriotic virtues and material benefits of small families. Positive incentives such as more farmland or preferred housing have been offered to couples with only one child, and fines or demotions have been meted out to those who violate the policy. In some places, workplace medics or local doctors monitor contraceptive use and women's fertility cycles, and a couple must have official permission to have a child. Defiance has sometimes led to forced abortion or sterilization.

The one-child campaign, the modernizing economy, and a comparatively strong record in improving educational and employment opportunities for women have all played a role in bringing China's population growth rate to about 0.8 percent per year. This figure is *very* low for a country at China's level of economic development. India, for example, has also had some success in promoting family planning, but its annual population growth rate is 1.6 percent, while Nigeria's is 2.4 percent. These may not seem like big differences, but consider this: at these respective growth rates, it will take eighty-seven years for China's population to double, whereas India's

population will double in forty-three years and Nigeria's in just twenty-nine years!

There have been some very serious problems with China's population policy. The compulsory, intrusive nature of the family planning program and the extensive use of abortion as one of the major means of birth control have led to some international criticism, which Beijing has rejected as interference in its domestic affairs.

Many farmers have evaded the one-child policy—for example, by not registering births—because the return to household-based agriculture has made the quantity of labor an important ingredient in family income. The still widespread belief that male children will contribute more economically to the family and that a male heir is necessary to carry on the family line causes some rural families to take drastic steps to make sure that they have a son. Female infanticide and the abandonment of female babies have increased dramatically, and the spread of ultrasound technology has led to large number of sex-selective abortions of female fetuses. As a result, China has an unusual gender balance among its young population: normally, 103 to 107 boys are born for every 100 girls, but China's last census, completed in 2000, showed a gender ratio of nearly 120 boys for every 100 girls and as high as 135 to 100 in some regions. As a result, there are hundreds of thousands (perhaps millions) of "missing girls" in China's population under the age of thirty. One estimate suggests that there are 70 million more males in China than females, and some worry this has already led to "bride stealing" and other kinds of trafficking in women.

Partly in response to rural resistance and international pressure, the Chinese government has relaxed its population policies somewhat; forced abortion is now infrequent, although sex-selective abortion is not. Rural couples are now often allowed to have two children. In the cities, where there has been more voluntary compliance with the policy because of higher incomes and limited living space, the one-child policy is still basically in effect.

Workers in the remaining state-owned enterprises still have rather generous health and pension plans, but employees in the rapidly expanding semiprivate and private sectors usually have few benefits.

The breaking of the iron rice bowl has motivated people to work harder in order to earn more money. But it has also led to a sharp increase in urban unemployment. An estimated 45 to 60 million workers have been laid off in recent years. Many are too old or too unskilled to find good jobs in the modernized and marketized economy, and China has very little in the way of unemployment insurance or social security for its displaced workers. The official unemployment rate is about 4 percent of the urban labor force, but it is generally believed to be at least twice that and to be as high as 40 percent in some parts of the country. China's health care system—once touted as a model for the Third World—is in shambles. Less than a quarter of the urban population, and only 10 percent of those who live in the rural area, have health insurance. The World Health Organization ranks China among the worst countries in terms of the allocation of medical resources.

Work slowdowns, strikes, and demonstrations (in some cases with tens of thousands of participants) are becoming more frequent, particularly in China's northeastern rust belt, where state-owned industries have been particularly hard hit. In the past, the CCP has not dealt gently with protesting workers: the army was ordered to crush the 1989 Tiananmen demonstrations partly because party leaders were alarmed by the large number of workers who had joined the protests under the banner of an unauthorized union. If unemployment continues to surge, labor unrest could be a political time bomb for China's communist party-state.

Market reforms have also opened China's cities to a flood of rural migrants. After the agricultural communes were disbanded in the early 1980s, many of the peasants who were not needed in the fields found work in the rapidly expanding township and village enterprises. But many others, no longer constrained by the strict limits on internal population movement enforced in the Mao era, headed to the urban areas to look for jobs. The more than 100 million people who make up this so-called "floating population" are mostly employed in low-paying temporary jobs such as unskilled construction work. These migrants are filling an important niche in China's changing labor market, but they are also putting increased pressure on urban housing and social services. Their presence in Chinese cities could become politically destabilizing if they find their economic aspirations thwarted by a stalled economy or if they are treated too roughly or unfairly by local governments, which often see them as intruders. With another 150 million un- or underemployed rural dwellers, the floating population is expected to keep growing for years to come.

China's economic boom has also created enormous opportunities for corruption. In a country in transition from a command to a market economy, officials still control numerous resources and retain power over many economic transactions from which large profits can be made. Bribes are common in this heavily bureaucratized and highly personalized system. Because the rule of law is often weaker than personal connections (called *guanxi* in Chinese), nepotism and cronyism are rampant. Recognizing the threat that corruption poses to its legitimacy, the government has repeatedly launched well-publicized campaigns against official graft, with severe punishment, including execution, for some serious offenders, but with little effect in curbing such nefarious practices.

The benefits of economic growth have reached most of China to one degree or another. But there has also been a significant rise in inequality—a contradiction for a country led by a party that still claims to believe in communist ideals. China's market reforms and economic boom have created sharp class differences, generally benefiting people who live in the cities much more than those in the countryside. There is also widening gap between the more developed coastal regions and the inland areas, although recent poverty alleviation programs, including a "Develop the West" campaign, have brought a little economic progress to some of poorest parts of the country. The PRC government has been touting what it calls the *xiaokang* (or "well-off society") model of development, which emphasizes not only achieving a higher average standard of living, but a more equitable distribution of income and basic social welfare, including health and education.

Gender inequalities also appear to have increased in some ways since the introduction of the market reforms. There is no doubt that the overall situation of women in China has improved enormously since 1949 in terms of social status, legal rights, employment, and education. Women have also benefited from rising living standards and expanded economic opportunities that the reforms have brought. But the trend toward marketization has not benefited men and women equally. In the countryside, it is almost always the case that only male heads of households sign contracts for land and other production resources, and therefore men dominate rural economic life. This is true despite the fact that farm labor has become increasingly feminized as many men move to jobs in rural industry or migrate to the cities. Only 1 percent of the leaders in China's 700,000 villages are women. Economic and cultural pressures have also led to an alarming suicide rate (the world's highest) among rural women. Over 70 percent (about 120 million) of illiterate adults in China are female. Although China has one of the world's highest rates of female urban labor participation, the market reforms have "strengthened and in some cases reconstructed the sexual division of labor, keeping urban women in a transient, lower-paid, and subordinate position in the workforce."[14] Women workers are the first to be laid off or are forced to retire early when a collective or state-owned enterprise downsizes.

Finally, the momentous economic changes in China have had serious environmental consequences. As in the former Soviet Union and East-Central Europe, China's environment suffered greatly under the old state socialist system, but in some ways, ecological damage has become even worse in the profit-at-any-cost atmosphere of the market reforms. Industrial expansion is fueled primarily by the use of highly polluting coal, which has made the air in China's cities and even many rural areas among the dirtiest in the world. Soil erosion, the loss of arable land, and deforestation are serious problems for the countryside. The dumping of garbage and toxic wastes goes virtually unregulated, and it is estimated that 80 percent of China's rivers are badly polluted. One of the most serious problems is a critical water shortage in north China due to urbanization and industrialization. Private automobile use is just starting to take off and will greatly add to the country's pollution concerns (and demand for more oil) in the very near future.

There are signs of increasing environmental awareness among China's citizens. A large number of green groups are active on the national and local levels, and in April 2005, a protest over chemical plant pollution in rural central China turned into a violent clash between villagers and armed riot police. The government has begun to enact policies to address some of these problems, and environmental protection is another goal of the *xiaokang* model of development. However, as one journalist with long experience in China observed, "It still seems that every environmentally friendly measure is offset by a greater number of abuses" in the quest for rapid economic development.[15]

Dealing with some of the negative consequences of fast growth and market reforms is one of the main challenges facing China's government. The ability of citizen associations—including labor, women's, and environmental organizations—to place their concerns about these problems on the nation's political agenda remains limited by the party's tight control of political life and by restrictions on the formation of autonomous interest groups (see Section 4).

China in the Global Economy

Deng Xiaoping's program for transforming the Chinese economy rested on two pillars: the market-oriented reform of the domestic economy and the policy of opening China to the outside world. The extensive internationalization of the Chinese economy in recent decades contrasts sharply with the semi-isolationist policy of economic self-reliance pursued by Mao Zedong.

China was not a major trading nation when Deng took power in 1978. Total foreign trade was around $20 billion (approximately 10 percent of GDP), and foreign investment in China was minuscule, since the stagnant economy, political instability, and heavy-handed bureaucracy were not attractive to potential investors from abroad.

In the early 1980s, China embarked on a strategy of using trade as a central component of its drive for economic development, following in some ways the model of export-led growth pioneered by Japan and **newly industrializing countries** (NICs) such as the Republic of Korea (South Korea). The essence of this model is to take advantage of low-wage domestic labor to produce goods that are in demand internationally and then to use the earnings from the sale of those goods to finance the modernization of the economy.

By 2004, China was the world's third largest trading nation (after the United States and Germany), with imports and exports totaling more than $1.1 trillion, an increase of about 35 percent from just the year before. China's main exports are office machines, data-processing and telecommunications equipment, clothing and footwear, toys, and sporting goods. For many products, China dominates the world market. For example, 75 percent of DVD players and microwave ovens come from the PRC, as do over 60 percent of the world's bicycles: nine out of ten bikes sold in the United States are made in China. The PRC imports mostly industrial machinery, technology and scientific equipment, iron and steel, and raw materials needed to support economic development. Despite having large domestic sources of petroleum and significant untapped reserves, China became a net importer of oil for the first time in 1993 because of the huge energy demands of its economic boom. And in 2002, in order to meet the voracious appetite for steel generated by a construction boom and a surge in automobile production, China surpassed the United States as the world's largest importer of that commodity, even though it already produces more steel than the United States and Japan combined.

Much of China's trade is in East Asia, particularly with Japan, South Korea, Taiwan, and Hong Kong (which is now administratively part of the PRC, but is a highly developed, capitalist economy; see "Global Connection: Hong Kong: From China to Britain—and Back Again").

The United States has also become one of the PRC's major trading partners and is now the biggest market for Chinese exports (over 20 percent of the total in 2003). In 2000, China surpassed Japan as the country with which the United States had the largest trade deficit (that is, imports exceed exports) by a small margin, but as Japan continued to be mired in a deep recession, the U.S. deficit with China ($162 billion in 2004) is now larger than it is with Japan ($75 billion). This huge imbalance has become a source of tension in U.S.-China relations, particularly because quite a few Americans think that the PRC is engaging in trade practices (such as undervaluing its currency) that give

its products an unfair advantage in global commerce. Some politicians, business leaders, and labor union officials, who also believe that Americans are losing jobs because U.S. companies are "outsourcing" production to China because of its very low labor costs, are calling for the government to impose restrictions on Chinese imports. But others point out how trade with the PRC benefits the U.S. economy—for example, by bringing inexpensive goods into stores that have saved American consumers hundreds of billions of dollars over the last decade or so. They also note that China uses some of its export earnings to buy U.S. government bonds. These bonds provide the U.S. government with revenue to finance America's large budget deficit, the result of spending on the war in Iraq and tax cuts enacted by the Bush administration. If China (and other nations) did not purchase these government bonds, U.S. interest rates (including mortgages) would probably rise. Rising interest rates could result in a slowdown in the U.S. economy, which would have a ripple effect throughout the global economy.

Foreign investment in the PRC has also skyrocketed. There was literally no investment from abroad in China during the Maoist era, since letting foreigners own property, employ Chinese workers, or take profits out of the country was considered an infringement of national sovereignty and dignity. China is now the world's largest absorber of foreign direct investment ($150 billion in 2004), and more than 400 of the world's 500 top corporations have operations in the PRC. Although foreign firms generally pay Chinese workers considerably more than the average manufacturing wage of about 60 cents per hour, the low cost of labor in China is still a major attraction to investors from abroad.

Another lure to foreign investment is the huge Chinese domestic market, particularly as disposable incomes rise, and corporations, like Coca-Cola, General Motors, and Starbucks, have poured huge amounts of money into China in an effort to attract Chinese consumers. American tobacco companies are hoping that China's 350 million smokers can make up for sharply declining cigarette sales in the United States: in 2005, Philip Morris signed an agreement with a Chinese company to jointly produce Marlboros (2 billion in the first year!) to be sold in China. China is itself becoming a foreign investor, and in a sign of just

Hong Kong became a British colony in three stages during the nineteenth century as a result of what China calls the "unequal treaties" imposed under military and diplomatic pressure from the West. Two parts of Hong Kong were ceded permanently to Britain in 1842 and 1860, respectively, but the largest part of the tiny territory was given to Britain in 1898 with a ninety-nine-year lease. It was the anticipated expiration of that lease that set in motion negotiations between London and Beijing in the 1980s over the future status of Hong Kong. In December 1984, a joint declaration was signed by the two countries in which Britain agreed to return all of Hong Kong to Chinese sovereignty on July 1, 1997. On that date, Hong Kong became a Special Administrative Region (SAR) of the People's Republic of China.

Britain ruled Hong Kong in a traditional, if generally benevolent, colonial fashion. A governor sent from London presided over an administration in which foreigners rather than the local people exercised most of the power. There was a free press, a fair and effective legal system, and other important features of a democratic system. In the last years of British rule, there were efforts to appoint more Hong Kong Chinese to higher administrative positions and expand the scope of elections in choosing some members of the colony's executive and representative bodies. The British, who controlled Hong Kong for over a century, were criticized for taking steps toward democratization only on the eve of their departure from the colony. They allowed only a small number of Hong Kong residents to emigrate to the United Kingdom before the start of Chinese rule.

Hong Kong flourished economically under the free-market policies of the British and became one of the world's great centers of international trade and finance, and now has the highest standard of living in Asia outside of Japan and Singapore. Hong Kong is also characterized by extremes of wealth and poverty. When it took over Hong Kong in 1997, China, under the principle of "one country, two systems," pledged not to impose socialism and to preserve capitalism in the HKSAR for fifty years. Because of the extensive integration of the economies of Hong Kong and southern China, the PRC has a strong motivation not to do anything that might destroy the area's economic dynamism.

Although the PRC took over full control of Hong Kong's foreign policy and has stationed troops of the People's Liberation Army in Hong Kong, Beijing has generally fulfilled its promise that the SAR will have a high degree of political as well as economic autonomy. Civil liberties, the independence of the judiciary, and freedom of the press have largely been maintained.

China has, nevertheless, made sure that it keeps a grip on power in Hong Kong. The SAR is headed by a chief executive, who along with other top civil servants must be approved by the PRC. Politicians favoring democracy in Hong Kong have a strong presence in the SAR's elected legislature, but the legislature itself is relatively powerless when it comes to policymaking. In a telling example of the tug of war over the direction of Hong Kong's political future, the PRC's plan to implement a law prohibiting "any act of treason, secession, sedition, subversion against the Central People's Government, or theft of state secrets" was withdrawn in 2004 after large-scale protests by those who worry that British colonialism in Hong Kong might be replaced by Chinese authoritarianism.

Hong Kong

Land area	401.5 sq mi/ 1,092 sq km (about six times the size of Washington, D.C.)
Population	6.9 million
Ethnic composition	Chinese, 95%; other, 5%
GDP at purchasing power parity (US$)	$235 billion
GDP per capita at purchasing power parity (US$)	$34,200
GDP growth rate (2004)	7.9%
Life expectancy	81.39
Infant mortality (per 1,000 live births)	2.97
Literacy	94%
Human Development Index (HDI) ranking (value) out of 177 countries:	23 (.903)

how far the PRC has come as an economic actor in the world of states, the Chinese Lenovo Group bought the majority stake in IBM's personal computer business in late 2004. In a much more controversial move in mid-2005, the partly government-owned China National Offshore Oil Company (CNOOC) became embroiled in a multibillion-dollar bidding war with Chevron to purchase Unocal, a relatively small American company with valuable oil and gas holdings in Southeast Asia and elsewhere. Although the Chinese company eventually withdrew its offer, the episode sparked a debate in Congress and the media about whether CNOOC's efforts to acquire Unocal was another example of globalization at work and the rise of China as a major economic power or a serious threat to the energy and military security of the United States.

The admission of the PRC to the World Trade Organization (WTO) in December 2001 was another significant step in the country's integration into the global economy. The WTO is the major international organization that oversees and regulates commerce between nations, and membership in it is a great benefit to any country that engages in foreign trade. The United States and other highly developed countries agreed to admit China only after they felt that its economy was more "market" than "state" dominated and that China would play by the rules of free trade.

In agreeing to the terms of joining the WTO, China had to promise to make fundamental changes in its trade practices and domestic economic policies. Most important is the further opening of the Chinese economy to foreign investment and competition. Tariffs (that is, taxes) on imported goods must be drastically cut, and sectors of the economy that have been largely closed to foreign companies, such as banking, insurance, and agriculture, will have to be unbarred. China's state-owned enterprises, government monopolies, and rural economy will likely find this step toward deeper globalization particularly challenging, but the advantages to the PRC are an expected large increase in foreign trade and investment.

China occupies an important, but somewhat contradictory, position in the global economy. On the one hand, the PRC's relatively low level of economic and technological development, compared to the industrialized countries, makes it very much a part of the Third World. On the other hand, the total output and rapid growth of its economy, expanding trade, and vast resource base (including its population) make it a potential economic superpower among nations. Indeed, that day may have already come: In mid-2005, the highly respected British weekly magazine, *The Economist,* ran a cover story entitled "How China Runs the World Economy" arguing that "Beijing, not Washington, increasingly takes the decisions that affect workers, companies, financial markets and economies everywhere."[16] In the years ahead, China is certain to become an even more active participant in the global economy. At the same time, international influences are likely to play an increasingly important role in China's economic and political development.

Section ❸ Governance and Policy-making

The People's Republic of China, Cuba, Vietnam, North Korea, and Laos are the only remaining communist party-states in the world. Like the Soviet Union before its collapse in 1991, the political systems of these countries are characterized by Communist Party domination of all government and social institutions, the existence of an official state ideology based on Marxism-Leninism, and, to varying and changing degrees, state control of key aspects of the economy. The CCP, which has about 70 million members, claims that only it can govern in the best interests of the entire nation and therefore has the right to exercise the "leading role" throughout Chinese society. Although China has moved sharply toward a market economy in recent decades, the CCP still asserts that it is building socialism with the ultimate objective of creating an egalitarian and classless communist society.

Organization of the State

"The force at the core leading our cause forward is the Chinese Communist Party," observed Mao Zedong in a speech given in 1954 at the opening session of China's legislature, the National People's Congress, which according to the constitution adopted at that meeting, was the "highest organ of state power" in the People's Republic.[17] Chairman Mao's statement was a blunt reminder that the party was in charge of the national legislature and all other government organizations. This same line was the very first entry in *The Little Red Book,* the bible of Mao quotes used by the Red Guards who ransacked the country in the name of ideological purity during the Cultural Revolution. Although many party members became targets of the Cultural Revolution, the prominence of this quotation reflected the fact that at the height of the movement's near anarchy, Mao and his supporters did not intend to call into question the primacy of Communist rule in China.

Even Deng Xiaoping, the architect of China's economic reforms, was unwavering in his view that the country should "never dispense with leadership by the party."[18] Despite the many fundamental changes that have taken place in recent decades, party leadership remains an unchallengeable principle of political life in China, and the nation's rulers still claim allegiance to communist ideology. Any analysis of governance and policymaking in China therefore must begin with a discussion of the ideology and power of the Communist Party.

Mao Zedong is said by the CCP to have made a fundamental contribution to communist ideology by adapting Marxism-Leninism to China's special circumstances, particularly its emphasis on the peasant-based revolution that brought the party to power. Mao's ideology ("Maoism") is officially referred to in China as "Mao Zedong Thought." The party continues to praise Mao, although they acknowledge that he made serious mistakes and that some of his ideas were wrong, such as his views about class struggle that led to the Cultural Revolution.

In 1997, the CCP added "Deng Xiaoping Theory" to its official ideology to reflect the late leader's role in justifying a self-proclaimed socialist country's use of market forces to promote the growth of the economy. And in 2002, when he retired as general secretary, even Jiang Zemin's ideas (the "Three Represents") about expanding the CCP to incorporate all sectors of Chinese society, including private entrepreneurs, were enshrined in the party constitution (see Section 4).

Although the focus of Chinese communism has shifted from an emphasis on revolutionary change to economic development, most people in China have lost faith in the ideology because of the CCP's erratic and repressive leadership over the past several decades, or else they simply consider ideology largely irrelevant to their daily lives. Many of those who join the party now do so mainly for career advancement. There are numerous other sources of beliefs and values in society, such as family and religion, that are more important to most people than the official ideology. But the latest Chinese communist variant of Marxism-Leninism still provides the framework for governance and policymaking and sets the boundaries for what, in the party's view, is permissible in politics.

The underlying organizing principles of China's party-state are clearly laid out in the PRC constitution, which is a totally different document from the party (CCP) constitution.[19] The preamble makes repeated reference to the fact that the country is under "the leadership of the Communist Party of China." Article 1 defines the PRC as "a socialist state under the people's democratic dictatorship" and declares that "disruption of the socialist system by any organization or individual is prohibited." Such provisions imply that the Chinese "people"—implicitly defined as those who support socialism and the leadership of the party—enjoy democratic rights and privileges; but the Chinese constitution also gives the CCP the authority to exercise dictatorship over any person or organization that it believes is opposed to socialism and the party.

China's constitution is less a governing document than it is a political statement, and constitutional change (from amendments to total replacement) during the last 50 years has reflected the shifting political winds in China. The character and content of the constitution in force at any given time bear the ideological stamp of the prevailing party leadership. For example, the constitution adopted in 1975 toward the end of the Cultural Revolution noted prominently the yet unfinished "struggle between the socialist road and the capitalist road," whereas the current PRC constitution (adopted in 1982) was amended in 1993 to replace references to the superiority of central planning and state ownership with phrases more consistent with capitalist economic reforms, including the statement (Article 15) that China "practices a socialist market economy."

The constitution of the People's Republic specifies the structures and powers of subnational levels of government, including the country's provinces, autonomous regions, and centrally administered cities. But China is not a federal system (like Brazil, Germany, India, Nigeria, and the United States), in which subnational governments have considerable policymaking autonomy. Provincial and local authorities operate "under the unified leadership of the central authorities" (Article 3), which makes China a unitary state (like France and Japan), in which the national government exercises a high degree of control over other levels of government.

The Executive

The government of the People's Republic of China is organizationally and functionally distinct from the Chinese Communist Party. For example, the PRC executive consists of both a premier (prime minister) and a president, whereas the CCP is headed by a general secretary. But there is no alternation of parties in power in China, and the Communist Party exercises direct or indirect control over all government organizations and personnel. All high-ranking government officials with any substantive authority are also members of the CCP. Therefore, real executive power in the Chinese political system lies with the top leaders and organizations of the CCP (see Table 1). The government of the PRC essentially acts as the administrative agency for carrying out and enforcing policies made by the party. Nevertheless, to fully understand governance and policymaking in China, it is necessary to look at the structure of both the Chinese Communist Party and the government of the People's Republic of China (the "state") and the relationship between the two.

The Chinese Communist Party

The constitution of the CCP specifies national and local party structures and functions, the distribution of authority among party organizations, the requirements

for joining, the behavior expected of members, and procedures for dealing with infractions of party rules. Despite such organizational and procedural details, individual power, factional maneuvering, and personal connections (*guanxi*) are ultimately more important than formal constitutional arrangements for understanding how the party works.

For example, Deng Xiaoping, who was indisputably the most powerful individual in China from 1978 until he became physically incapacitated a year or so before his death in 1997, never occupied any of the top executive offices in the party or the government. Even when he no longer played an active role in day-to-day governance, no major decision was made without his approval, and he was regularly referred to as China's "paramount leader." The sources of Deng's immense power came from informal factors, such as his seniority as one of the founders of the regime, his *guanxi* with other key political and military leaders, and his long advocacy of now widely supported ideas about how China should develop into a strong and modern nation.

Despite the persisting strong influence of retired elders (such as Jiang Zemin) and personal connections in Chinese politics, the formal structures of power have assumed greater importance for understanding who has power and how decisions are made. According to the CCP constitution, the "highest leading bodies" of the party are the National Party Congress and the Central Committee (see Figure 2). But its infrequent, short meetings (for one week every five years) and large size (more than 2,100 delegates) mean that the role of the Congress in the party is more symbolic than substantive. The essential function of the National Party Congress is to approve decisions already made by the top leaders and to provide a showcase for the party's current policies. For instance, the party congress that convened in November 2002 was a highly orchestrated celebration of Jiang Zemin's leadership, as well as the occasion for installing Hu Jintao as the new general secretary. There was little debate about policy and no contested voting of any consequence.

The Central Committee, which currently has 198 full and 158 alternate members, is the next level up in the pyramid of party power and consists of CCP leaders from around the country who meet annually

Table 1

Who's Who in Beijing: China's Most Important Party and State Leaders Since 1949		
Leader	Highest Positions Held	Comment
Mao Zedong (1893–1976)	CCP Chairman (1943–1976) PRC President (1949–1959) Military Commission Chair (1949–1976)	Became effective leader of the CCP in 1934–1935 during the Long March, although not elected chairman of the Politburo until 1943.
Liu Shaoqi (1898–1969)	PRC President (1959–1966) CCP Vice-Chairman (1949–1966)	Purged as a "capitalist roader" during the Cultural Revolution. Died in detention.
Zhou Enlai (1898–1976)	PRC Premier (1949–1976) PRC Foreign Minister (1949–1958) CCP Vice-Chairman (1949–1969; 1973–1976)	Longtime Mao ally, but a moderating influence during the Cultural Revolution. Architect of détente with U.S. in early 1970s.
Lin Biao (1907–1971)	CCP Vice-Chairman (1958–1971) PRC Vice-Premier (1954–1971) PRC Defense Minister (1959–1971)	One of Mao's strongest supporters in the Cultural Revolution. Allegedly killed in plane crash after failure of attempted coup against Mao.
Jiang Qing (1914–1991)	Deputy Director, Cultural Revolution Group (1966–1969) Member, CCP Politburo (1969–1976)	Former movie actress who married Mao in 1939. One of the leaders of the Cultural Revolution. Arrested after Mao's death in 1976 and sentenced to life in prison, where she died.
Hua Guofeng (1920–)	CCP Chairman (1976–1981) PRC Premier (1976–1980) Military Commission Chair (1976–1981)	Became CCP chairman after Mao's death and purge of Jiang Qing and her radical followers. Removed from power by Deng Xiaoping, who saw him as too weak and a neo-Maoist.
Deng Xiaoping (1904–1997)	PRC Vice-Premier (1952–1966; 1973–1976; 1977–1980) CCP Vice-Chairman (1975–1976; 1977–1987) Military Commission Chair (1981–1989)	Purged twice during Cultural Revolution. Became China's most powerful leader in 1978 and remained so until shortly before his death.
Jiang Zemin (1926–)	CCP General Secretary* (1989–2002) PRC President (1993–2003) Military Commission Chair (1989–2004)	Former Shanghai mayor promoted by Deng a safe choice to carry out his policies after Tiananmen crisis. Consolidated his own power after Deng's death in 1997.
Hu Jintao (1942–)	CCP General Secretary (2002–) PRC President (2003–) Military Commission Chair (2004–)	Chosen by Deng Xiaoping before his death to succeed Jiang Zemin as head of the CCP. A relatively young technocrat.

*The position of CCP chairman was abolished in 1982 and replaced by the general secretary as the party's top position.

for about a week. Members are elected for a five year term by the National Party Congress by secret ballot, and there is limited choice of candidates. Contending party factions may jockey to win seats, but the overall composition of the Central Committee is closely controlled by the top leaders to ensure compliance with their policies. The Central Committee elected in late 2002 continued the trend toward promoting younger and better-educated party members who are strong supporters of economic reform.

The Central Committee directs party affairs when the National Party Congress is not in session, but its

Figure 2

The Chinese Communist Party (CCP)

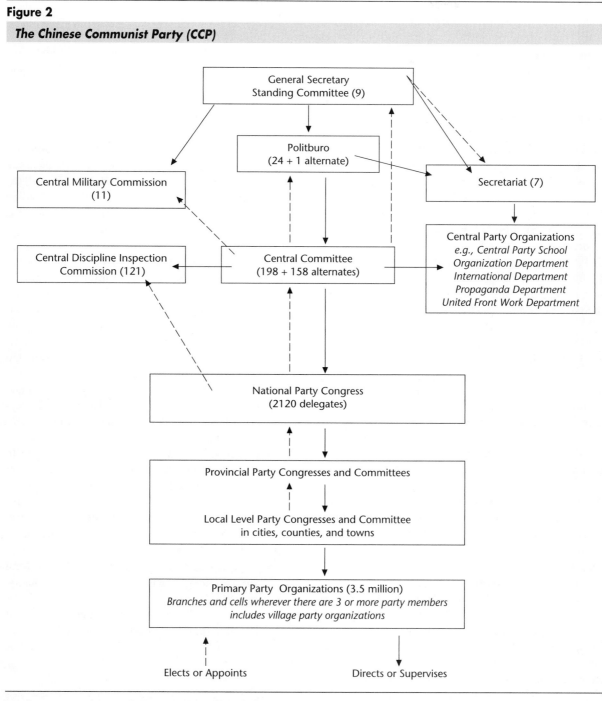

Numbers in parentheses refer to the number of members as of 2005.

size and short, infrequent meetings (called plenums) also greatly limit its effectiveness. However, Central Committee plenums and occasional informal work conferences do represent significant gatherings of the party elite, which can be a very important arena of political maneuvering and decision making.

The most powerful political organizations in China's communist party-state are the two small executive bodies at the very top of the CCP's structure: the Politburo (or Political Bureau) and its even more exclusive Standing Committee. These bodies are elected by the Central Committee from among its own members under carefully controlled conditions. The current Politburo has twenty-four members (plus one alternate), nine of whom also belong to the Standing Committee, the formal apex of power in the CCP. People who study Chinese politics scrutinize the membership of the Politburo and Standing Committee for clues about leadership priorities, the balance of power among party factions, and the relative influence of different groups in policymaking. The Politburo and Standing Committee are not responsible to the Central Committee or any other institution in any meaningful sense. The operations of these organizations are generally shrouded in secrecy. Most of their work goes on, and many of the top leaders live, in a high-security compound called Zhongnanhai ("Central and Southern Seas"), which is adjacent to the former imperial palace near Tiananmen Square. There is now a little more openness about the frequency (once a month) and subjects covered at Politburo meetings. Since becoming party leader, Hu Jintao has also regularized the practice of holding study sessions at which Politburo members are briefed on important policy issues by leading academic specialists.

Prior to 1982, the top position in the party was the chairman of the Politburo's Standing Committee, which was occupied by Mao Zedong (hence *Chairman* Mao) for more than three decades until his death in 1976. The title of chairman was abolished in 1982 to symbolize a break with Mao's highly personalistic and often arbitrary style of leadership. Since then, the party's leader has been the general secretary, who presides over the Politburo and the Standing Committee, a position most recently held by Jiang Zemin (1989–2002) and Hu Jintao (2002–present). Neither Jiang nor Hu have had the personal clout or charisma of either Deng or Mao and therefore have governed as part of a collective leadership that included their fellow members on the Standing Committee and Politburo.

Hu Jintao is said to be the core of the "fourth generation" of CCP leadership, while Jiang was the core of the "third generation." (Mao Zedong and Deng Xiaoping were, respectively, the core leaders of the first and second generations.) The transition of power from the Mao-Deng generations to the Jiang-Hu generations represents a shift from revolutionary to technocratic leadership. Indeed, both Jiang and Hu, as well as all the other currents members of the Politburo Standing Committee elected in 2002, were trained and worked as engineers before embarking on political careers.

Two other party organizations deserve brief mention. The Secretariat manages the day-to-day work of the Politburo and Standing Committee and coordinates the party's complex and far-flung structure with considerable authority in organizational and personnel matters. The Central Commission for Discipline Inspection is responsible for monitoring the compliance of party members with the CCP constitution and other rules. Recently, the commission has been used as a vehicle against corruption. In 2004, it disciplined 164,831 party members, including 15 at the ministerial level; most cases ended in some type of organizational punishment, such as demotion or expulsion from the party, but nearly 5,000 were turned over to judicial authorities for additional legal action.

Below the national level, the CCP has a hierarchy of local party organizations in provinces, cities, and counties, each headed by a party committee. There are also more than 3 million primary party organizations, called branches or cells, which are found in workplaces, government offices, schools, urban neighborhoods, rural towns, villages, and army units throughout the country. Local and primary organizations extend the CCP's reach throughout Chinese society and are designed to ensure the subordination of each level of party organization to the next higher level and ultimately to the central party authorities in Beijing.

The Government of the PRC

Government (or state) authority in China is formally vested in a system of people's congresses that begins

Former Chinese president and communist party leader Jiang Zemin confers with his successor, Hu Jintao, during a meeting of the National People's Congress in March 2003.   *Source:* © Reuters NewMedia, Inc. / Corbis.

with the National People's Congress at the top and continues in hierarchically arranged levels down through provincial people's congresses, municipal people's congresses, rural township people's congresses, and so on (see Figure 3). In theory, these congresses (the legislative branch) are empowered to supervise the work of the "people's governments" (the executive branch) at the various levels of the system, but in reality, government executives (such as cabinet ministers, provincial governors, and mayors) are ultimately subject to party authority rather than to the people's congresses. For example, the city of Shanghai has both a mayor and a party secretary, each with distinct and important power. But the party secretary's power is more consequential, as was reflected in 2001 when the popular mayor of Shanghai (himself a party member) was forced to resign as the result of a political dispute with the local party head.

The National People's Congress elects the president and vice president of China. But there is only one candidate, chosen by the Communist Party, for each office. The president's term is concurrent with that of the congress (five years), and there is a two-term limit. The position is largely ceremonial, although a senior party leader has always held it. As China's head of state, the president meets and negotiates with other world leaders. Jiang Zemin revived the practice that the leader of the CCP serves concurrently as PRC president, as Mao had done from 1949 to 1959. Hu Jintao followed Jiang's example and was elected

president of China at the National People's Congress in March 2003.

The premier (prime minister) is the head of the government and has authority over the bureaucracy and policy implementation. The premier is formally appointed by the president with the approval of the National People's Congress. But in reality, the Communist Party decides who will serve as premier, and that post has always been held by a very high-ranking member of the CCP Standing Committee. Like the president, the premier may serve only two five-year terms. Wen Jiabao, a geological engineer and a former vice premier in charge of agriculture, the financial system, flood control, and poverty alleviation, was chosen as premier in March 2003.

The Bureaucracy

The premier directs the State Council, which is constitutionally "the highest organ of state administration" (Article 85) in the PRC. The State Council is formally appointed by the National People's Congress, although its membership is determined by the party leadership. It functions much like the cabinet in a parliamentary system and includes the premier, a few vice premiers, the heads of government ministries and commissions, and several other senior officials.

The size of the State Council varies as ministries and commissions are created, merged, or disbanded to meet changing policy needs. At the height of the state

Figure 3

Government of the People's Republic of China

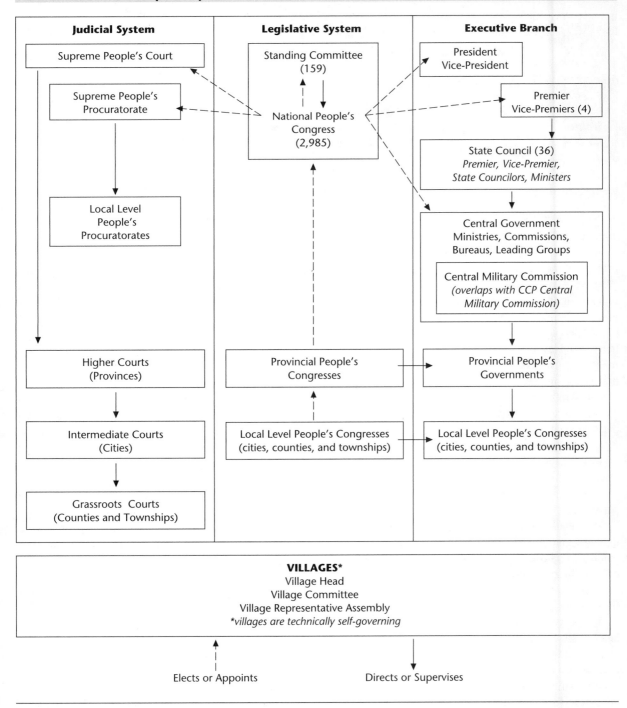

Numbers in parentheses refer to the number of members as of 2005.

socialist planned economy, there were more than one hundred ministerial-level officials. In the 1990s, there were forty ministries and commissions, and in 2003 the number was cut to twenty-eight, reflecting the decreased role of central planning and the administrative streamlining undertaken to make the government more efficient. The ministers run either functionally specific departments, such as the Ministry of Health, or organizations with more comprehensive responsibilities, such as the State Development and Reform Commission. Beneath the State Council is an array of support staffs, research offices, and other bureaucratic agencies charged with policy implementation. The work of the State Council (and the CCP Politburo) is supported by flexible issue-specific task forces called "leadership small groups." These informal groups bring together officials from various ministries and commissions in order to coordinate policymaking and implementation on matters that cross the jurisdiction of any single organization. Some groups, such the Central Leading Group on Foreign Affairs, are more or less permanent fixtures in the party-state structure, while others may be convened on an ad hoc basis, such the one that was formed to deal with the Severe Acute Respiratory Syndrome (SARS) public health crisis that China faced in 2003.

China's bureaucracy is immense in size and expansive in the scope of its reach throughout the country. The total number of **cadres** in the PRC—people in positions of authority who are paid by the government or party—is in the range of 40 million. A minority of these work directly for the government or the CCP. The remainder occupy key posts in economic enterprises (such as factory directors); schools (such as principals); and scientific, cultural, and other state-run institutions. Not all party members are cadres; in fact, most party members are ordinary workers, farmers, teachers, and so on. And most cadres are not party members, although party cadres ultimately have power over nonparty cadres. In 2001, the government announced a plan to reduce the size of the bureaucracy by 10 percent over the next five to ten years, particularly at the city, county, and township levels. There have also been substantive moves toward professionalizing the bureaucracy, particularly at the city level of government, by making more official positions subject to competition through civil service exams rather than the still-prevalent method of appointment from above.

One of the most significant administrative reforms of the post-Mao era—and one that is quite unprecedented in a communist party-state—has been the implementation of measures to limit how long officials can stay in their jobs. Depending on their position, both government and party cadres must now retire between the ages of sixty and seventy. A two-term limit has been set for all top cadres. In 1998, Premier Li Peng became the first central leader of the People's Republic to leave office at the end of a constitutionally specified term limit. But exceptions are still sometimes made for core leaders such as Jiang Zemin (born in 1926), who stayed on as CCP general secretary until he was seventy-six.

Other State Institutions

The Military and the Police

China's People's Liberation Army (PLA), which encompasses all of the country's ground, air, and naval armed services, is the world's largest military force, with about 2.3 million active personnel (down from nearly 4 million in 1989). In the early 2000s, the PRC had 2.18 active military personnel per 1,000 population, considerably smaller than the U.S. ratio of 4.70 per 1,000. The PLA also has a formal reserve of another 1 million or so and a backup people's militia of 12 to 15 million, which could be mobilized in the event of war, although the level of training and weaponry available to the militia are generally minimal. China has a Military Service Law that applies to all citizens between the ages of eighteen and twenty-two and gives the government the power to conscript both men and women as necessary to meet the country's security needs (although only males must register when they turn 18). But the military has not had to rely on conscription to fills its ranks since serving in the PLA is considered a prestigious option for many young people, particularly for rural youth who might not have many other opportunities for upward mobility.

The PRC has increased military spending by double-digit percentages nearly every year for more than a decade (12.6 percent in 2005) in order to modernize its armed forces and raise the pay of military personnel. China said that it spent $29.9 billion on defense in 2005, compared with $401.7 billion by the

United States. Many analysts think that the PRC vastly understates its defense budget and estimate that it is really closer to three times the official figures; still, China spends much less in total and vastly less per capita on military expenditures than does the United States.

The military has never held formal political power in the PRC, but it has been a very important influence on politics and policy. Ever since the days of the revolution and the civil war, there have been close ties between the political and military leaders of the CCP, with many top leaders (such as Mao and Deng) serving in both political and military capacities. One of the most famous quotes from Chairman Mao's writings, "Political power grows out of the barrel of a gun," conveyed his belief that the party needed strong military backing in order to win and keep power. However, the often overlooked second half of the quote, "Our principle is that the party commands the gun, and the gun must never be allowed to command the party," made the equally important point that the military had to be kept under civilian (that is, CCP) control.[20] Although there have been a few periods when the role of the military in Chinese politics appeared to be particularly strong (such as during the Cultural Revolution), the party has always been able to keep the "gun" under its firm command. The CCP extends its control of the PLA through a system of party committees and political officers who are attached to all military units.

There are no military officers on the party's most elite body, the Standing Committee, but two of the twenty-four full members of the Politburo are generals, and PLA representatives make up about 20 percent of the full members of the Central Committee. Nevertheless, the PLA continues to play a significant, if muted, role in Chinese politics. Military support remains a crucial factor in the factional struggles that still figure prominently in inner-party politics.

The key organizations in charge of the Chinese armed forces are the CCP and PRC Central Military Commissions (CMC). On paper, these are two distinct organizations, but, in fact, they overlap entirely in membership and function. The chair of the state Military Commission is "elected" by the National People's Congress, but is always the same person as the chair of the party CMC. The CMC chair is, in effect, the commander in chief of China's armed forces. This position has almost always been held by the most powerful party leader, for example, by Deng Xiaoping from 1981 to 1989, or his protégé, as was the case when Jiang Zemin took over the chairmanship in 1989 under Deng's auspices. Hu Jintao is the current chair of China's Central Military Commission.

China's internal security apparatus consists of several different organizations. The Ministry of State Security is responsible for combating espionage and gathering intelligence at home and abroad. A 1 million strong People's Armed Police (under the PLA) guards public officials and buildings, carries out some border patrol and protection, and is used to quell serious public disturbances, including worker or peasant unrest. The Ministry of Public Security is responsible for the maintenance of law and order, the investigation of crimes, and the surveillance of Chinese citizens and foreigners in China suspected of being a threat to the state. Local Public Security Bureaus are under the command of central ministry authorities in Beijing. In effect, then, China has a national police force stationed throughout the country. There are also local police forces, but they do little more than supervise traffic.

For people convicted of serious crimes, including political ones, the Ministry of Public Security maintains an extensive system of labor reform camps. These camps, noted for their harsh conditions and remote locations, are estimated to have millions of prisoners. They have, at times, become a contentious issue in U.S.-China relations because of claims that they use political prisoners as slave labor to produce millions of dollars worth of products (such as toys) that are then exported to U.S. and other foreign markets. China has agreed to curtail the export of prison-produced goods, but it maintains that productive work by prison inmates (common in many countries, including the United States) helps to rehabilitate prisoners and is a legitimate part of the penal system.

Public Security Bureaus have the authority to detain indefinitely people suspected of committing a crime without making a formal charge and can use administrative sanctions, that is, penalties imposed outside the court system, to levy fines or sentence detainees for up to four years of "re-education through labor." There is a special system of more than 300 labor camps for such detainees (estimated at 300,000), who include prostitutes, drug users, petty criminals, as well as some who might be considered political prisoners. But in a sign of the somewhat freer political environment, a few lawyers and scholars in China have begun openly claiming that administrative sanctions are contrary to the country's efforts to establish a fairer legal system.

The Judiciary

China has a four-tiered "people's court" system reaching from a Supreme People's Court down through higher (provincial-level), intermediate (city-level), and grassroots (county- and township-level) people's courts. The Supreme People's Court supervises the work of lower courts and the application of the country's laws, but it hears few cases and does not exercise judicial review over government policies. A nationwide organization called the "people's procuratorate" serves in the courts as public prosecutor and also has investigatory functions in criminal cases. Citizen mediation committees based in urban neighborhoods and rural villages play an important role in the judicial process by settling a large majority of civil cases out of court.

China's judicial system came under attack as a bastion of elitism and revisionism during the Cultural Revolution. The formal legal system pretty much ceased to operate during that period, and many of its functions were taken over by political or police organizations, which often acted arbitrarily in making arrests or administering punishments.

In recent decades, the legal system of the PRC has been revitalized. There are now more than 100,000 lawyers in China (by way of comparison, there are about a million in the United States), and legal advisory offices have been established throughout the country to provide citizens and organizations with legal assistance. Many laws and regulations have been enacted, including new criminal and civil codes, in the effort to regularize the legal system.

There has been an enormous surge in the number of lawsuits filed (and often won) by people against businesses, local officials, and government agencies. Chinese courts can provide a real avenue of redress to the public for a wide range of nonpolitical grievances, including loss of property, consumer fraud, and even unjust detention by the police.

China's criminal justice system works swiftly and harshly. Great faith is placed in the ability of an official investigation to find the facts of a case, and the outcome of cases that actually do come to trial is pretty much predetermined: there is a conviction rate of 98 to 99 percent for all criminal cases. Prison terms are long and subject to only cursory appeal. A variety of offenses in addition to murder—including, in some cases, rape and particularly serious cases of embezzlement and other "economic crimes"—are subject to capital punishment, which is carried out within days of sentencing by a single bullet in the back of the convicted person's head. Particularly large numbers of people are executed during the periodic government-sponsored anticrime "Strike Hard" campaigns. In 2004, China led the world in the application of the death penalty with about 3,500 executions, followed by Iran (159), Vietnam (64), and the United States (59).

Although the PRC constitution guarantees judicial independence, China's courts and other legal bodies remain under party control. The appointment of judicial personnel is subject to party approval, and the CCP can and does bend the law to serve its interests. Legal reform in China has been undertaken because China's leaders are well aware that economic development requires detailed laws, professional lawyers and judicial personnel, predictable legal processes, and binding documents such as contracts. China has, by and large, become a country where there is rule *by* law, which means that the party-state uses the law to carry out its policies and enforce its rule. But it is still far from having established the rule *of* law, in which everyone and every organization, including the Communist Party, is accountable and subject to the law.

Subnational Government

There are four main layers of state structure beneath the central government in China: provinces, cities, counties, and rural towns. There are also four very large centrally administered cities (Beijing, Shanghai, Tianjin, and Chongqing) and five autonomous regions, which are areas of the country with large minority populations (such as Tibet and Mongolia). Each of these levels has a representative people's congress that meets infrequently, and plays only a limited role in managing affairs in the area under its jurisdiction.

Subnational government organizations in China are under the supervision of both the next higher level of government and the Communist Party at their own level. For example, the organization in charge of education in one of China's provinces would be subject both to administrative supervision by the Ministry of Education in Beijing and to political control by the province's CCP committee. Such a system leads to complex and sometimes conflicting lines of authority within the Chinese bureaucracy. It also reinforces two key aspects of governance in the PRC: centralization and party domination. Nevertheless, since the 1980s, government administration in China has become increasingly decentralized as the role of central planning has been reduced and more power has been given to provincial and local authorities, particularly in economic matters. Efforts have also been made to reduce party interference in administrative work.

Despite decentralization, the central government still retains considerable power to intervene in local affairs when and where it wants. This power of the central authorities derives not only from their ability to set binding national priorities but also from their control over the military and the police, critical energy sources, resource allocation, and the construction of major infrastructure projects. A number of political scientists in China and abroad have suggested that the PRC, given its continental size and great regional diversity, would be better served by a federal system with a more balanced distribution of power between the national, provincial, and local levels of government, but such a move would be inconsistent with the highly centralized structure of a communist party-state.

Beneath the formal layers of state administration are China's 700,000 or so rural villages, which are home to the majority of the country's population. These villages, with an average population of 500–1,000 each, are technically self-governing and are not formally responsible to a higher level of state authority. In recent years, village leaders have been directly and competitively elected by local residents, and village representative assemblies have become more active in managing local affairs, trends that have brought an important degree of grass-roots democracy to village government (see Section 4). However, the single most powerful person in Chinese villages is still the local Communist Party leader (the party secretary) and the most powerful organization is the village party committee.

The Policy-making Process

At the height of Mao Zedong's power, many scholars described policy-making in China as a simple top-down "Mao-in-command" system. Then the Cultural Revolution led analysts to conclude that policy outcomes in the PRC were best understood as a result of factional and ideological struggles within the Chinese political elite. Now, a much more complex model, "fragmented authoritarianism," is often used to explain Chinese policy-making. This model recognizes that China is still fundamentally an authoritarian state and is far from being a democracy in which public opinion, party competition, media scrutiny, and independent interest groups have an impact on policy decisions. But it also takes into account that power in China has become much more dispersed, or fragmented, than it was during the Maoist era and sees policy as evolving from a complex process of cooperation, conflict, and bargaining among political actors at various levels of the system.[21] The decentralization of power that has accompanied economic reform has given provincial and local governments a lot more clout in the policy process, and the national focus on economic development has also led to the growing influence of nonparty experts and organizations in the policy loop.

The fragmented authoritarian model acknowledges that policymaking in China is still ultimately under the control of the Chinese Communist Party and that the top two dozen or so party leaders wield nearly unchecked power. The CCP uses a weblike system of organizational controls to make sure that the government bureaucracy complies with the party's will in policy implementation. In the first place, almost all key government officials are also party members. Furthermore, the CCP exercises control over the policy process through party organizations that parallel government agencies at all levels of the system. For example, each provincial government works under the watchful eye of a provincial party committee. In addition, the communist party maintains an effective presence inside every government organization through a "leading party group" that is made up key officials who are also CCP members.

The CCP also influences the policy process by means of the "cadre list," or as it was known in the Soviet Union where the practice was developed, the ***nomenklatura*** system. The cadre list covers millions of positions in the government and elsewhere (including institutions such as universities, banks, trade unions, and newspapers). Any personnel decision involving appointment, promotion, transfer, or dismissal that affects a position on this list must be approved by a party organization department, whether or not the person involved is a party member. In recent years, the growth of nonstate sectors of the economy and administrative streamlining have led to a reduction in the number of positions directly subject to party approval. Nevertheless, the *nomenklatura* system remains one of the major instruments by which the CCP tries to "ensure that leading institutions throughout the country will exercise only the autonomy granted to them by the party."[22]

No account of the policy process in China is complete without noting again the importance of *guanxi* ("connections"), the personal relationships and mutual obligations based on family, friendship, school, military, professional, or other ties. The notion of *guanxi* has its roots in Confucian culture and has long been an important part of political, social, and economic life in China. These connections are still a basic fact of life within the Chinese bureaucracy, where personal ties are often the key to getting things done. Depending on how they are used, *guanxi* can either help cut red tape and increase efficiency or bolster organizational rigidity and feed corruption.

In sum, the power of the Communist Party is the most basic fact of political life in China. Party domination, however, does not mean that the system "operates in a monolithic way"; in fact, it "wriggles with politics" of many kinds, formal and informal.[23] In order to get a more complete picture of governance and policymaking in China, it is important to look at how various influences, including ideology, factional struggles, bureaucratic interests, citizen input, and *guanxi,* shape the decisions ultimately made by Communist Party leaders and organizations.

Section ❹ Representation and Participation

The Chinese Communist Party claims to represent the interests of all the people of China and describes the People's Republic as a **socialist democracy** that it says is superior to democracy in capitalist countries where wealthy individuals and corporations dominate politics and policy-making despite multi-party politics. China's *socialist* democracy is based on the unchallengeable role of the CCP as the country's only ruling party and should not be confused with the *social* democracy of Western European center-left political parties, which is rooted in a commitment to competitive politics.

Representation and participation play important roles as instruments of socialist democracy in the PRC political system. There are legislative bodies, elections, and organizations like labor unions, all of which are meant to provide citizens with ways of influencing public policymaking and the selection of some government leaders. But such democratic elements in Chinese politics are strictly controlled and bounded by the CCP.

The Legislature

China's constitution grants the National People's Congress (NPC) the power to enact and amend the country's laws, approve and monitor the state budget, and declare and end war. The NPC is also empowered to elect (and recall) the president and vice president, the chair of the state Central Military Commission, the head of China's Supreme Court, and the procurator-general (something like the U.S. attorney general). The NPC has final approval over the selection of the premier and members of the State Council. At least on paper, these powers make China's legislature the most powerful branch of the government. In fact, these powers are exercised only in the manner allowed by the Communist Party.

The National People's Congress is a unicameral legislature. It is elected for a five-year term and meets annually for only about two weeks in March. Deputies to the NPC are not full-time legislators but remain in their regular jobs and home areas except for the brief time when the congress is in session. The size of the NPC is set by law prior to each five-year electoral cycle. The NPC that was elected in 2003 consisted of nearly 3,000 deputies. All the delegates, except those who represent the People's Liberation Army, are chosen on a geographic basis from China's provinces, autonomous regions, and major municipalities. About 73 percent of the deputies elected in 2003 were members of the CCP, while the others either belonged to one of China's few non-Communist (and powerless) political parties or had no party affiliation.

Workers and farmers made up about 18 percent of the deputies elected in 2003, intellectuals and professionals made up another 21 percent, government and party cadres accounted for a little under a third, 9 percent were from the military, and the remainder consisted of representatives of other occupational categories, such as entrepreneurs. Women made up 20 percent and ethnic minorities 14 percent of the deputies.

The annual sessions of the NPC are hailed with great fanfare in the Chinese press as an example of socialist democracy at work, but generally legislation is passed and state leaders are elected by an overwhelming majority. For instance, Hu Jintao was elected president of China in March 2003 by a vote of 2,937 for, 4 against, and 3 abstentions. Nevertheless, some debate and dissent do occur. For example, in 1992, about a third of NPC deputies either voted against or abstained from voting on the construction of the hugely expensive ($70 billion) and ecologically controversial Three Gorges dam project now being built on the Yangtze River. On very rare occasions, government legislative initiatives have even been defeated. But all NPC proceedings are subject to party scrutiny, and the congress never debates politically sensitive issues. The CCP also monitors the election process to make sure that no outright dissidents are elected as deputies.

Still, as economics has replaced ideology as the main priority of China's leaders, the NPC has become a much more significant and lively part of the Chinese political system than it was during the Mao era. Many NPC deputies are now chosen because of their ability to contribute to China's modernization rather than simply on the basis of political loyalty, and some have become a bit more assertive in expressing their opinions on various issues like corruption and environmental problems.

Political Parties and the Party System

China is usually called a one-party system because the country's politics are so thoroughly dominated by the Chinese Communist Party. In fact, China has eight political parties in addition to the CCP, but these parties neither challenge the basic policies of the CCP nor play a significant part in running the government, although they do sometimes provide advice in the policymaking process.

The Chinese Communist Party

The Chinese Communist Party has about 70 million members. The party has grown steadily since it came to power in 1949, when it had just under 4.5 million members. Only during the Cultural Revolution was there a sharp drop in membership due to the purge of "capitalist roaders" from party ranks, and many of those purged were welcomed back into the CCP after the death of Mao.

The CCP is the largest political party in the world in terms of total formal membership. But as with all other former and current ruling communist parties, its members make up a small minority of the country's population. CCP members are now about 5 percent of China's population, or about 8 percent of those over eighteen, the minimum age for joining the party.

The social composition of the CCP's membership has changed considerably in recent decades. In the mid-1950s, peasants made up nearly 70 percent of party membership. In 2002, a generic category that included "industrial workers, laborers in township enterprises, farmers, herdsman, and fishermen" accounted for only 45 percent of the CCP even though the party constitution still claims that "Members of the Communist Party of China are vanguard fighters of the Chinese working class imbued with communist consciousness" (Article 2). The majority of CCP members are not manual laborers of any sort, but are government officials, office workers, enterprise managers, military personnel, and professionals, including scientists, technical experts, and academics. In the last few years, the CCP has made an effort to get private entrepreneurs (capitalists) to join the party. This is quite a change from the Maoist era when any hint of capitalism was crushed. It is also a recognition of the increasing importance of the private sector in China's economy and a strategy by which the party hopes to prolong its rule by adapting to a rapidly modernizing society. But it will also likely change the social composition of the CCP and perhaps even lead to a gradual redefinition of the party's political role in China.

Women make up less than 20 percent of the CCP as a whole and only 2.5 percent of full members of Central Committee (and 14 percent of alternates) elected in 2002. There is one female member of the Politburo, Wu Yi, who is also a vice premier and former minister of foreign trade (and, by training, a petroleum engineer). There are no women on the party's most powerful organization, the Politburo Standing Committee.

Nearly 70 million people between the ages of fourteen and twenty-eight belong to the Communist Youth League, which serves as a training ground for party membership. Despite the fact that many Chinese believe that communist ideology is irrelevant to their lives and the nation's future, the CCP enrolls about 2 million new members each year. Being a party member still provides unparalleled access to influence and resources and remains a prerequisite for advancement in many careers in China, particularly in government.

China's Noncommunist Parties

The eight noncommunist political parties in the PRC are officially referred to as the "democratic parties," a designation meant to signify the role they play in representing different interests in the political process. This is meant to lend credibility to the CCP's claim that China is a democracy. Each noncommunist party draws its membership from a particular group in Chinese society. For example, the China Democratic League consists mostly of intellectuals, whereas the Chinese Party for the Public Interest draws on returned overseas Chinese and experts with overseas connections.

The democratic parties, all of which were founded before the CCP came to power, have a total membership of fewer than 500,000. These parties do not contest for power or challenge CCP policy. Their function is to provide advice to the CCP and generate support within their particular constituencies for CCP policies. Individual members of the parties may assume important government positions. But organizationally these parties are relatively insignificant and function as little more than "a loyal non-opposition."[24]

The main forum through which the noncommunist parties express their views on national policy is the Chinese People's Political Consultative Conference (CPPCC). The CPPCC is an advisory, not a legislative body, which according to its charter operates under the guidance of the Communist Party. It meets in full session once a year for about two weeks at the same time as the National People's Congress (NPC), which CPPCC members attend as nonvoting deputies. The large majority of the more than 2,000 delegates to the CPPCC are noncommunists, representing the "democratic parties" or various constituencies such as education, the arts, and medicine, But all delegates are chosen through a process supervised by the CCP, and a high-ranking party leader heads the CPPCC itself. CPPCC delegates are increasingly speaking out about national problems, but they do not express serious dissent from the party line on any matter. The severe prison sentences given to the activists who tried to establish an independent China Democratic Party in 1998 showed just how determined China's leaders are to prevent the formation of any political organization not subservient to the CCP.

Elections

Elections in the PRC are basically mechanisms to give the communist party-state greater legitimacy by allowing large numbers of citizens to participate in the political process under very controlled circumstances.

Most elections in China are "indirect' elections in which members of a one government body elect those who will serve at the next highest level. For example, provincial representatives to the National People's Congress are elected, not by all voters in the province, but by the deputies who are already serving in the provincial-level people's congress, who were, themselves elected by the county-level people's congresses in the province. Direct elections are most common at the village level, although there have been a few experiments with letting all eligible citizens choose officials and representatives at the next rung up the administrative ladder (the township). The authorities have been very cautious in expanding the scope of direct elections in order to prevent them from becoming a forum for dissent or a vehicle for the formation of an opposition party.

For several decades after the founding of the PRC, only one candidate stood for each office, so the only choice facing voters was to approve or abstain. Since the early 1980s, many direct and indirect elections have had multiple candidates for each slot, with the winner chosen by secret ballot. The nomination process has also become more open. Any group of more than ten voters can nominate candidates for an election, and there have been a significant number of cases where independently nominated candidates have defeated official nominees, although even independent candidates are basically approved by the CCP.

The most significant progress toward real democratic representation and participation in China has occurred in the rural villages. Laws implemented since the late 1980s have provided for the direct election of village committees, which are made up of local leaders (including the village head) who were previously appointed by and responsible to higher levels of government. These elections are, for the most part, multi-candidate and secret ballot, although they are still closely monitored by the village CCP committee. Village representative assemblies, with members chosen from each household or group of households, have taken a more active role in supervising the work of local officials and decision making in matters affecting community finances and welfare. Outside observers have been split on whether such direct grass-roots elections and the representative assemblies are seeds of real democracy in China or merely a facade designed by the Communist Party to appease international critics and give the rural population a way to express discontent with some officials without challenging the country's fundamental political organization.

Recent electoral reform has certainly increased popular representation and participation in China's government. But elections in the PRC still do not give citizens a means by which they can exercise effective control over the party officials and organizations that have the real power in China's political system. Top Chinese communist leaders, from Mao to now, have repeatedly rejected multiparty democracy as unsuited to China's traditions and conditions. In a major speech in 2004 marking his consolidation of power in the transition from Jiang Zemin, CCP general secretary and PRC president Hu Jintao said that indiscriminately copying western political systems would be a "blind alley" for China and that the "Communist Party of China logically came into the position to shoulder the historic mission of leading the Chinese people . . ."[25] There is little reason to think that this bottom-line framework for political representation and participation in China will change much in the foreseeable future.

Political Culture, Citizenship, and Identity

From Communism to Consumerism

Since its founding in 1949, the PRC's official political culture has been based on communist ideology, and the party-state has made extensive efforts to get people's political attitudes and behavior to conform to whatever was the currently prevailing version of Marxism-Leninism in the CCP. But this ideology has gone through such severe crises and profound changes during the turbulent decades of Communist rule that its future in China is seriously in doubt.

At the height of the Maoist era, Mao Zedong Thought was hailed as "an inexhaustible source of strength and a spiritual atom bomb of infinite power" that held the answer to all of China's problems in domestic and foreign policy.[26] By the mid-1970s, however, the debacles of the Mao years had greatly tarnished the appeal, to most people in China, not only of Maoism, but of communist ideology in general.

After Deng Xiaoping came to power in 1978, he set about trying to restore the legitimacy of the Communist Party through economic reforms and to revive communist ideology by linking it directly to China's development aspirations. After Deng's death in 1997, the CCP amended the party constitution to add "Deng Xiaoping Theory" to its official ideology. One key part of Deng's theory, often referred to under the rubric of "Building Socialism with Chinese Characteristics," was a major departure from Maoism in its central claim that, given China's relative poverty, the main task of the CCP was to promote economic development by any means necessary, even capitalist ones.

The other central components of Deng's ideology, which are fully consistent with Maoist theory and practice, are his so-called **Four Cardinal Principles:** upholding the socialist road, the people's democratic dictatorship, the leadership of the Communist Party, and Marxism-Leninism. In essence, then, Deng Xiaoping Theory is an ideological rationale for the combination of economic liberalization and party dictatorship that characterizes contemporary China.

In an effort to have himself placed on a historical pedestal equal to that of Deng and Mao, as he neared retirement Jiang Zemin offered his own variation on Chinese communism, the "Three Represents," which was said to sum up his contribution to the party's ideology. According to the, yet again, amended party constitution, the Three Represents depict the CCP as the faithful representative of the "development trend of China's advanced productive forces, the orientation of China's advanced culture, and the fundamental interests of the overwhelming majority of the Chinese people." This is a reaffirmation of Deng's emphasis on economic development, but it is also an ideological rationale for recruiting private entrepreneurs into the Communist Party and accommodating the many existing party members who have gone into private business (and often made large fortunes) in recent years. These so-called red capitalists are seen as the driving force in China's modernization, and the Three Represents theory is the latest ideological adaptation in the CCP's persistent claim to be a vanguard party that is best able and uniquely suited to lead the country to achieve its national and international objectives.

The CCP tries to keep communist ideology—now officially called "Marxism-Leninism, Mao Zedong Thought, Deng Xiaoping Theory, and the Important Thought of the Three Represents"—viable and visible by continued efforts to influence public opinion and socialization—for instance, by controlling the media and overseeing the educational system. Although China's media are much livelier and more open than during the Maoist period, there is no true freedom of the press. Reduced political control of the media has, to a large extent, meant only the freedom to publish more

entertainment news, human interest stories, local coverage, and some nonpolitical investigative journalism. The arts, in general, are the area of life in which there has been the greatest political change in China in recent years, in the sense that there is much less direct (but not totally absent) censorship. The Chinese film industry, for example, has emerged as one of the best in the world, with many of its directors, stars, and productions winning international acclaim.

Internet access is exploding in the PRC, with nearly 100 million users as of mid-2005 and Web connections available even in some quite remote towns. The government, worried about the potential influence of email and electronic information it cannot control, has blocked access to certain foreign websites, shut down unlicensed cyber cafés, which it likened to the opium dens of the past, and arrested people it has accused of disseminating subversive material over the Internet, including, in January 2005, a political essayist who was sentenced to five years in prison for subversion of state power and the socialist system.

Web access in China is tightly controlled by the licensing of just a few Internet Service Providers, who are themselves responsible for who uses their systems and how. A special state organization, with an estimated 50,000 employees, has been established to police the Internet, and the government is investing huge sums in developing (with technical assistance from western companies) stronger firewalls and monitoring systems. Microsoft, Yahoo, and Google have all been criticized by human rights organizations for agreeing to political restrictions on websites, news sources, chat rooms, and blogs in exchange for the right to do business in China. The Chinese party-state knows that cutting-edge technology is critical to its modernization plans—even the CCP has its own Web sites—and wants citizens to become computer literate; but, as with so much else in China, the party-state wants to define the way and dictate the rules.

Schools are one of the main institutions through which all states instill political values in their citizens. Educational opportunities have expanded enormously in China since 1949. Although enrollment rates drop sharply at the secondary school level, primary school enrollment is close to 100 percent of the age-eligible population (ages six to eleven). In Maoist China, students at all levels spent a considerable amount of time studying politics and working in fields or factories, and teaching materials were often overlaid with a heavy dose of political propaganda. Today, political study (recently with an emphasis on learning the "Three Represents") is a required but relatively minor part of the curriculum at all levels of education. Much greater attention is paid to urging students to gain the skills and knowledge they need to further their own careers and help China modernize.

Yet schools in China are by no means centers of critical or independent thinking, and teachers and students are still monitored for political reliability. In March 2005, a journalism professor at Beijing University (China's most prestigious) was fired for his public criticism of party censors, whom he compared to those in Nazi Germany. More than 80 percent of China's students between the ages of seven and fourteen belong to the Young Pioneers, an organization designed to promote good social behavior, patriotism, and loyalty to the party.

But efforts to keep communist ideology alive in China do not appear to be having much success with the younger generation. Alternative sources of socialization are growing in importance, although these do not often take expressly political forms because of the threat of repression. In the countryside, peasants have replaced portraits of Mao and other Communist heroes with statues of folk gods and ancestor worship tablets, and the influence of extended kinship groups such as clans often outweighs the formal authority of the party in the villages. In the cities, popular culture, including gigantic rock concerts, shapes youth attitudes much more profoundly than do party messages about the "Three Represents." Throughout China, consumerism and the desire for economic gain rather than communist ideals of self-sacrifice and the common good provide the principal motivation for much personal and social behavior. Many observers, both inside China and outside, have spoken of a moral vacuum in the country, which is not uncommon for a society that is undergoing such rapid, multifaceted change.

Religion, which was ferociously repressed during the Mao era, is attracting an increasing number of Chinese adherents. Buddhist temples, Christian churches, and other places of worship operate more freely than they have in decades. However, despite the fact that freedom of religion is guaranteed by the PRC constitution (as is the freedom not to believe in any religion), religious life is strictly controlled and limited to officially approved organizations and venues. Clergy of any religion who defy the authority of the party-state are still imprisoned. Clandestine Christian communities, called house churches, have sprung up in many areas of China among people who reject the government's control of religious life and are unable to worship in public. Though local officials sometime tolerate the existence of these churches, there have been numerous cases in which house church leaders and lay people have been arrested and the private homes where services are held have been bulldozed. The Chinese Catholic Church is prohibited from recognizing the authority of the pope, although there have been recent signs of a thaw between Beijing and the Vatican.

Citizenship and National Identity

China's citizens certainly have a strong sense of national identity in cultural terms. But their national identity in terms of what ties them to the state is going through a profound and uncertain transformation. Party leaders realize that most citizens are skeptical or dismissive of communist ideology and that appeals to socialist goals and revolutionary virtues no longer work to inspire loyalty. Therefore, the CCP has turned increasingly to patriotic themes to rally the country behind its leadership and goes to great lengths to portray itself as the best guardian of China's national interests. The official media put considerable emphasis on the greatness and antiquity of Chinese culture, with the not-so-subtle message that it is time for the Chinese nation to reclaim its rightful place in the world order—under the leadership of the CCP.

The party-state also does all it can to get political capital by touting its role in managing China's impressive economic achievements, winning the 2008 Summer Olympics for Beijing, and securing the return to China of territories like Hong Kong and Macao (a former Portuguese colony) that were lost long ago to Western imperialist powers. In the view of some, such officially promoted nationalist sentiments could lead to a more aggressive foreign and military policy, particularly, given the country's growing need for energy resources, toward areas such as the potentially oil-rich South China Sea, where the PRC's historical territorial claims conflict with those of other countries including Vietnam and the Philippines.

China's Non-Chinese Citizens

The PRC calls itself a multinational state with fifty-six officially recognized ethnic groups, one of which is the majority Han people. The defining elements of a minority group in China involve some combination of language, culture (including religion), and race that distinguish them from the Han. The fifty-five minorities number a little more than 100 million, or about 8.5 percent of the total population of the PRC. These groups range in size from 16 million (the Zhuang of southwest China) to about 2,000 (the Lhoba in the far west of the country). Most of these minorities have come under Chinese rule over many centuries through territorial expansion rather than through migration into China.

China's minorities are highly concentrated in the five autonomous regions of Guangxi, Inner Mongolia, Ningxia, Tibet, and Xinjiang, although only in the last two do minority people outnumber Han Chinese, who have been encouraged to migrate to these regions. The five autonomous regions are sparsely populated, yet they occupy about 60 percent of the total land area of the PRC. Some of these areas are resource rich, and all are located on strategically important borders of the country, including those with Vietnam, India, and Russia. In addition to the autonomous regions, which are the equivalent of provinces in the state structure, there are also numerous autonomous counties and other administrative units in many parts of the country where the majority or a large percentage of the population consists of ethnic minorities.

The Chinese constitution grants these autonomous areas the right of self-government in certain matters, such as cultural affairs, but their autonomy is in fact very limited, and the minority regions are kept firmly under the control of the central authorities. Minority peoples are given some latitude to develop their local economies as they see fit, religious freedom is generally respected, and the use of minority languages in the media and literature is encouraged, as is bilingual education. In order to keep the already small minority

populations from dwindling further, China's stringent family planning policy is applied much more loosely among minorities, who are often allowed to have two or more children per couple rather than the one-child prescribed limit for most Chinese.

There has been a concerted effort to recruit and promote minority cadres to run local governments in autonomous areas. But the most powerful individual in these areas, the head of the Communist Party, is likely to be Han Chinese; for example, the party secretary in all five autonomous regions is Han. Also, despite significant progress in modernizing the economies of the minority regions, these areas remain among the poorest in China.

The most extensive ethnic conflict in China has occurred in Tibet, which has been under Chinese military occupation since the early 1950s. Hu Jintao, the current president of the PRC and general secretary of the CCP, served as the party chief in Tibet from 1988 to 1992. This gives him vastly more personal experience in this troubled part of the country than any previous national leader. Some see this experience as a cause for optimism, while others are critical of Hu's record of enforcing repressive Chinese control of the region (see "Current Challenges: Tibet and China").

According to official PRC statistics, there are about 20 million Muslims in China (although some outside observers put the number at several times that). China's Muslims live in many parts of the country and are spread among several different ethnic minorities, the largest of which are the Hui (9 million) and Uyghur (8 million). The highest concentration of Muslims is in the far west of China in the Ningxia Hui and Xinjiang Uyghur autonomous regions, the latter of which borders the Islamic nations of Afghanistan and Pakistan and the Central Asian states of the former Soviet Union.

There is growing unrest among Uyghurs in Xinjiang (the more secular Hui are better integrated into Han Chinese society). The government has clashed with Uyghur militants who want to create a separate Islamic state of "East Turkestan" and have sometimes used violence, including bombings and assassinations, to press their cause. One of the reasons that the PRC became an eager ally of the United States in the post–September 11 war on terrorism was that it

Current Challenges: *Tibet and China*

Tibet is located in the far west of China on the border with India, Burma, Nepal, and Bhutan. It is a large area (about 470,000 square miles, which is nearly 13 percent of China's total area) and is ringed by some of the world's highest mountains, including the Himalayas and Mt. Everest. Ninety-three percent of Tibet's 2.6 million people are Tibetans, who are ethnically, linguistically, and culturally distinct from the Chinese. Another 3 million ethnic Tibetans live elsewhere in China, mostly in provinces adjacent to Tibet.

In the thirteenth century, Tibet became a theocracy in which absolute power was held by a Buddhist priest, called the Dalai Lama, who ruled the country with the help of other clergy and the aristocracy. Traditional Tibetan society was sharply divided between the tiny ruling class and the common people, most of whom were serfs living and working under difficult and often brutal conditions.

Tibet became subordinate to China in the early eighteenth century, although the Dalai Lama and other Tibetan officials continued to govern the country. After the collapse of China's imperial system in 1911, Tibet achieved de facto independence. However, Britain, which saw Tibet in the context of its extensive colonial rule in South Asia, exercised considerable influence in Tibetan affairs.

Shortly after coming to power in 1949, the Chinese Communists made known their intention to end foreign intervention in Tibet, which they, like previous Chinese governments, considered to be part of China. In 1951, the Dalai Lama agreed to the peaceful incorporation of Tibet into the People's Republic of China rather than face a full-scale military assault. Although some Chinese troops and officials were sent to Tibet, the Dalai Lama remained in a position of symbolic authority for much of the 1950s. In 1959, a widespread revolt against Chinese rule led to the invasion of Tibet by the People's Liberation Army. The Dalai Lama and over 50,000 of his supporters fled to exile in India, and Chinese rule was even more firmly established. In 1965, the Tibetan Autonomous Region was officially formed, but Chinese political and military officials have kept a firm grip on power in Tibet.

During the Maoist era, traditional Tibetan culture was suppressed by the Chinese authorities. Since the late 1970s, Buddhist temples and monasteries have been allowed to reopen, and Tibetans have gained a significant degree of cultural freedom; the Chinese government has also significantly increased investment in Tibet's economic development. However, China still considers talk of Tibetan political independence to be treason, and Chinese troops have violently crushed several anti-China demonstrations in Lhasa, the capital of Tibet.

The Dalai Lama is very active internationally in promoting the cause of independence for Tibet. In 1989, he was awarded the Nobel Peace Prize. He has met with several U.S. presidents (mostly recently with President Bush in September 2003), addressed Congress, and spoken widely at colleges and to other audiences in the United States. In 1999, the U.S. State Department appointed a special coordinator for Tibetan issues. The Chinese government considers these events as proof of tacit American support for Tibetan independence.

In recent years, high-level delegations from the Dalai Lama's government-in-exile have visited Beijing and Lhasa to further explore better relations. The Dalai Lama appears willing to return to Tibet and accept Chinese sovereignty in exchange for guarantees of real autonomy in managing local, particularly religious and cultural, affairs. But the PRC is fearful that his presence would incite greater opposition to Chinese rule and has rejected the Dalai Lama's offer of a compromise as a "disguised" plan to gain independence for Tibet. The two sides appear far from any agreement, and tensions between Tibetans and Chinese in Tibet remain high and potentially explosive.

allowed China to justify its crackdown on the Xinjiang-based East Turkestan Islamic Movement (ETIM), which Washington has included on its list of organizations connected to Osama bin Laden and al Qaeda.

China's minority population is relatively small and geographically isolated, and where ethnic unrest has occurred, it has been limited, sporadic, and easily quelled. Therefore, the PRC has not had the kind of intense identity-based conflict experienced by countries with more pervasive religious and ethnic cleavages, such as India and Nigeria. But it is possible that in the future, both domestic and global forces will cause issues of ethnic identity to become more visible and volatile on China's national political agenda.

Interests, Social Movements, and Protest

The formal structures of the Chinese political system are designed more to extend party-state control of political life than to facilitate citizen participation in politics. Therefore, people make extensive use of their personal connections (*guanxi*) based on kinship, friendship, and other ties to help ease their contacts with the bureaucrats and party officials who wield such enormous power over so many aspects of their lives.

Patron-client politics is also pervasive at the local level in China, as it is in many other developing countries where ordinary people have little access to the official channels of power. For example, a village leader (the patron) may help farmers (the clients) avoid paying some taxes by reporting false production statistics in exchange for their support to keep him in office. Such clientelism can be an important way for local communities to resist state policies that they see as harmful to their interests.

Organized interest groups and social movements that are truly independent of party-state authority are not permitted to influence the political process in any significant way. The CCP uses official "mass organizations" as one means to preempt the formation of autonomous groups and movements. Still, these organizations provide a way for interest groups to express their views on policy matters within strict limits.

China has numerous mass organizations formed around social or occupational categories, with a total membership in the hundreds of millions. Two of the most important mass organizations are the All-China Women's Federation, the only national organization representing the interests of women in general, and the All-China Federation of Trade Unions (ACFTU), to which about 90 million Chinese workers belong. Both federations are top-down, party-controlled organizations, and neither constitutes an independent political voice for the groups they are supposed to represent. But they do sometimes act as an effective lobby in promoting the nonpolitical interests of their constituencies. For example, the Women's Federation has become a strong advocate for women on issues ranging from domestic violence to economic rights, and the Trade Union Federation has pushed for legislation to reduce the standard workweek from six to five days. The ACFTU also represents individual workers with grievances against management, though it always does so within the context of its role as an organization whose first loyalty is to the Chinese communist party-state.

The AFCTU's relationship with Wal-Mart is a telling example of the kind of labor union it really is. The corporation (which imports more than $8 billion of Chinese goods for sale in the United States) does not allow unions to organize in its American stores, but it has agreed to let the AFCTU establish a branch in its several dozen stores in the PRC. As *The New York Times* put it, "Only in China, with its inimitable bend of Dickensian capitalism and authoritarian communism, has Wal-Mart found a union to its liking. And small wonder . . . the role of the state-sanctioned unions isn't to channel the discontent [of workers] into achievable gains; it's to contain it to the employer's benefit."[27]

Since the late 1990s, there has been a huge increase in the number of nongovernmental organizations (NGOs) less directly subordinate to the CCP than the traditional mass organizations. There is an enormous variety of national and local NGOs, including those that deal with the environment (such as the China Green Earth Volunteers), health (for instance, the China Foundation for the Prevention of STDs and AIDS), charitable work (such as the China Children and Teenagers Fund), and legal issues (for instance, the Beijing Center for Women's Law Services). These NGOs, which still must register with the government, have considerable latitude to operate within their functional areas without direct party interference *if* they steer clear of politics and do not challenge official policies.

Although the various representative bodies and other citizen organizations discussed in this section remain subordinate to the CCP, they should not be dismissed as inconsequential in China's political system. They do "provide important access points between the Party and the organized masses, which allow the voicing of special interests in ways that do not threaten Party hegemony and yet pressure the shaping of policy."[28]

Mechanisms of Social Control

While China has certainly loosened up politically since the days of Mao Zedong, the party-state's control mechanisms still penetrate to the basic levels of society and serve the CCP's aim of preventing the formation of groups or movements that might defy its authority. In the rural areas, the small-scale, closely knit nature of the village facilitates control by the local party and security organizations. The major means of control that has been used by the party-state in urban China, called the work unit (or *danwei*) system, is more complex. For most of the history of the People's Republic, almost all urban adults belonged to a work unit, and the *danwei* was the center of economic, social, and political life for most urban residents.

At the height of their influence, the work units were the source not only of a person's salary, but also of housing, health care, and other benefits. The *danwei* would hold mandatory meetings to discuss the official line on important policies or events, and its personnel department kept employment and political dossiers on every person who worked in that unit. If a person changed jobs, which often could be done only with the *danwei*'s approval, the dossier moved too. In these and other ways, the unit acted as a check on political dissent and social deviance. The *danwei* system is still in effect, particularly in economic, educational, and other organizations with official government ties, but its influence in people's daily lives is greatly diminished.

Residents' committees are another instrument of control in urban China. These neighborhood-based organizations, each of which cover 100–1,000 households depending on the size of the city, effectively extend the unofficial reach of the party-state down to the most basic level of urban society. They used to be staffed mostly by appointed retired persons (often elderly women), but now, as their functions shift from surveillance to service, many are led by younger and better educated residents, and in some places committee members are elected by their neighbors.

As Chinese society continues to change under the impact of economic reform and globalization, government control mechanisms are weakening. The growth of private enterprise, increasing labor and residential mobility, and new forms of association (such as discos and coffeehouses) and communication (for example, cell phones, email, fax machines) are just some of the factors that are making it much harder for the party-state to monitor citizens as closely as it has in the past.

Protest and the Party-State

The Tiananmen massacre of 1989 showed the limits of protest in China. The leadership was particularly alarmed at signs that a number of grass-roots organizations, such as the Beijing Federation of Autonomous Student Unions and the Beijing Workers' Autonomous Union, were emerging from the demonstrations. The success of Solidarity, the independent Polish workers' movement, in challenging the power of the Communist Party in Poland in the late 1980s was much in the minds of China's leaders as they watched the Tiananmen protests unfold. Severe repression was their way of letting it be known that what Deng Xiaoping referred to as the "Polish disease" would not be allowed to spread to China and that neither open political protest nor the formation of autonomous interest groups would be tolerated.

There have been no large-scale political demonstrations in China since 1989, and prodemocracy groups have been driven deep underground or abroad. Known dissidents are continuously watched, harassed, imprisoned, and, recently and more benevolently, expelled from the country, sometimes as a conciliatory diplomatic gesture. In late December 2002, one of China's leading democratic activists, Xu Wenli, was released and sent to the United States for medical care after spending sixteen of the previous twenty-one years in prison: he had been most recently sentenced to a thirteen-year jail term in 1998 for his efforts to organize an independent political party.

But repression has by no means put an end to all forms of citizen protest in the PRC. Ethnic protests occur sporadically on China's periphery. The biggest and most continuous demonstrations against the party-state in recent years have been carried out by the Falun Gong (literally, "Dharma Wheel Practice"). Falun Gong (FLG) is a spiritual movement that combines philosophical and religious elements drawn from Buddhism and Taoism with traditional Chinese physical exercises (similar to *tai chi*) and meditation. It was founded in the early 1990s by Li Hongzhi, a one-time low-level PRC government employee now living in the United States. The movement claims 70 million members in China and 30 million in more than seventy other countries: these numbers may be exaggerated, but there is no doubt that the FLG has an enormous following. Its promise of inner tranquility and good health has proven very appealing to a wide cross-section of people in China as a reaction to some of the side effects of rapid modernization, including crass commercialism, economic insecurity, and the rising crime rate.

The Chinese authorities, reacting to the movement's growing popularity, began a crackdown on Falun Gong in 1999. Ten thousand FLG followers responded that April by holding a peaceful protest outside the gates of Zhongnanhai, the walled compound in the center of Beijing where China's top leaders live and work. The government then outlawed Falun Gong and deemed it an "evil cult" that spread lies, fooled people to the point that they rejected urgently needed medical care, encouraged suicides, and generally threatened social stability. It is not only the movement's size that alarms the Chinese party-state but also its ability to communicate with and mobilize its members and spread its message through both electronic means and by word of mouth.

The intense suppression of Falun Gong has included destruction of related books and tapes, jamming of websites, and the arrest of thousands of practitioners, many of whom, the movement claims, have been not only jailed but also beaten (sometimes to death) and sent to psychiatric hospitals or labor camps. There have been a few small demonstrations by FLG followers in recent years, including one in Tiananmen Square in January 2001 that involved self-immolation by five believers. But, by and large, the crackdown seems to have been successful, or, at least, Falun Gong has decided not to overtly challenge the party-state for the time being.

Labor unrest is becoming more frequent in China, with reports of thousands of strikes and other actions in recent years. There have been big demonstrations at state-owned factories by workers angry about the ending of the iron rice bowl system, layoffs, the nonpayment of pensions or severance packages, and the arrest of grass-roots labor leaders. Workers at some foreign-owned enterprises have gone on strike to protest unsafe working conditions or low wages. Most of these actions have remained limited in scope and duration, so the government has usually not cracked down on the protesters and has, on occasion, actually pressured the employers to meet the workers' demands.

The countryside has also seen a rising tide of protest. In the poorer regions of the country—especially in central China—farmers have attacked local officials and rioted over corruption, exorbitant taxes and extralegal fees, and the government's failure to pay on time for agricultural products it has purchased. In areas that have tasted some of the fruits of China's economic growth, people have protested environmental damage done by factories whose owners care for little other than profit and illegal land seizures by greedy developers working in cahoots with local officials.

These protests have not spread beyond the locales where they started and have focused on farmers' immediate material concerns, not on grand-scale issues like democracy. They have usually been contained by the authorities through a combination of coercion and concessions to some of the farmers' demands. The government has lately become more open in acknowledging rural discontent, going so far as to issue a report saying that, in 2003, there were 58,000 protests in the countryside, involving more than three million people—an increase of 15 percent over the year before. However, in mid-2005, a front-page commentary published in the communist party's national newspaper, the *People's Daily,* and clearly aimed the wave of rural protest, reiterated the importance of maintaining stability above all else and warned that lawbreakers would face the full sanction of the law.

The overall political situation in China presents a rather contradictory picture. Although people are much freer in many ways than they have been in decades, repression can still be intense, and open political dissent is almost nonexistent. But there are many signs that the Chinese Communist Party is losing some of its ability to control the movements and associations of its citizens and can no longer easily limit access to information and ideas from abroad. Some forms of protest also appear to be increasing and may come to pose a serious challenge to the authority of the party-state.

Section ⑤ Chinese Politics in Transition

Political Challenges and Changing Agendas

Scenes from the Chinese Countryside

The economic and political circumstances of China's vast rural population differ dramatically depending on where in the countryside you look.[29]

Huaxi, Jiangsu Province. In many ways, this rural village looks like an American suburb: spacious roads lined with two-story townhouses, potted plants on doorsteps, green lawns, and luscious shade trees. Homes are air-conditioned and have leather living room furniture, studies with computers, and exercise rooms, and most families have at least one car. There's even a fifteen-story pagoda-style hotel to accommodate the visitors who come to see China's richest village.

Things were not always so prosperous in Huaxi. In the early 1980s, most villagers were farmers living in tiny houses and hoping to save enough money to buy a bicycle. Now the residents are entrepreneurs and investors, and have an annual per capita income of nearly $10,000 per year—more than thirty times the rural average—(plus dividends). This remarkable transformation began about two decades ago when the Maoist communes were dissolved and replaced with household-based farming. Under the leadership of a savvy leader (who was criticized as a "capitalist roader" during the Cultural Revolution), enough funds were accumulated to allow the establishments of a few village industries, and over the years these have expanded into an array of fifty-eight different enterprises, many of which are now staffed by migrants from poorer rural areas.

Nanliang, Shaanxi Province. This village is located in one of the areas known as China's Third World, where persistent poverty rather than growing prosperity is still the common lot in life. There are no townhouses here; per capita income is less than $50 a year, and most families live in one-room, mud-brick houses with no running water that they often share with pigs or other farm animals. One muddy waterhole is used for bathing—by both people and livestock. There are no paved roads. The children, dressed in grimy clothes and ragged cloth shoes, are not starving, but they do not seem to be flourishing either. Education, professional health care, and other social services are minimal or nonexistent. There is no industry, and the poor quality land barely supports those who work it. Tens of millions of Chinese peasants in villages like Nanliang remain mired in poverty and have benefited little from the country's economic boom.

Beihe, Shandong Province. This may be, in many ways, a rather typical Chinese village, nowhere near as wealthy as Huaxi nor as poor as Nanliang. Per capita income is about $600 per year, derived mostly from a number of small, privately-owned factories. Lots of residents have mobile phones and own consumer electronics. But they are worried. The local enterprises are struggling to survive fierce market competition, and the village-owned malt factory that once employed 200 workers has gone bankrupt. Many hope to revive village fortunes by leasing out land—its last remaining valuable commodity—to expanding businesses.

Daolin, Hunan Province. A few years ago, thousands of angry farmers marched on the township government headquarters to protest excessive taxes and the gross corruption of local officials. One farmer was killed and dozens injured when the police used clubs and tear gas to disperse the crowd. Shortly afterward, nine people suspected of being ringleaders of the protests were arrested. The demonstrations had been spurred by a grass-roots organization called Volunteers for Publicity of Policies and Regulations, formed to bring attention to local violations of a national law that limits taxes on farmers to 5 percent of their income. In many parts of rural China, villagers are subject to a wide range of arbitrary fees: charges for slaughtering pigs, for sending children to school, for permits to get married or to have a baby, for registering land, and for outhouse renovations—to name just a few. As a result of such local fees, Daolin's farmers were paying double the legal tax rate, which for people with an annual per capita income of only $170 was quite a burden. People were even more furious because the extra fees often went to support the wining and dining of township bureaucrats rather than for worthy local projects.

Beiwang, Hebei Province.   This was one of the first villages in China to establish a representative assembly and hold democratic elections for local officials. Among the first decisions made by the assembly was to reassign the contracts for tending the village's 3,000 pear trees. After the rural communes were disbanded in the 1980s, each of the five hundred or so families in the village was given six trees to look after under the new household responsibility system. The assembly, however, decided that it would be better to reassign the trees to a very small number of families who would care for them in a more efficient and productive manner.

The local Communist Party branch objected on the grounds that the village might lose much of the revenue that it earned from signing contracts with many households, which was used to pay for various public works projects such as road maintenance. The party was probably also concerned about the ideological implications of a less egalitarian distribution of the village's trees and the income derived from them. Nevertheless, assembly representatives were able to generate strong support in the village for their proposal, and the party branch agreed under pressure to recontract the trees to just eleven households. In a short time, pear production zoomed. The new system proved to be economically beneficial not only to the few families who looked after the trees but also to the village as a whole because of the local government's share of the increased profits.

The scenes just described make several important points about Chinese politics today. First, they remind us of the central role that China's rural areas will play in the nation's future. Most Chinese still live in the

countryside, and China's political and economic fate will be greatly influenced by what goes on there. These scenes also reflect the enormous diversity of the Chinese countryside: prosperity and poverty, mass protests and peaceful politics. It is very hard to generalize about such a vast and varied nation by looking at what is going on in only one small part of the country.

The scene from Beiwang reminds us that in China, as in other countries, not all politics involves matters of national or international significance. For many, perhaps most, Chinese, the question of who looks after the village pear trees matters more than what goes on in the inner sanctums of the Communist Party or the outcomes of U.S.-China presidential summits. The victory of the Beiwang representative assembly on the pear tree issue shows that even in a one-party state, the people sometimes prevail against those with power, and democracy works on the local level—as long as the basic principle of party leadership is not challenged.

The Huaxi scene is just one example of the astonishing improvement in living standards in much of rural China brought about by decollectivization and industrialization. But huge pockets of severe poverty, like that in Nanliang, still persist, especially in inland regions that are far removed from the more prosperous coastal regions. Most of rural China falls somewhere between the affluence of Huaxi and the extreme poverty of Nanliang. And it is in these in-between areas, such as Beihe and Daolin, where the combination of new hopes brought about by economic progress and the anger caused by blatant corruption, growing inequalities, stagnating incomes, and other frustrations may prove to be politically explosive.

Economic reform has yielded a better life and higher hopes for most of China's farmers. The CCP must now deal with the challenge of having to satisfy those hopes or risk the wrath of a social group that for decades has been the bedrock of the party's support.

Economic Management, Social Tension, and Political Legitimacy

The problems of China's rural areas are part of a larger challenge facing the country's leadership: how to sustain and effectively manage the economic growth on which the CCP's legitimacy as China's ruling party is now largely based. The party is gambling that continued solid economic performance will literally buy it legitimacy in the eyes of the Chinese people and that most citizens will care little about democracy if their material lives continue to get better.

Despite the overall success of the reforms, the Chinese Communist Party faces a number of serious challenges in governing the economy that will affect the party's political fortunes. Failure to keep inequality under control, especially between city and countryside, or to continue providing opportunities for advancement for the less well off could become a source of social instability and a liability for a political party that still espouses a commitment to socialist goals. One of the government's most formidable tasks will be to create enough jobs not only for the millions of workers who are expected to be laid off by the closure or restructuring of state-owned enterprises, but also for the ten million or so new entrants to the labor force each year. This situation will very likely be compounded by those displaced from companies that are no longer competitive in China's increasingly globalized economy.

The considerable autonomy gained by provinces and localities as a result of the decentralization of economic decision making has had important benefits for China's development, but it has also fostered a kind of regionalism that is a potential threat to the political control of the central government and coordinated national economic policy. China's communist party leaders will also have to decide how to further nurture the private sector, which is an established and dynamic part of the socialist market economy, yet still faces significant restrictions and daunting obstacles to growth. Corruption affects the lives of most people more directly than does political repression and has become so blatant and widespread that it is probably the single most corrosive force eating away at the legitimacy of the Chinese Communist Party.

Two issues—age and AIDS—illustrate the kinds of serious challenges that confront China's leaders with crucial policy choices that will have to be made in the very near future. Simply put, the age issue is that China "is unique in growing old before it has grown rich."[30] The country has a large and growing percentage of people over sixty-five and, because of its stringent population control policy, a shrinking percentage of working age population (sixteen to sixty-four). Most countries don't experience this kind of demographic "graying"

until they are much more affluent than China is or will be for several decades. The bottom line is that there is an urgent need for the government to plan for much better pension and senior citizen health care programs than are currently in place.

The spread of AIDS in China has the potential to turn into a major crisis. Recent surveys estimate the number of infected citizens to be between 850,000 and 1 million. Unless the current infection rate is slowed, predictions are that there could be 10 million AIDS victims in China by 2010.

AIDS first spread in China in the early 1990s among needle-sharing heroin users, mostly in the border regions of the west and southwest. It has since spread to all areas of the country through injecting drugs with contaminated needles and sexual activity, particularly prostitution. There was also an extensive outbreak of AIDS in several provinces among blood donors and their families. In these cases, poor farmers had sold their blood for cash at unscrupulous and unsafe collection stations run by local "entrepreneurs," doctors, and officials. Some villages in Henan province have an HIV infection rate of over 60 percent of the population.

The government has recently taken active steps to deal with the situation, including new laws regulating the blood supply, increased funding for AIDS prevention, support for AIDS awareness campaigns, improved access to cheaper drugs, and cooperation with international organizations. The premier, Wen Jiabao, made a well-publicized visit to AIDS patients in a Beijing hospital in December 2003 that reflected an unprecedented level of official acknowledgement of the disease. But responding effectively to AIDS will require concerted action on the national and local levels and the involvement of nongovernmental organizations and experts best equipped to address the root causes of the looming epidemic. As one authoritative article observed, "There are few countries in the world with a comparable level of governmental infrastructure and control, or that have experienced such steady and dynamic economic growth. China must muster the political will and resources to prevent this progress from quickly unraveling as a result of AIDS."[31]

A comparative study by the World Bank that was published in May 2005 concluded that China's "governance"—a composite category measuring corruption, government accountability and effectiveness, political stability, rule of law, and market-friendly policies—had actually declined in recent years.[32] Clearly, the leaders of the PRC will have to make some difficult policy choices in deciding how to manage China's rapidly modernizing economy and respond to its radically changing society.

China and the Democratic Idea

China has evolved in recent decades toward a system of what has been called "Market-Leninism," a combination of increasing economic openness and continuing political rigidity under the leadership of a ruling party that adheres to a remodeled version of communist ideology.[33] The major political challenges now facing the CCP and the country emerge from the sharpening contradictions and tensions of this hybrid system.

In the short run, the CCP's gamble that the country's economic boom would divert the attention of most Chinese from politics to profits has paid off. However, as the people of China become more secure economically, better educated, and more aware of the outside world, they are likely to become politically less quiescent. The steadily expanding class of private entrepreneurs may want political clout to match their economic wealth. Scholars, scientists, and technology specialists may become more outspoken about the limits on intellectual freedom. And the many Chinese citizens who travel or study abroad may find the political gap between their party-state and the world's growing number of democracies to be increasingly intolerable.

There are reasons to be both optimistic and pessimistic about the future of the democratic idea in China.[34] On the negative side, China's long history of bureaucratic and authoritarian rule and the hierarchical values of still-influential Confucian culture seem to be mighty counterweights to democracy. And although its political legitimacy may be weak and some aspects of its social control have broken down, the coercive power of China's communist party-state remains formidable. The PRC's relatively low per capita standard of living, a largely rural population and vast areas of extreme poverty, and state-dominated media and means of communications also impose some impediments to democratization. Finally, many in China are apathetic about politics or fearful of the violence and chaos that radical political change might unleash.

On the positive side, the impressive success of democratization in Taiwan in the past decade, including free and fair multiparty elections from the local level up to the presidency, strongly suggests that the values, institutions, and process of democracy are not incompatible with Confucian culture. And though it is still a developing country, China has a higher literacy rate, more extensive industrialization and urbanization, a faster rate of economic growth, and a larger middle class than most countries at its level of economic development—conditions widely seen by social scientists as favorable to democracy.

Despite the CCP's continuing tight hold on power, there have been a number of significant political changes in China that could be planting the seeds of democracy: the decentralization of political and economic power to local governments; the setting of a mandatory retirement age and term limits for all officials; the coming to power of younger, better educated, and more worldly leaders; the increasingly important role of the National People's Congress in the policymaking process; the introduction of competitive elections in rural villages; the strengthening and partial depoliticization of the legal system; tolerance of a much wider range of artistic, cultural, and religious expression; and the important freedom (unheard of in the Mao era) for individuals to be apolitical.

Furthermore, the astounding spread of the democratic idea around the globe has created a trend that will be increasingly difficult for China's leaders to resist. The PRC has become a major player in the world of states, and its government must be more responsive to international opinion in order to continue the country's deepening integration with the international economy and growing stature as a responsible and mature global power.

One of the most important political trends in China has been the resurgence of **civil society,** a sphere of independent public life and citizen association, which, if allowed to thrive and expand, could provide fertile soil for future democratization. The development of civil society among workers in Poland and intellectuals in Czechoslovakia, for example, played an important role in the collapse of communism in East-Central Europe in the late 1980s by weakening the critical underpinnings of party-state control.

The Tiananmen demonstrations of 1989 reflected the stirrings of civil society in post-Mao China. But the brutal crushing of that movement showed the CCP's determination to thwart the growth of civil society before it could seriously challenge Communist authority. But as economic modernization and social liberalization have deepened in the PRC, civil society has begun to stir again. Some stirrings, like the Falun Gong movement, have met with vicious repression by the party-state. But others, such as the proliferation and growing influence of nongovernmental organizations, have been encouraged by the authorities. Academic journals and conferences have recently had surprisingly open, if tentative, discussions about future political options for China, including multiparty democracy.

At some point, the leaders of the CCP will face the fundamental dilemma of whether to accommodate or, as they have done so often in the past, suppress organizations, individuals, and ideas that question the principle of party leadership. Accommodation would require the party-state to cede some of its control over society and allow more meaningful citizen representation and participation. But repression would likely derail the country's economic dynamism and could have terrible costs for China.

Chinese Politics in Comparative Perspective

As mentioned at the end of Section 1, students of comparative politics should find it particularly interesting to compare China with other nations from two perspectives. First, the People's Republic of China can be compared with other communist party-states with which it shares or has shared many political characteristics. Second, China can be compared with other developing nations that face similar economic and political challenges.

China as a Communist Party-State

Why has the Chinese communist party-state been more durable than other regimes of its type? The PRC's successful economic restructuring and the rapidly rising living standard of most of the people have saved the CCP from the kinds of economic crises that greatly weakened other Communist systems, including the Soviet Union. China's leaders believe that one of the biggest mistakes made by the last Soviet party chief, Mikhail Gorbachev, was that he went too far with political reform and not far enough with economic change, and they are convinced that their reverse formula is a key reason that they have not suffered the same fate.

The fact that the Chinese Communists won power through an indigenous revolution with widespread popular backing and did not depend on foreign military support for their victory also sets China apart from the situation of most of the now-deposed East-Central European communist parties. Although repression and corruption may be harming the popularity of the CCP, the party still has a deep reservoir of historical legitimacy among large segments of the population.

But China also has many things in common with other past and present communist party-states, including the basic features of what has been often called its totalitarian political system. **Totalitarianism** (a term also applied to fascist regimes such as Nazi Germany) describes a system in which the ruling party prohibits all forms of meaningful political opposition and dissent, insists on obedience to a single state-determined ideology, and enforces its rule through coercion and terror. Such regimes also seek to bring all spheres of public activity (including the economy and culture) and even many parts of its citizens' private lives (including reproduction) under the total control of the party-state in the effort to modernize the country and, indeed, to transform human nature. Maoist China was, in many ways, a classic totalitarian political system.

China offers an interesting comparative perspective on the nature of change in totalitarian systems. Partly because of their inflexibility, totalitarian regimes in Russia and East-Central Europe collapsed quickly and thoroughly, to be replaced by democracies in the 1990s. The CCP appears to be trying to save communist rule in China by abandoning or at least moderating many, if not all, of its totalitarian features. In order to promote economic development, the CCP has relaxed its grip on many areas of life, and citizens are now free to pursue their interests without state interference as long as they steer clear of sensitive political issues.

In this sense, the PRC has evolved from totalitarianism toward a less intrusive, but still dictatorial, "consultative authoritarian regime" that "increasingly recognizes the need to obtain information, advice, and support from key sectors of the population, but insists on suppressing dissent . . . and maintaining ultimate political power in the hands of the Party."[35] Thus, China seems, at least for the moment, to be going through a type of post-totalitarian transition characterized by bold economic and social reform that may, in time, nurture a transition to democracy, but that so far has helped sustain a still dictatorial political system.

China as a Third World State

The record of communist rule in China raises many issues about the role of the state in economic development. It also provides an interesting comparative perspective on the complex relationship between economic and political change in the Third World.

When the Chinese Communist Party came to power in 1949, China was a desperately poor country, with an economy devastated by a century of civil strife and world war. It was also in a weak and subordinate position in the post–World War II international order. Measured against this starting point, the PRC has made remarkable progress in improving the well-being of its citizens, building a strong state, and enhancing the country's global role.

Why has China been more successful than so many other nations in meeting some of major challenges of development? Third World governments have often served narrow class or foreign interests more than the national interest. Many political leaders in Africa, Asia, and Latin America have been a drain on development rather than a stimulus. The result is that Third World states have many times become defenders of a status quo built on extensive inequality and poverty rather than agents of needed change. In contrast, the PRC's recent rulers have been quite successful in creating what social scientists call a **developmental state,** in which government power and public policy are used effectively to promote national economic growth.

Whereas much of the Third World seems to be heading toward democracy without development—or at best very slow development—China seems to be following the reverse course of very fast development without democracy. There is a sharp and disturbing contrast between the harsh political rule of the Chinese communist party-state and its remarkable accomplishments in improving the material lives of the Chinese people. This contrast is at the heart of what one journalist has called the "riddle of China" today, where the government "fights leprosy as aggressively as it attacks dissent. It inoculates infants with the same fervor with which it arrests its critics. Partly as a result, a baby born in Shanghai now has a longer life expectancy than a baby born in New York City."[36] This "riddle" makes it difficult to settle on a clear evaluation of the overall record of Communist rule in China, particularly in the post-Mao era. It also makes it hard to predict the future of the Chinese Communist Party, since the regime's economic achievements could provide it with the support, or at least compliance, it needs to stay in power despite its serious political shortcomings.

The CCP's tough stance on political reform is in large part based on its desire for self-preservation. But in keeping firm control on political life while allowing the country to open up in other important ways, Chinese Communist Party leaders also believe they are wisely following the model of development pioneered by the newly industrializing countries (NICs) of East Asia such as South Korea, Taiwan, and Singapore.

The lesson that the CCP draws from the NIC experience is that only a strong "neoauthoritarian" government can provide the political stability and social peace required for rapid economic growth. According to this view, democracy—with its open debates about national priorities, political parties contesting for power, and interest groups squabbling over how to divide the economic pie—is a recipe for chaos, particularly in a huge and still relatively poor country But another of the lessons from the East Asian NICs—one that most Chinese leaders have been reluctant to acknowledge so far—is that economic development, social modernization, and global integration also create powerful pressures for political change from below and abroad. In both Taiwan and South Korea, authoritarian governments that had presided over economic miracles in the 1960s and 1970s gave way in the 1980s and 1990s to the democracy, largely in response to domestic demands.

China's dynamic economic expansion and social transformation over the last twenty-five years suggest that the PRC is in the early stages of a period of growth and modernization that will lead it to NIC status. However, in terms of the extent of industrialization, per capita income, the strength of the private sector of the economy, and the size of the middle and professional classes, China's development is still far below the level at which democracy succeeded in Taiwan and South Korea. Before concluding that the China's communist rulers will soon yield to the forces of modernization, it is important to remember that "authoritarian governments in East Asia pursued market-driven economic growth for decades without relaxing their hold on political power."[37]

Nevertheless, economic reform in China has already created groups and processes, interests and ideas that are likely to evolve as sources of pressure for more and faster political change. And the experience of the NICs and other developing countries suggests that such pressures will intensify as the economy and society continue to modernize. Therefore, at some point in the not-too-distant future, the Chinese Communist Party may again face the challenge of the democratic idea. How China's new generation of leaders responds to this challenge is perhaps the most important and uncertain question about Chinese politics in the early twenty-first century.

Key Terms

communist party-state
Marxism-Leninism
autonomous regions
guerrilla warfare
collectivization
socialism
Hundred Flowers Movement
Anti-Rightist Campaign
Great Leap Forward
communism
Great Proletarian Cultural Revolution
revisionism
command economy
socialist market economy
people's communes
household responsibility system
township and village enterprises
decentralization
iron rice bowl
guanxi
newly industrializing countries
cadres
nomenklatura
socialist democracy
Four Cardinal Principles
danwei
civil society
totalitarianism
developmental state

Suggested Readings

Bernstein, Thomas P., and Xiaobo Lü. *Taxation Without Representation in Contemporary Rural China.* Cambridge: Cambridge University Press, 2003.

Blecher, Marc J. *China Against the Tides: Restructuring Through Revolution, Radicalism, and Reform.* 2nd ed. New York: Continuum, 2003.

Chang, Jung, and Jon Halliday, *Mao: The Unknown Story.* New York: Random House, 2005.

Chang, Jung. *Wild Swans: Three Daughters of China.* New York: Simon & Schuster, 1996.

Dickson, Bruce J. *Red Capitalists in China: The Party, Private Entrepreneurs, and Prospects for Political Change.* Cambridge, Mass.: Cambridge University Press, 2003.

Gao Yuan. *Born Red: A Chronicle of the Cultural Revolution.* Stanford, Calif.: Stanford University Press, 1987.

Goldman, Merle. *From Comrade to Citizen: The Struggle for Political Rights in China.* Cambridge: Harvard University Press, 2005.

Gries, Peter Hays. *China's New Nationalism: Pride, Politics, and Diplomacy.* Berkeley: University of California Press, 2004.

Hutchings, Graham. *Modern China: A Guide to a Century of Change.* Cambridge: Harvard University Press, 2001.

Judd, Ellen R. *The Chinese Women's Movement Between State and Market.* Stanford, Calif.: Stanford University Press, 2002.

Kraus, Richard Curt. *The Party and the Arty in China: The New Politics of Culture.* Lanham, Md.: Rowman & Littlefield Publishers, 2004.

Lampton, David M. *Same Bed, Different Dreams: Managing U.S.-China Relations, 1989–2000.* Berkeley: University of California Press, 2001.

Lardy, Nicholas R. *Integrating China into the Global Economy.* Washington, D.C.: Brookings Institution Press, 2002.

Lieberthal, Kenneth. *Governing China: From Revolution to Reform.* 2nd ed. New York: W.W. Norton, 2003.

MacFarquhar, Roderick, ed. *The Politics of China: The Eras of Mao and Deng.* 2nd ed. Cambridge: Cambridge University Press, 1998.

Perry, Elizabeth J. *Challenging the Mandate of Heaven: Social Protest and State Power in China.* Armonk, N.Y.: M. E. Sharpe, 2002.

Saich, Tony. *Governance and Politics of China.* 2nd ed. New York: Palgrave Macmillan, 2004.

Solinger, Dorothy J. *Contesting Citizenship in Urban China: Peasant Migrants, the State, and the Logic of the Market.* Berkeley: University of California Press, 1999.

Spence, Jonathan. *Mao Zedong.* New York: Viking, 1999.

Spence, Jonathan D., and Annping Chin. *The Chinese Century: A Photographic History of the Last Hundred Years.* New York: Random House, 1996.

Unger, Jonathan. *The Transformation of Rural China.* Armonk, N.Y.: M. E. Sharpe, 2002.

Suggested Websites

China Links, Professor William A. Joseph, Wellesley College
www.wellesley.edu/Polisci/wj/China/chinalinks.html
Embassy of the People's Republic of China in the United States
www.china-embassy.org
Finding News About China
www.chinanews.bfn.org
PRC China Internet Information Center
www.china.org.cn
China Leadership Monitor
www.chinaleadershipmonitor.org

Endnotes

[1] "Beijing Win Divides World Opinion," CNN.com, http://www.cnn.com/2001/WORLD/asiapcf/east/07/13/beijing.win/.

[2] Mao Zedong, "Report on an Investigation of the Peasant Movement in Hunan," March 1927, in *Selected Readings from the Works of Mao Tsetung* (Beijing: Foreign Languages Press, 1971), 24.

[3] Maurice Meisner, *Mao's China and After: A History of the People's Republic*, 3rd ed. (New York: Free Press, 1999), 183.

[4] David Bachman, *Bureaucracy, Economy, and Leadership in China: The Institutional Origins of the Great Leap Forward* (Cambridge: Cambridge University Press, 1991), 2.

[5] Fareed Zakaria, "The Big Story Everyone Missed," *Newsweek*, December 30, 2002, 52.

[6] Interview on MSNBC "The Wall Street Journal Report with Maria Bartiromo," November 13, 2004, at http://www.state.gov/secretary/former/powell/remarks/38165.htm; U.S. Department of State, "Rice, Chinese Leaders Stress Constructive, Growing Relationship," March 20, 2005, at http://usinfo.state.gov/eap/Archive/2005/Mar/20-527426.html.

[7] "Rumsfeld issues a sharp rebuke to China on arms," *The New York Times*, June 4, 2005, p. A1; United States Department of Defense, Annual Report to Congress, *The Military Power of the People's Republic of China, 2005*, at http://www.defenselink.mil/news/Jul2005/d20050719china.pdf.

[8] See, for example, "When China Wakes," *Economist*, November 28, 1992; and Nicholas D. Kristof and Sheryl WuDunn, *China Wakes: The Struggle for the Soul of a Rising Power* (New York: Time Books, 1994).

[9] "When China Wakes," 3, 15.

[10] Barry Naughton, "The Pattern and Legacy of Economic Growth in the Mao Era," in Kenneth Lieberthal et al. (eds.), *Perspectives on Modern China: Four Anniversaries* (Armonk, N.Y.: M. E. Sharpe, 1991), 250.

[11] Deng Xiaoping first expressed his "cat theory" in 1962 in a speech, "Restore Agricultural Production," in the aftermath of the failure and famine of the Great Leap Forward. In the original speech, he actually quoted an old peasant proverb that refers to a "yellow cat or a black cat," but it is most often rendered "white cat or black cat." See *Selected Works of Deng Xiaoping (1938–1965)* (Beijing: Foreign Languages Press, 1992), 293.

[12] Kathleen Hartford, "Socialist Agriculture Is Dead; Long Live Socialist Agriculture! Organizational Transformation in Rural China," in Elizabeth J. Perry and Christine P. W. Wong (eds.), *The Political Economy of Reform in Post-Mao China* (Cambridge: Council on East Asian Studies, Harvard University, 1985), 55.

[13] Christine P. W. Wong, "China's Economy: The Limits of Gradualist Reform," in William A. Joseph (ed.), *China Briefing, 1994* (Boulder, Colo.: Westview Press, 1994), 50.

[14] Emily Honig and Gail Herschatter, *Personal Voices: Chinese Women in the 1980s* (Stanford, Calif.: Stanford University Press, 1988), 337.

[15] Jasper Becker, "China's Growing Pains," *National Geographic*, March 2004, p. 81.

[16] *The Economist*, July 28, 2005, p. 61.

[17] Mao Zedong, "Strive to Build a Great Socialist Country," September 15, 1954, in *Selected Works of Mao Tsetung*, vol. 5 (Beijing: Foreign Languages Press, 1977), 149.

[18] Deng Xiaoping, "Uphold the Four Cardinal Principles," March 30, 1979, in *Selected Works of Deng Xiaoping (1977–1982)* (Beijing: Foreign Languages Press, 1984), 178.

[19] The constitution of the People's Republic of China can be found on line at the website of the *People's Daily*, http://english.people.com.cn/constitution/constitution.html. The full text of the constitution of the Chinese Communist Party can be found at the website of the International Department of the CCP at: http://www.idcpc.org.cn/english/cpcbrief/constitution.htm.

[20] Mao Zedong, "Problems of War and Strategy," November 6, 1938, in *Selected Works of Mao Tsetung*, vol. 2 (Beijing: Foreign Languages Press, 1972), 224.

[21] Kenneth Lieberthal and David Michael Lampton (eds.), *Bureaucracy, Politics, and Decision-Making in Post-Mao China* (Berkeley: University of California Press, 1992).

[22] John P. Burns, *The Chinese Communist Party's Nomenklatura System: A Documentary Study of Party Control of Leadership Selection, 1979–1984* (Armonk, N.Y.: M. E. Sharpe, 1989), ix–x.

[23] Gordon White, *Riding the Tiger: The Politics of Economic Reform in Post-Mao China* (Palo Alto, Calif.: Stanford University Press, 1993), 20.

[24]James D. Seymour, *China's Satellite Parties* (Armonk, N.Y.: M. E. Sharpe, 1987), 87.

[25]"Copying Western Political Systems Would Lead to Blind Alley for China: Chinese President," *People's Daily,* September 15, 2004, http://english.people.com.cn/200409/15/eng20040915_157076.html.

[26]Lin Biao, "Foreword to the Second Edition," *Quotations from Chairman Mao Tse-tung* (Beijing: Foreign Languages Press, 1967), iii.

[27]Harold Meyerson, "Wal-Mart Loves Unions (In China)," *The New York Times*, December 1, 2004. I would like to thank my student, Michele Park, for drawing my attention to this example and article.

[28]James R. Townsend and Brantly Womack, *Politics in China,* 3rd ed. (Boston: Little, Brown, 1986), 271.

[29]The following scenes are extrapolated from Jonathan Watts, "In China's richest village," *The Guardian*, May 10, 2005; Wang Zhe, "Behind the Dream of a Village," *Beijing Review,* June 14, 2001, 13–16; Lu Xueyi, "The Peasants Are Suffering, the Villages Are Very Poor," *Dushu* (Readings), January 2001, in U.S. Embassy (Beijing, China), PRC Press Clippings, http:// www.usembassy-china.org.cn/sandt/peasantsuffering.html); Hannah Beech, "In Rural China, It's a Family Affair" Time/Asia, May 27, 2002; "The Silent Majority: A Rare Look inside a Chinese Village," *The Economist*, April 7, 2005; Erik Eckholm, "Heated Protests by Its Farmers Trouble Beijing," *New York Times,* February 1, 1999, A; Susan V. Lawrence, "Democracy, Chinese-Style: Village Representative Assemblies," *Australian Journal of Chinese Affairs,* no. 32 (July 1994): 61–68.

[30]*The Economist,* "A Survey of India and China," March 3, 2005.

[31]Joan Kaufman and Jun Jing, "China and AIDS—The Time to Act Is Now," *Science,* June 28, 2002, 2340.

[32]D. Kaufmann, A. Kraay, and M. Mastruzzi, *Governance Matters IV: Governance Indicators for 1996–2004.* (Washington, D.C.: The World Bank), 2004. Available at: http://www.worldbank.org/wbi/governance/pubs/govmatters4.html.

[33]Nicholas D. Kristof, "China Sees 'Market-Leninism' as Way to Future," *New York Times,* September 6, 1993, 1, 5.

[34]Many of the points in this section are based on Martin King Whyte, "Prospects for Democratization in China," *Problems of Communism* (May–June 1992): 58–69; Michel Oksenberg, "Will China Democratize? Confronting a Classic Dilemma," *Journal of Democracy* 9, no. 1 (January 1998): 27–34; and Minxin Pei, "Is China Democratizing?" *Foreign Affairs* 77, no. 1 (January– February 1998), 68–82.

[35]Harry Harding, *China's Second Revolution: Reform After Mao* (Washington, D.C.: Brookings Institution, 1987), 200.

[36]Nicholas D. Kristof, "Riddle of China: Repression as Standard of Living Soars," *New York Times,* September 7, 1993, A1, A10.

[37]Nicholas Lardy, "Is China Different? The Fate of Its Economic Reform," in Daniel Chirot (ed.), *The Crisis of Leninism and the Decline of the Left* (Seattle: University of Washington Press, 1991), 147.

CHAPTER 3

India

Atul Kohli and Amrita Basu

Republic of India

Land and People

Capital	New Delhi
Total area (square miles)	1,269,338 (slightly more than one-third the size of the U.S.)
Population	1.08 billion

Annual population growth rate (%)	1975–2002	1.9
	2003–2015	1.3

Urban population (%)	30	
Major languages* (%)	Hindi	40
	Telugu	8
	Bengali	8
	Marathi	7.3
	Tamil	6.0
	Urdu	5
	Gujarati	4
	Other	22

*Hindi is the national language and the principal language of 30 percent of the population; English has associate status but is the most important language for national, political, and commercial communications.

Religious affiliation (%)	Hindu	81.3
	Muslim	12
	Christian	2.3
	Sikh	1.9
	Buddhist and other	2.5

Economy

Domestic currency	Rupee (INR) US$1 = 46 INR (2004 average)
Total GNI (US$)	570.8 billion
GNI per capita (US$)	540
Total GNI at purchasing power parity (US$)	3.06 trillion
GNI per capita at purchasing power parity (US$)	2,880

GDP annual growth rate (%)	1983–1993	5.4
	1993–2003	5.9
	2002	4.1
	2003	6.0
	2004	6.2

GDP per capita average annual growth rate (%)	1983–1993	3.3
	1993–2003	4.1

Inequality in income or consumption (2000) (%)	Share of poorest 10%	3.9
	Share of poorest 20%	8.9
	Share of richest 20%	43.3
	Share of richest 10%	28.5
	Gini index (2000)	32.5

Structure of production (% of GDP)	Agriculture	23.6
	Industry	28.4
	Services	48

Labor force distribution (% of total)	Agriculture	60
	Industry	17
	Services	23

Exports as % of GDP	14.5
Imports as % of GDP	16.0

Society

Life expectancy at birth	64.35	
Infant mortality per 1,000 live births	56.29	
Adult illiteracy (% of population age 15+)	Male	30
	Female	52
Access to information and communications (per 1,000 population)	Telephone lines	38
	Mobile phones	6
	Radios	120
	Televisions	83
	Personal computers	5.8

Women in Government and the Economy

Women in the national legislature (2004)	
Lower house or single house (%)	8.3
Upper house (%)	12
Women at ministerial level (%)	10.1
Female economic activity rate (age 15 and above) (%)	42.4
Female labor force (% of total)	32.6

Estimated earned income (PPP US$)	Female	1,442
	Male	3,820

Composite Ratings and Rankings

Human Development Index (HDI) ranking (value) out of 177 countries:	127 (.595)
Gender-related Development Index (GDI) ranking (value) out of 144 countries:	103 (.572)
Gender Empowerment Measure (GEM) ranking (value) out of 78 countries:	N/A
Corruption Perception Index (CPI) ranking (value) out of 146 countries:	90 (2.8)

Environmental Sustainability Index (ESI) ranking (value) out of 146 countries:	101 (45.2)
Freedom in World Rating:	Free (2.5)

Political Organization

Political System Parliamentary democracy and a federal republic.

Regime History In 2004, the government was formed by the United Progressive Alliance; the Congress Party is the single largest party in the government and Manmohan Singh is prime minister.

Administrative Structure Federal, with 28 state governments.

Executive Prime minister, leader of the party with the most seats in the parliament.

Legislature Bicameral, upper house elected indirectly and without much substantial power; lower house, the main house, with members elected from single-member districts, winner-take-all.

Judiciary Independent constitutional court with appointed judges.

Party System Multiparty system. The Congress Party is the dominant party; the Bharatiya Janata Party (BJP) is the major opposition party.

Section ❶ The Making of the Modern Indian State

Politics in Action

Millions of Indians went to the polls in the seething summer heat of May 2004 and voted the ruling right-leaning Bharatiya Janata Party (or BJP, Indian People's Party) out of power. Back into power came India's venerable old centrist party, the Congress, but with a difference. Unlike in the earlier history of sovereign India, when the Congress was a hegemonic ruling force, now the Congress was a rump of its old self, ruling only with the support of various other parties, including India's main communist party, the Communist Party of India, Marxist (or CPM). However, the Congress Party's departure from old patterns also portended some novel developments for Indian democracy: Sonia Gandhi, heir to the dynastic rule of the Gandhi family, stepped aside and passed the mantle of power to Manmohan Singh. For the first time ever, India was ruled by a man who was not a leader of his own party nor that of the ruling alliance, but rather an incorruptible scholar, distinguished civil servant, and a member of the Sikh minority community.

National elections in India are dramatic moments that reveal salient themes of contemporary Indian politics. The 2004 elections underline at least three such themes. First and foremost is a fairly obvious observation that nevertheless raises a significant question: India continues to elect its rulers through regular elections. With over a billion people of diverse cultural

Sonia Gandhi elected in the 2004 national elections
Source: Amit Bhargava/Corbis

backgrounds, many of them very poor, how has India managed to maintain democratic institutions since gaining independence after World War II?

Second, competition for power in India continues to be intense, with no political party enjoying a position of unchallenged dominance. (This represents a strong contrast with the period of several decades following independence, when the Congress Party won election after election.) Neither of the two major electoral contenders, the Congress or the BJP, is at present able to muster anything close to a majority of parliamentary seats to form a government. As a centrist party, the Congress presently stands for secularism, economic liberalization, and mild redistribution of wealth. The BJP, by contrast, has in recent years been associated with the emergence of religious nationalism in India, especially championing antiminority politics. In addition to these two main contenders, other major competitors include the all-India CPM and nearly thirty regional parties with a presence in the parliament. The CPM, though communist in name and organization, has evolved into a social democratic party that accepts the limits of a market economy and of democracy, but nevertheless seeks greater benefits for India's numerous poor. The most recent elections that put Congress back at the helm, albeit supported by the communists, have been rightly interpreted as a victory—though quite possibly a temporary victory—for the forces of secularism and limited redistribution over the more conservative politics of the religious nationalists.

And finally, it should be noted that this political drama is unfolding against a background in which the national economy has been growing steadily but also becoming more unequal. For the last twenty-five years or so, the Indian economy has grown at some 5 to 6 percent annually. Similar to China's rapid expansion, this development has propelled India into the ranks of the world's fastest growing and potentially largest economies. In the last few years, India's economic success has attracted considerable scholarly attention. Books and articles appear frequently in the United States about the soaring number of call centers, technical support services, and software producers locating in India. Unfortunately, as in the case of China, India's growing wealth has been accompanied by growing inequalities along regional, rural-urban,

and class lines. Along with the question of how to manage ethnic conflicts and political fragmentation, the issue of how to ensure economic growth without debilitating inequalities has thus emerged as the most pressing political challenge in contemporary India.

Geographic Setting

India is a populous and geographically and culturally diverse country. Its large size, approximately 2,000 miles in both length and width, is rivaled in Asia only by China. Its rich geographic setting includes three diverse topographic zones (the mountainous northern zone, the basin formed by the Ganges River, and the peninsula of southern India) and a variety of climates (mountain climate in the northern mountain range; dry, hot weather in the arid, northern plateau; and subtropical climate in the south). Along with its neighbors Pakistan and Bangladesh, the region is physically isolated from the rest of Asia by the Himalayas to the north and the Indian Ocean to the east, south, and west. The northwest frontier is the only permeable frontier, and it is the route that successive invaders and migrants have used to enter this region.

With over 1 billion people, India is the country with the second largest population in the world, after its neighbor China. It is the world's largest democracy and the oldest democracy among the developing countries of Asia, Africa, and Latin America. India has functioned as a democracy with full adult suffrage since 1947, when it emerged as a sovereign nation-state, following the end of British colonial rule. The durability of Indian democracy is especially intriguing considering the diversity of Indian society. Some fourteen major languages and numerous dialects are spoken. India contains many different ethnic groups, a host of regionally concentrated tribal groups, as well as adherents of virtually the entire world's major religions. In addition to the majority Hindu population, India includes Muslims, **Sikhs,** Jains, Buddhists, Christians, and even several tiny Jewish communities. Furthermore, Indian society, especially Hindu society, is divided into myriad caste groupings. Although these are mainly based on occupation, they also tend to be closed social groups in the sense that people are born into, marry, and die within their caste. India is still largely an agrarian society; 70 percent of the population lives in far-flung villages in the rural areas. The major cities, Bombay (renamed Mumbai), Calcutta, and New Delhi, the national capital, are densely populated.

Critical Junctures

India is among the most ancient civilizations of the world, dating back to the third millennium B.C. The Indian subcontinent, comprising Pakistan, India, and Bangladesh, has witnessed the rise and fall of many civilizations and empires. Only five of the most recent legacies that have shaped present-day politics are reviewed here.

The Colonial Legacy (1757–1947)

Motivated by a combination of economic and political interests, the British started making inroads into the Indian subcontinent in the late seventeenth and early eighteenth centuries. Since 1526, large sections of the subcontinent had been ruled by the Mughal dynasty, which hailed from Central Asia and was Muslim by religion. As the power of the Mughal emperors declined in the eighteenth century, lesser princely contenders vied with one another for supremacy. In this environment, the British East India Company, a large English trading organization with commercial interests in India and strong backing from the British Crown, was able to play off one Indian prince against another, forming alliances with some, subduing others, and thus strengthening its control through a policy of divide and rule.

This informal empire was replaced in the mid-nineteenth century with a more formal one. After a major revolt by an alliance of Indian princes against growing British power, known as the Sepoy Rebellion or the Mutiny of 1857, the British Crown assumed direct control of India and retained it until 1947.

In order to consolidate its political and economic hold, the British created three main varieties of ruling arrangements. First, numerous small- to medium-sized states, as many as five hundred covering an area equal to two-fifths of the subcontinent, continued to be ruled throughout the colonial period by traditional Indian princes, the **Maharajas.** In exchange for accepting British rule, these Indian princes were allowed a relatively free hand within their realms. Second, in other parts of India, British indirect rule penetrated more deeply than in the princely states, for example, in the Bengal area (currently Bihar, West Bengal, and Bangladesh). In these regions, the British transformed traditional Indian elites, who controlled much agricultural land, into legal landlords, the *zamindars,* in exchange for periodic payments to the colonial administration. Third, the British established direct rule in the remaining regions of India, for example, in Bombay and the Madras presidencies (large areas around the cities of the same name), where British civil servants were directly responsible for collecting land taxes and adjudicating law and order.

Whatever its particular forms, British rule seldom reached very deep into Indian society, especially in rural areas, which were organized into countless relatively self-sufficient villages. Social life within villages was further divided by religiously sanctioned caste groups. Typically, a few landowning castes dominated many other castes lower in the ritual, occupational, and income hierarchies.

Critical Junctures in Modern India's Development	
1526	Mughal dynasty founded.
1612–1690	British East India Company establishes trading stations at Surat, Bombay, and Calcutta.
1757	Britain establishes informal colonial rule.
1857	Britain establishes formal colonial rule in response to Sepoy Rebellion.
1885	Indian National Congress is created.
1947	India achieves independence from Britain; India and Pakistan are partitioned; modern Indian state is founded.
1947–1964	Jawaharlal Nehru is prime minister.
1966–1984	Indira Gandhi is prime minister (except for a brief period from 1977 to 1980).
1999–2004	Bharatiya Janata Party government in power.
2004	Congress Party–dominated coalition government; the United Progressive Alliance comes to power.

The British sought to create a semblance of coherence in India through the creation of a central government that controlled and led these various territories and indigenous authority structures. Important instruments included the creation of an all-India civil service, police force, and army. Although at first only British nationals could serve in these institutions, with the introduction of modern educational institutions, some educated Indians were incorporated into government services. Unlike many other colonies, particularly in Africa, the British helped create a relatively effective state structure in India. When India emerged from British rule in 1947, it inherited, maintained, and expanded colonial institutions. The civil administration, police, and armed services in contemporary India continue to be organized along the principles established by the British colonialists in the last century. Thus, there is close continuity between the modern Indian state and the British colonial tradition.

The Nationalist Movement (1885–1947)

With the growth of commerce, education, and urbanization, groups of urban, educated upper-caste

Indian elites emerged as the new Indian leaders. They observed and closely interacted with their colonial rulers and often felt slighted by their treatment as second-class citizens. Even at this stage, a secular-religious divide was apparent. Some of them were Hindu nationalists who believed that a reformed Hinduism could provide a basis for a new, modern India. Others were attracted to British liberal ideas, which they invoked to seek greater equality with the British.

Two centuries of British colonial rule witnessed growing intellectual and cultural ferment in India. The British colonial rulers and traditional Indian elites had become allies of sorts, squeezing from the poor Indian peasantry resources that were simultaneously used to maintain the colonial bureaucratic state and support the conspicuous lifestyles of a parasitic landlord class. It was not long before Indian nationalists opposed these arrangements through the Indian National Congress (INC), which was actually formed by an Englishman in 1885. Its aim was to right the racial, cultural, and political wrongs of colonial rule. In its early years, the INC was mainly a collection of Indian urban elites who periodically met and petitioned India's British rulers, invoking liberal principles of political equality and requesting greater Indian involvement in higher political offices. The British largely ignored these requests, and over time, the requests turned into demands, pushing some nationalists into militancy and others into non-violent mass mobilization.

World War I was an important turning point for Indian nationalists. After the war, as great European empires disintegrated, creating new sovereign states in Europe and the Middle East, the principle of self-determination for people who considered themselves a nation gained international respectability. Indian nationalists were also inspired by the Russian revolution of 1917, which they viewed as a successful uprising against imperialism.

The man most responsible for helping to transform the INC from a narrow, elitist club to a mass nationalist movement was Mohandas Karamchand Gandhi, called Mahatma ("great soul") by his followers, one of the most influential and admirable leaders of the twentieth century. After becoming the leader of the INC in the 1920s, Gandhi successfully mobilized the middle classes, as well as a segment of the peasantry, into an anti-British movement that came to demand full sovereignty for India.

Three characteristics of the nationalist movement greatly influenced state building and democracy in India. First, the INC came to embody the principle of unity within diversity, which served India well in creating and maintaining a relatively stable political system. Because the INC became a powerful political organization committed to establishing an Indian nation, many conflicts could play themselves out within the INC without undermining its unity. Second, the nationalist movement gave rise to divisions as well as unity. The most serious conflict was between Hindus and Muslims. A segment of the Indian Muslim elite refused to accept the leadership of Gandhi and the INC, demanded separate political rights for Muslims, and called for an independent Muslim state when the INC refused.

The resulting division of the subcontinent into two sovereign states in 1947—the Muslim state of Pakistan and the secular state of India, most of whose citizens were Hindu—was turbulent and bloody. Millions of Muslims fled from India to Pakistan, and millions of Hindus fled the other way; over 10 million people migrated and nearly a million died in communal violence. The euphoria of independence in India was thus tempered by the human tragedy that accompanied the subcontinent's partition. The two countries have fought three wars since partition and, although there have been some significant recent initiatives to defuse tensions, relations between them remain frosty.

Third, the nationalist movement laid the foundations for democracy in India. Although Gandhi pioneered the use of civil disobedience to challenge British laws that he regarded as unjust, he did so on the basis of profound ethical commitments and nonviolent means. Many of the INC's prominent leaders, like Jawaharlal Nehru, were educated in England and were committed democrats. Moreover, the INC participated in limited elections allowed by the British, ran democratic governments with limited powers in various British-controlled Indian provinces, and chose its own leaders through internal elections. These preindependence democratic tendencies were valuable assets to Indian democracy.

During the 1920s and 1930s, Gandhi, Nehru, and other INC leaders were increasingly successful in

Leaders: *Mahatma Gandhi*

Born in 1869 in western India, Mohandas Gandhi studied law in London for two years and worked in Durban, South Africa, as a lawyer and an activist for twenty-one years before returning home to join the Indian nationalist movement. His work among the different communities in South Africa helped him to develop the political strategies of nonviolence, or *satyagraha* (grasp of truth). On his arrival in India in 1915, he set about transforming the Indian National Congress into a mass party by reaching out to the urban and rural poor, non-Hindu religious groups, and the scheduled castes, which he called *Harijans,* or Children of God. Following the British massacre of unarmed civilians gathered in protest in the Punjab (at Jallianwala Bagh, a location well-known in Indian history) in April 1919, Gandhi and Jawaharlal Nehru proposed a noncooperation movement. This required a boycott of British legal and educational institutions as well as British merchandise, for which were substituted indigenous, or *swadeshi,* varieties. (The image of Gandhi weaving his own cloth is familiar to many.) Gandhi believed that mass civil disobedience could succeed only if people were truly committed. The involvement of some Congress workers in a violent incident in 1922 greatly disturbed him, causing him to call off the noncooperation movement. Gandhi was strongly opposed to the partition of India along religious lines in 1947, but because he had resigned from Congress in 1934, his protests were ignored. Nevertheless, he dominated India's nationalist movement for more than two decades until he was assassinated in January 1948, five months after India achieved its goal of self-rule, or *swaraj,* by a Hindu extremist who thought Gandhi was overly sympathetic to Muslm interests.

Mahatma Gandhi, the leader of India's independence movement as he appeared at the head of a 200-mile march, staged in defiance of the statute establishing a government salt monopoly by the British colonial government in 1930.
Source: UPI/Bettmann.

mobilizing Indians in the anti-British nationalist movement for India's independence. The more successful the INC became, the more the British either had to repress it or make concessions—and they tried

both. However, World War II consumed Britain's energies, and the political, economic, and symbolic costs of colonization became extremely onerous. In order to gain Indian support for its war efforts, the

British promised Indians independence. Soon after the war, India became a sovereign state in August 1947.

The Nehru Era (1947–1964)

Within India, Jawaharlal Nehru, whom Gandhi favored, emerged as the leader of the new nation. Soon after, a militant member of the extremist anti-Muslim Hindu cultural organization, the *Rashtriya Swayam Sevak Sangh* (RSS), assassinated Gandhi, who had opposed partition and later ardently defended Muslims within India. Nehru became the uncontested leader of a new India, a position he maintained until his death in 1964. The years of Nehru's rule shaped the dominant patterns of India's future development.

Nehru's India inherited an ambiguous legacy from British rule: a relatively strong central government and a weak economy. Nehru, a committed nationalist and social democrat, sought to strengthen India's independence and national power and to improve its economy and the lives of the Indian poor. He used the governmental machinery that India had inherited to accomplish these tasks.

At independence, India was confronted with major political problems, including a massive inflow of refugees, war with Pakistan over the disputed state of Kashmir situated between the two countries, and the need to consolidate numerous Indian princely states into a coherent national state. Concerned about India's capacity to deal with such problems, Nehru and other leaders depended on and further strengthened the civil, police, and armed services that were legacies of colonial rule.

After independence, India adopted a democratic constitution and established a British-style democracy with full adult suffrage. Because political power now required winning elections, the INC had to transform itself from an opposition movement into a political party, the Congress Party. It was highly successful in doing so, in part by establishing a nationwide patronage system. Another important change in the decade following independence was the linguistic reorganization of states. As in the United States, the Indian constitution defines India as a federal system. The contentious political issue in the 1950s was the criterion by which regional groups could demand a state within the federal union. With Indians divided by the languages they speak, an obvious basis for the federal system was to organize constituent units based on language groups. Hindi is the most widely spoken Indian language; however, most Hindi speakers are concentrated in the north-central part of the country. Indians living in the south, east, and parts of the west speak a variety of other languages. Concerned about domination by Hindi speakers, many of these non-Hindi groups demanded a reorganization of the Indian union into linguistically defined states. Initially, Nehru resisted this demand, worried that linguistic states within a federation might become secessionist and demand sovereignty. As demands for linguistic states mounted, especially from south Indian groups, Nehru compromised in 1956: the new Indian union was organized around fourteen linguistically defined states. In the years that followed, additional states were carved out of existing ones, and there are now twenty-eight major states within India.

Another legacy of the Nehru era is noteworthy. Jawaharlal Nehru was an internationalist who wanted India to play a global role. Together with other postcolonial leaders of Asia and Africa, Nehru initiated what became known as the nonaligned movement, which united those countries wishing to maintain a distance from the two superpowers. India and many other developing countries viewed both Western capitalism and Soviet communism with suspicion. Under Nehru, India played a leadership role among other nonaligned developing countries while pursuing mixed economic policies at home that were neither fully capitalist nor fully socialist (see Section 2).

Nehru's initiatives put India firmly on a stable, democratic road. However, the strong, centralized state that Nehru created also had some negative long-term consequences. The new Indian state came to resemble the old British Indian state that Nehru and others had so vociferously opposed. The colonial state's tendency to favor landowning Indian elites carried over into the Nehru era. Powerful groups in the society, including elite bureaucrats, wealthy landowners, entrepreneurs, and leaders of well-organized ethnic movements, enjoyed a favored position. While Nehru and the Congress Party continued to maintain a

Leaders: *The Nehru-Gandhi Dynasty*

Jawaharlal Nehru

Jawaharlal Nehru was a staunch believer in liberal democratic principles. Along with Gandhi and others, he was at the forefront of India's nationalist movement against the British. When India became independent in 1947, Nehru became prime minister, as head of the Congress Party, and retained that position until his death in 1964. During this period, he established India as a socialist, democratic, and secular state in theory, if not always in practice. On the international front, he helped found the nonaligned movement, a forum for expressing the interests and aspirations of developing countries that did not want to ally with the United States or the Soviet Union during the cold war. Nehru attempted to set India on a rapid road to industrialization by establishing heavy industry. His efforts to effect redistribution of wealth through land reform were combined with an equally strong commitment to democratic and individual rights, such as the right to private property. Upon his death, India inherited a stable polity, a functioning democracy, and an economy characterized by a large public sector and an intricate pattern of state control over the private sector.

Indira Gandhi

Indira Gandhi (no relation to Mahatma Gandhi) became prime minister shortly after the death of her father, Jawaharlal Nehru, and dominated the Indian political scene until her assassination in 1984. Her years in power strengthened India's international position, but her domestic policies weakened the organizational structure of the Congress Party. Her tendencies toward centralization and the personalization of authority within the Congress and the concomitant use of demagogic rhetoric in electoral campaigns contributed to the erosion of the Congress Party. By defining the regional conflict in the Punjab and tensions with Pakistan as Hindu-Sikh and Hindu-Muslim problems, respectively, she contributed to further erosion of the party's secular base and to rising religious factionalism. Her decision to send troops into the holiest of the holy Sikh temples in Amritsar, in order to root out Sikh militants using the temple as a sanctuary, deeply alienated Sikhs, a small but important religious group in India. The ensuing bloodshed culminated in her assassination by one of her Sikh bodyguards in 1984. Her death ushered in a new generation of the Nehru-Gandhi dynasty, as her son Rajiv Gandhi served as prime minister until 1989.

---

pro-poor, socialist rhetoric, they generally failed to deliver on their promises.

The Indira Gandhi Era (1966–1984)

When Nehru died in 1964, the Congress Party was divided over the choice of a successor and hurriedly selected mild-mannered Lal Bahadur Shastri to be prime minister. When he died of a heart attack in 1966 and rivalry again broke out over his successor, party elites found a compromise candidate in Nehru's daughter, Indira Gandhi. They chose her to capitalize on the fact that as Nehru's daughter, she would help the Congress Party garner the electoral support it needed to remain in power. They also calculated that

she would be a weak woman who could be manipulated by competing factions within the party. They were right about the first point, but decisively wrong about the second.

As prime minister from 1966 to 1984, except for the brief period of 1977 to 1980, Indira Gandhi's rule had several long-term legacies for contemporary Indian democracy. First, Indian politics became more personalized, populist, and nationalist. During the late 1960s, the Bengali-speaking eastern half of Pakistan, which was separated from its western half by nearly 1,000 miles of Indian territory, demanded sovereignty. As violence escalated within Pakistan and refugees from East Pakistan began pouring into India, Gandhi ordered Indian forces to intervene. This led to the creation of the sovereign state of Bangladesh. Because the United States sided with Pakistan in that conflict (and the Soviet Union backed India), Indira Gandhi was able to mobilize Indian nationalist sentiment against both Pakistan and the United States. India's victory added to Indira Gandhi's popularity. She soon consolidated her leadership over the Congress Party, forcing out leaders who opposed her and replacing them with loyal allies. The result was to create a new Congress Party in her own image. Subsequently, she portrayed the old Congress elite as conservative defenders of the status quo who prevented her from helping the poor. Gandhi's populist rhetoric won her immense popularity among India's poor. From 1971 to 1984, she dominated Indian politics as much as Mahatma Gandhi or her father ever had.

A second legacy of Indira Gandhi's rule was to further centralize the Indian political system. During the Nehru era, local elites had helped select higher political officeholders, but in the 1970s, Indira Gandhi directly appointed officeholders at both the national and regional levels. Although this strategy enabled her to gain a firm grip over the party, it isolated her from broader political forces and eroded the legitimacy of local leaders.

A third important legacy of Indira Gandhi's rule was her failure to translate populist rhetoric into real gains for India's poor. She was unable to redistribute agricultural land from large landowners to those who worked the land or to generate employment, provide welfare, or improve access by the poor to education and medical services. Some analysts argue that she was never sincere in her commitment to the poor and that her populism was mainly a strategy for gaining votes. Given the magnitude of India's poverty, however, even sincere efforts faced a monumental task.

Indian politics became increasingly turbulent under Indira Gandhi, a fourth legacy of her rule. As her popularity soared, so did opposition to her. The old Congress elite denounced her demagogic political style, arguing that her government was corrupt; they began organizing mass demonstrations and strikes to press their case. In 1974, the political situation in India became unstable; with the opposition organizing general strikes, Indira Gandhi declared a national **Emergency,** suspended many democratic rights, and arrested most opposition leaders. The Emergency

lasted nearly two years, the only period since 1947 when India was not a democracy.

In 1977, Indira Gandhi rescinded the Emergency and called for national elections, confidently expecting that she would be reelected. To her surprise, she was soundly defeated, and for the first time since independence, a non-Congress government came to power. Various groups that had opposed Gandhi hastily joined together in a loosely organized party (the Janata Party). Indira Gandhi's authoritarian measures during the Emergency were so unpopular that the newly formed party was able to unite India's fragmented opposition groups and achieve electoral success. However, soon after the elections, Janata leaders became factionalized, and the Janata government collapsed. Indira Gandhi exploited the situation to regain power in the 1980 parliamentary elections.

Indira Gandhi's tenure in power between 1980 and 1984 was marked by a personal and populist political style, an increasingly centralized political system, failure to implement antipoverty policies, and growing political turbulence. However, she departed from her previous approach in two ways. The first was in the realm of the economy. During the 1970s, India's industrial establishment grew relatively slowly because the government spent too much on buying political support and too little on investment; incomes of the poor were not improving, and therefore demand for new products was limited; and excessive rules and regulations were counterproductive, both for domestic entrepreneurs and for integrating India into the world economy. With few means to rechannel government spending or improve the spending capacity of the poor, Gandhi started changing the rules that governed India's economy, especially embracing India's private sector as a means to improve economic performance.

The second important change concerns the strategy Indira Gandhi employed to achieve electoral support. Given her abandonment of appeals to socialism and secularism, which both she and her father had championed since the 1950s, Indira Gandhi needed to devise an alternative platform. In the early 1980s, she began to use religious appeals to mobilize India's Hindu majority. By introducing religion into politics, the Congress Party sowed the seeds for the growth of the Hindu nationalist BJP.

Another way that religious conflicts began to re-enter Indian politics in the early 1980s involved the growing conflict between the Sikh religious minority, based in the Punjab, and the national government. During the course of the conflict, Indian security forces invaded and extensively damaged the holiest Sikh shrine, the Golden Temple in the city of Amritsar, to attack Sikh militants besieged there. The anger that she provoked among Sikhs was so intense that she was assassinated in 1984 by one of her Sikh bodyguards.

Immediately after Gandhi's assassination, rampaging mobs of Hindus brutally murdered Sikhs in New Delhi, Kanpur, and other north Indian cities. Most of the 3,700 Sikh victims were poor. Some leading figures within the Congress Party orchestrated anti-Sikh violence. In this respect, it resembled the anti-Muslim violence organized by BJP party and state leaders in the following decade.

Indira's son, Rajiv Gandhi, won a landslide victory in the subsequent national elections as a result of the sympathy wave that his mother's assassination generated. He came to office promising clean government, a high-tech economy that would carry India into the next century, and reduced ethnic conflict. He was somewhat successful in ameliorating tensions in the state of Punjab. But Rajiv Gandhi inflamed tensions between Hindus and Muslims by sponsoring a law that placed Muslim women under the purview of the family. His leadership was marred by allegations of corruption concerning an arms deal between the Indian government and the Swedish Bofors company.

With Indira Gandhi's death, the tradition of powerful and populist prime ministers came to an end. India has since been facing governmental instability that began during the Indira Gandhi era. This was evident in increasing factionalism within the Congress Party, India's dominant party since independence. Moreover, other secular political parties proved unable to fill the vacuum in government caused by the Congress Party's disintegration. Since 1984, only three governments, the first two led by Congress, have lasted their full terms: under Rajiv Gandhi (1984–1989), Narasimha Rao (1991–1996), and Atal Behari Vajpayee (1999–2004).

Coalition Governments (1989 to the Present)

In not one of the six parliamentary elections since 1989 has a single party won an absolute majority of seats. A succession of largely unstable coalition and minority governments has ruled since then. Between 1998 and 2004, India was ruled by a BJP-led coalition government with Atal Behari Vajpayee as prime minister. The BJP was defeated in 2004 by a Congress Party government headed by Manmohan Singh.

The tendency for Indian elections to produce unstable or at best short-lived coalition governments at the national level has grown because no party has been able to fill the vacuum created by the old Congress Party's decline. Coalition governments at the national level and in most states have generally been hurriedly arranged and poorly conceived. The cement that binds coalitions together has been more negative than positive. For example, opposition to Congress brought governments to power in 1977. By the early 1990s, opposition to the BJP provided the major incentive for coalitional arrangements among regional and lower-caste parties. The BJP-led government elected in 1998 lasted a full term but ruled as a coalition, as does the present Congress government (see Table 1).

Table 1

Prime Ministers of India, 1947–Present

	Years in Office	Party
Jawaharlal Nehru	1947–1964	Congress
Lal Bahadur Shastri	1964–1966	Congress
Indira Gandhi	1966–1977	Congress
Morarji Desai	1977–1979	Janata
Charan Singh	1979–1980	Janata
Indira Gandhi	1980–1984	Congress
Rajiv Gandhi	1984–1989	Congress
V. P. Singh	1989–1990	Janata
Chandra Shekhar	1990–1991	Janata (Socialist)
Narasimha Rao	1991–1996	Congress
Atal Bihari Vajpayee	1996 (13 days)	BJP & allies
H. D. Deve Gowda	1996–1997	United Front
I. K. Gujral	1997–1998	United Front
Atal Bihari Vajpayee	1998–1999, 1999–2004	BJP & allies
Manmohan Singh	2004–	Congress & allies

Politics in India today is characterized by precarious coalition governments, weakened political institutions, and considerable political activism along class and ethnic lines. These developments have generated policies that range from limited action on the economic front to nationalist outbursts on the military front. Whether any party or charismatic leader capable of unifying the country across the salient cleavages will emerge remains to be seen.

India after September 11

The September 11 attacks on the United States have had an important impact on relations between India and the United States. The frosty relations between the two countries during the cold war had begun to improve under the Clinton administration, after the demise of the Soviet Union deprived India of her former ally. They further improved after September 11. A significant change occurred when India allowed the United States to establish a military presence in the country. India strongly supported the U.S. intervention in Afghanistan. With the overthrow of the Taliban and the establishment of the Hamid Karzai government, India established close diplomatic, civil, and commercial ties to the new Afghan government.

The United States has also become increasingly involved in trying to resolve regional conflicts within South Asia. It actively sought to negotiate Indo-Pakistan tensions over Kashmir, the civil war in Sri Lanka, and armed conflict between the monarchy and Maoist militants in Nepal.

Tensions between India and the United States increased in 2003 when India opposed the U.S. war against Iraq, on the grounds that it did not have UN backing. India continued to refuse to send in troops as part of a stabilizing force after the war ended in the absence of UN authorization. Yet strong forces continue to favor close ties between the two countries. The United States is India's largest trading partner, and there has recently been a substantial increase in U.S.-based transnational corporation investment in India. Since September 11, the United States has greatly increased its military presence in Asia and would like to gain greater access to the Indian Ocean and Persian Gulf, for which it needs India's cooperation. India thus has a prominent place in Washington's security strategy. The challenge for India will be how to strengthen ties with the United States without compromising its own regional ambitions and submitting to all of Washington's dictates.

Themes and Implications

Historical Junctures and Political Themes

India in a World of States.   India's domestic difficulties reflect and influence its changing status in the world of states. In an increasingly interdependent global political and economic system, India's attainment of nuclear weapons signaled the dawn of a new era. As a result, simmering historical tensions over territories such as Kashmir will need to be managed very carefully. India now shares borders with two nuclear powers, China and Pakistan, and has engaged in wars and periodic border skirmishes with both. India and Pakistan have a history of hostilities, and their politicians have exploited the tensions between them during domestic political crises. The challenge facing the Indian state is how to prevent domestic pressures from escalating into international conflicts.

Governing the Economy.   Successful economic performance is necessary for India to fulfill its national and domestic ambitions. Indian policymakers initially sought economic self-sufficiency through a policy of state-led industrialization focused on meeting the needs of its large internal market. This protectionist economic strategy had mixed results. Although it resulted in the development of some important basic industries, it also generated extensive inefficiencies and did little to alleviate the country's severe poverty. Like many other developing nations, India must adjust its economic strategy to meet the demands of increasingly competitive and interdependent global markets. Since about 1980, India's leaders have consistently sought to reform the Indian economy, with some favorable results. During the 1980s, these reforms consisted mainly of government incentives to India's established private sector to increase production. Since 1991, the reforms have opened the Indian economy to the outside world. The results include a growing economy but also growing inequalities. Among the daunting challenges facing Indian leaders is how to ensure sustained growth while sponsoring measures to reduce economic inequalities.

The Democratic Idea. The democratic idea has been sustained in India for over half a century, barring a short period of authoritarianism between 1977 and 1979. India can boast of a vibrant and vigilant civil society, periodic elections, unfettered media, and relatively autonomous courts and bureaucracy. However, these institutions have been corroded over the years. For example, Indira Gandhi's radical posturing brought turbulence to Indian democracy, damaged the economy, and never provided real benefits to the poor. Since the late 1980s, political parties have deployed electoral strategies that have exacerbated ethnic tensions. One challenge that India faces is how to balance an increasingly divided society with the demands of social, economic, and political citizenship for all. Further, since the vast majority of India's citizens are Hindu, political parties may be tempted to play the Hindu card and thereby marginalize India's minority religious communities. Indeed, this is precisely the scenario that brought the BJP to power in 1998.

India has recently become more democratic in some ways and less so in others. More groups with more diverse identities are participating in politics than ever before. They are joining a larger range of political parties from more diverse regions of the country. The Indian political class can no longer be identified with a single region, caste, and class. However, a key ingredient of democracy is the protection of minority rights, and on this count India is less democratic than in the past. Sikhs, Christians, and above all Muslims have suffered brutal attacks since the mid-1980s.

The Politics of Collective Identity. That there are intense conflicts around the issue of collective identity is not surprising in multicultural India. What is alarming is that mobilization of the electorate on ethnic grounds can corrode democratic values. Democracy is supposed to provide a level playing field for a tussle between different interests and identities. India faces the challenge of reconciling domestic electoral strategies of ethnic mobilization to capture power with moderation demanded in the exercise of such

power, all the while coping with demands of multiethnic and multiclass groups and sustaining economic growth.

Implications for Comparative Politics

Certain exceptional features of the Indian state have great significance for the study of comparative politics. First, India is a poor yet vibrant democracy. Despite widespread poverty and illiteracy, most Indians value their citizenship rights and exercise them vigorously. Theories of modernization have usually posited that democracy and economic growth are conjoined, but India stands out as an exception. At independence, the country was struggling with problems of nation building, poverty, and poor human development indicators, and was managing a transition to democracy. Against all odds, India became and remains a thriving democracy, an achievement especially striking when compared to the authoritarian fate of most other newly independent colonies in Asia and Africa.

Second, unlike other multiethnic states such as Yugoslavia and the former Soviet Union, which disintegrated with the advent of democracy, the Indian state has managed to remain fairly cohesive and stable—although this must be qualified by the severe turmoil at various times in the states of Assam, Punjab, Gujarat, and especially Kashmir. Indian politics thus offers a case study of the tempering influence of democracy on ethnic cleavages. Contrast the BJP's exclusionary rhetoric when it was in opposition with its rhetorical shift toward moderation after becoming India's ruling party. In an attempt to stabilize a fractious multiparty coalition government, the BJP was forced to put contentious religious issues such as the temple in Ayodhya on a back burner.

Third, as home to 1 billion people with diverse cultural, religious, and linguistic identities, Indian democracy offers an arena for testing and studying various theories and dilemmas of comparative politics. For instance, one dilemma in comparative politics is how multiethnic democracies can develop a coherent institutional system that gives representation to diverse interests without degenerating into authoritarianism or total collapse.

Fourth, theorists dealing with recent transitions to democracy in Latin America and Eastern Europe have puzzled over the question of what constitutes a consolidated democracy and how one achieves such consolidation. Here, a comparison of India with Pakistan is instructive. At independence, Pakistan adopted a centralized, authoritarian system, while India created a federal, parliamentary state. These decisions had critical implications. India has functioned as a democracy for all but two years since 1947, whereas Pakistan has functioned as an authoritarian state for most of the same period. Moreover, the Indian experience with authoritarianism during the Emergency era in the late 1970s and the resurgence of democratic norms when Indira Gandhi was voted out by an angry citizenry show the importance of elections. It also shows that the existence of democratic institutions and procedures can lead to the diffusion of democratic norms throughout the society.

Fifth, comparativists have focused on the dilemma of whether democracy and social equity can be achieved simultaneously in poor countries. The case of Kerala, a state in southern India, suggests an affirmative answer. Although one of the poorest states in India, Kerala has achieved near-total literacy, long life expectancy, low infant mortality, and high access to medical care. Kerala's development indicators compare favorably with the rest of India, other low-income countries, and even wealthy countries like the United States.

Finally, there is a lively debate in comparative politics concerning the impact of democracy on economic growth. While cross-national evidence remains inconclusive, India's record of steady growth of nearly 6 percent annually for nearly 25 years suggests the tantalizing possibility of successful economic management within the framework of a democracy. What can other emerging democracies learn from India's recent experience in growth promotion?

This discussion of critical junctures in Indian history highlights the central challenge of contemporary Indian politics: how to establish a coherent, legitimate government that will use its power to facilitate economic growth and equitable distribution. The former requires forming durable electoral coalitions without exacerbating political passions and ethnic conflicts. The latter requires careful implementation of policies that simultaneously help entrepreneurs produce goods and ensure a fair distribution of national income.

Section ❷ Political Economy and Development

At the time of independence, India was largely a poor, agricultural economy. Although it still has a very large agricultural sector and considerable poverty, India today also has a substantial industrial base and a vibrant middle class. Since the introduction of economic liberalization policies under Narasimha Rao's Congress government in 1991, all Indian governments have supported economic reform. Before discussing what liberalization entails, why it has become a priority, and what its implications are for Indian politics, we review the historical evolution of the Indian economy.

State and Economy

The Economy Under British Rule

During the colonial period, the Indian economy was largely agricultural, with hundreds of millions of poor peasants living in thousands of small villages, tilling the land with primitive technology, and producing at a low level of efficiency. The British, along with Indian landlords, extracted extensive land revenues, land taxes, and tributes from Indian princes. However, they reinvested only a small portion of this surplus into improving agricultural production. Most resources were squandered through conspicuous consumption by Indian princes and landlords or used to finance the expensive colonial government. The result of this mismanagement was that Indian agricultural productivity mostly stagnated in the first half of the twentieth century. For example, productivity in India was considerably lower in 1950 than in Japan or even China.

Some industry developed under colonial rule, but its scope was limited. The British sold manufactured goods to India in exchange for Indian raw materials.

Because the British economy was more advanced, it was difficult for Indians to compete successfully. Indigenous manufacturing, especially artisanal production, was ruined by the forced opening of the Indian market to British goods. Thus, the Indian economy at independence in 1947 was relatively stagnant, especially in agriculture. Some private sector industry did develop, but it constituted only a small proportion of the national economy.

The Economy After Independence

One of the central tasks facing Indian leaders after 1947 was to modernize the sluggish economy. During Nehru's rule, India adopted a model of development based largely on private property, although there was extensive government ownership of firms and government guidance of private economic activity. Nehru created a powerful planning commission that, following the Soviet model, made five-year plans for the Indian economy, outlining the activities in which government investment would be concentrated. Unlike the plans in communist party states, however, the Indian plans also indicated priority areas for private entrepreneurs, who remained a powerful force in the Indian economy.

The Indian government levied high tariffs on imports, arguing that new Indian industries, so long disadvantaged under colonial rule, required protection from foreign competitors. The government tightly regulated the start-up and expansion of private industries under the presumption that the government was the best safeguard of the public interests. This government-planned private economy achieved mixed results. It helped India create an impressive industrial base but did little to help the poor, and its protected industries were quite inefficient by global standards.

Nationalist in temperament, Nehru and other Congress Party leaders were suspicious of involving foreign investors in India's economic development. The government thus undertook a series of coordinated economic activities on its own. It made significant public sector investments to create such heavy industries as steel and cement; protected Indian entrepreneurs from foreign competition; where possible, further subsidized these producers; and finally, created elaborate rules and regulations controlling the activities of private

producers. As a result, India developed a substantial industrial base over the next few decades.

Congress leaders promised to redistribute land from landowners to tenants in order to weaken the former supporters of the colonial government and motivate the tillers of the land to increase production. Although some of the largest landowners were indeed eliminated in the early 1950s, poor tenants and agricultural laborers received very little land. Unlike the communist government in China, India's nationalist government had neither the will nor the capacity to undertake radical property redistribution. Instead, most of the land remained in the hands of medium- to large-sized landowners. Many became part of the Congress political machine in the countryside. This development further weakened the Congress Party's capacity to assist the rural poor and undermined its socialist commitments.

The failure of land reforms led to a new agricultural strategy in the late 1960s known as the **green revolution.** Instead of addressing land redistribution, the state sought to provide landowners with improved seeds and access to subsidized fertilizer. Because irrigation was essential for this strategy to succeed and because irrigation was assured only to larger farmers in some regions of India, the success of the green revolution was uneven. Production increased sharply in some areas, such as the Punjab, but other regions (and especially the poorer farmers in these regions) were left behind. Nevertheless, as a result of this strategy, India became self-sufficient in food (and even became a food exporter), thus avoiding the mass starvation and famines that had occurred in the past.

Between 1950 and 1980, the Indian government facilitated what has been described as **state-led economic development.** This development policy consisted of an expansion of the public sector, protection of the domestic sector from foreign competition, and rules and regulations to control private sector activity. Political leaders hoped to strengthen India's international position by promoting self-sufficient industrialization. To a great extent, the Indian government succeeded in achieving this goal. By 1980, India was a major industrial power able to produce its own steel, airplanes, automobiles, chemicals, military hardware, and many consumer goods. On the agricultural side, although land reforms had failed, the revised agricultural strategy had improved food production.

State-led development insulated the Indian economy from global influences. The strategy resulted in modest economic growth—not as impressive as that of Brazil, Mexico, or the Republic of Korea but better than that of many less developed countries. The main beneficiaries were the business classes, medium and large landowning farmers, and political and bureaucratic elites. A substantial urban middle class also developed during this phase. However, state-led development was associated with a number of problems. First, given the lack of competition, much industry was inefficient by global standards. Second, the elaborate rules and regulations controlling private economic activity encouraged corruption, as entrepreneurs bribed bureaucrats to get around the rules. And third, the focus on heavy industry directed a substantial portion of new investment into buying machinery rather than creating jobs. As a result, 40 percent of India's population, primarily poor tenant farmers and landless laborers, did not share in the fruits of this growth. And because population growth continued, the number of desperately poor people increased substantially during these decades.

Economic Liberalization

A number of global and national changes moved India toward **economic liberalization** beginning in the 1980s and accelerating after 1991. Throughout the 1980s, socialist models of development came under attack. Within India, political and economic elites were increasingly dissatisfied with India's relatively sluggish economic performance, especially compared with dynamic East Asian economies. For example, during the 1970s, whereas India's economy grew at the rate of 3.4 percent per year, South Korea's grew at 9.6 percent. New elites coming to power in India, less nationalist and socialist than their predecessors, interpreted the country's slow economic growth as a product of excessive governmental controls and of India's relative insulation from the global economy. India's business and industrial classes increasingly found government intervention in the economy more of a hindrance than a help. Realizing that poverty limited the possibility for expanding domestic markets, they increasingly sought to export their products.

India's economy has done relatively well since the 1980s, growing at 5 to 6 percent per year, a record especially noteworthy when compared to the dismal performance of many debt-ridden Latin American and African economies, such as Brazil and Nigeria. Some of this improved performance resulted from domestic liberalization that, since the 1980s, has enabled Indian entrepreneurs to operate with fewer government restrictions, and since 1991 from external liberalization that has further integrated India into the global economy. Economic performance has also been improved by public loans to small factory owners and farmers and by public investments in their enterprises. However, a large part of economic growth in the 1980s was based on increased borrowing from abroad, which represented a shift from a conservative fiscal policy. This expansionary fiscal policy, largely funded by foreign loans, was risky because India's exports to other countries did not grow very rapidly. For example, its exports during the 1980s grew at approximately 6 percent per year in comparison to 12 percent per year for both South Korea and China. As a result, the need to repay foreign loans put enormous pressure on the government toward the end of the decade. India was forced in the early 1990s to borrow even more from such international agencies as the International Monetary Fund (IMF) and the World Bank. In return for fresh loans, these international organizations required the Indian government to reduce its deficit through such controversial measures as reducing subsidies to the poor and selling government shares in public enterprises to the private sector. Critics allege that the government sold some public enterprises at prices well below their market value.

Liberalization has both a domestic and an international component. The government has sought to dismantle controls over private sector economic activities, especially in industry. More recently, new industries have been created, including oil and natural gas, transportation infrastructure, telecommunications, and power generation. The government has provided a variety of incentives to industry, including tax breaks, eliminating customs duties on the import of equipment, and underwriting losses.

Alongside government reforms aimed at opening up and privatizing the economy have been policy moves to cut the work force in public enterprises in order to reduce public spending and deficits. The government has announced measures to reduce the size of the work force by not filling vacancies when employees retire. The goal is to reduce the labor force in public enterprises by 2 percent a year, or 10 percent over five years. In 2002, the government sponsored a voluntary early retirement scheme for government employees.

The government has also sought to reduce workers' legal protections. Industrialists have demanded that the government revise a law requiring government authorization before firms can lay off workers or close factories that employ a minimum of a hundred workers; industry has demanded that the threshold be raised to a thousand. Industry has also called for easing restrictions on hiring temporary workers. In the face of this pressure, the government in 1999 appointed the Second Labor Commission to recommend reforming labor laws. The commission proposed replacing the forty-hour week with a sixty-four-hour week, abolishing employment security, enlarging possibilities for employing temporary workers, making government authorization of plant closures and cutbacks easier, and restricting workers' rights to form unions. Recent court decisions have also restricted workers' right to organize and strike, and have reduced traditional benefits.

The government's initiative has encountered spirited resistance. In 2001, unions prevented the privatization of the Uttar Pradesh State Electricity Board. The following year, in the largest action anywhere in the world against economic reforms, 10 million workers across the country went on strike to protest proposed changes to the labor laws and moves toward privatization.

There has also been opposition to economic liberalization from segments of Indian business. The BJP government that came to power in 1998 based much of its campaign on nationalist rhetoric. It gained support from powerful Indian businesses whose monopolies were threatened by imports and foreign investors. This reaction has slowed the liberalization process, especially when compared to countries in Latin America or Eastern Europe. While the present government remains committed to liberalization, the communists have slowed down the process of privatizing public enterprises.

To summarize, India's economy has grown at a relatively impressive annual growth rate since 1980, averaging between 5 and 6 percent (see Figure 1). While liberalizing economic policies may have contributed to this robust economic performance, their impact needs to be kept in perspective. Economic liberalization in India, especially external opening and privatization, has been relatively limited. Furthermore, liberalization policies have failed in their intentions of accelerating industrial growth. The significant growth of the Indian economy is most likely propelled by a number of other factors: the share of the slower growing agricultural economy in the overall economy continues to decline steadily, both the knowledge and the stock of modern technology continues to grow, and the closer relationship between government and business has increased the share of private investment in overall investment, thereby increasing production.

Reforms in Agriculture

India's agricultural production made steady and modest progress during the 1990s, helped by good rains during the decade. Weather patterns, especially the timeliness of seasonal rains (the monsoons), continue

Figure 1

Recent GDP Growth, 1997–2003

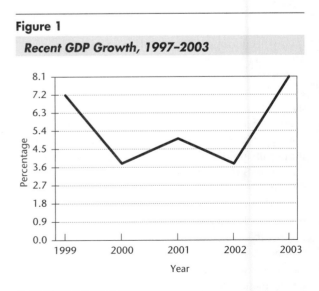

Source: World Bank National Accounts data, and OECD National Accounts data files. http://devdata.worldbank.org/data-query/SMChartExp.asp

to have significant bearing on Indian agriculture. Drought hit large parts of the countryside and affected agricultural production and employment opportunities in 2002. Unable to find work or buy food, people faced starvation and suicide, and mass migration occurred in Rajasthan, Madhya Pradesh, and other states. The victims were invariably from the poorest, lowest-caste segments of the rural population.

The impact of economic liberalization on agriculture has been growing. With the goal of reducing subsidies, the central government excluded millions of impoverished families just above the poverty line from receiving publicly subsidized food supplies. Furthermore, the government sharply increased the price of food sold under the public distribution system. Sixty million tons of food grain have been rotting in the storage centers of the Food Corporation of India because it is too costly for the poor to buy.[1]

The government's decision to remove restrictions on imports to conform to obligations under World Trade Organization (WTO) rules has important implications for the agrarian sector. Agricultural producers, such as coffee farmers in south India, are being harmed by increased imports. Just when prices of primary commodities are falling worldwide, and the United States and other industrialized countries have maintained trade barriers on agricultural products and subsidized their domestic farmers, India's agriculture economy is being opened up to global forces without safety nets in place.

Economic reforms have had mixed results thus far. India's foreign exchange reserves are much higher than they were in the past. Some industries, such as information technology, have taken off. The service sector is expanding and contributing significantly to India's economic growth. However, as noted earlier, economic liberalization is only partly responsible for robust economic growth. A variety of other long-term factors such as close relations between Indian business and the conservative government that occupied office until 2004 also help explain larger and more efficient private investments and economic growth.

Social Welfare Policy

India's poor are a diverse, heterogeneous, and enormous group constituting more than one-third of the population. Since independence, the percentage of the poor has been cut in half. However, because of India's rapid population growth, this advance has not been sufficient to reduce the absolute numbers of the poor, which increased from around 200 million in the 1950s to about 300 million in the new millennium. India has the sad distinction of having the largest number of poor people in the world. Nearly two-thirds of the Indian population and three-fourths of the poor live in rural areas. Urban poverty accounts for only one-fourth of the poor population, but the number of poor urban people, over 70 million, is staggering.

India's poorest people are illiterate women and children and untouchables and tribals. They include peasant farmers who own little land, agricultural tenants, landless laborers in villages, and those without regular jobs in cities who eke out a living on society's margins, often huddled into shantytowns that lack sanitary facilities and electricity or living on the streets of cities like Calcutta or Bombay.

Although most poor people are unorganized, they exercise political influence in several ways. First, their sizable numbers impel many Indian politicians to adopt populist or socialist electoral platforms. Second, because many of the poor share a lower-caste status (especially within specific states), they can have a considerable impact on electoral outcomes. In some states, notably West Bengal and Kerala, there is a long history of radical politics; the poor in these states are well organized by communist or socialist parties and periodically help elect left-leaning governments. Third, the anger and frustration of the poor provide the raw material for many social movements in India.

Over the years, Indian governments have undertaken various poverty alleviation programs. Some have been partly successful, but most have not. Redistribution of agricultural land to the poor was mostly a failure compared to results in China, where radical land redistribution was a key component of a successful assault on poverty. As a communist dictatorship, however, China used government coercion to implement property redistribution. In some Indian states, such as West Bengal and Kerala, elected communist governments have been somewhat successful in land redistribution. Overall, however, land reforms have proved to be nearly impossible in India's democracy.

India has very few Western-style welfare programs such as unemployment insurance, comprehensive public health programs, or guaranteed primary education. The size of the welfare problem is considerable and would tax the resources of any government. No Indian government has ever attempted to provide universal primary education, although there has been considerable internal and external pressure to do so.

One set of welfare-enhancing programs that has had modest success in India is public employment programs. They enable the national and state governments to sponsor the construction of roads and bridges and the cleaning of agricultural waterways. Because the rural poor are unemployed for nearly half the year when agricultural jobs are not available, public employment programs become a source of off-season employment and income. Many surveys have demonstrated that such programs help the poor, though mostly in the short run, and the programs rarely benefit the poorest citizens. In the 1990s, however, under the impact of liberalization policies, government budgets came under considerable pressure, creating a squeeze on public investments, especially in such areas as public employment. The present government is undertaking a reform of the employment guarantee scheme to provide employment to India's rural poor.

Many respected observers have repeatedly stated that development spending, public investment, and bank credit to the rural sector were crucial to economic growth in the 1980s and remain critical today. Food-for-work programs, however inefficient, leaky, and corrupt, not only deal with surplus stock but also help generate nonfarm employment, and consequently generate demand for local manufactures, stimulate industry, and hence help savings and investment.[2] Food-for-work spending was only $170 million in 2001, and budgeted at $259 million for 2002–2003, whereas public food stocks are valued at $10.6 billion. The food-for-work program was absorbed into the national rural employment guarantee scheme in the 2005 budget.

Society and Economy

Wealth and income present intense contrasts in Indian society. At the top, a small number of incredibly affluent Indians have made fortunes in basic business and industry. The wealth of the Ambanis, Tatas, and Birlas rival that of the richest corporate tycoons in the world. Below them, a much larger group, nearly 100 million Indians (approximately 10 percent) are relatively well off and enjoy a standard of living comparable to that of the middle classes in many developed countries. India has a sophisticated, technologically developed industrial sector that produces a variety of consumer products, military technologies, nuclear energy, computers, and computer software. For instance, India's nuclear explosions were the product of indigenous scientific and technological research.

India's lower middle classes, about half of all Indians, are mainly small farmers or urban workers. Relatively poor by global standards, they barely eke out a living. Finally, at the bottom of the class structure, between a quarter and a third of the population is extremely poor and is concentrated mostly in India's thousands of villages as landless laborers or as the urban unemployed in city slums. Low levels of literacy, poverty, and primitive technology characterize a good part of India's rural society.

India's large population continues to grow at a relatively rapid pace, and India will surpass China as the world's largest country in a few years. Since India already has more labor than it can use productively, rapid population growth hinders economic growth. Simply put, the more people, the more mouths there are to feed, and the more food and economic products must be produced simply to maintain people's standard of living.

Why does India's population continue to grow at such a rapid pace? The comparison with China provides part of the explanation. The communist-led Chinese government has pursued strict birth control policies of one child per family since the late 1970s. In part, coercion was used to implement these policies. The result was to reduce birthrates dramatically. India's democratic government, by contrast, has found it difficult to implement population control policies.

Coercion is not the only means of reducing population growth rates, however. By 2005, the national rate of population growth was around 1.68 percent per year, a figure that Kerala had achieved many years earlier. An important reason was that Kerala has one of the highest literacy rates, especially female literacy rates, in India. Whereas the average literacy rate in India is around 48 percent for females (and 70 percent for males), Kerala's female literacy rate is 90.92 percent. Literate women are more likely to marry later in life, exercise options in the work force, have some power in personal relationships, and practice birth control.

India is one of the few countries in the world that has a lower percentage of females than men; the ratio is 1.06 males to females. Indian society favors boys over girls, as evidenced by all social indicators, from lower female literacy and nutrition rates to lower survival of female versus male infants. Prejudice against girls is reinforced through such traditions as the dowry system (the Hindu custom of giving the groom and his family assets, a dowry, at the time of a daughter's wedding). These traditions, deeply rooted and slow to change, confine the majority of Indian women, particularly poor women, to a life of few opportunities.

India also has the world's largest population of child labor. Children are employed widely, not only in agricultural labor but also in such urban enterprises as match making and rug weaving and selling tea or sweets at train stations. Children usually work long hours at low wages. They cannot receive an education and consequently lose the chance for upward social mobility. The issue of child labor is closely related to India's failure to provide universal primary education (see Figure 2). If school-age children were required to be in school, they could not be readily employed as full-time laborers. Many Indian elites argue that in their poor country, compulsory primary education is an unaffordable luxury. However, this argument is not persuasive; many poor African countries have higher rates of primary school enrollments than does India (and recall the example of Kerala, among India's poorer states). The more likely obstacle to universal primary education is poverty and caste inequality. Many upper-caste elites do not see lower-caste children as their equals and do not consider the issue of educating lower-caste children a priority. Child labor is directly linked to poverty and survival, since many poor families see large families as a form of insurance. Yet for most poor families, a larger family also means not being able to invest in each child's education and depending on their children's labor for survival.

Figure 2

Educational Levels by Gender

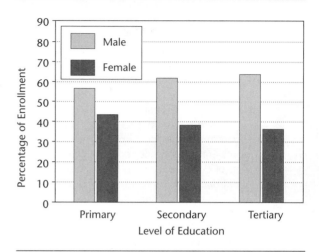

Source: UNESCO Institute for Statistics, http://www.uis.unesco.org/en/stats/stats

Caste issues pervade many other aspects of India's political and economic life (see "Institutional Intricacies: The Caste System"). First, by assigning people to specific occupations, it impedes the free movement of labor and talent. Although the link between caste and occupation has been weakening in India, especially in urban areas, it remains an important organizing principle for employment. Second, in the political arena, caste is a powerful force around which political groups and voting blocs coalesce. Because caste is usually organized at the local level, Indian politics often takes on a local and segmented quality. Related to this, caste cuts across class, making it difficult for labor, business, and other economic classes in India to act in a politically cohesive manner. Third, the Indian government often uses caste as a basis for **reservations,** the Indian version of affirmative action. The government reserves some jobs, admissions into universities, and similar privileges for members of specific underprivileged castes. This has become a highly contentious issue in Indian politics. And last, those who suffer the most in India's **caste system** are those at the bottom of the caste hierarchy: the untouchables. Nearly 10 percent of India's population, or some 90 million people, are categorized by the Indian census as belonging to the untouchables or scheduled

Institutional Intricacies: **The Caste System**

Originally derived from the Portuguese word *castas,* today the word *caste* inevitably evokes images of a rigid hierarchy that characterizes Indian society. In reality, however, castes are less immutable and timeless categories than suggested by the popular image.

Historically, the **caste system** compartmentalized and ranked the Hindu population of the Indian subcontinent through rules governing various aspects of daily life, such as eating, marriage, and prayer. Sanctioned by religion, the hierarchy of caste is based on a conception of the world as divided into realms of purity and impurity. Each hereditary and endogamous group (that is, a group into which one is born and within which one marries) constitutes a *jati,* which is itself organized by *varna,* or shades of color. The four main *varna* are the **Brahmin,** or priestly, caste; the Kshatriya, or

warrior and royal, caste; the Vaishyas, or trading, caste; and the Shudra, or artisan, caste. Each of these *varna* is divided into many *jatis* that often approximate occupational groups (such as potters, barbers, and carpenters). Those who were not considered members of organized Hindu society because they lived in forests and on hills rather than in towns and villages, or were involved in "unclean" occupations such as sweepers and leather workers were labeled **untouchables,** outcastes, or **scheduled castes.** Because each *jati* is often concentrated in a particular region, it is sometimes possible to change one's *varna* when one moves to a different part of the country by changing one's name and adopting the social customs of higher castes, for example, giving up eating meat. Some flexibility within the rigidity of the system has contributed to its survival over the centuries.

castes, as they are officially known. Notwithstanding considerable government efforts, the social stigma that members of this group suffer runs deep.

India in the Global Economy

After a prolonged colonial experience, nationalist India in the 1950s shunned economic links with the outside world. Although India pursued an active foreign policy as a leader of the **nonaligned bloc,** it was defensive in its economic contacts. A prolonged and successful nationalist movement help explain both India's urge to play a global political role and its desire to protect its economy from foreign influence. India's political and economic elites favored protectionism in trade and sought to limit foreign investment. Although three decades of this policy helped generate an industrial base and domestic capitalism, it gave rise to problems that led to economic liberalization, from which new problems arose.

During the decades of relatively autarkic development, powerful groups emerged with vested interests in maintaining the old order. Many bureaucrats abused

the system of government controls over private economic activities by accepting bribes to issue government licenses to start private businesses. Indian industry was often relatively inefficient because neither cheaper foreign goods nor foreign investors were readily allowed into India. Moreover, organized labor, especially in government-controlled factories, had a stake in maintaining inefficient factories because they offered a greater number of jobs. These well-entrenched groups resisted liberalization and threatened to throw their political weight behind opposition parties, making the ruling government hesitant to undertake any decisive policy shift.

However, not long after the liberalization of the domestic economy began in the 1980s, the government sponsored a significant shift toward integrating India into the international economy. Embracing globalization quickly bore fruit. Foreign investment soared from $100 million a year between 1970 and 1991 to nearly $4 billion annually between 1992 and 1998, to $4.3 billion in 2003. However, the level of foreign direct investment in India—0.6 to 0.7 percent of the annual gross domestic product (GDP)—remains relatively low; China and Brazil receive several times that volume each year.[3] Furthermore, because foreign investment focuses on the domestic market, it has not always facilitated export promotion, potentially a major benefit in poor countries.

One high-tech sector in which India has excelled is computer software. Indian firms and multinational corporations with operations in India take ample advantage of India's highly skilled and poorly paid scientific and engineering talent to make India a world leader in the production of software. India can boast the equivalent of the Silicon Valley in the boom area around Bangalore in southern India, home to a large number of software firms. Furthermore, within the past few years, transnational corporations have taken advantage of the fact that India's large number of scientifically trained graduates are fluent English-speakers. When Americans have a problem in operating their computer, cable television, or appliance, their call for help these days is likely to be answered by a technician in New Delhi or Bangalore.

Considerable pressure is being brought to bear on the Indian government to liberalize banking, insurance, and other services as part of the World Trade Organization's (WTO) agreement on trade in services. Over forty foreign banks operate independently in India, and the government is now allowing foreign holdings in Indian banks. It has also opened up the insurance sector to private and foreign investment. The result can be a mixed blessing. For example, foreign banks have focused on retail banking in profitable urban areas, ignoring less lucrative areas of lending. Small borrowers in agriculture and small-scale industrialists have found their access to bank lending curtailed. Loans to rural areas and poorer regions have fallen.

A significant component of India's performance in the international political economy concerns its regional context. India is a giant among the South Asian countries of Pakistan, Bangladesh, Sri Lanka, Nepal, and Bhutan, although its northern neighbor, China, is an even bigger and more powerful giant.

The effect of India's troubled relations with neighboring countries is a low level of regional economic interactions. Figure 3 compares exports as a percentage of gross national product (GNP) for India and its major trading partners; India's export quantity and rate

Figure 3

Exports of India and Its Trading Partners

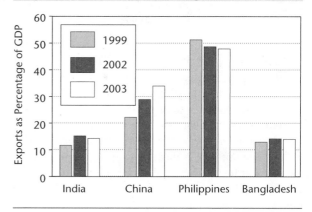

Source: World Bank Country at a Glance, www.worldbank.org/data/countrydata/countrydata.html

of growth are relatively low. As nations increasingly look to their neighbors for trade and investment, the pressure on India and its neighbors to increase economic contact is likely to grow. Some movement in this direction was already evident in the first half of the 1990s, especially toward China, but there is still a long way to go before South Asia develops an integrated zone of economic activity.

In conclusion, economic globalization has had a powerful and complex impact on India's economy and politics. India has recently been identified as a potential economic superpower of the twenty-first century. It is well-positioned to reap the benefits of a large, well-trained, highly skilled population willing to work for low wages, and a growing number of world-class corporations. Globalization has promoted the rapid expansion of a large middle class, whose members eagerly participate in the world's consumer culture. At the same time, however, globalization has increased economic inequality by generating more benefits for those in the middle and upper ranks of the income pyramid than for the rural and urban poor. One result was that the BJP's "India shining" proclamation fell on so many deaf ears in the 2004 elections. The challenge for the current Congress-dominated coalition is to devise ways for globalization to work for all.

Section ❸ Governance and Policy-Making

Organization of the State

India is a democratic republic with a parliamentary and federal system of government. The constitution adopted in 1950 created this system, and although there have been many profound changes since then in the distribution and use of power, the basic character of India's political system has remained unchanged. For much of this period, India has been a stable, democratic country with universal suffrage and periodic elections at local, state, and national levels. This continuity and democratic stability are remarkable among developing countries. To simplify a complex reality, Indian democracy has proved so resilient because its political institutions, while always under pressure, have been able to accommodate many new power challenges and to repress the most difficult ones.

India's constitution is lengthy. In contrast to the British constitution on which it is modeled, it is a written document that has been periodically amended by legislation. Among its special features, three are worth noting. First, unlike many other constitutions, the Indian constitution directs the government to promote social and economic equality and justice. The constitution thus goes beyond stipulating formal procedures of decision making and allocating powers among political institutions, and outlines policy goals. Although the impact of these constitutional provisions on government policies is limited, the provisions ensure that issues of welfare and social justice are not ignored. Second, the Indian constitution, like the U.S. Constitution, provides for freedom of religion and defines India as a secular state. This was an especially controversial issue in Indian politics during the late 1990s because the BJP was committed to establishing Hinduism as a state-sanctioned religion. And third, the constitution allows for the temporary suspension of many democratic rights under conditions of emergency. These provisions were used, somewhat understandably, during wars with Pakistan or China. But they have also been invoked, more disturbingly, to deal with internal political threats, most dramatically during the national Emergency from 1975 to 1977, when a politically vulnerable Indira Gandhi suspended many democratic rights and imprisoned her leading political opponents.

India's federal system is relatively centralized. The central government controls the most essential government functions such as defense, foreign policy, taxation, public expenditures, and economic planning, especially industrial planning. State governments formally control such policy areas as agriculture, education, and law and order within the states. Because they are heavily dependent on the central government for funds in these policy areas, however, the power of the states is limited.

India is a parliamentary democracy designed on the British model. The Indian parliament, known as the *Lok Sabha,* or House of the People, is the most significant political institution. The leader of the political party with the most seats in the *Lok Sabha* becomes the prime minister, who nominates a cabinet, mostly from the ranks of other members of parliament belonging to the ruling coalition. The prime minister and the cabinet, along with permanent civil servants, control much of the government's daily functioning. The prime minister is the linchpin of the system because effective power is concentrated in that office, where most of the country's important policies originate. By contrast, the office of the president is largely ceremonial. In periodic national elections, 544 members of the *Lok Sabha,* the lower house of the bicameral parliament, are elected. The *Lok Sabha* is much more politically significant than the **Rajya Sabha,** the upper house. The prime minister governs with the help of the cabinet, which periodically meets to discuss important issues, including any new legislation that is likely to be initiated. Individually, cabinet members are the heads of various ministries, for example, Foreign Affairs or Industry, that direct the daily work of the government and make up the permanent bureaucracy.

The Executive

The President and the Prime Minister

The president is the official head of the state and is elected indirectly every five years by an electoral college composed of elected representatives from the national and state governments. In most circumstances, the president acts on the advice of the prime minister and is thus not a very powerful political figure. The presidency is a ceremonial office, symbolizing the unity of the country, and it is supposedly above partisan politics. Under exceptional circumstances, however, especially when the selection of a prime minister becomes a complex issue, the president can play an important political role. For example, in the 1998 election, there was a hung parliament, with no party gaining a clear majority. The president then requested the party with the largest percentage of votes, the BJP, to show that it could muster enough allies to form a government.

The prime minister and other cabinet ministers are the most powerful political figures in India. Because they represent the majority party coalition in parliament, the passage of a bill is not as complicated a process as it can be in a presidential system, especially one with a divided government. The prime minister and the cabinet also head various ministries, so that after legislation is passed, they oversee its implementation. In practice, the permanent bureaucracy, especially the senior and middle-level bureaucrats, are responsible for policy implementation. Nevertheless, as in most other parliamentary systems, such as those in Britain, Germany, and Japan, there is considerable overlap in India between the executive and the legislative branches of the government, creating a greater degree of centralization of power than is initially evident. The duration of the prime minister's tenure in office has become steadily truncated over time. Between 1947 and 1984, except for a few brief interludes, India had only two prime ministers: Nehru and Indira Gandhi (see Table 1). This is nearly unique among democracies; it underlines the powerful hold that the Nehru-Gandhi family had on India's political imagination. Since then, there has been a more rapid turnover. Rajiv Gandhi, Indira Gandhi's son, succeeded his mother after her assassination in 1984. When he lost power four years later, there were short-lived governments under the leadership of V. P. Singh and Chandra Shekhar. Narasimha Rao lasted his full term in office. Atal Behari Vajpayee (1999–2004) served an entire term in office, unlike his previous truncated terms.

The method of selecting a prime minister in India is fairly complex. The original choice of Nehru was a natural one, given his prominent position in the nationalist movement and his relationship to founding father Mahatma Gandhi. The choice of Indira Gandhi was less obvious. She was chosen to head the Congress Party by a group of prominent second-tier party leaders because of her national name, which they calculated would reap handsome electoral rewards. A similar logic prevailed when Rajiv Gandhi was chosen by party elites to succeed his mother. Rajiv Gandhi benefited from the wave of sympathy generated by his mother's assassination, and he led the Congress Party back to power in 1984 with a handsome electoral majority.

Following Rajiv Gandhi's assassination, the Nehru-Gandhi family line appeared to have reached an end, since Rajiv Gandhi's wife, Sonia Gandhi, was of Italian background, and their children were too young to enter politics. In 1991, Narasimha Rao was brought back as an elder statesman who was non-threatening and acceptable to competing factions within the Congress Party. Both subsequent United Front prime ministers were compromise candidates who lacked the personality and power to manage their disparate coalitions. In 1998, the Congress Party attempted to resurrect its fortunes by choosing Sonia Gandhi to head their party, creating the possibility that the political rule of the Nehru-Gandhi family would continue. The gamble paid off in 2004 when Congress, headed by Sonia Gandhi, narrowly edged the BJP out of power. Although she declined to be prime minister, mainly to avoid controversy about her Italian origins, as head of the Congress Party, she wields significant power over the government.

The Cabinet

The prime minister chooses the cabinet, mostly from among the party's members elected to parliament. Seniority, competence, and personal loyalty are the main criteria that a prime minister takes into account when choosing cabinet ministers. Regional and caste representation at the highest level of government must also be considered. During Indira Gandhi's rule, personal loyalty was critical in the choice of senior ministers. Rajiv Gandhi, by contrast, put a high premium on competence, which unfortunately he equated with youth and technical skills, at the expense of political experience. Since Vajpayee was able to form a government only with the help of many smaller parties in 1999, the heads of these parties had to be accommodated, producing a vast, eclectic, and disparate cabinet.

The Bureaucracy

The prime minister and cabinet ministers run the government in close collaboration with senior civil servants. Each senior minister oversees what is often a sprawling bureaucracy, staffed by some very competent, overworked, senior civil servants and by many not-so-competent, underworked, lowly bureaucrats.

The **Indian Administrative Service** (IAS), an elite corps of top bureaucrats, constitutes a critical but relatively thin layer at the top of India's bureaucracy. The competence of the IAS is a central reason that India is moderately well governed. Because political leaders come and go, whereas senior civil servants stay, many civil servants possess a storehouse of knowledge and expertise that makes them very powerful. Higher-level civil servants in India reach their positions after considerable experience within the government. They are named to the IAS at a relatively young age, usually in their early twenties, by passing a highly competitive entrance exam. Some of India's most talented young men and women were attracted to the IAS during the 1950s and 1960s, reflecting the prestige that service in national government used to enjoy in Indian society. The attraction of the IAS has declined, however, and many talented young people now go into engineering or business administration, or leave the country for better opportunities abroad. Government service has become tainted as areas of corruption have developed and the level of professionalism within the IAS has eroded, mainly because politicians prefer loyalty over merit and seniority when making promotions. Nevertheless, the IAS continues to recruit very talented young people, many of whom become dedicated senior civil servants who still constitute the backbone of the Indian government.

Below the IAS, the level of talent and professionalism drops rather sharply. Within each ministry at the national level and in many parallel substructures at the state level, the bureaucracy in India is infamous for corruption and inefficiency. These problems contribute to the gap between good policies made at the top and their poor implementation at the local level.

Other State Institutions

The Military and the Police

Unlike the militaries in many other developing countries, say, Brazil and Nigeria, the Indian military has never intervened directly in politics. The Indian military, with more than 1 million well-trained and well-equipped members, is a highly professional organization. Over the years, the continuity of constitutional, electoral politics and a relatively apolitical military have come to reinforce and strengthen each other. Civilian politicians provide ample resources to the armed forces and, for the most part, let them function as a professional organization. The armed forces, in turn, obey the orders of democratically elected leaders, and although they lobby to preserve their own interests, they mostly stay out of the normal tumble of democratic politics.

Since the 1970s, two factors have weakened this well-institutionalized separation of politics and military. First, during Indira Gandhi's rule, loyalty to political leaders became the key criterion for securing top military jobs. This policy tended to politicize the military and narrow the separation between politics and the military.

Second, there were growing regional and ethnic demands for secession (see Section 4). As these demands became more intense in some states, notably in Kashmir, and as militants began to resort to armed conflict, occasionally with the help of India's often-hostile neighbor Pakistan, the Indian government called in the armed forces. However, soldiers are not trained to resolve political problems; rather, they are trained to use force to secure compliance from reluctant political actors. As a result, not only have democratic norms and human rights been violated in India, but the distance between politics and the military has narrowed.

A similar trend toward politicization and deprofessionalization has occurred in India's sprawling police services, but with a difference. The Indian police organization was never as professionalized as the armed forces, and the police services come under the jurisdiction of state governments, not the central government. Because state governments are generally less well run than the national government, the cumulative impact is that the Indian police are not apolitical civil servants. State-level politicians regularly interfere in police personnel issues, and police officers in turn regularly oblige the politicians who help them. The problem is especially serious at lower levels. The police are widely regarded as easily bribed and often allied with criminals or politicians. In some states, such as Bihar and Uttar Pradesh, police often take sides in local conflicts instead of acting as neutral arbiters or enforcers of laws. When they take sides, they tilt the power balance in favor of dominant social groups such as landowners or upper castes or the majority Hindu religious community.

In addition to the regular armed forces and the state-level police forces, paramilitary forces, controlled by the national government, number nearly half a million men. As Indian politics became more turbulent in the 1980s, paramilitary forces steadily expanded. Because the national government calls on the regular armed forces only as a last resort in the management of internal conflicts and because state-level police forces are not very reliable, paramilitary forces are viewed as a way to maintain order. A large, sprawling, and relatively ineffective police service remains a problematic presence in Indian society.

The Judiciary

An independent judiciary is another component of India's state system. But unlike Britain, where the judiciary's role is limited by parliamentary sovereignty, a fundamental contradiction is embedded in the Indian constitution between the principles of parliamentary sovereignty and judicial review. Over the years, the judiciary and the parliament have often clashed, with the former trying to preserve the constitution's basic structure and the latter asserting its right to amend the constitution (see "Institutional Intricacies: The Executive Versus the Judiciary"). The judiciary comprises an apex court, atop a series of national courts, high courts in states, and lower courts in districts.

The supreme judicial authority is the Supreme Court, comprising a chief justice and seventeen other judges, appointed by the president, but as in most other matters of political significance in India, only on the advice of the prime minister. Once appointed, judges cannot be removed from the bench until retirement at age sixty-five. The caseload on the Supreme Court, as on much of the rest of the Indian legal system, is extremely heavy, with a significant backlog.

The main political role of the Supreme Court is to ensure that legislation conforms to the intent of the constitution. Because the Indian constitution is very detailed, however, the need for interpretation is not as great as in many other countries. Nevertheless, there are real conflicts, both within the constitution and in India's political landscape, that often need to be adjudicated by the Supreme Court. For example, the constitution simultaneously protects private property and urges the government to pursue social justice. Indian leaders have often promulgated socialist legislation, for example, requiring the redistribution of agricultural land. Legislation of this nature is considered by the Supreme Court because it potentially violates the right to private property. Many Supreme Court cases have involved the conflict between socialistically inclined legislation and constitutional rights. Cases involving other politically significant issues, for instance, rights of religious minorities such as Muslims and the rights of women, also periodically reach the Supreme Court.

Like many other Indian political institutions, the Supreme Court lost much of its autonomy in the 1980s. The process began during Indira Gandhi's rule, when she argued that the court was too conservative and an obstacle to her socialist program. To remedy this shortcoming, she appointed many pliant judges, including the chief justice. The Supreme Court itself more or less complied with her wishes during the two years of Emergency (1975–1977), when the political and civil rights of many Indians were violated. No such dramatic instance of a politicized Supreme Court has recurred since the late 1970s.

The Supreme Court often functions as a bulwark for citizens against state invasiveness, as is evident from many landmark civil rights judgments. The Court introduced a system of public interest litigation

Institutional Intricacies: *The Executive Versus the Judiciary*

Over the years, the Supreme Court has clashed head to head with the parliament as a result of the contradiction between principles of parliamentary sovereignty and judicial review that is embedded in India's constitution. For instance, during the early years of independence, the courts overturned state government laws to redistribute land from landlords (*zamindars*), saying that the laws violated the *zamindars'* fundamental rights. In retaliation, the parliament passed the first of a series of amendments to the constitution to protect the executive's authority to promote land redistribution. But matters did not end there. The Supreme Court responded by passing a judgment stating that the parliament did not have the power to abrogate fundamental rights. In 1970, the court also invalidated the bank nationalization bill and a presidential order abolishing privy purses (including titles and privileges of former rulers of India's princely states). In retaliation, the parliament passed a series of amendments that undercut the Supreme Court's rulings, thus moving the power balance toward parliamentary sovereignty. The Supreme Court responded that the court still reserved for itself the discretion to reject any constitutional amendments passed by parliament on the grounds that the amendments could not change the constitution's basic structure. During the Emergency period, the parliament passed yet another amendment that limited the Supreme Court's judicial review to procedural issues. The Janata government in the post-Emergency era, however, reversed these changes, thus reintroducing the tension between the executive and judiciary.

Since the 1980s, the courts have increasingly functioned as a bulwark for citizens by protecting their civil liberties from state coercion. For instance, since 1993, it has enforced a policy of compensating victims of violence while in police custody. In 1985, the Supreme Court upheld a verdict finding two people guilty of murdering their wives on the grounds that the dowry was insufficient and sentenced them to life imprisonment. In the mid-1980s, the Supreme Court clashed with parliament on its interpretation of personal law over the Shah Bano case. In India, personal law falls under the purview of religion, although an individual can choose secular alternatives. However, a woman married under religious law cannot seek divorce or alimony under secular law. Neither Muslim nor Hindu personal law entitles women to alimony. The British colonial government had passed a law that required divorced men to provide maintenance to their ex-wives. Shah Bano, a destitute seventy-five-year-old woman abandoned and later divorced by her husband, filed for maintenance under this law. The Supreme Court upheld Shah Bano's right to maintenance on the grounds that secular laws transcended personal law (religious law). The parliament, succumbing to pressures from religious leaders, passed a bill excluding Muslim women from the purview of secular laws.

The battle between the executive and the judiciary has compromised the autonomy of the courts. The judiciary has been affected by the general malaise of institutional decay that has affected Indian politics over the years. The backlog of cases has grown phenomenally, while expeditious judgment of cases has declined dramatically.

---

that enabled bonded laborers, disenfranchised tribal people, the homeless, and indigent women to redress their claims. In recent years, the Supreme Court has defended environmental causes. To protect the Taj Mahal, India's most treasured national monument, from damage by air pollution, it ordered the closure of 212 nearby businesses that had chronically violated environmental regulations. It similarly shut down almost 200 polluters along the Ganges River. The Court enforced clean water and air laws in New Delhi in 1996–1997 by ordering that polluting cars and buses be removed from the roads and by shutting down polluting enterprises. It required central and state governments to prevent starvation by releasing food stocks and to promote education by providing school lunches and daycare facilities.

Compared to other large, multiethnic democracies, India has generally shown great respect for the pillars of civil rights: a free and lively press, legal protections for citizens' rights, and an independent judiciary. India's media, especially its newspapers and magazines, are as free as any in the world. They represent a wide variety of viewpoints, engage in vigorous investigative reporting and analysis, and maintain pressure for public action. The combination of a vocal intellectual stratum and a free press is a cherished element in India's democracy.

Nevertheless, India's tradition of a strong, interventionist state has enabled the government to violate civil liberties, and the trend since the mid-1980s has been troubling. Global events conjoined with national ones resulted in a restriction of civil liberties in the aftermath of September 11. The BJP-led government used the war against terrorism as justification for depicting proindependence groups in Kashmir and Muslim groups throughout India as terrorists. Soon after September 11, the Indian government banned the Students Islamic Movement of India (SIMI), the students' wing of the radical Islamic Jamaat-e-Islami political party in Pakistan. However, the government did not ban the Bajrang Dal, the militant organization with ties to the Visva Hindu Parisad that has repeatedly organized anti-Muslim violence, most recently in Gujarat in 2002.

After September 11, the Indian government issued the Prevention of Terrorism Ordinance (POTO), later enacted into law by parliament. Its definition of terrorism was extremely vague, and a citizen need not have committed a specific act to be charged under POTO: conspiring, attempting to commit, advocating, abetting, advising, or inciting such acts was punishable with penalties ranging from stiff prison sentences to death. Membership in a terrorist organization was punishable with life imprisonment. Confessions made to police officers were admissible as evidence in courts, contrary to ordinary law, and confessions were brutally extracted in Indian police stations. The right to bail was severely restricted. An accused person could be kept in police custody for one month and imprisoned for six months without charges.[4] In certain regions, merely possessing firearms was punishable with life imprisonment.

Predictably, the government primarily used POTO against Muslims and political dissidents. The largest number of arrests took place in India's newest state, Jharkhand, where members and supporters of Marxist-Leninist groups were incarcerated under POTO. By 2002, twenty-three organizations, including Marxist-Leninist parties such as the CPI (ML)–People's War Group, and the Maoist Communist Center had been banned under POTO. The new government has demonstrated greater commitment to the protection of civil liberties than its predecessor. Shortly after Manmohan Singh became prime minister, the cabinet approved the repeal of POTO on grounds that it had been misused. Instead it amended existing laws to tackle terrorism. Whereas POTO placed the burden of proof on the accused, the amended act shifts it back to the prosecutor.

Subnational Government

Under India's federal system, the balance of power between the central and state governments varies by time and place. In general, the more powerful and popular the central government and prime minister are, the less likely states are to pursue an independent course. During the rule of Nehru and especially under Indira Gandhi, the states were often quite constrained. By contrast, weaker central governments, like the BJP-led alliance that took office in 1999, or the Congress-led alliance that took office in 2004, enlarge the room for state governments to maneuver. When state governments are run by political parties other than the national ruling party—and this is often true in contemporary India—there is considerable scope for center-state conflict. For example, a popular communist government in West Bengal has often disagreed with the national government in New Delhi, charging it with discriminatory treatment in the allocation of finances and other centrally controlled resources.

While the political parties at the national and the state levels may differ, the formal structure of the twenty-eight state governments parallels that of the national government. The chief minister of each state heads the state government. The chief minister is the leader of the majority party (or the party with most seats) in the lower house of the state legislature. The chief minister appoints cabinet ministers who head various ministries staffed by a state-level, permanent bureaucracy. The quality of government below the national level is often poor, contributing to regional and ethnic conflicts.

In lieu of a president, each state has a governor, appointed by the national president. The governors, like the president, are supposed to serve on the advice of the chief minister, but in practice, they often become independently powerful, especially in states where the national government is at odds with the state government or where state governments are unstable. Governors can dismiss elected state governments and proclaim temporary presidential rule if they determine state governments to be ineffective. When this happens, the elected government is dissolved, and the state is governed from New Delhi until fresh elections are called and a new government is elected. Although this provision is intended to be a sensible constitutional option, an intrusive national government has often used it for partisan purposes.

The power struggle between the central government and the states is ongoing. With many Indian states inhabited by people with distinctive traditions and cultures, including language, and with conflicting political parties in power at the national and state levels, central-state relations can be fueled by substantial political and ethnic conflicts.

In recent years, Indian politics has become increasingly regionalized. Three new states were formed in 2000 out of existing states. Furthermore, states have become increasingly autonomous economically and politically. As a result of economic liberalization, states have acquired rights and opportunities to seek out investors independent of the national government. One consequence is that regional inequalities are widening as states like Haryana, Punjab, Maharashtra, Gujarat, Andhra Pradesh, Karnataka, and Tamil Nadu, have aggressively sought investments while some of the largest and poorest states in the north and east have fallen behind.

The twenty-eight states of India's federal system have also come to play an increasingly important role in national governance. In each of the national elections since 1989, parties based in a single state have been key to the success of coalition governments. According to the Election Commission's classification of parties, in the five national elections between 1991 and 2004, the vote share of national parties

(those with a base in many states) dropped from 80.91% in 1991 to 67.98% in 1998 and the proportion of seats they controlled 86% in 1991 to 72% in 1998. By contrast, parties based in single states increased their percentage share of the votes from 17 to 27 percent and their seats from 16 to 29 percent. Since 1989, every coalition government has depended on regional parties for its survival. This development has double-edged implications for democracy. On the one hand, governing coalitions that are established by disparate parties with little ideological or programmatic cohesion are likely to be unstable. On the other hand, national governments are less likely than they were in the past to seek the dismissal of state governments because national governments are likely to be composed of regional political parties.

The *panchayats,* which function at the local, district, and state levels, represent the most important attempts at the devolution of power. The *panchayats* are a precolonial institution that was responsible historically for adjudicating conflicts and presiding over community affairs in the rural areas. In 1959, the Indian government introduced a three-tier model of *panchayats,* linked together by indirect elections. However, it gave the *panchayats* meager resources, for members of parliament and the legislative assembly saw them as potential rivals to their authority. By the mid-1960s, the *panchayats* were stagnating and declining.

Some states revived the *panchayats* on their own initiative. In 1978, the communist government of West Bengal overhauled the *panchayat* system by providing for direct elections and giving them additional resources and responsibilities. Other states followed suit. In 1992, the government amended the constitution to enable all states to strengthen the *panchayats,* although states were free to create their own models. It envisaged the *panchayats'* primary role as implementing development programs and encouraging greater local involvement in government. The amendment stipulated that *panchayat* elections would be held every five years and made provisions for reserving 33 percent of the seats for women and seats proportional to the population for scheduled castes and tribes. In the first elections held under the new framework (in 1993), 700,000 women were elected to office. Most states met and several exceeded the 33 percent women's reservations at all three levels.

The abilities of women who were elected to the *panchayats* varied widely. Women who had a prior history of political activism were most likely to use the *panchayats* to benefit women. Some were responsible for the *panchayats'* sponsoring important local development projects. Others sought *panchayat* action on behalf of women over issues like marriage, divorce, and alcoholism. However, most women elected to the *panchayats* had no prior history of activism and became tokens who were silenced, marginalized, and, in extreme situations, even harassed and attacked. Many women ran for election in order to represent the interests of powerful men. In some cases, when women threatened male candidates, they were accused of sexual immorality. Women were often ignorant about the functions of the *panchayats* and relied on their husbands for advice.

More generally, the resources and planning capabilities of the *panchayats* are relatively limited. State legislatures determine how much power and authority the *panchayats* can wield. Very few states have engaged in a serious devolution of the *panchayats'* development functions. Most *panchayats* are responsible for implementing rural development schemes but not devising them. Policy is made at the national and state levels. Although considerable resources pass through them, local governments have little discretion over how they are allocated. Local political elites, bureaucrats, and influential citizens often siphon off a large share of public funds and determine where projects will be located, who gets a contract, and who is hired on public projects. Thus, many local governments in India tend to be corrupt, ineffective, and wasteful. City streets are not kept clean, potholes are not repaired, irrigation canals are not properly maintained, and rural schools are so poorly built that they leak as soon as the monsoons start.

The Policy-Making Process

Major policies in India are made by the national government, in New Delhi. The prime minister and senior cabinet ministers are generally responsible for initiating policies. Behind the scenes, senior civil servants in each ministry, as well as in cross-ministry offices like the prime minister's secretariat and the planning commission, play a critical role in identifying problems, synthesizing data, and presenting to political leaders alternative solutions and their implications. After decisions have been made at the highest level, many require new legislation. Because the prime minister usually has a clear majority in parliament, passage of most legislation is ensured, except in extremely controversial areas.

The real policy drama in India occurs early on, when major bills are under consideration, and during the process of implementation. Consider economic liberalization policies, which represented a major policy change. The new course was formulated at the highest level of government, involving only a handful of senior ministers and bureaucrats. To reach the decision, however, a fairly complex set of political activities took place. Decision makers consulted some of the most important interest groups, such as associations of Indian businessmen and representatives of international organizations like the World Bank and the IMF. Others, including those who might be adversely affected, were heard; organized labor, for example, might call a one-day general strike (it actually did) to warn the government that any attempt to privatize the public sector would meet considerable resistance. Newspapers, magazines, and intellectuals also expressed support or opposition. Political parties got into the act. Members of the ruling party, the Congress in this case, did not necessarily support the political thinking of their own leaders at the early stage; rather, they worried about the political implications of policies for intraparty power struggles and future elections. Opposition parties, in turn, worried about the interests of their constituents. These pressures modified the policy that the government eventually adopted.

After policies have been adopted, their implementation is far from assured. Continuing with the liberalization example, some aspects of the new policy package proved easier to implement than others. Changing the exchange rate (the value of the Indian rupee in relation to the U.S. dollar) was relatively easy to implement because both the policy decision and its implementation require the actions of only a handful of politicians and bureaucrats. By contrast, the attempts to simplify the procedures for Indian or foreign business executives to create new business enterprises proved far more complicated. Implementation of such policies involves layers of bureaucrats, most of whom benefit from the control they already exercise. When forced to relinquish power, many dragged their feet and, where possible, sabotaged the newly simplified procedures.

Another example is the policies aimed at improving the standard of living for the Indian poor. Since the 1960s, the national government has attempted to redistribute agricultural land and create public works programs to help India's rural poor. The national government set the broad outlines for land reforms and allocated funds for public works programs but left refinement of these policies, as well as their implementation, to state governments. State governments vary in terms of social classes in the state, ruling party coalitions, and quality of their bureaucracies. The result is that the implementation of antipoverty policies within India has been quite uneven.

Attempts to generate extra employment for the rural poor through public works projects (such as road construction and canal cleaning) have been somewhat more successful than land redistribution policies because they do not involve any direct confiscation of property. The main issues in the implementation of these policies are the quality of projects chosen, whether they target the poor, and how honestly they are completed. Because the quality of local governments in implementing national policies varies (although it is rarely very high), many of the funds spent on poverty alleviation programs have been wasted. Public works policies have been most effectively implemented in the states of Maharashtra and West Bengal, where there is considerable political pressure from caste or class politics, and in some southern states, where the local bureaucracy is more efficient.

To review, the policy-making process in India, though relatively centralized, takes into account various interests and frequently produces well-developed policies. By contrast, the process of implementation is quite decentralized and relatively ineffective. Sound policy ideas and positive intentions do not reach fruition because policies are diluted at the state level and because of lackluster implementation.

Section ❹ Representation and Participation

Over the years, India has become a participatory democracy, as previously excluded social groups such as the poor, the landless, and backward castes entered the political arena and used their influence to shape the political process. In the early years of independence, the Congress Party mobilized most groups. However, in recent years, there has been a proliferation of political parties that have appealed to the Indian masses on ethnic grounds (particularly caste and religion), a trend initiated by Indira Gandhi. Simultaneously, the adoption of the democratic idea in the institutional sphere led to an explosion of social movements in civil society. Poor women have marched on the streets of Andhra Pradesh demanding prohibition of the sale of liquor (because of the economic toll it inflicts and its role in domestic violence), while poor tribals in Maharashtra have protested their displacement by the construction of large dams. The democratic idea is so deeply rooted that today thousands of nongovernmental organizations function in the country, representing causes ranging from welfare issues, to the environment, to human rights. Some social movements have transformed themselves into political parties, while others militantly oppose the established political system. Thus, ironically, while Indian democracy has become more truncated in some respects as it has experienced institutional decline and decay, it has flourished in other respects through the growth of popular participation within and outside the party system.

The Legislature

A good place to begin the discussion of representation and participation in a democracy is with the legislature. The Indian parliament is bicameral, consisting of the *Rajya Sabha* and the *Lok Sabha*. Although the government dominates the parliament, election to the *Lok Sabha* is of vital importance. First, the outcome of parliamentary elections determines which party coalition will control the government. Second, although members of parliament are unable to influence policies directly, they enjoy considerable status, personal access to resources, and influence over allocations of government monies and contracts within their constituencies.

Elections to the *Lok Sabha* must be held at least every five years, but, as in other parliamentary systems, the prime minister may choose to call elections earlier. India is divided into 544 electoral districts of roughly equal population, each of which elects and sends one representative to the national parliament by a first-past-the-post electoral system. The major political parties nominate most candidates. Elections in India are won or lost mainly by parties, especially by party leaders, so most legislators are beholden to party leaders for securing a party ticket. Success in elections therefore does not depend on having an independent power base but on belonging to a party whose leader or whose programs are popular. Given the importance of the party label for nominations, members of parliament maintain strong voting discipline in the *Lok Sabha.* The main business of the *Lok Sabha* is to pass new legislation as well as to debate government actions. Although members sometimes introduce bills, the government introduces most new legislation. After bills are introduced, they are assigned to parliamentary committees for detailed study and discussion. The committees report the bills back to the *Lok Sabha* for debate, possible amendment, and preliminary votes. They then go to the *Rajya Sabha,* the upper house, which is not a powerful chamber; it generally approves bills passed by the *Lok Sabha.* Most members of the *Rajya Sabha* are elected indirectly by state legislatures. After any final modifications by the *Rajya Sabha,* bills return to the *Lok Sabha* for a third reading, after which they are finally voted on in both houses and forwarded to the president for approval.

To understand why the *Lok Sabha* does not play a significant independent role in policymaking, keep in mind that (1) the government generally introduces new legislation; (2) most legislators, especially those belonging to the Congress Party, are politically beholden to party leaders; and (3) all parties use party whips to ensure voting along party lines. One implication of parliament's relative ineffectiveness is that routine changes in its social composition do not have significant policy consequences. Whether members of parliament are business executives or workers, men or women, members of upper or lower castes is not likely to lead to dramatic policy shifts. Nevertheless, groups in society derive satisfaction from having one of their own in the parliament, and dramatic shifts in social composition are bound to influence policy.

The typical member of parliament is a male university graduate between forty and sixty years old. Over the years, there have been some changes in the social composition of legislators. For example, legislators in the 1950s were likely to be urban men and were often lawyers and members of higher castes. Today, nearly half the members of parliament come from rural areas, and many have agricultural backgrounds. Members of the middle castes (the so-called backward castes) are also well represented today. These changes reflect some of the broad shifts in the distribution of power in Indian society. By contrast, the proportion of women and of poor, lower-caste individuals in the parliament remains low. The representation of women in parliament has not increased much from the 4.4 percent (or 22 women) in the first parliament (1952–1957) to 8.8 percent (48 women) in the 1998 elections, to 8.3 percent (45 women) in the lower house of parliament and 11.57 percent in the upper house of parliament in 2004 (see Figure 4).

Figure 4

Women in Parliament

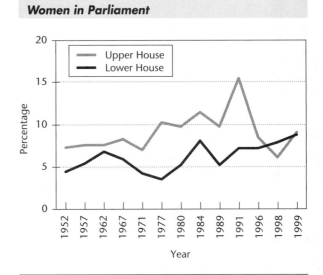

Source: India Together, http://indiatogether.org/manushi/issue116/Table-1.htm

Successive governments since 1996 have supported a constitutional amendment guaranteeing at least 33 percent reserved seats for women in Parliament and the legislative assemblies. However, although most political parties have endorsed the bill in their election manifestos, they have not supported its passage in Parliament. It was defeated most recently in December 2000, when a range of parties expressed either ambivalence or opposition to it. As a compromise measure, then Home Minister L. K. Advani supported the chief election commissioner's proposal to require all political parties to reserve 33 percent of their nominations for women contestants. Critics fear that political parties will nominate women in unwinnable constituencies. Thus far, parties' records in nominating women candidates have been poor. In the 1996 parliamentary elections, for example, political parties allotted less than 15 percent of the total number of tickets to women. Women constitute only 10 to 12 percent of the membership of political parties.[5]

There has been far more resistance to state and national reservations for women by political parties than by the broad public. One survey found that 75 percent of women and 79 percent of men favor the active participation of women in politics, and 75 percent of men and women favor reservations in legislative bodies. Parties that represent the lower middle castes have opposed the reform because it makes no provision for reservations on a caste basis.

Political Parties and the Party System

Political parties and elections are where much of the real drama of Indian politics occurs. Parties in control of a majority of seats in the national or state parliaments form the national or state governments and control government resources. Parties thus devote substantial political energy to contesting and winning elections. Since independence, the party system has evolved from being dominated by the Congress Party to one in which Congress is among the major parties but far from dominant (see Table 2). Thus, what began as virtually a one-party system has evolved into a real multiparty system, with three main political tendencies: centrist, center-left, and center-right. Within this framework, there are at least four potentially significant national parties and countless regional parties

competing for power. The four parties with significant national presence are the Congress, the Janata Party, the BJP, and the Communist Party of India (Marxist; CPM). Whereas the CPM is a left-leaning party and the BJP is a religious, right-leaning one, both Congress and the Janata are more or less centrist parties. Furthermore, coalitions among these parties have occurred in the past. For example, the Janata Party joined forces with the CPM and other smaller parties in the 1996 elections to form the United Front and was able to form two short-lived left-leaning governments. The CPM is a supporter of the United Progressive Alliance government, which came to power in 2004. Further, the major parties are unable to form a government on their own but must stitch together coalitions that include many small, usually regionally based parties. As one would expect, there are feverish negotiations among coalition parties over the allocation of cabinet positions and the policies that the governing coalition will pursue.

The Congress Party

Congress was India's premier political party until the 1990s. Many aspects of this party have already been discussed because it is impossible to analyze Indian politics without referring to its role. To summarize briefly, the Congress Party built its electoral network by creating patrons who would mobilize electoral support for the party during elections. Once in power, the Congress Party would channel government resources to these people, further enhancing their local position and ensuring their support.

This patronage system (some call it machine politics) worked quite well for the Congress Party for nearly two decades. Nevertheless, even when the party was electorally successful, this strategy generated internal contradictions. The pro-poor Congress Party of India, with a socialist shell, came to be internally dominated by high-caste, wealthy Indians.

By the early 1950s, with Nehru at its helm, Congress was the unquestioned ruling party of India. Over the years, especially since the mid-1960s, this hegemony came to be challenged. By the time Indira Gandhi assumed power in 1966, the old Congress Party had begun to lose its political sway, and anticolonial nationalism was fading. The spread of

Table 2

Major Party Election Results

	1991 %	1991 Seats	1996 %	1996 Seats	1998 %	1998 Seats	1999 %	1999 Seats	2004 %	2004 Seats
Congress	37.3	225	29	143	25.4	140	28.4	112	26.69	145[a]
BJP & Allies	19.9	119	24	193	36.2	250	41.3	296	35.91	189
Janata	10.8	55	Joined with UF		Joined with UF		1	1	Joined with Congress	
United Front	—	—	31	180	20.9	98	—	—	—	—
Communists[b]	—	48	Joined with UF		Joined with UF		5.4	32	7.0	53
Others							23.9	107	19.9	78

[a]The more relevant figures in 2004 for Congress and allies were 35.82 and 219, respectively.

[b]Includes both the CPM and the CPI.

Source: India Today, July 15, 1991, March 16, 1998; *Economic Times* website http://economictimes.indiatimes.com; and *The Hindu*, May 20, 2004.

democratic politics mobilized many poor, lower-caste citizens who depended less and less on village big men for political guidance. As a result, numerous regional parties started challenging Congress's monopoly on power. Weather-related food shortages in the mid-1960s also hurt the Congress Party in the 1967 elections.

Indira Gandhi sought to reverse the decline in the Congress's electoral popularity through mobilizing India's vast majority, the poor, by promising poverty alleviation as the core of her political program. This promise struck a popular chord, propelling Indira Gandhi to the top of India's political pyramid. Her personal success, however, came at a cost to the party. The old Congress split into two parties, with one branch, the Congress (O), becoming moribund and leaving the other, Congress (I) (the "I" stands for Indira) to inherit the position of the old undivided Congress. Nevertheless, the Congress Party formed all governments from independence to 1989, with just one interlude, when the Janata Party formed the government (1977–1980). Since 1989 Congress headed governments from 1991 to 1996 and returned to power again in 2004.

Prior to Indira Gandhi's prime ministership, rank-and-file party members elected the lowest-level Congress Party officers, who in turn elected officers at higher levels of the party organization, up to the position of the party leader, who was the prime minister

during the long period when the Congress formed the government. Indira Gandhi reversed this bottom-up party structure by creating a top-down party in which leaders appointed party officers. With some modifications, including some limited internal party elections, this is basically how the contemporary Congress Party is organized. The top-down structure enables the leaders to control the party, but it is a major liability when grassroots support is necessary. As the nation's oldest party, the Congress continues to attract substantial electoral support. If this support ever declined sharply, most likely the party rank-and-file would demand its reorganization.

Whereas Congress during the 1970s had a left-of-center, pro-poor political platform, beginning in 1984 it moved toward the ideological center under Rajiv Gandhi (see Section 2). For much of the 1980s and the 1990s, the Congress Party tilted right-of-center, championing issues of economic efficiency, business interests, and limited government spending over the rights of the poor and the working people and over social questions of health, education, and welfare. However, under Sonia Gandhi's leadership, Congress has moved somewhat to the left.

As a nationalist party, the Congress Party is intimately associated with the stability of the Indian nation and the state in Indian political culture. Regardless of its economic program, therefore, the Congress has always attracted support from diverse social groups: rich and poor, upper and lower castes, Hindus and Muslims, northerners and southerners. Nevertheless, elections in the 1990s indicate that Congress has lost some of its traditional constituencies among the poor, lower castes, and Muslims.

The Janata Party

The Janata Party, India's other centrist party, formed short-lived national governments in 1977, 1989, and together with other parties through the United Front in 1996 and 1997. The Janata Party, however, is not so much a political party as an umbrella for various parties and factions that change with the political circumstances. The Janata Party was created in 1977 when several small parties that opposed Indira Gandhi's Emergency hurriedly united to contest her and, much to their own surprise, won the national elections. This loose coalition lasted only a little over two years, when conflicting leadership ambitions tore it apart.

During the late 1980s, the Janata Party enjoyed another brief term as a national government under the leadership of a breakaway Congress leader, V. P. Singh. With these appeals, the party won enough seats in the national parliament to form a minority government in 1989. Once again, factionalism overwhelmed any attempt at a stable government, and this second attempt with a non-Congress-led government collapsed after a little over two years. Since then, the Janata Party has been able to survive only under the umbrella of the United Front, which is a collection of smaller parties, including the CPM.

The Janata Party has a very weak organizational structure and lacks a distinctive, coherent political platform. To distinguish itself from Congress, it claims that it is more Gandhian, a reference to Mahatma Gandhi's vision that modern India should be more decentralized and village oriented, and less pro-Brahmin. Although most of its efforts at political self-definition have not been very successful, V. P. Singh undertook one major policy initiative while in power that identified the Janata Party with a progressive cause. This was the acceptance of the Mandal Commission's recommendation that India's **other backward classes,** generally, the middle, rural castes that constitute a near majority in the Indian countryside, be provided substantial reservations (or reserved access) to government jobs and educational institutions. The government's acceptance of this recommendation produced a nationwide outburst of riots and violence led by upper castes, who felt threatened. The uproar eventually contributed to the downfall of V. P. Singh's government. Nevertheless, Singh's acceptance of what has been called "Mandal" associated the Janata Party with the interests of the backward castes. How strongly backward castes will continue to identify with this party in the future is unknown. For now, the Janata Party is viewed, especially in north-central India, as a party of small, rural agriculturalists who generally fall somewhere in the middle of the rigid caste hierarchy between Brahmins and untouchables.

The Bharatiya Janata Party (BJP)

The BJP, one of the major political parties in contemporary India, is a direct descendant of the Jana Sangh Party, which entered the Indian political scene in 1951. The Jana Sangh joined the Janata Party government in 1977 but then split off and formed the BJP in 1980. The BJP is a right-leaning, Hindu-nationalist party, the first major party to mobilize explicitly on the basis of religious identity and to often adopt an anti-Muslim stance. In comparison to both the Congress and the Janata, the BJP is better organized; it has disciplined party members, who after a prolonged apprenticeship become party cadres, and the authority lines within the party are relatively clear and well respected.

The party is closely affiliated with many related organizations, the most significant of which is the RSS. Most BJP leaders were at one time members of the Rashtriya Swayam Sevak Sangh, which recruits young people (especially educated youth in urban areas) and involves them in a fairly disciplined set of cultural activities, including the study of a chauvinistic reinterpretation of India's "great Hindu past." These young people, uniformed in khaki shorts and shirts, can often be seen in Indian cities doing group exercises in the mornings and evenings and singing songs glorifying India's Sanskritic civilization (Sanskrit is the classical language in which some of the ancient Hindu scriptures are written). Recalling the pursuits of right-wing fascist groups of interwar Europe, the activities of these youth groups, seemingly no more than an appeal to cultural pride, dismay many non-Hindu minorities and Indian liberals, who fear the havoc that cultural pride can produce.

Those traditionally attracted to the Jana Sangh and the BJP were mainly urban, lower-middle-class groups, especially small traders and commercial groups. As long as this was its main source of support, the BJP remained a minor actor on the Indian political scene. Since the mid-1980s, however, the BJP has widened its base of support appreciably by appealing to Hindu nationalism, especially in north-central India. The decline in the Congress Party's popularity created a vacuum that the BJP was well positioned to fill. Moreover, the BJP found in Indian Muslims a convenient scapegoat for the frustrations of various social groups and successfully mobilized Hindus in an attempt to create a religiously oriented political force where none had existed before. The electoral success of the BJP in 1989 and 1991 and its formation of the government in 1999 underscore the party's rapid rise to power. The BJP's early efforts resulted in its ruling four states from 1991 to 1993, although it lost power in three of the four in 1993. During the 1999 parliamentary elections, the BJP scored a major success and formed the national government, only to lose power again in 2004.

The BJP's growth in the 1980s and 1990s represented a break with past traditions. In the aftermath of independence, the RSS and its affiliated organizations were widely regarded as divisive, anti-Muslim organizations. The BJP's predecessor, the *Bharatiya Jana Sangh,* responded to its stigmatization by adopting a relatively moderate, centrist position through the 1984 elections, when it won only two seats in parliament. Its fortunes began to rise after the 1989 elections, when it emerged as the third-largest party after the Congress and Janata parties. In 1991, the BJP held the second largest number of seats in parliament. To capitalize on the Hindu support it had been mobilizing, the BJP joined the RSS and VHP in a campaign questioning the legitimacy of the Babri Masjid (a Muslim mosque) in Ayodhya that was designed to shore up anti-Muslim sentiments. BJP leaders argued that the mosque at Ayodhya, a place of worship for India's Muslims, had been built on the birthplace of the Hindu god Rama. On December 6, 1992, thousands of Hindus, encouraged by the BJP, stormed and demolished the mosque. Seventeen hundred people were killed in the accompanying riots.

Six years later, as a result of the failures of other parties to lead effective governments, the BJP formed a governing coalition, the National Democratic Alliance, led by Prime Minister Atal Behari Vajpayee. However, its mismanagement of the economy soon generated a popular backlash against the BJP. The BJP government collapsed in 1999, just thirteen months after taking power.

However, the BJP formed a new electoral coalition, again headed by Atal Behari Vajpayee; it was elected in 1999 and lasted a full term, until 2004. It was more broadly based than previous BJP-led coalition governments because it attracted the support of regionally based political parties in various states. The result not only strengthened the BJP's hold on power but also strengthened trends toward the regionalization of Indian politics.

Another reason for the greater strength of the BJP-led government in 1999 was its cultivation of a more moderate, centrist stance. In 1996, most political parties shunned an alliance with the BJP, for it was tainted by its militant identity. Even in 1998, the BJP put together a governing coalition with great difficulty. In 1999, the BJP went to great lengths to project Atal Behari Vajpayee as a moderate, centrist leader. Moreover, the National Democratic Alliance platform shelved contentious issues that identified it with the interests of Hindus over and against those of religious minorities. None of this, however, proved sufficient for the BJP to maintain power. In 2004, the BJP projected itself as the sponsor of "shining India," with a robust economy and nuclear might. Congress's commitment to secularism and the poor, along with its more deft approach to coalition building, won the day instead.

The BJP has never fully swung to the political center or abdicated its militance, even when in power. It continues to retain strong ties to the RSS and periodically demonstrates its commitment to constructing a temple in Ayodhya. The most striking evidence of this was the BJP's complicity in riots in Gujarat in 2002 and its reluctance to act decisively to bring the guilty to trial in their aftermath.

The riots in Gujarat in early 2002 were among the worst that India has experienced in the post-independence period. The catalyst for the violence was an attack on a trainload of Hindu pilgrims returning from Ayodhya, in which fifty-nine Hindus were killed. In the weeks that followed, Hindu groups engaged in a campaign of terror against the Muslim population of Gujarat in which over a thousand people were killed. The rampage was a particularly grave challenge to democratic principles because it was sanctioned by leading political officials of the BJP state government in Gujarat. Unlike riots of the past, which were an urban phenomenon, this one spread to the villages and gained the support of scheduled castes and tribals. The violence often included sexual assaults on women. However, with tacit support from the national government, the BJP government in Gujarat called for early elections in 2002 and won a landslide victory by capitalizing on the electoral support of Hindus that it had mobilized during the riots.

A number of factors have prevented the BJP from moving in a wholly centrist direction. The first and most important concern is its close ties to the RSS and the Hindu religious organization, the *Visva Hindu Parishad* (VHP). Since its formation in 1964, the VHP has sought to strengthen Hindu identity in a chauvinist and exclusionary fashion. In the 1960s, its activities centered on converting Muslims, who, it claimed, had been forcibly converted to Hinduism. In the 1980s, it became active around the construction of the temple in Ayodhya.

There are clearly some important differences in the orientation of these organizations. The RSS is committed to economic nationalism, the BJP to liberalization. The VHP has been implicated in violence, whereas the BJP has promised stability. Despite these differences, the BJP has maintained a close relationship to the RSS and the VHP. The RSS has intervened to mend rifts within the party in various states. It has helped ensure that the BJP, unlike most Indian political parties, has never split. Moreover, it is hard to imagine a complete rupture between the RSS and the BJP: the highest-ranking BJP members are of RSS backgrounds, and many have continuing ties to the RSS. The BJP's relationship to the VHP, though conflictual at times when the BJP is in office, has also been close. RSS and VHP activists have regularly participated in the electoral campaigns of the BJP in state and general elections. Moreover, the riots that the VHP has engineered have polarized the electorate along Hindu-Muslim lines in a way that benefited the BJP.

The BJP's continuing commitment to privileging the interests of the Hindu majority, evident in response to the Gujarat riots, the temple construction in Ayodhya, and policies in Kashmir, has increased the vulnerability of the Muslim community. Although the BJP has consistently proclaimed its attachment to secular principles, it has taken steps to undermine the conditions under which secularism flourishes. Its promises of providing clean, honest governance have been marred in recent years by charges of corruption by high-ranking officials, in the discriminatory distribution of relief after a massive earthquake in Gujarat in 2001, in evidence that the army engaged in corruption after a border clash with Pakistan in 1999, and in patterns of bribery in defense procurement in 2001.

The Communist Party of India (CPM)

The CPM is an offshoot of the Communist Party of India, which was formed during the colonial period and has existed nearly as long as the Congress Party. Although the contemporary CPM has a national presence in that it nearly always elects representatives to the *Lok Sabha,* its political base is concentrated in two of India's states, West Bengal and Kerala. These states have often been ruled by the CPM, and they often elect *Lok Sabha* members who run on a CPM ticket.

The CPM is a disciplined party, with party cadres and a hierarchical authority structure. Other than its name and internal organization, however, there is nothing communist about the CPM; rather, it is a social democratic party like the British Labour Party or the German Social Democratic Party. The CPM accepts the framework of democracy, regularly participates in elections, and often wins them in West Bengal and Kerala. In these two states, the CPM enjoys the support of the lower-middle and lower classes, both factory workers and poorer peasants. Within the national parliament, CPM members often strongly criticize government policies that are likely to hurt the poor. On occasion, the CPM joins with other parties against the BJP, as it did in the 1996 elections by joining the United Front. At present, the CPM lends its support to the Congress government in power but has not formally joined the government. Where the CPM runs state governments, for example, in West Bengal and Kerala, it has provided a relatively honest and stable administration. It has also pursued a moderate but effective reform program, ensuring the rights of agricultural tenants (such as preventing their evictions), providing services to those living in shantytowns, and encouraging public investments in rural areas.

Elections

Elections in India are a colossal event. Nearly 500 million people are eligible to vote, and close to 300 million do so. The turnout rate in the 1990s of over 60 percent was considerably higher than in the United States, although it declined to 58 percent in 2004. The level of technology used in both campaigning and the conduct of elections is fairly low. Television plays an increasingly important role, but much campaigning still involves face-to-face contact between politicians and the electorate. Senior leaders fly around the country, making speeches to millions of potential supporters at political rallies held in tiny villages and district towns. Lesser politicians and thousands of party supporters travel the dusty streets, accompanied by blaring music and political messages from loudspeakers.

Given the high rate of illiteracy, pictures of party symbols are critical: a hand for the Congress (I); a lotus for the BJP; a hammer and sickle for the CPM. Illiterate voters signify their vote for a candidate in the polling booth by putting thumb marks on one of these symbols. During the campaign, therefore, party representatives work very hard to associate certain individuals and election platforms with specific symbols. A typical election slogan is, "Vote for the hammer and sickle because they stand for the rights of the working people."

India's electoral system, like the British system, is a first-past-the-post system. A number of candidates compete in an electoral district; the candidate with the most votes wins. This system privileges the major political parties. It also generates considerable pressure

Source: Danish Small/Reuters/Corbis.

for opposition parties to ally against the government. In practice, however, given the differences among opposition parties and the considerable clash of leadership ambitions, many parties compete, favoring the candidates of the larger parties.

One of the pillars of Indian democracy is its system of open, honest elections. Credit for this goes in part to the Election Commission, a constitutionally mandated central body that functions independently of the executive. Particularly since 1991, with the appointment of a respected chief, the Election Commission has defended free and fair elections.

Political Culture, Citizenship, and Identity

The only generalization that can be made about Indian political culture is that in such a large and culturally diverse country, no single set of cultural traits is shared by the entire population. Nevertheless, three important tendencies are worth noting. These political cultural traits reflect India's hybrid political style, as a rigid, hierarchical, and village-oriented old civilization adapts itself to modern socioeconomic changes, especially to democratic politics.

One important tendency is that India's political and public spheres are not sharply divided from personal and private spheres of activity. The idea that public office is not a legitimate means for personal enrichment or for furthering the interests of family members or of personal associates is not yet fully accepted in India. As a result, there is fairly widespread misuse of public resources for personal gain, that is, widespread corruption in political life. The positive aspect of this tendency is the high level of political involvement by the citizenry in public life.

Second, the Indian elite are extremely factionalized. The roots of such behavior are complex, reflecting India's fragmented social structure. Although some important exceptions exist, generally the personal political ambitions of Indian leaders prevent them from pursuing such collective goals as forming cohesive political parties, running a stable government, or focusing on problems of national development. In contrast to many East Asian countries, where the norms of consensus are powerful and political negotiation is often conducted behind closed doors, politics in India veers toward the other extreme, and open disagreements and conflicts are the norm.

The third and possibly most important political cultural tendency that deserves mention concerns the fragmentation of political life in India. Indian society is highly segmented. Different regions have different languages and cultures; within regions, villages are poorly connected with each other; and within villages, different castes often live in isolation from one another. Politics is often fragmented along caste lines, but even caste grievances tend to remain local rather than becoming national or even regional. Some observers of India find this segmented quality of Indian politics a blessing because it localizes problems, facilitating political stability, but others find it a curse because it stymies the possibility of national reforms to improve the lot of the poorest members of society.

Democracy is relatively well established in India. Most Indians value their citizenship rights and, in spite of poverty and illiteracy, exercise them with vigor. However, the spread of democratic politics can simultaneously fuel political conflicts. The spread of democracy is undermining many of India's political

givens, including some of the most rigid hierarchies, and has begun to produce new political patterns.

The most significant of these recent developments concerns identity politics. Region, language, religion, and caste all help Indians define who they are. Such differences have generated political cleavages in India, underlining the importance and yet the malleability of collective identities. Some of these identity conflicts remained dormant when Nehru's secular nationalism and Indira Gandhi's poor-versus-rich cleavage defined the core political issues. In the 1980s and 1990s, however, with the relative decline of the Congress Party and with developments in telecommunications and transportation that have made people more aware of each other's differences, identity-based political conflicts have mushroomed in India.

Two of the more significant conflicts deserve mention. First, caste conflicts, formerly confined to local and regional politics, have taken on a national dimension in recent years. For example, groups of backward castes had made a political mark in many states, but prior to Mandal, they were seldom a cohesive factor in national politics. V. P. Singh hoped to create a powerful support base out of these disparate groups. However, the move backfired. The threatened upper castes reacted sharply with demonstrations, riots, and political violence. Not only did this disruption contribute to the downfall of Singh's government, but it also converted the conflict between castes from a local and regional issue to a divisive national issue.

The second identity-based political conflict that has reemerged has pitted Hindus and Muslims against each other. Tensions between these religious communities go back several centuries, when Muslim rulers from Central Asia established the Moghul dynasty in India. Stories and memories of the relative greatness of one community over the other, or of atrocities and injustices unleashed on one community by the other, abound in India's popular culture. For the most part, these legends may fan low-level hostilities but they do not prevent peaceful coexistence. However, political circumstances, especially political machinations by ambitious leaders, can inflame these tendencies and instigate overt conflict. This is what has happened since the mid-1980s, as the BJP has whipped up anti-Muslim sentiments in an effort to unite disparate Hindu groups into a political force. The resulting aggression against Muslims illustrates the dangers of identity-based political passions.

There are many poor or otherwise frustrated social groups in India whose anger is available for political mobilization. Whether the BJP will succeed in tapping this anger in the longer term cannot be predicted. What can be said is that democracy and large pockets of social frustration provide a combustible mix that will continue to generate unexpected outcomes in Indian politics.

Interests, Social Movements, and Protest

India has a vibrant tradition of political activism that has both enriched and complicated the workings of democracy. Social movements, nongovernmental organizations (NGOs), and trade unions have put pressure on the state to be attentive to the interests and needs of underprivileged groups and have checked its authoritarian tendencies.

Among the groups that are politically active, labor has played a significant but not leading role. Labor unions are politically fragmented, particularly at the national level. Instead of the familiar model of one factory/one union, several political parties often organize within a single factory. Above the factory level, several labor organizations compete for labor's support. The government generally stays out of labor-management conflicts. India's industrial relations are thus closer to the pluralist model practiced in Anglo-American countries than to the corporatist model of Mexico. The political energies of unions are channeled into frequent local battles involving strikes, demonstrations, and a peculiarly Indian protest technique called *gherao,* which entails workers' encircling and holding executives of the firm hostage until their demands are met.

Social movements, the most important form of civil society activism, date back to the mid-1970s. During the period of the national Emergency (1975–1977) when the government imprisoned members of the opposition, activists came together to form political parties and social movements, often with close ties to one another. In 1977, the Gandhian Socialist leader Jai Prakash Narain organized the movement for total democracy that ultimately brought about the downfall of Congress and the election of the

Janata Party. A decade later, V. P. Singh resigned from Congress and formed the *Jan Morcha* (Peoples' Front), an avowedly nonpolitical movement that brought new groups into politics and helped bring the National Front to power in 1989.

Social movements continued to grow and assume new organizational forms in the 1980s. Some engaged in grassroots activism, and others worked more closely with the state. The number of NGOs also expanded. Until the early 1980s, when Indira Gandhi was prime minister, the state was distrustful of what is commonly known in India as the voluntary sector and sought to restrict its activities. When Rajiv Gandhi came to power, he attempted to cultivate a closer relationship with NGOs, for he recognized their potential for taking over some of the development work that the state had traditionally performed. Over the years, financial support for NGOs from the national government has steadily increased. During the seventh five-year plan (1985–1990), the federal government spent about US$11 million each year through NGOs; by 2002 this had increased to over $44 million annually. Today, there are 20,000 voluntary organizations listed with the Ministry of Home Affairs, and the actual number is much higher. The most significant social movements organized around either distinctive themes or identities include the women's movement, the environmental movement, the farmers' movement, and the *dalit* (a term of pride used by untouchables) movement. In recent years, there has also been the growth of antinuclear and civil liberties activism. The large number and extensive activities of social movements make India quite distinctive among developing countries.

The environment movement is organized by educated urban activists and some of India's poorest and most marginal groups. Their activism has been spurred by the magnitude of the country's environmental crisis and the ineffectiveness of its environmental laws. India suffers from severe air pollution in large cities and contaminated lakes and rivers. The shortage of drinking water is worsened by salinization, water overuse, and groundwater depletion. The emission of carbon dioxide has contributed to the greenhouse effect, leading to an increase in temperature, a rise in the sea level, and the destruction of coastal croplands and fisheries. Commercial logging, fuel wood depletion, and urbanization have caused serious problems of deforestation, which is associated with droughts, floods, and cyclones.

Successive governments have chosen to promote increased production at the expense of environmental protection. Effective enforcement of environmental laws and policies would put many firms out of business and slow down economic growth. Moreover, it would be very time-consuming and difficult for the government to monitor and control all small-scale industries. Although the Congress Party sponsored most of India's environmental laws, it also catered to the interest of big business at the expense of environmental protection. The United Front parties have been strong supporters of environmental issues but have tended to target only big business rather than small businesses. The BJP has explicitly favored business interests over environmental concerns. Thus, the major sources of support for environmental protection have been social movements and NGOs.

The Chipko movement against deforestation in the Himalayas, which emerged in the early 1970s, has been one of the longest-lasting movements against deforestation and has influenced similar forms of activism in other regions of the country. Large-scale protest at the 1984 Union Carbide disaster in Bhopal demanded greater compensation for victims of the gas leak, as well as more environmental regulations to prevent similar disasters in the future. This resulted in the creation of the Central Pollution Control Board in 1986 and a series of environmental statutes, regulations, and protocols.

The largest and most significant environmental movement in India has protested the construction of the Sardar Sarvodaya Dam in western India. The Narmada Bachao Andolan (NBA) has organized opposition to the construction of the dam on grounds that it will benefit already prosperous regions to the detriment of poor regions, lead to the large-scale displacement of people, and put in place vastly inadequate resettlement schemes. A large proportion of those who would be displaced are tribals who do not possess land titles. The movement has galvanized tens of thousands of people to engage in nonviolent protest to oppose the construction of the dam. The protest caused the World Bank to rescind promised loans, but the Indian government is still pursuing the project.

Women and questions of gender inequality have been at the forefront of environmental struggles like the Chipko and Narmada movements. The 1980s also witnessed the formation of a number of autonomous urban women's organizations. They campaigned

Playcards protesting the construction of the Sardar Sarrodaya Dam

Source: Tom Pietrasik/Corbis

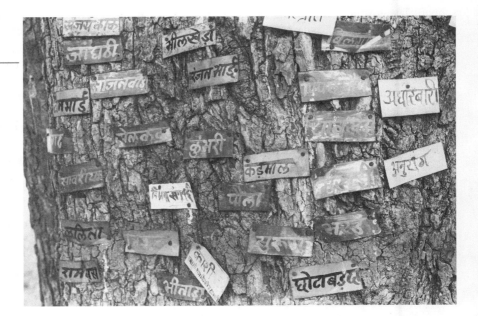

around rape in police custody, dowry murders, *sati* (the immolation of widows on their husbands' funeral pyres), female feticide (through the use of amniocentesis), media misrepresentation of women, harmful contraception dissemination, coercive population policies, and, most recently, the adverse impact of the economic reforms.

The *dalit* movement looks back to Dr. Balasaheb Ambedkar, the *dalit* author of the Indian constitution, as the founding father of the movement. He was responsible for the creation of the Republican Party in the late 1960s. The disintegration of the party gave rise to the emergence of a radical youth movement that called itself the Dalit Panthers. The movement demanded that *dalits* be treated with dignity, and provided better educational opportunities. Today, the *dalit* movement reflects dalits' growing aspirations for electoral power and public office.

Kanshi Ram formed the Bahujan Samaj Party (BSP) in 1989 with the goal of achieving political power for the *dalits*. The BSP experienced significant growth in the 1990s. With a share of 4.7 percent of the national vote in 1998 and 4.2 percent in 1999, it is almost as strong as the CPM (5.4 percent). Its strength is mainly confined to Uttar Pradesh, where it has oscillated between playing ally and enemy to the BJP. In 2002, the BJP became a minority coalition partner to the BSP in UP in order to broaden its support base among lower-caste Hindus. However, this alliance collapsed by the following year. Amidst its aspirations to exercise power in India's largest state, the BSP has forsaken its earlier commitments to social justice and the eradication of class inequality.

Other small lower-caste parties and movements have been active in Maharashtra and Tamil Nadu. However, none of these parties is able to play a national role other than participating in and influencing electoral alliances. Moreover, these parties have confined themselves to seeking political power for *dalits* and lack a broader vision of social transformation. Tensions have emerged within the *dalit* community. Some of the poorer and lower-status *dalits* feel that the better-off, higher-status *dalits* have benefited from reservations at their expense. Radical sections within the *dalit* movement argue that *dalits* ought not to depend entirely on reservations or the state, but

should initiate a mass movement of their own that highlights issues of employment, education, and landlessness.

Three important developments have influenced the character and trajectory of social movements in recent years. First, many social movements have been drawn into a closer relationship to the state and to electoral politics. In the past, social movements tended to be community based and issue-specific. Once they had achieved some success, around, say, the felling of forest trees, the construction of a dam, or higher prices for agricultural subsidies, the movement would subside. Although many social movements continue to be confined by their focus, duration, and geographic reach, some of them have sought to overcome these difficulties by engaging in electoral politics. The *dalit* movement and Hindu nationalism are two of the most important examples. Participation in electoral politics has in turn shaped and influenced these movements' goals. Other movements have sought to work with particular branches of the state. The women's movement, for example, has worked closely with the bureaucracy and the courts. In part because of the closer relationship between social movements and the state, an enduring broad left-wing formation consisting of left-wing parties and social movements has not emerged. By contrast, Hindu nationalists, particularly under the auspices of the VHP, have sustained their strong connections to the BJP.

Second, the growth of the religious right has confronted left-wing social movements with a serious challenge and dilemma. Unlike some regions of the world where the religious right and the secular left disagree on most issues, the situation in India is more complex. Segments of the religious right, like parts of the left, oppose economic liberalization and globalization. For example, both feminists and Hindu nationalists oppose the commodification of women's bodies that occurs in the media and in international beauty pageants. Similarly, the women's movement has put on the back burner its demand for a uniform civil code that would provide equal treatment of men and women of all religious communities under the law because the BJP has made this very demand, albeit for very different reasons. Furthermore, several social movements have abandoned a commitment to poverty alleviation and embraced the state-initiated shift toward the market.

Third, many NGOs and social movements have developed extensive transnational connections. The consequences for social movements have been double-edged. On the positive side, funding from foreign sources has been vital to the survival of NGOs and social movements. India lacks a tradition of donating to secular-philanthropic causes, and corporate funding is limited and tightly controlled. However, organizations receiving foreign funding are often viewed with suspicion and have difficulty establishing their legitimacy. Moreover, foreign funding has created a sharp division between activists with and without access to foreign donors.

If these developments have complicated the agendas of social movements, there is also a potential for NGOs and social movements to grow stronger. There are greater opportunities than ever before for social movement and NGO activists to take advantage of the resources that the state is making available. Some groups have already done this by putting candidates up for elections at the local level, as we have seen in the case of the *panchayats*. Furthermore, the BJP's defeat in the 2004 elections in part because its claims of "India shining" so blatantly contradicted persistent poverty and inequality, coupled with the relatively strong performance of left-of-center parties, may well revitalize movements of the most underprivileged groups.

September 11th, the war in Iraq, and changing relations with the United States have not significantly reshaped collective political identities and action in India. On the one hand, the BJP's attempt to play the anti-Muslim card after September 11th was quite unsuccessful, as evidenced by its electoral defeat in 2004. Furthermore, the fact that Indo-U.S. relations improved immediately after September 11th did not prevent the Indian government from later opposing the U.S. intervention in Iraq and rejecting U.S. attempts to elicit Indian assistance. While economic globalization has intensified political cleavages related to who wins and loses from globalization, this factor is quite unrelated to India's geopolitical situation.

To review, political participation over the years in India has broadened in scope and deepened in intensity. A single-party system dominated by the Congress Party has slowly been supplanted by a multiparty system of parties on the left and the right. Similarly, old hierarchies of caste have eroded in Indian society, and upper castes cannot readily control the political behavior of those below them. The result is that many groups in society increasingly feel empowered and hope to translate this new consciousness and sense of efficacy into material gains by influencing government policies.

Section ⑤ Indian Politics in Transition

Political Challenges and Changing Agendas

As a large country with a legitimate government and sizable armed forces, India has not readily been influenced by external forces. For example, India tested nuclear bombs in 1998 and successfully withstood international condemnation and sanctions. However, in an increasingly interdependent global economic context, India has become far more vulnerable to global pressures. The changing geopolitical environment in the aftermath of the September 11th terrorist attacks has drawn India into closer relations with the United States. India today must confront major challenges at home and abroad if it is to preserve and strengthen its democratic institutions and improve its economic performance.

Kashmir Within a World of States

Of all the challenges that India has faced since independence, among the most enduring and intractable is its relationship to Kashmir, the state located in northern India on the border with Pakistan. The roots of conflict within Kashmir have often been attributed to the ethnic and religious diversity of the state, which is roughly 65 percent Muslim and 35 percent Hindus and other minorities. The non-Muslim minorities—Hindus, Sikhs, and Buddhists, who are concentrated in the areas of the state called Jammu and Ladakh—largely wish to live under Indian sovereignty. The Kashmir Valley, which is predominantly Sunni Muslim, is mostly in favor of Kashmir's becoming an independent country or part of Pakistan. However, separatist sentiments cannot be explained primarily by ethnic differences. Rather, one must ask what led many Kashmiri Muslims to become progressively radicalized against India.

Heightened separatist, fundamentalist, and terrorist activities have resulted from the frustrations many Kashmiris have experienced as a result of the central government's actions. At independence, Nehru promised that a referendum in Kashmir would decide the status of the region. However, the Indian government has never honored this pledge, mainly because it has feared a proindependence vote. With the partial exceptions of 1947–1953 and 1977–1984, Kashmir has been directly ruled from New Delhi. This has hindered democratic participation and institutional development in the state. As demands for independence grew, so too did the repressive actions of the Indian state, leading to spiraling cycles of insurgent militance and state-sanctioned violence. Pakistan also contributed significantly to the insurgency by training and supporting the militants. Whether the fate of Kashmiris can be resolved through democratic means is an open question.

More than any other conflict, the Kashmir dispute is triggered and sustained by the international context. The timing of Indian independence and simultaneous partition of the subcontinent into India and Pakistan fueled tensions in Kashmir and created uncertainty over its status within the Indian union. Superpower rivalry in the cold war deterred India and Pakistan from reaching an agreement on the status of Kashmir.

The problem of Kashmir reveals the limits of Indian democracy, for the national government has ruled Kashmir more undemocratically than any other state in India, through a combination of repression, direct control, and manipulation to install unrepresentative governments. The constant rigging of elections has prevented the development of free and autonomous competition among political parties. While elections were held in most parts of the country from 1952 onward, in Kashmir elections to the legislative assembly were held in only 1962 and to the

parliament only in 1967. Most elections in Jammu and Kashmir were fraudulent. The elections in 2002 and 2004 were partial exceptions. Although the police and army forced people to vote, in part in response to the separatists' **call** for an electoral boycott, they were more open and inclusive than previous elections.

The other serious impediment to resolving the Kashmir dispute is continuing tensions between India and Pakistan. These tensions are one of the important reasons for the two countries' high military expenditures (see Figure 5). Relations between the two countires have periodically swung from terrible to moderately good—only to decline again. After a military confrontation in 1999, followed by a thaw, relations again took a turn for the worse in 2001.

Soon after September 11, there was an exchange of fire on the border between the two countries. Relations plummeted further after October 1, 2001, done with an attack by groups from Pakistan on the Jammu and Kashmir legislative assembly and, far more serious, an attack on the Indian parliament later that year. India charged that the attacks on a key political institution were orchestrated by Pakistan. Following the attack on parliament, India prepared for war with Pakistan by massing over one million troops near the

Figure 5

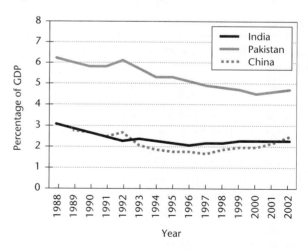

Source: Information from the Stockholm International Peace Research Institute (SIPRI), Military Expenditure Database, http://first.sipri.org/index.php?page=step3&compact=true

Pakistani border. Pakistan responded in kind, and for several weeks, nuclear conflagration seemed a distinct possibility. Intense intervention by the United States helped to defuse the situation, and Pakistan and India withdrew most of their troops from the border. Since then the United States has worked behind the scenes to pressure Pakistan to restrain terrorists within its borders. The two countries subsequently restored full diplomatic ties, exchanged ambassadors, restored air travel links and, of great symbolic significance, resumed cricket matches.

Nuclear Power Status

Soon after the BJP first came to power in May 1998, it fulfilled an electoral promise by gatecrashing the nuclear club. When it set off a nuclear test, it triggered a nuclear arms race in South Asia. Although the Indian government cited regional threats from China and Pakistan as the key reason to develop nuclear weapons, the decision to become a nuclear state can also be traced directly to the evolution of Indian democracy since the late 1980s. Electoral mobilization along ethnic lines (religious, language, or caste) in an atmosphere of economic turmoil and poverty prompted political parties to mobilize Indians' national pride, thereby deflecting attention from domestic economic and political problems. Within a few weeks of India's nuclear test, Pakistan responded by testing its own bomb. Worldwide condemnation swiftly followed as many countries, including the United States, imposed economic and technology sanctions on both India and Pakistan.

One major political challenge for India is how to negotiate with the rest of the world, particularly the United States, on its emergence as a nuclear weapons state. The United States and other parts of the international community have sought to enforce a universal nonproliferation agreement. The Vajpayee and the Clinton administrations engaged in several rounds of delicate arms control talks in which Clinton tried to persuade India to sign the Comprehensive Test Ban Treaty (CTBT) and the Nuclear Non-Proliferation Treaty (NPT) in exchange for completely lifting U.S. sanctions. India opposed the NPT on the grounds that it was unfair to nonnuclear countries because it did not establish a procedure for eventual phase-out of nuclear weapons by the nuclear powers. In 1998, India announced its intention to sign the CTBT if talks with the United States ended successfully and also signaled its willingness to join other nuclear control groups. In 1999, India and Pakistan agreed to continue a moratorium on further nuclear tests.

The Manmohan Singh government took a dramatic step towards defusing tensions around the nuclear issue after its election in 2004. While emphasizing that decisions about India's nuclear programs must be made domestically and should not be subject to externally imposed sanctions, Singh emphasized India's nonproliferation record and its commitment to preventing the proliferation of weapons of mass destruction. Parliament voted to propose a stricter regime of external transfers and tighter controls to prevent international leakages. When Manmohan Singh and George W. Bush met in Washington, D.C., in September 2004, they issued a joint statement emphasizing the commitment of the two countries to work together to stop the proliferation of weapons of mass destruction. In July 2005 they agreed that India could secure international help for its civilian nuclear reactors while retaining its nuclear arms. This agreement paved the way for removing a U.S. ban on nuclear technology sales to India.

How India confronts challenges on the nuclear front is closely tied to its success in several other areas, including resolution of the Kashmir dispute, the management of increasing ethnic tensions, and its economic performance.

The Challenge of Ethnic Diversity

The future of Indian democracy is closely bound up with how the country confronts the growing political impact of ethnic identities. Mobilized ethnic groups seeking access to state power and state-controlled economic resources are a basic component of the contemporary Indian political scene. Caste, language, and religion all provide identities around which political mobilization can be galvanized. Identification with a group is heightened by the democratic context, in which parties and leaders freely choose to manipulate such symbols. When studying Indian politics, it is difficult to separate interest- and identity-based politics. For example, caste struggles in India are simultaneously struggles for identity, power, and wealth. Identity politics in India is likely to be characterized by two trends: considerable political ferment, with a variety of dissatisfied groups making demands on parties and governments, and pressure on political parties to broaden their electoral appeal to disadvantaged groups, especially those belonging to the middle and lower strata, many of whom are very poor. India's political leaders will thus continue to experience pressures to expand their support base by promising economic improvements or manipulating nationalist symbols. Under what conditions will such political forces engage in constructive rather than destructive actions? Will democracy succeed in merely tempering the effect of such forces, or will it in the long run promote a positive channeling of identity politics? Answers to these questions partly hinges on India's economic performance.

Economic Performance

India's economic experience is neither a clear success nor a clear failure. If many African countries have done poorly economically and many East Asian countries (prior to 1997) have had dramatic successes, India falls somewhere in the middle. Three conditions may explain this outcome. The first is the nature and the quality of the government for promoting economic growth. In this, India has been fortunate to have enjoyed relatively good government since independence: its democratic system is mostly open and stable, its most powerful political leaders are public spirited, and its upper bureaucracy is well trained and competent. These positive attributes stand out in comparison with many African countries, such as Nigeria.

The second condition concerns India's strategy for economic development. India in the 1950s chose to insulate its economy from global forces, limiting the role of trade and foreign investment and emphasizing the role of government in promoting self-sufficiency in heavy industry and agriculture. The positive impact of this strategy was that India now produces enough food to feed its large and growing population while it simultaneously produces a vast range of industrial goods. This strategy, however, was not without costs. Most of India's manufactured goods are produced rather inefficiently by global standards. India sacrificed the additional economic growth that might have

come from competing effectively in global markets and by selling its products abroad. It also gave up another area of potential economic growth by discouraging foreign investment. And last, during the phase of protective industrialization, India did little to alleviate its staggering poverty: land redistribution failed, job creation by heavy industries was minimal, and investment in the education and health of the poor was minuscule in relation to the magnitude of the problem. The poor also became a drag on economic growth because they were unable to buy goods and stimulate demand for increased production and because an uneducated and unhealthy labor force is not a productive labor force.

Yet despite this sluggish past, India's economy over the last quarter of a century has grown handsomely. As discussed earlier, the main forces propelling this change have been a closer relation between respective Indian governments and Indian business groups, liberalization of the economy, and integration in the global economy. This steady growth, however, is not without problems. A variety of inequalities are growing. As a result, India's numerous poor are not benefiting as much from growth as they might. The reduction in public spending has hurt the poor by limiting their access to publicly funded education and health services. Reconciling continuing growth with rapid poverty alleviation remains a pressing challenge.

Indian Politics in Comparative Perspective

Given its large size, diversity, and vibrant social and political system, India is an exceptionally good case study for analyzing themes of general significance in comparative politics. In this concluding section, we first examine the implications of the study of India for comparative politics and then assess how Indian politics and its economy will influence developments in a regional and global context.

Some comparative scholars suggest that citizens' widespread desire to exercise some control over their government is a potent force encouraging democracy. This assumption is clearly illustrated in India. Although democracy was introduced to India by its elites, it has established firm roots within society. A clear example is when Indira Gandhi declared

Emergency rule (1975–1977) and curtailed democratic freedoms. In the next election, in 1977, Indian citizens decisively voted Indira Gandhi out of power, registering their preference for democratic rule. Most Indians value democracy and use its institutions to advance their claims.

Comparativists debate whether democracy or authoritarianism is better for economic growth. In the past, India did not compare well with the success stories of East Asian and Chinese authoritarian-led countries. India's impressive economic growth in recent years reopens these old debates. Moreover, the collapse in the late 1990s of several East Asian economies and the subsequent rise of instability within those societies makes a study of Indian democracy more relevant to understanding the institutional and cultural factors underpinning economic stability in the long run.

Another theme has been to assess the implications of establishing democracy in multiethnic societies. The rising tide of nationalism and the breakup of the Soviet Union and Yugoslavia, among others, have prompted closer examination of how and why India continues to exist as a cohesive entity. By studying India's history, particularly the post-1947 period, comparativists could explore questions of how cleavages of caste, religion, and language in India balance one another and cancel the most destructive elements in each. Comparativists have also puzzled about the conditions under which multiple and contradictory interests could be harnessed within a democratic setup to generate positive economic and distributional outcomes. Here, the variable performance of different regions in India can serve as a laboratory. For instance, two communist-ruled states, Kerala and West Bengal, have (to a certain extent) engaged in land redistribution policies. An examination of factors such as the role of the mobilizing parties and the interaction between the landless poor and the entrenched landed elite could provide answers. The main elements of the Kerala model are a land reform initiative that abolished tenancy and landlord exploitation, effective public food distribution that provides subsidized rice to low-income households, protective laws for agricultural workers, pensions for retired agricultural laborers, and a high rate of government employment for members of low-caste communities.

Another question engaging comparativists is whether success in providing education and welfare inevitably leads to success in the economic sphere. Again, the case of Kerala provides pointers for further research. Kerala scores high on human development indicators such as literacy and health, and its economy has also grown in recent years.

What are the international and domestic challenges that India faces at the dawn of the twenty-first century? How will it cope with its new-found status as a nuclear power? How can it prevent further escalation of conflict in the region that could end in a nuclear conflagration? A worst-case scenario would be a conventional war with Pakistan that could escalate into a nuclear war. Domestically, both countries are wracked with ethnic tensions, one with a military dictatorship and the other with an elected coalition government. In an attempt to hold on to power, the leaders of each country could try to divert attention toward a national security threat from its neighbor, a ploy that has been used effectively in the past by politicians in both countries. The history of three wars between India and Pakistan, the simmering tensions over Kashmir, and both countries' possession of nuclear arms could prompt a nuclear war. The challenge for India is to establish a stable relationship with its nuclear neighbors, Pakistan and China, that would eschew proliferation of their nuclear and ballistic missiles arsenals and engage in constructive diplomatic and economic cooperation. India's history of wars with both countries is not an encouraging starting point, but the engagement of Western powers in generating a dialogue between these countries is a portent for the future. The recent initiation of people-to-people contacts and resumption of talks among leaders provides grounds for optimism. Whether such overtures will result in fruitful negotiations on Kashmir and on economic cooperation in the region remains to be seen. Answers to these questions depend at least in part on domestic political developments.

For nearly sixty years, democracy in India has been a double-edged sword. Winning elections involves attracting votes. While avoiding authoritarianism, the practice of democracy, particularly electoral politics, has worsened ethnic relations between Hindus and Muslims, upper and lower castes, and north and south. With the spread of democracy, many dissatisfied groups are finding their voices and becoming politically mobilized. The challenge for Indian politics is how to repair the divide within a democratic framework. Current voter emphasis on good governance and sound economic management rather than on religious or nationalistic issues might transform electoral platforms in the twenty-first century. Will India be able to manage its domestic tensions and enlarge social, political, and economic rights for its citizens?

Another challenge for India is how to combine its global ambitions of becoming a strong power with its program for economic liberalization. The increasing interdependence of global economies as manifested in global effects of the 1997 East Asian crisis and the dependence of developing countries on investor confidence and external aid should not be underestimated. While India was protected from the East Asian debacle because of the partially closed nature of its economy, the country nevertheless suffered some economic blows in the aftermath of becoming nuclear when economic sanctions resulted in the loss of billions of dollars in foreign aid. However, the Indian economy recovered relatively quickly. Even with modest liberalization, India is now attracting considerable foreign investment and growing at an impressive rate. The Indian case nevertheless embodies the tensions inherent in combining democracy with economic liberalization. Political parties in India face pressures to expand their support base by promoting contradictory economic improvements or by manipulating nationalist symbols. But simultaneously, these promises clash with the task of economic liberalization. The challenge faced by Indian governments is how to combine the task of economic liberalization with the conflicting demands of electoral politics.

How India reconciles its national political ambitions, domestic political demands for greater economic redistribution, and global pressures for an efficient economy will affect its influence on regional and global trends. Will India be able to capitalize on some of its positive achievements, such as the long-standing democratic ethos framed by functioning institutions, a vibrant civil society and media, and a growing middle class imbued with the desire to succeed economically? Or will it be crippled by ethnic hostility resulting in inaction at best and total disintegration of the country at worst? The current trends indicate a scenario of two-party rule, with either a

BJP-led or a Congress-led coalition ruling at the center. There also seems to be some room for optimism with regard to voter needs and interests on the international and domestic fronts. Public opinion polls show an overwhelming number of people in India and Pakistan want improved relations between the two countries. On the domestic side, the preoccupation of voters with secularism, equitable distribution, and economic management was evident from the results of the 2004 national elections. Of course, balancing the demands of simultaneously achieving equity and efficiency generates its own problems. Understanding the ways in which India meets these challenges will be of enormous interest to students of comparative politics in the years to come.

Key Terms

Sikhs
Maharajas
zamindars
Emergency (1975–1977)
green revolution
state-led economic development
economic liberalization
reservations
caste system
Brahmin

untouchables
scheduled castes
nonaligned bloc
Lok Sabha
Rajya Sabha
Indian Administrative Service
panchayats
other backward classes

Suggested Readings

Bardhan, Pranab. *The Political Economy of Development in India.* New Delhi: Oxford University Press, 1984.

Basu, Amrita. *Two Faces of Protest: Contrasting Modes of Women's Activism in India.* Berkeley: University of California Press, 1992.

———, and Kohli, Atul, eds. *Community Conflicts and the State in India.* New Delhi: Oxford University Press, 1998.

Bayly, C. A. *The New Cambridge History of India: Indian Society and the Making of the British Empire.* Vol. 2, no. 1. Cambridge: Cambridge University Press, 1988.

Brass, Paul R. *The New Cambridge History of India: The Politics of India Since Independence.* Vol. 4, no. 1. Cambridge: Cambridge University Press, 1990.

———, *The Production of Hindu-Muslim Violence in Contemporary India.* Madison: University of Wisconsin Press, 2005.

Carras, Mary C. *Indira Gandhi: In the Crucible of Leadership.* Boston: Beacon Press, 1979.

Chatterjee, Partha, ed. *State Politics in India*. New Delhi: Oxford University Press, 1997.

Dreze, Jean, and Amartya, Sen, eds. *Economic Development and Social Opportunity*. New Delhi: Oxford University Press, 1995.

Frankel, Francine. *India's Political Economy, 1947–2004: The Gradual Revolution*. New Delhi: Oxford University Press, 2005.

Gopal, Sarvepalli. *Jawaharlal Nehru: A Biography*. Vols. 2 and 3. New Delhi: Oxford University Press, 1984.

Graham, Bruce. *Hindu Nationalism and Indian Politics*. Cambridge: Cambridge University Press, 1990.

Hardgrave, Robert L., Jr., and Kochanek, Stanley A. *India: Government and Politics in a Developing Nation*. 4th ed. New York: Harcourt Brace Jovanovich, 1986.

Hasan, Zoya. *Quest for Power: Oppositional Movements and Post-Congress Politics in Uttar Pradesh*. Delhi: Oxford University Press, 1998.

Jaffrelot, Christophe. *The Hindu Nationalist Movement and Indian Politics, 1925 to the 1990s: Strategies on Identity Building, Implantation and Mobilization*. New York: Columbia University Press, 1996.

Jalal, Ayesha. *Democracy and Authoritarianism in South Asia*. Cambridge: Cambridge University Press, 1995.

Jalan, Bimal. *India's Economic Crisis: The Way Ahead*. New Delhi: Oxford University Press, 1991.

Jenkins, Rob. *Regional Reflections: Contemporary Politics Across India's States*. New Delhi: Oxford University Press, 2004.

Kohli, Atul. *Democracy and Discontent: India's Growing Crisis of Governability*. Cambridge: Cambridge University Press, 1991.

———. *State Directed Development: Political Power and Industrialization in the Global Periphery*. Cambridge: Cambridge University Press, 2004.

———. *The State and Poverty in India: The Politics of Reform*. Cambridge: Cambridge University Press, 1987.

———, ed. *The Success of India's Democracy*. Cambridge: Cambridge University Press, 2001.

Misra, B. B. *Government and Bureaucracy in India: 1947–1976*. New Delhi: Oxford University Press, 1986.

Nayar, Baldev Raj. *India's Mixed Economy*. Bombay: Popular Prakashan, 1989.

Ray, Raka, and Katzenstein, Mary, eds. *Social Movements in India: Poverty, Power and Politics*. Lanham, MD: Rowman and Littlefield, 2005.

Rothermund, Dietmar. *An Economic History of India: From Pre-Colonial Times to 1986*. London: Croom Helm, 1988.

Rudolph, Lloyd, and Rudolph, Susanne. *In Pursuit of Lakshmi: The Political Economy of the Indian State*. Chicago: University of Chicago Press, 1987.

Sarkar, Sumit. *Modern India: 1885 to 1947*. Madras: Macmillan, 1983.

Varshney, Ashutosh. *Ethnic Conflict and Civic Life: Hindus and Muslims in India*. New Haven, Conn.: Yale University Press, 2002.

———, ed. *India and the Political Economy of Developing Countries: Essays in Honor of Myron Weiner*. New Delhi: Sage Publishers, 2004.

Weiner, Myron. *The Child and the State in India*. Princeton, N.J.: Princeton University Press, 1992.

———. *The Indian Paradox: Essays in Indian Politics*. New Delhi: Sage, 1989.

Wilkinson, Steven. *Votes and Violence: Electoral Competition and Ethnic Riots in India*. Cambridge: Cambridge University Press, 2004.

Suggested Websites

BJP Party
www.bjp.org
Economic and Political Weekly, a good source of information on Indian politics
www.epw.org.in
Frontline, a magazine with coverage of Indian politics
www.flonnet.com
Hindu, an English daily paper in India
www.hinduonnet.com
Hindustan Times
www.hindustantimes.com
Directory of Indian government websites
goidirectory.nic.in
Sabrang Communications, providing coverage of human rights issues in India
www.sabrang.com

Endnotes

[1] Madhura Swaminathan, "Food Security: No Panacea?" *Frontline*, October 14–27, 2000; Jayati Ghosh, "Wasted Food, Wasted Opportunities?" *Frontline*, September 30–October 13, 2000.

[2] Prabhat Patnaik, "Budget 2002: The Poverty of Economic Policy?" *Frontline*, March 16–29, 2002.

[3] *Times of India*, September 7, 2002.

[4] People's Union for Democratic Rights, Resisting POTO, People's Union for Democratic Rights, "No Vakeel, No Daleel, No Appeal," *Delhi*, November 2001, pp. 5–9; also see V. Venkatesan, "Terror Through Ordinance," *Frontline*, November 23, 2001, pp. 26–29, and Gautam Navlakha, "POTO: Taking the Lawless Road," *Economic and Political Weekly*, December 8, 2001, pp. 4520–4522.

[5] Shirin M. Rai, "Gender and Representation: Women MPs in the Indian Parliament," in Anne Marie Goetz, ed., *Getting Institutions Right for Women and Development* (London: Zed Books, 1997), p. 105.

CHAPTER 4

Mexico

Merilee S. Grindle

United Mexican States

Land and People

Capital	Mexico City	
Total area (square miles)	756,066 (about 3 times the size of Texas)	
Population	104.96 million	
Annual population growth rate (%)	1975–2002	2.0
	2002–2015 (projected)	1.2
Urban population (%)	75.2%	
Major language(s) (%)	Spanish	94.1
	Mayan, Nahuatl, and other indigenous languages	5.9
Religious affiliation (%)	Roman Catholic	89
	Protestant	6
	Other	5

Economy

Domestic currency	Peso (MXN) US$1: 11.29 MXN (2005)	
Total GNI (US$)	637.2 billion	
GNI per capita (US$)	6,230	
Total GNI at purchasing power parity (US$)	918.5 billion	
GNI per capita at purchasing power parity (US$)	8,980	
GDP annual growth rate (%)	1983–1993	2.4
	1993–2003	3.2
	2002	0.7
	2003	1.3
	2004	4.1
GDP per capita average annual growth rate (%)	1983–1993	0.4
	1993–2003	1.7
Inequality in income or consumption (2000) (%)	Share of poorest 10%	1.0
	Share of poorest 20%	3.1
	Share of richest 20%	59.1
	Share of richest 10%	43.1
	Gini Index (2000)	54.6
Structure of production (% of GDP)	Agriculture	4
	Industry	27.2
	Services	68.9
Labor force distribution (% of total)	Agriculture	18
	Industry	24
	Services	58
Exports as % of GDP	28.4	
Imports as % of GDP	30.1	

Society

Life expectancy at birth	74.94	
Infant mortality per 1,000 live births	21.69	
Adult literacy (%)	Male	94
	Female	90.5
Access to information and communications (per 1,000 population)	Telephone lines	147
	Mobile phones	255
	Radios	330
	Televisions	283
	Personal computers	82.0

Women in Government and the Economy

Women in the national legislature		
Lower house or single house (%)		22.6
Upper house (%)		15.6
Women at ministerial level (%)		11.1
Female economic activity rate (age 15 and above) (%)		40.2
Female labor force (% of total)		32
Estimated earned income (PPP US$)	Female	4,915
	Male	12,967

Composite Rankings and Ratings

2004 Human Development Index ranking (value) out of 177 countries	53
Gender-related Development Index (GDI) ranking (value) out of 144 countries	53 (.802)
Gender Empowerment Measure (GEM) ranking (value) out of 78 countries	34 (.563)
Corruption Perception Index (CPI) ranking (value) out of 146 countries	64 (3.6)
Environmental Sustainability Index (ESI) ranking (value) out of 146 countries	95 (46.2)
Freedom in World rating	Free (2.0)

Political Organizations

Political System   Federal republic.

Regime History   Current form of government since 1917.

Administrative Structure   Federal with 31 states and a federal district.

Executive   President, elected by direct election with a six-year term of office; reelection not permitted.

Legislature   Bicameral Congress. Senate (upper house) and Chamber of Deputies (lower house); elections held every three years. There are 128 senators, 3 from each of the 31 states, 3 from the federal (capital) district, and 32 elected nationally by proportional representation for six-year terms. The 500 members of the Chamber of Deputies are elected for three-year terms from 300 electoral districts, 300 by simple majority vote and 200 by proportional representation.

Judiciary Independent federal and state court system headed by a Supreme Court with 11 justices appointed by the president and approved by the Senate.

Party System Multiparty system. One-party dominant (Institutional Revolutionary Party) system from 1929 until 2000. Major parties: National Action Party, Institutional Revolutionary Party, and the Democratic Revolutionary Party.

Section ❶ The Making of the Modern Mexican State

Politics in Action

On December 1, 2000, Vicente Fox Quesada became president of Mexico. Although most of the inauguration ceremony followed long-established tradition, the event was historic. For the first time in seventy-one years, the president of Mexico did not represent the Institutional Revolutionary Party (PRI, pronounced "pree"), which had governed the country without interruption since 1929. Fox assumed the presidency under the banner of the National Action Party (PAN, pronounced "pahn"), a center-right party that had long opposed the PRI. He won the election largely because the old civil-authoritarian system could no longer ensure political stability, economic progress, and responsiveness to the demands of a society that was increasingly characterized by inequality.

The inauguration of Fox signaled a new stage in Mexico's quest for democracy. Under the PRI, political conflict had been largely limited to internal struggles within the party, and those who questioned its monopoly of power were usually co-opted into quiescence with promises and benefits, or they were quietly but effectively repressed. The regime was sometimes called "the perfect dictatorship." For several decades, this system produced political stability and economic growth. Yet, increasingly during the 1980s and 1990s, Mexicans began to press for fairer elections and more responsive public officials. They demanded the right of opposition parties to compete for power on an equal basis with the PRI. They argued that the president had too much power and that the PRI was riddled with corruption. By 2000, a significant number of

the country's 100 million citizens wanted political change.

Just six years before, in 1994, despite widespread disillusionment with the political system, PRI candidate Ernesto Zedillo had easily won the presidency. At that time, many voters feared that political change might bring violence and instability more than they feared politics as usual under the continuation of a PRI government. And having spent all their lives under the PRI, some citizens remembered the party's triumphs of decades past and continued to support it. By 2000, however, a majority of the voters had had enough. Yet it was natural that they should be concerned about what government under the PAN would bring. Along with trepidation about change, many were expecting a great deal from the new government—more open political debate, more open government, more capacity to influence public policies, more economic growth, improved public services. President Fox had his job cut out for him.

Today, Mexicans are proud that their country has demonstrated its ability to move toward more democratic politics. Yet political and economic dissatisfaction continues to characterize the country. Regime change did not bring much evidence of improved capacity to respond to the needs of many. For elites, the opportunities of globalization have provided unprecedented wealth and cosmopolitan lifestyles. Yet indicators of increased poverty are everywhere. At least a quarter of the population lives on less than two dollars a day. The public education and health systems struggle to meet demand. In the countryside, the peasant population faces destitution. In urban areas, the poor are forced to find meager sources of income however they can.

Thus, the advent of the Fox administration drew attention to ongoing and interrelated challenges of Mexico's development:

- Would a country with a long tradition of authoritarian government be able to sustain a democratic political system in the face of increasing demands and high expectations?
- Would a country that had long sought economic development through government activism and the domestic market be able to compete effectively in a competitive, market-driven global economy?
- Would a country long noted for severe inequalities between the rich and the poor be capable of providing better living standards for its growing population?

Geographic Setting

Mexico is one of the most geographically diverse countries in the world, encompassing snow-capped volcanoes, coastal plains, high plateaus, fertile valleys, rain forests, and deserts within an area slightly less than three times the size of Texas. To the north, it shares a 2,000-mile-long border with the United States, to the south, a 600-mile-long border with Guatemala and a 160-mile-long border with Belize. Two imposing mountain ranges run the length of Mexico: the Sierra Madre Occidental to the west and the Sierra Madre Oriental to the east. As a result, the country is noted for peaks, plateaus, and valleys that produce an astonishing number of microclimates and a rich diversity of plants and animals. Mexico's varied geography has historically made communication and transportation between regions difficult and infrastructure expensive. The mountainous terrain tends to limit large-scale commercial agriculture to irrigated fields in the northern part of the country, while the central and southern regions produce a wide variety of crops on small farms. Soil erosion and desertification are major problems because of the steep terrain and unpredictable rainfall in many areas. The country is rich in oil, silver, and other natural resources, but it has long struggled to manage those resources wisely.

The human landscape is equally dramatic. With some 100 million inhabitants, Mexico is the world's eleventh most populous country—the second-largest nation in Latin America after Portuguese-speaking Brazil and the largest Spanish-speaking nation in the world. Sixty percent of the population is *mestizo,* or people of mixed **Amerindian** and Spanish descent. About 30 percent of the population claims indigenous (Amerindian) descent, although only about 6 percent of the population speaks an indigenous language rather than Spanish. The rest of the population is made up of Caucasians and people with other backgrounds. The largest **indigenous groups** are the Maya in the south and the Náhuatl in the central regions, with well over 1 million members each. There are also dozens and perhaps hundreds of smaller linguistic and social groups throughout the country. Although Mexicans pride themselves on their Amerindian heritage, problems of racism and classism run deep.

Mexico was transformed from a largely rural to a largely urban country in the second half of the twentieth century, with over 75 percent of the population now living in urban areas. Mexico City has become one of the world's largest cities, with about 20 million inhabitants.[1] Annual population growth has slowed to about 1.4 percent, but society continues to adjust to the baby boom of the 1970s and early 1980s as these twenty- to thirty-year-olds seek jobs and form families. Migration both within and beyond Mexico's borders has become a major issue. Greater economic opportunities in the industrial cities of the north lead many men and women to seek work there in the *maquiladoras,* or assembly industries. As a result, border cities like Tijuana and Ciudad Juárez have experienced tremendous growth in the past twenty years. Many job seekers continue on to the United States, lured by a larger job market and higher wages. The problem repeats itself in reverse on Mexico's southern border, with many thousands of Central Americans looking for better prospects in Mexico and beyond.

Critical Junctures

Mexicans are deeply affected by the legacies of their collective past, including centuries of colonialism and decades of political instability after the end of Spanish rule. The legacies of the distant past are still felt, but the most formative event in the country's modern history was the Revolution of 1910. Mexico

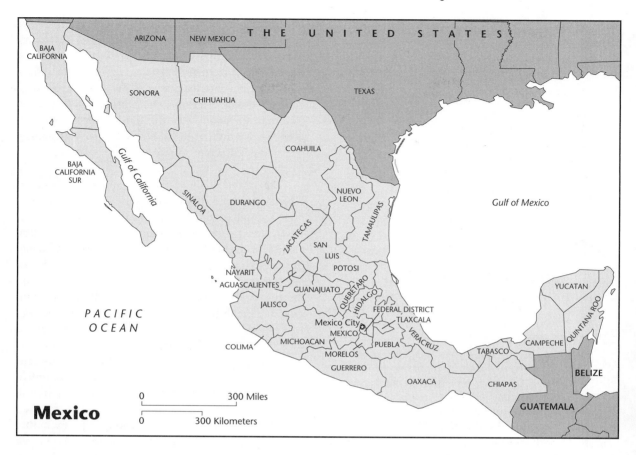

Mexico

experienced the first great social revolution of the twentieth century, a conflict that lasted for more than a decade and claimed the lives of as many as 1 million people. The revolution was fought by a variety of forces for a variety of reasons, which made the consolidation of power that followed as significant as the revolution itself. The institutions and symbols of the current political regime emerged from these complex conflicts.

Independence and Instability (1810–1876)

Spain ruled Mexico for three centuries, administering a vast economic, political, and religious empire in the interests of the imperial country, its kings, and its representatives in North America (see "Global Connection: Conquest or Encounter?"). Colonial policy was designed to extract wealth from the territory then known as New Spain and to limit the

possibilities for Spaniards in the New World to benefit from agriculture, commerce, or industry without at the same time benefiting the mother country. It was also designed to ensure commitment to the Roman Catholic religion and the subordination of the Amerindian population.

In 1810, a parish priest in central Mexico named Miguel Hidalgo called for an end to Spanish misrule. At the head of a motley band of insurgents, he began the first of a series of wars for independence that pitted rebels against the Spanish Crown for eleven years. Although independence was gained in 1821, Mexico struggled to create a stable and legitimate government for decades after. Liberals and conservatives, federalists and centralists, those who sought to expand the power of the church and those who sought to curtail it, and those who wanted a republic and those who wanted a monarchy were all engaged in the battle for Mexico's soul during the nineteenth century. Between

Critical Junctures in Mexico's Political Development	
1521	Spaniards led by Hernán Cortés capture the Aztec capital, initiating three centuries of colonial rule.
1810–1821	War of independence from Spain
1876–1911	Dictatorship of Porfirio Díaz
1910–1920	Mexican Revolution
1917	Mexican Constitution
1929	Plutarco Elías Calles founds PRI.
1934–1940	Presidency of Lázaro Cárdenas; entrenchment of corporatist state
1968	Massacre of Tlaltelolco; hundreds of protesting students killed
1978–1982	State-led development reaches peak with petroleum boom and bust.
1982	Market reformers come to power in PRI.
1988	Carlos Salinas is elected amid charges of fraud.
1989	First governorship is won by an opposition party.
1994	NAFTA goes into effect; uprising in Chiapas; Colosio assassinated.
1996	Political parties agree on electoral reform.
1997	Opposition parties advance nationwide; PRI loses absolute majority in congress for first time in its history.
2000	PRI loses presidency; Vicente Fox of PAN becomes president, but without majority support in congress.

of Veracruz. With considerable loss of civilian lives, U.S. forces marched toward Mexico City, where they engaged in the final battle of the war at Chapultepec Castle. An 1848 treaty gave the United States title to what later became the states of Texas, New Mexico, Utah, Nevada, Arizona, California, and part of Colorado for about $18 million, leaving a legacy of deep resentment toward the United States, which many Mexicans still consider to be the "Colossus of the North."

The loss in this war did not make it any easier to govern Mexico. Liberals and conservatives continued their struggle over issues of political and economic order and, in particular, the power of the Catholic Church. The Constitution of 1857 incorporated many of the goals of the liberals, such as a somewhat democratic government, a bill of rights, and limitations on the power of the church. The constitution did not guarantee stability, however. In 1861, Spain, Great Britain, and France occupied Veracruz to collect debts owed by Mexico. The French army then continued on to Mexico City, where it subdued the weak government, and established the rule of Emperor Maximilian (1864–1867). Conservatives welcomed this respite from the liberal rule. Benito Juárez returned to the presidency in 1867 after defeating and executing Maximilian. Juárez, a Zapotec Indian from Oaxaca who came to be a liberal hero, is still hailed in Mexico today as an early proponent of more democratic government.

The Porfiriato (1876–1911)

Over the next few years, a popular retired general named Porfirio Díaz became increasingly dissatisfied with what he thought was a "lot of politics" and "little action" in Mexico's government. After several failed attempts to win and then take the presidency, he finally succeeded in 1876. His dictatorship lasted thirty-four years and was at first welcomed by many because it brought sustained stability to the country.

Díaz imposed a highly centralized authoritarian system to create political order and economic progress. Over time, he came to rely increasingly on a small clique of advisers, known as *científicos* (scientists), who wanted to adopt European technologies and values to modernize the country. Deeply disdainful of the

1833 and 1855, thirty-six presidential administrations came to power.

Adding insult to injury during this disorganized period, Mexico lost half its territory to the United States. Its northern territory of Texas proclaimed and then won independence in a war ending in 1836. Then the Lone Star Republic, as Texas was then called, was annexed by the United States in 1845, and claims on Mexican territory north of the Rio Grande were increasingly heard from Washington. On the basis of a dubious claim that Mexico had invaded U.S. territory, the United States declared war on its southern neighbor in 1841. The war was first fought along what was later to become the border between the two countries, and then, in 1847, the U.S. army invaded the port city

Global Connection: *Conquest or Encounter?*

The year 1519, when the Spanish conqueror Hernán Cortés arrived on the shores of the Yucatán Peninsula, is often considered the starting point of Mexican political history. But the Spanish explorers did not come to an uninhabited land waiting to be excavated for gold and silver. Instead, the land that was to become New Spain and then Mexico was home to extensive and complex indigenous civilizations that were advanced in agriculture, architecture, and political and economic organization—civilizations that were already over a thousand years old. The Mayans of the Yucatán and the Toltecs of the central highlands had reached high levels of development long before the arrival of the Europeans. By 1519, diverse groups had fallen under the power of the militaristic Aztec Empire, which extended throughout what is today central and southern Mexico.

The encounter between the Europeans and these indigenous civilizations was marked by bloodshed and violence. The great Aztec city of Tenochtitlán—the site of Mexico City today—was captured and largely destroyed by the Spanish conquerors in 1521. Cortés and the colonial masters who came after him subjected indigenous groups to forced labor; robbed them of gold, silver, and land; and introduced flora and fauna from Europe that destroyed long-existing aqueducts and irrigation systems. They also brought alien forms of property rights and authority relationships, a religion that viewed indigenous practices as the devil's work, and an economy based on mining and cattle—all of which soon overwhelmed existing structures of social and economic organization.

Within a century, wars, savage exploitation at the hands of the Spaniards, and the introduction of European diseases reduced the indigenous population from an estimated 25 million to 1 million or fewer. The Indian population took three hundred years just to stop decreasing after the disaster of the conquest.

Even so, the Spanish never constituted more than a small percentage of the total population, and massive racial mixing among the Indians, Europeans, and to a lesser extent Africans produced a new *raza*, or *mestizo* race. This unique process remains at once a source of pride and conflict for Mexicans today. What does it mean to be Mexican? Is one the conquered or the conqueror? While celebrating Amerindian achievements in food, culture, the arts, and ancient civilization, middle-class Mexico has the contradictory sense that to be "Indian" nowadays is to be backward. Many Amerindians are stigmatized by mainstream society if they speak a native dialect. But perhaps the situation is changing, with the upsurge of indigenous movements from both the grass roots and the international level striving to promote ethnic pride, defend rights, and foster the teaching of Indian languages.

The collision of two worlds resonates in current national philosophical and political debates. Is Mexico a Western society? Is it colonial or modern? Third or First World? South or North? Is the United States an ally or a conqueror? Perhaps most important, many Mexicans at once welcome and fear full integration into the global economy, asking themselves: Is globalization the new conquest?

---

vast majority of the country's population, Díaz and the *científicos* encouraged foreign investment and amassed huge fortunes. During this period, known as the *Porfiriato*, this small elite group monopolized political power and reserved lucrative economic investments for itself. Economic and political opportunities were closed off for new generations of middle- and upper-class Mexicans, who became increasingly resentful of the greed of the Porfirians and their own lack of opportunities.

The Revolution of 1910 and the Sonoran Dynasty (1910–1934)

In 1910, conflict broke out as reformers sought to end the dictatorship. Díaz had pledged himself to an open election for president, and in 1910, Francisco I. Madero, a landowner from the northern state of Coahuila, presented himself as a candidate. The slogan "Effective Suffrage, No Reelection" summed up the reformers' goals in creating opportunities for a new class of politically ambitious citizens to move into positions of power. When this opposition swelled, Díaz jailed Madero and tried to repress growing dissent. But it was too late. The clamor for change forced Díaz into exile. Madero was elected in 1911, but he was soon using the military to put down revolts from reformers and reactionaries alike. When Madero was assassinated during a **coup d'état** in 1913, political order in the country virtually collapsed.

At the same time that middle-class reformers struggled to displace Díaz, a peasant revolt that focused on land claims erupted in the central and southern states of the country. This revolt had roots in legislation that made it easy for wealthy landowners and ranchers to claim the lands of peasant villagers. Encouraged by the weakening of the old regime and driven to desperation by increasing landlessness, villagers armed themselves and joined forces under a variety of local leaders. The most famous of these was Emiliano Zapata, who amassed a peasant army from Morelos, a state in southern Mexico. Zapata's manifesto, the Plan de Ayala, became the cornerstone of the radical agrarian reform that would be incorporated into the Constitution of 1917.

In the northern part of the country, Francisco (Pancho) Villa rallied his own army of workers, small farmers, and ranch hands. He presented a major challenge to the national army, now under the leadership of Venustiano Carranza, who inherited Madero's middle-class reformist movement and eventually became president. Villa's forces recognized no law but that of their chief and combined military maneuvers with banditry, looting, and warlordism in the territories under their control. In 1916, troops from the United States entered Mexico to punish Villa for an attack on U.S. territory. Although this badly planned, poorly executed military operation failed to locate Villa, the presence of U.S. troops on Mexican soil resulted in increased public hostility toward the United States, against which feelings were already running high because of a 1914 invasion of Veracruz.

The Mexican Constitution of 1917 was forged out of the diverse and often conflicting set of interests represented by the various revolutionary factions. The document established a formal set of political institutions and guaranteed citizens a range of progressive social and economic rights: agrarian reform, social security, the right to organize in unions, a minimum wage, an eight-hour workday, profit sharing for workers, universal secular education, and adult male suffrage. Despite these socially advanced provisions, the constitution did not provide suffrage for women, who had to wait until 1953 to vote in local elections and 1958 to vote in national elections. In an effort to limit the power of foreign investors, the constitution declared that only Mexican citizens or the government could own land or rights to water and other natural resources. It also contained numerous articles that severely limited the power of the Roman Catholic Church, long a target of liberals who wanted Mexico to be a secular state. The signing of the document signaled the formal end of the revolution and the intent of the contending parties to form a new political regime. Despite such noble sentiments, violence continued as competing leaders sought to assert power and displace their rivals. By 1920, a modicum of stability had emerged, but not before many of the revolutionary leaders—including Zapata and President Carranza—had been assassinated in struggles over power and policy. There were, however, occasional outbreaks of violence among local warlords during the twenties.

Despite this violence, power was gradually consolidated in the hands of a group of revolutionary leaders from the north of the country. Known as the Sonoran Dynasty, after their home state of Sonora, these leaders were committed to a capitalist model of economic development. Eventually, one of the Sonorans, Plutarco Elías Calles, emerged as the *jefe máximo,* or supreme leader. After his presidential term (1924–1928), Calles managed to select and dominate his successors from 1929 to 1934. The consolidation of power under his control was accompanied by extreme **anticlericalism,** which eventually resulted in warfare between the government and the conservative leaders of the Catholic Church and their followers.

In 1929, Calles brought together many of the most powerful contenders for leadership, including

In 1914, Pancho Villa (right) met with Emiliano Zapata in Mexico City to discuss the revolution and their separate goals for its outcome.   *Source:* Robert Freck/Odyssey/Chicago.

many regional warlords, to create a political party. The bargain he offered was simple: contenders for power would accommodate each other's interests in the expectation that without political violence, the country would prosper and they would be able to reap the benefits of even greater power and economic spoils. They formed a political party, whose name was changed in 1938 and again in 1946, to consolidate their power; and for the next seven decades, Calles's bargain was effective in ensuring nonviolent conflict resolution among elites and the uninterrupted rule of the Institutional Revolutionary Party (PRI) in national politics.

Although the revolution was complex and the interests contending for power in its aftermath were numerous, there were five clear results of this protracted conflict. First, the power of traditional rural landowners was undercut. But in the years after the revolution, wealthy elites would again emerge in rural areas, even though they would never again be so powerful in national politics nor would their power be so unchecked in local areas. Second, the influence of the Catholic Church was strongly curtailed. Although the church remained important in many parts of the country, it no longer participated openly in national political debates. Third, the power of foreign investors was severely limited; prior to the

revolution, foreign investors had owned much of the country's land as well as many of its railroads, mines, and factories. Henceforth, Mexican nationalism would shape economic policymaking. Fourth, a new political elite consolidated power and agreed to resolve conflicts through accommodation and bargaining rather than through violence. And fifth, the new constitution and the new party laid the basis for a strong central government that could assert its power over the agricultural, industrial, and social development of the country.

Lázaro Cárdenas, Agrarian Reform, and the Workers (1934–1940)

In 1934, Plutarco Elías Calles handpicked Lázaro Cárdenas, a revolutionary general and former state governor, as the official candidate for the presidency. The *jefe máximo* fully anticipated that Cárdenas would go along with his behind-the-scenes management of the country and that the new president would continue the economic policies of the postrevolutionary coalition. To his great surprise, Cárdenas executed a virtual coup that established his own supremacy and sent Calles packing to the United States for an "extended vacation."[2] Even more unexpectedly, Cárdenas mobilized peasants and workers in pursuit of the more radical goals of the 1910 revolution. He encouraged peasant associations to petition for land and claim rights promised in the Constitution of 1917. During his administration, more than 49 million acres of land were distributed, nearly twice as much as had been parceled out by all the previous postrevolutionary governments combined.[3] Most of these lands were distributed in the form of **ejidos** (collective land grants) to peasant groups. **Ejidatarios** (those who acquired *ejido* lands) became one of the most enduring bases of support for the government. Cárdenas also encouraged workers to form unions and demand higher wages and better working conditions. He established his nationalist credentials in 1938 when he wrested the petroleum industry from foreign investors and placed it under government control.

During the Cárdenas years (1934–1940), the bulk of the Mexican population was incorporated into the political system. Organizations of peasants and workers, middle-class groups, and the military were added to the official party, and the voices of the poor majority were heard within the councils of government, reducing the risk that they would become radicalized outside them. In addition, the Cárdenas years witnessed a great expansion of the role of the state as the government encouraged investment in industrialization, provided credit to agriculture, and created infrastructure.

Lázaro Cárdenas continues to be a national hero to Mexicans, who look back on his presidency as a period when government was clearly committed to improving the welfare of the country's poor. His other legacy was to institutionalize patterns of political succession and presidential behavior that continue to set standards for Mexico's leaders. He campaigned extensively, and his travels took him to remote villages and regions, where he listened to the demands and complaints of humble people. Cárdenas served a single six-year term, called a *sexenio,* and then relinquished full power to his successor—a pattern of presidential succession that still holds in Mexican politics. Cárdenas's conduct in office created hallowed traditions of presidential style and succession that all subsequent national leaders have observed.

The Politics of Rapid Development (1940–1982)

Although Cárdenas had directed a radical reshuffling of political power in the country, his successors were able to use the institutions he created to counteract his reforms. Ambitious local and regional party leaders and leaders of peasants' and workers' groups began to use their organizations as pawns in exchange for political favors. Gradually, the PRI developed a huge patronage machine, providing union and *ejido* leaders with jobs, opportunities for corruption, land, and other benefits in return for delivering their followers' political support. Extensive chains of personal relationships based on the exchange of favors allowed the party to amass far-reaching political control and limit opportunities for organizing independent of the PRI. These exchange relationships, known as **clientelism,** became the cement that built loyalty to the PRI and the political system.

This kind of political control enabled post-Cárdenas presidents to reorient the country's development away from the egalitarian social goals of the 1930s toward a development strategy in which the state actively encouraged industrialization and the accumulation of wealth. Initially, industrialization created jobs and made available a wide range of basic consumer goods to Mexico's burgeoning population. Economic growth rates were high during the 1940s, 1950s, and 1960s, and Mexicans flocked to the cities to take advantage of the jobs created in the manufacturing and construction industries. By the 1970s, however, industrial development policies were no longer generating rapid growth and could not keep pace with the rapidly rising demand for jobs.

The country's economy was in deep crisis by the mid-1970s. Just as policymakers began to take actions to correct the problems, vast new amounts of oil were discovered in the Gulf of Mexico. Soon, rapid economic growth in virtually every sector of the economy was refueled by extensive public investment programs paid for with oil revenues. Based on the promise of petroleum wealth, the government and private businesses borrowed huge amounts of capital from foreign lenders, who were eager to do business with a country that had so much oil. Unfortunately for Mexico, international petroleum prices plunged sharply in the early 1980s. Almost overnight, there was no more credit to be had and much less money from petroleum to pay for economic expansion or the interest on the debts incurred in preceding years. Mexico plunged into a deep economic crisis that affected many other countries around the world.

Crisis and Reform (1982–2001)

This economic crisis led two presidents, Miguel de la Madrid (1982–1988) and Carlos Salinas (1988–1994), to introduce the first major reversal of the country's development strategy since the 1940s. New policies were put in place to limit the government's role in the economy and to make it easier for Mexican producers to export their goods. This period clearly marked the beginning of a new effort to integrate Mexico more fully into the global economy. In 1993, by signing the **North American Free Trade Agreement (NAFTA),** which committed Mexico, the United States, and Canada to the elimination of trade barriers among them, Mexico's policymakers signaled the extent to which they envisioned that the future prosperity of

Mexican presidential candidates are expected to campaign hard, traveling to remote locations, making rousing campaign speeches, and meeting with citizens of humble origins. Here, presidential candidate Vicente Fox Quesada is on the campaign trail. *Source:* R. Kwiotek/Zeitenspiegel/Corbis/Sygma.

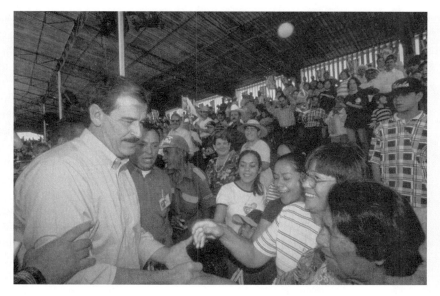

their country would be linked to that of its two neighbors to the north.

The economic reforms of the 1980s and 1990s were a turning point for Mexico and meant that the country's future development would be closely tied to international economic conditions. A major economic crisis at the end of 1994, in which billions of dollars of foreign investment fled the country, was indicative of this new international vulnerability. The peso lost half of its value against the dollar within a few days, and the government lacked the funds to pay its debt obligations. Suddenly, Mexico's status among nations seemed dubious once more, and the country felt betrayed by outgoing President Salinas, convinced that he had patched together a shaky house of cards only long enough to get himself out of office. The Mexican economy shrank by 6.2 percent in 1995, inflation soared, taxes rose while wages were frozen, and the bank system collapsed. The United States orchestrated a $50 billion bailout, $20 billion of which came directly from the U.S. Treasury. Faced with limited options, the administration of Ernesto Zedillo (1994–2000) implemented a severe and unpopular economic austerity program, which restored financial stability over the next two years.

Economic crisis was exacerbated by political concerns. On January 1, 1994, a guerrilla movement, the Zapatista Army of National Liberation (EZLN),

seized four towns in the southern state of Chiapas. The group demanded land, democracy, indigenous rights, and an immediate repeal of NAFTA. Many citizens throughout the country openly supported the aims of the rebels, pointing out that the movement brought to light the reality of two different Mexicos: one in which the privileged enjoyed the fruits of wealth and influence and another in which citizens were getting left behind because of poverty and repression. The government and the military were also criticized for inaction and human rights abuses in the state.

Following close on the heels of rebellion came the assassination of the PRI's presidential candidate, Luis Donaldo Colosio, on March 23, 1994, in the northern border city of Tijuana. The assassination shocked all citizens and shook the political elite deeply. The murder opened wide rifts within the PRI and unleashed a flood of speculation and distrust among the citizenry. Many Mexicans were convinced that the assassination was part of a conspiracy of party "dinosaurs," political hardliners who opposed any kind of democratic transformation.[4] Although that has never been proved, speculation about who was behind the assassination has continued to this day. Fear of violence helped provide the PRI with strong support in the August 1994 elections.

The PRI was able to remain in power, but these shocks provoked widespread disillusionment and frustration with the political system. Many citizens, especially in urban areas, decided that there was no longer any reason to support the PRI. Buoyed by a 1996 electoral reform, the opposition made important gains in the legislative elections the following year. For the first time in modern Mexican history, the PRI lost its absolute majority in the Chamber of Deputies, the lower house of the national legislature. Since then, the congress has shown increasing dynamism as a counterbalance to the presidency, blocking executive decisions, demanding unrestricted information, and initiating new legislation. In addition, opposition parties have won important governorships and mayorships. The 2000 election of Vicente Fox as the first non-PRI president in seven decades was the culmination of this electoral revolution.

The Fox Presidency and Post–September 11 Mexico (2001 to the Present)

When Vicente Fox entered Los Pinos, the official residence of the Mexican president, in December 2000, hopes were high that his administration would transform the country, consolidating the progress towards democracy that had been made, while also improving public services and reducing poverty. However, Fox found it difficult to bring about the changes that he had promised to the Mexican people. The difficulties faced by the new president as he attempted to implement his ambitious agenda arose in part because he and his team lacked experience in addressing the challenges of governance on a national scale. However, a bigger problem for Fox was that new structural factors placed significant limits on the president's ability to secure approval for his policies. Because he lacked the compliant congressional majority and the close relationship with his party that his PRI predecessors had enjoyed, Fox was unable to overcome opposition to many of his initiatives. Proposals for a reform of the tax code and for the restructuring of the government-controlled electricity corporation went down to defeat, and the president was subjected to catcalls and heckling when he made his annual reports to the congress.

With his legislative agenda stalled, Fox hoped that achievements in international policy would enhance his prestige at home. He was particularly hopeful that a close personal connection with the new U.S.

president, George W. Bush, would facilitate an agreement under which a greater number of Mexicans would be able to migrate to the United States and work there. During his first months in office, Fox had good reasons to be optimistic that he might be successful in building a more constructive relationship with Mexico's powerful neighbor. Bush had indicated that building a partnership with Mexico would be an important component of his foreign policy program, and the two governments initiated talks on a possible migration accord in 2001.

The events of September 11, 2001, dramatically changed the outlook, however. After the terrorist attacks on the World Trade Center and the Pentagon, top U.S. officials immediately turned their attention away from Mexico and Latin America and toward Afghanistan and the Middle East, diminishing the prospects for significant breakthroughs in U.S.-Mexican relations. It did not help that some in Washington felt that Mexico had been slow to express its solidarity with the United States in the wake of the attacks. The possibility of an agreement on migration disappeared as Washington moved to assert control over its borders and to restrict access to the United States. In the months that followed, Mexican officials cooperated with their U.S. counterparts in efforts designed to improve security at border crossings between the two nations, but many in Mexico City were frustrated that no progress was being made on issues like migration that were important to their country.

In 2002, Mexico began a two-year term as a member of the United Nations Security Council. The Fox administration intended the country's return to the council after a twenty-year absence to signal the desire of a democratic Mexico to play a larger role in international affairs. Serving on the Security Council presented the Mexican government with a new set of dilemmas, however. Deliberations at the UN headquarters in New York focused increasingly on U.S. proposals for the use of force against Iraq. The Bush administration, aware of Mexico's close economic ties with the United States and of Fox's personal friendship with the U.S. president, believed that Mexico could be convinced to support its position on the issue. Public opinion in Mexico was so deeply opposed to an invasion of Iraq, however, that Fox's government decided to reject U.S.-sponsored resolutions on the subject. The U.S. officials who had counted on Mexican support were bitterly disappointed, but what they had failed to realize was that memories of past U.S. invasions and occupations still made questions involving national sovereignty very sensitive in Mexico and that any Mexican government that effectively sponsored a U.S. attack on a smaller, weaker country would have to confront a tremendous backlash. This episode, and the Fox administration's post-9/11 foreign policy more generally, show that nationalism and ambivalence about Mexico's proximity to the United States remained important factors in the country's politics at the beginning of the twenty-first century.

Themes and Implications

Historical Junctures and Political Themes

The modern Mexican state emerged out of a popular revolution that proclaimed goals of democratic government, social justice, and national control of the country's resources. In the chaotic years after the revolution, the state created conditions for political and social peace. By incorporating peasants and workers into party and government institutions, and by providing benefits to low-income groups during the 1930s, it became widely accepted as legitimate. In encouraging considerable economic growth in the years after 1940, it also created a belief in its ability to provide material improvements in the quality of life for large portions of the population. These factors worked together to create a strong state capable of guiding economic and political life in the country. Only in the 1980s did this system begin to crumble.

In its external relations, Mexico has always prided itself on ideological independence from the world's great powers. For many decades, its large population, cultural richness, political stability, and front-line position regarding the United States prompted Mexico to consider itself a natural leader of Latin America and the developing world in general. After the early 1980s, however, the government rejected this position in favor of rapid integration into a global economy. The country aspired to the status enjoyed by the newly industrialized countries of the world, such as South Korea, Malaysia, and Taiwan. While the reforms of the 1980s and 1990s, and especially NAFTA, have advanced this goal, many citizens are concerned that the government has accepted a position of political, cultural, and economic subordination to the United States.

Mexico enjoyed considerable economic advancement after the 1940s, but economic and political crises after 1980 shook confidence in its ability to achieve its economic goals and highlighted the conflict between a market-oriented development strategy and the country's philosophical tradition of a strong and protective state. The larger questions of whether a new development strategy can generate growth, whether Mexican products can find profitable markets overseas, whether investors can create extensive job opportunities for millions of unemployed and part-time workers, and whether the country can maintain the confidence of those investors over the longer term continue to challenge the country.

Politically, after the Revolution of 1910, the country opted not for true democracy but for representation through government-mediated organizations within a **corporatist state,** in which interest groups became an institutionalized part of state structure rather than an independent source of advocacy. This increased state power in relation to **civil society.** The state took the lead in defining goals for the country's development and, through the school system, the party, and the media, inculcated in the population a broad sense of its legitimate right to set such goals. In addition, the state had extensive resources at its disposal to control or co-opt dissent and purchase political loyalty. The PRI was an essential channel through which material goods, jobs, the distribution of land, and the allocation of development projects flowed to increase popular support for the system or to buy off opposition to it.

This does not mean that Mexican society was unorganized or passive. Indeed, many Mexicans were actively involved in local community organizations, religious activities, unions, and public interest groups. But traditionally, the scope for challenging the government was very limited. At the same time, Mexico's strong state did not become openly repressive except when directly challenged. On the contrary, officials in the government and the party generally worked hard to find ways to resolve conflicts peacefully and to use behind-the-scenes accommodation to bring conflicting interests into accord.

By the 1980s, cracks began to appear in the traditional ways in which Mexican citizens interacted with the government. As the PRI began to lose its capacity to control political activities and as civic groups increasingly insisted on their right to remain independent from the PRI and the government, the terms of the state-society relationship were clearly in need of redefinition. The administration of President Zedillo signaled its willingness to cede political power to successful opposition parties in fair elections, and electoral reform in 1996 and competitive elections in 1997 were significant steps that led to the defeat of the PRI in 2000. Mexico's future stability depends on how well a more democratic government can accommodate conflicting interests while at the same time providing economic opportunities to a largely poor population.

Implications for Comparative Politics

The Mexican political system is unique among developing countries in the extent to which it managed to institutionalize and maintain civilian political authority for a very long time. In a world of developing nations wracked by political turmoil, military coups, and regime changes, the PRI regime established enduring institutions of governance and conditions for political stability. Other developing countries have sought to emulate the Mexican model of stability based on an alliance between a dominant party and a strong development-oriented state, but no other government has been able to create a system that has had widespread legitimacy for so long. Among developed nations, perhaps Japan comes closest to this model. The PRI's revolutionary heritage, as well as its ability to maintain a sense of national identity, were important factors in accounting for its political continuity.

Currently, Mexico is a nation undergoing significant political change without widespread violence, transforming itself from a corporatist state to a democratic one for the first time in its long history. At the same time, it struggles to resolve the conflicts of development through integration with its North American neighbors. Mexico has been categorized as an upper middle-income developing country, and its per capita income is comparable to countries such as Latvia, Malaysia, South Africa, and Chile.[5] It has made significant strides in industrialization, which accounts for about 27.2 percent of the country's gross domestic product (GDP). Agriculture contributes about 4.0 percent to GDP, and services contribute some 68.9 percent.[6] This structure is very similar to the economic profiles of Argentina, Brazil, Poland, and Hungary. But unlike those countries, Mexico is oil rich. The government-owned petroleum industry is a ready source of revenue and foreign exchange, but this commodity also makes the economy extremely vulnerable to changes in international oil prices.

Mexico's industrial and petroleum-based economy gives the country a per capita income higher than those of most other developing nations. If income were spread evenly among all Mexicans, each would receive $6,230 annually—far more than the per capita incomes of Nigeria ($320), India ($530), and China ($1,100), but considerably less than those of France ($24,770), Germany ($25,250), Britain ($28,350), and Mexico's wealthy neighbor, the United States ($37,500).[7] Of course, income is not spread evenly. Mexico suffers from great inequalities in how wealth is distributed, and poverty continues to be a grim reality for millions of Mexicans. The way the country promoted economic growth and industrialization is important in explaining why widespread poverty has persisted and why political power is not more equitably distributed.

Section ❷ Political Economy and Development

State and Economy

During the years of the Porfiriato (1876–1911), Mexico began to produce some textiles, footwear, glassware, paper, beer, tiles, furniture, and other simple products. At that time, however, policymakers were convinced that Mexico could grow rich by exporting its raw materials to more economically advanced countries. Their efforts to attract domestic and international investment encouraged a major boom in the production and export of products such as henequin (for making rope), coffee, cacao (cocoa beans), cattle, silver, and gold. Soon, the country had become so attractive to foreign investors that large amounts of land, the country's petroleum, its railroad network, and its mining wealth were largely controlled by foreigners. Nationalist reaction against the power of these foreign interests played a significant role in the tensions that produced the Revolution of 1910.

In the postrevolutionary Mexican state, this nationalism combined with a sense of social justice inspired by popular revolutionary leaders such as Zapata. Mexicans widely shared the idea that the state had the responsibility to generate wealth for all its citizens. As a result, the country adopted a strategy in which the government guided the process of industrial and agricultural development. Often referred to as **state capitalism,** this development strategy relied heavily on government actions to encourage private investment and reduce risks for private entrepreneurs. In the twenty years following the revolution, many of those concerned about the country's development became convinced that economic growth would not occur unless Mexico could industrialize more fully. They argued that reliance on exports of agricultural products, minerals, and petroleum—called the agro-export model of development—forced the country to import manufactured goods, which, over the long term, would always cost more than what was earned from exports. Mexico, they believed, should begin to manufacture the goods that it was currently importing.

Import Substitution and Its Consequences

Between 1940 and 1982, Mexico pursued a form of state capitalism and a model of industrialization known as import substitution, or **import substituting industrialization (ISI).** Like Brazil and other Latin American countries during the same period, the government promoted the development of industries to supply the domestic market by encouraging domestic and international investment; providing credit and tax incentives to industrialists; maintaining low rates of inflation; and keeping wage demands low through subsidized food, transportation, housing, and health care for workers. It also fostered industrialization by establishing state-owned steel mills, electric power generators, ports, and petroleum production and by using tariffs and import licenses to protect Mexican

industries from foreign competition. These policies had considerable success. Initially, the country produced mainly simple products like shoes, clothing, and processed foods. But by the 1960s and 1970s, it was also producing consumer durables (refrigerators, automobiles, trucks), intermediate goods (steel, petrochemicals, and other products used in the manufacturing process), and capital goods (heavy machinery to produce manufactured items).

Mexican agriculture was also affected by this drive to industrialize. With the massive agrarian reform of the 1930s (see Section 1), the *ejido* had become an important structure in the rural economy, accounting for half the cultivated area of the country and 51 percent of the value of agricultural production by 1940. After Cárdenas left office, however, government policymakers moved away from the economic development of the *ejidos*. They became committed instead to developing a strong, entrepreneurial private sector in agriculture. For them, "the development of private agriculture would be the 'foundation of industrial greatness.'"[8] They wanted this sector to provide foodstuffs for the growing cities, raw materials for industry, and foreign exchange from exports. To encourage these goals, the government invested in transportation networks, irrigation projects, and agricultural storage facilities. It provided extension services and invested in research. It encouraged imports of technology to improve output and mechanize production. Since policymakers believed that modern commercial farmers would respond better to these investments and services than would peasants on small plots of land, the government provided most of its assistance to large landowners.

The government's encouragement of industry and agriculture set the country on a three-decade path of sustained growth. Between 1940 and 1950, GDP grew at an annual average of 6.7 percent, while manufacturing increased at an average of 8.1 percent. In the following two decades, GDP growth rates remained impressive, and manufacturing growth continued to outpace overall growth in the economy. In the 1950s, manufacturing achieved an average of 7.3 percent growth annually and in the 1960s, 10.1 percent annually. Agricultural production grew rapidly as new areas were brought under cultivation and green revolution technology (scientifically improved seeds, fertilizers, and pesticides) was extensively adopted on large farms. These were years of great optimism as foreign investment increased, the middle class grew larger, and indicators for health and welfare steadily improved. Even the poorest Mexicans believed that their lives were improving. Table 1 presents data that summarize a number of advancements during this period. So impressive was Mexico's economic performance that it was referred to internationally as the Mexican Miracle.

While the government took the lead in encouraging industrialization, it was not long before a group of domestic entrepreneurs developed a special relationship with the state. Government policies protected their products through high tariffs or special licensing requirements, limiting imports of competing goods. Business elites in Mexico received subsidized credit to invest in equipment and plants; they benefited from cheap, subsidized energy; and they rarely had to pay taxes. These protected businesses emerged as powerful players in national politics. In the 1940s and 1950s, they led a set of industry-related interest groups that worked to promote and sustain favorable policies. With this organizational foundation, groups like the chambers of industry, commerce, and banking began to play increasingly important roles in government policymaking. They were able to veto efforts by the government to cut back on their benefits, and they lobbied for even more advantages. The government remained the source of most policy initiatives, but generally it was not able to move far in the face of opposition from those who benefited most from its policies.

Workers also became more important players in national politics. As mentioned in Section 1, widespread unionization occurred under Cárdenas, and workers won many rights that had been promised in the Constitution of 1917. Cárdenas organized the

Table 1

Mexican Development, 1940–2003

	1940	1950	1960	1970	1980	1990	2003
Population (thousands)	19,815	26,282	38,020	52,771	70,416	88,598	102,300
Life expectancy (years)[b]	–	51.6	58.6	62.6	67.4	68.9	73.6
Infant mortality (per 1,000 live births)	–	–	86.3	70.9	49.9	42.6	23.0
Illiteracy (% of population age 15 and over)	–	42.5	34.5	25.0	16.0	12.7	9.0
Urban population (% of total)	–	–	50.7	59.0	66.4	72.6	75.0
Economically active population in agriculture (% of total)	–	58.3	55.1	44.0	36.6	22.0	18.0[a]

	1940–1950	1950–1960	1960–1970	1970–1980	1980–1990	1990–2003
GDP growth rate (average annual percent)	6.7	5.8	7.6	6.7	1.6	1.3
Per capita GDP growth rate	–	–	3.7	3.7	–0.7	–0.2

[a]2001

[b]Five-year average.

Sources: Statistical Abstract for Latin America (New York: United Nations, Economic Commission for Latin America, various years); Roger Hansen, *The Politics of Mexican Development* (Baltimore, Md.: Johns Hopkins University Press, 1971); *Statistical Bulletin of the OAS*. World Bank Country Data for Mexico, http://www.worldbank.org/data/countrydata/countrydata.html; World Bank, World Development Indicators.

unions into the Confederation of Mexican Workers (CTM), which became the most powerful voice of organized labor within the PRI. The policy changes initiated in the 1940s, however, made the unions more dependent on the government for benefits and protection; the government also limited the right to strike. Despite the fact that unions were closely controlled, organized workers continued to be an elite within the country's working classes. Union membership meant job security and important benefits such as housing subsidies and health care. These factors helped compensate for the lack of democracy within the labor movement. Moreover, labor leaders had privileged access to the country's political leadership and benefited personally from their control over jobs, contracts, and working conditions. In return, they guaranteed labor peace.[9]

In agriculture, those who benefited from government policies and services were primarily farmers who had enough land and economic resources to irrigate and mechanize, as well as the capacity to make technological improvements in their farming methods and crops. By the 1950s, a group of large, commercially oriented farmers had emerged to dominate the agricultural economy.[10] Like their urban counterparts in business, they became rich and powerful. These rural landowners also became firm supporters of the continuation of government policies that provided them with special advantages.

There were significant costs to this pattern of economic and political development. Most important, government policies eventually limited the potential for further growth.[11] Industrialists who received extensive subsidies and benefits from government had few incentives to produce efficiently. High tariffs kept out foreign competition, further reducing reasons for efficiency or quality in production. Importing technology to support industrialization eventually became a drain on the country's foreign exchange. In addition, the costs of providing benefits to workers increased beyond the capacity of the government to generate revenue, especially because tax rates were kept low as a further incentive to investors. Mexico's tax rates, in fact, were among the lowest in the world, and opportunities to avoid payment were extensive. Eventually, the ISI strategy became less effective in generating new jobs, as industrialists moved from investing in labor-intensive industries such as processed foods and textiles to capital-intensive industries such as automobiles, refrigerators, and heavy equipment.

Moreover, as the economy grew, and with it the power of industrial, agricultural, and urban interests, many were left behind. The ranks of the urban poor grew steadily, particularly from the 1960s on. Mexico developed a sizable **informal sector**—workers who produced and sold goods and services at the margin of the economic system and faced extreme insecurity. By 1970, a large proportion of Mexico City's population was living in inner-city tenements or squatter settlements surrounding the city.[12]

Also left behind in the country's development after 1940 were peasant farmers. Their lands were often the least fertile, plot sizes were minuscule, and access to markets was impeded by poor transportation and exploitive middlemen who trucked products to markets for exorbitant fees. Farming in the *ejido* communities, where land was held communally, was particularly difficult. Because *ejido* land could not be sold or (until the early 1980s) rented, *ejidatarios* could not borrow money from private banks because they had nothing to pledge as collateral if they defaulted on their payments. Government banks provided credit, but usually only to those who had political connections. The government invested little in small infrastructure projects throughout the 1960s, and agricultural research and extension focused on the large-farm sector. Not surprisingly, the *ejido* sector consistently reported low productivity.

Increasing disparities in rural and urban incomes, coupled with high population growth rates, contributed to the emergence of rural guerrilla movements and student protests in the mid- and late 1960s. The government was particularly alarmed in 1968, when a student movement openly challenged the government on the eve of the Mexico City Olympic Games. Moreover, by the early 1970s, it was becoming evident that the size of the population, growing at a rate of some 3.5 percent a year, and the structure of income distribution were impeding further industrial development. The domestic market was limited by poverty; many Mexicans could not afford the sophisticated manufactured products the country would need to produce in order to keep growing under the import substitution model.

The Mexican government had hoped that industrialization would free the economy from excessive dependence on the industrialized world, and particularly on the United States, making the country less subject to abrupt swings in prices for primary commodities. Industrialization, however, highlighted new vulnerabilities. Advanced manufacturing processes required ever more foreign investment and imported technology. Concern grew about powerful multinational companies, which had invested heavily in the country in the 1960s, and about purchasing foreign technology with scarce foreign exchange. By the late 1960s, the country was no longer able to meet domestic demand for basic foodstuffs and was forced to import increasingly large quantities of food, costing the government foreign exchange that it could have used for better purposes. By the 1970s, some policymakers had become convinced that industrialization had actually increased the country's dependence on advanced industrial countries and particularly on the United States.

Sowing the Oil and Reaping a Crisis

In the early 1970s, Mexico faced the threat of social crisis brought on by rural poverty, chaotic urbanization, high population growth, and the questioning of political legitimacy. The government responded by increasing investment in infrastructure and public industries, regulating the flow of foreign capital, and increasing social spending. It was spending much more than it generated, causing the public internal debt to grow rapidly and requiring heavy borrowing abroad. Between 1971 and 1976, inflation rose from an annual average of 5.3 percent to almost 16 percent, and the foreign debt more than tripled. In response to mounting evidence that its policies could not be sustained, the government devalued the peso in 1976 to encourage exports and discourage imports. It also signed a stabilization agreement with the International Monetary Fund (IMF) to reduce government spending, increase tax collection, and control inflation. Little progress was made in changing existing policies, however, because just as the seriousness of the economic situation was being recognized, vast new finds of oil came to the rescue.

Between 1978 and 1982, Mexico was transformed into a major oil exporter. As international oil prices

A farmer with a hat labeled "rural misery" hangs his shirt on a cactus: "Welcome, Mr. President." Among those who have benefited least from the government's development policies are the rural poor.
Source: Ausencias y Presencias Gente de Ayer y Hoy en su Tinta: Problematica Politica, Social, Vista por un Cartoonista Potosino by Luis Chessal, Unversidad Autonoma de San Luis Potosi, Mexico, 1984.

rose rapidly, from $13.30 per barrel in 1978 to $33.20 per barrel in 1981, so too did the country's fortunes, along with those of other oil-rich countries such as Nigeria, Iran, Indonesia, and Venezuela. The administration of President José López Portillo (1976–1982) embarked on a policy to "sow the oil" in the economy and "administer the abundance" with vast investment projects in virtually all sectors and major new initiatives to reduce poverty and deal with declining agricultural productivity. Oil revenues paid for much of this expansion, but the foreign debt also mounted as both public and private sectors borrowed heavily to finance investments and lavish consumer spending.

By 1982, Mexico's foreign debt was $86 billion, and the peso was seriously overvalued, making Mexican products more expensive on the world market. Oil accounted for 77.2 percent of the country's exports, causing the economy to be extremely vulnerable to changes in oil prices. And change they did. Global overproduction brought the international price for Mexican petroleum down to $26.30 a barrel in 1982 and to even lower levels in the years that followed. Revenues from exports declined dramatically. At the same time, the United States tightened its monetary policy by raising interest rates, and access to foreign credit dried up. Wealthy Mexicans responded by sending vast amounts of capital out of the country just as the country's international creditors were demanding repayment on their loans. In August 1982, the government announced that the country could not pay the interest on its foreign debt, triggering a crisis that reverberated around the world. The impact of these conditions on the Mexican economy was devastating. GDP growth in 1982 was –0.6 percent and fell to –4.2 percent the following year.

The economic crisis had several important implications for structures of power and privilege in Mexico. First, faith in the import substitution policy was destroyed. The crisis convinced even the most diehard believers that import substitution created inefficiencies in production, failed to generate sufficient employment, cost the government far too much in subsidies, and increased dependency on industrialized countries. In addition, the power of interest groups and their ability to influence government policy declined. Bankruptcy and recession exacted their toll on the fortunes of even large entrepreneurs. As economic hardship affected their members, traditional business organizations lost their ability to put strong pressure on the government.

Similarly, the country's relatively privileged unions lost much of their bargaining power with government over issues of wages and protection. Union leaders loyal to the PRI emphasized the need for peace and order to help the nation get through tough

times, while inflation and job loss focused many of the country's workers on putting food on the table. A shift in employment from the formal to the informal economy further fragmented what had once been the most powerful sector of the party. Cuts in government subsidies for public transportation, food, electricity, and gasoline created new hardships for workers. The combination of these factors weakened the capacity of labor to resist policy changes that affected the benefits they received.

In addition, new voices emerged to demand that the government respond to the crisis. During the recession years of the 1980s, wages lost between 40 and 50 percent of their value, increasingly large numbers of people became unemployed, inflation cut deeply into middle-class incomes, and budgets for health and education services were severely cut back. A wide variety of interests began to organize outside the PRI to demand that government do something about the situation. Massive earthquakes in Mexico City in September 1985 proved to be a watershed for Mexican society. Severely disappointed by the government's failure to respond to the problems created by death, destruction, and homelessness, hundreds of communities organized rescue efforts, soup kitchens, shelters, and rehabilitation initiatives. A surging sense of political empowerment developed, as groups long accustomed to dependence on government learned that they could solve their problems better without government than with it.[13]

Moreover, the PRI was challenged by the increased popularity of opposition political parties, one of them headed by Cuauhtémoc Cárdenas, the son of the country's most revered president, Lázaro Cárdenas. The elections of 1988 became a focus for protest against the economic dislocation caused by the crisis and the political powerlessness that most citizens felt. Carlos Salinas, the PRI candidate, received a bare majority of 50.7 percent, and opposition parties claimed widespread electoral fraud.

New Strategies: Structural Reforms and NAFTA

Demands on the Salinas administration to deal with the economic and political crisis were extensive. At the same time, the weakening of the old centers of political power provided the government with a major opportunity to reorient the country's strategy for economic development. Between 1988 and 1994, the mutually dependent relationship between industry and government was weakened as new free-market policies were put in place. Deregulation gave the private sector more freedom to pursue economic activities and less reason to seek special favors from government. A number of large government industries were reorganized and sold to private investors. A constitutional revision made it possible for *ejidatarios* to become owners of individual plots of land; this made them less dependent on government but more vulnerable to losing their land. In addition, financial sector reforms that changed laws about banking and established a stock exchange encouraged the emergence of new banks, brokerage firms, and insurance companies.

Salinas pursued, and Zedillo continued, an overhaul of the federal system and the way government agencies worked together. Called the New Federalism, it was an attempt to give greater power and budgetary responsibilities to state and local governments, which had been historically very weak in Mexico. Beginning with education and health, the presidents hoped decentralization would make government more efficient and effective. Additionally, the central bank, the institution responsible for making national monetary policy, became independent from the government in 1994, although exchange rates are still determined by the finance ministry.

Among the most far-reaching initiatives was NAFTA. This agreement with Canada and the United States created the basis for gradual introduction of free trade among the three countries. These changes were a major reversal of import substitution and economic intervention that had marked government policies in the past. However, the liberalization of the Mexican economy and opening of its markets to foreign competition increased the vulnerability of the country to changes in international economic conditions. These factors, as well as mismanaged economic policies, led to a major economic crisis for the country at the end of 1994 and profound recession in 1995. NAFTA has meant that the fate of the Mexican economy is increasingly linked to the health of the American economy. For example, the economic strength of Mexico's northern neighbor sheltered the country from the contagion of the 1997–1998 Asian financial crisis, while the economic cooldown in the United States slowed growth in Mexico in the early 2000s.

Society and Economy

Mexico's economic development has had a significant impact on social conditions in the country. Overall, the standard of living rose markedly after the 1940s. Rates of infant mortality, literacy, and life expectancy have steadily improved. Provision of health and education services expanded until government cutbacks on social expenditures in the early 1980s. Among the most important consequences of economic growth was the development of a large middle class, most of whom live in Mexico's numerous large cities. By the 1980s, a third or more of Mexican households could claim a middle-class lifestyle: a steady income, secure food and shelter, access to decent education and health services, a car, some disposable income and savings, and some security that their children would be able to experience happy and healthy lives.

These achievements reflect well on the ability of the economy to increase social well-being in the country. However, the impressive economic growth through the early 1970s and between 1978 and 1982 could have produced greater social progress. In terms of standard indicators of social development—infant mortality, literacy, and life expectancy—Mexico fell behind a number of Latin American countries that grew less rapidly but provided more effectively for their populations. Costa Rica, Colombia, Argentina, Chile, and Uruguay had lower overall growth but greater social development in the period after 1940. These countries paid more attention to the distribution of the benefits of growth than did Mexico. Moreover, rapid industrialization has made Mexico City one of the most polluted cities in the world, and in some rural areas, oil exploitation left devastating environmental damage.

Mexico's economic development also resulted in a widening gap between the wealthy and the poor and among different regions in the country. Although the poor are better off than they were in the early days of the country's drive toward industrialization, they are worse off when compared to middle- and upper-income groups. In 1950, the bottom 40 percent of the country's households accounted for about 14 percent of total personal income, while the top 30 percent had 60 percent of total income.[14] In 2000, it is estimated, the bottom 40 percent accounted for about 10.3 percent of income, while the top 40 percent shared 78.1 percent.[15] As the rich grew richer, the gap between the rich and the poor increased.

Among the poorest are those in rural areas who have little or no access to productive land. Harsh conditions in the countryside have fueled a half-century of migration to the cities. Nevertheless, some 25 million Mexicans continue to live in rural areas, many of them in deep poverty. Many work for substandard wages and migrate seasonally to search for jobs in order to sustain their families. Among rural inhabitants with access to land, almost half have five hectares or less. This land is usually not irrigated and depends on erratic rainfall. It is often leached of nutrients as a result of centuries of cultivation, population pressure, and erosion. The incidence of disease, malnutrition, and illiteracy is much higher in Mexico's rural areas than in urban areas. When the rebels in Chiapas called for jobs, land, education, and health facilities, they were clearly reflecting the realities of life in much of the country.

Poverty has a regional dimension in Mexico. The northern areas of the country are significantly better off than the southern and central areas. In the north, large commercial farms using modern technologies grow fruits, vegetables, and grains for export. The U.S. border, the principal destination of agricultural products, is close at hand, and transportation networks are extensive and generally in good condition. Moreover, industrial cities such as Monterrey and Tijuana provide steady jobs for skilled and unskilled labor. Along the border, a band of manufacturing and assembly plants, called *maquiladoras,* provides many jobs, particularly for young women who are seeking some escape from the burdens of rural life or the constraints of traditional family life.

In the southern and central regions of the country, the population is denser, the land poorer, and the number of *ejidatarios* eking out subsistence greater. Transportation is often difficult, and during parts of the year, some areas may be inaccessible because of heavy rains and flooding. Most of Mexico's remaining indigenous groups live in the southern regions, often in remote areas where they have been forgotten by government programs and exploited by regional bosses for generations. The conditions that spurred the Chiapas rebellion are found throughout the southern states.

The economic crisis of the 1980s had an impact on social conditions in the country as well. Wages declined by about half, and unemployment soared as businesses collapsed and the government laid off workers in public offices and privatized industries. The informal sector expanded rapidly. Here, people eked out a living by hawking chewing gum, umbrellas, sponges, candy, shoelaces, mirrors, and a variety of other items in the street; jumping in front of cars at stoplights to wash windshields and sell newspapers; producing and repairing cheap consumer goods such as shoes and clothing; and selling services on a daily or hourly basis. While the informal sector provides important goods and services, conditions of work are often dangerous, and uncertainty as to where the next peso will come from is endemic.

The economic crisis of the 1980s also reduced the quality and availability of social services. Expenditures on education and health declined after 1982 as the government imposed austerity measures. Salaries of primary school teachers declined by 34 percent between 1983 and 1988, and many teachers worked second and even third jobs in order to make ends meet. Per capita health expenditures declined from a high of about $19 in 1980 to about $11 in 1990. Although indicators of mortality did not rise during this troubled decade, the incidence of diseases associated with poverty—malnutrition, cholera, anemia, and dysentery—increased. The crisis began to ease in the early 1990s, however, and many came to believe that conditions would improve for the poor. The government began investing in social services. When a new economic crisis occurred, however, unemployment surged, and austerity measures severely limited investments. Despite considerable recovery in the late 1990s, wages remain low for the majority of workers while taxes and the cost of living have increased.

Mexico in the Global Economy

The crisis that began in 1982 altered Mexico's international policies. In response to that crisis, the government relaxed restrictions on the ability of foreigners to own property, reduced and eliminated tariffs, and did away with most import licenses. Foreign investment was courted in the hope of increasing the manufacture of goods for export. The government also introduced a series of incentives to encourage the private sector to produce goods for export. In 1986, Mexico joined the General Agreement on Tariffs and Trade (GATT), a multilateral agreement that seeks to promote freer trade among countries that later became the basis for the World Trade Organization (WTO), and in the 1990s and early 2000s Mexico signed trade pacts with many countries in Latin America, Europe, and elsewhere.

The government's effort to pursue a more outward-oriented development strategy culminated in the ratification of NAFTA in 1993, with gradual implementation beginning on January 1, 1994. This agreement is important to Mexico. In 2000, 89 percent of the country's exports were sent to the United States, and 74 percent of its imports came from that country.[16] Access to the U.S. market is essential to Mexico and to domestic and foreign investors. NAFTA signaled a new period in U.S.-Mexican relations by making closer integration of the two economies a certainty.

NAFTA also entails risks for Mexico. Domestic producers worry about competition from U.S. firms. Farmers worry that Mexican crops cannot compete effectively with those grown in the United States; for example, peasant producers of corn and beans have been hard hit by the availability of lower-priced U.S.-grown grains. In addition, many believe that embracing free trade with Canada and the United States indicates a loss of sovereignty. Certainly, Mexico's economic situation is now more vulnerable to the ebb and flow of economic conditions in the U.S. economy. Some are also concerned with increasing evidence of "cultural imperialism" as U.S. movies, music, fashions, and lifestyles increasingly influence consumers. Indeed, for Mexico, which has traditionally feared the power of the United States in its domestic affairs, internationalization of political and economic relationships poses particularly difficult problems of adjustment.

On the other hand, the United States, newly aware of the importance of the Mexican economy to its own economic growth and concerned about instability on its southern border, hammered together a $50 billion economic assistance program composed of U.S., European, and IMF commitments to support its neighbor when crisis struck in 1994. The Mexican government imposed a new stabilization package that contained austerity measures, higher interest rates, and limits on wages. Remarkably, by 1998, Mexico had paid off all of its obligations to the United States.

Globalization is also stripping Mexico of some of the secrecy that traditionally surrounded government decision making, electoral processes, and efforts to deal with political dissent. International attention increasingly focuses on the country, and investors want clear and up-to-date information on what is occurring in the economy. The Internet and email, along with lower international telephone rates, are increasing information flows across borders. The government can no longer respond to events such as the peasant rebellion in Chiapas, alleged electoral fraud, or the management of exchange rates without considering how such actions will be perceived in Tokyo, Frankfurt, Ottawa, London, or Washington.

Section ❸ Governance and Policy-Making

Mexico is a federal republic, although until the 1990s, state and local governments had few resources and a limited sphere of action when compared with the national level. Under the PRI, the executive branch held almost all power, while the legislative and judiciary branches followed the executive's lead and were considered rubber-stamp bodies. During the years of PRI hegemony, the government was civilian, authoritarian, and corporatist. Currently, Mexico has multiparty competitive elections, and power is less concentrated in the executive branch and the national government. Since the mid-1980s, great efforts have been made to reinvigorate the nation's laws and institutions and to make the country more democratic.

Organization of the State

According to the supreme law of the land, the Constitution of 1917, Mexico's political institutions resemble those of the United States. There are three branches of government, and a set of checks and balances limits the power of each. The congress is composed of the Senate and the Chamber of Deputies. One hundred twenty-eight senators are elected, three from each of the country's thirty-one states; three from the Federal District, which contains the capital, Mexico City; and another thirty-two elected nationally by **proportional representation.** The 500 members of the Chamber of Deputies are elected from 300 electoral districts—300 by simple majority vote and 200 by proportional representation. State and local governments are also elected. The president, governors, and senators are elected for six years, and deputies (representatives in the lower house) and municipal officials are elected for three.

In practice, the Mexican system is very different from that of the United States. The constitution is a very long document that is easily amended, especially when compared to that of the United States. It lays out the structure of government and guarantees a wide range of human rights, including familiar ones such as freedom of speech and protection of the law, but also economic and social rights such as the right to a job and the right to health care. Economic and social rights are acknowledged but in practice do not reach all of the population. Although there has been some decentralization of power, the political system is still much more centralized than that of the United States. Congress is now more active as a decision-making arena and as a check on presidential power, but the executive remains central to initiating policy and managing political conflict.

The Executive

The President and the Cabinet

The presidency is the central institution of governance and policymaking in Mexico. Until the 1990s, the incumbent president always selected who would run as the PRI's next presidential candidate, appointed officials to all positions of power in the government and

the party, and often named the candidates who almost automatically won elections as governors, senators, deputies, and local officials. Even with a non-PRI incumbent, the president continues to set the broad outlines of policy for the administration and has numerous resources to ensure that those policy preferences are adopted. Until the mid-1970s, Mexican presidents were considered above criticism in national politics and revered as symbols of national progress and well-being. While economic and political events of the 1980s and 1990s diminished presidential prestige and politicians are showing an increasing willingness to stand up to the chief executive in today's multiparty system, the extent of presidential power remains a legacy of the long period of PRI ascendance.

Mexican presidents have a set of formal powers that allows them to initiate legislation, lead in foreign policy, create government agencies, make policy by decree or through administrative regulations and procedures, and appoint a wide range of public officials. More important, informal powers provide them with the capacity to exert considerable control. The president manages a vast patronage machine for filling positions in government and initiates legislation and policies that were, until recently, routinely approved by the congress. When Vicente Fox became president in 2000, he promised many fewer personnel changes in government than under previous incumbents. He promised more open government and greater diversity among his cabinet and other appointees. His powers have been curtailed to some degree by a more forceful congress and his administration's lack of experience in governing.

Under the PRI, presidents were always male and almost always members of the outgoing president's cabinet. Four of the five presidents who served between 1946 and 1976 had previously been ministers of the interior, with responsibility for the maintenance of law and order in the country. With the expansion of the government's role in economic development, candidates in the 1970s and 1980s were selected from the ministries that managed the economy. José López Portillo (1976–1982) had been minister of finance, and Miguel de la Madrid (1982–1988) and Carlos Salinas (1988–1994) had served as ministers of planning and budgeting. The selection of Luis Donaldo Colosio, who had been minister of social development and welfare, was thought by political observers to signal renewed concern with social problems. When Colosio was assassinated in 1994, the selection of Ernesto Zedillo, who had first been minister of planning and budgeting and then minister of education, was interpreted as reflecting an ongoing concern with social issues and as an effort to maintain the policies of economic liberalization that Salinas had introduced. With the victory of the PAN in 2000, this long tradition came to an end. Prior to running for president, Vicente Fox had been in business and had served as the governor of the state of Guanajuato.

Mexican presidential candidates since the mid-1970s have had impressive educational credentials and have tended to be trained in economics and management rather than in the traditional field of law. Presidents since López Portillo have had postgraduate training at elite institutions in the United States. By the 1980s, a topic of great debate in political circles was the extent to which a divide between *políticos* (politicians) and *técnicos* (**technocrats**) had emerged within the national political elite. Among the old guard of the PRI, there was open skepticism about the ability of young technocrats like Carlos Salinas and Ernesto Zedillo to manage political conditions in the country. During the presidential campaign of 1994, considerable efforts were made to stress the more humble origins of Colosio and Zedillo and the fact that they had had to work hard to get an education. Under Fox, the ties of the president to business elites raised similar fears that the government would not respond to the concerns of everyday citizens.

Once elected, the president moves quickly to name a cabinet. Under the PRI, he usually selected those with whom he had worked over the years as he rose to political prominence. He also used cabinet posts to ensure a broad coalition of support; he might, for example, appoint people with close ties to the labor movement, business interests, or some of the regional strongholds of the party. Only in rare exceptions were cabinet officials not active members of the PRI. When the PAN assumed the presidency, the selection of a cabinet and close advisers was more difficult. Until then, the party had elected officials only to state and local governments and to congress. As a consequence, the range of people with executive experience to whom Fox could turn was limited. He appointed U.S.-trained economists for his economic team and business executives for many other important posts. Few of these appointees had close ties to the PAN, and few had prior experience in government. Over the years, few women have been selected for ministry-level posts—there are a handful of examples in recent administrations—and thus far they have only presided over agencies with limited influence over decision making, like the ministries of tourism, ecology, and foreign relations.

The president has the authority to fill numerous other high-level positions, which allows him to provide policy direction and keep tabs on what is occurring throughout the government. The range of appointments that a chief executive can make means that the beginning of each administration is characterized by extensive turnover of positions, and as a result progress on the president's policy agenda can be slow during his first year in office as newly appointed officials learn the ropes and assemble their staffs. The president's power to make appointments provides him with the capacity to build a team of like-minded officials in government and ensure their loyalty to him. This system traditionally served the interests of presidents and the PRI well; under the PAN, given the limited number of its partisans who have experience at national levels, the system has not guaranteed the president as much power over the workings of the executive branch. In addition, with pressure mounting for a less politicized civil service in a more democratic Mexico, Fox committed himself to retaining qualified people in their positions and making many fewer changes than was customary.

Mexican presidents, though powerful, are not omnipotent. They must, for example, abide by a deeply held constitutional norm, fully adhered to since 1940, by stepping down at the end of their term, and they must adhere to tradition by removing themselves from the political limelight to allow their successors to assume full presidential leadership. All presidents, regardless of party, must demonstrate their loyalty to the myths and symbols of Mexican nationalism, such as the indigenous roots of much of its culture and the agrarian origins of the revolution, and they must make a rhetorical commitment to social justice and sovereignty in international affairs. Moreover, in the 1990s, President Zedillo relinquished a number of the traditional powers of the presidency. He announced, for example, that he would not select his PRI successor but would leave it up to the party to determine its candidate. In doing so, however, he created considerable conflict and tension as the PRI had to take on unaccustomed roles and as politicians sought to fill the void left by the "abandonment" of presidential power. Fox inherited a system in which he was expected to set the policies and determine the priorities for a very wide range of government activity. Without a strong party in congress to back him or many experienced people in his government, he was often unable to deliver. In the absence of strong presidential leadership, Mexico's government often seemed to flounder.

The Bureaucracy

Mexico's executive branch is large and powerful. Almost 1.5 million people work in the federal bureaucracy, most of them in Mexico City. An additional 1 million work for the large number of state-owned industries and semiautonomous agencies of the government. State and local governments employ over 1.5 million people.

Officials at lower levels in the bureaucracy are unionized and protected by legislation that gives them job security and a range of benefits. At middle and upper levels, most officials are called "confidence employees"; they serve as long as their bosses have confidence in them. These officials have been personally appointed by their superiors at the outset of an administration. Their modest salaries are compensated for by the significant power that they can have over public affairs. For aspiring young professionals, a career in government is often attractive because of the challenge of dealing with important problems on a daily basis. Some employees also benefit from opportunities to take bribes or use other means to promote their personal interests.

The Para-Statal Sector

The **para-statal** sector—composed of semiautonomous or autonomous government agencies, many of which produce goods and services—was extremely large and powerful in Mexico. Because the government provided significant support for the development of the economy as part of its post-1940 development strategy, it engaged in numerous activities that in other countries are carried out by the private sector. Thus, until the Salinas administration, the country's largest steel mill was state-owned, as were the largest fertilizer producer, sugar mills, and airlines. In addition, the national electricity board still produces energy and supplies it at subsidized prices to industries. The state-owned petroleum company, PEMEX, grew to enormous proportions in the 1970s and 1980s under the impact of the oil boom. NAFIN, a state investment corporation, provides a considerable amount of investment capital for the country. At one point, a state marketing board called CONASUPO was responsible for the importation and purchase of the country's basic food supplies, and in the 1970s, it played a major role in distributing food, credit, and farm implements in rural areas.

This large para-statal sector was significantly trimmed by the economic policy reforms that began in the 1980s. In 1970, there were 391 para-statal organizations in Mexico. By 1982, their number had grown to 1,155, in part because of the expansion of government activities under presidents Echeverría and López Portillo and in part because of the nationalization of private banks in 1982. Shortly afterward, concerted efforts were made to privatize many of these industries, including the telephone company, the national airlines, and the nationalized banks. By 1994, only 215 state-owned industries remained, and efforts continued to sell or liquidate many of them. However, some core components of the para-statal sector will likely remain in government hands for the foreseeable future because an influential bloc of nationalist political actors insist on the symbolic importance of public ownership of key industries. The Fox government, a partisan of the private sector, raised the possibility of privatizing PEMEX and the electricity board, but quickly retreated to very partial measures in the face of extensive opposition to private ownership of the "national patrimony."

Other State Institutions

The Military

Mexico is one of only a few countries in the developing world, particularly in Latin America, to have successfully marginalized the military from centers of political power. Although former military leaders dominated Mexican politics during the decades immediately after the Revolution of 1910, Calles, Cárdenas, and subsequent presidents laid the groundwork for civilian rule by introducing the practice of rotating regional military commands so that generals could not build up geographic bases of power. In addition, postrevolutionary leaders made an implicit bargain with the military leaders by providing them with opportunities to engage in business so that they did not look to political power as a way of gaining economic power. After 1946, the military no longer had institutional representation within the PRI and became clearly subordinate to civilian control. No military officer has held the presidency since that time.

This does not mean that the military has existed outside politics. It has been called in from time to time to deal with domestic unrest: in rural areas in the 1960s, in Mexico City and other cities to repress student protest movements in 1968, in 1988 in the arrest of a powerful labor leader, in 1989 to break a labor strike, in 1990 to deal with protest over electoral fraud, in Chiapas beginning in late 1994, and to manage the Mexico City police in 1997. The military was also called in to deal with the aftermath of the earthquake in Mexico City in 1985, but its inadequate response to the emergency did little to enhance its reputation in the eyes of the public. In recent years, the military has been heavily involved in efforts to combat drug trafficking, and rumors abound about deals struck between military officials and drug barons. Such fears were confirmed when General Jesús Gutierrez Rebollo, the head of the antidrug task force, was arrested in 1997 on accusations of protecting a drug lord. When the PAN government made it possible for citizens to gain greater access to government information, it was discovered that the military had been involved in political repression, torture, and killing in the 1970s and 1980s. The scandal created by such revelations further lowered its reputation.

Whenever the military is called in to resolve domestic conflicts, some Mexicans become concerned that the institution is becoming politicized and may come to play a larger role in political decision making. Thus far, such fears have not been realized, and many believe that as long as civilian administrations are able to maintain the country's tradition of stability, the military will not intervene directly in politics. The fact that the country successfully observed the transfer of power from the PRI to the PAN also has increased a sense that the military will remain subordinate to civilian control.

The Judiciary

Unlike Anglo-American legal systems, Mexico's law derives from the Roman and Napoleonic tradition and is highly formalized and explicit. The Constitution of 1917 is a lengthy document that has been amended many times and contains references to a wide range of civil rights, including items as broad as the right to a healthy environment. Because Mexican law tends to be very explicit and because there are no punitive damages allowed in court cases, there are fewer lawsuits than in the United States. One important exception to this is the *amparo,* whereby individual citizens may ask for a writ of protection claiming that their constitutional rights have been violated by specific government actions or laws.

There are federal and state courts in Mexico. The federal system is composed of the Supreme Court, which decides the most important cases in the country; circuit courts, which take cases on appeal; and district courts, where all cases enter the system. As in the United States, Supreme Court justices are nominated by the president and approved by the Senate. Since most of the important laws in Mexico are federal, state courts have played a subordinate role. However, this is changing. As Mexican states become more independent from the federal government, state law has been experiencing tremendous growth. In addition, there are many important specialized federal courts, such as labor courts, military courts, and electoral courts.

Like other political institutions in Mexico, the judiciary was for many decades politically, though not constitutionally, subordinate to the executive. The courts occasionally slowed the actions of government by issuing *amparos;* however, in almost every case in which the power of government or the president was at stake, the courts ruled on the side of the government. The Zedillo administration tried to change this by emphasizing the rule of law over that of powerful individuals. Increasing interest in human rights issues by citizens' groups and the media has added pressure to the courts to play a stronger role in protecting basic freedoms. Zedillo's refusal to interfere with the courts' judgments also strengthened the judiciary. This trajectory continued under Fox. Nevertheless, the judicial system remains the weakest branch of government.

Subnational Government

As with many other aspects of the Mexican political system, regional and local government in Mexico is quite different from what is described in the constitution. Mexico has a federal system, and each state has its own constitution, executive, unicameral legislature, and judiciary. Municipalities (equivalent to U.S. counties) are governed by popularly elected mayors and councils. But most state and municipal governments are poor. Most of the funds they command are transferred to them from the central government, and they have little legal or administrative capacity to raise their own revenue. States and localities also suffer greatly from the lack of well-trained and well-paid public officials. As at the national level, many jobs are distributed as political patronage, but even officials who are motivated to be responsive to local needs are generally ill equipped to do so. Since the early 1990s, the government has made several serious efforts to decentralize and devolve more power to state and local governments. At times, governors and mayors have resisted such initiatives because they meant that regional and local governments would have to manage much more complex activities and be the focus of demands from public sector workers and their unions. Local governments were also worried that they would be unable to acquire the budgetary resources necessary to carry out their new responsibilities.

There are exceptions to this picture of regional and local government impoverishment and lack of capacity. The governments of some northern states, such as Nuevo León, have been more responsive to local needs and better able to administer public services. In such states, local municipalities have become famous for the extent to which they differ from the norm in most of Mexico. The city of Monterrey, for example, has a reputation for efficient and forward-looking municipal government. Much of this local capacity can be credited to a regional political tradition that has stressed independence from—and

even hostility to—Mexico City and the PRI. In addition, states and localities that have stronger governments and a tradition of better service tend to be areas of greater wealth, largely in the north of the country. In these cases, entrepreneurial groups and private citizens have often invested time and resources in state and local government.

Until 1988, all governors were from the PRI, although many believe that only electoral fraud kept two governorships out of the hands of an opposition party in 1986. Finally, in 1989, a non-PRI governor assumed power in Baja California, an important first. By late 2005, 13 states and the Federal District were governed by parties other than the PRI. Also, municipalities have increasingly been the focus of authentic party competition. As opposition parties came to control these levels of government, they were challenged to improve services such as police protection, garbage collection, sanitation, and education. PRI-dominated governments have also tried to improve their performance because they are now more threatened by the possibility of losing elections.

The Policy-Making Process

The Mexican system is very dependent on the quality of its leadership and on presidential understanding of how economic and social policies can affect the development of the country. As indicated throughout this chapter, the six-year term of office, the *sexenio,* is an extremely important fact of political life in Mexico. New presidents can introduce extensive change in positions within the government. They are able to bring in "their" people, who build teams of "their" people within ministries, agencies, and party networks. This generally provides the president with a group of high- and middle-level officials who share a general orientation toward public policy and are motivated to carry out his goals. When the PRI was the dominant party, these officials believed that in following presidential leadership, they enhanced their chances for upward political mobility. In such a context, even under a single party, it was likely that changes in public policies could be introduced every six years, creating innovation or discontinuity, or both. As indicated, the limited experience of the PAN in executive office and the increasing role of congress in policymaking meant that the influence of the president on government became less strong after 2000. Nevertheless, Mexicans continue to look to the president and the executive branch for policy leadership.

Together with the bureaucracy, the president is the focal point of policy formulation and political management. Until 1997, the legislature always had a PRI majority and acted as a rubber stamp for presidentially sponsored legislation. Since then, the congress has proven to be a more active policymaker, blocking and forcing the negotiation of legislation, and even introducing its own bills. The president's skills in negotiating, managing the opposition, using the media to acquire public support, and maneuvering within the bureaucracy can be important for ensuring that his program is fully endorsed.

Significant limits on presidential power occur when policy is being implemented. In fact, in areas as diverse as the regulation of working conditions, antipollution laws, tax collection, election monitoring, and health care in remote rural areas, Mexico has extremely advanced legislation on the books. Yet the persistence of unsafe factory conditions, pollution in Mexico City, tax evasion, electoral fraud, and poor health care suggests that legislation is not always translated into practice. At times, policies are not implemented because public officials at the lower levels disagree with them or make deals with affected interests in order to benefit personally. This is the case, for example, with taxes that remain uncollected because individuals or corporations bribe officials to overlook them. In other cases, lower-level officials may lack the capacity or skills to implement some policies, such as those directed toward improving education or rural development services. For various reasons, Mexican presidents cannot always deliver on their intentions. Traditionally, Mexican citizens have blamed lower-level officials for such slippage, but exempting the president from responsibility for what does or does not occur during his watch has become much less common since the 1970s.

Section ❹ Representation and Participation

How do citizen interests get represented in Mexican politics, given the high degree of centralization, presidentialism, and, until recently, PRI domination? Is it possible for ordinary citizens to make demands on government and influence public policy? In fact, Mexico has had a relatively peaceful history since the revolution in part because the political system offers some channels for representation and participation. Throughout this long history, the political system has emphasized compromise among contending elites, behind-the-scenes conflict resolution, and distribution of political rewards to those willing to play by the formal and informal rules of the game. It has also responded, if reluctantly and defensively, to demands for change.

Often, citizens are best able to interact with the government through a variety of informal means rather than through the formal processes of elections, campaigns, and interest group lobbying. Interacting with government through the personal and informal mechanisms of clientelism usually means that the government retains the upper hand in deciding which interests to respond to and which to ignore. For many interests, this has meant "incorporation without power."[17] Increasingly, however, Mexican citizens are organizing to alter this situation, and the advent of truly competitive elections has increased the possibility that citizens who organize can gain some response from government.

The Legislature

Students in the United States are frequently asked to study complex charts explaining how a bill becomes a law because the formal process of lawmaking affects the content of legislation. Under the old reign of the PRI in Mexico, while there were formal rules that prescribed such a process, studying them would not have been useful for understanding how the legislature worked. Because of the overwhelming presence of this political party, opposition to presidential initiatives by Mexico's two-chamber legislature, the Senate and the Chamber of Deputies, was rarely heard. If representatives did not agree with policies they were asked to approve, they counted on the fact that policy implementation was flexible and allowed for after-the-fact bending of the rules or disregard of measures that were harmful to important interests.

Members of the Mexican congress are elected through a dual system of "first past the post" (that is, the candidate with the most votes wins) and proportional representation. Each state elects three senators. Two of them are determined by majority vote, and the third is determined by whichever party receives the second highest number of votes. In addition, thirty-two senators are determined nationally through a system of proportional representation that awards seats based on the number of votes cast for each party. Senators serve six-year terms. The same type of electoral system works in the Chamber of Deputies, with 300 selected on the basis of majority vote and 200 additional representatives chosen by proportional representation. Deputies are elected for three-year terms. Representation in congress has become somewhat more diverse since the end of the 1980s. In 2004, women held 15.6 percent of seats in the Senate and 22.6 percent in the Chamber of Deputies. Some representatives also emerged from the ranks of community activists who had participated in activities such as urban popular movements.

The PRI's grip on the legislature was broken in 1988. The growing strength of opposition parties, combined with legislation that provided for greater representation of minority parties in the congress, led to the election of 240 opposition deputies (out of 500) that year, depriving the PRI of the two-thirds majority it needed for major pieces of legislation or constitutional amendments. After that, when presidential legislation was sent to the chamber, the opposition challenged the tradition of legislative passivity and insisted on real debate about issues. The two-thirds PRI majority was returned in 1991—amid allegations of voter fraud—and presidentialism was reasserted. Nevertheless, the strong presence of opposition parties continued to encourage debate as PRI delegates were challenged to defend proposed legislation. The 1994 elections returned a clear PRI majority of 300 deputies, but in 1997, the PRI lost this majority when 261 deputies were elected from opposition parties. For

the first time in its history, the PRI did not have an absolute majority in the Chamber of Deputies. The party composition of the Chamber of Deputies and the Senate after the elections of 2003 is shown in Figure 1.

Since the late 1990s, the role of congress in the policy process has been strengthened considerably.[18] The cost of greater power sharing between the executive and the legislature, however, has been to stall the policy process. Several important pieces of legislation were stalled under President Zedillo. Even PRI legislators became more willing to slow or alter presidential initiatives. Under the Fox administration, relations with congress have been even more confrontational. The president lacks a party majority in congress and had a difficult time promoting his investment plan, labor code reform, and the liberalization of the energy sector. In a first-ever use of congressional power, in 2002, the Senate, angry over differences with the president about U.S.-Mexico relations, greatly embarrassed Fox by denying him the required permission to travel outside of Mexico for a visit to the United States and Canada. As a consequence of this kind of muscle flexing, congressional committees that once were important only for their control over patronage have acquired new relevance, and committee members and chairs are becoming somewhat more like their U.S. counterparts in terms of the power they can wield. Party caucuses have also emerged as centers of power in the legislature. In addition, interest groups, which before 1997 had scant interest in lobbying for legislative action because the legislature did not make important decisions, have increased their activities in congress. Thus, as a genuine multiparty system has emerged, the Mexican congress has become a more important forum for a variety of political voices and points of view.

Political Parties and the Party System

Even under the long reign of the PRI, a number of political parties existed in Mexico. By the mid-1980s, some of them were attracting more political support, a trend that continued into the 1990s and 2000s. Electoral reforms introduced by the López Portillo, de la Madrid, Salinas, and Zedillo administrations made it easier for opposition parties to contest elections and win seats in the legislature. In 1990, an electoral

Figure 1

Congressional Representation by Party, 2003

Chamber of Deputies   Senate

PRI = Partido Revolucionario Institucional
PAN = Partido Acción Nacional
PRD = Partido de la Revolución Democrática
PVEM = Partido Verde Ecologista de México
PT = Partido del Trabajo
Convergencia = Convergencia por la Democracia

Source: CIA World Factbook, http://www.cia.gov/cia/publications/factbook/geos/mx.html; see also http://www.senado. gob.mx and http://www.camaradediputados.gob.mx.

commission was created to regulate campaigns and elections, and in 1996 it became fully independent of the government. Now all parties receive funding from the government and have access to the media. In addition to the PRI, two other political parties have demonstrated the capacity to win substantial support in elections.

The PRI

Mexico's Institutional Revolutionary Party (PRI) was founded by a coalition of political elites who agreed that it was preferable to work out their conflicts within an overarching structure of compromise than to continue to resort to violence. In the 1930s, the forerunner of the PRI (the party operated under different names until 1946) incorporated a wide array of interests, becoming a mass-based party that drew support from all classes in the population. Over seven decades, its

principal activities were to generate support for the government, organize the electorate to vote for its candidates, and distribute jobs and resources in return for loyalty to the system.

Until the 1990s, party organization was based largely on the corporate representation of class interests. Labor was represented within party councils by the Confederation of Mexican Workers (CTM), which includes industry-based unions at local, regional, and national levels. Peasants were represented by the National Peasant Confederation (CNC), an organization of *ejido* and peasant unions and regional associations. The so-called popular sector, comprising small businesses, community-based groups, and public employees, had less internal cohesion but was represented by the National Confederation of Popular Organizations (CNOP). Of the three, the CTM was consistently the best organized and most powerful. Traditionally, the PRI's strongest support came from the countryside, where *ejidatarios* and independent small farmers were grateful for and dependent on rewards of land or jobs. As the country became more urbanized, the support base provided by rural communities remained important to the PRI but produced many fewer votes than were necessary to keep the party in power.

Within its corporate structures, the PRI functioned through extended networks that distributed public resources—particularly jobs, land, development projects, and access to public services—to lower-level activists who controlled votes at the local level. In this system, those with ambitions to public office or to positions within the PRI put together networks of supporters from above (patrons), to whom they delivered votes, and supporters from below (clients), who traded allegiance for access to public resources. For well over half a century, this system worked

extremely well. PRI candidates won by overwhelming majorities until the 1980s (see Figure 2). Of course, electoral fraud and the ability to distribute government largesse are central explanations for these numbers, but they also attest to an extremely well-organized party. Although the PRI became much weaker in the 1980s and 1990s, it was still the only political party that could boast a network of constituency organizations in virtually every village and urban community in the country. Its vast political machinery also allowed it to monitor events, even in remote areas.

Within the PRI, power was centralized, and the sector organizations (the CTM, the CNC, and the CNOP) responded primarily to elites at the top of the political pyramid rather than to member interests. Over time, the corporate interest group organizations, particularly the

Figure 2

PRI Support in Congressional Elections, 1946–2003

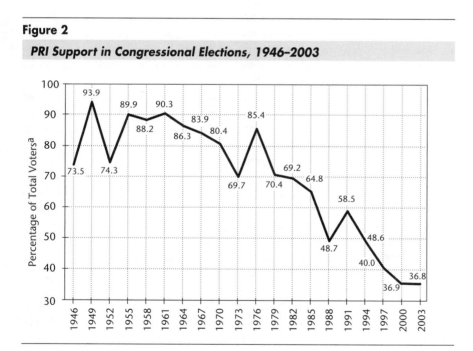

Sources: For 1946–1988: Juan Molinar Horcasitas, *El Tiempo de la legtimidad: Elecciones, autoritarismo y democracia en México* (México, D.F.: Cal y Arena, 1991). For 1991: Secretaría Nacional de Estudios, Partido Acción Nacional, *Análisis del Proceso Federal Electoral 1994, 1995.* For 1994: Instituto Federal Electoral, *Estadística de las Elecciones Federales de 1994, Compendio de Resultados* (Mexico, D.F., 1995). For 1997: http://www.ife.org.mx/ ww-worge/tablas/mrent.htm. For 2000 and 2003: Instituto Federal Electoral, http://www. ife.org.mx. Figures for 2003 include votes received by the Alianza para Todos (Alliance for Everyone), which brought the PRI and the much smaller PVEM together on a single ticket in some states.

CTM and the CNC, became widely identified with corruption, bossism, centralized control, and lack of effective participation. By the 1980s, new generations of voters were less beholden to patronage-style politics and much more willing to question the party's dominance. When the administrations of de la Madrid, Salinas, and Zedillo imposed harsh austerity measures, the PRI was held responsible for the resulting losses in incomes and benefits. Simultaneously, as the government cut back sharply on public sector jobs and services, the PRI had far fewer resources to distribute to maintain its traditional bases of support. Moreover, it began to suffer from increasing internal dissension between the old guard—the so-called dinosaurs—and the "modernizers" who wanted to reform the party.

Until 1988, PRI candidates easily won election to the presidency (see Table 2). After that year, however, the PRI was challenged by parties to the right and left, and outcomes were hotly contested by the opposition, which claimed fraudulent electoral practices. In 1994, Zedillo won primarily because the opposition was not well organized and failed to present a program other than its opposition to the PRI. Presidents Salinas and Zedillo also distanced themselves from the party during their administrations, giving the first clear signals in PRI history that there was a distinction between the party and the government.

As the PRI faced greater competition from other parties and continued to suffer from declining popularity, efforts were made to restructure and reform it. The CNOP was replaced by an organization that sought to incorporate a wide array of non-class-based citizen and neighborhood movements. In 1990, membership rules were altered to allow individuals and groups not identified with its corporate sector organizations to join. In addition, regional party organizations gained representation at the national level. Party conventions were introduced in an effort to democratize the internal workings of the party, and some states and localities began to hold primaries to select PRI candidates, a significant departure from the old system of selection by party bosses.

The PRI continues to face a difficult future. Voters are younger, better educated, more middle class, and more likely to live in urban areas than they were in the days of the PRI's greatest success—the 1940s, 1950s, and 1960s. The 1988 presidential elections demonstrated the relevance of changing demographic conditions when only 27.3 percent of the population of Mexico City voted for the PRI candidate and only 34.3 percent of the population in other urban areas supported him. By 2003, support for the party had fallen so far in the nation's capital that only 11.8 percent of voters in the Federal District cast their ballots for PRI congressional candidates. With the vast majority of the country's population now living in cities, the PRI will have to win the support of more urban voters in order to remain a relevant political force. That task looks all the more difficult after the historic election of 2000. Not only did opposition campaigns tap into a deep well of resentment against evidence of corruption and mismanagement in the PRI, but Fox's victory stripped the party of the aura of invincibility that had helped to cement its dominance of Mexican politics for decades.

In the immediate aftermath of the PRI's defeat, many analysts wondered how the party would be able to survive as an effective organization. Some predicted that the party would fall apart without one of its own in the presidency. However, public disappointment over Fox's inability to deliver on his promises of far-reaching change has allowed the PRI to remain a significant part of the Mexican political landscape. In recent years, despite initial uncertainty about the long-term direction of the party and a few defections, the PRI has for the most part remained disciplined and unified under the leadership of Roberto Madrazo, a former governor who is seen as representing the organization's old guard. The party has fared well in state and local elections, even winning back the governorship in the state of Chihuahua (in 1998 and 2004) and the mayor's office in Tijuana (2004), both places that were considered to be strongholds of the PAN. The PRI also continues to be the largest party in both chambers of the Mexican congress. Whether or not the PRI can return to the pinnacle of political power in Mexico by reoccupying the presidency remains to be seen.

The PAN

The National Action Party (PAN) was founded in 1939 to represent interests opposed to the centralization and anticlericalism of the PRI. It was founded by those who believed that the country needed more than

Table 2

Voting in Presidential Elections, 1934–2000

Year	Votes for PRI Candidate[a]	Votes for PAN Candidate	Votes for All Others[b]	Turnout (% Voters Among Eligible Adults)[c]
1934	98.2%	—	1.8%	53.6%
1940	93.9	—	6.1	57.5
1946	77.9	—	22.1	42.6
1952	74.3	7.8%	17.9	57.9
1958	90.4	9.4	0.2	49.4
1964	88.8	11.1	0.1	54.1
1970	83.3	13.9	1.4	63.9
1976[d]	93.6	—	1.2	29.6
1982	71.0	15.7	9.4	66.1
1988	50.7	16.8	32.5[e]	49.4[f]
1994	50.1	26.7	23.2	77.16
2000	36.1	42.5[g]	19.2[h]	64.0

[a]From 1958 through 1982, includes votes cast for the Partido Popular Socialista (PPS) and the Partido Auténtico de la Revolución Mexicana (PARM), both of which regularly endorsed the PRI's presidential candidate. In 1988, they supported opposition candidate Cuauhtémoc Cárdenas.

[b]Excludes annulled votes; includes votes for candidates of nonregistered parties.

[c]Eligible population base for 1934 through 1952 includes all males ages 20 and over (legal voting age: 21 years). Both men and women ages 20 and over are included in the base for 1958 and 1964 (women received the franchise in 1958). The base for 1970–1988 includes all males and females ages 18 and over (the legal voting age was lowered to 18, effective 1970).

[d]The PRI candidate, José Lopez Portillo, ran virtually unopposed because the PAN failed to nominate a candidate. The only other significant candidate was Valentín Campa, representing the Communist Party, which was not legally registered to participate in the 1976 election. More than 5 percent of the votes were annulled.

[e]Includes 31.1 percent officially tabulated for Cuauhtémoc Cárdenas.

[f]Estimated using data from the Federal Electoral Commission. However, the commission itself has released two different figures for the number of eligible voters in 1988. Using the commission's larger estimate of eligible population, the turnout would be 44.9 percent.

[g]Votes cast for Alianza por el Cambio, formed by the Partido Acción Nacional (PAN) and the Partido Verde Ecologista de Mexico (PVEM).

[h]Includes votes cast for Alianza por México, formed by the Partido de la Revolución Democrática (PRD), the Partido del Trabajo (PT), Convergencia por la Democracia, the Partido Alianza Social (PAS), and the Partido de la Sociedad Nacionalista (PSN).

Sources: From *Comparative Politics Today: A World View*, 4th ed. by Gabriel Almond and G. Bingham Powell, Jr. Copyright ©1988. Reprinted by permission of Addison-Wesley Educational Publishers, Inc. For 1994: Instituto Federal Electoral, *Estadística de las Elecciones Federales de 1994, Compendio de Resultados* (Mexico, D.F., 1995). For 2000: Instituto Federal Electoral, www.ife.org.mx.

one strong political party and that opposition parties should oppose the PRI through legal and constitutional actions. Historically, this party has been strongest in northern states, where the tradition of resistance to Mexico City is also strongest. It has also been primarily an urban party of the middle class and is closely identified with the private sector. The PAN has traditionally campaigned on a platform endorsing greater regional autonomy, less government intervention in the economy, reduced regulation of business, clean and fair elections, rapprochement with the Catholic Church, and support for private and religious education. When PRI governments of the 1980s and 1990s moved toward market-friendly and export-oriented policies, the policy differences between the two parties were significantly reduced. Nevertheless, a major difference of perspectives about religion continued to characterize the two parties. The PAN has always favored a closer relationship with the Catholic Church, and President Fox's public protestations of faith, including kissing Pope John Paul II's ring when the pontiff visited Mexico in 2002, raised many an eyebrow in a system long noted for its commitment to secularism.

For many years, the PAN was able to elect only 9 to 10 percent of all deputies to the national congress and capture control of a few municipal governments. Then, in the early 1980s, and especially after President López Portillo nationalized the banks, opposition to centralism and state control of the economy grew more popular. The PAN began to develop greater capacity to contest elections at higher levels of government. In particular, the party gained popularity among urban middle-class voters, won elections in several provincial cities, and came close to winning governorships in two states. In 1989, it won its first governorship, in the state of Baja California. In the 1994 elections, the PAN's candidate garnered 26 percent of the presidential vote, more than it had won in any previous election, and the party won 25 seats in the Senate and 119 in the Chamber of Deputies. In 1997, the party's legislative delegation grew to 33 senators and 121 deputies, and those numbers rose again in 2000, to 53 and 224, respectively. By late 2005, the PAN controlled the governorships in nine states, and in one more the governor had been elected as the candidate of an alliance between the PAN and another political party (see below). And, of course, the PAN won the presidency in 2000 with 42.7 percent of the total vote.

The PAN has traditionally set relatively high standards for activism among its party members; as a consequence, the membership of the party has remained small, even as its capacity to attract votes has grown. In their efforts to control the development of the party, its leaders have had a difficult relationship with the PAN standard bearer, Vicente Fox. As Fox's national political profile expanded while serving as the governor of the state of Guanajuato, leaders of the party became concerned that he would emerge as a favorite for the presidency. They considered him to be an opportunistic newcomer to the party, and they worked to limit his ability to run for office, forcing him to look for other sources of financing his campaign. In 1997, the "Friends of Fox" organization began to raise funds and promote his candidacy for president, and at the same time, the traditional leaders of the party were weakened significantly when the PAN made a poor showing in electoral contests. Fox gained in popularity throughout the country, and in 1999, the party had little option but to nominate him as its candidate. The Friends of Fox continued to provide the most important source of campaign support, however, and when Fox won the presidential election, the PAN organization was weak and not at all united in backing him. Furthermore, although the party made a very good showing in elections for the Chamber of Deputies and the Senate, it did not have a majority in either chamber.

President Fox hoped that mid-term congressional elections in 2003 would return a PAN majority, making it possible for him to push ahead with various initiatives that had been stalled by the legislative branch. Instead, many voters expressed their frustration with the administration's lack of effectiveness by casting their ballots for non-PAN candidates. The party's representation in the Chamber of Deputies dropped substantially, from 224 seats to 151. With Fox constitutionally barred from seeking a second term, the PAN will have to find a new presidential candidate in the 2006 elections.

The PRD

Another significant challenge to the PRI has come from the Democratic Revolutionary Party (PRD), a populist and nationalist alternative to the PRI whose policies are left of center. Its candidate in the 1988 and 1994 elections was Cuauhtémoc Cárdenas, the son of Mexico's most famous and revered president. He was a PRI insider until party leaders virtually ejected him for demanding internal reform of the party and a platform emphasizing social justice. In the 1988 elections, Cárdenas was officially credited with winning 31.1 percent of the vote, and his party captured 139 seats in the Chamber of Deputies. He benefited from massive political defection from the PRI and garnered support from workers disaffected with the boss-dominated unions as well as from peasants who remembered his father's concern for agrarian reform and the welfare of the poor.

Even while the votes were being counted, the party began to denounce widespread electoral fraud and claim that Cárdenas would have won if the election had been honest. The PRD challenged a number of vote counts in the courts and walked out on the inaugural speech given by the PRI's Salinas. Considerable public opinion supported the party's challenge. In the aftermath of the 1988 elections, then, it seemed that the PRD was a strong contender to become Mexico's second most powerful party. It was expected to have a real chance in future years to challenge the PRI's "right" to the presidency.

However, in the aftermath of these elections, the party was plagued by internal divisions over its platform, leadership, organizational structure, and election strategy. By 1994, it still lagged far behind the PRI and the PAN in establishing and maintaining the local constituency organizations needed to mobilize votes and monitor the election process. In addition, the PRD found it difficult to define an appropriate left-of-center alternative to the market-oriented policies carried out by the government. While the claims that such policies ignored the need for social justice were popular, policies to respond to poverty that did not imply a return to unpopular government intervention were difficult to devise. In the aftermath of the Colosio assassination, citizens also became more alarmed about violence, and some were concerned that the level of political rivalry represented by the PRD threatened the country's long-term political stability. In the 1994 elections, Cárdenas won only 17 percent of the votes, although the PRD elected seventy-one deputies and eight senators.

Thanks to the government's continued unpopular economic policies and the leadership of a successful grass-roots mobilizer named Andrés Manuel López Obrador, who was elected to head the party in 1996,

the PRD began to stage a remarkable turnaround. Factional bickering was controlled, and organizational discipline increased. In addition, the PRD proved successful in moving beyond its regional strongholds and established itself as a truly national party. In 1997, the party increased its share of seats to 125 in the Chamber of Deputies and 16 in the Senate. Most important, Cárdenas became the first popularly elected mayor of Mexico City, providing him and the party with an opportunity to demonstrate their ability to govern. By this time, the PRD had managed to shed some of its reputation as a "one-horse show" and had won two governorships. In 2000, López Obrador was elected mayor of Mexico City with 39.5 percent of the vote, signaling again the political importance of the capital city. In the presidential race, Cárdenas ran again, but he was able to garner only 16.5 percent of the vote. The party's performance in the legislative race was equally disappointing. The PRD retained 16 seats in the Senate, but lost 58 in the Chamber of Deputies, holding only 67 seats.

The party's fortunes improved somewhat in 2003, when the size of its delegation in the Chamber of Deputies rose to 97. Although the problem of factional infighting had still not been completely resolved by 2005, by then four states and the Federal District were governed by the PRD. Another governor had been elected as the representative of a coalition between the PRD and the PAN, which put aside their divergent ideologies and worked together on the local level to unseat the PRI in the rural, traditional state of Chiapas.

Thanks largely to its control over the capital city and the existence of PRD administrations on the municipal level in parts of the country, the party was able to boast that about a quarter of the country's population lived under a PRD government. Although it continues to occupy fewer offices than the other two major parties, the party is still considered a significant contender for political power in Mexico, with Mexico City Mayor Andrés Manuel López Obrador seen by many as a front-runner in the 2006 presidential elections.

Other Parties

There are a number of smaller parties that contest elections in Mexico. In 2003, the Green Ecologist

Party of Mexico (PVEM), the Labor Party (PT), and Convergence for Democracy (Convergencia) each won between 2.3 and 4.0 percent of the vote for congressional seats. A handful of even smaller parties garnered less than 1 percent of the vote apiece. Since Mexican law requires parties to receive at least 2.5 percent of the vote to be able to compete in future elections, the long-term viability of some of these organizations is very doubtful. Small parties usually do win a few of the seats in the Chamber of Deputies and the Senate that are filled by proportional representation. Also, these groups sometimes wield influence on national politics by forming alliances with the larger parties, either endorsing their candidates for president or governor in national and state elections or backing a single slate of candidates for congress. For example, the PVEM joined with the PAN in the Alliance for Change to back Fox's bid for the presidency in 2000, while the PT, Convergencia, and two even smaller parties formed the Alliance for Mexico to support the PRD's candidate, Cuauhtémoc Cárdenas. In the congressional elections of 2003, the PVEM entered into another alliance, this time with the PRI, and in many states, candidates from the two parties ran for office as members of the Alliance for Everyone. Because these small parties often appear to be opportunistic in the shifting alliances that they make, and because a few of the most insignificant parties apparently exist only to tap into the public funding that finances election campaigns in Mexico, many Mexicans have a low regard for some of these organizations.

Elections

Each of the three main political parties draws voters from a wide and overlapping spectrum of the electorate. Nevertheless, a typical voter for the PRI is likely to be from a rural area or small town, to have less education, and to be older and poorer than voters for the other parties. A typical voter for the PAN is likely to be from a northern state, to live in an urban area, to be a middle-class professional, to have a comfortable lifestyle, and to have a high school or even a university education. A typical voter for the PRD is likely to be young, to be a political activist, to have an elementary or high school education, to live in one of the central states, and to live in a small town or an urban area. As we have seen, the support base for the PRI is the most vulnerable to economic and demographic changes in the country. Voting for opposition parties is an urban phenomenon, and Mexico continues to urbanize at the rate of 3 percent per year. This means that in order to stay competitive, the PRI will have to garner more support from urban areas. It must also be able to appeal to younger voters, especially the large numbers who are attracted to the PRD and the PAN.

Elections are becoming more competitive and fairer in Mexico. Electoral reforms introduced by the López Portillo, de la Madrid, Salinas, and Zedillo administrations made it easier for opposition parties to contest elections and win seats in the legislature. In 1990, an electoral commission was created to regulate campaigns and elections, and in 1996 it became fully independent from the government. Now all parties receive government funding and have guaranteed access to the media. These and other laws that limit campaign spending and campaign contributions were a response to demands that the government level the playing field between the PRI and the other parties. Voter registration was reformed to ensure that fraud would be more detectable. Election monitoring was also strengthened, and another reform increased the chances for opposition parties to win representation in the Senate. Beginning in 1994, elections have been much fairer, and subsequent congressional, state, and municipal elections reinforced the impression that electoral fraud is on the wane in many areas. The PAN's victory in 2000 substantially increased this impression. Some state and local elections continue to be questioned, however, especially in rural areas in the south, where local PRI bosses remain powerful.

Political Culture, Citizenship, and Identity

Most citizens in Mexico demonstrate overall commitment to the political system while expressing considerable criticism—and often cynicism—about how it works and how equitable it is. Many criticize corruption in government and the PRI, but remain proud that their country has become more democratic.

Institutional Intricacies: *Campaigning with Comic Books*

In the more democratic Mexico that has emerged since the 1990s, political leaders have found that they must find new and imaginative ways to communicate with voters and to seek their backing. As the effectiveness of the clientelist networks that guaranteed PRI hegemony for so many years declines, candidates for public office and government officials are increasingly turning to strategies used in other democratic systems to win support for themselves and their programs. For example, public opinion polling and elaborate marketing plans are now becoming important tools for Mexican politicians who previously relied on patronage and strategies of co-optation and accommodation to achieve their goals.

Even as they adopt some of the methods used by their counterparts in other countries, however, some politicians are also reaching out to their constituents in a distinctly Mexican way: through comic books. Though the comic books published by officials and aspirants to higher office tend to be less lurid and suggestive than the enormously popular pocket-sized publications sold at newsstands throughout the country, they reach a wide audience since they are generally distributed free of charge.

Mexico City Mayor Andrés Manuel López Obrador of the left-of-center Democratic Revolutionary Party (PRD) was among the first to use a comic book to trumpet his accomplishments. In a series entitled *Stories of the City*, the popular head of the government of the Federal District is depicted as a defender of the poor and downtrodden residents of the capital. Later, when allegations of corruption in his administration threatened to derail the mayor's bid for the presidency in 2006, the municipal government issued another edition of *Stories of the City* to expose what it called "the dark forces against López Obrador." The comic book reiterated the populist mayor's claim that elites and hidden special interests were attempting to manufacture scandals that would prevent him from reaching Los Pinos.

President Vicente Fox also recognized the potential usefulness of comic books as a means of disseminating his political message. In 2002, faced with the widespread perception that the Fox administration had failed to bring about substantial change, the president's office commissioned a comic book called *July 2nd: Now Nobody Will Stop Change in Mexico!* in which a group of university students convince skeptical classmates that the date of Fox's election—July 2, 2000—was a historic milestone for Mexico. After discussing the various achievements of the Fox administration, the students conclude that the president "always speaks openly, is honest, and works every day for the good of all Mexicans." At a time when Fox was seen by many as weak and ineffectual, *July 2nd* represented an unconventional effort to convince Mexicans that the president was getting results.

Mexican political comic books have even had an impact in the realm of international affairs. When the Mexican foreign ministry issued a comic book–style *Guide for the Mexican Migrant* late in 2004, a number of U.S. legislators complained that the Mexican government appeared to be offering its citizens tips on how to flout American immigration laws. Although the publication noted that the safest way to travel abroad was with a passport and a visa, it also explained how to avoid dehydration when passing through remote desert regions and how to reduce the danger of drowning when crossing rivers. The guide also advised migrants not to call attention to themselves and to avoid loud parties once they were across the border. Despite the outcry that arose over the publication in certain circles in Washington, D.C., the Mexican Foreign Ministry insisted that the guide had been prepared for humanitarian reasons, inasmuch as many migrants had lost their lives trying to reach the United States in recent years.

Politicians and government agencies alike have recognized that comic books can be an effective way to reach a large number of Mexican citizens. The speed with which publications of this sort have proliferated shows the resourcefulness of Mexican political actors as they seek to adapt to a new political landscape that is more competitive and open and that places more of a premium on successful communication with the citizenry.

Most Mexicans have a deep familiarity with how their political system works and the ways in which they might be able to extract benefits from it. They understand the informal rules of the game in Mexican politics that have helped maintain political stability despite extensive inequalities in economic and political power. Clientelism has long been a form of participation in the sense that through their connections, many people, even the poorest, are able to interact with public officials and get something out of the political system. This kind of participation emphasizes how limited resources, such as access to health care, can be distributed in a way that provides maximum political payoff. This informal system is a fundamental reason that many Mexicans continued to vote for the PRI for so long.

However, new ways of interacting with government are emerging, and they coexist along with the clientelistic style of the past. An increasing number of citizens are seeking to negotiate with the government on the basis of citizenship rights, not personal patron-client relationships. The movements that emerged in the 1980s sought to form broad but loose coalitions with other organizations and attempted to identify and work with reform-oriented public officials. Their suspicion of traditional political organizations such as the PRI and its affiliates also led them to avoid close alliances with other parties, such as the PAN and the PRD.

As politics and elections became more open and competitive, the roles of public opinion and the mass media have become more important. In the past, public opinion polling was often contaminated by the dominance of the PRI, and some polling organizations were even subsidized by the party or the government. Increasingly, however, even the PRI and the government are interested in objective information and analysis of public opinion. These data have influenced the content and timing of government decisions and the development of strategies in election campaigns. In 1994 and 2000, politicians, citizens, and political activists closely followed the popularity polls of the three major candidates for president, and party officials monitored how the image of their contender could be molded to capture higher voter approval ratings. Because extensive public opinion polling is comparatively new in Mexico, it is difficult to assess how attitudes toward government have changed over time. Surveys indicate that public confidence in government fell sharply during the 1980s but rebounded somewhat in the 1990s. Fewer Mexicans claim a party preference today than in the past, and the percentage of citizens who identify with the PRI has dropped dramatically in recent years.

Today, the media play an important role in public opinion formation in Mexico. In the past, it was not easy for newspapers, magazines, or radio and television stations to be openly opposed to the government. For many years, the government used access to newsprint, which it controlled, to reward sympathetic news coverage and penalize coverage it considered hostile. In addition, the government and ambitious officials paid stipends to reporters who covered their activities favorably. A considerable amount of the revenue of newspapers and other media organizations came from advertising placed by the government. Each of these mechanisms was used to encourage positive reporting of government activities and the quashing of stories that reflected ill on the party or the administration, without resorting to outright government control of the media.

As with other aspects of Mexican politics, the media began to become more independent in the 1980s, enjoying a "spring" of greater independence and diversity of opinion.[19] There are currently several major television networks in the country, and many citizens have access to CNN and other global networks. The number of newspapers is expanding, as is their circulation, and several news magazines play the same role in Mexico that *Time* and *Newsweek* do in the United States. Citizens in Mexico today clearly hear a much wider range of opinion and much greater reporting of debates about public policy and criticism of government than at any time previously.

Interests, Social Movements, and Protest

The Mexican system has long responded to groups of citizens through pragmatic **accommodation** to their interests. This is one important reason that political tensions among major interests have rarely escalated into the kind of serious conflict that can threaten stability. Where open conflict has occurred, it has generally been met with efforts to find some kind of compromise solution. Accommodation has been particularly apparent in response to the interests of business. Mexico's development strategy encouraged the growth of wealthy elites in commerce, finance, industry, and agriculture (see Section 2). Although these elites were the primary beneficiaries of the country's development, they were never directly incorporated into the PRI. Instead, they represent themselves through a set of business-focused interest groups and personal relationships with influential officials. Through these networks, business organizations and individuals seek policies favorable to their interests.

Labor has been similarly accommodated within the system. Wage levels for unionized workers grew fairly consistently between 1940 and 1982, when the economic crisis caused a significant drop in wages. At the same time, labor interests were attended to in terms of concrete benefits and limitations on the rights of employers to discipline or dismiss workers. Union leaders controlled their rank and file in the interest of their own power to negotiate with government, but at the same time, they sought benefits for workers who continued to provide support for the PRI. The power of the union bosses has declined, in part because the unions are weaker than in the past, in part because union members are demanding greater democratization, and in part because the PRI no longer monopolizes political power.

Under the PRI, accommodation was often coupled with **co-optation** as a means of incorporating dissidents into the system so that they did not threaten its continuity. In 1968, for example, students protesting against authoritarianism, poverty, and inequity challenged the government just prior to the opening of the Olympic Games. The government responded with force—in one instance killing several hundred students in Mexico City—sparking even greater animosity. When Luis Echeverría became president in 1970, he recruited large numbers of the student activists into his administration. He also dramatically increased spending on social services, putting many of the young people to work in expanding antipoverty programs in the countryside and in urban slums. Through these actions, a generation of political and social activists was incorporated into the system, and there was some accommodation to their concerns. We also know now that his government allowed the military to kidnap, arrest, torture, and kill some political dissidents.

Despite the strong and controlling role of the PRI in Mexico's political history, the country also has a tradition of civic organizations that operate at community and local levels with considerable independence from politics. Local village improvement societies, religious organizations, and sports clubs are widespread. Many of their activities are not explicitly political, although they may have political implications in that they encourage individuals to work together to find solutions to problems or to organize around common interests. Other organizational experiences are more clearly political. The student movement of 1968 provided evidence that civil society in Mexico had the potential to contest the power of the state. The emergence of independent unionism in the 1970s was another indication of renewed willingness to question the right of the state to stifle the dissenting voices.

The economic crisis of 1982 combined with this civic tradition to heighten demands for assistance from the government. In October 1983, as many as 2 million people participated in a civic strike to call attention to the economic crisis and demand a forceful government response. In urban areas, citizen groups demanded land rights in squatter settlements, as well as housing, infrastructure, and urban services, as rights of citizenship rather than as a reward for loyalty to the PRI.[20] In the aftermath of the 1985 earthquake, citizen groups became especially dynamic in demanding that government respond to the needs of citizens without reference to their history of party loyalty.[21] Many also became active in groups that share concerns about quality-of-life issues such as clean air and safe neighborhoods (see "Citizen Action: Urban Popular Movements").

In subsequent years, a variety of groups in Mexico have continued to organize around middle-class and urban issues. Women, with a strong cultural role as caretakers of the home, have begun to mobilize in many cities to demand community services, equal

Citizen Action: **Urban Popular Movements**

In October 1968, hundreds of students and working-class people took to the streets of Mexico City to protest high unemployment and the authoritarianism of the government. What began as a peaceful rally in Tlaltelolco Plaza ended in a tragedy when government troops opened fire on the crowd and killed more than two hundred people. The political activism of the students heralded the birth of urban popular movements in Mexico. The massacre in Tlaltelolco became a symbol of a government that was unwilling or unable to respond to citizen demands for economic and political equity. The protest movements sparked by the events of 1968 sought to transcend class boundaries and unite voices around a range of urban issues, from housing shortages to inadequate urban services, to lack of land, to centralized decision making. Such social movements forged new channels for poor and middle-class urban residents to express their needs. They also generated forums for demanding democratic government that the traditional political system was not providing. In May 1980, the first national congress of urban movements was held in Monterrey in northern Mexico.

Urban popular movements, referring to activities of low- and modest-income (popular) groups, gained renewed vitality in the 1980s. When the economic crisis resulted in drastic reductions of social welfare spending and city services, working- and middle-class neighborhoods forged new coalitions and greatly expanded the national discussion of urban problems. The Mexico City earthquake of 1985 encouraged the formation of unprecedented numbers of grass-roots movements in response to the slow and poorly managed relief efforts of the government. Turning to each other, earthquake victims organized to provide shelter, food, and relocation. The elections of 1988 and 1994 provided these groups with significant opportunities to press parties and candidates to respond to their needs. They insisted on their rights to organize and protest without fear of repression or co-optation by the government or the PRI. As the opposition parties expanded rapidly, some leaders of urban movements enrolled as candidates for public office.

Urban popular movements bring citizens together around needs and ideals that cut across class boundaries. Neighborhood improvement, the environment, local self-government, economic development, feminism, and professional identity have been among the factors that have forged links among these groups. As such identities have been strengthened, the need of the political system to negotiate and bargain with a more independent citizenry has increased. Urban popular movements have helped to transform political culture on the most local level, one reason the PAN was able to garner so many votes in the 2000 election.

---

pay, legal equality, and opportunities in business traditionally denied them.[22] Religious groups, both Catholic and Protestant, have begun to demand greater government attention to problems of poverty and inequity, as well as more government tolerance of religious education and religious practices. In the early 1990s, the government's social development program, which many critics claim was a ploy by President Salinas to win back respect for his government after the flawed elections of 1988, helped organize thousands of grass-roots organizations and possibly contributed to a trend towards broader mobilization independent of PRI clientelist networks.[23] In 1997 and 2000, unprecedented numbers of citizens volunteered their time to civic associations that observed the vote to ensure, ballot box by ballot box, that the votes were counted accurately. Where this occurred, mostly in urban areas, there were few accusations of fraud.

In the countryside, too, rural organizations demanded greater independence from government and the leaders of the PRI and the CNC (the national peasant association) in the 1980s.[24] In addition to

Mexicans demonstrate for better housing in Mexico City's central plaza. *Source:* Robert Freck/Odyssey/Chicago.

greater access to land, they demanded better prices for the crops they produced, access to markets and credit, development of better infrastructure, and the provision of better education and health services. They began to form alliances with other groups. Since 1994, the rebels in Chiapas have become a focal point for broad alliances of those concerned about the rights of indigenous groups (ethnic minorities) and rural poverty. Indigenous groups have also emerged to demand that government be responsive to their needs and respectful of their traditions. Overall, then, civil society in Mexico is becoming more pluralist and less easily controlled, and there is broader scope for legitimate protest, opposition, and dissent.

Section ⑤ Mexican Politics in Transition

Political Challenges and Changing Agendas

Mexico confronts a world of increasing interdependence among countries. For all countries, economic integration raises issues of national sovereignty and identity. Mexicans define themselves in part through a set of historical events, symbols, and myths that focus on the country's troubled relationship with the United States. Among numerous national heroes and martyrs are those who distinguished themselves in confrontations with the United States. The myths of the Revolution of 1910 emphasize the uniqueness of the country in terms of its opposition to the capitalists and militarists of the northern country. In the 1970s, Mexicans were encouraged to see themselves as leading Third World countries in arguing for enhanced bargaining positions in relation to the industrialized countries of the north. This view stands in strong contrast to more recent perspectives touting the benefits of an internationally oriented economy and the undeniable post-NAFTA reality of information, culture, money, and people flowing back and forth across borders.

The country's sense of national identity is affected by international migration. Of particular importance in the Mexican case is labor migration. Every year, large numbers of Mexicans enter the United States as workers. Many return to their towns and villages with new values and new views of the world. Many stay in the United States, where Hispanics have become the largest ethnic population in the country. Most continue to believe that Mexican culture is preferable to American culture, which they see as excessively materialistic and violent. Although they believe that Mexico is a better place to nurture strong family life and values, they are nevertheless strongly influenced by U.S. mass culture, including popular music, movies, television programs, fast food, and consumer goods (see "Global Connection: Mexican Migration to the United States").

The inability of the Mexican economy to create enough jobs pushes additional Mexicans to seek work in the United States, and the cash remittances that migrants abroad send home to their families and communities are now almost as important a source of income for Mexico as PEMEX's oil sales. However, the issues surrounding migration have become even more complex since the attacks of September 11, 2001. Hopes for a bilateral accord that would permit more Mexicans to enter and work in the United States legally evaporated after U.S. officials suddenly found themselves under greatly increased pressure to control the country's borders. Illegal immigration has not abated, however, and Mexican

Global Connection: Mexican Migration to the United States

The contrast between the poverty of much of the developing world and the prosperity of industrialized nations is nowhere on more vivid display than it is along the 2,000-mile-long border between Mexico and the United States. Because of the economic disparities that exist between the two neighboring countries, Mexicans with limited opportunities at home have long been venturing north of the border in search of jobs and a higher standard of living. The money that these migrants send back to Mexico helps to sustain not just their own families but entire regions that have been left behind by the country's uneven pattern of growth and development. As the number of the Mexican migrants seeking opportunities abroad has grown in recent years, their presence in the United States has come to have profound ramifications for the politics of both nations.

Mexicans began moving to the United States in substantial numbers late in the nineteenth century, and their ranks grew as many fled the chaotic conditions that had been created by the Revolution of 1910. Although some of these early migrants found work in northern industrial centers such as Chicago, most settled in the border states of California and Texas, where they joined preexisting Mexican communities that had been there since the days when the American southwest had been part of Mexico. Even greater numbers of migrants began to arrive during World War II, when the U.S. government allowed Mexican workers, known as *braceros,* to enter the country to help provide much-needed manpower for strategic production efforts. The *bracero* program remained in place after the war, and under it, a predominantly male Mexican workforce provided seasonal labor to U.S. employers, mostly in the agricultural sector.

After the *bracero* program came to an end in 1964, Mexicans continued to seek work in the United States, despite the fact that most then had to enter the country illegally. To a large extent, the U.S. government informally tolerated the employment of undocumented migrants until the 1980s, when policymakers came under pressure to assert control over the border. The 1986 Immigration Reform and Control Act (IRCA) allowed migrants who had been in the United States for a long period of time to gain legal residency rights, but it called for tighter controls on immigration in the future.

However, rather than cutting off the movement of Mexicans into the United States, IRCA and subsequent efforts to deter illegal immigration simply turned a pattern of seasonal migration into a flow of migrants that settled permanently north of the border. Before 1986, most Mexican migrant workers left their families at home and worked in the United States for only a few months at a time before returning to their country with the money they had earned. But many of the seasonal migrants who gained amnesty under IRCA then sent for their families to join them, creating a more permanent immigrant community. Also, with increased vigilance and new barriers making the crossing of the border more difficult, more of the migrants who arrived in the United States decided to remain there rather than risk apprehension by traveling back and forth between the two countries. High-profile efforts to patrol the border around urban areas such as San Diego and El Paso led migrants to use more remote crossing points, and although the number of Mexicans who died trying to reach the United States rose as many attempted to travel through the desolate deserts of Arizona, the overall rate of illegal immigration was not affected by the government's crackdown.

In the 1990s, growing Mexican communities in the United States spread into areas such as North Carolina, Georgia, Arkansas, and Iowa, where few Mexicans had lived before. They also became increasingly mobilized politically as they organized to resist anti-immigrant voter initiatives such as Proposition 187 in California in 1994 and Proposition 200 in Arizona in 2004, both of which threatened to cut off social services for undocumented migrants. At the same time, their political importance in Mexico has reached unprecedented heights as officials at all levels of government there

(continued)

Global Connection: *Mexican Migration to the United States (cont.)*

recognize the critical importance to the Mexican economy of the $16.6 billion that the country receives each year in remittances from migrants working in other countries. Mexican governors, mayors, and federal officials now regularly visit representatives of migrant groups in the United States, often seeking their support and funding for projects at home. Moreover, a 1996 law allowing Mexicans to hold dual citizenship could allow

many Mexican migrants to have a voice in the governance of both the country of their birth as well as the country where they now reside. In 2005, Mexican legislators finally approved a system under which registered Mexican voters living abroad could participate in federal elections using mail-in ballots, and it is easy to imagine that this huge group could play a decisive role in future electoral contests.

officials continue to try to convince their counterparts in Washington that allowing more migrants to cross the border legally would actually enhance U.S. security by reducing the number of unauthorized crossings. Whether or not the U.S. government approves, the difference in wages between the United States and Mexico will persist for a long time, which implies that migration will also persist.

There is disagreement about how to respond to the economic challenges that Mexico faces. Much of the debate surrounds the question of what integration into a competitive international economy really means. For some, it represents the final abandonment of Mexico's sovereignty. For others, it is the basis on which future prosperity must be built. Those who are critical of the market-based, outward-oriented development strategy are concerned about its impact on workers, peasants, and national identities. They argue that the state has abandoned its responsibilities to protect the poor from shortcomings of the market and to provide for their basic needs. They believe that U.S. and Canadian investors have come to Mexico only to find low-wage labor for industrial empires located elsewhere, and they argue that those investors will not hesitate to abandon Mexico for even lower-wage countries such as China when the opportunity arises. They see little benefit in further industrial development based on importation of foreign-made parts, their assembly in Mexico, and their

export to other markets. This kind of development, they argue, has been prevalent in the *maquiladoras,* or assembly industries, many of which are located along the U.S.-Mexico border. Those who favor closer integration with Canada and the United States acknowledge that some foreign investment does not promote technological advances or move the work force into higher-paying and more skilled jobs. They emphasize, however, that most investment will occur because Mexico has a relatively well-educated population, the capacity to absorb modern technology, and a large internal market for industrial goods.

In addition to the economic challenges it faces, Mexico provides a testing ground for the democratic idea in a state with a long history of authoritarian institutions. The democratic ideas of citizen rights to free speech and assembly, free and fair elections, and responsive government are major reasons that the power of the PRI came under so much attack beginning in the 1980s. Currently, Mexico is struggling with opening up its political institutions to become more democratic. Vicente Fox, for example, promised to make information about government activities much more widely available to the population, and extensive files about violent military and police repression of political dissent in the past have been made available to citizens. The government also created the independent National Human Rights Commission, which has been active in protecting citizens' rights (see "Current Challenges: Human Rights in Mexico"). However, efforts to bring about greater transparency in the Mexican political system have sometimes run up against obstacles as government ministries have resisted pressures to release sensitive documents and as investigations into the - repressive activities of the PRI regime in decades past have been stymied. These setbacks leave some Mexicans skeptical of claims that a truly open, democratic political culture is being forged. Mean-while, when Fox demonstrated little capacity to set priorities and communicate a vision for his government, many government agencies found it difficult to act, given a long history of dependence on presidential leadership. This has left many citizens with questions about the effectiveness of democratic institutions.

Centralization of power and decision making is another legacy that Mexico is trying to revise. Countries around the globe increasingly recognize that the

Current Challenges: *Human Rights in Mexico*

The government of Vicente Fox (2000–2006) committed itself to opening up government and improving the state of human rights in Mexico. In the past, the government had been able to limit knowledge of its repressive actions, use the court system to maintain the political peace, and intimidate those who objected to its actions. The president appointed human rights activists to his cabinet and ordered that secret police and military files be opened to public scrutiny. He instructed government ministries to supply more information about their activities and the rights that citizens have to various kinds of services. He also invited the United Nations to open a human rights office in Mexico. He encouraged the ratification of the Inter-American Convention on Enforced Disappearance of Persons. The government also sought to protect the rights of Mexicans abroad, and the United States and Mexico have established a working group to improve human rights conditions for migrants.

The results of these actions have been dramatic. For the first time, Mexicans learned of cases of hundreds of people who had "disappeared" as a result of police and military actions. In addition, citizens have come forward to announce other disappearances, ones they were unwilling to report earlier because they feared reprisals. In 2002, former president Luis Ech\ererría was brought before prosecutors and questioned about government actions against political dissent in 1968 and 1971, a kind of accountability unheard of in the past. The National Human Rights Commission has been active in efforts to hold government officials accountable and to protect citizens nationally and abroad from repetitions of the abuses of the past.

Yet challenges to human rights accountability remain. Opening up files and setting up systems for prosecuting abusers need to be followed by actions to impose penalties on abusers. The judicial system is weak and has little experience in human rights cases. In addition, action on reports of disappearances, torture, and imprisonment has been slowed by contention about civil and military jurisdictions. In an embarrassing revelation to the government, Amnesty International reported several cases of disappearances that occurred after Fox assumed leadership of the country. There were also reports of arbitrary detentions and extrajudicial executions. In October 2001, Digna Ochoa, a prominent human rights lawyer, was shot. In the aftermath of this assassination, the government was accused of not doing enough to protect her, even when it was widely known that she had been targeted by those opposed to her work. Human rights activists claimed that police and military personnel, in particular, still had impunity to the laws. The strength of the Fox administration was tested in these events, and although human rights were much more likely to be protected than in the past, the government continued to have a long way to go in safeguarding the rights of indigenous people, political dissidents, migrants, gays and lesbians, and poor people whose ability to use the judicial system is limited by poverty and lack of information.

solutions to many policy problems lie at regional and local levels. While the government has introduced the decentralization of a number of activities and services, state and municipal governments are struggling to meet the demands of citizens who want competence, responsiveness, and accountability from their local and regional public officials.

Improving social conditions is an important challenge for Mexico. While elites enjoy the benefits of sumptuous lifestyles, education at the best U.S. universities for their children, and luxury travel throughout the world, large numbers of Mexicans remain ill educated, poorly served with health care, and distant from the security of knowing that their basic needs for food, shelter, and employment can be met. The Chiapas rebellion of 1994 made the social agenda a topic of everyday conversation by reminding Mexicans that some people lived in appalling conditions with little hope for the future.

As in the United States, some argue that the best solutions to these problems are economic growth and expanded employment. They believe that the achievement of prosperity through integration into the global economy will benefit everyone in the long run. For this to occur, however, they insist that education will have to be improved and made more appropriate for developing a well prepared work force. They also believe that improved education will come about when local communities have more control over schools and curricula and when parents have more choice between public and private education for their children. From their perspective, the solution to poverty and injustice is fairly clear: more and better jobs and improved education.

For those critical of the development path on which Mexico embarked in the 1980s and 1990s, the problems of poverty and inequity are more complex. Solutions involve understanding the diverse causes of poverty, including not only lack of jobs and poor education but also exploitation, geographic isolation, discriminatory laws and practices, as well as the disruptive impact of migration, urbanization, and the tensions of modern life. In the past, Mexicans looked to government for social welfare benefits, but their provision was deeply flawed by inefficiency and political manipulation. The government consistently used access to social services as a means to increase its political control and limit the capacity of citizens to demand equitable treatment. Thus, although many continue to believe that it is the responsibility of government to ensure that citizens are well educated, healthy, and able to make the most of their potential, the populace is deeply suspicious of the government's capacity to provide such conditions fairly and efficiently.

Finally, Mexico is confronting major challenges of adapting newly democratic institutions to reflect ethnic and religious diversity and provide equity for women in economic and political affairs. The past decade has witnessed the emergence of more organized and politically independent ethnic groups demanding justice and equality from government. These groups claim that they have suffered for nearly 500 years and that they are no longer willing to accept poverty and marginality as their lot. The Roman Catholic Church, still the largest organized religion in the country, is losing members to Protestant sects that appeal particularly to the everyday concerns of poor Mexicans. Women, who make up 32 percent of the formal labor force but 40 percent of professional and technical workers, are becoming more organized, but they still have a long way to go before their wages equal those of men or they have equal voice in political and economic decisions.

Mexican Politics in Comparative Perspective

Mexico faces many of the same challenges that beset other countries: creating equitable and effective democratic government, becoming integrated into a global economy, responding to complex social problems, and supporting increasing diversity without losing national identity. Indeed, these were precisely the challenges that the United States faced at the millennium, as did India, Nigeria, Brazil, Germany, and others. Mexico confronts these challenges within the context of a unique historical and institutional evolution. The legacies of its past, the tensions of the present, and the innovations of the future will no doubt evolve in ways that continue to be uniquely Mexican.

What will the future bring? How much will the pressures for change and the potential loss of national identity affect the nature of the political system? In 1980, few people could have foreseen the extensive economic policy reforms and pressures for democracy that Mexico would experience in the next two decades. Few would have predicted the defeat of the PRI in the elections of 2000. In considering the future of the country, it is important to remember that Mexico has a long tradition of relatively strong institutions. It is not a country that will easily slip into sustained political instability. A tradition of constitutional government, a strong presidency, a political system that has incorporated a wide range of interests, little military involvement in politics, and a deep sense of national identity: these are among the factors that need to be considered in predicting the political consequences of democratization, economic integration, and greater social equality in Mexico.

Mexico represents a pivotal case of political and economic transition for the developing world. If it can successfully bridge the gap between its past and its future and move from centralization to effective local governance, from regional vulnerability to global interdependence, and from the control of the few to the participation of the many, it will set a model for other countries that face the same kind of challenges.

Key Terms

mestizo

Amerindian

indigenous groups

maquiladoras

coup d'état

anticlericalism

ejidos

ejidatarios

sexenio

clientelism

North American Free Trade Agreement (NAFTA)

corporatist state

civil society

state capitalism

import substituting industrialization (ISI)

informal sector

proportional representation

technocrats

para-statal

accommodation

co-optation

Suggested Readings

Babb, Sarah L. *Managing Mexico: Economists from Nationalism to Neoliberalism.* Princeton, N.J.: Princeton University Press, 2001.

Bethell, Leslie, ed. *Mexico Since Independence.* Cambridge: Cambridge University Press, 1991.

Castañeda, Jorge G. *Perpetuating Power: How Mexican Presidents Were Chosen.* New York: New Press, 2000.

Chand, Vickram K. *Mexico's Political Awakening.* Notre Dame, Ind.: University of Notre Dame Press, 2001.

Collier, Ruth Berins. *The Contradictory Alliance: State-Labor Relations and Regime Change in Mexico.* Berkeley: University of California Press, 1992.

Cook, Maria Lorena, Middlebrook, Kevin J., and Molinar, Juan (eds.). *The Politics of Economic Restructuring in Mexico.* San Diego: Center for U.S.-Mexican Studies, University of California, 1994.

Cornelius, Wayne A. "Nation-Building, Participation, and Distribution: The Politics of Social Reform Under Cárdenas." In Gabriel A. Almond, Scott Flanagan, and Robert J. Mundt (eds.), *Crisis, Choice, and Change: Historical Studies of Political Development.* Boston: Little, Brown, 1973.

Cornelius, Wayne A., Eisenstadt, Todd A., and Hindley, Jane (eds.). *Subnational Politics and Democratization in Mexico.* San Diego: Center for U.S.-Mexican Studies, University of California, 1999.

Davidow, Jeffrey. *The U.S. and Mexico: The Bear and the Porcupine.* Princeton, N.J.: Markus Wiener Publishers, 2004.

Dominguez, Jorge I., and Lawson, Chappell H. (eds.). *Mexico's Pivotal Democratic Election: Candidates, Voters, and the Presidential Campaign of 2000.* Stanford, Calif.: Stanford University Press, 2004.

Durand, Jorge, Douglas S. Massey, and Emilio A. Parrado. "The New Era of Mexican Migration to the United States," *The Journal of American History* 86: 2 (September 1999)

Foweraker, Joe, and Craig, Ann L. (eds.), *Popular Movements and Political Change in Mexico.* Boulder, Colo.: Lynne Rienner, 1990.

Grindle, Merilee S. *Challenging the State: Crisis and Innovation in Latin America and Africa.* Cambridge: Cambridge University Press, 1995.

Harvey, Neil. *The Chiapas Rebellion: The Struggle for Land and Democracy.* Durham, N.C.: Duke University Press, 1998.

Krauze, Enrique. *Mexico, Biography of Power: A History of Modern Mexico, 1810-1996.* Trans. by Hank Heifetz. New York: HarperCollins, 1997.

Lawson, Chappell H. *Building the Fourth Estate: Democratization and the Rise of a Free Press in Mexico.* Berkeley: University of California, 2002.

Levy, Daniel C., and Bruhn, Kathleen. *Mexico: The Struggle for Democratic Development.* Berkeley: University of California Press, 2001.

Lustig, Nora. *Mexico: The Remaking of an Economy.* 2nd ed. Washington, D.C.: Brookings Institution, 1998.

Meyer, Michael C., Sherman, William L., and Deeds, Susan M. *The Course of Mexican History*. 7th ed. New York: Oxford University Press, 2002.

Paz, Octavio. *The Labyrinth of Solitude: Life and Thought in Mexico*. New York: Grove Press, 1961.

Preston, Julia, and Dillon, Samuel. *Opening Mexico: The Making of a Democracy*. New York: Farrar, Straus and Giroux, 2004.

Salinas de Gortari, Carlos. *México: The Policy and Politics of Modernization*. Trans. by Peter Hearn and Patricia Rosas. Barcelona: Plaza & Janés Editores, 2002.

Suárez-Orozco, Marcelo, ed. *Crossings: Mexican Immigration in Interdisciplinary Perspective*. Cambridge: Harvard University Press, 1998.

Ugalde, Luis Carlos. *The Mexican Congress: Old Player, New Power*. Washington, D.C.: Center for Strategic and International Studies, 2000.

Womack, John, Jr. *Zapata and the Mexican Revolution*. New York: Vintage Books, 1968.

Suggested Websites

Office of the President (in Spanish and English)
www.presidencia.gob.mx
Secretariat of Foreign Relations (in Spanish and English)
www.sre.gob.mx
El Universal newspaper (in Spanish and English)
estadis.eluniversal.com.mx/noticiash.html
The Mexico Project, National Security Archive
www2.gwu.edu/~nsarchiv/mexico
Washington Post (registration required, free)
**www.washingtonpost.com/wp-dyn/world/americas/
    northamerica/mexico**
Federal Electoral Institute (in Spanish only)
www.ife.org.mx/InternetCDA/HOME/home.jsp

Endnotes

[1] This figure represents an estimate of the metropolitan area of Mexico City, which extends beyond the official boundaries of the city.

[2] An excellent history of this event is presented in Wayne A. Cornelius, "Nation-Building, Participation, and Distribution: The Politics of Social Reform Under Cárdenas," in Gabriel A. Almond, Scott Flanagan, and Robert J. Mundt (eds.), *Crisis, Choice and Change: Historical Studies of Political Development* (Boston: Little, Brown, 1973).

[3] Michael C. Meyer and William K. Sherman, *The Course of Mexican History*, 5th ed. (New York: Oxford UP, 1995), 598–599.

[4] Although the self-confessed "lone gunman" was jailed, the ensuing investigation raised concerns about a possible conspiracy involving party and law enforcement officials as well as drug cartels. Rumors circulated about a cover-up scandal. Eventually, skepticism about the integrity of the inquiry was so great that President Salinas called for a new investigation. At this point, little remains known about what exactly happened in Tijuana and why.

[5] United Nations Development Programme, *Human Development Report* (2004), http://hdr.undp.org/reports/global/2004/pdf/hdr04_HDI.pdf.

[6] World Bank, *World Development Indicators* database, August 2004, http://www.worldbank.org/data/countrydata/ countrydata.html.

[7] World Bank, *World Development Report, 2001* (New York: Oxford University Press, 2001).

[8] Merilee S. Grindle, *State and Countryside: Development Policy and Agrarian Politics in Latin America* (Baltimore: Johns Hopkins University Press, 1986), 63, quoting President Avila Camacho (1940–1946).

[9] Kevin J. Middlebrook (ed.), *Unions, Workers, and the State in Mexico* (San Diego: Center for U.S.-Mexican Studies, University of California Press, 1991).

[10] Grindle, *State and Countryside,* 79–111.

[11] For a description of this process, see Carlos Bazdresch and Santiago Levy, "Populism and Economic Policy in Mexico," in Rudiger Dornbusch and Sebastian Edwards (eds.), *The Macroeconomics of Populism in Latin America* (Chicago: University of Chicago Press, 1991), 72.

[12] For an assessment of the mounting problems of Mexico City and efforts to deal with them, see Diane E. Davis, *Urban Leviathan: Mexico City in the Twentieth Century* (Philadelphia: Temple University Press, 1994).

[13] Joe Foweraker and Ann L. Craig (eds.), *Popular Movements and Political Change in Mexico* (Boulder, Colo.: Lynne Rienner, 1989).

[14] Roger Hansen, *The Politics of Mexican Development* (Baltimore: Johns Hopkins University Press, 1971), 75.

[15] World Bank, *World Development Indicators, 2004*, 61.

[16] Economist Intelligence Unit, *Country Commerce, Mexico* (London: EIU, September 2001), 43.

[17] Daniel Levy and Gabriel Székely, *Mexico: Paradoxes of Stability and Change* (Boulder, Colo.: Westview Press, 1983), 100.

[18] See Luis Carlos Ugalde, *The Mexican Congress: Old Player, New Power* (Washington, D.C.: Center for International and Strategic Studies, 2000).

[19] See Chapell H. Lawson, *Building the Fourth Estate: Democratization and the Rise of a Free Press in Mexico* (Berkeley: University of California Press, 2002).

[20]Susan Eckstein (ed.), *Power and Popular Protest: Latin American Social Movements* (Berkeley: University of California Press, 1989).

[21]Wayne A. Cornelius and Ann L. Craig, "Politics in Mexico," in Gabriel Almond and G. Bingham Powell (eds.), *Comparative Politics Today,* 5th ed. (Boston: Scott Foresman, 1992), 502.

[22]Foweraker and Craig, *Popular Movements and Political Change in Mexico.*

[23]Jonathan Fox and Gustavo Gordillo, "Between State and Market: The Campesinos' Quest for Autonomy," in Wayne A. Cornelius, Judith Gentleman, and Peter H. Smith (eds.), *Mexico's Alternative Political Futures* (San Diego: Center for U.S.-Mexican Studies, University of California Press, 1989).

[24]Wayne A. Cornelius, Ann L. Craig, and Jonathan Fox (eds.), *Transforming State-Society Relations in Mexico: The National Solidarity Strategy* (San Diego: Center for U.S.-Mexican Studies, University of California Press, 1994).

CHAPTER 5

Brazil

Alfred P. Montero

Federative Republic of Brazil

Land and People

Capital	Brasilia	
Total area (square miles)	3,286,500 (slightly smaller than the United States)	
Population	176.6 million	
Annual population growth rate (%)	1975–2002	1.8
	2002–2015 (projected)	1.0
Urban population (% of total)		82.2
Ethnic composition (% of total)	White (includes Portuguese, German, Italian, Spanish, Polish)	53.7
	Mixed white and black	38.5
	Black	6.2
	Other (includes Japanese, Arab, Amerindian)	1.6
Major language(s)	Portuguese	
Religious affiliation (%)	Roman Catholic (nominal)	73.6
	Protestant	15.4
	Spiritualist	1.3
	Bantu/voodoo	0.3
	Other	1.8
	Unspecified	0.2
	None	7.4

Economy

Domestic currency	real (BRL)	
	US$1 = BRL 2.9251 (2004)	
Total GNI (US$)	479.5 billion	
GNI per capita (US$)	2,720	
Total GNI at purchasing power parity (US$)	1.326 trillion	
GNI per capita at purchasing power parity (US$)		7,510
GDP annual growth rate (%)	1983–1993	2.4
	1993–2003	2.3
	2002	–1.9
	2003	–0.2
	2004	5.1
GDP per capita average annual growth rate (%)	1983–1993	0.6
	1993–2003	1.0
Inequality in income or consumption (2001)	Share of poorest 10%	0.7
	Share of poorest 20%	2.4
	Share of richest 20%	63.2
	Share of richest 10%	46.9
	Gini Index	59.3

Structure of production (% of GDP)	Agriculture	10.1
	Industry	38.6
	Services	51.3
Labor force distribution (% of total)	Agriculture	20
	Industry	14
	Services	66
Exports as % of GDP	16.9	
Imports as % of GDP	13.1	

Society

Life expectancy	68.7	
Infant mortality per 1,000 live births	33	
Adult literacy (% of population age 15+)	Female	86.6
	Male	86.3
Access to information and communications (per 1,000 population)	Telephone lines	218
	Mobile phones	167
	Radios	433
	Televisions	349
	Personal computers	62.9

Women in Government and the Economy

Women in the National Legislature		
Lower house or single house (%)		8.6
Upper house (%)		12.3
Female professional and technical workers (% of total)		62
Women at ministerial level		3
Female economic activity rate (age 15 and above)		43.7
Female labor force (% of total)		36
Estimated earned income (PPP US$)	Female	4,594
	Male	10,879

Composite Rankings and Ratings

2002 Human Development Index ranking (value) out of 173 countries	73
Human Development Index (HDI) ranking (value) out of 177 countries	72 (.775)
Gender-related Development Index (GDI) ranking (value) out of 144 countries	60 (.768)
Gender Empowerment Measure (GEM) ranking (value) out of 78 countries	N/A
Corruption Perception Index (CPI) ranking (value) out of 146 countries	59 (3.9)

Environmental Sustainability Index (ESI) ranking (value) out of 146 countries	11 (66.2)
Freedom in World rating	Free (2.5)

Political Organization

Political System Federal republic, presidential with separation of powers.

Regime History Democratic since 1946 with periods of military authoritarianism, especially 1964–1985.

Administrative Structure Federal, with 26 states plus the Federal District, which also functions as a state. Subnational legislatures are unicameral. State governments have multiple secretariats, the major ones commonly being economy, planning, and infrastructure. The states are divided into municipalities (over 5,500), with mayors and councilors directly elected.

Executive President, vice president, and cabinet. The president and vice president are directly elected by universal suffrage in a two-round runoff election for four-year terms. Since 1998, the president and vice president may run for a second term.

Legislature Bicameral: The Senate is made up of three senators from each state and from the Federal District, elected by plurality vote for an eight-year term; the Chamber of Deputies consists of representatives from each state and from the Federal District, elected by proportional vote for a four-year term.

Judiciary Supreme Court, High Tribunal of Justice, regional courts, labor courts, electoral courts, military courts, and state courts. Judiciary has financial and administrative autonomy. Most judges are appointed for life.

Party System Multiparty system including several parties of the right, center-left, and left. Elections are by open-list proportional representation. There is no restriction on the creation and merging of political parties.

Section ❶ The Making of the Modern Brazilian State

Politics in Action

In May 1997, thousands of Brazilians gathered outside the stock exchange in Rio de Janeiro while hundreds more collected inside the building. All were waiting for the beginning of an auction of *Companhia Vale do Rio Doce* (CVRD), a mining conglomerate that was Brazil's largest public firm. The sale of Vale, as the company is known, was the latest in a series of **privatization** moves that began in the early 1990s with the sale of Brazil's steel mills, fertilizer firms, and utility companies. Fifty-two state enterprises had already been sold, and now it was Vale's turn. For the Brazilians gathered outside the stock exchange, this event meant much more than a sale: a cherished piece of Brazil's past was being lost to the faceless market. Vale represented memories of the Brazilian economy that blossomed after World War II with ambitious industrialization projects led by large public firms. Now, all of that was under attack by "greedy capitalists" intent on exploiting the patrimony of the Brazilian people for personal gain. For the students, workers, and professionals who joined to protest the sale of the mining giant, it was too much to take. Minutes before the auction gavel fell, tempers flared. The angry crowd pushed against police barricades. Some threw punches; others were hurled to the floor and trampled; many would leave with bloodied faces. Everyone felt the painful defeat. The old Brazil was dead.

For those inside the stock exchange, the sale of Vale meant the birth of a new Brazil. By agreeing to privatize one of the most recognizable symbols of Brazilian industry, the country's leaders were embracing the importance of the market in modernizing Brazil. Despite its past successes, the state could no longer guarantee Vale or any other industrial firm the resources needed to become competitive in global markets. By putting Vale up for sale, Brazil's political leadership was guaranteeing that the firm would have a future. The new owners of Vale were young Brazilian industrialists and bankers as well as international investors, including U.S. firms such as NationsBank and the financier George Soros. Unlike most other Brazilian firms, which are family owned, the new Vale would be owned by shareholders and operated by professional administrators, much as major U.S. and

European multinational firms are. Nothing less would befit the world's largest exporter of iron ore. The new Vale was emblematic of the new Brazil: modern, competitive, and linked to global markets.

The opposition to the auctioning of Vale revealed aspects of the new Brazil. Only a week before the sale, opponents had filed 135 separate lawsuits in state courts to halt the privatization. In response, squads of lawyers for the National Development Bank, the federal agency responsible for organizing the sale of Vale, had traveled to the far corners of Brazil to defeat each and every lawsuit. The absence of a centralized and effective system for adjudicating disputes of this type reflects the inherently political failures of Brazilian politics today: getting things done on reform and policymaking in general is a slow, conflict-driven process. Political institutions disperse power so that enacting fundamental change is difficult.

Geographic Setting

Brazil is larger than the continental United States and occupies two-thirds of South America. It borders all the other countries of South America except Ecuador and Chile. The population of 170 million is concentrated in the urban southern and southeastern regions, with more than 15 million inhabitants in Greater São Paulo alone. This density contrasts with the northern, sparsely populated rain forest regions of the Amazon. Overall, Brazil's 18.2 inhabitants per square kilometer makes it less densely populated than the United States, France, or Britain.

The physical geography of Brazil is diverse, including thick rain forest in the Amazon valley, large lowland swamps known as the *pantanal* in the central western states, and vast expanses of badlands known as the *sertão* in the north and northeast. The country is rich in natural resources and arable land. The Amazon has an abundance of tropical fruit and minerals; the central and southern regions provide most of the country's iron ore and coal; offshore and onshore sources of petroleum in Rio de Janeiro and the northeast coastline are also significant. Brazil's farmlands are particularly fertile, including large soy-producing areas, coffee in Rio de Janeiro and in São Paulo, and sugar and other agriculture along the narrow stretch off the northeast coast. The Amazon's climate is wet,

the *sertão* is dry, and the agricultural areas of the central, southeastern, and southern regions are temperate.

Centuries of voluntary and involuntary immigration of Europeans and Africans contributed to the emergence of an ethnically mixed society. Although this complexity makes any classification scheme precarious, the National Brazilian Institute of Geography and Statistics (IBGE) claims that 57 percent of the population is white, 37 percent is *pardo* (brown or mulatto), 6 percent is black, and 0.6 percent is Asian.[1] These numbers probably ignore people of mixed race, from indigenous and white parents, who are known as *mestizos* but are sometimes classified erroneously as being white or *pardo*. The indigenous people who live in the vast Amazon basin are estimated to number 250,000.[2] The Asian population is dominated by people of Japanese descent who immigrated, mostly to São Paulo, after 1925. Numbering over 2 million, this community of Japanese descendants is the largest outside Japan.

Like other ethnically plural societies such as India, Mexico, Nigeria, Russia, Iran, and the United States, Brazil is a unique blend of distinct cultural influences. Portuguese as the common language helps keep Brazilians united, and unlike the people of India, Iran, and Nigeria, Brazilians are not greatly divided over religious differences. Roman Catholicism was imposed by Portuguese colonial rule, then reinforced by immigration from Catholic Italy, Spain, and Portugal at the end of the nineteenth century. In recent years, evangelical Protestants have made inroads and now compose about 11 percent of the population. Afro-Brazilian and indigenous religions also operate alongside the Catholic liturgy throughout Brazil.

Critical Junctures

The Brazilian Empire (1822–1889)

Europeans first arrived in Brazil in 1500 with an expedition led by the Portuguese explorer Pedro Alvares Cabral. Unlike the other countries of Latin America, Brazil was a Portuguese colony, not a Spanish one. So it was spared the violent wars of independence that coincided with the comparatively more spasmodic collapse of the Spanish colonial system during the 1810s and 1820s. Brazilian independence was declared peacefully by the Crown's own agent in the colony.

In 1808, when Napoleon Bonaparte invaded Spain and Portugal, the Portuguese king, João VI, and his court escaped to Brazil. After the defeat of Napoleon, Dom João returned to Portugal to reclaim his throne, but he left his son, Dom Pedro, behind in Rio de Janeiro as prince regent. In September 1822, Dom Pedro declared Brazil independent and took the new title of emperor of Brazil. In 1824, a constitution was drafted, making Brazil the only constitutional monarchy in the Americas. In 1840, Dom Pedro I's son, Dom Pedro II, assumed the throne.

The Brazilian empire's chief concern was keeping control of such a large territory. The solution was to centralize authority in the emperor, who acted as a **moderating power** (*poder moderador*), mediating conflicts among the executive, legislative, and judicial branches of government and powerful landowning elites, known as the landed **oligarchy.** This centralization of authority provided a contrast with the other postcolonial Latin American states, which suffered numerous conflicts among territorially dispersed strongmen called *caudillos.*

In contrast with its neighbors, imperial Brazil enjoyed several features of a functioning representative democracy: regularity of elections, the alternation of parties in power, and scrupulous observation of the constitution. In substance, however, liberal institutions only regulated political competition among the rural, oligarchical elites, reflecting the interests of a privileged minority and not the larger Brazilian population.

Critical Junctures in Brazil's Political Development

1822	Dom Pedro I declares himself emperor of Brazil, peacefully ending three hundred years of Portuguese colonial rule.
1824	Constitution drafted
1888	Abolition of slavery
1889	Dom Pedro II, who assumed throne in 1840, is forced into exile; landowning elites establish an oligarchical republic
1891	A new constitution establishes a directly elected president.
1930	Getúlio Vargas gains power after a coup led by military and political leaders. His period of dictatorship (1937–1945) is known as the New State.
1945	Vargas calls for general elections. General Eurico Dutra of the Social Democratic Party wins.
1950	Vargas is elected president. Scandals precipitate his suicide in 1954.
1956	Juscelino Kubitschek becomes president.
1960	Jânio Quadros becomes president.
1961	Quadros resigns. João Goulart gains presidency despite an attempted military coup.
1964	A military coup places power in the hands of successive authoritarian regimes.
1984	*Diretas Já!*, a mass mobilization campaign, calls for direct elections.
1985	Vice-presidential candidate José Sarney becomes president on the sudden death of elected president Tancredo Neves.
1988	A new constitution grants new social and political rights.
1989	Fernando Collor is elected president.
1992	Collor is impeached; Vice President Itamar Franco assumes presidency.
1994	Fernando Henrique Cardoso is elected president after his Real Plan controls inflation.
1998	Cardoso is relected.
1999	The Real Plan weathers a financial crisis.
2002	Lula da Silva is elected president.

The Old Republic (1889–1930)

The next critical juncture in Brazilian history occurred in 1889 with the peaceful demise of the empire, the exile of Dom Pedro II, and the emergence of a republic ruled by the landowning oligarchy (the Old Republic). The decline of slavery and the rise of republicanism were the main forces that ended the empire. Britain's ban of the slave trade in 1850 and Brazil's abolitionist movement gradually wore away slavery as an institution until it was abolished in 1889. Socioeconomic changes also paved the way for abolition. The dynamic coffee economy, concentrated in the state of São Paulo, had grown impressively since the 1830s. Unlike the plantation sugar economy of the northeast, coffee did not require the use of slave labor. By this time, too, liberal political values in opposition to the centralization of political authority had taken root among the coffee oligarchy.

The Old Republic (1889–1930) consolidated the political rise of the coffee oligarchy and a small urban industrial class and commercial elite linked to the coffee trade. The constitution of 1891, which was inspired by the U.S. model, established a directly elected president as the head of government, guaranteed the separation of church and state, and expanded the franchise to include all literate males (about 3.5 percent of the population before 1930). The **legitimacy** of the republican political system was established on governing principles that were limited to a privileged few, but no longer determined by the hereditary rights of the emperor. Power was decentralized to the states, which gained greater authority to formulate policy, spend money, levy taxes, and maintain their own militias.

Although the republican elite went further than the empire's elite in expressing liberal ideas in the constitution, most Brazilians continued to reside in rural areas where the landed oligarchy vigorously suppressed dissent. As in the southern United States and in Mexico, landed elites manipulated local political activity. The colonels, as these elites were called in Brazil, assumed extensive extralegal authority to gather their poor workers and "vote them" (use their votes to guarantee the election of officials favored by the local colonels). This process became widely known as *coronelismo.*

The ties that developed between the patron (the landowner) and the client (the peasant) during the Old Republic became the basis of modern Brazilian politics. In return for protection and occasional favors, the client did the bidding of the patron. As urbanization and the growth of the state's administrative and bureaucratic agencies proceeded, the process of trading favors and demanding action was transformed and became known as **clientelism.** *Coronelismo* in rural areas and clientelism in urban areas were extended to the politics of the national state. In this way, the state was dominated by **patrimonialism**—the injection of private interests into public policymaking.

In contrast to the centralization of power during the empire, the Old Republic consecrated the power of local elites. The **politics of the governors** empowered regional elites, mainly from the coffee and cattle regions, who dominated national politics. Three states in particular emerged as key players: São Paulo (coffee), Minas Gerais (coffee and ranching), and Rio Grande do Sul (ranching). The presidency alternated so regularly among them that this period of Brazilian political history is referred to as the rule of *café com leite* ("coffee with milk"), reflecting the dominance of the São Paulo coffee and Minas Gerais cattle elites.

The 1930 Revolution

The Great Depression of the 1930s upset the economic and political base of the Old Republic. As world demand for coffee plummeted, the coffee and ranch elites faced their worst crisis. Worker demonstrations and a resurgent Brazilian Communist Party challenged the legitimacy of the Old Republic. Among the ranks of discontented political elites, a figure emerged who would change the shape of Brazilian politics for the rest of the century: Getúlio Vargas (see "Leaders: Getúlio Dornelles Vargas").

After a disputed presidential campaign in 1930, Vargas came to power as the head of what he called a new "revolutionary government." He moved swiftly to crush middle-class and popular dissent and built a political coalition around a new economic project of industrialization led by the central government and based on central state resources. In contrast to the Old Republic, Vargas insisted on controlling the regional governments by replacing all governors (except in Minas Gerais) with handpicked allies (**interventores**). The center of gravity of Brazilian politics swung back to the national state.

Vargas believed he could win the support of these groups by answering their demands in a controlled way. They would be allowed to participate in the new political order, but only as passive members of state-created and state-regulated unions and associations. This model of government was **state corporatism.** It rejects the idea of competition among social groups by having the state arbitrate all conflicts. For instance, when workers requested increases in their wages, state agencies would determine to what extent such demands were answered and how business would pay for them.[3]

By 1937, Vargas had achieved a position of virtually uncontested power. During the next eight years, Vargas consolidated his state corporatist paradigm with labor codes, the establishment of public firms to produce strategic commodities such as steel and oil, and paternalistic social policies. Packaged with nationalist fervor, these policies were collectively called the **New State** (*Estado Novo*).

The New State was decidedly authoritarian. Vargas, who was called *pai do povo* (father of the people), could not be upstaged by competing political images and organizations. Brazilian society would be linked directly to the state and to Vargas as the state's primary agent. Although the New State's constitution had fascist overtones, Vargas's policies were as much inspired by the New Deal of U.S. President Franklin D. Roosevelt as by fascist Italy or Nazi Germany.[4] The new regime expanded the existing rudimentary social insurance and pension programs into a broad welfare and health care system for urban workers. Although unemployment insurance was not envisaged by the new laws, workers were provided with insurance against occupational accidents, illness, and death. Vargas created a Ministry of Labor and labor courts to regulate and solve conflicts between employers and labor. The armed forces experienced marked improvements in professional standards of

Leaders: *Getúlio Dornelles Vargas*

Getúlio Dornelles Vargas (1883–1954) came from a wealthy family in the cattle-rich southernmost state of Rio Grande do Sul. Vargas's youth was marked by political divisions within his family between federalists and republicans, conflicts that separated Brazilians during the Old Republic and particularly in Rio Grande do Sul, which had a strong regional identity. Political violence, which was common in the state's history, also affected Vargas's upbringing. His two brothers were each accused of killing rivals, one at the military school in Minas Gerais that Getúlio attended with one of his older siblings. After a brief stint in the military, Vargas attended law school in Porto Alegre, where he excelled as an orator. Like many others in his generation, his university education was incomplete. He supplemented his studies by reading many books published in other countries.

After graduating in 1907, he began his political career as a district attorney. Later, he served as majority leader in the state senate. In 1923, Vargas was elected federal deputy for Rio Grande do Sul, and in 1924 he became leader of his state's delegation in the Chamber of Deputies. In 1926, he made another political career change when he was named finance minister for the Washington Luis administration (1926–1930). He served for a year before winning the governorship of his home state. Never an ideologue, Vargas embraced a highly pragmatic style of governing that made him one of Brazil's most popular politicians by the end of the 1920s.

Vargas's powerful political position as governor of Rio Grande do Sul catapulted him into national prominence in 1929. The international economic crisis compelled several regional economic oligarchies to unite in opposition to the coffee and financial policies of the government. The states, including the state of São Paulo, divided their support between two candidates for the presidency: Julio Prestes, who was supported by President Luis, and Vargas, head of the opposition. The two states of Minas Gerais and Rio Grande do Sul voted as a bloc in favor of

Vargas, but he lost the 1930 election. Immediately after this loss, a conspiracy among discontented military and political leaders led to the coup of October 1930, which installed Vargas in power.

No other figure in Brazilian political history has ever affected the country as much as Getúlio Vargas. His New State launched a series of reforms that established the terms on which Brazilian society would be linked to the state for decades. Even today, his political legacy continues in the form of state agencies and laws protecting workers.

Getúlio Vargas as president in 1952. *Source:* Hulton/Getty Archive by Getty Images.

Source: For more on Vargas's life, see Robert M. Levine, *Father of the Poor? Vargas and His Era* (New York: Cambridge University Press, 1998).

promotion and conduct through the establishment of the Superior War College (*Escola Superior de Guerra*).[5]

The Populist Republic (1945–1964)

The ever-growing mobilization of segments of the working and middle classes as well as U.S. diplomatic pressure forced Vargas, in 1943, to call for full democratic elections to be held in December 1945. Three political parties emerged to contest the election: the Social Democratic Party (PSD) and the Brazilian Labor Party (PTB) were pro-Vargas, while the National Democratic Union (UDN) stood against him. The PSD and the PTB, which operated in alliance, were both creations of the state, while the UDN brought together various regional forces committed to a return to liberal constitutionalism. By October 1945, the bitterness of the campaign led the military to force Vargas's resignation, two months before the general election.

The turn to democracy in 1946 fell far short of breaking with the past. The new 1946 constitution guaranteed periodic elections but the most important economic and social policies were still decided by the state bureaucracy and not by the national legislature.

Populism, not democracy, became the defining characteristic of the new political order. In Brazil, the terms *populist* and *populism* refer to politicians, programs, or movements that seek to expand citizenship to previously disenfranchised sectors of society in return for political support. Populist governments tend to grant benefits to guarantee support, but they discourage lower-class groups from creating autonomous organizations. Populists also do not regard themselves as accountable to the people.

Vargas returned to power after he was elected in 1950. Brazilian workers supported him for his promises to improve the social insurance system. However, economic limitations and opposition claims that he was preparing a new dictatorship made Vargas politically vulnerable.[6] Vargas was soon swept up in a bizarre scandal involving the attempted assassination of a popular journalist. The crisis drove Vargas to take his own life on August 24, 1954.

Under Vargas's democratic successor, Juscelino Kubitschek (in office from 1956 to 1960), the economic picture improved. Brazilian industry expanded tremendously in the 1950s. Kubitschek was a master of political symbolism and **nationalism.** His administration promoted images of a new and bigger Brazil, capable of generating "fifty years of development in five." Chief among these symbols of the new Brazil was Kubitschek's decision to move the country's capital from Rio de Janeiro to a planned city called Brasília. The building of this utopian city acted as a political symbol to rally support among Brazil's business popular classes for Kubitschek's developmentalist policies.

The presidents who followed Kubitschek's term proved much less competent.[7] Jânio Quadros, elected in 1960, resigned months later with little explanation. His successor, João Goulart, embarked on an ill-fated campaign for structural reforms, mainly of the educational system and agrarian reform. But he faced an increasingly polarized situation as peasant league movements, students, and professional organizations organized protests, strikes, and illegal seizures of land. As right-wing organizations battled leftist groups in the streets of the capital, the military's distrust of Goulart convinced them to end Brazil's experiment with democratic populism in March 1964.

The Rise of Bureaucratic Authoritarianism (1964–1985)

The military government that came to power in 1964 installed what the Argentine sociologist Guillermo O'Donnell termed **bureaucratic authoritarianism (BA).**[8] These authoritarian regimes emerge in response to severe economic crises and are led by the armed forces and key civilian allies, most notably professional economists, engineers, and administrators. Repression in Brazilian BA varied from combinations of mild forms that constricted civil rights and other political freedoms and harsher forms that included wholesale censorship of the press through institutional acts, torture of civilians, and imprisonment without trial. The first and the last two military rulers, Castelo Branco (1964–1967), Ernesto Geisel (1974–1979), and João Figueiredo (1979–1985) presented less violent forms of authoritarianism, whereas the rule of Artur Costa e Silva (1967–1969) and of Emilio Médici (1969–1974) encompassed the worst forms of physical repression.

Brazil's capital, Brasília. The planned city was designed by the world-famous Brazilian architect Oscar Niemeyer.
Source: Georges Holton/Photo Researchers.

Initially, the military government envisioned a quick return to civilian rule and even allowed the continuation of democratic institutions, though in a limited form. After being purged in 1964 of the BA's opponents, the national congress continued to function and direct elections for federal legislators and most mayors (but not the president or state governors) were held at regular intervals. In November 1965, the military abolished all existing political parties and replaced them with only two: the National Renovation Alliance, or ARENA, and the Brazilian Democratic Movement, or MDB. ARENA was the military government's party, and MDB was the "official" party of the opposition. Former members of the three major parties joined one of the two new parties.[9]

Although these democratic institutions were more than pro forma, their powers were severely limited. The military government used institutional decrees to legislate the most important matters, thereby stopping the congress from having an important voice. Few civilian politicians could speak out directly against the military for fear of being removed from office.

In economic policy, the military reinforced the previous pattern of state interventionism. The government actively promoted **state-led development** by creating hundreds of state corporations and investing millions in established public firms such as Vale. Under military leadership, Brazil implemented one of the most successful economic development programs among newly industrialized countries. Often called the "Brazilian miracle," these programs demonstrated that, like France, Germany, and Japan in earlier periods, a developing country could create its own economic miracle.

The Transition to Democracy and the First Civilian Governments (1974–2001)

After the oil crisis of 1973 set off a wave of inflation around the world, the economy began to falter. Increasing criticism from Brazilian business led Geisel and Figueiredo to sustain a gradual process of democratization.[10] Initially, these leaders envisioned only a liberalizing, or opening (*abertura*), of the regime that would allow civilian politicians to compete for political office. As was later the case with Gorbachev's *glasnost* in the Soviet Union, however, control over the process of liberalization gradually slipped from their hands and was captured by organizations within civil society. In 1974, the opposition party, the MDB, stunned the military government by increasing its representation in the Senate from 18 to 30 percent and in the Chamber of Deputies from 22 to 44 percent. These numbers did not give it a majority, but the party did capture a majority in both chambers of the state legislatures in the most important industrialized southern and southeastern states.[11]

Abertura accelerated in the following years. The opposition made successive electoral gains and used them to get concessions from the government. The most important of these concessions was the re-establishment of direct elections for governors in 1982, political amnesty for dissidents, the elimination of the government's power to oust legislators from political office, and the restoration of political rights to those who had previously lost them. The gubernatorial elections of November 1982 sealed the fate of promilitary candidates as opposition gubernatorial candidates won landslide victories in the major states.

The military, which wanted to maintain as much control over the succession process as possible, preferred to have the next president selected within a restricted electoral college. Mass mobilization campaigns sought the right to elect the next president directly. The *Diretas Já!* ("Direct Elections Now!") movement, comprising an array of social movements, opposition politicians, and labor unions, expanded in size and influence in 1984.[12] Their rallies exerted

tremendous pressure on the military at a moment when the question of who would succeed General Figueiredo was not clear. The military's fight to keep the 1984 elections indirect alienated civilian supporters of the generals, many of whom broke with the regime and backed an alliance (the Liberal Front) with Tancredo Neves, the candidate of the opposition PMDB, or Party of the MDB. Neves's victory in 1984, however, was marred by his sudden death on the eve of the inauguration. Vice President José Sarney became the first civilian president of Brazil since 1964.

The sequence of events that led to Sarney's presidency was a keen disappointment to those who had hoped for a clean break with the authoritarian past. Most of the politicians who gained positions of power in the new democracy hailed from the former ARENA or its misleadingly named successor, the Democratic Social Party (PDS). Most of these soon joined Sarney's own PMDB or its alliance partner, the Party of the Liberal Front (PFL).[13]

A chance for fundamental change appeared in 1987 when the national Constituent Assembly met to draft a new constitution. Given the earlier success of the opposition governors in 1982, state political machines became important players in the game of constitution writing. The state governments petitioned for the devolution of new authority to tax and spend. Labor groups also exerted influence through their lobbying organization. Workers demanded constitutional protection of their right to strike and called for an extension of the right to public employees, who had previously been prohibited from engaging in such activism. The constitution also granted workers the right to create their own unions without authorization from the Ministry of Labor.[14] As a whole, the constitution guaranteed a rich array of social and political rights, yet it also left vestiges from the corporatist past, including protection of public firms in petroleum (Petrobrás) and telecommunications from foreign investment and privatization.

The other primary issue of the day was inflation. Soon after Sarney's rise to power, annual rates of inflation began to skyrocket. The government invoked several stabilization plans to stop the explosion of prices, but to no avail. By the presidential elections of

1989, the first since the 1960s to be held as direct elections for that post, Brazilian society was calling for a political leader who would remedy runaway inflation and remove corrupt and authoritarian politicians from positions of power.

Rising from political obscurity, an ex-governor from Alagoas, a small state in the poor northeast, Fernando Collor de Mello, became president. Collor and his small party, the Party of National Reconstruction (PRN), had fought a grueling campaign against the popular left-wing labor leader and head of the Workers' Party (*Partido dos Trabalhadores,* or PT), Luiz Inácio "Lula" da Silva (see "Citizen Action: The Workers' Party" in the "Political Parties and the Party System" section later in this chapter). To counteract Lula's appeal among the Brazilian people, Collor's campaign rhetoric appealed to the poor, known as the *descamisados* ("shirtless ones"), who were attracted by his attacks against politicians and the social problems caused by bureaucratic inefficiency. A skillful campaigner on television, Collor convinced Brazilians that he could "kill inflation with one shot" and get rid of the "maharajahs"—corrupt public servants who collected massive salaries but did little work.

The Collor presidency was a critical juncture as the government's economic team began the privatization of state enterprises, deregulation of the economy, and the reversal of decades of policies that had kept Brazil's markets closed to the rest of the world. Yet Collor failed to solve the nagging problem of inflation and, ironically, was soon accused of bribery and influence peddling and was impeached in September 1992, an ignominious end for the first directly elected president since the 1960s.

Collor's impeachment brought to the presidency Itamar Franco, a well-known politician in Minas Gerais who was less well known at the national level as Collor's vice president. Despite a high level of uncertainty during Franco's first year, including rumors of a military coup that was allegedly in the works in 1993, his government played an important stabilizing role. Perhaps his most important decision was to support his minister of finance, Fernando Henrique Cardoso, a sociologist and senator from São Paulo, in a plan to conquer inflation. In July 1994, Cardoso implemented the Real Plan, which created a new currency, the *real*. Monthly inflation fell from 26 percent to 2.82 percent in October 1994 (see Section 2).

Cardoso rode the success of the Real Plan to the Brazilian presidency, beating out Lula of the PT in 1994 and again in 1998 to become the first Brazilian president to be re-elected. After his inauguration in January 1995, Cardoso proved adept at keeping inflation low and consolidating some of the structural reforms of the economy. As the tale of Vale suggests, privatization moved forward. Other reforms, however, remained stuck in congress, including crucial reforms of the tax system. Brazil's budget and trade deficits increased, and financial crises in Asia and Russia in 1997 and 1998 eventually led to a crisis in the Real Plan. In January 1999, after weeks of foreign investors taking money out of the country, the value of the *real* collapsed. The currency soon stabilized, and hyperinflation did not return. The country also weathered the financial calamity of the Argentine economy's meltdown after December 2001 without turning back on any of the structural reforms implemented during the 1990s.

After September 11, 2001

The events of September 11 and the collapse of the Argentine economy produced a fundamental crisis of confidence in Brazil. The fate of the economy now hinged on events across the border and in the United States. As one of Brazil's top three export markets and as its chief partner in the common market of the south (Mercosul, see Section 2), Argentina's crisis threatened to destabilize the recovery of the *real*. Meanwhile, the economic and diplomatic repercussions from Washington's war on terror threatened to displace social and economic priorities in Brazil's relations with the United States. Diplomacy with Washington became particularly embittered over the Bush administration's insistence on going to war with Iraq and its heavy-handed approach to dealing with foreigners, Brazilians included, who had to go through demeaning checks at American airports.

The election of Lula da Silva as president in October 2002 reflected a response to the need to put the social agenda ahead of the American focus on security. Lula claimed frequently in international meetings that "poverty is the most devastating weapon of mass destruction." Lula's election also reflected the maturation of democracy. Once a proponent of socialism, Lula embraced Cardoso's reform agenda. He passed major social security reforms in 2003 and 2004, but then suffered from the same inefficiencies of his predecessor when his reforms became stuck in Congress during the run-up to municipal elections in late 2004. In 2005, Lula's government became mired in a widening corruption scandal involving Workers' Party leaders accused of bribing legislators for their votes on reform. The crisis threatened Lula's presidency and its lofty aspirations to continue in power after the 2006 presidential elections.

Themes and Implications

Historical Junctures and Political Themes

In the world of states, both international and domestic factors have influenced the Brazilian state's structure, capacity, and relations with society. During the days of the empire, international opposition to slavery forced powerful oligarchs to turn to the state for protection. The coffee and ranch economies that provided the material base for the power of the Old Republic were intricately tied to Brazil's economic role in the world. Even the *Estado Novo,* with its drive to organize society, was democratized by the defeat of fascism in Europe. The return to democracy during the 1980s was also part of a larger global experience, as authoritarian regimes gave way all over Latin America, Eastern Europe, southern Europe, and the Soviet Union.

Within Brazil, the state adjusted to changes in the distribution of power; the rise of new, politically active social classes; and the requirements of development. The federal state saw power shift regularly between the central and subnational governments. These swings between centralizing periods, such as the empire and the *Estado Novo*, to decentralizing experiences, such as the Old Republic and the more recent transition to democracy, punctuated many of the critical junctures of Brazilian politics.

The inclusion of new political actors such as the working and middle classes reshaped the Brazilian

state during the twentieth century. Vargas's New State provided mechanisms for mobilizing and organizing workers and professionals. Populist democracy later provided these social segments protection from unsafe working environments, the effects of eroding wages, and the prohibitive expense of health care. Public firms such as Vale employed hundreds of thousands of Brazilians and dramatically altered the development possibilities of the country. Not surprisingly, during the 1980s and 1990s, neoliberal reforms dramatically altered the role of the Brazilian state and its relations with society (see Section 2).

State-led growth established the essential foundation for the governing of the economy. Developmentalism transformed Brazil from a predominantly agrarian economy into an industrialized economy. To be sure, growth was poorly distributed, and the social problems that emerged from it remain at the heart of the country's ongoing struggles with democracy.

Regarding the democratic idea, Brazil certainly has the institutions of a democracy, but in many ways, decades of patrimonialism, populism, and corporatism undermine these institutions. Brazilian politicians typically cultivate personal votes (they are known as **personalist politicians**) and avoid following the rule of parties or alliances. Many switch parties several times in a political career. As a result, Brazilian political parties are extremely weak. Personalism in Brazilian politics persists because it is well rewarded.

Even with these enduring shortcomings in democracy, Brazilians prefer this form of government. They appreciate that democracy gives them more say in public policymaking. Thousands of new political groups, social movements, civic networks, and economic associations have emerged in recent years. The Brazilian state is highly decentralized into twenty-six states, a federal district, and over 5,500 municipalities. Each of these centers of power has become a locus of demand-making by citizens and policymaking by elites. Under these circumstances, centralized rule following the model of the New State or the bureaucratic authoritarian period is impossible and undesirable today.

Collective identities remain uncertain in Brazil, although Brazilians are now more commonly linked through their place in the democratic order. Who are the Brazilians? has always been a vexing question, no less so now that Brazil's borders are becoming obsolete in a world of heavy flows of international commerce, finance, and ideas. One common response to the question is that the symbols of the Brazilian nation continue to tie Brazilians together: carnival, soccer, samba, and bossa nova. Yet even as these symbols have become more prevalent, they have also lost some of their meaning because of commercialization and export as part of a tourist-attracting image of Brazil. Catholicism is a less unifying force today as Pentecostalism and evangelism have eaten into the church's membership. Women have improved both their social position and their political awareness as gender-based organizations have become a more important resource of civil society. Yet even here, Brazil remains an extremely patriarchal society: women are expected to balance motherhood and other traditional roles in the household, even while they are pressured by economic need to produce income.

Perhaps race, more than any other form of identity, remains the most difficult issue to understand in Brazilian politics and society. Racial identity continues to divide Brazilians, but not in the clearcut manner it divides blacks and whites in the United States. These categories are multiple and often they coalesce due to racial mixing in ways that defy the kind of stark, black–white segregation in the United States.

Like race, class continues to separate Brazilians. Economic reforms and the erosion of populist redistribution have caused social gaps to widen further, making Brazil a highly fragmented society. Although it is one of the world's ten wealthiest economies, with a gross domestic product over US$588 billion, that wealth is poorly distributed. Like India, Brazil's social indicators such as income distribution, infant mortality, and nutrition consistently rank near the bottom in the world of states. Income disparities mirror racial differences since the poor are represented by mostly blacks and mulattos, and the rich are almost invariably white. The poverty of the north and northeast also contrasts with the more industrialized and prosperous southeastern and southern states.

Implications for Comparative Politics

As a large, politically decentralized, and socially fragmented polity, Brazil presents several extraordinary challenges to the study of comparative politics. First, the Brazilian state is an anomaly. It has been both highly centralized and decentralized during different periods of its history. In each of these periods, the state produced lasting political legacies that have both strengthened and weakened its capacity for promoting development, democracy, and social distribution. Although political centralization has been an important factor in making the French state strong, decentralized states such as the United States and German federations have also proven to be successful formulas for government. The Brazilian case is a laboratory for evaluating which approach is likely to be more successful in other large, decentralized states in the developing world, such as China and India and, until recently, Russia.

While the complexity of the Brazilian state represents one problem area, the weakness of the country's democratic institutions suggests another, and perhaps more troubling, concern. Along with Russia, Brazil demonstrates how the lack of coherent party systems and electoral institutions can endanger democracy. In contrast to the highly organized polity of Germany and the strength of parties in parliamentary democracies like the United Kingdom and Japan, Brazil's experience highlights how anemic representative institutions can weaken democracy.

Paradoxically, as Brazil developed economically and made its way back to democracy in the 1980s, it also became a more socially unequal country. Established democracies like India and transitional democracies like Mexico and Russia have also experienced the reality that democratization does not improve the distribution of wealth. Finally, the complex divisions afflicting Brazilians' collective identities challenge all attempts to address the country's problems. Yet even today, Brazilians and outside observers continue to treat the country as a singular unit. In this regard, Brazil presents a puzzle for theories about collective identities: How has such a socially fragmented society remained a coherent whole for so long?

Section ❷ Political Economy and Development

Like most other countries in the developing world, Brazil's politics has always been shaped by the country's quest for economic and social development. Two processes in particular have left enduring legacies: the pattern of state intervention in the domestic market and the effects of external economic change. Historically, these two factors have influenced each other. External economic crises—world depressions, fluctuations in the price of exported goods such as coffee, upsurges in the prices of imported goods—have compelled the Brazilian state to intervene in the domestic economy through protection, subsidies, and even the production of goods that it previously imported. In turn, policies aimed at promoting the industrial growth of the country have made Brazil one of the newly industrialized countries of the world, alongside Mexico, India, and China.

In order to clarify how political and economic development have been intertwined in Brazil, this section explores the state-led model of development, considers how the domestic effects of the state-led model and its reform generated enormous social costs, and discusses the international capitalist forces that shaped domestic economic policy and society.

State and Economy

Like its Latin American neighbors, Brazil's economic development prior to the New State was based on **export-led growth,** that is, on the export of agricultural products such as sugar, cotton, coffee, and, for a short time in the early 1900s, rubber. In the nineteenth century, coffee emerged as the engine of growth in the Brazilian economy. By the time of the Old Republic, a strong demand for Brazilian coffee in Europe and North America gave the country a virtual monopoly in the global market. Cotton, sugar, and cereals continued to be important export products too, but they were secondary to coffee. By 1919, coffee composed 56 percent of Brazil's total exports. Only five years later, that figure jumped to 75 percent.[15]

The dominance of coffee ensured that the Old Republic would keep Brazil active in the world market with minimal state involvement in promoting the export-led economy. Export receipts provided a reservoir of capital to build railroads, power stations, and other infrastructure. These investments, in turn, spurred the growth of some light industries, mostly in textiles, footwear, and clothing. With ample domestic capital, public finance was relegated to a minor role.

The Brazilian state's involvement in the economy became far more **interventionist** during the 1930s when the Great Depression caused international demand for coffee to decline. As exports fell, imports of manufactured goods also declined. The incentives that were produced by the crisis led Brazilian manufacturers to replace these goods with domestically produced ones. These forces prompted **import substitution industrialization (ISI),** a model of development that promoted domestic industrial production of previously imported manufactured goods. Initially, large doses of state intervention were not necessary. The initial phase of ISI—the so-called light, or easy, phase—focused on manufactured products that required little capital or sophisticated technology. Most of these industries, such as textiles and food processing, were labor intensive and created jobs. Although these conditions did not require large infusions of state capital, Vargas's New State provided limited subsidies and tariff protection to nascent ISI sectors.

At the end of World War II, new ideas about Third World development came to be popular among various international agencies. The new goal was to "deepen" the ISI model by promoting heavy industry and capital-intensive production. In Brazil, as in Argentina, Mexico, and India, a new generation of **state technocrats**—experts in economic development—took an active role in designing new policies. Inspired by the texts of the United Nations Economic Commission for Latin America (ECLA), these technocrats targeted particular industrial sectors as strategic.[16] Then, through the use of industrial policies including planning, subsidies, and financial support, state agencies promoted the quick growth of these sectors.

Brazil was the epitome of ECLA-style **developmentalism,** the ideology and practice of state-sponsored growth, during the 1950s in Latin America. More than any other Latin American state, the Brazilian state was organizationally capable of implementing industrial policies to deepen ISI. New bureaucratic structures, such as a national development bank and national public firms, were created during the first and second Vargas governments to produce as well as to regulate industrial growth. The producer state promoted private investment by extracting and distributing raw materials for domestic industries at prices well below the international market level. These lower prices were in effect subsidies to domestic industry. Other firms linked to sectors of the economy receiving these supports would benefit in a chain reaction.

Although growth rates achieved impressive levels during the 1950s and early 1960s and even higher levels in the 1970s (see Table 1), it was during this period that the first serious contradictions of ISI emerged.[17] Protection fostered noncompetitive, inefficient production because it removed incentives for competition. Although industries grew, they did so by depending too heavily on public subsidies. ISI also became import-intensive. Businesses used subsidized finance to import technology and machinery. The government helped these firms by overvaluing the currency to make import prices cheaper. This overvaluation of the currency hurt export earnings, which were necessary to pay for imports. As a result, the export sector could not supply the state with much-needed revenues to sustain growth, prompting the government to print money, which in turn led to inflation. Under the Goulart government (1961–1964), the economy's capacity to import and export dwindled, and stagnation set in. The economic crisis that soon followed contributed to the coup of 1964 and Goulart's fall.

The failures of ISI during the 1960s inspired new thinking about development, at least in Brazilian and other Latin American academic circles. The so-called dependency school, whose adherents were known as *dependencistas,* emerged in the social sciences around the idea that underdeveloped or "peripheral" countries faced tremendous obstacles to achieving sustained levels of industrialization and growth in a world

Table 1

Governing the Economy: GDP Growth Rates, 1940–2003

1940–1949	5.6%
1950–1959	6.1
1960–1969	5.4
1970–1979	12.4
1980–1989	1.5
1990–1996	2.1
1997–2000	0.8
2001–2003	1.0

Source: Brazilian Institute of Geography and Statistics (IBGE), *Anuario Estatístico Brasilero* (Rio de Janeiro: IBGE, various years).

dominated by "core" economies in North America and Western Europe. ISI's failures, the *dependencistas* argued, were due to the ill-fated attempt to adjust marginally the inherently exploitative structure of world markets. Pursuing capitalist development only favored the core economies, so the *dependencistas* advocated (vaguely) de-linking Brazil from the world economy. This early attack on what we today call globalization inspired a new generation of progressive thinkers, among them the sociologist and future president Fernando Henrique Cardoso, who became one of the preeminent proponents of a variant of the dependency argument. The fall of Brazilian democracy, however, would provide little opportunity for these groups to take their ideas out of the universities.

The rise of the military governments in 1964 led to reform but eventually to an attempt to deepen ISI through state-led development methods. From 1964 to 1985, the state continued to promote industrialization, especially the production of consumer durable goods such as automobiles, televisions, refrigerators, and machinery for the domestic market. Multinational firms also invested and transferred technology to these and other new industries. Table 2 highlights the important contribution of industry to the Brazilian gross domestic product.

Para-statals, also known as public or state firms, played an important role in the military's development model. Large-scale projects in shipbuilding, mining, steel, oil, bauxite, and aluminum were financed and

Table 2

**Governing the Economy:
Sector Composition of the GDP, 1970–2000**

Year	Agriculture	Industry	Services
1970	11.55%	35.87%	52.59%
1980	10.16	40.99	48.84
1990	9.26	34.20	56.54
2000	9.00	29.00	62.00

Source: IBGE and Werner Baer, *The Brazilian Economy:
Growth and Development,* 4th ed. (New York: Praeger,
1994), 382–383. Copyright © 1995 by Werner Baer.
Reprinted by permission of Greenwood Publishing Group,
Inc. All rights reserved.

managed by bureaucratic agencies and state firms, and often including foreign companies. Peter Evans, an American political economist, insightfully characterized these complex relations among the state, foreign investors, and domestic capitalists as a "triple alliance."[18] The state, however, remained the dominant partner.

In the 1970s, Brazil's military leaders realized that, in order to finance the huge public expenditures of national industrial policy, international financial markets would have to play a role. The military also began to emphasize primary exports such as coffee, iron ore, cereals, and other agricultural products. Policies designed to increase agricultural productivity and technological modernization were expanded. The export of agricultural surplus and the sale of food products in the internal market were facilitated by a growing agribusiness sector. Spurred on by state subsidies, agribusiness supplied new resources and management for previously inefficient agricultural subsectors. One of the most unusual agribusiness ventures occurred in the 1970s, when the military government introduced a plan to use sugarcane alcohol as a fuel source. Northeast agribusiness boomed during these years as the sugar economy became tied to the dynamic industrial economy of the southern and southeastern regions.

The Environmental Costs of State-Led Growth

The impressive growth of industry and agriculture was concentrated in the central and southern regions of Brazil. Centers of growth in the states of São Paulo, Minas Gerais, Rio de Janeiro, and Rio Grande do Sul became the locomotives of the country's development and sites of environmental degradation. As capital-intensive industries became more common in Brazil, ecologically destructive technologies were used without much regulation. Before the mid-1970s, Brazilian policymakers were unconcerned with the emission of toxic waste into the ground at major industrial zones, air pollution in overgrown urban areas, or pesticide and chemical fertilizer use in agricultural regions.

The environmental costs of these attitudes became clear in the 1970s. Guanabara Bay and the Paraiba do Sul River basin, both in Rio de Janeiro state, were brought to the brink of biological death. Urban pollution in São Paulo devastated the Tietê River, which runs through the city, making it no better than a toxic waste dump in some areas and threatening the health of millions. By far the worst tragedy was in Cubatão, an industrial city 60 kilometers east of metropolitan São Paulo. There, petrochemical industries and steel mills wreaked havoc on the environment, pumping 1,102 tons of pollutants into the surrounding ecological system each day. The conditions in the residential area of Cubatão became so bad that by 1981, one city council member reported that he had not seen a star in twenty years.[19] Thousands reported becoming afflicted with tuberculosis, pneumonia, bronchitis, emphysema, asthma, and cancer. Forty of every one thousand babies in Cubatão were stillborn.

Big development projects reached the forests of the Amazon River basin in the 1970s with Vale do Rio Doce's Carajás mining work in the eastern Amazon. This and other industrial projects threatened the tropical forests, as did cattle ranching, timber extraction, and slash-and-burn agriculture by poor farmers, a practice that allowed frequent rains to leech nutrients from the soil and prevent the return of tropical habitats. By the 1980s, it was clear that the primary result of these practices was the deforestation of the Amazon.

Brazil's worsening environmental problems received official attention after 1972, when the United Nations held its Conference on the Human Environment. Soon afterward, Brazil created an environmental secretariat, and in 1981 the government established the National Environmental Council (CONAMA), which included officials from national and state government, and representatives from business, professional, and environmental groups. State governments also established their own environmental agencies and passed important legislation.[20] In 1975, São Paulo passed a comprehensive antipollution law. The cleanup of Cubatão began in 1983.

Partly as a result of the return to democracy in 1984, new environmental movements within and outside Brazil began to influence official and public opinion on the costs of resource degradation. Much attention was brought to these problems when the Brazilian government successfully persuaded the United Nations to hold its 1992 Conference on the Environment in Rio de Janeiro, a follow-up to the 1972 conference. Thousands of delegates and hundreds of **nongovernmental organizations** gathered in Rio to discuss global environmental problems that were virtually all present in Brazil.[21]

Despite the attention the Rio conference brought to the issue, rates of deforestation, pollution, and resource degradation fell only briefly after 1992 and have since returned to historically high levels. Because of their expense, Brazilian business has shown only passing interest in the use of clean technologies. In the third international UN conference on the environment, held in Kyoto, Japan, in 1997, Brazil was joined by the rest of the developing world in deflecting the finger of blame for ecological problems.

The Fiscal System

In developed countries such as the United States, Germany, France, and Britain, governments can use tax policy to punish polluters. In Brazil, however, tax collection has been notoriously weak, making this a less useful instrument to regulate business or individuals. As the Brazilian economy became more complex after the 1960s, new opportunities for evading taxes emerged. An **informal economy** of small firms, domestic enterprises, street vendors, and unregistered employees proliferated, virtually outside the domain of the taxable economy. In some cases, these enterprises grew to a substantial size, accounting for the distribution of everything from artisans' goods to professional services. Legally registered companies began to subcontract unregistered professionals to render services beyond the reach of the tax system.

Although reliable information is lacking, economists estimate that the informal economy could be as large as half of Brazil's gross domestic product (about US$300 billion) and it may employ about 30 million to 45 million people. Figures on tax evasion in both the formal and informal sectors estimate that federal coffers lose over $70 billion a year.

Other problems developed for the tax system after the transition to democracy. The new constitution of 1988 decentralized the fiscal structure by allowing the states and municipalities to expand their collection of taxes and to receive larger transfers of funds from Brasília. Significant gaps emerged in tax collection responsibilities and public spending as a result of these changes. Although the central state spent less than it collected in taxes between 1960 and 1994, Brazil's 5,500 municipal governments spent several times more than they collected. Subnational governments also gained more discretion over spending since the destination of most of these funds was not predetermined by the federal government. The governors also used public banks held by the state governments to finance expenditures, thus expanding their debt. By 1992, the states held almost half of Brazil's total debt.

The Collor administration began to reverse some of the adverse effects by threatening to cut off federal debt servicing and to close down regional banks. Efforts to increase tax receipts to 25 percent of GDP helped to stave off a fiscal meltdown.[22] But it was the Cardoso administration's efforts at recovering federal tax revenues and reducing the fiscal distortions produced by Brazil's federal structure that made the greatest difference. Tax evasion was slowed, as the federal tax collection agency was expanded and its surveillance powers enhanced. Legislation in 1994 and 1998 allowed the federal government to employ more discretion over transfers of funds constitutionally earmarked for the state and municipal governments and to cap the states' ability to acquire debt. This allowed the federal government to exert leverage on state governments to control their spending. Brasília also shifted more spending responsibilities in health care, housing, and social policy to subnational governments. This has allowed the federal government to reduce its own spending and to control how the states spend their resources. The most important reform in this area, the Fiscal Responsibility Law, which was passed in 2000, set strict limits on federal, state, and municipal expenditures, but its enforcement is still in doubt. Given still large civil service payrolls (often these constitute more than 70 percent of state and municipal revenues), governments are hard-pressed to implement the law. The National Confederation of Municipalities estimates that 80 percent of Brazil's mayors and sixteen of twenty-seven states are not in compliance with the law's strict requirements. These problems are at the center of Brazil's mounting public debt, which now hovers over 60 percent of GDP, and they have played a role in the country's recent financial crises (see Figure 1).

In 2003, Lula's government passed a tax reform that permitted increases in seven federal taxes and simplified the tax code. Other aspects of tax reform, however, remained unfulfilled. Legislation to address fiscal competition among the states, the simplification and unification of the states' value-added tax, and efforts to reduce the overall tax burden on business (currently 35 percent) were postponed for 2005 and beyond. The government also failed to do something about the weight of taxes, such as sales taxes, that fall more heavily on the poor.

The Problem of Inflation

Inflation deserves special mention in Brazil, for in no other country, with the possible exceptions of Germany and Argentina, has this phenomenon had such a lasting impact on a country's politics. In Brazil, inflation accompanied state-led development, especially after 1974. The Brazilian state, business, and unions all distorted the value of goods and services by manipulating prices, interest rates, and wages. After the transition to democracy, successive attempts to control inflation fell apart as different interest groups attempted to retain these controls. No fewer than seven "stabilization" plans designed to control prices between 1985 and 1994 fell apart, sometimes generating "hyperinflation" (600 percent or more annual inflation). Figure 2 illustrates this terrible track record.

The Sarney, Collor, and Franco governments sought to control the growth in prices by setting the value of some basic products and freezing wages while the government reduced spending. The plans all failed. Once fixed prices could not be maintained or government spending could not be restrained or wages were increased in accordance with monthly inflation rates, the inflationary spiral would heat up.

Only Cardoso's Real Plan proved successful in reining in inflation. The Real Plan anchored the real,

Figure 1

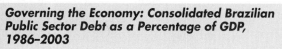

Governing the Economy: Consolidated Brazilian Public Sector Debt as a Percentage of GDP, 1986–2003

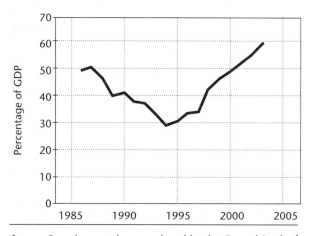

Source: Based on numbers produced by the Central Bank of Brazil.

Figure 2

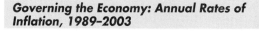

Governing the Economy: Annual Rates of Inflation, 1989–2003

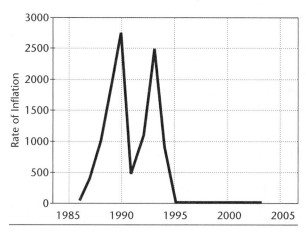

Source: Author's design based on Brazilian Central Bank figures, 2005.

the new currency, to the dollar. Unlike a similar plan in Argentina, the Real Plan did not fix the real to the dollar strictly but allowed it to float within bands, thus achieving more flexibility in the exchange rate. This is one of the main reasons that the real was able to weather the kind of financial turmoil that led the Argentine economy to ruin in 2001–2002.

Paradoxically, the Real Plan's formula for success proved to be a source of weakness. Soon after the Mexican *peso* crisis of December 1994, Central Bank managers in Brasília became convinced that the *real* was overvalued, just as the *peso* had been before its crash. Overvaluation made exports more expensive abroad, raised the costs of production, and made imports cheaper. Brazil's trade deficit rose by more than 140 percent after 1995 and foreign investors became antsy following financial crises in Asia and Russia in 1997–1998. Even Cardoso's signing of a US$42 billion bailout sponsored by the International Monetary Fund (IMF) in November 1998 could not avoid a crisis. The *real* fell by more than 50 percent against the dollar in January 1999. Despite the devaluation, hyperinflation did not return, and the government was successful in moderating the growth in public spending through reforms such as the Law of Fiscal Responsibility. Nevertheless, the growth in the massive public debt, which has continued under Lula's presidency, remains a concern for the long-term stability of the currency.

Society and Economy

Brazil's astounding levels of industrialization during the 1950s, 1960s, and 1970s had lasting effects on the urban population. In 1950, 35 percent of the population lived in urban areas. By 1980, that number had increased to 68 percent. During the same period, employment in industry jumped from 14 percent to 24 percent, while employment in agriculture declined from 60 percent to 30 percent. Import substitution had created these jobs by expanding the size of both the working and the middle classes. Service-sector professionals like lawyers, doctors, and private teachers soon found clients as the domestic consumer market grew along with the working class.

Nevertheless, the number of jobs created in the industrial sector did not begin to absorb the huge number of unemployed Brazilians. Many of the new jobs required skilled and semiskilled specialized labor. Metallurgy, automobile production, and mining did not provide many opportunities for the large numbers of unskilled workers in the Brazilian labor market. In the late 1980s and 1990s, even skilled workers faced losing their jobs because of intense industrial restructuring. During the 1990s, manufacturing jobs fell by 48 percent and unemployment in metropolitan areas rose above 18 percent. Service-sector employment increased, but not enough to make up for industrial job losses. These jobs also paid less and offered fewer protections from arbitrary dismissal.

Industrialization also failed to eradicate the racial inequalities inherited from slavery. Despite the impressive industrial development of Brazil, Afro-Brazilians continued to make less than their white colleagues and had fewer opportunities for upward mobility. According to one study, nonwhite men and women in Brazil have made real gains in their income because of improvements in education and occupation, but the gap separating nonwhite income from white income remains significant.[23] On average, blacks make 41 percent and mulattos make 47 percent of what whites make.

Women constitute 28 percent of the economically active population in Brazil and continue to enter the labor market in record numbers. In 2003, over half of all women were in the work force as compared with 73 percent of all men. Brazil also ranks second only to the United States in the percentage of women in top management positions (44 percent to 46 percent in the United States). Working women typically have more years of schooling than men, but they still receive lower salaries for the same job. Women make 57 percent of what men make. Afro-Brazilian women, who are doubly disadvantaged by race and gender, are more likely to have underpaid and menial work. For example, over 90 percent of domestic servants are black women.

The uneven effects of industrialization patterns and other demographic and policy factors discussed below have all worked against the equalization of income distribution in Brazil. Compared with other developing countries, including Mexico and India, Brazil has the worst structure of income distribution in the world (see Table 3).

Table 3

Governing the Economy: Brazilian Income Distribution in Comparative Perspective

			Percentage of Total Income Received		
Country	*Year*	*10% Richest*	*20% Richest*	*40% Poorest*	*20% Poorest*
Peru	2000	37.2%	60.2%	6.5%	2.2%
China	2001	33.1	50.0	9.0	4.7
United States	2000	29.9	45.8	10.7	5.4
India	2000	27.4	41.6	12.3	8.9
France	1995	25.1	40.2	12.6	7.6
Britain	1999	28.5	44.0	11.4	6.1
Brazil	1998	46.7	64.4	5.7	2.0
Chile	2000	47.0	62.2	6.6	3.3
Mexico	2000	43.1	59.1	7.2	3.1
Germany	2000	22.1	36.9	13.7	8.5
Poland	1999	27.4	42.5	11.8	7.3

Source: World Bank, *World Development Indicators 2004* (Washington, D.C.: World Bank, 2004), 60–62.

The Welfare System

In a country of startling social inequalities, welfare policy plays a remarkably minor role in the lives of most Brazilians. Although welfare and education expenditures constitute about 11 percent of the GDP, among the highest levels in the world, the money has not improved Brazil's mediocre welfare state. Unlike the systems in Britain, France, Germany, and Japan, Brazil's welfare system has not reduced the high level of poverty or helped the majority of the poor.

Brazil supports a public school system as well as a health, retirement, and social assistance system that includes funds for unemployment relief. Salaried workers are entitled to benefits such as health care, worker's compensation, retirement pensions, paid vacations, and overtime pay, yet only an estimated 15 percent of the Brazilian population qualify for these benefits. Workers in the informal sector, who are normally undocumented, cannot collect welfare since technically the federal government does not consider them employed. Corruption, clientelism, and outright waste make the welfare system incapable of delivering benefits to the people who need them the most.[24]

Part of the problem is that more people need welfare than actually contribute to the welfare state. Today, only half of the 70 million people who are economically active contribute to the welfare system. That means that the government must finance the shortfall with debt.

Between 1960 and 2000, while the population doubled, the number of retired people multiplied eleven-fold. As a result, retirement benefits and pensions currently exceed the salaries of working employees by 30 percent. The average retirement age for public employees is 57 for men and 54 for women, although recent reforms hope to increase this average. The fiscal problems of the pension system fall most heavily on the public system. While developed economies spend just 1.7 percent of GDP on public pensions, Brazil spends almost three times that number, and its retirement age population is only 40 percent that of the developed economies. More than 70 percent of all income transfers are retirement benefits that go to middle-class and upper-class individuals, including politicians, judges, and military officers. The indigent receive only 1.5 percent of these monies. Such imbalances deepen the social disparities evident in Brazil.

In the fall of 2003, the Lula government scored its first reform victory by passing the first phase of social security reform, which raised the minimum retirement age, placed stricter limits on benefit ceilings, reduced survivor benefits, and taxed pensions and benefits. Issues including the taxation of social security benefits for judges and military officers and the reduction of survivor benefits for the latter group became stumbling blocks in cross-party negotiations. These and other issues became the basis for government concessions, including reducing proposed cuts, so that the total annual savings produced by the reform were less than half of the original target. Some of Lula's other bold new social reforms have captured headlines but have been modest in their implementation. The government initiated its "Zero Hunger" program, a centerpiece of Lula's 2002 presidential campaign, by distributing monthly cash disbursements to qualified families, but the first stage of Zero Hunger was limited to a few municipalities in the north. The government's "Zero Illiteracy" program promised to wipe out the functional illiteracy that currently plagues 38 percent of the population by 2006. Its implementation in 1,768 municipalities and the recruitment of 56,000 "literacy agents" including university students is a good sign of the government's commitment. Yet the program currently covers less than half of all municipalities.

Agarian Reform

The restructuring of the rural economy in the 1960s and 1970s altered the rural social structure. The growing role of agribusiness created jobs for some segments of the rural working class, while it crowded out small landowners. After 1964, various state welfare programs were launched in the agricultural sector: retirement policies for low-income producers, pension plans for rural workers, and financial support to community rural associations. These policies played a prominent role in breaking landowners' political and economic control of the rural population. During the 1970s and 1980s, rural workers were organized into rural unions that received welfare transfers from the state—medical plans, job security, and protection of wages against inflation.

Landownership in Brazil remains concentrated in the hands of only 1 percent of the landowning class. The arable land held by this small group of owners (about 58,000) is equal to the size of Venezuela and Colombia combined. Over 3 million other farmers survive on only 2 percent of the country's land. An additional 4.5 million Brazilians are farm laborers or squatters who own no land. In the 1980s and 1990s, several landless peasant movements grabbed headlines by sanctioning illegal land invasions and coming to blows with rural landowners and police. Among the most important of these groups, the Landless Workers' Movement (*Movimento dos Sem-Terra,* or MST) attracted the most attention by seizing some 1.38 million acres.

The Cardoso administration responded to these problems by expropriating some unproductive estates and settling 186,000 families on them. Perhaps sensing that the Lula government would be more sympathetic, the MST dramatically increased the rate of land invasions in 2003–2005. Lula promised to resettle 60,000 families, but budgetary realities made actual redistributions fall well short of this target. MST rhetoric and direct action will continue to escalate tensions and test the Lula government's commitment to fiscal austerity and modest social reform.

Any serious effort to address rural poverty will affect urban poverty. Through rural-to-urban migration, the landless poor have swelled the rings of poverty that surround Brazil's major cities. During the 1950s and 1960s, the growth of industry in the south and southeast enticed millions to migrate to the states of São Paulo, Minas Gerais, and Rio de Janeiro in the hopes of finding new economic opportunities. The rapidity of rural-to-urban migration was striking. Over 31 million people migrated to these cities during the 1960s and 1970s. By 1991, 75 percent of Brazil's population was living in urban areas.

The flood of migrants to urban areas and the growth of urban populations created terrible social problems. The pressures on Brazilian cities for basic services such as sanitation, education, and transportation soon overwhelmed the budgets of municipalities and state governments. Poor people were left to their own devices. Squatters soon took government land, settling on the outskirts of the major cities. They built huge shantytowns called *favelas* around cities like Rio and São Paulo.

Regional disparities in income worsened during this period. The military governments addressed this problem by transferring revenues from the industrialized south and southeast to the poor north and northeast, where many of their supporters were based. The federal government subsidized communication and

Favelas in Rio de Janeiro.   *Source:* © Mar Valdecantos.

transportation in the poorer regions and created new state agencies to implement regional developmental projects. These policies had mixed results. The contribution of poor regions to GDP increased. The growth rate of the central and western regions was spurred on by agribusiness activities, mineral exploration, and financial services. The economic gap between regions narrowed, but social and income disparities within the underdeveloped regions increased.[25] Industrialization in the poorer regions was capital intensive and therefore labor saving but did not create jobs. Only the most skilled workers in these regions benefited from these changes. Poor agricultural management, ecological destruction, the murder of native Brazilians due to the need to expropriate land for mining and agriculture, and corruption all weakened the distributive effect of these policies.

Today, the northern and northeastern regions remain much poorer than those in the south and southeast. Whereas 15 percent of the population in the southeast subsist under the poverty line, more than 50 percent of the inhabitants of the northeast are below that marker. The life expectancy of a northeasterner—fifty-eight years—is nine years below that of a resident of São Paulo state (sixty-seven years) and fifteen years below that of a resident of Rio Grande do Sul (seventy-three years).[26]

Brazil in the Global Economy

As the financing needs of state-led industrialization outstripped the resources of the national development bank and domestic bankers, the deepening of ISI required Brazil to pursue international sources of credit. During the late 1960s and the 1970s, private lenders were eager to provide loans to Brazil and other fast-growing countries. As a result, Brazil became the largest single debtor country in the developing world.

External events had a hand in creating and then managing Brazil's external debt. By the end of the 1970s, the world economy had been hit with two oil price shocks that sent inflation rates soaring in the United States and other industrialized countries. Many of these countries also held Brazilian debt. As the central banks in Europe and the Federal Reserve in the United States ratcheted interest rates upward to force prices back down, Brazil's interest payments soared.[27]

After Mexico declared a moratorium on interest payments in 1982, private investors began to shun Brazil and other Latin American debtors. During the 1980s, the so-called Lost Decade of slow growth and debt crisis, the IMF and the World Bank became important suppliers of badly needed credit. But only debtors who promised to take concrete steps to reduce inflation, open their domestic markets to foreign competition, promote exports, and privatize state industries were eligible for help.

Brazil, along with Argentina and Peru, rejected these conditions. The Sarney government refused to implement the free-market policies demanded by the international financial institutions. In 1987, his government took the ultimate gamble in resisting creditors by declaring a moratorium on debt repayment, a move that sent a signal to investors that Brazil would control its own reform agenda on its own terms. The moratorium, however, did not last. It was lifted a few months later under intense pressure from the international financial community. Opposition to the moratorium within the country was also great in the business community, which feared that such aggressive action would scare off foreign investors and ruin the country's already tattered credit rating.

Collor reversed course. Partly in response to pressure from international creditors and partly in recognition that Sarney's alternative policies had failed, he agreed to put Brazil on the path of free-market policies with reforms that included the privatization of state enterprises and the deregulation of the economy. These domestic changes were reflected externally as Collor began to normalize relations between Brazil and the multilateral agencies, especially the IMF.

The liberalization of markets opened Brazilian industry to higher degrees of foreign competition. As a result, the competitiveness of domestic firms emerged as a core problem. Brazilian industrial productivity reached its lowest levels in 1992, when, on a list of fifty countries, Brazil was ranked forty-ninth, just ahead of Pakistan. One 1997 study showed that the overall productivity of Brazilian industry runs at only 27 percent of the U.S. level.[28] Although productivity levels improved by 7 percent after 1992, inherent inefficiencies caused by poor infrastructure, untrained labor, and lack of access to technology and capital continue to create obstacles to higher growth. The average Brazilian worker has only six years of schooling, half as much as the average worker in Japan or the United States.

How Brazil will fare in an increasingly interconnected and competitive global marketplace will also depend on its external political relations. Brazil's trade relations with the United States. have been particularly conflictual. Both countries tangled over Brazilian exports of steel, soy, orange juice, and other products during the 1980s and especially in recent years. The political climate was less charged during the American presidential administrations of George H. W. Bush and Bill Clinton, when international free-trade accords, such as the North American Free Trade Agreement (NAFTA), received the support of both Washington and most Latin American governments. During the Summit of the Americas in Miami in December 1994, the leaders of the United States, Central America, the Caribbean (except Cuba), and South America agreed to form a Free Trade Area of the Americas (FTAA) by the year 2005. In November 2003 and then again in 2004, Brazil and the United States agreed to ease the way toward an implementation of the FTAA in 2005. Brazil won an important concession in having the United States negotiate directly with the Market of the South (Mercosul), Brazil's own subhemispheric trade block in 2004. (See "Global Connection: Governing the Economy in a World of States: MERCOSUL.") But it lost on the key issue of negotiating American subsidies for agriculture, an issue Washington insists can only be handled at the Doha trade round of the World Trade Organization (WTO).

Brazil's degree of commitment to the international free-trade system will likely expand in the coming years with the growing importance of its export sector. Since 1998, Brazil has turned a record current account deficit of $33 billion into a surplus of $33 billion in December 2004. Trade has grown with developing countries such as China and India as fast as it has with Europe and the United States, suggesting that Brazil is becoming one of the major manufacturing and agrindustry nodes in the globalized system of production and consumption.

Domestic and international opposition to globalization will constrain the Lula presidency from pursuing even further integration. Brazil's persistent fiscal problems will keep the specter of the IMF around as Lula attempts to satisfy the Fund's macroeconomic requirements. That will fuel more attacks by unions and antiglobalization activists like those who appeared at the annual World Social Forum in Porto Alegre, Brazil. Yet Lula's government has also found ways of working in partnership with international financial and multilateral institutions. During his first year as president, Lula signed agreements with the World Bank and the Inter-American Development Bank to create and fund new social assistance programs. Following on the Zero Hunger program, new family stipend programs will funnel some $2 billion to 11 million families by 2006.

Global Connection: *Governing the Economy in a World of States: MERCOSUL*

After several years of negotiating the Treaty of Asunción, Brazil, Argentina, Paraguay, and Uruguay inaugurated MERCOSUL, a regional common market group, in January 1995. Under MERCOSUL (Mercosur in Spanish), Brazil and its trade partners agreed to reduce tariffs on imports from signatories gradually until 2006, when the 10,000 items that make up the tariff listings of all four countries must conform to a common external tariff (CET) regime.

During the negotiations over the Treaty of Asunción between March 26, 1991, and MERCOSUL's inauguration, trade among the partners increased from 8 to 20 percent, making the case for a subhemispheric common market stronger. After a rough start due to the Mexican peso crisis, the signatories reaffirmed their commitment to forge the common market. Efforts to remove gradually tariff protections and nontariff protections, such as regulations that slow the flow of trade, proceeded with few disruptions.

At the center of MERCOSUL's evolution is the long list of products that the CET targets. However, the signatories are allowed to exclude up to 300 items (399 in Paraguay) as exceptions to the CET. The partners also agreed to numerous dispute-resolution mechanisms to avoid conflicts that might threaten the free-trade group.

MERCOSUL is only the latest in a list of common market schemes in Latin America. In 1960, the Latin American Association of Free Trade (ALALC) initiated a process for forming a common market in twelve years. Although this goal was unfulfilled because of persistent differences among the group's members, intraregional trade increased from 7.7 percent in 1960 to 13.8 percent in 1980. Subhemispheric common market groups unconnected to ALALC also emerged as the Andean Group in 1969 (Bolivia, Colombia, Ecuador, and Venezuela) and the Central American Common Market in 1960 (Costa Rica, Guatemala, El Salvador, Honduras, and Nicaragua). ALALC was replaced in 1980 with the Latin American Integration Association (ALADI). Unlike ALALC's mission of forming a common market, ALADI's goal was to foster the formation of preferential trade agreements among subhemispheric groups. These efforts received their most important boost soon after the administration of George H. W. Bush delivered its Enterprise for the Americas Initiative (EAI) in 1990, a plan of lofty goals for hemispheric economic integration, which are being implemented now through the Free Trade Area of the Americas (FTAA). Soon after the EAI was announced, the existing regional groups and a new wave of other groups formed preferential organizations. Besides MERCOSUL, the most important of these was the North American Free Trade Agreement (NAFTA), initiated on January 1, 1994.

MERCOSUL differs from NAFTA in several ways. First, it is designed to be a common market among developing countries and not, as NAFTA is, a tripartite free-trade area organized to reduce tariffs primarily across the U.S.-Mexico border. Second, MERCOSUL can evolve in ways unimagined in NAFTA, such as the creation of a common currency. Finally, MERCOSUL can and has negotiated free-trade agreements with other global blocks such as the European Union (EU). This gives these four developing countries more leverage on the international level. Mexico's interests as a developing country are arguably not given the same priority by its trade partners in NAFTA.

MERCOSUL also differs markedly from the EU. Because the EU is a supranational organization, its members shift important sovereign areas of policy such as commercial; competition; increasingly justice and home affairs; and for the members of the euro zone, monetary policy to Brussels. The signatories of MERCOSUL do not envision more than a commercial and perhaps monetary agreement, and all this is negotiated multilaterally. MERCOSUL does not have an executive body such as the EU Commission that regulates the behavior of members. It has dispute resolution mechanisms, but nothing like the European Court of Justice whose decisions are binding on EU members.

Like its predecessors, MERCOSUL was a product and a cause of increased commercial

(continued)

integration among its signatories. Since its creation, MERCOSUL has contributed to a threefold increase in trade among its members. The common market, however, is in dire straits now in the wake of the Argentine financial crisis and continued economic instability in Brazil, Uruguay, and Paraguay. MERCOSUL is also at a crossroads regarding the role it will play in the continuing FTAA process. President Lula da Silva will likely attempt to use Brazil's leadership within

MERCOSUL to extract concessions from Washington on the type and pacing of trade liberalization in the hemisphere.

Source: Lia Valls Pereira, "Tratado de Assunção: Resultados e Perspectivas," in Antônio Salazar P. Brandão and Lia Valls Pereira, eds., *Mercosul: Perspectivas da Integração* (Rio de Janeiro: Fundação Getúlio Vargas, 1996), 11.

Section ③ Governance and Policy-Making

Organization of the State

The institutions of the Brazilian state have changed significantly since independence. Even so, a number of institutional legacies have endured and continue to shape Brazilian politics. The most important is the centralization of state authority in the executive. Paradoxically, a second legacy is the decentralized federal structure of the Brazilian state. The constitution of 1988 attempted to construct a new democratic order but left these contradictory tendencies in place. The president retained the authority to legislate on social and economic matters, but new powers governing the implementation of these policies were devolved to the state and municipal governments. As a result, the 1988 constitution was simultaneously the focus of much hope and intense attack. It was to be the governing document for the new democracy, but it became an instrument used to confound political and economic reform. Since it was the result of the bargaining of many different groups, it failed to provide a coherent vision of how institutions should be structured and what functions they should have. The separation of powers remains ill-defined, allowing ad hoc and informal arrangements to determine the boundaries of official authority.

Some generalizations about the organization of the Brazilian state can be made. First, the church and state are officially separated. The Catholic Church never controlled any portion of the state apparatus or directly influenced national politics as it did in other Catholic countries, including Spain. This does not mean, however, that the Catholic Church plays no role in Brazilian politics (see Section 4).

Second, Brazil has a presidential system of government. The directly elected president is the head of state, head of government, and commander in chief of the armed forces. The Brazilian state has traditionally placed vast power in the hands of the executive. Although the executive is one of three branches of government (the legislature and the judiciary being the other two), Brazilian presidents have traditionally been less bound by judicial and legislative constraints than their European or North American counterparts. Brazilian constitutions have granted the executive more discretion than the other branches in enforcing laws or in making policy. The legislature and the judiciary historically have played secondary roles.

The Brazilian state does not have the checks and balances of the U.S. government system. It differs also from the semipresidentialism of France. Brazil's executive and the bureaucracy manage most of the policymaking and implementation functions of government. Both the federal legislature and the state governments look to the president and, in economic matters, to the minister of the economy for leadership on policy. The heads of the key agencies of the economic bureaucracy—the ministers of the economy and of planning, the president of the Central Bank, and the head of the national development bank—have more discretion over the details of policy than the president does. Although some Brazilian presidents have delegated less to bureaucratic agencies, recent presidents have had little choice but to delegate, given the growing complexity of economic and social policy. Ultimate authority nevertheless remains in the hands of the president, who may replace the cabinet ministers.

Although the Brazilian president is the dominant player among the three branches of government, the powers of the legislature and the judiciary are becoming stronger. Since the transition to democratic rule in 1985, these institutions have become critical to democracy. The 1988 constitution gave many oversight functions to the legislature and judiciary, so that much presidential discretion in economic and social policy is now subject to approval by either the legislature or the judiciary, or both. This gives these branches of government some independence and leverage over the presidency, although this power is not often employed effectively. Centralizing traditions are still strong in Brazil, making the obstacles to the deconcentration of executive power enormous.

A third generalization that may be offered on the Brazilian state is that it is decentralized. Like Germany, Mexico, India, and the United States, the Brazilian state has a federal structure. The country's 26 states are divided into 5,500 municipal governments. Most of the country's presidents have relied on subnational bases of power to stay in office. The presidents of the Old Republic and even Getúlio Vargas counted on the support of local clientelist political machines led by self-interested governors and mayors.

With the transition to democracy, these "barons of the federation," as one study calls them, became a crucial source of political support for legislators as well as presidents.[29] By controlling indispensable reservoirs of patronage through their powers of appointment and spending, governors and even some mayors can wield extraordinary influence. In recent years,

attempts to mollify this subnational constituency have watered down key pieces of reform legislation.

Seen as a whole, political decentralization, which was accelerated with the constitution of 1988, has further fragmented the Brazilian polity. At the same time, some subnational governments have become an important source of innovative policymaking.[30] Average Brazilian citizens have more access to their municipal and state governments than they do to their federal representatives, which suggests that decentralization may eventually strengthen democracy by making political elites more accountable to their local constituencies.

The Executive

A majority of delegates to the 1987 National Constituent Assembly that drafted the new democratic constitution favored the creation of a parliamentary system. President Sarney, who did not want to see his powers reduced, used his support among the governors to lobby against the parliamentary option. The best he could do was force the members of the assembly to defer the issue to a plebiscite in 1993. Yet the plebiscite, envisioned by the Constitution's Framers as the climactic event that would determine Brazil's political structure, ended by giving a stamp of approval to the existing presidential system.

In 1993, the campaign to retain presidentialism succeeded in convincing people that the parliamentary option was little more than a trick to "take the right to vote away from the people." The concept of a parliamentary system that would allow a prime minister to be elected by legislative elites and not directly by the citizenry seemed contrary to what Brazilians had fought for during the long struggle for democracy. Brazilians did not want to lose the ultimate check on the presidency: direct elections by voters every four years. Popular elections will now present a crucial test for presidents wishing to pursue their agendas for another four years.

If parliamentary government seemed a far-off goal, rules designed to rein in the power of the federal executive still found their way into the 1988 constitution. In part as a reaction to the extreme centralization of executive authority during military rule, the delegates restored some of the congressional prerogatives that existed prior to 1964, and they granted new ones. Among the new ones were oversight over economic policy and the right of consultation on executive appointments. Executive decrees, which allowed the president to legislate directly, were replaced by "provisional measures" (MPs) (also known as "emergency measures"). MPs preserved the president's power to legislate for thirty days, at the end of which congress can pass, reject, or allow the provisional law to expire. President Sarney and his successors got around this restriction by reissuing their "provisional measures" indefinitely; yet to become law, they would need to survive a two-thirds vote of both houses of the congress. Finally, the 1988 constitution limited the president to a single term, a provision common to Latin American constitutions. In 1997, however, Cardoso succeeded in passing a constitutional amendment that removed the one-term rule, allowing him and twenty-two governors to run again in 1998. This expansion of presidential power was later met with a restriction on the power to reissue provisional measures, which both houses of Congress passed in 2001.

Despite these new constraints, Brazilian presidents were still able to use emergency measures with considerable success because of the sorry state of the economy. Given crisis conditions, how could Congress deny the president the right to railroad through much-needed reform legislation? Some presidents articulated such arguments with great frequency. Collor, for example, severely abused these powers. In his first year in office, Collor handed down 150 emergency measures. Technically, this meant that the country experienced a crisis situation every forty-eight hours.[31] Worse still, the Supreme Tribunal, the highest court in Brazil, did little to curb this obvious abuse of constitutional authority by the president. The use of presidential discretionary power has only reinforced the powers of the executive to legislate.[32] Even with the restrictions passed in 2001, over 80 percent of all legislation originates in the executive branch.

The president also retains extremely valuable powers of appointment over the huge Brazilian bureaucracy, particularly at the ministerial level. Among them are broad powers to select and dismiss close associates and select ministers for the armed forces according to the merit system prevailing in their respective branches. For most other positions, the president usually appoints ministers from groups of his long-time cronies and collaborators, or from any of the existing parties. Although these appointees are not as cohesive a group as the presidential *camarillas* in Mexico, the close-knit and often personal networks binding the Mexican president and his chief ministers and advisors, this comparison illustrates the importance of personal ties to the president in Brazil. Under the 1988 constitution, the president must negotiate with congress and some powerful groups (such as business associations, labor unions, bar associations) over certain positions in the cabinet, mainly those responsible for economic policymaking. Presidential appointments are also often crafted to reward or entice the leaders of parties in Congress to support the executive's reform agenda.

Among the chief cabinet posts, the ministries of Economy (also called Finance during certain administrations) and Planning have had extraordinary influence. Since the beginning of the military governments, the Ministry of Economy has had more authority than any other executive agency of the state. These powers grew in response to the economic problems of the 1980s and the reform agenda of the 1990s. As a result of their control of the federal budget and the details of economic policy, recent ministers of the economy have had levels of authority typical of a prime minister in a parliamentary system. For example, the success of Cardoso in the 1994 presidential campaign was due in large part to his effective performance as Itamar Franco's minister of economy.

The Bureaucracy: State and Semipublic Firms

Bureaucratic agencies and public firms have played key roles in Brazilian economic and political development during the twentieth century. After 1940, the state created a large number of new agencies and public enterprises. Many of these entities were allowed to accumulate their own debt and plan development projects without undue influence from central ministries or politicians. Public firms became a key part of the triple alliance of state, foreign, and domestic capital that governed the state-led model of development. Yet it was the state that dominated this alliance. By 1981, ten of the top twenty-five enterprises in Brazil were owned by the federal government, and eight others were owned by state governments. Public expenditures as a share of GDP increased from 16 percent in 1947 to more than 32 percent in 1969, far higher than in any other Latin American country except socialist Cuba.[33]

Much of this spending (and the huge debt that financed it) was concentrated on development projects, many of gigantic proportions. Key examples include the world's largest hydroelectric plant, Itaipú; Petrobrás's petroleum processing centers; and steel mills such as the gargantuan National Steel Company in Volta Redonda, Rio de Janeiro; and Vale do Rio Doce, which maintains interests in sectors as diverse as mining, transport, paper, and textiles. Under the past three military governments (Médici, Geisel, and Figueiredo), dozens of other projects were completed, including the trans-Amazonian highway, the Tucuruí hydroelectric plants, the Açominas metallurgy park, and the National Nuclear Reactor Program. These and hundreds of more modest projects accounted for much of the country's industrial production. On the eve of the debt crisis in 1982, the top thirty-three projects, including those just listed, absorbed US$88 billion in external debt, employed 1.5 million people, and added $47 billion to the GDP.

Managing the planning and finance of these projects required enormous skill. Several public agencies were responsible, but the National Bank for Economic and Social Development (*Banco Nacional de Desenvolvimento Economico e Social,* or BNDES) stands out as an important coordinator. Founded by Vargas in the early 1950s, the BNDES played a key role in channeling public funds to industrial projects. Among the bank's greatest achievements was the creation of an automobile sector based on subsidized public steel; foreign assemblers such as Ford, General Motors, and Volkswagen; and domestic suppliers of parts and labor. Under President Juscelino Kubitschek, the BNDES implemented an industrial policy in automobiles called the Plan of Goals (*Plano de Metas*), which coordinated domestic and international resources to create the largest automobile industry in Latin America.[34]

The experience of the BNDES demonstrated that despite Brazil's clientelist legacies, the Brazilian bureaucracy could function effectively. Meritocratic advancement and professional recruitment granted these agencies some autonomy from political manipulation.

Such agencies were considered islands of efficiency in a state apparatus characterized by patronage and corruption.[35]

Other state and semipublic firms, however, were rife with clientelism. Civilian and military leaders often appointed their supporters as the heads of these enterprises, positions with quite generous salary and retirement packages. Many public firm managers took advantage of their positions to dole out government contracts to associates and even to their own companies in the private sector.

The fiscal crisis of the 1980s put severe strains on the entire economic bureaucracy, but some things failed to change. The 1988 constitution did not alter significantly the concentration of power in the economic bureaucracy that made developmentalism with clientelism possible. In fact, the new constitution reinforced certain bureaucratic monopolies by codifying them as rights. For example, the state's control over petroleum, natural gas, the exploration of minerals, nuclear energy, and telecommunications was protected constitutionally. These sectors could not be privatized, much less sold to foreign governments or multinational companies.

What the writers of the new constitution did do in response to the fiscal crisis was place new restraints on the activity of state-directed industries. The fiscal independence of state firms was curtailed with restrictions on the amount of debt they could incur. The constitution imposed additional obstacles to the creation of public firms, including the requirement that congress approve any new state enterprises proposed by the executive branch.

Some of the constitutional protections of the public firms lasted only a few years. After his election in 1989, Fernando Collor began a sweeping reform of Brazil's public bureaucracy, beginning with the privatization of large public firms in steel, chemicals, and mining. In 1990, his government launched the National Destatization Program (*Programa Nacional de Destatização,* PND). Under the PND, more than US$39 billion in public firms were sold ($8.5 billion in the steel sector alone) by 2004. Although the program slowed under the Franco administration, the Cardoso administration went even further. The government convinced the Congress to amend the constitution to remove the public monopoly on petroleum refining, telecommunications, and infrastructure, making these sectors available for auction. Electricity distribution, cellular phone bands, and the octopus-like structure of Vale were put up for privatization. In 1998, much of the public telecommunications sector was privatized, bringing in about $24 billion.

Paradoxically, the agency at the center of the privatization process in Brazil is the BNDES, which is also the agency most responsible for developmentalism. Faced with the fiscal crisis of the 1980s, BNDES managers adopted a new perspective on the state's role in the economy. Instead of targeting industries and spending large sums to promote them, its new mission was to provide financing to productivity-enhancing investments such as new technology and labor retraining, outlays that promise to make firms soon to be privatized and already privatized more competitive in international markets.[36] As a result, the economic bureaucracy in Brazil continues to play a crucial role in the country's development.

The Military and the Police

The military is another significant arm of the state. Like many other South American militaries, the Brazilian armed forces retain substantial independence from civilian presidents and legislators. Brazil has suffered numerous coups; those in 1930 and 1964 were critical junctures, while others brought in care-taker governments that eventually ceded to civilian rule. Although the military's grip on power was never as tight as in Argentina during the murderous "Dirty War" governments (1976–1983), the generals have maintained influence in Brazilian politics, blocking policies they do not like and lobbying on behalf of those they favor.

The military's participation in Brazilian politics became more limited, if still quite expansive, following the transition to democracy. Several laws governing areas of policymaking affecting the armed forces gave the military broad prerogatives to "guarantee internal order" and to play a "tutelary role" in civilian government. During the Sarney administration, members of the armed forces retained cabinet-level rank in areas of importance to the military, such as the ministries of the armed forces and the nuclear program. Military officers also kept middle- and lower-level positions in public firms and bureaucratic agencies. Most important, the armed forces were successful in securing amnesty for human rights abuses committed during the preceding authoritarian regime. In an effort to professionalize the armed forces and keep them in the barracks, the Collor government slashed the military budget, which reduced the resource autonomy the military enjoyed during the authoritarian period. Collor also replaced the top generals with officers who had few or no connections to the authoritarian regime and were committed to civilian leadership. Collor's reforms were helped by the decline of the country's arms industry, which lost key markets for ordnance, tanks, and guns in the Middle East during the 1980s. The collapse and privatization of these military industries gave civilians more control over the generals.[37] One recent test of civilian authority was the successful removal of the commandant of the Brazilian Air Force, Brigadier Walter Werner Bräuer, for alleged involvement in drug trafficking, money laundering, and organized crime activities. Despite public demonstrations by air force officers supporting Bräuer, congressional investigations continued, and the general was dismissed at the end of 1999.

The military police are only nominally controlled by state governors; they are trained, equipped, and managed by the armed forces, which also maintain a separate judicial system to try officers for wrong-doing. The state police consists of two forces: the civil police force, which acts as an investigative unit and is not completely uniformed, and the uniformed military police force, which maintains order.

During the 1990s, economic crisis and press coverage made urban crime one of the most important political issues facing the country. Perhaps the most telling indicator of the rising level of violence is the fact that over fifty mayors were assassinated in Brazil between 1990 and 2000. Murders, kidnappings, rapes, and violent robberies are the talk of nightly news programs, and these subjects often dominate citizens' lists of chief concerns.

The specter of criminal violence has shocked Brazilians into voting for politicians who promise them better police security. Yet as more attention has focused on the use of police resources, Brazilians have learned that these forces themselves are often part of the problem. Despite official oversight of police authorities, in practice the military and civil police forces in many cities of the northeast, in São

Paulo, and in Rio de Janeiro often act abusively. Cases of arbitrary detention, torture, corruption, and systematic killings by Brazilian police have received much international attention. Human rights investigations have found that off-duty police officers are regularly hired by merchants and assorted thugs to kill street urchins whom they accuse of theft. One study in Rio de Janeiro between 1993 and 1996 showed that police officers shoot to kill rather than to disable.[38] The majority of victims were shot in the shoulders or the head; in 40 of the 697 cases, the victims were shot in the back of the head in gangland execution style. The victims were mostly young black men and boys, and had no criminal records whatsoever. Other studies have shown that at least 10 percent of the homicides in Rio de Janeiro and São Paulo are committed by the police.[39] That is double the rate of any U.S. city.

The federal police force is a small unit of approximately 3,000 people. It operates like a combined U.S. Federal Bureau of Investigation, Secret Service, Drug Enforcement Agency, and Immigration and Naturalization Service. Under the authority of the executive, the federal police are responsible for providing security to public officials, cracking down on drug rings, administering customs regulations, and investigating federal crimes. The demands placed on this single agency have caused some Brazilian politicians to propose that the federal police be split up into more specialized units, as in the U.S. system.

Other State Institutions

The Judiciary

The Brazilian judiciary is composed of a network of state courts, which have jurisdiction over state matters, and a federal court system, not unlike the one in the United States, which maintains jurisdiction over federal crimes. A supreme court (the Supreme Federal Tribunal), similar in jurisdiction to the U.S. Supreme Court but lacking a clear judicial review authority over the other branches of government, acts as the final arbiter of court cases. The eleven justices are appointed by the president and confirmed by an absolute majority of the Senate. The Superior Court of Justice, with thirty-three sitting justices, operates under the Supreme Federal Tribunal as an appeals

court. Matters requiring interpretation of the Constitution go to the Supreme Federal Tribunal. The military maintains its own court system. Most judges in the Brazilian judicial system serve for life.

The judiciary is designed to adjudicate political conflicts as well as civil and social conflicts. The Electoral Supreme Tribunal (*Tribunal Supremo Electoral,* TSE) has exclusive responsibility for the organization and oversight of all issues related to voting. The seven-member TSE is composed of three justices elected from the members of the Supreme Federal Tribunal, two from the Superior Court of Justice, and two nominated by the president from a group of six attorneys of notable ability who are selected by the Supreme Federal Tribunal. The seven justices on the TSE serve for two years, and they have the power to investigate charges of political bias by public employees, file criminal charges against persons violating electoral laws, and scrutinize and validate electoral results. In addition to these constitutional provisions, under electoral law and its own regulations, the TSE monitors the legal compliance of electoral campaigns and executive neutrality in campaigns. The integrity of the tribunal in the conduct of elections has remained very high, making fraud relatively rare in national elections. The TSE is assisted in this process by a system of regional electoral courts that oversee local elections.

As in the rest of Latin America, penal codes established by legislation govern the powers of judges. This makes the judiciary less flexible than its North American counterparts, which operate on case law, but it provides a more effective barrier against judicial activism—the tendency of the courts to render broad interpretations of the law. The main problem in the Brazilian system has been the lack of judicial review. Lower courts are not obliged to follow the precedents of the STF or STJ. The judicial branch is independent from politics but its various courts can be too independent of one another, making for an ambiguous structure of judicial oversight.

In recent years, the judiciary has been severely criticized for its perceived unresponsiveness to Brazil's social problems and the persistent corruption in the lower courts. These problems are particularly apparent in rural areas, where impoverished defendants are often denied the right to a fair trial by powerful landowners, who have undue influence over judges and procedures. Children are especially victimized; courts have refused to hear cases prosecuting those who profit from child prostitution, pornography, and murder of street urchins.

Official corruption in the judiciary is an important and high-profile issue. The federal police initiated "Operation Anaconda" in São Paulo in 2003 to root out corrupt judges who sold writs of habeas corpus and other "services" to defendants. The operation exposed a crime ring implicating eleven federal judges, police officers, and other agents of the court system. Such events escalated tensions between the presidency and the judiciary. Lula retained the upper hand in that struggle as opinion surveys showed that the judiciary is considered the most corrupt and least reliable of institutions in Brazil. But the president's fortunes changed in 2005 when allegations by one political party leader associated with the government accused leaders of the PT, many with offices in the presidential palace, of bribing legislators for their votes in Congress.

A more everyday indicator of systemic corruption is the difficulty that citizens face in prosecuting the police. In the state of Rio de Janeiro, between January 1996 and July 1997, 68 percent of cases in military court involving the police were withdrawn without a hearing because of insufficient evidence (which is often destroyed by the police) or because of the police's favorite excuse: that the defendant was injured or killed "while resisting arrest." Although federal legislation in 1996 granted civil courts jurisdiction over such matters, paradoxically the power to investigate these crimes was left in the hands of the police.

The Supreme Tribunal's reluctance to act on these matters leaves little hope for change in the short term. Judicial reform has thus far focused on beefing up the Supreme Tribunal's judicial review functions, avoiding the more difficult question of restructuring the judiciary to eliminate corruption.

Restructuring of the judiciary continues to receive attention. Proposals for reform include subjecting judges to external control through periodic elections. Members of the judiciary deeply resent and fear such a prospect. They argue that it would push the institution into the kind of partisanship that has marred policy debates on key social and political issues. Others view the structure of the judiciary and its approach to interpreting and implementing laws as the central obstacles to accomplishing policy goals. Like the Brazilian bureaucracy, the judiciary has a complex structure, with multiple jurisdictions at different levels of government. The problems inherent in this complex network of adjudication were made clear during the privatization of Vale, when opposition groups in different states and jurisdictions were able to use the local courts to create numerous obstacles to the sale.

Subnational Government

The structure of subnational politics in Brazil consists of a governor; his chief advisers, who also usually lead key secretariats such as economy and planning; and a unicameral legislature, which is often dominated by the supporters of the governor. Governors are elected to four-year terms and, under the 1997 amendment of the 1988 constitution, may run for a second term.

State and municipal governments wield tremendous influence in Brazilian politics. Since the days of the Old Republic, governors and mayors have been essential sources of support for presidents and federal legislators. This "politics of the governors" expanded with the transition to democracy. The 1982 elections created the first opportunity since the inauguration of the military regime for Brazilians to elect their governors directly, which made these subnational politicians crucial standard-bearers of the transition. This lent legitimacy to the governors' campaign to decentralize fiscal resources in the form of taxes and federal transfers.

The 1988 constitution provided much of what the governors and mayors wanted. First, the states and municipalities were promised a larger share of tax revenues. At the same time, however, the governors and mayors were successful in deflecting Brasília's attempts to devolve additional spending responsibilities to subnational government, particularly in the areas of education, health, and infrastructure. The governors also proved successful in protecting state banks from a major overhaul, which was greatly needed, given that these financial institutions continued to fund irresponsible subnational spending by accumulating huge debts that the federal government agreed to roll over.

During the Collor administration, the federal government began to regain much of the fiscal authority it had lost to the states and municipalities. The Central Bank made good on its threats to intervene in bankrupt state banks and to privatize them. The federal government also refused to roll over state debt without a promise of reform, including the privatization of money-losing utility companies. The Cardoso administration required states and municipalities to finance a larger share of social spending, including education and health care. At the same time, new legislation empowered Brasília to claim more discretionary authority over fiscal transfers and tax revenues that had previously devolved to subnational governments.

Despite these efforts, Brazilian presidents must continue to negotiate the terms of reform with governors as much as with the congress. Lula met with the twenty-seven governors repeatedly during 2003 and 2004 to work out the details of fiscal reform. One of the reasons why the supposed savings his reform created were limited was that the president had to concede shares of new taxes and cede control of some state revenues that might otherwise have been used to contain spending and reduce the mounting federal debt.

Although most subnational politics are still preoccupied with the distribution of political favors in return for fiscal rewards, certain governors and mayors have devised innovative solutions to Brazil's social and economic problems. One recent study of the state of Ceará in the poor northern region has demonstrated that even the most underdeveloped subnational governments can produce important policies to promote industrial investment, employment, and social services.[40] Mayors affiliated with Lula's PT have had much electoral success (more than doubling their number between 2000 and 2004 to lead 411 cities) based on a solid record of effective local government. Such examples are a reminder that the quality of political leadership matters greatly in determining how well subnational governments are run.

The Policy-Making Process

Although policy-making continues to be fluid and ambiguous in Brazil, certain domains of policy are clearly demarcated. Foreign policy, for example, is exclusively within the purview of the executive branch. Political parties and the Congress in general still have only inconsistent power over investment policies. Because most legislation originates in the executive branch, bureaucratic agencies retain command over the details of social and economic policies.

The process of making policy in Brazil can be characterized by one common quality: the tendency of clientelism to inject itself at every stage, from formulation and decision making to implementation. Established personal contacts often shape who benefits from policymaking, a hallmark of clientelistic practice. Quid pro quos, nepotism, and other kinds of favoritism, if not outright corruption, regularly obstruct or distort policymaking.[41] For example, politicians often give radio station licenses to their cronies in return for favorable political coverage.

Complex formal and informal networks linking the political executive, key agencies of the bureaucracy, and private interests tend to be the chief players in clientelist circles. One of Cardoso's contributions to sociology before he became involved in Brazilian politics was his characterization of these clientelistic networks as **bureaucratic rings.** For Cardoso, the Brazilian state is highly permeable, fragmented, and therefore easily colonized by private interests that make alliances with mid-level bureaucratic officers. By shaping public policy to benefit these interests, bureaucrats gain the promise of future employment in the private sector. While in positions of responsibility, bureaucratic rings are ardent defenders of their own interests. Because they are entrenched and well connected throughout the Brazilian bureaucracy, few policies can be implemented without the resources and support of the most powerful bureaucratic rings. These rings represent one of the most enduring forms of established clientelistic exchange in the Brazilian state.

One example of the role of bureaucratic rings is the creation of large development projects. The politics surrounding these decisions were often intense. Governors and mayors wanted lucrative public projects to be placed in their jurisdictions; private contractors yearned for the state's business; and politicians positioned themselves for all the attendant kickbacks, political and pecuniary.[42] Although the days of huge development projects are over, the public sector still formulates policy and allocates resources under the influence of bureaucratic rings.

Among the key sources of influence external to the state is organized business. Unlike business associations in some Asian and West European countries, Brazilian business groups have remained independent of corporatist ties to the state. There is no Brazilian version of the French agricultural association *Fédération Nationale des Syndicats d'Exploitants Agricoles* (FNSEA) or the para-public institutions of the Federal Republic of Germany. Business associations have also remained aloof from political parties. Brazil has nothing akin to Mexico's National Action Party (*Partido Acción Nacional,* or PAN), a party that claims to represent a large portion of the business class. That does not mean, however, that Brazilian business interests are not organized. Lobbying by Brazilian entrepreneurs is common, and their participation in bureaucratic rings is legendary. Few major economic policies are passed without the input of the Federation of São Paulo Industries (*Federação das Industrias do Estado de São Paulo,* or FIESP). Other business groups, some that have broken off from FIESP, continue to defend their interests energetically as Brazil reforms its economy.

The country's labor confederations and unions have had less consistent access to policymaking. Although unions were once directly organized and manipulated by the corporatist state, they gained autonomy in the late 1970s and the 1980s. From then on, they sought leverage over policymaking through outside channels, such as the link between the *Central Única dos Trabalhadores* (CUT, Workers' Singular Peak Association) and Lula da Silva's Workers' Party. Attempts to bring labor formally into direct negotiations with business and the state have failed. Shortly after assuming power, Sarney initiated talks among business, government, and representatives of the major labor federations. These talks quickly broke down. Widening cleavages within the Brazilian union movement tended to split sectors of organized labor, causing some segments to refuse to be bound by any agreement. Later, during the Collor administration, a second attempt at tripartite negotiation, called the "sectoral chambers," took place in the São Paulo automotive sector. These talks produced some noteworthy accords, but the chambers did not last because of opposition from the Ministry of Economy and other agencies. These experiences contrast sharply with the legacy of co-determination in Germany and other formulas for maintaining collective bargaining with state mediation in West European countries.

Policy implementation is also highly politicized. Debate and lobbying do not stop in Brazil once laws are enacted. Policy implementation is a subject of perpetual bargaining. One popular phrase, *o jeito brasileiro* ("the Brazilian way"), captures this aspect of Brazilian politics.[43] The Brazilian way is to scoff at the law and find a way around it. If one wants to get something without really paying for it, one asks for a *jeito*—a momentary suspension or exception to the rules. Paradoxically, *jeito* can be the source of great efficiency in Brazilian society, but it carries a heavy price in that the rule of law is not respected. Therefore, reform of the policymaking process will require more than restrictions on clientelism and legislative and judicial oversight of suspected bureaucratic rings. It will require a shift in thinking about the role of law in Brazilian society.

Section ❹ Representation and Participation

The most enduring aspect of contemporary Brazilian political institutions is the capacity of minority interests to block institutional change. The fragmentation of legislative politics, the weaknesses of political parties, and the interests of particular politicians and their clientelistic allies make enacting reform on behalf of the national interest extremely difficult. Getting things done involves the political use of public resources. Politicians and parties that are most capable of dispensing patronage and cultivating clientele networks are the most successful in the Brazilian system. While this benefits some voters who are the periodic recipients of these favors and resources, more often than not, the main beneficiaries are a small number of elite economic and political interests who develop ongoing relationships with legislators, governors, and presidents. Representation, therefore, is weak in Brazil.

The transition to democracy, however, coincided with an explosion of civil society activism and mobilization. The expansion of voting rights and the involvement of gender and ethnic groups, urban social movements, and environmental and religious organizations in Brazilian politics expanded greatly the range of political participation. Nonetheless, political institutions up to this point in Brazilian political history have failed to reconcile these contradictory forces between the deficiencies of representation and the expansion of political participation.

The Legislature

The 594-member national legislature is bicameral, consisting of an upper house, the Senate with 81 members, and a lower house, the Chamber of Deputies with 513 members. Each state and the federal district elects three senators by simple majority. Senators serve for eight-year terms and may be reelected without limits. Two-thirds of the Senate is elected at one time, and the remaining one-third is elected four years later. Senatorial elections are held concurrently with those for the Chamber of Deputies, which places all of its seats up for election after each four-year cycle. Federal deputies may be reelected without limits. The number of members in the Chamber of Deputies is, in theory, proportional to the population of each state and the federal district. Each state is allowed a minimum of eight and a maximum of seventy deputies, regardless of population.

Both houses of the legislature have equal authority to make laws. In all cases, each chamber can propose or veto legislation passed by the other. Bills go back and forth between houses without going through a conference committee of the two chambers, as in the United States. Once the bill is passed by both houses, the president may sign it into law, reject it as a whole, or reject it in part. The legislature can override a presidential veto with a majority of the vote in both houses during a joint session, but such instances are rare. Constitutional amendments must be passed twice by three-fifths of the votes in each house of congress. Amendments may also be passed by an absolute majority in a special unicameral constituent assembly proposed by the president and created by both houses

of congress. The Senate retains authority to try the president and other top officials, including the vice president and key ministers and justices, for impeachable offenses. It also has the power to approve appointments to high offices, including justices of the high courts, heads of diplomatic missions, and the directors of the Central Bank.

Complex constitutional rules for determining representation in the legislature favor sparsely populated states, especially in the north. Because these states are the most numerous in the federal system, voters from small states tend to be overrepresented in the legislature by as much as 33 times more per voter than are voters in São Paulo. If seats were allocated on a strictly proportional order, then São Paulo should have 114 seats and Roraima would have one. Instead, São Paulo has seventy and Roraima has eight. The least populated states are also the poorest and most rural in Brazil. Typically, they have been political bases for conservative landowning interests and, more recently, agribusiness. After 1964 the military cultivated support among conservative rural groups by granting statehood to sparsely populated territories in the north and northeast, reinforcing their overrepresentation in the Chamber. These precedents continued into the democratic period and largely explain why conservative landowners and agribusiness elites maintain positions of great influence in the Brazilian congress.

In contrast to the presidency, the Brazilian legislature has rarely played a dominant role in the country's politics. In part, that is due to the ability of the president to impose policy through corporatism and populism. However, the congress must accept some of the blame. Many senators and deputies are more interested in cultivating and dispensing patronage than in representing and being accountable to the voters. As a result, representatives have never organized their parties or large segments of the population in support of national policy. Only the rarest of exceptions exist to this rule of Brazilian congressional politics.

Legislators view their service primarily as a means to enhance their own income with generous public pensions and through kickbacks earned in the dispensing of political favors. Election to the federal legislature is often used as a steppingstone to even more lucrative, especially executive, posts.[44] After the presidency, the governorships of the industrialized states are the most coveted positions. Appointment to head any of the premier ministries and state firms also ranks high, since these are choice positions from which to distribute and receive favors. Although many members of congress are independently wealthy, most come from the middle or upper middle classes; most of these have much to gain from appointment to well-paid posts in the executive and the para-statal enterprises. Ethnic minorities and women are poorly represented in their ranks. A mere 3 percent of seats in the congress are held by Afro-Brazilians. Only 6 percent of the seats in the Chamber and 7 percent of those in the Senate are held by women. Lula's cabinet includes three women from the PT.

The Congress has largely failed to use the expanded powers granted by the 1988 constitution. Lack of a quorum to vote is a frequent problem, and recently acquired powers have provided greater opportunities for some legislators to practice corruption and backroom dealing, conditions that have helped to break down party loyalties and reinforce the self-serving nature of congressional politics. The many deficiencies of the Brazilian legislature were magnified in recent years by several corruption scandals. Before 2005, the most serious case involved a handful of senators and deputies who were accused of embezzling from regional development projects or directly from the national treasury. Now that the Lula government has been targeted for corrupt dealings with legislators, the Congress has once again been criticized for its lack of accountability.

One response to legislative corruption has been to use parliamentary commissions of inquiry to review cases of malfeasance by elected officials. Testimony before a congressional commission by the party leader making the most sweeping accusations of bribery against the Lula government enraptured the nation during the summer of 2005. Although these temporary committees have demonstrated some influence, most notably the parliamentary commission of inquiry that investigated Collor and recommended his impeachment, they have not always produced results. The temporary committees work alongside sixteen permanent legislative committees that treat issues as diverse as taxation and human rights. These committees, however, are not nearly as strong as the major

committees in the U.S. Congress. Due to the self-interested focus of Brazilian politicians and the related weakness of political parties, legislative committees, both temporary and permanent, often fail to conclude an investigation or find solutions to persistent dilemmas in policy.

Political Parties and the Party System

The Brazilian political party system is one of the most mercurial in the world. Party names, affiliations, and the structure of party alliances are constantly in flux. This is nothing new in Brazilian political history. Like many of the country's current problems, party instability stretches back to the New State of Getúlio Vargas and the centralization of politics in the Brazilian state. State corporatism and populism were hostile to the development of independent party organizations. Political parties, when they did emerge, were created by state managers. Populist redistribution reinforced these tendencies, as workers and the middle class became accustomed to asking what they would receive from a politician in return for support. Except for members of the Communist Party and other extreme organizations, Brazilian voters did not develop a strong sense of political identity linked to established parties.

Many of the traditional weaknesses of the party system were reinforced after the transition to democracy, making parties even more anemic. The rules governing the party system made it easier for politicians to switch parties, virtually at will. A distinguished analyst of Brazilian politics, Scott Mainwaring, found that the 559 representatives of the 1987–1991 legislature had belonged to an average of over three parties during the five years of the legislature.[45] Politicians switched parties to increase their access to patronage. The rules of the electoral system even created incentives for politicians to ignore party labels. Brazil's experience with **proportional representation (PR),** which is used to elect federal and state deputies, is particularly important in this regard. (See "Institutional Intricacies: Proportional Representation.")

Brazil's mix of presidentialism and multiparty democracy creates other problems for the country's system of representation. Given the political fragmentation of the legislature and the weakness of the party

Institutional Intricacies: *Proportional Representation*

Proportional representation was introduced in Brazil in 1932 and was later reaffirmed by the military governments. Unlike Mexico, Britain, and the United States, but like many of the European parliamentary democracies, Brazil is divided into electoral districts that choose more than one representative. The ability to choose more than one representative means that a broader range of voices may be heard in elected offices.

Minority parties can make alliances to pass the threshold of votes needed to achieve representation. Proportional representation may be based on either a closed-list or an open-list system. In a closed-list PR, the party selects the order of politicians, and voters cannot cross party lines. Because voters are effectively choosing the party that best represents them, this system encourages party loyalty among both the electorate and individual politicians. In an open-list PR system, the voters have more discretion and can cross party lines. Brazil's PR system is open-list. Voters cast single ballots for either a party label, which adds to the party's total for determining representation, or for individuals. No names appear on Brazilian ballots, so voters must write in their choices.

Electoral districts for the election of state and federal deputies are entire states in Brazil. In any given election, there may be between six and seventy federal deputies and from twelve to eighty-four state deputies running for office. With few limits on how many individuals and parties may run in the same electoral district, crowded fields discourage party loyalty and emphasize the personal qualities of candidates, who must stand out in the minds of voters. Party affiliations do little to reduce the confusion of the average Brazilian voter as he or she is confronted with dozens of names for each position. Worse still, the open-list

PR system creates incentives for politicians to ignore party labels, because voters can cross party lines with ease. That even leads to politicians from the same party running against each other for the same position within a district.

Open-list proportional representation explains why there are so many parties in Brazil. With so much emphasis on the personal qualities of politicians, ambitious individuals can ignore the established party hierarchies while achieving elected office. They need only create their own parties or form alliances to get on the ballot and gain enough votes to qualify for representation. As a result, Brazil has the most fragmented party system in Latin America and one of the most fragmented in the world.

As if the open-list PR system were not distorting enough, Brazilian electoral law also allows incumbents to keep their party affiliation and remain on the ballot for the next election. This provision strips political parties of any control over their members: an incumbent may ignore the party's interests while in office but still must be kept on the ballot during the next contest.

Brazil's electoral system differs from other open-list proportional representation systems in that state, not national, parties select legislative candidates. In most cases, Brazilian governors exert tremendous influence over who can be elected. This further weakens national party leaders, who remain beholden to governors who can reward them with supportive nominees or rivals.

Source: Scott Mainwaring, "Brazil: Weak Parties, Feckless Democracy," in Scott Mainwaring and Timothy R. Scully, eds., *Building Democratic Institutions: Party Systems in Latin America* (Stanford, Calif., Stanford University Press, 1995), 375.

system, presidents are unable to maintain majority alliances in congress, a requirement for stability in a multiparty system. In parliamentary systems, the party in power has an absolute majority or stands at the head of an alliance of parties that compose a majority. As a result, the ruling party or alliance can implement a programmatic approach to legislation. By contrast, in Brazil the president has never been able to maintain a supraparty alliance in congress. More often, Brazilian presidents have attempted to govern above parties, dispensing favors to key congressional politicians to get legislation approved. Alternatively, presidents have not been shy about railroading reform through congress by using their discretionary authorities. As Timothy Power, a scholar of presidential authority in Brazil, has noted, "The [presidential] pen is mightier than the congress."[46]

In the midst of Brazil's confusing party system, a number of political organizations have emerged over the last few years. These parties can be defined ideologically, although the categories are not as internally consistent or as cut and dry as they might seem (see Table 4). Brazilian political parties are internally eclectic.

Political parties on the right currently defend neoliberal economic policies designed to shrink the size of the public sector. They support the reduction and partial privatization of the welfare state. A majority advocate a liberal trade policy and support Mercosul, but a substantial minority press for protectionism and the continuation of subsidies, particularly in agriculture. No party of the right has yet emerged as a solid defender of neoliberal restructuring of the economy, although scholars have detected a significant trend in favor of these policies among the parties on the right. On constitutional reform, right-wing parties are fairly united in favor of rolling back social spending; they also advocate electoral reform—specifically, the establishment of a majority or mixed, rather than purely proportional, district voting system, although this is contentious within the rightist cohort.

A loose set of conservative parties currently struggles for the mantle of the right. In front of the pack is the PFL (Party of the Liberal Front), one of the largest parties in the Senate and the Chamber and an organization that generally is in opposition to President Lula. Many small parties with low to moderate levels of representation in congress ally themselves with right-wing and center-right parties or advocate right-wing issues; the Brazilian Labor Party (PTB), the Brazilian Progressive Party (PPB), and the evangelistic Liberal Party (PL) are examples.

The two other large parties in congress are the PMDB (Party of the Brazilian Democratic Movement, the successor to the old MDB) and the PSDB (the Party of Brazilian Social Democracy, originally an offshoot

Table 4

The Democratic Idea: The Major Parties in Brazil

Conservative/Right-Wing Parties

PFL: *Partido da Frente Liberal* (Party of the Liberal Front)

PL: *Partido Liberal* (Liberal Party)

PPB: *Partido Progressista Brasileiro* (Brazilian Progressive Party)

Centrist Parties

PMDB: *Partido do Movimento Democrático Brasileiro* (Party of the Brazilian Democratic Movement)

PSDB: *Partido da Social Democracia Brasileira* (Party of Brazilian Social Democracy)

PTB: Partido Trabalhista Brasileiro (Brazilian Labor Party)

Populist/Leftist Parties

PT: Partido dos Trabalhadores (Workers' Party)

PSB: *Partido Socialista Brasileiro* (Brazilian Socialist Party)

PCdoB: *Partido Comunista do Brasil* (Communist Party of Brazil)

PDT: Partido Democrático Trabalhista (Democratic Labor Party)

PPS: Partido Popular Socialista (ex-Partido Comunista Brasileiro) (Popular Socialist Party)

of the PMDB and Cardoso's party). These parties, while having disparate leftist and rightist elements, tend to dominate the center and center-left segment of the ideological spectrum. Along with the PFL, these have been the key governing parties during the democratic era. Some scholars argue that these parties have formed a disciplined proreform bulwark in congress for Cardoso especially; hence, they are "government parties."[47] Other scholars argue that although these parties seem to vote coherently in favor of reform, these votes are infrequent and, more important, they are the product of the president's dispensing large amounts of patronage to particular politicians to manufacture a coherent vote.[48] Yet there is agreement that these parties have become ideologically more cohesive in favor of neoliberal reform, and hence they can be characterized as being on the right or center-right.[49]

Political parties on the left advocate reducing deficits and inflation but also maintaining the present size of the public sector and improving the welfare state. Left-oriented parties want to expand the state's role in promoting and protecting domestic industry. On constitutional reform, they support the social rights guaranteed by the 1988 constitution.

On the left, the most important party continues to be the Workers' Party (PT). (See "Citizen Action: The Workers' Party.") Since 1985 the PT has occupied much of the left's political space, marginalizing already peripheral parties such as the Brazilian Socialist Party (PSB), the Brazilian Communist Party (PCB—renamed the Popular Socialist Party, or PPS, in 1992), and the Communist Party of Brazil (PCdoB). The Democratic Labor Party (PDT), a populist organization, advocates Vargas-era nationalism and state-led development. The PPS is led by Ciro Gomes, a former finance minister (under Itamar Franco) and governor of Ceará. Gomes ran for president in 1998 and 2002 but did not make it to the second round in either contest. In 2003, Lula appointed him Minister of National Integration, a position that the president hoped would keep Gomes's party on the government's side in congress.

As might be expected, the proliferation of political parties has only added to the incoherence of legislative politics. Currently, no party has more than 24 percent of the seats in either house of congress (see Figures 3 and 4). Cardoso's multiparty alliance of the PSDB-PFL-PTB-PPB controlled 57 percent of the vote in the lower house and 48 percent in the upper house. Lula's alliance of his PT, the PL, and some of the leftist and center-left parties might provide a "governing coalition" similar in size to Cardoso's, but not without centrist and even center-right support, especially in the senate. Party switching, merging, and clientelism also make the loyalty of these "pro-government" parties remarkably soft. Consistency of support is difficult to maintain as turnover in the Chamber is high, with 50 to 60 percent of the members being replaced with each election. This reality has reinforced the common claim of the executive to be the only source of political order in the Brazilian democratic system.

Lula's rise to power has changed some aspects of the dominant alliance patterns, but fundamental problems with legislative coherence continue. Lula's PT

Figure 3

Share of Seats of the Major Parties in the Chamber of Deputies, February 2003 Congress

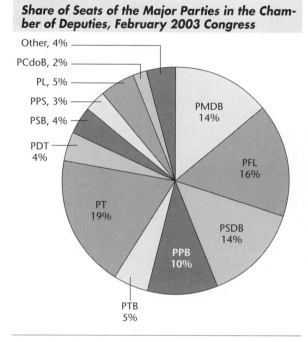

Source: Data from final TSE numbers.

Figure 4

Share of Seats of the Major Parties in the Senate, February 2003 Congress

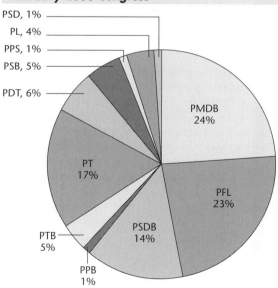

Source: Data from final TSE numbers.

Citizen Action: *The Workers' Party*

The creation of the Workers' Party (PT) in the early 1980s was a remarkable development in Brazilian history. The PT was founded by workers who had defied the military government and engaged in strikes in São Paulo's metalworking and automobile industries in 1978 and 1979. Although the PT began with a working-class message and leftist platform, its identity broadened during the 1980s and early 1990s. The party and its leader, Luiz Inácio "Lula" da Silva, increasingly campaigned for the support of the middle class, the rural and urban poor, and even segments of business and the upper classes. Unlike previous populist parties in Brazil, the PT aimed both to bring previously excluded groups into the political arena and to change the status quo substantively.

Lula da Silva ran for the presidency four times: in 1989, 1994, 1998, and 2002. In 1989, he qualified for, but lost, the runoff to Collor. In 1994 and 1998, he was beaten during the first round by Cardoso. In 1998, the PT forged an electoral alliance with Leonel Brizola's left-populist PDT, as well as with other leftist parties, including the PSB, PCdoB, and the PCB. Despite a unified leftist ticket, da Silva captured 31.7 percent of the vote to Fernando Henrique Cardoso's 53.1 percent. Lula did much better in 2002, beating Cardoso's designated successor, José Serra, in the second round with 61.3 percent, the largest share for any presidential winner in the democratic period. The party's electoral success is a product of its demonstrated capacity for clean and effective government at all levels in Brazil's federal system.

As Margaret Keck, an American scholar of the PT, argues, the party was a novel development because it sought to represent the interests of workers and the poor. This had never before been attempted by a political organization that operated independently from the state. The PT also tries to be an internally democratic party. Its leaders respect the views of grassroots organizers and

ensure that their voices are heard in the party's decision making.

Luiz Inácio "Lula" da Silva, founder of the Workers' Party and Brazilian president (2002–2006). *Source:* © Jornal do Brasil, August 19, 1998, Alexandre Sassaki.

Source: Margaret Keck, *The Workers' Party and Democratization in Brazil* (New Haven, Conn.: Yale University Press, 1992), 219–220.

has forged a somewhat stable congressional alliance that includes parties on the right and center-right (PL, PTB) and on the left (PSB, PPS, PCdoB) in favor of his reform agenda. For example, the passage of the first phases of social security reform in 2003 reflected relatively coherent support among the progovernment parties during the roll-call votes on these reform packages. Even the fractious PMDB, which increased its interests in acquiring cabinet positions and working with Lula in congress, voted for the government's policies. These votes also reflected the weakness of the opposition parties. Over 43 percent of the opposition PFL and PSDB deputies voted for the social security reforms. Yet Lula's first "victories" also underscored the Achilles' heel of relying on the support of undisciplined parties. Defections from the government parties, including four notable PT members who were expelled from the party in December 2003, made congressional support unreliable. For example, the roll-call votes on the first phase of social security reform in the Chamber suffered over 56 defections out of approximately 350 deputies from the government coalition parties. The reforms would not have passed the required three-fifths majority threshold without PFL and PSDB votes, parties that nominally are not allied to the government.

Elections

Because of urbanization and economic modernization, the Brazilian electorate grew impressively after 1945. Improved literacy and efforts by political parties to expand voter registration increased the number of citizens eligible to vote. All illiterates were given the right to vote in 1985, the voting age was reduced from 18 to 16 in 1988, and voting was made compulsory for those 18 and older, except for illiterates and citizens over seventy. The Brazilian electorate stands at 106 million and regularly votes (for example, turnout in the October 2002 presidential vote was 82.2 percent in the first round and 79.5 percent in the second round).

The expansion of the Brazilian electorate coincided with the proliferation of political organizations and movements dedicated to marshaling popular support. Mass appeal became an important element in campaigns and political alliances. With the return to democracy in the 1980s, newly independent labor unions and special-interest organizations emerged, making new alliances in civil society possible.

Nevertheless, the richness of political organization was restrained by the legacies of state-centered structures of social control. Despite the transition to democracy, state corporatism continued to govern important segments of the Brazilian polity. Some political parties lacked staying power, as well as many of the new social movements and political organizations that

helped end the military government. Clientelism continued to fragment the legislature and weaken other democratic institutions.

Contests for public office in Brazil are dominated by the rules of proportional representation (PR), which distorts democratic representation as well. Everything, from federal legislative to municipal council positions, is distributed to ensure proportionality among political parties. In addition to its effects on the party system, open-list PR (see "Institutional Intricacies: Proportional Representation") weakens the incentives for politicians to listen to the electorate. Given the multiplicity of parties, the unbalanced apportionment of seats among the states, and the sheer size of some electoral districts, candidates often have few incentives to be accountable to their constituency. In states with hundreds of candidates running in oversized electoral districts, the votes obtained by successful candidates are often scattered, limiting the accountability of those elected. In less populated states, there are more seats and parties per voter; the electoral and party quotients are lower. As a result, candidates often alter their legal place of residence immediately before an election in order to run for a safer seat, compounding the lack of accountability.

As in all other modern nations, the media play a key role in Brazilian political campaigns. With the *abertura,* political parties gained the right to air electoral propaganda on radio and television. All radio stations and TV channels are required to broadcast, at no charge, two hours of party programming each day during a campaign season. The parties are entitled to an amount of time on the air proportional to their number of votes in the previous election.

In recent years, elections, particularly presidential contests, have become touchstones of the country's progress in building democracy. The 1989 presidential election gave Brazilians their first opportunity to elect the president directly. Collor's (PRN) selection became an important precedent that further strengthened Brazilian democracy. Ironically, his impeachment two years later also promoted democracy because it reinforced the rule of law and enhanced the oversight functions of the congress. Fernando Henrique Cardoso's election in 1994 and reelection in 1998 repeated and reinforced the 1989 precedent of direct elections for the presidency. Although elections cannot guarantee democracy, recent contests have shown how far Brazilian democracy has come in little over a decade.

Seen from the perspective of average Brazilians, however, the situation is a bit more complex. Although most Brazilians are suspicious of authoritarianism and wary of the return of the military or any other form of dictatorship, they seem to be disappointed with the results of democracy. The weakness of political parties, coupled with the persistence of clientelism and accusations of corruption even against previously squeaky clean parties such as the PT, has disillusioned average Brazilians with their country's politics. According to opinion polls, support for democracy as a viable system of government is under 50 percent nationwide. Brazilians vote, but they disparage politics and politicians regularly. For example, in the October 2002 presidential elections, 9.7 million voters turned in blank or spoiled ballots, a common indicator of voter discontent in Brazil. It should also be noted that these characteristics of the voters pervade all class, ethnic, and gender groups. Those who vote and those who return spoiled ballots come from every walk of life. Lula's voters in 2002 were generally those who voted for Cardoso in 1994 and 1998.

Political Culture, Citizenship, and Identity

The notion of national identity describes a sense of national community that goes beyond mere allegiance to a state, a set of economic interests, regional loyalties, or kinship affiliations. The cultivation of a national identity occurs through a process of nation building during which a set of national symbols, cultural terms and images, and shared myths consolidates around historical experiences that define the loyalties of a group of people.

Several developments made Brazilian nation building possible. Unlike nation formation in culturally, linguistically, and geographically diverse Western Europe, Africa, and Asia, Brazil enjoyed a homogeneous linguistic and colonial experience. As a result, Brazilian history largely avoided the ethnic conflicts that have become obstacles to nation building in Eastern Europe, Nigeria, and India. Immigrants added their ideas and value systems at the turn of the century, but they brought no compelling identities that could substitute for an overarching national consciousness.

Regional secessionist movements were uncommon in Brazilian history and were short-lived episodes when they did emerge in the twentieth century.

Despite Brazil's rich ethnic makeup, racial identities in Brazil have seldom been the basis for political action. In part, this was the result of the historical myth that the country was racially mixed. Therefore, a singular racial consciousness emerged around the spurious idea that Brazil was a racial democracy. Even in the face of severe economic and political oppression of native peoples, Afro-Brazilians, and Asians, the myth of racial democracy has endured in the national consciousness. As a result, the unique contributions of different ethnic groups were not appreciated.

Brazilian literature, political discourse, and history textbooks reinforced the myth of racial democracy. For example, the famous Brazilian historian Gilberto Freyre, in his book *The Masters and the Slaves,* described the evolution of social relations among blacks and whites since colonial times, but he treated the underlying reality of racial conflict as an issue of secondary importance.[50] For such intellectuals, miscegenation had diminished racial differences and made conflict unlikely. This thinking buttressed the false belief that prejudice and discrimination were lacking among whites, blacks, indigenous peoples, and mulattos.

Like the myth of racial democracy, the major collective political identities in Brazilian history have sought to hide or negate the real conflicts in society. For example, the symbols and images of political nationalism tended to boost the quasi-utopian visions of the country's future development. Developmentalists under the military governments and democratic leaders such as Kubitschek espoused optimism that "Brazil is the country of the future." In the face of severe fiscal, social, and political problems, Brazilians continue to have faith in their country, even when their confidence in their politicians and democratic institutions has been shaken.

Gendered identities are another significant dimension of Brazilian politics. And as with racial identities, socioeconomic realities belie the widely perceived view that women have equal citizenship with men. Brazilian women make only 70 percent of what men make and black women do even worse at 40 percent.

Carnival in Brazil, the world's largest floor show, is also an insightful exhibition of allegories and popular myths about the country, its people, and their culture.
Source: Bettmann/ Corbis.

Only 7 percent of women with university degrees earn more than twenty times the minimum wage (about $75 per month), as compared to 28 percent of men. In rural areas, women are substantially disadvantaged in the granting of land titles. Female heads of families are routinely passed over by official agencies distributing land titles to favor oldest sons, even when these are minors. Thirty-four percent of illiterate women earn the minimum wage or less, versus 5 percent of illiterate males. Despite women's improved economic, social, and political importance, progress on women's issues is slow. This situation has sparked more women's activism, but more commonly, it has led to feelings of pervasive disempowerment.

The persistence of optimistic myths about the country in the face of socioeconomic and political realities often set the stage for angry disengagement from politics. This reflects a weak system of political socialization. Pervasive corporatism and populism in twentieth-century Brazilian politics, and the current crisis in these forms of mobilizing popular support,

have limited Brazilians' avenues for becoming more involved in politics. The weakness of political parties is one problem. But an underfunded primary and secondary educational system and a largely uncritical media leave most Brazilians without the resources to become more politically aware. Brazil's illiteracy rate of 16.7 percent remains one of the highest in Latin America and is a key obstacle to mobilizing the electorate. The frenetic nature of political change in Brazil has confused the citizenry, further breaking down whatever continuous political identities might emerge. Perhaps the ultimate reflection of these distressing tendencies is the cynical joke among Brazilians that "Brazil is the country of the future and *always will be.*"

The political sentiments of Brazilian society are actually quite static because most Brazilians feel powerless to change their fates. Brazilians have always considered liberal democratic institutions, particularly individual rights, as artificial or irrelevant. Although this view may appear cynical, it is a deeply ingrained notion in Brazilian political culture. Since the end of the nineteenth century, Brazilians have made a distinction between the "legal" Brazil—that is, the formal laws of the country—and the "real" Brazil—what actually occurs. A prime example was the turn-of-the-twentieth-century liberal democracy, which concealed the patronage-ridden interior of Brazilian politics. Brazilian intellectuals developed the phrase *para ingles ver* ("for the English to see") to describe the notion that liberal democracy had been implanted to impress foreign observers, hiding the fact that real politics would be conducted behind the scenes. As Brazil struggles to balance the interests of foreign investors with those of its own people, many Brazilians continue to believe that much of the politics they observe is really "for the English to see."

One of the key outcomes of the sense of powerlessness among the majority of Brazilians was the belief that the state should organize society. This idea helped to justify both the Vargas dictatorship in 1937 and the military rule that followed the coup of 1964. The primacy of the state manifested itself in Brazilian political culture. The notion that the state had a duty to provide for its citizens' welfare placed the state at the center of the Brazilian polity and put the president at the center of the state. It should be clear, based on this analysis, that both society and the state in Brazil developed a set of core ideas that favored the establishment of a strong central government with an overbearing presidentialism. These ideas were not just imposed on Brazilians by savvy politicians; they were the product of many decades of social and political conflict.

During the redemocratization process, new trends in Brazilian political culture emerged. Most segments of Brazilian society came to embrace "modernization with democracy," even if they would later raise doubts about its benefits. The Catholic Church played an important role in promoting democracy. During the transition, a number of Catholic political organizations and movements aided by the church organized popular opposition to the military governments. After the transition, archbishops of the Catholic Church helped assemble testimonials of torture victims. The publication of these depositions in the book *Nunca Mais* (*Never Again*) fueled condemnation of the authoritarian past. In this way, an establishment that previously had been associated with social conservatism and political oppression became a catalyst of popular opposition to authoritarianism.

Another trend that developed during and after the transition to democracy was the growth of a profound distrust of the state. Brazilians began to doubt the ability of the state to find solutions to the country's economic and social problems. Business groups assailed the failures of state-led development, while labor unions claimed that corporatist management of industrial relations could not satisfy the interests of workers. As a result, Brazilians became increasingly receptive to fringe voices that promised to eradicate the previous economic-political order. By 1989, most Brazilians were willing to trust a little-known politician, Fernando Collor, who told the electorate what they wanted to hear. Collor swore to go to war against indolent state employees, corrupt politicians, and inefficient state enterprises. The results were, at least in part, disastrous. By ceding their authority to an untested figure like Collor, Brazilians failed one of the most important tests of democracy: ensuring that elected officials will be accountable to the electorate. In the end, antistatism proved hostile to democracy.

A third trend in Brazilian political culture can be seen among the most elite segments of society. Soon after the transition to democracy, many journalists, economists, politicians, intellectuals, and entrepreneurs began to embrace the notion that national institutions could be adjusted incrementally to strengthen democracy and promote economic growth. Constitutional, administrative, and economic reform became priorities of politicians such as Fernando Henrique Cardoso.

For average Brazilians, the dynamics of institutional tinkering are virtually unintelligible. The electorate must feel substantial change, primarily in their pocketbooks. Cardoso was able to deliver in 1994 when his Real Plan reduced inflation and increased the buying power of most Brazilians. That success gave him the popular support he needed to become president and launch an array of institutional reforms. In 1998, facing another presidential contest and with his reforms stuck in congress, Cardoso barely beat out Lula. Although his poll ratings make Lula the most popular president in recent memory, the progress of his reform agenda will also ultimately dictate whether the voters will support him for re-election in 2006.

The task of selling even the most complex sets of policies to a population with weak political socialization and poor general education has become central to gaining and maintaining political power in Brazil. This problem has placed a premium on the adept management of the media, particularly radio and television. The Brazilian media are free to criticize the government, and most of the broadcast businesses are privately owned. Although there is significant government influence over the resources necessary for media production and the advertising revenue from government campaigns, there is no overt government censorship, and freedom of the press is widely and constitutionally proclaimed. The largest media organizations are owned by a small group of conglomerates. The Globo network is Brazil's preeminent media empire and one of the five largest television networks in the world. It has been formidable in shaping public opinion; some believe it played a prominent role in Collor's election in 1989. Conglomerates like Globo play favorites and, in return, they expect licensing concessions from their political friends.

Unlike the situation in the United States, the events of 9/11 did not fundamentally change Brazilian political culture or its views of the nation's sense of security or vulnerability. Having fought against the military regime's torture and arbitrary killings—a kind of state terrorism—in their own country, Brazilians are very aware that democracy and decency have enemies capable of the greatest cruelty. Many Brazilians also live with a number of everyday terrors—poverty, hunger, disease, and violence—that they regard as far more dangerous than terrorism. In this context, American insistence that Brazil toe Washington's foreign policy line on Iraq and the war on terror often backfires. Brazilians resent such overtures, which only spark the people's nationalism.

Interests, Social Movements, and Protest

Despite the growing disengagement of most Brazilians from politics and the country's legacy of state corporatism, autonomous collective interests have been able to take positions of importance in the political landscape. The role of business lobbies, rural protest movements, and labor unions, particularly those linked to the Workers' Party, are all examples of how Brazilian civil society has been able to break through the vise of state corporatism and social control.

As noted, the Catholic Church was actively engaged in organizing grass-roots movements during and after the transition to democracy. After the profound changes in Catholic doctrine brought about by the Second Vatican Council in the early 1960s, the church in Brazil became more active in advocating social and political reform. The Brazilian church, through the National Conference of Brazilian Bishops (CNBB), produced an array of projects to improve literacy, stimulate political awareness, and improve the working and living conditions of the poor. Although some conservative segments of the Brazilian church reacted violently against the church's "messing in politics," the CNBB pressed on.

One well-known outcome of these changes was the development of liberation theology, a doctrine that argued that religion had to free people at the same time from their sins and from social injustice. In Brazil, this thinking was associated with the Franciscan theologian Leonardo Boff. During the *abertura*, this doctrinal shift sought to relate theology to Brazilian reality by having priests become directly involved in improving the lot of poor Brazilians by defending their social and political needs.[51] By organizing community-based movements to press for improved sanitation, clean water, basic education, and, most important, freedom from oppression, Catholic groups mobilized millions of citizens. Among the Brazilian church's most notable accomplishments was the development of an agrarian reform council in the 1970s, the Pastoral Land Commission. The commission called for the extension of land tenure to poor peasants. The Brazilian church also created ecclesiastical community movements to improve conditions in the *favelas*.

In the mid-1970s, Brazil witnessed a historic awakening of social and political organization: grass-roots popular movements; new forms of trade unionism; neighborhood movements; professional associations of doctors, lawyers, and journalists; entrepreneurial associations; and middle-class organizations. At the same time, a host of nongovernmental organizations (NGOs) became more active in Brazil; among them were Amnesty International, Greenpeace, and native Brazilian rights groups. Domestic groups active in these areas increasingly turned to the NGOs for resources and information, adding an international dimension to what was previously an issue of domestic politics.

Women's organizations played a significant role in popular urban social movements during the 1970s. By the 1980s, women were participating in and leading popular initiatives on a wide variety of issues related to employment and the provision of basic services. Many of these organizations enlisted the support of political parties and trade unions in battles over women's wages, birth control, rape, and violence in the home. Although practically absent in employers' organizations, women are highly active in rural and urban unions. Out of the country's 5,324 urban unions, 14.8 percent have elected women directors. Fewer women are leaders of rural unions (6.6 percent), but they compose 78 percent of active membership. In recent years, Brazilian women have created over 3,000 organizations to address their issues. Included in this total are special police stations (*delegacias de defesa da mulher,* DDMs) dedicated to addressing crimes against women. The DDMs have emerged in major Brazilian cities, and particularly in São Paulo, where their performance has been mixed.

Women's groups have seen their power increase as more women have joined the work force: 39 percent of women now work outside the home. That figure is higher than in Mexico (22 percent) and Argentina (33 percent). More than 20 percent of Brazilian families are supported exclusively by women. The share of domestic servants in the female work force has declined from 32 percent to 20 percent over the past ten years, suggesting that traditional roles for women have not absorbed the increase in the female work force.

Women have also made some strides in representative politics and key administrative appointments. Since 2000, the first women on the board of directors of the Central Bank and the Supreme Court took their positions of power. Women in formal politics have in recent years become mayor of major cities such as São Paulo and a woman, Roseanna Sarney, sustained a major candidacy for president in 2002 until corruption allegations derailed it. The number of women with seats in congress nearly doubled following the election of October 2002, but the rate remains one of the lowest in Latin America nonetheless.

In contrast to the progress of women's movements, a politically significant organization to address racial discrimination has not emerged. This fact is especially surprising because Brazil is one of the world's most racially mixed countries. Only during the 1940s did some public officials and academics acknowledge that prejudice existed against blacks. At that time, the problems of race were equated with the problems of class. Given the absence of legally sanctioned discrimination since the abolition of slavery in 1888, prejudice came to be viewed as class based, not race based. Attacking class inequality was thus considered a way to address prejudice against blacks. This belief seemed plausible because most poor Brazilians are either *pardo* (mulatto) or black. But it might be just as logical to suggest that they are poor because they are black. In any case, the relationship between race and class in Brazil is just as ambiguous as it is in the United States and other multiethnic societies.

Some analysts believe that a gradual and peaceful evolution of race relations is possible. Others argue that as a consequence of white domination, blacks lack the collective identity and political organization necessary to put race relations on the political agenda. Both sides seem to agree, however, that although poverty and color are significantly correlated, overt confrontation among races is uncommon. Ironically, this may explain why no serious national discussion of race relations has ever emerged in Brazil.

The rights of Brazil's indigenous peoples, the Indians of the Amazon, remain at the center of the debate on the country's most pressing social problems. Over the past half-century, the development of the Amazon has threatened the cultures and lives of Indians. For example, members of the Ianomami, a tribe with one of the largest reserves in Brazil, are frequently murdered by miners so they can gain access to mines in Indian territory. During the military government, the national Indian agency, FUNAI, turned a blind eye to such abuses with its claim that indigenous cultures represented "ethnic cysts to be excised from the body politic."[52] With the *abertura,* many environmental NGOs defended the human rights of indigenous people as part of their campaign to defend the

Amazon and its people. The end of military rule and the economic crisis of the 1980s slowed exploitation of the Amazon.

The 1988 constitution recognized the rights of indigenous peoples for the first time, creating large reserves for tribes like the Ianomami. Yet these protections were eroded when President Cardoso, under pressure by landowning conservative allies from the northeast, implemented a policy to allow private interests to make claims on over half of all indigenous lands. Miners, loggers, and land developers invade native lands, often with destructive consequences for the ecology and indigenous people. Allied against these interests are members of the Workers' Party, a coalition of indigenous groups known as COIAB, and church-based missionary organizations. The Kayapó and their resistance to large-scale development projects in the Amazon are a key example of how environmental, labor, and indigenous issues are melding together to form a powerful grass-roots campaign. Members of the Kayapó tribe have been successful in politically disrupting damming and mining projects through mass media campaigns.[53] Their struggle continues, but without more federal protection Amazonian Indians will continue to be threatened.

The sprouting of movements, associations, and interest groups may seem impressive, but they represent specific constituencies. Most Brazilians do not bother to participate in parties, movements, and unions because the basic functions of government such as security, justice, education, and health care simply do not reach them. When confronted with immediate deprivations, many Brazilians avoid organized and peaceful political action, often taking to the streets in sporadic riots. These events are usually sparked by changes in utility and transport prices, but they do not last for more than a few hours. Such events demonstrate that many Brazilians feel they have only two choices in the face of unresponsive political and state organizations: violent protest or passivity.

Section ⑤ Brazilian Politics in Transition

Political Challenges and Changing Agendas

As the financial and monetary crisis that began in Asia in late 1997 continued to scare foreign investors throughout the developing world, Fernando Henrique Cardoso appeared on a Cable News Network (CNN) business show in December. The Brazilian president proclaimed his country a safe place for foreign money, a stable and growth-oriented economy sure to remain immune from the economic difficulties afflicting Asia. Several years later, after his triumphant victory in the October 2002 presidential elections, Lula da Silva appeared at the World Economic Forum in Davos, Switzerland, the most important meeting of the major economic decision makers in the world. Lula repeated many of the ideas Cardoso once espoused on CNN: Brazil is ready to take off as a major economy and a global power. This was striking since Lula had previously been known as a representative of the trade unions and an ardent critic of "neoliberal reform." What explained this transformation?

The investors gathered at Davos knew something that the viewers of Cardoso on CNN did not know back in 1997. In the years between Cardoso's interview and Lula's election victory, Brazil had weathered its own economic crisis in January 1999 and emerged with relatively low inflation and otherwise good economic fundamentals, but in shaky fiscal health and with many of Cardoso's erstwhile reforms still stuck in congress. Due to these realities, Lula had no choice, those at Davos would say, but to embrace the pragmatism of Cardoso by attempting to convey the image of a political moderate and a friend of market-oriented reform. Like Cardoso, Lula talked up his dedication to a stable macroeconomic policy, open markets, sustained structural reforms such as privatization, and the need to balance social justice concerns with fiscal realities. To those gathered at Davos who were already suspicious of the ex-labor leader's personal commitment to reforms that he had long regarded as a betrayal of Brazil's people, Lula's words would have to backed up by action.

Since the president's appearance at Davos in 2002, he has lived up to those ideas, often antagonizing his more militant leftist supporters in the process. Lula's sustained dedication to meeting and exceeding IMF deficit targets, his government's strategic but nonetheless positive engagement with the United States on trade issues, and the partnering of Brazil's new social policies with the resources of multilateral agencies are all testament to Lula's belief that Brazil must engage the global marketplace rather than turn from it.

At the same time, there are serious costs to the presidential strategy of reforming the Brazilian political and economic structure in order to become more competitive in global markets. To curry center-right support, the Brazilian president has had to embrace the very mechanisms of clientelism that are at the heart of many of the inefficiencies that create a deadlock on the country's democratic institutions. Given a weak party system and constitutional requirements that all amendments must be passed twice by 60 percent majorities in both houses of congress, clientelism has become the presidency's most powerful mechanism for cultivating support in order to piece together large, fractious majorities needed to pass particular reform bills. It is not surprising then that some party officials affiliated with the PT and other government parties may have stepped over the line recently and employed corrupt practices to guarantee support for legislation.

This strategy has created serious paradoxes for the Lula presidency. Despite his criticism of Cardoso's tendency to kowtow to clientelistic interests, many of them in the conservative parties and in the poorest regions of Brazil where opposition to agrarian reform and social distribution is strongest, Lula has also depended upon the support of some of these forces to pass reform legislation. While Lula has not gone to the expensive lengths Cardoso did in buying the support of governors and political machines in congress with promises of spending, his reforms have suffered the watering down effect that comes with making politically expedient concessions to secure passage. And like his predecessor, Lula has done little to reinforce the discipline of political parties or reduce the fragmentation of the legislature. The expulsion of rebel members of his own PT demonstrates his commitment to partisan discipline in his own party, but the absence of electoral reform reflects Lula's pragmatic realization that his party must work with much less-disciplined allies on the center-left and center-right. If accusations of corruption continue to dog his presidency and the PT, and if the president and his party do not survive a deepening political crisis, the final cost of Lula's strategy may be considered too dear.

Despite the heady rhetoric of Cardoso's 1994 presidential campaign and the rising expectations of long-frustrated social democrats inside and outside Brazil, his administration offered little in the way of changing Brazilian politics for the long haul. Cardoso made only token progress on the country's persisting social inequalities. The Real Plan reduced the eroding effect of hyperinflation on the incomes of the poor, boosting consumption for millions of Brazilians. But other policies were less effective. Economic liberalization caused thousands of Brazilian firms to shave their labor costs, putting hundreds of thousands out of work. Privatization, for example, put an estimated 546,000 out of work as sold-off firms downsized to become viable market actors. As urban unemployment has increased, so too have urban violence and crime. The government distributed more land to poor people in rural areas, but these efforts failed to make a dent in Brazil's concentrated system of land tenure. Some innovations in health reform and education emerged regarding improving the availability of anti-HIV drugs and state-level experiments, respectively, but wider reforms received only lip service from the administration. The Lula presidency's mixture of modest social reform with a sustained commitment to fiscal probity and open markets will continue to build on Cardoso's accomplishments, but like his predecessor, Lula will not be able to generate vast social and political structural change. Pragmatism in the face of mounting problems seems to be the theme of both the Cardoso and Lula presidencies.

Both the fiscal and the environmental limits to Brazil's economic development have been stretched almost to their breaking points. Even without a significant downturn in the global economy, the fate of the Brazilian economy is being threatened by the state's burgeoning indebtedness, the inability to cut public spending, and the social and ecological costs of the maldistribution of income and the abuse of natural resources. The tendency to see solutions to Brazil's economic problems in terms of promoting exports and enlarging the economy deepens these problems. Considering that many of Brazil's exports are still extractive (such as iron ore and lumber), these recommendations place ever more pressure on the country's ecology.

The fragile ecosystem of the Amazon is in particular danger. Despite all of the attention the Amazon's natural value is given in the international media, in Brazil, "Amazonian defense"—the securing of the porous and vegetation-covered borders of Brazil's north from the encroachment of drug cartels and illegal miners—gets more attention than the "defense of the Amazon." The work of Brazilian and international NGOs in the Amazon is still relatively a recent—since the democratic transition—phenomenon, while development and security concerns are much older. And the work of these groups inevitably confronts the popular, nationalist sentiment that international actors cannot tell Brazilians what to do with "their Amazon basin."

The challenges facing Brazil and the way that the country's political leaders have chosen to deal with them are similar to experiences elsewhere. The Brazilian state lacks the resources to promote development as it did during the days of Vargas, Kubitschek, and military rule. As the needs of the Brazilian citizenry grow, the state appears less capable, and political leaders less willing, to respond. With the advent of the Real Plan, the priorities have been to attract foreign capital, boost export earnings, and favor the highest bidders in the privatization of public firms. The developmentalist state lives on only in some BNDES policies. Like former state-led industrializers India, Mexico, and France, Brazil has turned in the neoliberal direction, limiting the state's role in the economy. This shift in the state's organization reminds us of the importance of our theme of highlighting critical junctures in state formation.

In contrast to the corporatist and populist role of the state, the moderating power in Brazilian history, the central state has become a far more passive agent in society. Brazilian workers no longer negotiate labor issues with state mediation, as they still do in Germany. Instead, labor unions, when they are capable, negotiate directly with business. In most cases, given high urban unemployment, the interests of business usually prevail. Urban workers receive little or no compensation from the state when they suffer layoffs or reductions in their salaries and workplace benefits. Most rural workers, the millions in the informal sector, and minorities are in an even more precarious position, as they lack the few benefits and protections enjoyed by salaried urban workers. The weakness of the judiciary, the abusive use of police authority, and the tendency to vigilantism and class conflict in poor, rural areas reinforce the anemia of a civil society that increasingly discounts its role in politics.

In this context, Brazilian democracy has suffered greatly, the importance of which we highlighted in our theme of the democratic challenge. The poor feel doubly divorced from politics, both socially and politically disenfranchised from a process they view as unresponsive to their needs. Over time, this sense of disengagement has turned into open doubt about the utility of democracy itself. Stories of official corruption and the popular assumption that politicians' priority is their own pocketbook reinforce the idea that representatives are unaccountable to their constituencies. The weakness of political party loyalties and the fragmentation of interests compound the problem of accountability. By contrast, much stronger democracies such as Germany, the United States, France, and Britain rely on well-defined rules that force political leaders to be accountable to other branches of government and to their own constituencies. Brazil's example has shown how difficult it is to embrace the democratic idea without these structures.

Although some of Brazil's problems are unique, many take the same form as elsewhere. Like all other major economies in the world, Brazil's is well integrated into the global economy. Despite the country's current problems with monetary stability and debt, Brazil is one of the world's key platforms for agricultural production and manufacturing. Brazil's share of the world market in iron ore, textiles, footwear, steel, machine parts, and autos makes it an important hub in the multinational production of several industrial products. It is a crucial supplier of raw materials as well as a large market for multinational producers. It has advantages few other developing countries enjoy. This also means, however, that Brazilian firms and workers (not to mention the public sector itself) must be able to adapt to greater competition from abroad and the needs of foreign capital. Given the speed with which technology outpaces itself, the pressure to train workers, boost productivity, and enhance research and development has grown tremendously. Brazil is struggling just to keep pace with globalization.

As globalization and democratization have made Brazilian politics less predictable, older questions about what it means to be Brazilian have re-emerged. Brazil highlights the point made in the Introduction about our theme on political identities, the point that such identities are often reshaped in changed circumstances. What it means to be Brazilian has become a more complex question given the way that Brazil, like the rest of the world, has been bombarded by foreign consumer images. Democracy has given ordinary Brazilians more of a voice, and they have used it to express and shape their own understandings, but mostly on local issues, not at the national level. Women, nongovernmental organizations, Catholics, Pentecostals, blacks, landless peasants, and residents of *favelas* have all organized in recent years around social and cultural issues. On the one hand, these movements have placed additional pressure on an already weakened state to deliver goods and services. On the other hand, these groups have supplied alternatives to the state by providing their own systems of social and cultural support. Because the domain of the state in other countries is constrained by the need to compete in the global economy, space is created for nonstate actors to provide goods and services that were previously produced by the state. What is missing in all of this is a sense of the "national question." How are all these disparate groups linked? Do they have a common, national interest?

One very recent development involves the way that Brazilian elites see the role of the country in forging a counterweight to the hegemonic power of the United States. In both Brazil's engagement with the United States in trade policy (in FTAA and the WTO) as well as in security and other diplomatic relations, Lula's approach has been summed up by his foreign minister, Celso Amorim, as "benign restraint." Following this policy, Brazil opposes the United States on issues such as the war in Iraq and American agricultural subsidies, but it cooperates with Washington in the war against terrorism and regional integration. Lula's government is committed to fighting terrorism but it is unwilling to ignore social justice or to bend to the security policies of the United States. It remains to be seen whether this strategy will produce a coherent Brazilian self-image of the country's role in the world of states.

Brazilian Politics in Comparative Perspective

The most important lesson that Brazil offers for the broader study of comparative politics is that fragmented polities threaten democracy, social development, and nation building. The Brazilian political order is fragmented on several levels. The central state is fragmented by conflicts between the executive and the legislature, divided alliances and self-interested politicians in the congress, decentralized government, and an indecisive judiciary with a complicated structure and an uncertain mission. Political parties are fragmented by clientelism and electoral rules that create incentives for politicians and voters to ignore party labels. Finally, civil society itself is fragmented into numerous, often conflictual, organizations, interest groups, professional associations, social movements, churches, and, most important, social classes and ethnic identities.

In some societies that are similarly fragmented, such as the United States and India, institutions have been successful in bridging the gaps between individualistic pursuits and the demand of the people for good government. Rich systems of social organization and reciprocity that are linked to the state through political parties, parliaments, and even informal associations strengthen democracy in these countries. Where these systems are faulty, as they are in Brazil, fragmentation reinforces the weakness of the state and the society.

Recent Brazilian politics shows that a weak state deepens the citizenry's sense that all politics is corrupt. Although corruption is present in all polities to some degree, it does not by itself produce the angry disengagement from politics that has emerged in Brazil. Much more is wrong with the Brazilian political order. Police brutality, judicial incompetence, and the inability of bureaucratic agencies to respond to social demands have just as powerful an effect in legitimizing civil disengagement.

These problems only reinforce the importance of creating systems of accountability to reduce the corruption, police abuse, and bureaucratic incompetence that have given rise to these doubts. Unfortunately, the English word *accountability* has no counterpart in either Portuguese or Spanish. Given Brazil's (and Latin America's) long history of oligarchical rule and social exclusion, the notion of making elites accountable to the people is so alien that the languages of the region lack the required vocabulary. Systems of accountability must be built from the ground up; they must be nurtured in local government and in community organizations and then in the governments of states and the central state. The judiciary, political parties, the media, and organizations of civil society must be able to play enforcement and watchdog roles. These are the building blocks of accountability, and the accountability of political elites is the fulcrum of democracy.

Without a system of elite accountability, representation of the citizenry is impossible. The 60 percent of the Brazilian population that is classified as poor or close to poor has few autonomous organizations to pressure government. More than business, labor, or professional groups, the poor depend on their elected officials to find solutions to their problems. Brazilian politicians have shown that through demagoguery and personalism, they can be elected. But being elected is not the same as guaranteeing a constituency its right to be represented. For this to occur, institutions must make political elites accountable to the people who elected them. When that condition is met, genuine representation of citizens' interests becomes possible.

Lula's success in reducing hunger, poverty, and inequality—the most important goals of his presidency—has been mixed. "Zero Hunger," education reforms started under Cardoso, modest land reform, and other trademark targeted public spending have improved the lives of hundreds of thousands of Brazilians. But Brazil's social inequalities are too deep and the number of poor too legion for these efforts to have made more than a dent thus far.

Part of the problem is that these concerns require great political unity, but Brazil's experience confirms that political fragmentation can have a virulent effect on a country's sense of national purpose. Collective identities, by definition, require mechanisms that forge mutual understandings among groups of people.

Fractured societies turn to age-old ethnic identities that, as the India-Pakistan and Nigerian experiences demonstrate, can produce destructive, internecine conflict. In Brazil, such extreme conflict has been avoided, but the divisive effects of a fragmented polity on collective identities are serious nonetheless. Divided by class, poor Brazilians continue to feel that politics holds no solutions for them, so they fail to mobilize for their rights. Blacks, women, and Indians share some of the same interests because they are paid less than white men are for the same kind of work. Yet few national organizations have been able to unite a coalition of interest groups to change business practices in this regard. Finally, all Brazilians should be concerned with the clearing of rain forests, the pollution of rivers and lakes, and the destruction of species, yet the major political parties and the congress seem incapable of addressing these issues on behalf of future generations. Such national concerns continuously take a back seat to the self-interests of politicians in Brazil.

Perhaps the most serious effect of political fragmentation on Brazil has involved the struggle to achieve the country's interests in an increasingly competitive, global marketplace. While globalization forces all countries, and particularly developing countries, to adapt to new technology, ideas, and economic interests, it also lets states take advantage of the opportunity to attract investment. Given the weakness of the Brazilian state, the social dislocation produced by industrial restructuring (such as unemployment), and the current instability of the international investment climate, Brazil maintains only an ambiguous vision of its role in the global capitalist order. Although Brazilian business, some unions, and key political leaders speak of the need to defend Brazil's interests in the international political economy, the country has few coherent strategies. Such questions are inherently complex and politically difficult, perhaps no less so in Brazil than in France. But dealing with these issues requires a somewhat consistent policy created by a political leadership with clear ideas about the interests of the country. In Brazil's fragmented polity, developing such unambiguous strategies is difficult.

Acting now on behalf of Brazil's interests in the world of states must be a priority of the Lula presidency. In the world since September 11, 2001, issues of security are outpacing matters of equity and development. Lula's government is committed to fighting terrorism, but it is unwilling to ignore social justice or to bend to the security policies of the United States. The fact in 2003 that the Brazilians began to fingerprint Americans traveling to the country in response to the Bush administration's policy of doing the same to foreigners with visas traveling through American airports is evidence that the Lula government retains its autonomy and remains committed to its policy of "benign restraint."

Finally, Brazil's experience with economic restructuring and democratization will continue to influence countries undergoing similar transformations in Latin America and the rest of the developing world. As a large and resource-rich country, Brazil presents a useful case for comparison with other big developing countries such as Mexico, Russia, India, and China. Its evolving federal structure, as well as its efforts to manage its resources while dealing with environmental costs, can inform similar processes in these countries.

As a transitional democracy, Brazil can provide insights into which governance systems work better than others. As a negative example, Brazil's ongoing experiment with presidentialism, multiparty democracy, and open-list PR may well confirm the superiority of alternative parliamentary systems in India and Germany or presidentialism in France and the United States. As a positive example, Brazil's experiences with keeping a diverse country united through trying economic times will have much to teach Russia and Nigeria, since these countries too are weighed down by the dual challenges of economic reform and nation building.

Within Latin America, Brazil continues to consolidate its position as the preeminent economy of the region. Through MERCOSUL, Brazil exerts authority on commercial questions, and with its continued dominance of the Amazon basin, the country's political elite retains the world's attention when they speak on environmental issues in the developing world. Brazil's experiences with balancing the exigencies of neoliberal economic adjustment with the sociopolitical realities of poverty will keep it at center stage as the World Bank and the IMF and the region's political, economic, and academic leaders discuss the possibilities for a new model of development.

Brazil may not be "the country of the future," but it is a country with a future. None of the maladies of Brazilian politics and social development is immune to improvement. If political reform is consolidated in the next few years, the groundwork will have been laid for transforming Brazil into a country that deserves the respect of the world.

Key Terms

privatization	personalist politicians
moderating power	export-led growth
oligarchy	interventionist
legitimacy	import substitution
clientelism	industrialization (ISI)
patrimonialism	state technocrats
politics of the governors	developmentalism
interventores	*para-statals*
state corporatism	nongovernmental
New State	organizations
populism	informal economy
nationalism	*favelas*
bureaucratic	bureaucratic rings
authoritarianism (BA)	proportional
state-led development	representation (PR)
abertura	

Suggested Readings

Alvarez, Sonia. *Engendering Democracy in Brazil.* Princeton, N.J.: Princeton University Press, 1990.

Ames, Barry. *The Deadlock of Democracy in Brazil: Interests, Identities, and Institutions in Comparative Politics.* Ann Arbor: University of Michigan Press, 2001.

Baer, Werner, ed. *The Brazilian Economy: Growth and Development.* 4th ed. New York: Praeger, 1995.

Dean, Warren. *With Broadax and Firebrand: The Destruction of the Brazilian Atlantic Forest.* Berkeley: University of California Press, 1995.

Evans, Peter B. *Dependent Development: The Alliance of Multinational, State, and Local Capital in Brazil.* Princeton, N.J.: Princeton University Press, 1979.

Furtado, Celso. *The Economic Growth of Brazil: A Survey from Colonial to Modern Times.* Berkeley: University of California Press, 1963.

Keck, Margaret. *The Workers' Party and Democratization in Brazil.* New Haven, Conn.: Yale University Press, 1992.

Kingstone, Peter R., and Power, Timothy J., eds. *Democratic Brazil: Actors, Institutions, and Processes.* Pittsburgh: University of Pittsburgh Press, 2000.

Lamounier, Bolivar. "Brazil Towards Parliamentarism?" In Juan Linz and Valenzuela Arturo, eds., *The Failure of Presidential Democracy.* Baltimore: Johns Hopkins University Press, 1994.

Mainwaring, Scott. *Rethinking Party Systems in the Third Wave of Democratization: The Case of Brazil.* Stanford: Stanford University Press, 1999.

Matta, Roberto da. *Carnivals, Rogues, and Heroes: An Interpretation of the Brazilian Dilemma.* Notre Dame, Ind.: University of Notre Dame Press, 1991.

Roett, Riordan. *Brazil: Politics in a Patrimonial Society.* 4th ed. New York: Praeger, 1992.

Scheper-Hughes, Nancy. *Death Without Weeping: The Violence of Everyday Life in Brazil.* Berkeley: University of California Press, 1992.

Schneider, Ben Ross. *Politics Within the State: Elite Bureaucrats and Industrial Policy in Authoritarian Brazil.* Pittsburgh: University of Pittsburgh Press, 1991.

Skidmore, Thomas E. *Black into White: Race and Nationality in Brazilian Thought.* Durham, N.C.: Duke University Press, 1993.

———. *The Politics of Military Rule in Brazil, 1964–85.* New York: Oxford University Press, 1988.

Stepan, Alfred. *Rethinking Military Politics: Brazil and the Southern Cone.* Princeton, N.J.: Princeton University Press, 1988.

———, ed. *Democratizing Brazil: Problems of Transition and Consolidation.* New York: Oxford University Press, 1989.

Tendler, Judith. *Good Government in the Tropics.* Baltimore: Johns Hopkins University Press, 1997.

Weyland, Kurt. *Democracy Without Equity: Failures of Reform in Brazil.* Pittsburgh: University of Pittsburgh Press, 1996.

Suggested Websites

LANIC database, University of Texas-Austin, Brazil Resource page
lanic.utexas.edu/la/brazil/
U.S. Library of Congress Country Study Page for Brazil
lcweb2.loc.gov/frd/cs/brtoc.html
Political Resources for Brazil, Political Database of the Americas, Georgetown University
cfdev.georgetown.edu/pdba/Countries/countries.cfm?ID=43
SciELO Brazil, Searchable Database of Full-Text Articles on Brazil

www.scielo.br
National Development Bank of Brazil, Searchable Database of Documents on Brazilian Economy and Development (many in English)
www.bndes.gov.br/english/default.asp

Endnotes

[1] IBGE (Instituto Brasileiro de Geografia e Estatística), *PNAD–Síntese do Indicadores da Pesquisa Básica da PNAD de 1981 a 1989* (Rio de Janeiro: IBGE, 1990). For more on Brazil's multiclassification system, see George Reid Andrews, *Blacks and Whites in São Paulo, Brazil, 1888–1988* (Madison: University of Wisconsin Press, 1991).

[2] See Bertha K. Becker and Claudio A. G. Egler, *Brazil: A New Regional Power in the World Economy: A Regional Geography* (New York: Cambridge University Press, 1992), 5; and Terence Turner, "Brazil: Indigenous Rights vs. Neoliberalism," *Dissent* (Summer 1996): 67.

[3] For a complete treatment of state corporatism in Brazil during this period, see Ruth Berins Collier and David Collier, *Shaping the Political Arena: Critical Junctures, the Labor Movement, and Regime Dynamics in Latin America* (Princeton, N.J.: Princeton University Press, 1991), 169–195.

[4] Robert M. Levine, *Father of the Poor? Vargas and His Era* (New York: Cambridge University Press, 1998), 8–9.

[5] For an analysis of this "new professionalism," see Alfred Stepan, *The Military in Politics: Changing Patterns in Brazil* (Princeton, N.J.: Princeton University Press, 1971).

[6] Thomas E. Skidmore, *Politics in Brazil, 1930–1964: An Experiment in Democracy* (New York: Oxford University Press, 1967), 101.

[7] Maria do Carmo Campello de Souza, *Estado e Partidos Políticos no Brasil (1930 a 1964)* (São Paulo: Editora Alfa-Omega, 1975).

[8] Guillermo O'Donnell, *Modernization and Bureaucratic-Authoritarianism: Studies in South American Politics* (Berkeley: Institute of International Studies, University of California, 1973).

[9] Thomas E. Skidmore, *The Politics of Military Rule in Brazil, 1964–85* (New York: Oxford University Press, 1988), 49.

[10] Leigh A. Payne, *Brazilian Industrialists and Democratic Change* (Baltimore: Johns Hopkins University Press, 1994), chap. 4.

[11] For an analysis of these critical elections, see Bolivar Lamounier, "Authoritarian Brazil Revisited: The Impact of Elections on the Abertura," in Alfred Stepan, ed., *Democratizing Brazil: Problems of Transition and Consolidation* (New York: Oxford University Press, 1989).

[12] Margaret Keck, *The Workers' Party and Democratization in Brazil* (New Haven, Conn.: Yale University Press, 1992), 219–220.

[13]Timothy J. Power, *The Political Right in Postauthoritarian Brazil: Elites, Institutions, and Democratization* (University Park: Pennsylvania State University Press, 2000).

[14]Margaret Keck, "The New Unionism in the Brazilian Transition," in Stepan, *Democratizing Brazil,* 284.

[15]See Celso Furtado, *The Economic Growth of Brazil: A Survey from Colonial to Modern Times* (Berkeley: University of California Press, 1963).

[16]For a more complete treatment of how developmentalist ideas cultivated in ECLA affected policy choices in Brazil, see Kathryn Sikkink, *Ideas and Institutions: Developmentalism in Brazil and Argentina* (Ithaca, N.Y.: Cornell University Press, 1991).

[17]More complete treatment of the ISI experience can be found in Albert O. Hirschman, *A Bias for Hope: Essays on Development and Latin America* (New Haven, Conn.: Yale University Press, 1971).

[18]Peter B. Evans, *Dependent Development: The Alliance of Multinational, State, and Local Capital in Brazil* (Princeton, N.J.: Princeton University Press, 1979).

[19]These and other examples of ecological destruction are analyzed in Werner Baer and Charles C. Mueller, "Environmental Aspects of Brazil's Development," in Werner Baer, ed., *The Brazilian Economy: Growth and Development,* 4th ed. (New York: Praeger, 1995).

[20]For more on state environmental efforts, see Barry Ames and Margaret E. Keck, "The Politics of Sustainable Development: Environmental Policy Making in Four Brazilian States," *Journal of Interamerican Studies and World Affairs* 39, no. 4 (Winter 1998), 1–40.

[21]Kathryn Hochstetler, "The Evolution of the Brazilian Environmental Movement and Its Political Roles," in Douglas Chalmers, Carlos M. Vilas, Katherine R. Hite, Scott B. Martin, Kerianne Piester, and Monique Segarra, eds., *The New Politics of Inequality in Latin America: Rethinking Participation and Representation* (New York: Oxford University Press, 1997).

[22]Alfred P. Montero, "Devolving Democracy? Political Decentralization and the New Brazilian Federalism," in Peter R. Kingstone and Timothy J. Power, eds., *Democratic Brazil: Actors, Institutions, and Processes* (Pittsburgh: University of Pittsburgh Press, 2000).

[23]Peggy A. Lovell, "Race, Gender, and Development in Brazil," *Latin American Research Review* 29, no. 3 (1994), 7–35.

[24]Kurt Weyland, *Democracy Without Equity: Failures of Reform in Brazil* (Pittsburgh: University of Pittsburgh Press, 1996).

[25]Wilson Cano, "Concentración, desconcentración y descentralización en Brasil," in José Luis Curbelo, Francisco Alburquerque, Carlos A. de Mattos, and Juan Ramón Cuadrado, eds., *Territorios en Transformación: Análisis y Propuestas* (Madrid: Fondo Europeo de Desarrollo Regional, 1994).

[26]Leonardo Guimarães Neto, "Desigualdades Regionais e Federalismo," in Rui de Britto Álvares Affonso and Pedro Luiz Barros Silva, eds., *Desigualdades Regionais e Desenvolvimento* (São Paulo: FUNDAP, 1995).

[27]Jeffry A. Frieden, *Debt, Development, and Democracy: Modern Political Economy and Latin America, 1965–1985* (Princeton, N.J.: Princeton University Press, 1991), 54–65.

[28]Diana Jean Schemo, "The ABC's of Business in Brazil," *New York Times,* July 16, 1998, B1, 7.

[29]Fernando Luiz Abrúcio, *Os Barões da Federação: O Poder dos Governadores no Brasil Pós-Autoritário* (São Paulo: Editora HUCITECU, 1998).

[30]Alfred P. Montero, *Shifting States in Global Markets: Subnational Industrial Policy in Contemporary Brazil and Spain* (University Park: Pennsylvania State University Press, 2002).

[31]Timothy J. Power, "Politicized Democracy: Competition, Institutions, and 'Civic Fatigue' in Brazil," *Journal of Interamerican Studies and World Affairs* 33, no. 3 (Fall 1991), 75–112.

[32]Argelina Figueiredo and Fernando Limongi, "O Congresso e as Medidas Provisórias: Abdicação ou Delegação?" *Novos Estudos CEBRAP* 47 (1997): 127–154.

[33]Thomas J. Trebat, *Brazil's State-Owned Enterprises: A Case Study of the State as Entrepreneur* (New York: Cambridge University Press, 1983).

[34]Helen Shapiro, *Engines of Growth: The State and Transnational Auto Companies in Brazil* (New York: Cambridge University Press, 1994).

[35]Peter B. Evans, "Predatory, Developmental, and Other Apparatuses: A Comparative Political Economy Perspective on the Third World State," *Sociological Forum* 4, no. 4 (1989), 561–587.

[36]Alfred P. Montero, "State Interests and the New Industrial Policy in Brazil: The Case of the Privatization of Steel, 1990–1994," *Journal of Interamerican Studies and World Affairs* 40, no. 3 (Fall 1998), 27–62.

[37]Wendy Hunter, *Eroding Military Influence in Brazil: Politicians Against Soldiers* (Chapel Hill: University of North Carolina Press, 1997).

[38]Paulo Sérgio Pinheiro, "Popular Responses to State-Sponsored Violence in Brazil," in Chalmers et al., eds., *The New Politics of Inequality in Latin America.*

[39]Human Rights Watch, *Police Brutality in Urban Brazil* (New York: Human Rights Watch, 1997), 13.

[40]Judith Tendler, *Good Government in the Tropics* (Baltimore: Johns Hopkins University Press, 1997).

[41]For a study of how these exceptions have emerged in Brazil, see Barbara Geddes, *Politician's Dilemma: Building State*

Capacity in Latin America (Berkeley: University of California Press, 1994).

[42]Ben Ross Schneider, *Politics Within the State: Elite Bureaucrats and Industrial Policy in Authoritarian Brazil* (Pittsburgh: University of Pittsburgh Press, 1991).

[43]Lívia Neves de H. Barbosa, "The Brazilian Jeitinho: An Exercise in National Identity," in David J. Hess and Roberto A. DaMatta, eds., *The Brazilian Puzzle: Culture on the Borderlands of the Western World* (New York: Columbia University Press, 1995).

[44]Barry Ames, *The Deadlock of Democracy in Brazil: Interests, Identities, and Institutions in Comparative Politics* (Ann Arbor: University of Michigan Press, 2001).

[45]Scott Mainwaring, "Brazilian Party Underdevelopment in Comparative Perspective," *Political Science Quarterly* 107 (1993).

[46]Timothy J. Power, "The Pen Is Mightier Than the Congress: Presidential Decree Power in Brazil," in John M. Carey and Mathew S. Shugart, eds., *Executive Decree Authority: Calling Out the Tanks or Just Filling Out the Forms* (New York: Cambridge University Press, 1998).

[47]See Argelina C. Figueiredo and Fernando Limongi, "Presidential Power, Legislative Organization, and Party Behavior in Brazil," *Comparative Politics* 32 (January 2000): 151–170.

[48]See Ames, *Deadlock of Democracy.*

[49]See Power, *The Political Right in Postauthoritarian Brazil.*

[50]See especially Gilberto Freyre, *The Mansions and the Shanties: The Making of Modern Brazil* (New York: Knopf, 1963), chap. 12.

[51]Ralph Della Cava, "The 'People's Church,' the Vatican, and Abertura," in Stepan, *Democratizing Brazil.*

[52]Turner, "Brazil: Indigenous Rights vs. Neoliberalism," 67.

[53]William H. Fisher, "Megadevelopment, Environmentalism, and Resistance: The Institutional Context of Kayapó Indigenous Politics in Central Brazil," *Human Organization* 53, no. 3 (1994), 220–232.

CHAPTER 6

Nigeria

Darren Kew and Peter Lewis

Federal Republic of Nigeria

Land and People

Capital	Abuja	
Total area (square miles)	356,669 (more than twice the size of California)	
Population	135.7 million	
Annual population growth rate (%)	1975–2002	2.9
	2002–2015 (projected)	2.2
Urban population (%)	47	
Ethnolinguistic composition (% of population)	Hausa-Fulani	26
	Yoruba	21
	Igbo (Ibo)	18
	Ijaw	7
	Other	28

Note: There are more than 250 ethnic groups in Nigeria.

Official Language	English	
Religious affiliation (%)	Muslim	48
	Christian	45
	Indigenous	7

Economy

Domestic currency	Naira (NGN) US$1 = 132.89 NGN (2004 av.)	
Total GNI (US$)	47.5 billion (2002)	
GNI per capita (US$)	350 (2002)	
Total GNI at purchasing power parity (US$)	122.6 billion	
GNI per capita at purchasing power parity (US$)	950	
GDP annual growth rate (%)	1983–1993	4.9
	1993–2003	2.9
	2002	1.5
	2003	10.7
	2004	6.2
GDP per capita average annual growth rate (%)	1983–1993	1.9
	1993–2003	0.3
Inequality in income or consumption (1996–1997) (%)	Share of poorest 10%	1.6
	Share of poorest 20%	4.4
	Share of richest 20%	55.7
	Share of richest 10%	40.8
	Gini Index (1996–1997)	50.6
Structure of production (% of GDP)	Agriculture	36.3
	Industry	30.5
	Services	33.3

Labor force distribution (% of total)	Agriculture	70
	Industry	10
	Services	20
Exports as % of GDP	50.0	
Imports as % of GDP	40.9	

Society

Life expectancy at birth	42.0	
Infant mortality per 1,000 live births	87	
Adult literacy (% of population age 15+) (%)	Male	75.7
	Female	60.6
Access to information and communications (per 1,000 population)	Telephone lines	5
	Mobile phones	4
	Radios	200
	Televisions	68
	Personal computers	6.8

Women in Government and Economy

Women in the national legislature (2003)		
Lower house or single house (%)		6.4
Upper house (%)		3.7
Women at ministerial level (2001) (%)		22.6
Female economic activity rate (age 15 and above) (%)		47.8
Female labor force (% of total)		38
Estimated earned income (PPP US$)	Female	562
	Male	1,322

Composite Ratings and Rankings

Human Development Index ranking (value) out of 177 countries	151 (.466)
Gender-related Development Index (GDI) ranking (value) out of 144 countries	122 (.458)
Gender Empowerment Measure (GEM) ranking (value) out of 78 countries	N/A
Corruption Perception Index (CPI) ranking (value) out of 146 countries	144 (1.6)
Environmental Sustainability Index (ESI) ranking (value) out of 146 countries	98 (45.4)
Freedom in World Rating	Partly Free (4.0)

Political Organization

Political System   Democracy.

Regime History   Democratic government took office in May 1999, after sixteen years of military rule. The most recent national elections were held in 2003.

Administrative Structure   Nigeria is a federation of thirty-six states, plus the Federal Capital Territory (FCT) in Abuja. The three tiers of government are federal, state, and local. Actual power is centralized under the presidency and the governors.

Executive   U.S.-style presidential system, under Olusegun Obasanjo.

Legislature   A bicameral civilian legislature was elected in April 2003. The 109 senators are elected on the basis of equal representation: three from each state, and one from the FCT. The 360 members of the House of Representatives are elected from single-member districts.

Judiciary   The Nigerian judicial system resembles that of the United States with a network of local and district courts as well as state-level courts. The state-level judiciaries are subordinate to the Federal Court of Appeal and the Supreme Court of Nigeria, which consists of fifteen appointed associate justices and the chief justice. Every state of the federation can also opt to establish a system of Islamic law (shari'a)

courts for cases involving only Muslims in customary disputes (divorce, property, etc.); the secular courts, however, retain supreme jurisdiction at the federal level if any conflict arises over which system to use. Most Nigerian states feature such courts, which share a Federal *Shari'a* Court of Appeal in Abuja. Twelve northern states since 1999 have also instituted the *shari'a* criminal code, which allows for amputation for stealing, stoning to death for adultery, and other extreme sentences. Non-Muslim states may also set up customary courts, based on local traditional jurisprudence.

Party System   Thirty parties have been registered by the Nigerian electoral commission since 2002. The largest are the People's Democratic Party (PDP), the All Nigerian People's Party (ANPP), the Alliance for Democracy (AD), and the All Progressive Grand Alliance (APGA). PDP won the presidency, majorities in both houses of the National Assembly, as well as a majority of governorships, state assemblies, and local governments.

Section ❶ The Making of the Modern Nigerian State

Politics in Action

Olusegun Obasanjo took office as president in May 1999 amid tremendous domestic and international goodwill as Nigeria's first elected civilian leader in nearly twenty years. Flanked by Nelson Mandela and other global dignitaries, Obasanjo boldly stated his intentions to reform the corrupt Nigerian state, reverse its economic decline, and restore the nation's international stature. A succession of oppressive, thieving military leaders in the 1980s and 1990s had stolen billions from the national coffers, leaving this oil-rich nation in tremendous debt and making it an international pariah; 130 million Nigerians looked to Obasanjo to rectify the political sins of the past and pull them out of impoverishment. The president promised to do both, and in 1999 he set out with an ambitious political agenda.

Three years later, the National Assembly set out to impeach him. Members of Obasanjo's own party, including the Speaker of the House, sponsored the resolution to instigate impeachment proceedings. The legislators spoke publicly of the president's

unconstitutional behavior, but in private they were more outraged by his heavy-handed methods (including attempts to make ad hoc changes to election laws, and efforts to unseat contentious legislative leaders), aggravated by the fact that he refused to disburse their personal allowances for the year.

President Obasanjo's struggles with the National Assembly are symptomatic of the larger obstacles his government faces in trying to revive the dysfunctional Nigerian state. His ambitious agenda has run aground on the many contradictions in governance left by years of military rule, including a disproportionately powerful presidency married to an inexperienced legislature, all enmeshed in a web of rivalries among various powerbrokers and their supporters. In addition, the young democracy faces the challenge of managing the country's contentious ethnic and religious diversity in conditions of scarcity and weak institutions. Furthermore, years of economic decline and political corruption have left most Nigerians with little patience for Obasanjo's fragile, internally divided government to deliver significant progress. The military left power in 1999 a discredited institution, but it is slowly rebuilding, and the clock is ticking against the civilians: Will public frustrations with the slow pace of reform hold off long enough for democracy to consolidate sufficiently to meet even minimal public expectations?

Nigeria encapsulates many characteristics that more broadly identify Africa. These opposing forces are rooted in the constant struggle in Nigeria between **authoritarian** and democratic governance, the push for development amidst persistent underdevelopment, the burden of public corruption, and the pressure for accountability. Nigeria, like all other African countries, has sought to create a viable nation-state out of the social incoherence created by its colonial borders. Over 250 competing ethnic groups, crosscut by two major religious traditions, have repeatedly clashed over economic and political resources, as well as issues of administrative and legal identity. All of these factors combine to produce the political entity known as Nigeria with low levels of popular **legitimacy** and **accountability,** and a persistent inability to meet the most basic needs of its citizens. The country therefore provides a crucible in which to examine questions of democracy and authoritarianism, the pressures and management of ethnic conflict, and economic underdevelopment brought about by both colonial oppression and independent Nigeria's mismanagement of its vast resources.

Much about Nigeria is contentious. Since gaining independence from British colonial rule in 1960, Nigeria has undergone several political transitions, from democratic governments to autocratic regimes, both military and civilian, and from one military regime to another. It has experienced six successful coups and many unsuccessful attempted coups (most recently in 2004), and it was torn by three years of civil war that claimed over 100,000 military and over 1 million civilian casualties. Against this background, Nigeria today remains essentially an **unfinished state** characterized by instabilities and uncertainties.

Nigeria reached another critical turning point in 1999 when a military government transferred power to civilians for the second time since the British left in 1960. The civilians held their own elections in 2003 for the first time since 1983, when the elections were so flawed that the public welcomed a military coup. The 2003 elections were also deeply flawed. Will

Nigeria return to the discredited path of authoritarianism and greater underdevelopment, or will the civilian leadership rise to achieve a consolidated democracy and sustainable growth?

Geographic Setting

Nigeria, with 130 million people inhabiting 356,669 square miles, ranks as the most populous nation in Africa and among the ten largest in the world. A center of West African regional trade, culture, and military strength, Nigeria is bordered by four countries—Benin, Niger, Chad, and Cameroon, all of them Francophone—and by the Gulf of Guinea in the Atlantic Ocean to the south. The modern country of Nigeria, however, like nearly all the other contemporary states in Africa, is not even a century old.

Nigeria was a British colony from 1914 until its independence on October 1, 1960, although foreign domination of much of the territory had begun in the mid-nineteenth century. Nigeria's boundaries had little to do with the borders of the precolonial African societies in the territory that the British conquered. Instead, these boundaries merely marked the point where British influence ended and French began. Britain ruled northern and southern Nigeria as two separate colonies until 1914, when it amalgamated its Northern and Southern Protectorates. In short, Nigeria was an arbitrary creation reflecting British colonial interests. The consequences of this forced union of myriad African cultures and ruling entities under one political roof remain a central feature of Nigerian political life today.

Nigeria's location in West Africa, its size, and its oil-producing status have made it a hub of regional activity. Demographically, it overwhelms the other fifteen countries in West Africa, with a population that is nearly 60 percent of the region's total. Moreover, Nigeria's gross domestic product (GDP) typically represents more than half of the total GDP for the entire subregion.

Nigeria's ethnic map can be divided into six inexact areas or "zones." The northwest (or "core North") is dominated by Nigeria's single largest ethnic group, the Hausa-Fulani, two formerly separate groups that over the past century have largely merged. The northeast is a minority region, the largest of whom are the Kanuri. Both regions in the north are predominantly Muslim.

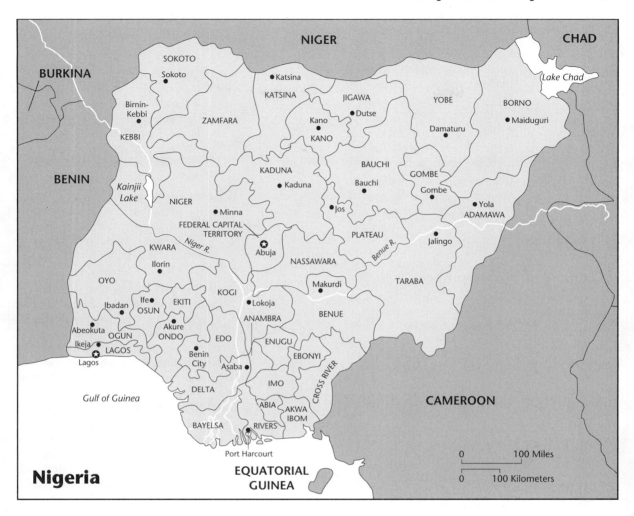

Nigeria

A large swath of territory stretching across the center of the country, called the Middle Belt, is also home to a wide range of minority groups of both Muslim and Christian faiths. The southwest (referred to as the Western Region in the First Republic) is dominated by the country's second largest ethnic group, the Yoruba, who are approximately 40 percent Muslim, 50 percent Christian (primarily Protestant), and 10 percent practitioners of Yoruba traditional beliefs. The southeast (which formed the hub of the First Republic's Eastern Region) is the Igbo homeland, Nigeria's third largest group, who are primarily Christian, and where Protestant evangelical movements have become popular. Between the Yoruba and Igbo regions of the south is the southern minority zone, which stretches across the Niger Delta areas and east along the coast as far as Cameroon.

Critical Junctures

A number of critical junctures have shaped the character of the Nigerian state and illustrate the difficult path that the country has taken during the past half-century. Nigeria's recent history reflects influences from the precolonial period, the crucial changes wrought by British colonialism, the post-colonial alternation of military and civilian rule, and the economic collapse since 1980, precipitated by Nigeria's political corruption and its overreliance on the petroleum industry.

Critical Junctures in Modern Nigerian Political Development

1960   Independence. Nigeria consists of three regions under a Westminster parliamentary model. Abubakar Tafawa Balewa, a northerner, is the first prime minister.

January 1966   Civilian government deposed in coup. General Aguiyi Ironsi, an Igbo, becomes head of state.

July 1966   Countercoup is led by General Yakubu Gowon (an Anga, from the Middle Belt) with aid from northern groups.

1967–1970   Biafran civil war

July 1975   Military coup deposes Gowon; led by General Murtala Muhammed, a northerner.

February 1976   Murtala Muhammed assassinated in failed coup led by Middle Belt minorities. Muhammed's second-in-command, General Olusegun Obasanjo, a Yoruba, assumes power.

September 1978   New constitution completed, marking the adoption of the U.S. presidential model in a federation with 19 states.

October 1979   Elections held. A majority in both houses is won by NPN, led by northern/Hausa-Fulani groups. Alhaji Shehu Shagari is elected Nigeria's first executive president.

December 1983   Military coup led by General Muhammadu Buhari, a northerner.

August 1985   Buhari is overthrown by General Ibrahim B. Babangida, a Middle Belt Muslim, in a palace coup. Babangida promises a return to democracy by 1990, a date he delays five times before being forced from office.

June 12, 1993   Moshood Abiola wins presidential elections, but Babangida annuls the election eleven days later.

August 1993   Babangida installs Ernest Shonekan as "interim civilian president" until new presidential elections could be held later that autumn.

November 1993   Defense Minister General Sani Abacha seizes power in a coup. Two years later he announces a three-year transition to civilian rule, which he manipulates to have himself nominated for president in 1998.

July–Sept. 1994   Prodemocracy strike by the major oil union, NUPENG, cuts Nigeria's oil production by an estimated 25 percent. Sympathy strikes ensue, followed by arrests of political and civic leaders.

June 1998   General Abacha dies; succeeded by General Abdulsalami Abubakar, a Middle Belt Muslim from Babangida's hometown. Abubakar releases nearly all political prisoners and installs a new transition program. Parties are allowed to form unhindered.

1999   Former head of state Olusegun Obasanjo and his party, the PDP, sweep the presidential and National Assembly elections, adding to their majority control of state and local government seats. The federation now contains thirty-six states.

November 1999   Zamfara state in the North is the first of twelve to institute the *shari'a* criminal code. That same month, President Obasanjo sends the army to the Niger Delta town of Odi to root out local militias, leveling the town in the process.

2000   Communal conflicts erupt in Lagos, Benue, Kaduna, and Kana states at different times over localized issues.

Spring 2002   The Supreme Court passes several landmark judgments, overturning a PDP-biased 2001 electoral law, and ruling on the control of offshore oil and gas resources. In November the Court opens the legal door for more parties to be registered.

August 2002	The National Assembly begins impeachment proceedings against President Obasanjo over budgetary issues. The matter ends by November, with the president apologizing.
July 2003	Rogue police units stage a coup in Anambra State, temporarily arresting the governor. The putsch soon collapses, but Anambra becomes a war zone between the governor and the state's political kingpin, who has family ties to the president.
May 2004	Politically motivated ethnic violence in Plateau State spreads to Benue and Kano states. The government imposes emergency rule in Plateau State, which ends in November.
March 2005	The presidency convenes a national political reform conference to debate the structure of the federation and to refine the constitution.

The Precolonial Period (800–1900)

Much of Nigeria's precolonial history before 1000 A.D. has been reconstructed from oral histories, since literate cultures evolved much later. In contrast to the peoples of the forest belt to the south, the more open terrain in the north, with its need for irrigation, encouraged the early growth of centralized states. Such states from the eighth century included Kanem-Bornu in the northeast and the Hausa states in the northwest. Another attempt at state formation led to the emergence of a Jukun kingdom, which by the end of the seventeenth century was a tributary state of the Bornu Empire.

A major element that shaped the course of events in the savanna areas of the north was trade across the Sahara Desert with northern Africa. Trade brought material benefits as well as Arabic education and Islam, which gradually replaced traditional spiritual, political, and social practices. In 1808, the Fulani, who came from lands west of modern Nigeria through a holy war (*jihad*) led by Uthman dan Fodio, established an Islamic empire, the Sokoto Caliphate. Portions of the region to the south, the present day Middle Belt,

were able to repel the *jihad* and preserve their independence and religious diversity. The Sokoto Caliphate used Islam and a common language, Hausa, to forge unity out of the disparate groups in the north. The Fulani Empire held sway until British colonial authority was imposed on northern Nigeria by 1900.

Toward the southern edge of the savanna lived such groups as the Tiv, whose political organization seldom extended beyond the village level. Within such societies, politics was generally conducted along kinship lines, and the fundamental political unit was the extended family. Political authority was diffuse rather than centralized, such that later Western contacts described them as "stateless," or **acephalous societies.** Because they lacked complex political hierarchies, these societies escaped much of the upheaval experienced under colonialism by the centralized states, and they retained much of their autonomy.

The development of collective identities in southern Nigeria was equally complex. Groups included the highly centralized Yoruba empires and kingdoms of Oyo and Ife; the Edo kingdom of Benin in the Midwest; the acephalous societies of the Igbo to the east; and the trading city-states of the Niger Delta and its hinterland, peopled by a wide range of ethnicities.

Several precolonial societies had democratic elements that scholars speculate might have led to more open and participatory polities had they not been interrupted by colonialism. Governance in the Yoruba and Igbo communities involved principles of accountability: rulers could not disregard the views and interests of the governed or they would risk revocation of consent and loss of their positions. Another element was representation, defined less in terms of formal procedures for selecting leaders, and more in terms of assurances that rulers adhered to culturally mandated principles and obligations that forced them to seek out and protect the interests of their subjects.

Among the Islamic communities of the north, political society was highly structured, reflecting local interpretations of Qur'anic principles. Leadership structures were considerably more hierarchical than those of the south, dominated by a few educated elites in positions of authority. In addition (although some of the pre-Islamic indigenous beliefs showed deference to important women spirit leaders), women were consigned to a subordinate position in systems

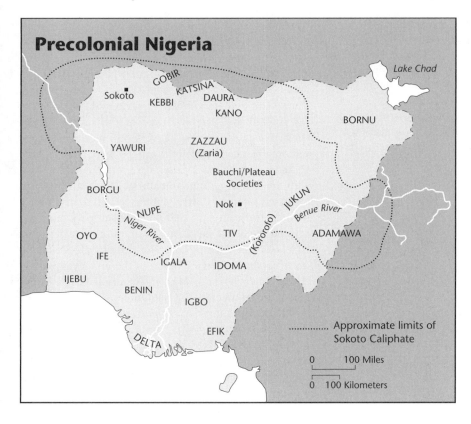

Precolonial Polities and Societies. *Source:* K. Michael Barbour, Julius Oguntoyinbo, J.O.C. Onyemelukwe, and James C. Nwafor, *Nigeria in Maps* (New York: Africana Publishing Company, 1982), 37.

of governance. The Islamic Fulani Empire was a confederation in which the rulers, **emirs,** owed allegiance to the sultan, who was the temporal and spiritual head of the empire. The sultan's powers, in turn, were circumscribed by the obligation to observe the principles of Islam in fulfilling his duties.

Colonial Rule and Its Impact (1860–1945)

Competition for trade and empire drove the European imperial powers further into Africa after 1860. Colonial rule deepened the extraction of Nigeria's natural resources and the exploitation of Nigerian labor, according to the economic and political requisites of Britain, the governing power. Colonialism left its imprint on all aspects of Nigeria's existence, bequeathing political and economic systems that have left enduring imprints on development and governance.

Where centralized monarchies existed in the north, the British ruled through a policy known as **indirect rule,** which allowed traditional structures to persist as subordinates to the British governor and a small administrative apparatus. Where more dispersed kingships ruled, as among the Yoruba, or where acephalous societies existed, particularly among the Igbo and other groups in the southeast, the colonizers either strengthened the authority of traditional chiefs and kings or appointed **warrant chiefs** (who ruled by warrant of the British Crown), weakening the previous practices of accountability and participation.

The British played off ethnic and social divisions to keep Nigerians from developing organized political resistance to colonial rule, and where resistance did develop, the colonizers were not afraid to employ repressive tactics, even as late as the 1940s. Yet the British also promoted the foundations of a democratic political system before they left in 1960. This dual standard left a conflicted democratic idea: formal democratic institutions yet an authoritarian political culture. Colonialism also strengthened the collective identities of Nigeria's multiple ethnic groups by fostering political competition among them, primarily among the three largest: the Hausa-Fulani, Yoruba, and Igbo.

Divisive Identities: Ethnic Politics Under Colonialism (1945–1960)

Based on their experience under British rule, leaders of the anticolonial movement came to regard the state as an exploitative instrument, and its control as an opportunity to pursue personal and group interests rather than broad national interests. Thus, when the British began to negotiate a gradual exit from Nigeria, the semblance of unity that had existed among the anticolonial leaders prior to the 1950s soon evaporated, and intergroup political competition became increasingly fierce.

Nigerian leaders quickly turned to ethnicity as the preferred vehicle to pursue competition and mobilize public support. The three largest ethnic groups, the Hausa-Fulani, Igbo, and Yoruba, though each a minority, together comprise approximately two-thirds of Nigeria's population, and they have long dominated the political process. By pitting ethnic groups against each other for purposes of divide and rule and by structuring the administrative units of Nigeria based on ethnic groups, the British ensured that ethnicity would be the primary element in political identification and mobilization.

Nigerian ethnic groups, championed by educated local elites, rallied followers based on common ethnic identity and challenged the colonial administration, while also competing with rivals from other ethnic groups. Initially, ethnically based associations were concerned with nonpolitical issues: promoting mutual aid for housing and education, as well as sponsoring cultural events. With the encouragement of ambitious leaders, however, these groups took on a more political character. Nigeria's first political party, the National Council of Nigeria and the Cameroons (later the National Convention of Nigerian Citizens, NCNC), initially drew supporters from across Nigeria. As the prospects for independence increased, however, indigenous elites began to divide along ethnic lines to mobilize support for their differing political agendas.

Recognizing the multiethnic character of their colony, the British divided Nigeria into a federation of three regions with elected governments in 1954. Each of the regions soon fell under the domination of one of the major ethnic groups and their respective parties. The Northern Region came under the control of the Northern Peoples Congress (NPC), dominated by Hausa-Fulani elites. In the southern half of the country, the Western Region was controlled by the Action Group (AG), which was controlled by Yoruba elites. The Igbo, the numerically dominant group in the Eastern Region, were closely associated with the NCNC, which became the ruling party there. Thus, ethnic and regional distinctions of modern Nigeria were reinforced in divisive ways during the transition to independence.[1]

Chief Obafemi Awolowo, leader of the AG, captured the sentiment of the times when he wrote in 1947 that "Nigeria is not a nation. It is a mere geographical expression. There are no 'Nigerians' in the same sense as there are 'English,' 'Welsh,' or 'French.' The word 'Nigerian' is merely a distinctive appellation to distinguish those who live within the boundaries of Nigeria from those who do not."[2]

The First Republic (1960–1966)

The British granted Nigeria independence in 1960 to an elected parliamentary government. Nigerians adopted the British Westminster model at the federal and regional levels, in which the chief executive, the prime minister, was chosen by the majority party. Northerners came to dominate the federal government by virtue of their greater population, based on the 1952–1953 census. The ruling coalition for the first two years quickly turned into a northern-only grouping when the NPC achieved an outright majority in the legislature. Having benefited less from the economic, educational, and infrastructural benefits of colonialism, the northerners who dominated the First Republic set out to redistribute resources to their benefit. This NPC policy of "northernization" brought them into direct conflict with their southern counterparts, particularly the Yoruba-based AG and later the Igbo-dominated NCNC.

When an AG internal conflict led to a political crisis in the Western regional assembly in 1962, the NPC-led national government seized the opportunity

Nigeria, 1955

Lake Chad

NORTHERN REGION

To Nigeria 1961

Niger River

Benue River

WESTERN REGION

EASTERN REGION

To Nigeria 1961

To Cameroon 1961

0   100 Miles

0   100 Kilometers

Nigeria in 1955: Divided into Three Federated Regions. The administrative division of Nigeria into three regions later became the basis for ethnoregional conflicts. (Note: At the time of independence, the southeastern part of the country, which had been governed as a trust territory, opted to become part of independent Cameroon; two northern trust territories opted to become part of independent Nigeria.)
Source: K. Michael Barbour, Julius Oguntoyinbo, J.O.C. Onyemelukwe, and James C. Nwafor, *Nigeria in Maps* (New York: Africana Publishing Company, 1982), 39.

to subdivide the Western (largely Yoruba) Region in two—diluting Yoruba political power. Violence escalated among the Yoruba factions in the West as the NPC-dominated government engaged in extensive political corruption. A fraudulent census, falsified ballots in the general elections, widespread violence, and intimidation of supporters and candidates alike ensured the NPC a tarnished victory in 1965.

Rivalries intensified as the NPC sat atop an absolute majority in the federal parliament with no need for its former coalition partner, the NCNC. Nnamdi Azikiwe, the NCNC leader who was also president in the First Republic (then a largely symbolic position), and Tafawa Balewa, the NPC prime minister, separately approached the military to ensure that if it came to conflict, they could count on its loyalty. Thus, "in the struggle for personal survival both men, perhaps inadvertently, made the armed forces aware that they had a political role to play."[3]

Civil War and Military Rule (1966–1979)

With significant encouragement from contending civilian leaders, a group of largely Igbo officers seized power in January 1966. Aguiyi Ironsi, also an Igbo, became head of state by dint of being the highest-ranking

officer rather than a coup plotter. His announced aim was to end violence in the Western Region and to stop political corruption and abuses by the northern-dominated government by centralizing the state apparatus, thereby replacing the federation with a unitary state. Although Ironsi claimed to be ethnically plural in his outlook, other Nigerians, particularly northerners, were deeply suspicious of his revocation of federalism. A second coup in July 1966 killed General Ironsi and brought Yakubu Gowon, a Middle Belt Christian, to power as a consensus head of state among the non-Igbo coup plotters.[4]

Because many northern officials had been killed in the initial coup, a tremendous backlash against Igbos flared in several parts of the country during 1966, especially after the second coup. Igbo migrant laborers were persecuted in the north, and ethnic violence sent many Igbos fleeing to their home region in the east. By 1967, the predominantly Igbo population of eastern Nigeria attempted to secede and form its own independent nation, named Biafra. The secessionists wanted to break free from Nigeria, believing that the north, by virtue of its greater numbers, would permanently lock the other regions out of power. General Gowon built a military-led government of national unity in what remained of Nigeria (the North and West) and, after a bloody three-year war of attrition and starvation tactics, defeated Biafra by January 1970. The conflict exacted a heavy toll on Nigeria's populace, including at least a million deaths.

After the war, Gowon presided over a policy of national reconciliation, which proceeded fairly smoothly with the aid of growing oil revenues. In order to dilute the power of the "big three" ethnic groups, he broke the four-region federation into twelve states, later increased to nineteen by his successor. He also oversaw an increase in the armed forces from about 10,000 men in 1966 to nearly 250,000 by 1970. Senior officers reaped the benefits of the global oil boom in 1973–1974, and corruption was widespread. Influenced by the unwillingness of the military elite to relinquish power and the spoils of office, Gowon opted to postpone a return to civilian rule, which he had pledged originally to complete by 1976. He was overthrown in 1975 by Murtala Muhammad, who promptly reactivated the transition program.

Muhammed was committed to the restoration of democracy, but he was assassinated in 1976. General Olusegun Obasanjo, Muhammad's second-in-command who took power after the assassination, peacefully ceded power to an elected civilian government in 1979, which became known as the Second Republic. Obasanjo retired but would later reemerge as a civilian president in 1999.

The Second and Third Republics, and Predatory Military Rule (1979–1999)

The president of the 1979–1983 Second Republic, Shehu Shagari, and his ruling National Party of Nigeria (NPN, drawn largely from the First Republic's northern-dominated NPC), did little to assuage the mistrust between the various parts of the federation, or to stem rampant corruption. Regional and ethnic polarization persisted, the economy deteriorated rapidly, and the conspicuous misconduct of politicians and political parties eroded the legitimacy of civilian rule. Four years of factional infighting, weak leadership, declining public services, chronic economic mismanagement, a steady parade of corruption scandals, and growing political violence increased public restiveness toward the civilian regime. The NPN captured outright majorities in the 1983 state

General Olusegun Obasanjo was the Nigerian head of state who supervised the transition to civilian rule from 1976 to 1979. In 1995 he was arrested and convicted in a secret trial in connection with an alleged attempt to overthrow the regime of General Abacha. After his release, he won the presidency in 1999 as a candidate for the PDP. *Source:* Bettmann/Corbis.

and national elections through massive fraud and violence. The last vestiges of popular tolerance dissipated, and a few months later the military, led by Major General Muhammadu Buhari, seized power.

When General Buhari refused to pledge a rapid return to democratic rule and failed to revive a plummeting economy, his popular support wavered, and in August 1985 General Ibrahim Babangida seized power. Although Babangida quickly announced a program of transition to democratic rule, he and his cohort engaged in an elaborate series of stalling tactics in order to extend their tenure in office. What promised to be the dawn of a Third Republic ended in betrayal when Babangida annulled the presidential election of June 12, 1993, which should have preceded a full withdrawal of the military from the political scene. In stark contrast to all prior elections since independence, the 1993 election was widely acclaimed as fair (despite military restrictions on the scope of competition), and was evidently won by Yoruba businessman Chief Moshood Abiola. The annulment provoked angry reactions from a population weary of postponed transitions, lingering military rule, and the deception of rulers. Babangida could not resist pressures to resign, but he did manage to hand-pick his successor, Ernest Shonekan, to head a civilian caretaker government with no mandate or public foundation.

General Sani Abacha, who had been installed by Babangida as defense minister in the caretaker regime, seized power from Shonekan in November 1993. Shonekan's government, never regarded by the public as legitimate, was vulnerable to increasing agitation from both civilian and military ranks, providing an opportunity for Abacha to remove the caretaker council. As head of state, General Abacha prolonged the now established tradition of military dominance, combining repression with frequent public promises to restore constitutional democracy. Like Babangida, Abacha announced a new program of transition to civilian rule and regularly delayed the steps in its implementation. He cracked down on political opposition, severely constricted civil liberties and political rights, and fomented corruption on a stupendous scale. Only Abacha's sudden death in June 1998 saved the country from certain crisis, as his scheme to orchestrate the outcome of the transition to produce his own "election" as president became clearer. General Abdulsalami Abubakar, Abacha's successor, quickly established a new transition program and promptly handed it over to an elected civilian government led

General Sani Abacha, a prominent member of Nigerian military regimes since December 1983, took over the government in November 1993, disbanded all elective institutions, and suppressed opposition forces. His death in June 1998 was celebrated in the streets; he and his close supporters looted billions of U.S. dollars from the nation's coffers. *Source:* AP/Wide World Photos.

by President Olusegun Obasanjo and the People's Democratic Party (PDP) in May 1999.

The Fourth Republic (1999 to the Present)

Obasanjo was called out of retirement by the leaders of the PDP to run for president for several reasons. Many Yorubas felt that their group had long been cheated of the presidency by northern elites, especially when Moshood Abiola's 1993 election victory was annulled. Yet most northern leaders did not trust the prominent Yoruba politicians. Obasanjo, although a Yoruba, handed power as military head of state in 1979 to the northerner Shehu Shagari at the dawn of the Second Republic. The northern political establishment then concluded that Obasanjo was a Yoruba candidate they could trust. In addition, many perceived that an ex-military leader could better manage the thorny task of keeping the armed forces in the barracks once they left power.

Yet Obasanjo was initially unpopular among his own people, and he assumed the presidency in 1999 with few Yoruba votes in an election marred by irregularities at the polls. Nonetheless, he claimed a broad mandate to arrest the nation's decline by reforming the state and economy. Within weeks, he electrified the nation by retiring all the military officers who had held positions of political power under previous military governments, seeing them as the most likely plotters of future coups.

Obasanjo began to address the manifold issues surrounding the stagnant economy. The critical oil sector was targeted for new management, while the president lobbied foreign governments to forgive Nigeria's massive debts. The minimum wage was raised significantly, a "truth and reconciliation" commission was set up to address past abuses, an anticorruption commission addressed previous misconduct as well as current offenses, and a special commission was created to channel a greater portion of oil revenues back to the impoverished and environmentally ravaged Niger Delta region, where oil is extracted. Civil society groups thrived on renewed political freedom, and the media grew bold in exposing corrupt practices in government, forcing a Speaker of the House of Representatives and two Senate presidents to resign.

Despite his ambitions for reform, Obasanjo had political debts to his party, and his first cabinet included many of the corrupt politicians who had brought down the nation's previous republics and had colluded with Generals Babangida and Abacha in the 1980s and 1990s. Veteran politicians along with newcomers at all levels of government grew increasingly bold in lining their own pockets with public funds. Obasanjo's political survival, notably his bid for reelection in 2003, required many of these same politicians to deliver the support of their constituencies, rendering the president's anticorruption machinery largely dormant in his first term, and bringing his reform agenda to a halt.

Having surrounded himself with politicians for whom he held little trust, Obasanjo largely kept his own counsel on matters of state. The president was openly disdainful of the National Assembly, and he eventually faced two motions to impeach him. After weeks of tense negotiations, the impeachment drive relented.

Having avoided impeachment, President Obasanjo secured renomination from his party in the 2003 elections through a series of political accommodations with key party barons. The PDP political machinery charged with organizing the election effort engaged in widespread electoral malpractices. In the states of the Niger Delta and the southeast, the ruling party brazenly rigged the elections, while in other regions, the veracity of election outcomes were highly questionable. There were also questions about a number of opposition victories in the northern and northeastern states that they controlled.

Political deals and sharp election practices saved the president's second term and secured the PDP's dominance, but public confidence in the president and the new democratic system plummeted in the wake of the second election. Political feuds led to political upheavals in the states, and the declaration of a state of emergency in violence-wracked Plateau state. Faced with increasing political turmoil and social conflict, the president called a National Political Reform Conference in early 2005, ostensibly to review the constitution and the structure of the federation, with the unstated goal of shoring up his government's sagging legitimacy.

Themes and Implications

Historical Junctures and Political Themes

Federalism and democracy have been important strategies in Nigeria for realizing "unity in diversity" (the national motto), with the goals of building a coherent nation-state out of over 250 different ethnic groups and blending democratic values with accountable government. In reality, the legacy of colonial rule and many years of military domination have yielded a unitary system in federal guise: a system with an all-powerful central government surrounded by weak and economically insolvent states.

When the military returned to the barracks in 1999, it left an overdeveloped executive arm at all levels of government—federal, state, and local—at the expense of weak legislative and judicial institutions. Unchecked executive power under the military, and a dominant executive under the civilians, has encouraged the arbitrary exercise of authority, accompanied by patronage politics, which sap the economy of its vitality, prevent accountability, and undermine the rule of law.

Since the return of democratic rule, the state governments, the National Assembly, and the judiciary have been whittling away at the powers of the national executive. The president, however, remains the dominant figure in Nigerian politics.

Nigeria in the World of States: Oil Dependence and Decline.   Although Nigeria enjoys economic and military power within the West African region, on a global level, it is marginalized and vulnerable. Nigeria, with its natural riches, has long been regarded as a potential political and economic giant of Africa. Yet the World Bank lists it among the poorest 20 percent of the countries of the world, with a GDP per capita of just over $300. Instead of independent growth, today Nigeria depends on unpredictable oil revenues, sparse external loans, and aid—a victim of its leaders' bad policies and poor management. Owing to neglect of agriculture, Nigeria moved from self-sufficiency in the production of basic foodstuffs in the mid-1960s to heavy dependence on imports less than twenty years later. Manufacturing activities, after a surge of investment by government and foreign firms in the 1970s,

suffered from inefficiency and disinvestment in subsequent decades, sagging to levels not seen since independence.

Nigeria's economy remains dependent on oil, and its heavy indebtedness gives foreign creditors and the International Monetary Fund (IMF) considerable leverage over its macroeconomic policies. Years of predatory military rule made Nigeria a political and economic pariah in the 1990s, and deteriorating political institutions made the country a way station for international drug trafficking to the United States and for international commercial fraud. Although the most recent accession of democratic government ended the nation's political isolation, its economy remains subject to the vicissitudes of the international oil market. The government has been favored in the short term by high oil prices and increasing U.S. consumption of Nigerian oil and gas, but there has been no effective restructuring or diversification of the petroleum monoculture.

Governing Nigeria's Economy.   Nigeria's oil dependence is a symptom of deeper structural problems. The very concept of the state was introduced into the colony in large part to restructure and subordinate the local economy to European capitalism. The Nigerian colonial state was conceived and fashioned as **interventionist,** with broad license to intrude into major sectors of the economy and society. The principal goals of the British colonial enterprise were to control the Nigerian economy and to marshal the flow of resources from the colonies to the metropole. A secondary concern was the creation of an economy hospitable to free markets and private enterprise. Nigeria's interventionist state extended its management of the economy, including broad administrative controls and significant ownership positions in areas as diverse as agriculture, banking, commerce, manufacturing, transportation, mining, education, health, employment, and, eventually, oil and natural gas.

After independence in 1960, Nigeria's civilian and military rulers alike expanded the interventionist state, which came to dominate all facets of the nation's economic life. Successive governments began in the late 1980s to reverse this trend, but privatization and economic reform have been piecemeal at best. President Obasanjo promised to sell off government interests in the telephone, power, and oil sectors, although the state remains by far the largest source of economic activity. The new regime's efforts to promote better macroeconomic management and to root out endemic corruption have not borne results in the form of economic growth, employment, or the reduction of poverty.

Democratic Ideas Amid Colonialism and Military Rule.   Colonialism introduced a cultural dualism—a clash of customs, values, and political systems—between the traditions of social accountability in precolonial society, and emerging Western ideas of individualism. These pressures weakened indigenous democratic bases for the accountability of rulers and responsibility to the governed, along with age-old checks on abuses of office. Although the colonial rulers left Nigeria with the machinery of parliamentary democracy, they largely socialized the local population to be passive subjects rather than responsive participants. Even as colonial rule sought to implant democracy in principle, in practice it bequeathed an authoritarian legacy to independent Nigeria. Military rule continued this pattern from 1966 to 1979 and again from 1983 to 1999, as juntas promised democratization yet governed with increasing severity.

This dualism promoted two public realms to which individuals belonged: the communal realm, in which people identified by ethnic or subethnic groups (Igbo, Tiv, Yoruba, and others), and the civic realm under the colonial administration and its successors in which citizenship was universal.[5] The realms influenced each other, but the communal realm was usually stronger in certain respects than the civic realm, posing Nigerians a loyalty dilemma: Does one serve the interests of one's ethnic group or those of a greater Nigeria? Because the colonial state and its "civic" realm began as an alien, exploitative force, Nigerians came to view the state as the realm from which rights must be extracted, duties and taxes withheld, and resources plundered (see Section 4), whereas morality was reserved for the ethnic or communal realm. Military regimes in the postcolonial era continued this pattern, and when they left in 1999, the democratic government faced the task of governing amid strong communal loyalties and an amoral civic realm.

In addition to suffering the burden of two public realms, the democratic idea in Nigeria has also been filtered through deep regional divisions. The British policy of indirect rule had profoundly different effects on the northern and southern regions. The south experienced both the benefits and burdens of colonial occupation. The coastal location of Lagos, Calabar, and their regions made them important hubs for trade and shipping activity, around which the British built the necessary infrastructure—schools (promoting Christianity and Western education), roads, ports, and the like—and a large African civil service to facilitate colonialism. In northern Nigeria, where indigenous hierarchical political structures were better established, the British used local structures and left intact the emirate authorities and Islamic institutions of the region. The north consequently received few infrastructural benefits, little Christian missionary activity, and its traditional administration was largely preserved.

A pattern of uneven development resulted, with the south enjoying the basis for a modern economy and exposure to democratic institutions and the north remaining largely agricultural and monarchical. These disparities between northern and southern Nigeria propelled northern leaders in the First and Second Republics to secure control of the federal government in order to redistribute resources to the north, while military rulers selectively colluded with northern elites and manipulated their fears and weathered southern resentments.

Despite these setbacks, the democratic idea remained vibrant across Nigeria throughout even the darkest days of military rule, and it remains strong even as frustrations rise over the imperfections of the current democratic government. Nigeria's incredible diversity continually demands constant processes of negotiation and protections of interests that democracy promises, albeit after a difficult period of transition.

Nigeria's Fragile Collective Identity.   This division between north and south is overlaid with hundreds of ethnic divisions across the nation, which military governments and civilians alike have been prone to manipulate for selfish ends. Over three decades after the Biafran civil war, Nigeria often seems as divided as it was in the prelude to that conflict. Fears of another civil war rose during the mid-1990s.

These many cultural divisions have been continually exacerbated by the triple threats of **clientelism,** corruption, and unstable authoritarian governing structures, which together foster ethnic group competition and hinder economic potential.[6] Clientelism is the practice by which particular individuals or segments receive disproportionate policy benefits or political favors from a political patron, usually at the expense of the larger society. In Nigeria, patrons are often linked to clients by ethnic, religious, or other cultural ties, and these ties have generally benefited only a small elite. By fostering political competition along cultural lines, clientelism tends to undermine social trust and political stability, which are necessary conditions for economic growth. Clientelism thus reduces the state to an arena of struggle over distribution of the "national cake" among primarily ethnic clients rather than serving as a framework of governance.

Despite the prevalence of ethnicity as the primary form of political identity and the accompanying scourge of ethnic-based clientelism, the idea of Nigeria has taken root among the country's ethnic groups over forty years of independence. Most public discourse does not question the idea of a single cohesive country, but instead revolves around finding an equitable balance among different ethnic groups within the context of a united Nigeria. This can be seen in recent calls from some organizations for a "national conference" to restructure the federation. Most Nigerians enjoy many personal connections across ethnic and religious lines, and elites in both the north and the south have significant business activities throughout the country. Nevertheless, ethnicity remains a critical flashpoint that has led to localized ethnic violence on many occasions, and politicians continue to use ethnic identification to forward their political objectives, often divisively.

Implications for Comparative Politics

The saying that "as Nigeria goes, so goes the rest of sub-Saharan Africa" may again be relevant. With a population of over 130 million growing at nearly 3 percent annually, Nigeria is by far the largest country in Africa and among the ten most populous countries in the world. One out of every five black Africans is Nigerian. Unlike most other countries on the continent, Nigeria has the human and material resources to overcome the vicious cycle of poverty and **autocracy.** Hopes for this breakthrough, however, have been regularly frustrated over four decades of independent rule. If Nigeria, with its vast resources, cannot succeed in breaking this cycle, what does that mean for the rest of sub-Saharan Africa?

Nigeria remains the oldest surviving federation in Africa, and it has managed through much travail to maintain its fragile unity. That cohesion has come under increasing stress, and a major challenge is to ensure that Nigeria does not ultimately collapse. One fact is certain: Nigeria's multiethnic, multireligious, multiclass, and multiregional nature makes it an especially valuable case for the study of social cleavages in conflict and cooperation. Even the United States, which is nearing a demographic transition from a white majority, can learn from Nigeria's efforts to find unity amid cultural diversity.

Nigeria's past failures to sustain democracy and economic development also render it an important case for the study of resource competition and the perils of corruption, and its experience demonstrates the interrelationship between democracy and development. Democracy and development depend on leadership, political culture, institutional autonomy, and the external economic climate; Nigeria has much to teach us on all these topics.

At this stage, it is uncertain whether Nigeria will return to the path of autocracy, underdevelopment, and fragmentation or continue on a course toward democratic consolidation and national construction. In the following sections, we will explore these issues and evaluate how they may shape Nigerian politics in the years ahead.

Section ❷ Political Economy and Development

We have seen how colonialism bequeathed Nigeria an interventionist state and how governments in the postindependence period continued this pattern.

The state became the central fixture in the Nigerian economy, stunting the private sector and encumbering industry and commerce. As the state began to unravel in the late 1980s and 1990s, leaders grew more predatory, plundering the petroleum sector, the nation's remaining source of revenues, and preventing the nation's vast economic potential from being realized.

State and Economy

Through direct ownership of industry and services or through regulation and administrative control, the Nigerian state plays the central role in making decisions about the extraction, deployment, and allocation of scarce economic resources. Any major economic activity involves the state in some way, whether through licenses, taxes, contracts, legal provisions, trade and investment policy, or direct involvement of government agencies. The state's premier role in the economy arises from control of the most productive sectors, particularly the oil industry. Most of the nation's revenues, and nearly all of its hard currency, are channeled through the government. The discretion of leaders in spending those earnings, known as **rents,** forms the main path for channeling money through the economy. Consequently, winning government contracts—for supplies, construction, services, and myriad functions connected to the state—becomes a central economic activity, and those who control the state become the gatekeepers of contracting, licenses, and other areas of economic gain. [7]

As individuals, groups, and communities jostled for state control or access, economic and social life became thoroughly politicized and consumed by **rent-seeking** behavior, best understood as competition over politically regulated economic gains (rents), which are furnished to those with political connections. In most societies, access to the state and its leadership confers some economic advantages, but it can literally be a matter of life and death in impoverished countries like Nigeria.

Perhaps 70 percent of Nigerians struggle along without such access, surviving on petty trade and subsistence agriculture—the so-called informal sector of the economy—where taxes and regulation rarely reach. A number of analysts estimate that the Nigerian informal sector can be valued at approximately 20 percent of the entire Nigerian GDP, much of it earned through cross-border trade.

Origins of Economic Decline

In the colonial and immediate postcolonial periods, Nigeria's economy was centered on agricultural production for domestic consumption as well as for export. Peasant producers were induced by the colonial state to produce primary export commodities—cocoa in the west, palm oil in the east, and groundnuts and cotton in the north—through direct taxation, forced cultivation, and the presence of European agricultural firms. Despite the emphasis on exports, Nigeria was self-sufficient in food production at the time of independence. Vital to this effort was small-scale local production of sorghum and maize in the north and cassava and yams in the south. Some rice and wheat were also produced. It was not until later in the 1960s that emphasis shifted to the development of nonfood export crops through large-scale enterprises.

Nearly exclusive state attention to large-scale, nonfood production meant that small farmers were left out and received scant government support. Predictably, food production suffered, and food imports were stepped up to meet the needs of a burgeoning population. Despite such government neglect, agriculture was the central component of the national economy in the First Republic. A combination of three factors effectively undermined the Nigerian agricultural sector.[8] The first was the Biafran War (1967–1970), which drastically reduced palm oil production in the east, where the war was concentrated. Second, severe drought in 1969 produced a famine from 1972 through 1974. Finally, the development of the petroleum industry caused a total shift in economic focus from agriculture (in terms of both labor and capital investment) to petroleum production. Agricultural export production plummeted from 80 percent of exports in 1960 to just 2 percent by 1980. To compensate for widening food shortfalls, food imports surged by 700 percent between 1970 and 1978.

With the 1970s boom in revenues from oil, Nigeria greatly increased its expenditures on education, defense, and infrastructure. The university system was expanded, roads and ports were built, and industrial and office buildings were constructed. Imports of capital goods and raw materials required to support this expansion rose more than seven-fold between 1971 and 1979. Similarly, imports of consumer goods rose dramatically (600 percent) in the same period as an increasingly wealthy Nigerian elite developed a taste for expensive imported goods.[9] By 1978, the Nigerian government had outspent its revenues and could no longer finance many of its ambitious projects; consequently, the government was forced to borrow money to make up the deficit, causing external debt to skyrocket.

The acceleration in oil wealth was mirrored by a corresponding increase in corruption. Many public officials became very wealthy by setting up joint ventures with foreign oil companies. Other officials simply stole public funds for their own benefit. The economic downturn of the 1980s created even greater incentives for government corruption, and the Babangida and Abacha administrations became infamous for avarice. A Nigerian government commission reported that some $12.2 billion had been diverted to special off-budget accounts between 1988 and 1993. These funds were supposedly earmarked for national security and infrastructure, but they were never audited, and their expenditure remains entirely unaccounted.[10] Within three years of seizing power in 1993, General Abacha allowed all of Nigeria's oil refineries to collapse, forcing this giant oil-exporting country into the absurd situation of having to import refined petroleum. Abacha's family members and friends, who served as fronts, shamelessly monopolized the contracts to import this fuel in 1997. Elsewhere outside the oil sector, small-time scam artists proliferated such that by 2002, Internet scams had become one of Nigeria's top five industries, earning over $100 million annually.

In sum, the oil boom was a double-edged sword for Nigeria. On the one hand, it has generated tremendous income; on the other, it has become a source of external dependence and has badly skewed the Nigerian economy. Since the early 1970s, Nigeria has relied on oil for over 90 percent of its export earnings and about three-quarters of government revenues, as shown in Table 1. Hasty, ill-managed industrial and infrastructural expansion under both military and civilian regimes, combined with the neglect of the agricultural sector, further weakened the Nigerian economy. As a result, the economy was unable to compensate for the sharp fall in world oil prices after 1981 and descended into crisis.

From 1985 to the Present: Deepening Economic Crisis and the Search for Solutions

Structural Adjustment. The year 1985 marked a turning point for the Nigerian state and economy. It ushered in Ibrahim Babangida's eight-year rule and revealed the economy's precarious condition. Within a year of wresting power from General Buhari in August 1985, the Babangida regime developed an economic **structural adjustment program (SAP)** with the active support of the World Bank and the IMF (also referred to as the **international financial institutions,** or **IFIs**). The decision to embark on the SAP was made against a background of increasing economic constraints arising from the continued dependence of the economy on waning oil revenues, a growing debt burden, **balance of payments** difficulties, and lack of fiscal discipline.[11] (See "Global Connection: Structural Adjustment Programs.")

The large revenues arising from the oil windfall enabled the state to increase its involvement in direct production. Beginning in the 1970s, the government created a number of para-statals (state-owned enterprises; see Section 3) including large shares in major banks and other financial institutions, manufacturing, construction, agriculture, public utilities, and various services. Although the government has since sold many of its para-statals, the state remains the biggest employer as well as the most important source of revenue, even for the private sector. By the 1980s, the public bureaucracy in Nigeria had swollen to over 3 million employees (most employed by the federal and state governments), representing more than 60 percent of employment in the modern, formal sector of the economy.

Privatization, which is central to Nigeria's adjustment program, means that state-owned businesses would be sold to private (nonstate) investors, domestic or foreign. Privatization is intended to generate revenue, reduce state expenditures for loss-making operations, and improve efficiency. Expectations that privatization would encourage Nigerian and foreign

Table 1

Oil Sector Statistics, 1970–2003

	Annual Output (million barrels)	Average Price Index	Oil Exports as Percent of Total Exports	Government Oil Revenue (Naira millions)	Percent of Total Revenue
1970	396	37	58	166	26
1971	559	43	74	510	44
1972	643	40	82	767	54
1973	750	39	83	1,016	60
1974	823	162	93	3,726	82
1975	651	109	93	4,271	77
1976	756	115	94	5,365	79
1977	761	115	93	6,081	76
1978	692	100	89	4,556	62
1979	840	237	93	8,881	81
1980	753	220	96	12,353	81
1981	525	225	97	8,563	70
1982	470	212	99	7,814	66
1983	451	200	96	7,253	69
1984	508	190	97	8,268	74
1985	544	180	97	10,915	75
1986	534	75	94	8,107	66
1987	464	90	93	19,027	76
1988	507	60	91	20,934	77
1989	614	87	95	41,334	82
1990	–	125	–	–	–
1991	–	80	–	–	–
1992	714	79	98	164,078	86
1993	720	62	91	162,102	84
1994	733	70	85	160,192	79
1995	705	65	95	244,902	53
1996	783	95	95	266,000	51
1997	803	85	95	250,000	80
1998	700	62	90	248,500	70
1999	1,950	–	–	–	76
2000	2,040	–	–	–	65
2001	2,083	–	98	1,668,000	79
2002	2,068	–	94	1,884,000	80
2003*	2,291	–	91	2,194,000	78

*Projected.

Sources: Output is from *Petroleum Economist* (1970–1989); price index and exports are from IMF, *International Financial Statistics* (1970–1984) and from Central Bank of Nigeria, *Annual Reports* (1985–1989); revenues are from Central Bank of Nigeria, *Annual Reports* (various years). From Tom Forrest, *Politics and Economic Development in Nigeria* (Boulder: Westview Press, 1993), 134. 1990s statistics are from the Nigerian Federal Office of Statistics, *Annual Abstract of Statistics: 1997 Edition,* from the 1998 IMF *Annual Report,* and from Vision 2010, *Report of the Vision 2010 Committee: Main Report* (Abuja: Federal Government of Nigeria, September 1997). Nigerian Economic Summit Group, *Economic Indicators* (Vol. 8, no. 2, April–June 2002). Compilation and some calculations by Darren Kew.

Global Connection: *Structural Adjustment Programs*

The solutions to Nigeria's economic woes depend, in the first instance, on its own people and government, but assistance must also come from outside its borders. In addition to bilateral (country-to-country) assistance, multilateral economic institutions are a key source of loans, grants, and other forms of development aid. Two multilateral institutions that have become familiar players on the African economic scene are the International Monetary Fund (IMF) and the World Bank. These international financial institutions (IFIs) were established after World War II to provide short-term credit facilities to encourage growth and expansion of trade and longer-term financing packages to rebuild the countries of war-torn Europe. Today, the functions of the IFIs have adapted and expanded to meet contemporary needs, including efforts to stabilize and restructure faltering economies. One area of emphasis by the IFIs, particularly among African countries, is the structural adjustment program (SAP).

Assistance from the World Bank and the IMF comes with many strings attached, which typically include SAPs. These rigorous programs, which are intended to reduce government intervention and develop free markets, call for immediate austerity measures by recipient governments. SAPs generally begin with currency devaluation and tariff reductions. These actions are followed by measures aimed at reducing budget deficits, restructuring the public sector (particularly employment practices), privatizing state-owned enterprises, agricultural reform (especially raising producer prices), and the reduction of consumer subsidies on staple foods. The social and economic hardships of these programs, particularly in the short term, can be severe. SAPs result in considerable economic, and frequently social, dislocation; dramatic price increases in foodstuffs and fuel, rising unemployment, and new fees for public services are seldom popular with the general population.

At Babangida's insistence, Nigeria's SAP was developed and deployed in 1986 independently of the IMF. The program was, however, endorsed by the IFIs, making Nigeria eligible to receive disbursements of funds from the IMF and the World Bank and to reschedule $33 billion of external debt with the Paris and London clubs of lenders. Ironically, Nigeria's SAP was in many regards more rigorous than an initial program designed by the IMF. Like SAPs elsewhere, the Nigerian program was designed to encourage economic liberalization and promote private enterprise in place of a reliance on state-owned enterprises and public intervention. The logic was that competition leads to more efficient products and markets. Recovery among Africa's struggling economies has, however, been limited. Africa's economic problems are deeply entrenched; although an economy may be stabilized relatively quickly, comprehensive structural adjustment takes considerably longer. Nigeria's SAP—in part because of the popular reaction to austerity measures, corruption in its implementation, and the complicating factor of unstable military rule—generally failed to revitalize the economy and achieve its stated goals. The final years of the Babangida administration (1985–1993) saw a marked slippage in the reform program, and the Abacha regime continued that trend. Abacha did enact a number of economic policies in 1995 and 1996 that lowered inflation, stabilized the exchange rate, and fostered mild GDP growth, but by 1997, these achievements had been squandered. President Obasanjo has sought to uphold the overall policies of SAP without calling it such, including attempts to end subsidies on fuel and to complete the privatization of the major government para-statals.

---

investments in manufacturing have been largely disappointed. On a domestic level, Nigerian entrepreneurs have found that trading, government contracting, and currency speculation offer more reliable yields than manufacturing. Potential foreign investors remain hesitant to risk significant capital in an environment characterized by political and social instability, unpredictable economic policies, and endemic corruption.

Only a few attractive areas such as telecommunications, utilities, and oil and gas are likely to draw significant foreign capital.

Economic Planning.   Beginning in 1946, when the colonial administration announced the ten-year Plan for Development and Welfare, national plans have been prepared by ministries of finance, economic development, and planning. Five-year plans were the norm from 1962 through 1985, when their scope was extended to fifteen years. The national plan, however, has not been an effective management tool. The reasons are the absence of an effective database for planning and a great lack of discipline in plan implementation. The state strives to dictate the pace and direction of economic development, but lacks the tools and political will to deliver on its obligations.

Nigerian and foreign business leaders revived dialogue with government on economic direction with the 1994 establishment of the annual Nigerian Economic Summit Group (NESG). This differed from previous planning efforts in that it was based on the coequal participation of government and private sector representatives. Two years later, General Abacha initiated the Vision 2010 process (see "Current Challenges: From Vision 2010 to NEEDS"). Participants in Vision 2010 advocated reductions in government's excessive role in the economy with the goals of increasing market efficiency and reducing competition for control of the state. The Obasanjo administration accepted much of the Vision 2010 agenda at the outset of its first term, although it did not say so publicly because of the plan's association with General Abacha's predatory regime. Many of the private sector participants in Vision 2010 continue to meet regularly through the Economic Summit. Advice from the NESG continues to influence the economic policies of both the Obasanjo administration and the National Assembly.

President Obasanjo opened his second term in office in 2003 with a renewed focus on economic reform and development. His appointment of a bold, reformist economic team won the praise of international financial institutions, and the president unveiled an ambitious package of economic reforms combined with social development initiatives, called the National Economic Empowerment and Development Strategy (NEEDS). In addition to stable macroeconomic policy,

especially promising developments have included a restructuring of the banking sector by the new governor of the Central Bank of Nigeria, and the activities of a second anticorruption agency established by the president, the Economic and Financial Crimes Commission (EFCC). Since its foundation in 2003, the EFCC has already indicted a cabinet minister, the inspector general of the police (the head of the nation's police force), and the governor of Plateau State—a far more successful record than Obasanjo's first anticorruption commission, the ICPC, which since its establishment in 2000 has yet to prosecute a single prominent figure.

Ambitious goals followed by lackluster implementation plagued the reform agenda in the president's first term, and many problems must still be overcome in the economy: low investment, low capacity utilization, unreliable distribution, stifling corruption, and overregulation. Average annual GDP growth rates were negative from 1981 through 1987 and have risen only moderately above the rate of population growth since Obasanjo took office in 1999. Consumption and investment have also recorded negative growth (see Table 2). Buoyant oil revenues have helped to float the economy, though poverty has not significantly diminished, and there remain basic questions about the sustainability of growth without a more diversified productive foundation.

Nigeria's heavy foreign debt exacerbates the nation's economic stagnation (see Table 3). President Obasanjo made debt relief one of his highest priorities on taking office in 1999 and promptly undertook numerous visits to the capitals of Europe, Asia, and the United States to urge the governments of those countries to forgive most of Nigeria's obligations. For a long time, his pleas fell largely on deaf ears as Nigeria's National Assembly showed little inclination to spend within the nation's means and the president himself showered funds on wasteful projects such as a half-billion-dollar soccer stadium. Nigeria, once considered a country likely to achieve self-sustaining growth, now ranks among the more debt-distressed countries in the developing world. It cannot earn enough from the export of goods to service its foreign debt—which eats over a quarter of the national budget—and also meet the basic needs of the population. After persistent international lobbying, along with progress on economic reforms during Obasanjo's second term, Nigeria eventually secured an agreement

Current Challenges: *From Vision 2010 to NEEDS*

In the early 1990s, concerned with the nation's economic decline, a number of the larger Nigerian businesses and key multinational corporations decided to pursue new initiatives. With the involvement of then head of state Ernest Shonekan, they arranged the first Economic Summit, a high-profile conference that advocated numerous policies to move Nigeria toward becoming an "emerging market" that could attract foreign investment along the lines of the high-performing states in Asia.

Shortly after the first Economic Summit, however, General Abacha took control and continued the ruinous economic approach of Babangida's later years. The Economic Summit meanwhile continued to meet annually. After his flawed 1994 budget sent the Nigerian economy into a tailspin, Abacha was ready to listen to the summit participants. He accepted several of their recommendations, and by 1996 the economy began to make modest gains. Therefore, when key members of the summit proposed Vision 2010, General Abacha seized the opportunity presented and endorsed it in September 1996. Chief Shonekan was named the chair.

Through Vision 2010, the government pledged to adopt a package of business-promoting economic reforms, while business pledged to work toward certain growth targets consistent with governmental priorities in employment, taxation, community investment, and the like. Along with government and business leaders, key figures were invited to participate from nearly all sectors of society, including the press, nongovernmental organizations, youth groups, marketwomen's associations, and others. Government-owned media followed Vision 2010's pronouncements with great fanfare, while the private media reviewed them with a healthy dose of skepticism regarding Abacha's intentions and the elitist nature of the exercise. Vision 2010's final report called for

- restoring democratic rule
- restructuring and professionalizing the military
- lowering the population growth rate

- rebuilding education
- meaningful privatization
- diversifying the export base beyond oil
- supporting intellectual property rights
- central bank autonomy

Whatever its merits, Vision 2010 was imperiled because of its association with Abacha. When the new Obasanjo administration took office in 1999 lacking a comprehensive economic plan of its own, however, it quietly approached Shonekan for the detailed recommendations and data produced by Vision 2010. Consequently, the general economic strategy and objectives of Vision 2010 are largely echoed in those of the current government. The Economic Summit, meanwhile, continues to provide annual assessments of the Nigerian economy and critical economic advice to policy makers.

President Obasanjo repackaged and developed many of these goals into a new economic initiative for his second term, the National Economic Empowerment and Development Strategy (NEEDS). NEEDS lists several ambitious objectives for restructuring the Nigerian economy. First is government reform, particularly in terms of anti-corruption, greater transparency, rule of law, and contract enforcement, which are all important political institutional supports for a properly functioning economy. Second, NEEDS seeks to spur private sector development through a renewed privatization effort, infrastructure development, agricultural support, and industrial expansion. In addition, NEEDS targets the development concerns of the nation's poor majority, through government assistance for Nigeria's ailing health, education, unemployment, and anti-poverty programs. Since announcing these efforts in 2003, however, the Obasanjo administration has been slow to implement them, although it has promised a number of redoubled initiatives toward these goals for 2005.

Source: Vision 2010 Final Report, September 1997; Federal Government of Nigeria, the *National Economic Empowerment and Development Strategy,* March 2004.

Table 2

Selected Economic Indicators, 1980–2003

	Real GDP (Naira billions) (1993 = 100)	GDP (% Growth)	Manufacturing Capacity Utilization (%)*	Inflation Rate (%)
1980	96.2	5.5	70.1	9.9
1985	68.9	9.4	37.1	5.5
1990	90.3	8.1	40.3	7.4
1991	94.6	4.8	42.0	13.0
1992	97.4	3.0	41.8	44.6
1993	100.0	2.7	37.2	57.2
1994	101.0	1.3	30.4	57.0
1995	103.5	2.2	29.3	72.8
1996	106.9	3.3	32.5	29.3
1997	111.1	3.9	–	8.5
1998	113.3	2.0	–	9.0
1999	114.4	1.0	–	6.7
2000	118.8	3.8	–	6.9
2001	123.5	4.0	–	18.9
2002	127.7	3.4	–	16.9
2003	133.1	4.2	–	13.5

GDP % Growth

1976–1986	–1.3
1987–1997	1.6

*Manufacturing capacity utilization is the average (across the economy) percentage of full production capabilities at which manufacturers are producing.

Sources: Vision 2010. *Report of the Vision 2010 Committee: Main Report.* Abuja: Federal Government of Nigeria, September 1997; World Bank, "Nigeria at a Glance," 1998 (www.worldbank.org) the 1998 IMF *Annual Report.* Nigerian Economic Summit Group, *Economic Indicators* (Vol. 8, no. 2, April–June 2002).

Table 3

Nigeria's Total External Debt (millions of US$; current prices and exchange rates)

1975–1979	1980	1981	1982	1983
3,304	8,934	12,136	12,954	18,540
1984	**1985**	**1986**	**1987**	**1988**
18,537	19,551	24,043	31,193	31,947
1989	**1994**	**1995**	**1996**	**1997**
32,832	34,000	35,010	33,442	32,906
1999	**2000**	**2001**	**2002**	**2003**
29,358	34,134	33,766	33,723	33,740

Nigeria's Debt Compared to its Earnings:

	1976	1986	1996	1997	1999
Total Debt/GDP	3.7	109.9	72.0	63.1	83.8
Total Debt Service/ Exports	3.7	28.4	15.2	15.9	204

	2000	2001	2002	2003
Total Debt/GDP	97.3	86.9	76.5	72.6
Total Debt Service/ Exports	147.6	147	177.5	159.5

Sources: UNDP, World Bank, *African Development Indicators* (Washington, D.C.: World Bank, 1992), 159; UNDP *1998 Human Development Report*; World Bank, "Nigeria at a Glance," 1998 (www.worldbank.org). Nigerian Economic Summit Group, *Economic Indicators* (Vol. 8, no. 2, April–June 2002).

for a substantial reduction of the country's debt. In June 2005, the Paris Club of official creditors approved a package of debt repayments, repurchases and write-offs that would effectively reduce Nigeria's external debt by 90 percent within two years. Obasanjo's efforts in the international arena appeared to be paying dividends,

Social Welfare.   Given the continued decline in its economic performance since the early 1980s, it is not surprising that Nigeria's social welfare has suffered greatly as well. Since 1986, there has been a marked deterioration in the quantity and quality of social services, complicated by a marked decline in household incomes (see Table 4). The SAP program and subsequent austerity measures emphasizing the reduction of state expenditures have forced cutbacks in spending on social welfare.

Budgetary austerity and economic stagnation have hurt vulnerable groups such as the urban and rural poor, women, the young, and the elderly. Indeed, Nigeria performs poorly in meeting basic needs: life expectancy is barely above forty years, and infant mortality is estimated at more than 80 deaths per

Table 4

**Index of Real Household Incomes of Key Groups 1980/81–1986/87, 1996, 2001
(Rural self-employed in 1980/81 = 100)**

	1980/81	1981/82	1982/83	1983/84	1984/85	1985/86	1986/87	1996*	2001*
Rural self-employed	100	103	95	86	73	74	65	27	32
Rural wage earners	178	160	147	135	92	95	84	48	57
All rural households	105	107	99	89	74	84	74	28	33
Urban self-employed	150	124	106	94	69	69	61	41	48
Urban wage earners	203	177	164	140	101	101	90	55	65
All urban households	166	142	129	109	80	80	71	45	53

*Estimated, based on 1980/81 figures adjusted for a 73 percent drop in per capita GDP from 1980 to 1996, and an 18 percent increase in per capita GDP from 1996 to 2001. The FOS lists annual household incomes for 1996 as $75 (N 6,349) for urban households and $57 (N 4,820) for rural households, suggesting that the gap between urban and rural households is actually 19 percent closer than our estimate.

Sources: National Integrated Survey of Households (NISH), Federal Office of Statistics (FOS) consumer price data, and World Bank estimates. As found in Paul Collier, *An Analysis of the Nigerian Labour Market,* Development Economics Department Discussion Paper (Washington, D.C.: World Bank, 1986). From Tom Forrest, *Politics and Economic Development in Nigeria* (Boulder: Westview Press, 1993), 214. 1996 data from FOS *Annual Abstract of Statistics: 1997 Edition,* p. 80.

1,000 live births. Nigeria's provision of basic education is also inadequate. Moreover, Nigeria has failed to develop a national social security system, with much of the gap filled by family-based networks of mutual aid. President Obasanjo took an important step in meeting basic needs when he raised the minimum wage nearly tenfold in 1999. Since wage levels had hardly been raised in years despite the inflation of the previous decade, the gains for workers with formal sector jobs were more meager than the increase suggests. Moreover, most Nigerians do not have access to formal sector jobs, and roughly 70 percent of the population must live on less than a dollar per day.

The provision of health care and other social services—water, education, food, and shelter—remains woefully inadequate in both urban and rural areas. Beyond the needless loss of countless lives to preventable and curable maladies, Nigeria's neglect of the health and social net will likely bear more bitter fruit. The nation stands on the verge of an AIDS epidemic of catastrophic proportions. The United Nations estimates—conservatively—that HIV infection rates are at approximately 6 percent of the population and are likely to spread to 10 percent by the end of the decade, dooming perhaps 15 million Nigerians. The government has made AIDS a secondary priority, leaving much of the initiative to a small group of courageous but underfunded nongovernmental organizations. The Obasanjo administration began providing subsidized antiretroviral medications through a small number of clinics in 2002, and in early 2005 announced that it planned to raise the numbers of patients with access to these medications from 14,000 to 100,000, but several million Nigerians are estimated to be HIV positive.

Society and Economy

Because the central government in Nigeria controls access to most resources and economic opportunities, the state has become the major focus for competition among ethnic, regional, religious, and class groups.[12] A partial explanation for the failure of economic strategies can be found within Nigerian society itself—a complex mix of contending ethnic, religious, and regional constituencies.

Ethnic and Religious Cleavages

Nigeria's ethnic relations have generated tensions that sap the country's economy of much needed vitality.[13]

Competition among the largest groups is centered on access to national economic and political resources. The dominance of the Hausa-Fulani, Igbo, and Yoruba in the country's national life, and the conflicts among political elites from these groups, distort economic affairs. Religious cleavages have also affected economic and social stability. Some of the federation's states in the far north are populated mainly by Muslims, whereas others, particularly in the middle and eastern parts of the south, are predominantly Christian.

Government ineptitude (or outright manipulation), and growing Islamic and Christian assertion, have heightened conflicts between adherents.[14] Christians have perceived past northern-dominated governments as being pro-Muslim in their management and distribution of scarce resources as well as in their policy decisions, some of which jeopardized the secular nature of the state. These fears have increased since 1999, when several northern states instituted expanded versions of the Islamic legal code, the *shari'a*. For their part, Muslims now fear that President Obasanjo, a born-again Christian, is tilting the balance of power and thus the distribution of economic benefits against the north. The decline in the Nigerian economy also contributed to the rise of Christian and Muslim fundamentalisms, which have spread among unemployed youths and others in a society suffering under economic collapse. Disputes over economic and political issues have sometimes escalated into physical attacks on Christians, Muslims, and members of ethnic groups resident outside their ethnoreligious homelands

Northern-led governments after independence, fearing a "southern tyranny of skills,"[15] sought to use the political clout of their numerical majority to keep the south in check and to redistribute resources to the north. Early military governments (1966–1979) tried to maintain some measure of ethnic and religious balance, but the Babangida regime in the 1980s became increasingly northern-dominated and more willing than any of its predecessors to manipulate Nigeria's ethnic divisions. General Abacha's regime tilted overwhelmingly in favor of northerners, specifically Hausa-Fulani, in its membership. Numerous attacks were perpetrated against prominent southern civilians, particularly Yoruba, often using Abacha's secret hit squads. His regime also closed universities and detained a number of activists, particularly in the south.

Other groups were adversely affected by Abacha's rule. The Ogoni, Ijaw, and other southern minorities of the oil-producing regions were brutalized by military and police forces when they protested the scant oil revenues remitted to the region, as well as the environmental degradation from the irresponsible oil industry. The Ogoni in particular were organized through the Movement for the Survival of the Ogoni People (MOSOP), under the leadership of internationally renowned writer and environmentalist Ken Saro-Wiwa. The military's abrupt hanging of Saro-Wiwa and eight Ogoni compatriots in 1995 following a kangaroo trial was widely criticized as "judicial murder" by human rights groups, and led to Nigeria's suspension from the Commonwealth (an international organization composed of Britain and its former colonies). A subsequent UN mission of inquiry declared the executions illegal under both Nigerian and international law.

MOSOP under Saro-Wiwa effectively blended claims for **self-determination,** which in this case meant increased local political autonomy and national political representation, with concerns over oil industry pollution in the Niger Delta, primarily on the part of global oil giant Royal Dutch/Shell, as a platform to forge alliances with international environmental and human rights organizations. Many other Niger Delta minority groups have subsequently followed MOSOP's lead in pushing for a combination of self-determination, political rights, environmental concerns, and demands for greater control over the oil pumped from their lands.

Since the return of democracy in 1999, many ethnic-based and religious movements have taken advantage of renewed political freedoms to organize around their interests and to press the government to address their grievances. Some mobilization has been peaceful, but many armed groups have also formed, at times with the encouragement or complicity of the mainstream political movements. In the oil-producing regions, these militias live off oil "bunkering": tapping into pipelines, siphoning oil, and reselling it on the black market. While armed gangs are primarily responsible, there have been allegations of complicity by members of the armed forces and senior officials.

Youths from the Niger Delta minorities, primarily the Ijaw, have occupied Shell and Chevron facilities on several occasions to protest their economic marginalization. One spectacular incident on an offshore oil platform in 2002 saw a group of local women stage a peaceful takeover using a traditional form of protest: disrobing in order to shame the oil companies and local authorities. Some of these protests have ended peacefully, although a large-scale upheaval in the Warri region in 2003 caused the deaths of several policemen, soldiers, and oil workers. The Obasanjo government has periodically responded to these incidents and other disturbances with excessive force. After Ijaw militias killed several policemen in the village of Odi in late 1999, the military subsequently flattened the village, raping and killing many innocent people. Army units committed similar retaliatory atrocities in 2001 among villages in the Middle Belt state of Benue, when ethnic militias apparently killed several soldiers engaged in a peacekeeping mission during an interethnic dispute.

In the Niger Delta, the struggle of the minority communities with the federal government and multinational oil corporations has been complicated by clashes among the minority groups themselves over control of land and access to government rents. Fighting among the Ijaws and the Itsekiris near Warri in 2003 claimed more than 100 lives. Ethnic-based mobilization, including the activities of militias and vigilante groups, has increased across the country since the transition to civilian rule. Political leaders have sometimes built alliances with such groups and are increasingly using them to harass and even kill political opponents. These practices have reached a dangerous threshold in the Niger Delta, where an ethnic militia attacked a state capital in late 2004 and forced the flight of the governor, who was originally instrumental in organizing the militia and used them to rig his re-election in 2003. The president ultimately mediated among these warlords and offered them an amnesty package for disarming.

These divisive practices overshadow certain positive aspects of sectional identities. For example, associations based on ethnic and religious affinities often serve as vehicles for mobilizing savings, investment, and production, such as informal credit associations. Sectional groups such as the Igbo *Ohaneze* or the Yoruba *Afenifere* have also advocated more equitable federalism and continued democratic development.

These groups, which form an important foundation of civil society, have continued to provide a vehicle for political expression while also reflecting the divisive pressures of Nigeria's cultural pluralism.

Gender Differences

Although the Land Use Act of 1978 stated that all land in Nigeria is ultimately owned by the government, land tenure in Nigeria is still governed by traditional practice, which is largely patriarchal. Despite the fact that women, especially from the south and Middle Belt areas, have traditionally dominated agricultural production and form the bulk of agricultural producers, they are generally prevented from owning land, which remains the major means of production. Trading, in which women feature prominently, is also controlled in many areas by traditional chiefs and local government councilors, who are overwhelmingly male.

Women have not succeeded in transforming their economic importance into political clout, but important strides are being made in this direction. Their struggle to achieve access to state power is a reflection of several factors. Women's associations in the past tended to be elitist, urban based, and mainly concerned with issues of trade, children, household welfare, and religion. The few that did have a more political orientation have been largely token appendages of the male-dominated political parties or instruments of the government. An example of the latter was the Better Life Program, directed by the wife of Babangida, and its successor, the Family Support Program, directed by Abacha's wife. Women are grossly underrepresented at all levels of the governmental system; only eight (of 469) national legislators are women.[16]

Reflecting the historical economic and educational advantages of the south, women's interest organizations sprouted in southern Nigeria earlier than in the north. Although these groups initially focused generally on nonpolitical issues surrounding women's health and children's welfare, organizations like Women in Nigeria began to form in the 1980s with explicit political goals, such as getting more women into government and increasing funds available for education.

As in the south, northern women's NGOs at first focused on less politicized issues, but by the end of the 1990s, explicitly political organizations emerged such as the 100 Women Groups, which sought to elect 100 women to every level of government. Northern groups also showed tremendous creativity in using Islam to support their activities, which was important considering that tenets of the religion have been regularly used by Nigerian men to justify women's subordinate status. Women's groups in general have been more dynamic in developing income-generating projects to make their organizations and constituents increasingly self-reliant, compared with male-dominated NGOs that depend heavily on foreign or government funding.

Nigeria in the Global Economy

At the international level, the Nigerian state has remained comparatively weak and dependent on Western industrial and financial interests. The country's acute debt burden, now set to be reduced, is roughly three-quarters the value of its annual GDP, while Nigeria is reliant on the developed industrial economies for finance capital, production and information technologies, basic consumer items, and raw materials. Mismanagement, endemic corruption, and the vagaries of international commodity markets have largely squandered the country's economic potential. Apart from its standing in global energy markets, Nigeria has receded to the margins of the global economy.

Nigeria and the Regional Political Economy

Nigeria's aspirations to be a regional leader in Africa have not been dampened by its declining position in the global political economy. Nigeria was a major actor in the formation of the **Economic Community of West African States (ECOWAS)** in 1975 and has carried a disproportionately high financial and administrative burden for keeping the organization afloat. Under President Obasanjo's initiative, ECOWAS voted in 2000 to create a parliament and a single currency for the region as the next step toward a European Union–style integration. These lofty goals will take years of concerted efforts from the region's troubled governments to become a reality, and the lackluster results of past integration efforts do not bode well for success.

Nigeria was also the largest contributor of troops to the West African peacekeeping force, the ECOWAS Monitoring Group (known as ECOMOG). Under Nigerian direction, the ECOWAS countries dispatched ECOMOG troops to Liberia from 1990 to 1997 to restore order and prevent the Liberian civil war from destabilizing the subregion. Ironically, despite military dictatorship at home, Nigerian ECOMOG forces invaded Sierra Leone in May 1997 to restore its democratically elected government, a move generally endorsed by the international community. The United Nations assumed leadership of the operation in 1999, but Nigeria continues to contribute troops. Nigeria under President Obasanjo has also sought to mediate crises in Guinea-Bissau, Togo, and Ivory Coast, and in Congo and Zimbabwe outside the ECOWAS region.

Because it is the largest economy in the West African subregion, Nigeria has at times been a magnet for immigration. At the height of the 1970s oil boom, many West African laborers, most of them Ghanaians, migrated to Nigeria in search of employment. When the oil-based expansion ceased and jobs became scarce, Nigeria sought to protect its own workers by expelling hundreds of thousands of West Africans in 1983 and 1985. Many Nigerians now flock to the hot Ghanaian economy for work and to countries across the continent, including far-off South Africa.

Nigeria and the Political Economy of the West

Nigeria's global influence peaked in the 1970s at the height of the oil boom. Shortly after the 1973–1974 global oil crisis, Nigeria's oil wealth was perceived by the Nigerian elite as a source of strength. In 1975, for example, Nigeria was selling about 30 percent of its oil to the United States and was able to apply pressure to the administration of President Gerald Ford in a dispute over Angola.[17] By the 1980s, however, the global oil market had become a buyers' market. Thereafter, it became clear that Nigeria's dependence on oil was a source of weakness, not strength. The depth of Nigeria's international weakness became more evident with the adoption of structural adjustment in the mid-1980s. Given the enormity of the economic crisis, Nigeria was compelled to seek IMF/World Bank support to improve its balance of payments and facilitate economic restructuring and debt rescheduling, and it has had to accept direction from foreign agencies ever since.

In addition to its dependence on oil revenues, Nigeria remains dependent on Western technology and expertise for exploration and extraction of its oil reserves. Nevertheless, oil can be an important political resource. For example, after General Babangida cancelled presidential elections in 1993, pressure by U.S. and European oil companies on their home governments ensured that severe economic sanctions on Nigeria were not imposed. The United States is now turning toward Nigerian oil to diversify its supply base beyond the Middle East, which should improve Nigerian government revenues but may not significantly alter the overall dependency of the economy.

Nigeria remains a highly visible and influential member of the Organization of Petroleum Exporting Countries (OPEC), selling on the average 2 million barrels of petroleum daily and contributing approximately 8 percent of U.S. oil imports. Britain, France, and Germany each have over $1 billion in investments. Nigeria's oil wealth and its great economic potential have tempered the resolve of Western nations in combating human rights and other abuses, notably during the Abacha period from 1993 to 1998.

Although President Obasanjo enjoyed much goodwill among Western governments when he assumed office, they were hesitant to discuss cancellation of Nigeria's enormous debt without some evidence of fiscal responsibility. Given the government's inconsistency in this regard, international donors remained largely unmoved, until economic reforms gained momentum midway through the administration's second term.

The West has nevertheless been supportive of the return of Nigerian leadership across Africa. Together with President Thabo Mbeki of South Africa, Obasanjo

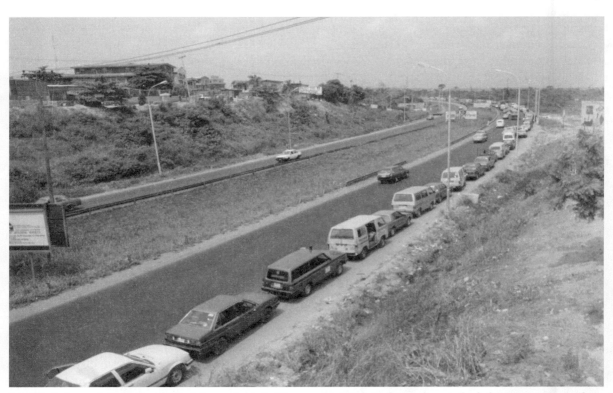

Despite being sub-Saharan Africa's largest crude oil exporter, Nigeria faces chronic fuel shortages. General Abacha allowed the nation's four refineries to collapse, forcing the country into the absurd situation of importing fuel—through middlemen who gave enormous kickbacks to Abacha and his family. Shortages have resurfaced periodically since 1999. *Source:* Jay Oguntuwase-Asope, *The Guardian* (Lagos), August 12, 1998.

was instrumental in convincing the continent's leaders to transform the OAU into the African Union (AU) in 2002, modeled on European-style processes to promote greater political integration across the continent. The AU's first item of business, largely promoted by Mbeki and Obasanjo, was to endorse the New Partnership for Africa's Development (NEPAD), through which African governments committed good governance and economic reforms in return for access to Western markets and financial assistance. NEPAD remains a central element in Nigerian and South African foreign policy, but their hesitancy to apply pressure for reforms in important countries, such as Zimbabwe, has led to significant ambivalence toward NEPAD among Western governments.

Despite its considerable geopolitical resources, Nigeria's economic development profile is bleak. Nigeria is listed very close to the bottom of the UNDP's Human Development Index (HDI), 142 out of 174, behind India and Haiti. Gross national product (GNP) per capita in 2001 was $300, less than 2 percent of which was recorded as public expenditures on education and health, respectively. These figures compare unfavorably with the $860 per capita GNP for China and $390 per capita for India. On the basis of its per capita GDP, the Nigerian economy is the nineteenth poorest in the world in a 1997 World Bank ranking. For comparative purposes, the same study ranks Ghana as thirty-first poorest and India twenty-seventh.

Section ❸ Governance and Policy-Making

The rough edges of what has been called the "unfinished Nigerian state" can be seen in its institutions of governance and policy-making. What seemed like an endless political transition under the Babangida and Abacha regimes was rushed through in less than a year by their successor, Abdulsalami Abubakar. President Obasanjo thus inherited a government that was close to collapse, riddled with corruption, unable to perform basic tasks of governance, yet facing high public expectations to deliver rapid progress.

Organization of the State

The National Question and Constitutional Governance

After four decades as an independent nation, Nigerians are still debating the basic political structures of the country, who will rule and how, and indeed, even if the country should remain united. They call this fundamental governance issue the "national question." How is the country to be governed given its great diversity? What should be the institutional form of the government? How can all sections of the country work in harmony and none feel excluded or dominated by the others? Nigerian leaders have attempted to answer these questions in various ways. Since independence,

one path has been reliance on Anglo-American models of democracy and constitutionalism. Another path has been military domination. Nigeria has stumbled along under hybrids of these two tendencies. As a consequence, the country has produced many constitutions but has yet to entrench constitutionalism.

Since the amalgamation of northern and southern Nigeria in 1914, the country has drafted nine constitutions—five under colonial rule (in 1922, 1946, 1951, 1954, and 1960) and four after colonial rule: the 1963 Republican Constitution, the 1979 Constitution of the Second Republic, the 1989 Constitution intended for the Third Republic, and the current 1999 Constitution, which essentially amended the 1979 version. Although huge sums were spent on constitution making by the Babangida and Abacha regimes, Nigeria actually conducted national elections in 1998–1999 without a settled constitutional document. Public pressure to revise the 1999 constitution has remained strong, and the president inaugurated a National Political Reform Conference in early 2005 to recommend changes in the constitution and the structure of the federation. The conference lacked broad legitimacy, however, since the president appointed delegates and the ruling party and presidential allies have significant influence over the deliberations. Consequently, a number of political parties and civil society groups condemned the conference, and threatened to hold their own national "confab" later in the year.

In contrast, Nigerian constitutions have earned little respect from military or civilian leaders, who have often been unwilling to observe legal and constitutional constraints. Governance and policymaking in this context are conducted within fragile institutions that are swamped by personal and partisan considerations. Military rule bolstered these tendencies and personalized governance and policymaking. With this in mind, we will discuss key elements of recent periods of military rule, their continued influence in the present, and the young institutions of the Fourth Republic.

Federalism and State Structure

Nigeria's First Republic experimented with the parliamentary model, in which the executive is chosen directly from the legislative ranks. The First Republic was relatively decentralized, with the locus of political power in the three federal units: the Northern, Eastern, and Western Regions. The Second Republic constitution, which went into effect in 1979, adopted a U.S.-style presidential model. The Fourth Republic continues with the presidential model: a system with a strong executive who is constrained by a system of checks and balances on authority, a bicameral legislature, and an independent judicial branch charged with matters of law and constitutional interpretation.[18]

Like the United States, Nigeria also features a federal structure comprising 36 states and 774 local government units empowered to enact their own laws within their individual jurisdictions, but limited in scope by the constitution and federal laws. Together, these units constitute a single national entity with three levels of government. The judicial system also resembles that of the United States with a network of local and district courts, as well as state-level courts.

Under a true federal system, the formal powers of the different levels of government would be derived from the constituent members of the federation, such as the states. In Nigeria, by contrast, these institutions have been created top-down, by military fiat. The military left a 1999 constitution that retains enormous powers in the federal government, and the executive in particular. In addition, so many years of military rule left a pattern of governance—a political culture—that retains many authoritarian strains despite the formal democratization of state structures.

The control of oil wealth by this centralized command structure has further cemented economic and political control in the center, resulting in a skewed federalism in which states enjoy nominal powers, but in reality are totally dependent on the central government. The powers of the state and local governments are delineated by the federal constitution, and they receive virtually their entire budget from the federally determined share of the oil revenues.

Another aspect of federalism in Nigeria has been the effort to arrive at some form of elite accommodation to moderate some of the more divisive aspects of cultural pluralism. A similar practice, known as "federal character," was introduced into the public service and formally codified by the 1979 constitution, while ethnic quotas have long been observed by the armed forces. (See "Current Challenges: Nigeria's Federal Character.")

Because federal character is also perceived as a tool of ethnic management, disputes about its application have tended to focus on ethnic representation rather than on representation of state interests. Although this principle was originally regarded as a positive Nigerian contribution to governance in a plural society, its application has tended to intensify rather than to reduce intergroup rivalries and conflicts. In recent years, there have been calls for the use of merit over federal character in awarding public sector jobs. (See "Current Challenges: Federalism in Nigeria.")

The Executive

Evolution of the Executive Function

In the Second Republic, the earlier parliamentary system was replaced by a presidential system based on the American model. The president was chosen directly by the electorate rather than indirectly by the legislature, based on a widespread belief that a popularly elected president could serve as a symbol of national unity. The framers of the Second Republic's constitution believed that placing the election of the president in the hands of the electorate, rather than parliament, would mitigate a lack of party discipline in the selection of the executive.

Current Challenges: **Nigeria's Federal Character**

Federal character, in principle, is an affirmative action program to ensure representation of all ethnic and regional groups, particularly in the civil service. Although *federal character* is regarded as a euphemism for *ethnic balancing,* in practice it has provoked ethnic instability, rivalry, and conflict. Federal character goes beyond federalism in the traditional Western and territorial sense. Federalism as a principle of government has a positive connotation (especially with regard to mitigating ethnic conflict); however, federal character elicits the unevenness and inequality in Nigerian politics, especially when it comes to the controversial use of ethnic-based quotas in hiring, the awarding of government contracts, and the disbursement of political offices.

The pursuit of ethnic balancing has had numerous ill effects, several of which are identified by Nigerian scholar Peter Ekeh.[*] Federal character has created benefit-seeking and autonomy-seeking groups in areas where they did not previously exist. Second, federal character and federalism have overloaded the political system in terms of personnel and other costs. Federal character has also "invaded the integrity of the public bureaucracy" by ignoring merit. Finally, the thirty-six states that currently exist in Nigeria are vying for control of the center in order to extract the greatest benefits, using ethnic quotas as a lever. None of these conditions is likely to change in the near future. Federal character, and everything that goes with it, appears to be a permanent part of Nigeria's political and social landscape.

[*]See Peter Ekeh, "The Structure and Meaning of Federal Character in the Nigerian Political System," in Peter Ekeh and Eghosa E. Osaghae (eds.), *Federalism and the Federal Character in Nigeria* (Ibadan: Heinemann, 1989).

Current Challenges: **Federalism in Nigeria**

The federal system has historically enjoyed wide support within Nigeria. With the "national question" unanswered, however, the federal structure endures increasing strain. At the conclusion of the civil war in 1970, many assumed that the question of national unity had been finally settled. Attempts to include clauses on the right to secede in the constitutions of 1979 and 1989 were roundly rejected by the drafting committees. Yet the most recent transition period featured a number of public debates about partition, particularly among the Yoruba, while other groups have continually lamented their political marginalization. Questions have also been raised as to whether Nigeria will continue to be a secular state and persist as a federation if it is to accommodate the country's ethnic, cultural, and religious heterogeneity.

To resolve these issues, some Nigerians have called for a national conference to review the basis of national unity and even to consider the restructuring of Nigeria into a loose confederation of autonomous states, perhaps along the lines of the First Republic. Such calls were ignored by the military, which foreclosed any debate on the viability of a united Nigeria, thus maintaining the geographic status quo. After resisting pressures for a national conference, President Obasanjo surprised the public by convening the National Political Reform Conference in early 2005. He insists that national unity is nonnegotiable, but several proposals to restructure the federation and to alter Nigeria's presidential system have been advanced. A number of political leaders and civil society groups have criticized the conference as being overly beholden to the president, and some groups are threatening to hold their own national conference as well.

The Second Republic's experiment with presidentialism lasted for only four years before it was ended by the 1983 coup. Although some Nigerian intellectuals call for a return to parliamentarism, the presidential model has become entrenched in the nation's political arena. The return of military rule in 1983 further concentrated power in the hands of the chief executive. Thus, when Obasanjo took office, the first elected Nigerian president since Shehu Shagari in 1983, he inherited an executive structure that towered above all other arms of the federal government, far beyond the careful balance envisioned when the model was adopted in 1979.

The Executive Under Military Rule

The leadership styles among Nigeria's seven military heads of state varied widely. The military regime of General Gowon (1966–1975) was initially consensual, with major national decisions made by a council of officers from across the federation, but the head of state clung to power for several years after the war; his authority declined while he increasingly relied on a small group of advisers. Generals Muhammad and Obasanjo ruled through expanded collegial institutions, though their executive control was strengthened in practice. General Buhari, after ousting the civilian Second Republic, made no pretense of political transition, and instituted stern authoritarian control.

After a few years of relatively consensual governance, the Babangida regime (1985–1993) drifted into a more personalized and repressive mode of governance. Abacha (1993–1998) exceeded his predecessors in his harsh autocratic rule. General Abubakar, in contrast, moved quickly to relax political controls, institute a rapid democratization program, and curb the abuses of the security services. Nearly all military leaders have talked of "transitions to democracy," though only Generals Obasanjo and Abubakar fulfilled the pledge of yielding power to an elected government.

Under military administrations, the president, or head of state, made appointments to most senior government positions.[19] Since the legislature was disbanded, major executive decisions (typically passed by decrees) were subject to the approval of a ruling council of high-level military officers. By the time of Abacha's Provisional Ruling Council (PRC), however, this council had become virtually a rubber stamp for the ruler. Given the highly personalistic character of military politics, patron-client relationships flourished during this period. Not surprisingly, ethnic, religious, and regional constituencies have paid close attention to the pattern of appointments to the executive branch.

The military was structurally weakened during its long years in power, having been politicized and divided by these patron-client relationships. Under Babangida and Abacha, the military was transformed from an instrument that guarantees national defense and security into another predatory apparatus, one more powerful than political parties. Four decades after the first military coup of January 1966, most Nigerians now believe that the country's political and economic development has been profoundly hampered by military domination and misrule. Within days of his taking office in 1999, President Obasanjo retired over ninety military officers who had held political offices (such as military governorships) under the previous military juntas, seeing them as the most likely plotters of future coups. While there have been media reports of several coup plots, the military establishment has apparently remained loyal and outside of politics.

In addition, President Obasanjo has paid close attention to keeping the military professionally oriented—and in the barracks. Because he is an ex-military head of state himself, this should not be surprising. U.S. military advisers and technical assistance have been invited to redirect the Nigerian military toward regional peacekeeping expertise—and to keep them busy outside of politics. So far, this strategy seems effective, but the military remains a threat should the civilians fail to gain popular approval.

The Obasanjo Administration

As noted earlier, President Obasanjo's first six months in office were marked by a number of initiatives to reform the armed forces, revitalize the economy, address public welfare, and improve standards of governance.

Prominent among these priorities, the president sought to root out misconduct and inefficiency in the public sector. His initial appointments to manage the oil industry drew early praise for their clean management and contracting policies, and the persistent fuel scarcities of the Abacha years abated. Soon, however, familiar patterns of clientelism and financial kickbacks for oil licenses resurfaced. Obasanjo proposed an anticorruption commission with sweeping statutory powers to investigate and prosecute public officials. Delayed in its establishment, the commission had little impact, and was accused by detractors of being a political tool of the presidency. A second anticorruption commission founded in 2003, the Economic and Financial Crimes Commission (EFCC), has had an impressive record of indictments, as discussed in Section 2.

In response to calls by civil society groups for some accounting for the injustices committed during years of military rule, Obasanjo set up the Peace and Reconciliation Commission in 1999. Unlike the famous Truth and Reconciliation Commission set up by South Africa at the end of the apartheid years, the Nigerian Commission did not have the power to grant amnesty in exchange for admissions of guilt, which would better ensure that testimony would be accurate. The stories and mutual recriminations of former Abacha henchmen riveted the nation in nightly television broadcasts and created high political drama. The commission conducted some of its most sensitive inquiries in secret, and submitted its report confidentially to the president, who refused to make its findings public. The report, however, was leaked to several civil society organizations who promptly published it.

A major impediment to reform came from the ruling party itself. The PDP is a collection of powerful politicians from Nigeria's First and Second Republics, many of whom had grown rich from their complicity with the Babangida and Abacha juntas. These "big men" approached Obasanjo and engineered political machines that delivered him the 1999 election victory, through a poll marked by numerous procedural violations. As apparent reward for this support, Obasanjo filled his cabinet with many of these dubious political kingpins and did not scrutinize their handling of ministry budgets. With a difficult re-election bid in 2003, these fixers again delivered a victory for the president and the PDP, accomplished through massive fraud in a third of Nigeria's states, and questionable practices in at least another third of the country. Not surprisingly, allegations of corruption at the highest levels of the Obasanjo administration have increased, and several high officials at the cabinet and gubernatorial levels

have been investigated. Personal differences between President Obasanjo and PDP leaders in the National Assembly, particularly the Speaker of the House, meanwhile, led them to instigate impeachment proceedings against the president in mid-2002, as will be discussed in Section 4.

An important area of attention has been the conflict-ridden Niger Delta. The president's initial goodwill from visiting the region and meeting local leaders, including youths, soon turned to hostility when he refused to negotiate claims by delta communities for greater control of the revenues from oil drilled on their lands. Instead, he proposed a Niger Delta Development Commission (NDDC) to disburse the 13 percent of oil revenues constitutionally mandated to return to the delta states. Community groups rejected the plan, governors of the Niger Delta states took Obasanjo to court, and youth militias returned to harassing the police, stealing oil, and kidnapping oil workers for ransom. One such attack killed several policemen in November 1999, whereupon military units destroyed the village of Odi and massacred many of its inhabitants.[20] The NDDC was slow to take shape and had little impact on the region's development. Meanwhile, ethnic militias, living off stolen oil, continue to grow bolder and more restive. Violence in Delta State in 2003 shut down nearly 40 percent of the country's oil exports for several days.

The fraud in the 2003 elections undermined the PDP government's legitimacy and signaled to "big men" across Nigeria that any method to achieve power was acceptable in Nigerian politics. Shortly after the governor of Anambra state was "elected" in a race that was by all accounts rigged—President Obasanjo himself later publicly admitted as much—the governor sought to distance himself from the "godfather" who had rigged the election for him. After the governor was abducted and released by rogue police officers, Anambra was reduced to a war zone between supporters of the governor and those of his patron. Obasanjo and other PDP leaders sought to mediate, but tellingly, the president refused to give the governor police protection or to arrest his political adversary.

A similar struggle between the governor of Plateau State (whose most recent election was also tainted) and other big men turned violent, as both sides used ethnic and religious grievances to incite communities across these divides. Christian attacks on Muslim communities in the town of Yelwa in May 2004 prompted revenge attacks by Muslims against Christians in several Middle Belt states and in Kano, forcing the president to declare a state of emergency in Plateau and to impose a military administrator for six months. Surprisingly, President Obasanjo restored the governor to office once the emergency was lifted, despite the fact that the British government had subsequently brought charges of money laundering against the governor.

The events in Anambra and Plateau states, as well as the chaos in the Niger Delta region, demonstrated deficits of legitimacy for the government as well as the democratic system. As Nigeria's political elites continue to flout the rules of the system, it is inevitable that patronage, coercion, and personal interest will drive policy more than the interests of the public. The

president sought to renew his reform agenda in 2005 with high-profile anticorruption and economic reform policies, but the titanic struggles of the big men at all levels of Nigerian politics continue to dilute and undermine the impact of these reforms. The president's occasional ambivalence about legal restraints on his own powers, as in the case of Plateau State, also offsets his own reform agenda.

The Bureaucracy

The bureaucracy touches upon all aspects of Nigerian government. The colonial system relied on an expanding bureaucracy to govern Nigeria. As government was increasingly "Africanized," the bureaucracy became a way to reward individuals in the patrimonial system (see "Current Challenges: Prebendalism").

Current Challenges: **Prebendalism**

Prebendalism, the peculiarly Nigerian version of corruption, is the disbursing of public offices and state rents to one's ethnic-based clients.* It is an extreme form of clientelism that refers to the practice of mobilizing cultural and other sectional identities by political aspirants and officeholders for the purpose of corruptly appropriating state resources. Prebendalism is an established pattern of political behavior that justifies the pursuit of and the use of public office for the personal benefit of the officeholder and his clients. The official public purpose of the office becomes a secondary concern. As with clientelism, the officeholder's clients comprise a specific set of elites to which he is linked, typically by ethnic or religious ties, and this linkage is key to understanding the concept. There are thus two sides involved in prebendalism, the officeholder and the client, and expectations of benefits by the clients (or supporters) perpetuate the prebendal system.

As practiced in the Babangida and Abacha eras, when official corruption occurred on an unprecedented scale, prebendalism deepened sectional cleavages and eroded the resources of the state. It also discouraged genuinely productive

activity in the economy and expanded the class of individuals who live off state patronage.

As long as prebendalism remains the norm of Nigerian politics, a stable democracy will be elusive. These practices are now deeply embedded in Nigerian society and are therefore more difficult to uproot. The corruption resulting from prebendal practices is blamed in popular discourse for the enormous overseas flight of capital into private accounts. The lion's share of the $12.2 billion windfall of the early 1990s is believed to have been pocketed by Babangida and senior members of his regime, an example of the magnitude of the systematic pilfering of public resources. General Abacha continued this pattern and diverted $5 billion from the Nigerian central bank. There are so many current officeholders in Nigeria who indulge in corrupt practices that Transparency International regularly lists Nigeria among the most corrupt countries.

---

*Richard Joseph, *Democracy and Prebendal Politics in Nigeria: The Rise and Fall of the Second Republic* (Cambridge: Cambridge University Press, 1987) 55–68.

Bureaucratic growth was no longer determined by function and need; increasingly, individuals were appointed on the basis of patronage, ethnic group, and regional origin rather than merit.

It is conservatively estimated that federal and state government personnel increased from a modest 72,000 at independence to well over 1 million by the mid-1980s. The salaries of these bureaucrats presently consume roughly half of government expenditures, which after another 30 percent or more for debt servicing leaves a paltry 10 percent or so for the other responsibilities of government, from education and health care to building the roads.

Para-statals

Among the largest components of the national administration in Nigeria are numerous state-owned enterprises, or **para-statals.** Para-statals in Nigeria are corporate enterprises, owned by the state, created for specific commercial and social welfare services. They are a hybrid, somewhere between institutions that engage in traditional government operations, such as customs or the postal service, and those in the private sector that operate primarily for profit. Para-statals are similar to private enterprises in having their own boards of directors. In principle, they are autonomous of the government that established them. In reality, however, such autonomy is limited since their boards are politically appointed and ultimately answerable to the government. In general, para-statals are established for several reasons. First, they furnish public facilities, including water, power, telecommunications, ports, and other transportation. A second rationale for the establishment of para-statals is the need to accelerate economic development by controlling the commanding heights of the economy, including steel production, petroleum and natural gas production, refining, petrochemicals, fertilizer, and certain areas of agriculture. Third, para-statals are intended to provide basic utilities and services to citizens at low costs, held below the levels that would be needed by private firms to generate profit. Finally, there is a nationalist dimension that relates to issues of sovereignty over sectors perceived sensitive for national security.

Para-statals such as agricultural commodity boards and the Nigerian National Petroleum Corporation (NNPC) have served as major instruments of the interventionist state. They have been used to co-opt and organize business and societal interests for the purpose of politically controlling the economy and dispensing state largesse. These enterprises are major instruments of patronage and rent seeking. In Nigeria, as in the rest of Africa, most para-statal enterprises are a tremendous drain on the economy. It is not surprising, therefore, that one of the major requirements of the economic structural adjustment program discussed in Section 2 is the privatization of most of these enterprises. Privatizing the para-statals remains a central part of reform strategy under the Obasanjo administration. The telecommunications and power industries are already up for sale, and the administration has promised to sell parts of the oil industry.

Other State Institutions

Other institutions of governance and policymaking, including the federal judiciary and subnational governments (incorporating state and local courts), operate within the context of a strong central government dominated by a powerful chief executive.

The Judiciary

At one time, the Nigerian judiciary enjoyed relative autonomy from the executive arm of government. Aggrieved individuals and organizations could take the government to court and expect a judgment based on the merits of their case. This situation changed as each successive military government demonstrated a profound disdain for judicial practices, and eventually it undermined not only the autonomy but also the very integrity of the judiciary as a third branch of government.

The Babangida and Abacha regimes, in particular, issued a spate of repressive decrees disallowing judicial review. Clauses were regularly inserted in government decrees barring any consideration of their legality by the courts, as well as any actions taken by government officials under them. Other methods included intimidation by the security services, the creation of parallel special military tribunals that could dispense with various legal procedures and due process, and disrespect for courts of record.

Through the executive's power of appointment of judicial officers to the high bench, as well as the executive's control of funds required for the running of the judiciary, the government can dominate the courts at all levels. In addition, what was once regarded as a highly competent judiciary has been undermined severely by declining standards of legal training as well as by bribery.

The decline of court independence reached a new low in 1993 when the Supreme Court, in what some analysts labeled "judicial terrorism," endorsed a government position that literally placed all actions of the military executive beyond the pale of judicial review. The detention and hanging of Ken Saro-Wiwa and eight other Ogoni activists in 1995 (see Section 2) underscored the politicization and compromised state of the judicial system. With the return of civilian rule, however, the courts have slowly begun to restore some independence and credibility. The Supreme Court in particular has returned as a critical player in national political development after years of docility and self-imposed irrelevance. In early 2002, it passed two landmark judgments. The first struck down a 2001 election law that would have prevented new parties from contesting the national elections in 2003—a decision that contravened the wishes of the president and the ruling party. The Court also decided against the governors of Nigeria's coastal states over control of the vast offshore gas reserves, declaring these to be under the jurisdiction of the federal government.

State and Local Judiciaries. The judiciaries at the state level are subordinate to the Federal Court of Appeal and the Supreme Court. Some of the states in the northern part of the country with large Muslim populations maintain a parallel court system based on the Islamic *shari'a* (religious law). Similarly, some states in the Middle Belt and southern part of the country have subsidiary courts based on customary law. Each of these maintains an appellate division. Otherwise, all courts of record in the country are based on the English common law tradition, and all courts are ultimately bound by decisions handed down by the Supreme Court.

How to apply the *shari'a* has been a source of continuing debate in Nigerian politics. For several years, some northern groups have participated in a movement to expand the application of *shari'a* law in predominantly Muslim areas of Nigeria, and some even have advocated that it be made the supreme law of the land. Prior to the establishment of the Fourth Republic, *shari'a* courts had jurisdiction only among Muslims in civil proceedings and in questions of Islamic personal law. In November 1999, however, the northern state of Zamfara instituted a version of the *shari'a* criminal code, which included cutting off hands for stealing, and stoning to death for those (especially women) who committed adultery. Eleven other northern states adopted the criminal code by 2001, prompting fears among Christian minorities in these states that the code might be applied to them and creating a divisive national issue. Although the *shari'a* criminal code appears to contradict Nigeria's officially secular constitution, the administration has so far been unwilling to take these states to court and appears to be pushing for a political solution.

State and Local Government

Because the creation of new states and local governments opens new channels to the oil wealth accumulated at the federal level, localities and groups are constantly clamoring for further subdivision. Periodic changes in these federal arrangements, including the creation of new states and the addition of a third level of local government, has generally occurred under nondemocratic auspices of colonial and military rule. Sensing opportunities to buy support for their regimes, Babangida and Abacha nearly doubled the number of states and tripled that of local governments (see Table 5). Although they touted these moves as answering the "national question" by increasing opportunities for local self-determination, the limited fiscal and political autonomy of these units has in fact bolstered central government control. Several states have added local governments since 2000, but the federal government has argued that they do not have the constitutional authority to do so.

The Nigerian experience has promoted a distributive approach to federalism. The lofty claims for federalism as a way of promoting unity through diversity are lost amid the intense competition among local communities and elites for access to national patronage, which

Table 5

Political Divisions, 1963–1996

1963	1967	1976	1987	1991	1996
					(Northwest zone)
Northern Region	North Central	Kaduna	Kaduna	Kaduna	Kaduna
			Katsina	Katsina	Katsina
	Kano	Kano	Kano	Kano	Kano
				Jigawa	Jigawa
	North Western	Sokoto	Sokoto	Sokoto	Sokoto
					Zamfara
				Kebbi	Kebbi
					(North-Central zone)
		Niger	Niger	Niger	Niger
	Benue-Plateau	Benue-Plateau	Benue-Plateau	Benue	Benue
				Plateau	Plateau
					Nassarawa
		Abuja	Abuja	FCT (Abuja)[c]	FCT (Abuja)
	West Central	Kwara	Kwara	Kwara	Kwara
				Kogi[a]	Kogi
					(Northeast zone)
	North Eastern	Bauchi	Bauchi	Bauchi	Bauchi
					Gombe
		Borno	Borno	Borno	Borno
				Yobe	Yobe
		Gongola	Gongola	Adamawa	Adamawa
				Taraba	Taraba
					(Southeast zone)
Eastern Region	East Central	Anambra	Anambra	Anambra	Anambra
				Enugu	Enugu
					Ebonyi
		Imo	Imo	Imo	Imo
				Abia	Abia
					(South-south zone)
	South Eastern	Cross River	Cross River	Cross River	Cross River
			Akwa Ibom	Akwa Ibom	Akwa Ibom
	Rivers	Rivers	Rivers	Rivers	Rivers
					Bayelsa
					(Southwest zone)
Mid-West Region	Mid-Western	Bendel	Bendel	Edo	Edo
				Delta	Delta
Western Region	Western	Ogun	Ogun	Ogun	Ogun
		Ondo	Ondo	Ondo	Ondo
					Ekiti
		Oyo	Oyo	Oyo	Oyo
				Osun	Osun
Lagos[b]	Lagos	Lagos	Lagos	Lagos	Lagos

[a]Kogi state was created by combining parts of Benue and Kwara states.

[b]Lagos was excised from the Western Region in 1954 and became the federal capital. In 1967, it also became capital of the new Lagos State, which included Badagry, Ikeja, and Epe districts from the Western Region.

[c]Abuja replaced Lagos as the federal capital in December 1991, although its boundaries were first delineated in the 1970s.

Source: Tom Forrest, *Politics and Economic Development in Nigeria* (Boulder, Colo.: Westview Press, 1993), 214; Darren Kew.

comes in the form of oil revenues that are collected, and then appropriated or redistributed, by the federal administration through the states. (See Table 6.)

State governments are generally weak and dependent on federally controlled revenues. Most of them would be insolvent and unable to sustain themselves without substantial support from the central government because of the states' weak resource and tax base. About 90 percent of state incomes are received directly from the federal government, which includes a lump sum based on oil revenues, plus a percentage of oil income based on population. The states and local governments, however, must generate more resources of their own to increase the efficiency of both their administrations and private economic sectors. In

all likelihood, only Lagos and Kano states could survive without federal subsidies.

In response to the proliferation of states, the political parties have turned to the notion of six zones in Nigeria, correlated roughly with the major ethnic regions in the country: Hausa-Fulani, Igbo, Yoruba, and three minority-dominated areas. Political appointments are roughly balanced among the six zones and rotate over time.[21] For instance, the presidency is currently held by the southwest (Yoruba) zone; the next president, by informal agreement, will likely be from one of the Middle Belt minorities, the Northeast, or from the South-South zone—the Niger Delta.

In the same way that states depend on federal handouts, local governments have remained dependent

Table 6

Percentage Contribution of Different Sources of Government Revenue to Allocated Revenue, 1980–2003

	Oil Revenue Petroleum Profits Tax	Mining Rents and Royalties	Nonoil Revenue Customs and Excise Duties	Others	Total
1980	58.1	25.7	12.3	3.9	100.0
1981	55.5	19.6	20.4	4.5	100.0
1982	44.5	27.3	21.5	6.7	100.0
1983	35.7	33.4	18.9	12.0	100.0
1984	44.8	32.4	15.2	7.6	100.0
1985	47.8	30.0	14.7	7.5	100.0
1986	40.5	25.3	14.6	19.6	100.0
1987	50.6	25.4	14.3	9.7	100.0
1988	46.7	31.5	15.9	5.9	100.0
	Oil Revenues (Combined)		Nonoil Revenue	Other	Total
1992	86.2		8.4	5.4	100.0
1993	84.0		8.0	8.0	100.0
1994	79.3		9.1	11.6	100.0
1995	53.2		8.1	38.7*	100.0
1996	51.1		10.6	38.3*	100.0
2001	79.7		17.6	2.7	100.0
2002	78.6		19.4	2.0	100.0
2003	78.1		19.9	2.0	100.0

*Beginning in 1995, the Nigerian government began including surplus foreign exchange as federally collected revenue in its accounting.

Sources: Federal Ministry of Finance and Economic Development, Lagos. From Adedotun Phillips, "Managing Fiscal Federalism: Revenue Allocation Issues," *Publius: The Journal of Federalism,* 21, no. 4 (Fall 1991), p. 109. Nigerian Federal Office of Statistics, *Annual Abstract of Statistics: 1997 Edition.* Nigerian Economic Summit Group, *Economic Indicators* (Vol. 8, no. 2, April–June 2002).

on both state and federal governments. This practice has continued despite the 1988 reforms of the local government system initiated by the Babangida regime, supposedly to strengthen that level of government. Dissatisfaction with local government performance persists, and President Obasanjo appointed a high-level committee to recommend reforms, which has yielded little concrete action. The current National Political Reform Conference may issue new proposals.

The state and local governments have the constitutional and legal powers to raise funds through taxes. However, Nigerians share a pronounced unwillingness, especially those in self-employment, trade, and other informal sector activities, to pay taxes and fees to a government with such a poor record of delivering basic services. The result is a vicious cycle: government is sapped of resources and legitimacy and cannot adequately serve the people. Communities, in turn, are compelled to resort to self-help measures to protect these operations and thus withdraw further from the reach of the state. Because very few individuals and organizations pay taxes, even the most basic government functions are starved of resources (see Table 7).

The return of democratic rule has meant the return of conflict between the state and national governments, much like during the Second Republic (1979–1983). The primary vehicle for conflict since 1999 has been a series of "governors' forums," one for the seventeen southern governors, one for the nineteen northern governors, and one for all thirty-six governors. Ad hoc committees on specific issues have also arisen. Southern governors have been particularly active in asserting greater legal control over the resources in their states (such as oil) and over the offshore oil and gas reserves. Much as at the national level, the state-level executives have far more power than their legislatures. These state assemblies, however, have not been docile, and on several occasions they have moved to impeach their state governors.

A number of governors, particularly in the Igbo-dominated southeast, have turned to armed militias and vigilante groups to provide security in their states and to intimidate political opponents. Many of these groups were initially local responses to the corrupt and ineffective police force, but several of the governors have sensed the larger political usefulness of these groups. Consequently, and disturbingly, political assassinations and violence increased as the 2003 elections approached. Some of these militias in the Niger Delta have turned on their former masters, on

Table 7

Share of Total Government Expenditure (%)

	1961	1965	1970	1975	1980	1987	1992	1996	2001	2002
Federal Government	49	53	73	72	66	75	72	74	57	52.3
State Government	51	47	27	28	34	25	28*	26*	24	26
Local Government**	–	–	–	–	–	–	–	–	20	21.7
Total Expenditure (millions Naira)	336	445	1,149	10,916	21,349	29,365	128,476	327,707	1,008,780	1,111,950

* Note that 67% of state spending in 1992 and 49% of it in 1996 came from federal government oil earnings, part of which are allocated annually to all the states roughly in proportion to their population size.

**Local government expenditures are included in state government figures in 1961 and 1965, and federal figures from 1970 through 1996.

Sources: Central Bank of Nigeria, Annual Report and Statement of Accounts; Federal Office of Statistics, Abstract of Annual Statistics (Lagos: Federal Government Printer, 1961, 1965, 1970, 1975, 1980, 1987, and 1997). From Izeubuwa Osayimwese and Sunday Iyare, "The Economics of Nigerian Federalism: Selected Issues in Economic Management," *Publius: The Journal of Federalism*, 21, no. 4 (Fall 1991), p. 91. Nigerian Economic Summit Group, Economic Indicators (Vol. 8, no. 2, April–June 2002). 1990s percentage calculations by Darren Kew.

one occasion forcing the Rivers State governor to flee to Abuja for protection.

The Policy-Making Process

Nigeria's prolonged experience with military rule has resulted in a policy process based more on top-down directives than on consultation, political debate, and legislation. Several years of democratic government have seen important changes, as the legislatures, courts, and state governments have begun to force the presidency to negotiate its policies and work within a constitutional framework.

First, we must explore how military rule shaped policymaking in Nigeria. Because of their influence in recruitment and promotions, as well as through their own charisma or political connections, senior officers often developed networks of supporters of the same or lower rank, creating what is referred to as a "loyalty pyramid."[22] Once in power, the men at the top of these pyramids in Nigeria gained access to tremendous oil wealth, passed on through the lower echelons of the pyramid to reward support. Often these pyramids reflect ethnic or religious affiliations (see the discussions of corruption in Section 2 and **prebendalism** in Section 3) such as the "Kaduna Mafia" of northern elites, but pyramids like the "Babangida" or "Abacha Boys" included a patchwork of officers beyond their ethnic circle. In addition, the well-developed pyramids had allies or personal connections in the bureaucracy and business. The personal ambitions of leaders commonly eclipsed the corporate mission of the military, Personal goals and interests became the defining characteristic of the regime and its policies, with the only check on personal power being another coup.

General Babangida signified a turning point within the military as national concerns were increasingly subsumed by personal ambitions.[23] He was a master at playing the different loyalty pyramids against each other, lavishing the nation's oil wealth on friends and buying the support of opponents he could not crush. Once in power, General Abacha made little pretense of accommodating other factions, instead ruthlessly centralizing nearly all government decision making and spreading little patronage.

Abacha's personal plunder of the nation's revenues dispelled the notion that the military was a cohesive,

nationalist institution capable of governing Nigeria any more efficiently than the civilians. A parallel structure of junior officers loyal to Abacha acted as his gatekeepers, circumventing and humiliating the military's normal chain of command. General Abubakar thus took the reins of a military that was divided and demoralized. Abubakar was more of a professional than his predecessors, purging the government of "Abacha boys" and swiftly returning the country to civilian rule. Despite having returned to the barracks, others in the military may well yearn for their turn at the top.

Because the military dominated Nigeria for three-quarters of its independent existence, civilian politics bears a strong resemblance to the politics of loyalty pyramids among the military.[24] Many of the current civilian politicians belonged to the loyalty pyramids of different military men—as bureaucrats, members of military cabinets, business partners to exploit Nigeria's oil wealth, and so on. Now that the politicians are in power, some of them former military officers, they are taking up the reins of the civilian portions of these pyramids, while they undoubtedly retain some influence with military figures.

Nigerians often refer to the politicians who sit atop these civilian loyalty pyramids as "big men." Unlike the military leaders, however, the civilian big men do not typically have access to formal coercive instruments, so to maintain their pyramids they must rely on financial kickbacks and promises of rents from the state: government jobs, contracts, and so on. (Section 4 discusses these clientelistic and prebendal patterns of the loyalty pyramids in greater detail.)

Thus, in patterns reminiscent of the struggles among military loyalty pyramids, the policymaking process today in Nigeria under democratic rule is a function of the clash of interests among the big men and their clients. The vice president, party leaders of the PDP, many of the ministers, and leaders in the National Assembly are all big men vying for larger rents from the state and increased influence and status. Ironically, Obasanjo was not a "big man" when he was elected; he rode to power on the backs of these big men and their supporters who are now in intense competition with each other.

Civilian policymaking in present-day Nigeria centers largely on presidential initiative in proposing reform policies, which are then filtered through the interests of the "big men." Invariably, their agendas conflict with those of the president and with each other, and policies are consequently blocked or significantly altered. Frequently, the reformist agenda is stalled or ineffectual. The president became increasingly adept at navigating these interests in his first term, but soon enough the reformist agenda took a back seat to his own concern for reelection. On this point his ministers were agreed, and policymaking by the administration was harnessed to the goal of getting the president reelected by any possible means. After the elections, the president turned back to a reform agenda, though these policies remain mired in the competition of interests among the big men of the political class.

Section ❹ Representation and Participation

Representation and participation are two vital components in modern democracies. Nigerian legislatures have commonly been sidelined or reduced to subservience by the powerful executive, while fraud, elite manipulation, and military interference have marred the party and electoral systems. Consequently, Nigerian society has found modes of participation outside the official structures. An important focus of this section will therefore be unofficial (that is, nongovernmental) methods of representation and participation through the institutions of civil society. The institutions of political society include such entities as parties, constitutions, and legislatures, while those of **civil society** include professional associations, trade unions, religious organizations, and various interest groups.

The patterns outlined in this section reflect the complexities of the relationship between representation and participation. Formal representation does not necessarily enhance participation. In fact, there are situations in which the most important modes of political participation are found outside institutional channels such as elections and legislatures—or even in opposition to them.

The Legislature

Not surprisingly, Nigeria's legislature has been a victim of the country's political instability. Legislative structures and processes historically suffered abuse, neglect, or peremptory suspension by the executive arm. As a consequence, the politicians who took office at the state and federal levels in 1999 had little understanding, and less experience, of legislative functions and responsibilities. In addition, they stood in the shadow of the overly powerful executive that had dominated Nigerian politics under the military.

Until the first coup in 1966, Nigeria operated its legislature along the lines of the British Westminster model, with an elected lower house and a smaller upper house composed of individuals selected by the executive. For the next thirteen years of military rule, a Supreme Military Council performed legislative functions by initiating and passing decrees at will. During the second period of civilian rule, 1979–1983, the bicameral legislature was structured similar to the U.S. system, with a Senate and House of Representatives (together known as the National Assembly) consisting of elected members.

Election to the Senate is on the basis of equal state representation, with three senators from each of the thirty-six states, plus one senator from the federal capital territory, Abuja. The practice of equal representation in the Senate is identical to that of the United States, except that each Nigerian state elects three senators instead of two. Election to the Nigerian House of Representatives was also based on state representation but weighted to reflect the relative size of each state's population, again after the U.S. example. Only eight women were elected in 1999 to sit in the Fourth Republic's National Assembly. This reflects the limited political participation of Nigerian women in formal institutions, as discussed in Section 2.

An innovation added during the failed transition to the Third Republic is that local government structures now enjoy greater autonomy from control by the state governments. The federal executive has, however, dominated other branches of government, partly as a consequence of military rule, and also by virtue of the strong fiscal centralization of the oil-based state.

Thus, Nigerian legislatures under military government were either powerless (as during the brief sitting of the Assembly in 1992–1993) or nonexistent. Even under previous elected civil administrations, however, Nigerian legislatures were subjected to great pressure by the executive and never assumed their full constitutional role. Because the executive and majority interests in the National Assembly belonged to the same party, influence has been easily exercised through party machines and outright bribery. This situation has been exacerbated by legislative dependence on the executive for their allowances and the resources to meet the relentless demands from their constituents for jobs, contracts, and other favors. This is the critical difference between the Nigerian and U.S. systems: in Nigeria, the president controls and disburses public revenues, which the Assembly only influences by its right to pass the budget. The U.S. Congress, by contrast, controls the public purse.

The National Assembly that took office in 1999 therefore began its work with great uncertainty over its role in Nigerian politics. Both the House and the Senate were controlled by the People's Democratic Party (PDP), as was the presidency. Thus, many observers expected the familiar pattern of executive dominance of the legislature through the party structures to continue as it had under the Second and Third Republics.

Initially, these expectations were fulfilled. Legislators spent most of their time clamoring for their personal spending funds to be disbursed by the executive. Some of their first acts were to vote themselves pay raises and exorbitant furniture expenditures (thus provoking a protest strike by trade unions). Other legislators tested the waters for the first time with a variety of radical bills that never emerged from committee, including one that would have asked the United States to invade Nigeria if the military staged another coup. The first Speaker of the House was forced to resign when a newspaper discovered that he had lied about his age and was too young to run for office. Three Senate presidents were also forced to resign when the media unearthed evidence of irregularities and corruption. The president, meanwhile, referred to legislators as "small boys" and rarely accorded them the respect of an equal branch of government.

Gradually, however, the National Assembly began to fight back and gain some relevance. The one constitutional power of the Assembly that President Obasanjo could not circumvent was the authority to approve the national budget. In 2001, negotiations between the president and Assembly leaders over the budget became deadlocked, and it was eventually passed several months after it was due. The 2002 budget negotiations were even more bruising, and the president was ultimately forced to sign a budget higher than the revenues expected for that year. When oil revenues dipped even lower than expected, Obasanjo unilaterally chose to disburse only a portion of the budgeted funds to programs of his choosing. Among the funds withheld were those for the National Assembly. In August 2002, the House and the Senate, including members of Obasanjo's own party, began impeachment proceedings against the president. A face-saving compromise, and an apology from the president, was reached through a combination of negotiation and reported side payments to key legislators.

The impeachment move was not so much a serious attempt to remove the president as it was a statement to Obasanjo that he had to deal with the legislature with respect and as an equal partner in governance. The motives of legislators were hardly pure, since most were primarily concerned with getting their personal slices of the budget, but the president had clearly overstepped his constitutional role by arbitrarily choosing which portions of the budget he would respect. Some of the big men in the Assembly, particularly the Speaker of the House, had personal grudges against Obasanjo that were also at play in the impeachment move. Overall, however, the legislature emerged strengthened from the encounter.

The president, however, ensured that this victory for the institution came at a heavy price for its members: Nearly 80 percent of legislators elected in 1999 were not returned in 2003—not because their constituents voted them out, but because they were removed in the PDP primaries, a process that President Obasanjo and the governors largely controlled. Not taking any chances, the PDP leadership even went so far as to have a court reverse the 2003 election results against one of their defeated candidates and then to have the man elected Senate president. Despite these efforts to ensure a more compliant leadership in the

National Assembly, the president has been more respectful of the prerogatives of the legislature in his second term, and legislators continue to demonstrate that they have their own minds on budget matters and significant legislation.

Legislatures at the state level face a similar imbalance of power with the governors, who control large local bureaucracies and disburse the funds received from the federally shared revenues. The politics of these state assemblies have been chaotic and often vicious, with behavior ranging from throwing chairs to storming the assembly hall with supporters, and increasingly, the use of political violence.

The Party System and Elections

An unfortunate legacy of the party and electoral systems after independence was that political parties were associated with particular regions and ethnic groups.[25] The tendency to perceive politics as a zero-sum (or winner-take-all) struggle for access to scarce state resources encouraged political and social fragmentation. Unlike Ghana, Mexico and, to some extent, India, Nigeria did not develop an authoritarian dominant-party system after independence, which might have transcended some of these social cleavages. Instead, the multiparty system deepened existing social divisions.

Nigeria's use of a first-past-the-post plurality electoral system produced legislative majorities for parties with strong ethnic and regional identities. Nigerian parties during the First Republic were dominated by the largest ethnic group in each of the three regions. During subsequent democratic experiments, many of the newer parties could trace their roots to their predecessors in the first civilian regime. In consequence, parties were more attentive to the welfare of the regions from which they drew their support than to the development of Nigeria as a whole. Control of the center, or special political access, assured claims to substantial financial resources. In a polity as potentially volatile as Nigeria, these tendencies intensified political polarization and resentment among the losers.

In the Second Republic, the leading parties shared the same ethnic and sectional support, and often the same leadership, as the parties prominent in the first civilian regime. The Unity Party of Nigeria, UPN (mainly Yoruba), was headed by former Action Group leader Chief Obafemi Awolowo; the Nigerian Peoples Party, NPP (mainly Igbo), was led by Nnamdi Azikiwe (formerly of the NCNC); the Peoples Redemption Party, PRP (centered in Kano city in northern Nigeria), was led by Mallam Aminu Kano; while the Great Nigeria Peoples Party, GNPP (organized around the Kanuri northeast), was a newer tendency under Waziri Ibrahim. The dominant party in the Second Republic, the National Party of Nigeria (NPN), brought together a diverse cross-ethnic coalition under a predominantly northern leadership that had been previously associated with the Northern People's Congress (NPC). In its wavering steps toward the civilian Third Republic, General Babangida announced a landmark decision in 1989 to establish only two political parties by decree.[26] The state provided initial start-up funds, wrote the constitutions and manifestos of these parties, and designed them to be "a little to the right and a little to the left," respectively, on the political-ideological spectrum. Interestingly, the elections that took place under these rules from 1990–1993 indicated that, despite their inauspicious beginnings, the two parties cut across the cleavages of ethnicity, regionalism, and religion, demonstrating the potential to move beyond ethnicity.[27] The Social Democratic Party (SDP), which emerged victorious in the 1993 national elections, was an impressive coalition of Second Republic party structures, including elements of the former UPN, NPP, PRP, and GNPP. The opposing National Republican Convention (NRC) was seen as having its roots in northern groups that were the core of the National Party of Nigeria (NPN).

Table 8 shows historical trends in electoral patterns and communal affiliations. As clearly outlined, northern-based parties dominated the first and second experiments with civilian rule. Given this background, it is significant that Moshood Abiola was able to win the presidency in 1993, the first time in Nigeria's history that a southerner electorally defeated a northerner. Abiola, a Yoruba Muslim, won a number of key states in the north, including the hometown of his opponent. Southerners therefore perceived the decision by the northern-dominated Babangida regime to annul the June 12 elections as a deliberate attempt by the military and northern interests to maintain their decades-long domination of the highest levels of government.

Table 8

Federal Election Results in Nigeria, 1959–2003

Presidential Election Results, 1979–2003

	Victor (% of the vote)	Leading Contender (% of the vote)
1979	Shehu Shagari, NPN (33.8)	Obafemi Awolowo, UPN (29.2)
1983	Shehu Shagari, NPN (47.3)	Obafemi Awolowo, UPN (31.1)
1993	M.K.O. Abiola, SDP (58.0)	Bashir Tofa, NRC (42.0)
1999	Olusegun Obasanjo, PDP (62.8)	Olu Falae, AD/APP alliance (37.2)
2003	Olusegun Obasanjo, PDP (61.9)	Mohammadu Buhari, ANPP (31.2)

Parties Controlling the Parliament/National Assembly (Both Houses) by Ethno-Regional Zone, First to Fourth Republics

		Northwest	North-Central	Northeast	Southwest	South-South	Southeast
First	1959	**NPC**	**NPC** (NEPU)	**NPC**	AG	AG	NCNC*
	1964–65	**NPC**	**NPC**	**NPC**	NNDP* (AG)**	NNDP* (AG)**	NCNC
Second	1979	**NPN**	PRP **(NPN, UPN)**	GNPP **(NPN)**	UPN **(NPN)**	**NPN** (UPN)	NPP*
	1983	**NPN**	**NPN** (PRP)	**NPN**	UPN **(NPN)**	**NPN**	NPP**
Third	1992	**NRC**	SDP **(NRC)**	SDP **(NRC)**	SDP	**NRC** (SDP)	**NRC**
Fourth	1999	**PDP** (APP)	**PDP**	**PDP** (APP)	AD **(PDP)**	**PDP** (APP)	**PDP**
	2003	ANPP **(PDP)**	ANPP **(PDP)**	**PDP** (ANPP)	**PDP** AD	**PDP** (ANPP)	**PDP** (APGA)

Boldfaced: Ruling party

Italicized: Leading opposition

*: Coalition with ruling party

**: Coalition with opposition

National Assembly and State Level Elections

Senate	1999	2003
PDP	63	73
APP/ANPP	26	28
AD	20	6

House	1999	2003
PDP	214	213
APP/ANPP	77	95
AD	69	31
Other		7

Table 8 (continued)

Federal Election Results in Nigeria, 1959–2003

Governorships	1999	2003
PDP	21	28
APP/ANPP	9	7
AD	6	1
State Houses of Assembly	*1999*	*2003*
PDP	23	28
APP/ANPP	8	7
AD	5	1

List of Acronyms Used in Table 8

AG	Action Group
AD	Alliance for Democracy
ANPP	All Nigerian Peoples Party (formerly APP)
APGA	Alll People's Grand Alliance
APP	All People's Party
GNPP	Great Nigerian Peoples' Party
NAP	Nigerian Advance Party
NCNC	National Convention of Nigerian Citizens (formerly National Council of Nigeria and the Cameroons)
NEPU	Northern Elements Progressive Union
NNDP	Nigerian National Democratic Party
NPC	Northern People's Congress
NPF	Northern Progressive Front
NPN	National Party of Nigeria
NPP	Nigerian People's Party
NRC	National Republican Convention
PRP	People's Redemption Party
PDP	People's Democratic Party
SDP	Social Democratic Party
UPN	Unity Party of Nigeria

Old Roots and New Alignments: The PDP and the Other Parties of the Fourth Republic

Nigerians generally reacted with anger to General Abacha's 1993 coup and his subsequent banning of the SDP and NRC, although party members themselves, with few exceptions, offered a muted response. Southern-based human rights and prodemocracy groups, in alliance with student unions and other organizations, launched street demonstrations, and trade union strikes brought the economy to a halt by mid-1994. With the unions crushed and Abiola in jail by the end of 1994, Abacha started his own transition program in October 1995. It featured a series of elections from the local to the federal levels over the following three years in a manner reminiscent of the Babangida program. In late 1996, the Abacha government registered only five parties, most of whose members had no public constituency and little political experience. By the time local government elections were held in January 1997, the few people who did vote had little idea for whom they were voting; some of the candidates confessed publicly that they had never seen their party's manifesto.

During 1997, the five parties, branded by the opposition as "five fingers of a leprous hand," began to clamor for General Abacha to run for president. Public participation in state assembly elections in December 1997 was abysmal, as each of the parties proclaimed, one after another, that Abacha was their candidate. The presidential election scheduled for August 1998 was reduced to a mere referendum, endorsed by the chief justice of the Supreme Court as legally permissible. The "transition" process had become a travesty.[28] Once Abacha's plan to be certified as president became a certainty, domestic opposition increased. A group of former governors and political leaders from the north (many former NPN and PRP members) publicly petitioned Abacha not to run for president. They were later joined by colleagues from the south, forming what they called the Group of 34 (G-34). Human rights and prodemocracy organizations began again to form alliances to organize protests, and critical press coverage recovered some of its former boldness. Even General Babangida voiced his opposition to Abacha's continuing as president. The only real obstacle to Abacha's plan for "self-succession" was whether the military would allow it.

Although there had been frequent rumors of Abacha's ill health, his death on June 8, 1998, was still a great surprise. The following day, General Abubakar, chief of Defense Staff, was sworn in as head of state. Shortly afterward, he promised a speedy transition to democracy and began releasing political prisoners. There were immediate calls for Chief Abiola's release and his appointment to head an interim government of national unity. Abiola's fatal heart attack a month after Abacha's death raised considerable suspicion, since Abiola had remained the sole obstacle to a fresh political process and new elections, which the military establishment clearly preferred. The political process, however, proceeded apace. New parties quickly formed, and even Yoruba political leaders agreed to participate, although they insisted that the next president should be a Yoruba to compensate their people for having been robbed of their first elected presidency.

Once again, political associations centered on well-known personalities, and intense bargaining and mergers took place. The G-34, the prominent group of civilian leaders who had condemned Abacha's plans to perpetuate his power, created the People's Democratic Party (PDP) in late August, minus most of their Yoruba members, who joined the Alliance for Democracy (AD). At least twenty more parties applied for certification to the electoral commission (INEC); many of them were truly grass-roots movements, including a human rights organization and a trade union party.

To escape the ethnic-based parties of the First and Second Republics, INEC required that parties earn at least 5 percent of the votes in twenty-four of the thirty-six states in local government elections in order to advance to the later state and federal levels. This turned out to be an ingenious way of reducing the number of parties, while obliging viable parties to broaden their appeal. The only parties to meet INEC's requirements were the PDP, AD, and the All Peoples Party (APP); the APP included a mixture of groups from the Middle Belt, the southeast, and the far north. With the big men of the PDP backing him, General Obasanjo went on to defeat an AD/APP alliance candidate, Chief Olu Falae, also Yoruba, in the presidential contest in February 1999.

These parties rely on elite-centered structures established during previous civilian governments and transition programs, and demonstrate the cross-ethnic alliances that have animated politics over the last quarter-century. The PDP includes core members of the northern established NPN, the northern progressive PRP, and the Igbo-dominated NPP of the Second Republic, as well as prominent politicians from the Niger Delta. The APP (now ANPP) drew from the Second Republic's GNPP, a party dominated by the Kanuri and groups from the Middle Belt, and also features southern politicians who had prominent roles in the Abacha-sponsored parties. The ANPP is also a multiethnic collection, drawing northern politicians of royal lineage, northeastern and Middle Belt minorities, Igbo business moguls, and southern minority leaders. The AD, however, is as Yoruba-centered as its predecessors, the UPN in the Second Republic and the AG in the First Republic. Yet like these earlier parties, it has attracted dynamic politicians from other areas. The rise of multiethnic political parties, however, is one of the most significant democratic developments of the Fourth Republic.

The haste of the Abubakar-supervised electoral process benefited civilian politicians and recently retired military officers with access to substantial financial resources. The civil society groups that led much of the struggle against the Abacha dictatorship found themselves at a disadvantage in trying to influence the processes of party formation and development. Thus, the leaders of the political parties in the Fourth Republic essentially represent alliances of convenience among powerful individuals, the big men who retain their own resource and client bases, while lacking a common ideology or clear policy agenda. The parties stand for little beyond the interests of their leading patrons, and loyalties among their members are weak, as are their connections to the wider populace. The Fourth Republic has enjoyed no real opposition movement at the national level. The PDP came together sufficiently to dominate the 2003 elections, but thereafter its internal divisions resurfaced, and the many competing interests of its leaders have continued to threaten party unity.

The Independent National Electoral Commission (INEC) complicated matters in 2002 when it registered three new political parties, each of them pragmatic alliances among disgruntled politicians from the existing parties, primarily the PDP. Late in 2002, the Supreme Court overruled the INEC's restrictive policies on registering parties, and dozens of new parties were permitted to contest the 2003 elections. In all, some thirty associations participated at the polls. Revealing its pro-Abacha roots, the ANPP nominated as its 2003 presidential candidate former head of state, General (retired) Muhammadu Buhari, a well-known supporter of the *shari'a* movement. The AD declined to nominate a 2003 presidential candidate in exchange for a PDP promise not to mount serious challenges against other AD candidates in the Yoruba region. The PDP, however, reneged on the backroom deal and defeated the AD at all levels in five of the six southwestern states in 2003.

Faced with the absolute dominance of the PDP in the 2003 elections, the other parties apart from the ANPP formed the Conference of Nigerian Political Parties (CNPP). The CNPP has subsequently been more vocal than the ANPP in its opposition to PDP policies. For their part, the ANPP, which holds seven of the northern governorships, has generally shown more interest in working with the PDP and the president than in playing the role of loyal opposition. Unless the PDP implodes, there appears to be no clear challenger to its dominance for the 2007 elections.

Political Culture, Citizenship, and Identity

Society is mobilized and represented politically by legislatures, political parties, trade unions, and elements of civil society. In the process, these institutions help to shape, organize, and express political culture and identities, thus nurturing qualities of citizenship. During long periods of military rule, these institutions were proscribed and disbanded (in the case of legislatures and political parties) or muzzled (in the case of labor unions). Their roles were filled at times by other groups and institutions, including ethnic and religious organizations, the mass media, and professional and trade groups. In many of these circles, the state is regarded as a distant entity of questionable legitimacy. The state's unwillingness or inability to deliver appropriate services, the rampant corruption among officials, and the prevalence of authoritarian rule have fostered a political culture of apathy and alienation among many Nigerians, accompanied by militant opposition among particular communities and groups.

Military rule left Nigeria with strong authoritarian influences in its political culture. Most of the younger politicians of the Fourth Republic came of age during military rule and naturally learned the business of politics from Abacha, Babangida, and their military governors. Nigeria's deep democratic traditions discussed in Section 1 remain vibrant among the larger polity, but they are in constant tension with the values imbibed during years of governance when political problems were often solved by military dictate, power, and violence rather than by negotiation and respect for law. This tension was manifest in the irony that the leading presidential contenders in 2003 were all former military men, one of whom—Buhari—was the ringleader of the 1983 coup that overthrew the Second Republic.

Modernity Versus Traditionalism

The terrain of political culture, citizenship, and identity is a contested arena within Nigeria. The interaction of modern (colonial, Western) elements with traditional (precolonial, African) practices has created the tensions of a modern sociopolitical system that rests uneasily on traditional foundations. Nigerians straddle two worlds, each undergoing constant evolution. On one hand, the strong elements in communal societies that promoted accountability have been weakened by the intrusion of Western culture oriented toward individuality. On the other hand, the modern state has been unable to free itself fully from rival ethnic claims organized around narrow, exclusivist constituencies.

As a result, exclusivist identities continue to dominate Nigerian political culture and to define the nature of citizenship.[29] Individuals tend to identify with their immediate ethnic, regional, and religious (or subethnic, subregional, and subreligious) groups rather than with state institutions, especially during moments of crisis. Nigerians usually seek to extract as many benefits as possible from the state but hesitate when it comes to performing basic civic duties such as paying taxes or taking care of public property. Entirely missing from the relationship between state and citizen in Nigeria is a fundamental reciprocity—a working social contract—based on the belief that there is a common interest that binds them.

Religion

Religion has been a persistent basis of conflict in Nigerian history. Islam began to filter into northeast Nigeria in the eleventh and twelfth centuries, spread to Hausaland by the fifteenth century, and greatly expanded in the early nineteenth century. In the north, Islam first coexisted with, then gradually supplanted, indigenous religions. Christianity arrived in the early nineteenth century, but expanded rapidly through missionary activity in the south. The amalgamation of northern and southern Nigeria in 1914 brought together the two regions and their belief systems.

These religious cultures have consistently clashed over political issues such as the secular character of the state. The application of the *shari'a* criminal code in the northern states has been a focal point for these tensions. For many Muslims, the *shari'a* represents a way of life and supreme (personal) law that transcends secular and state law; for many Christians, the expansion of *shari'a* law threatens the secular nature of the Nigerian state and their position within it. The pull of religious versus national identity becomes even stronger in times of economic hardship. The Babangida period corresponded to a rise in both Islamic fundamentalist movements and evangelical Christian fundamentalism that has continued through the present. Where significant numbers of southern Christians are living in predominantly Muslim states (for example, Kaduna State), many clashes have erupted, with great loss of life and the extensive destruction of churches, mosques, and small businesses.

The Press

The plural nature of Nigerian society, with the potential to engender a shared political culture, can be seen in virtually all aspects of public life. The Nigerian press, for instance, has long been one of the liveliest and most irreverent in Africa. The Abacha regime moved to stifle its independence, banning several publications and threatening the suspension of others. In this regard, Abacha was following the example of his predecessor, Babangida, especially during the final years of his rule. A northern paper, the *New Nigerian,* published in Kaduna, succumbed at times to overt sectionalism. The fact that the media are sometimes regarded as captives of ethnic and regional constituencies has weakened their capacity to resist attacks on their rights and privileges. Significantly, most of the Nigerian press has been based in a Lagos-Ibadan axis in the southwestern part of Nigeria and has frequently been labeled "southern." Recently, however, independent television and radio stations have proliferated around the country, and forests of satellite towers now span Nigerian cities to support the boom in Internet cafés and telecommunications. The freer environment of democracy has also allowed investigative journalism to flourish. Several legislative leaders have been brought down by timely media exposés of their misconduct, and other public figures, including prominent governors, cabinet officers, and the inspector-general of police, are being scrutinized in the press.

Interests, Social Movements, and Protest

Political attitudes, political culture, and sectional identities are still dominated and defined largely by elite, urban-based interests. These interests include ethnic as well as professional and associational groups. The few nonelite groups, such as urban-based marketwomen's associations, often serve as channels for disseminating the decisions and agendas of elite groups. In essence, nonelite and rural elements continue to be marginalized and manipulated by elites and urban groups. Lacking competence in the language of public discourse, namely, English, and access to financial networks, nonelites have difficulty confronting, on their own, the decision-making centers of the state and society.

Elite and nonelite Nigerians alike come together in civic organizations and interest groups such as labor unions and student and business associations. Because the political machinery was in the hands of the military, Nigerian citizens sought alternative means of representation and protest in an effort to affect political life. Historically, labor has played a significant role in Nigerian politics, as have student groups, some women's organizations, and various radical and populist organizations. Business groups have frequently supported and colluded with corrupt civilian and military regimes. In the last year of the Abacha regime, however, even the business class, through mechanisms like Vision 2010, began to suggest an end to such arbitrary rule. The termination of military rule has seen civil society groups flourish across Nigeria.

Labor

Organized labor has played an important role in challenging governments during both the colonial and postcolonial eras in several African countries, Nigeria among them. Continuous military pressure throughout the 1980s and 1990s forced a decline in the independence and strength of organized labor in Nigerian politics. The Babangida regime implemented strategies of **state corporatism** designed to control and co-opt various social forces such as labor. When the leadership of the Nigerian Labour Congress (NLC), the umbrella confederation, took a vigorous stand against the government, the regime sacked the leaders and appointed conservative replacements. Prodemocracy strikes in mid-1994 by the National Petroleum Employees Union (NUPENG) and other sympathetic labor groups significantly reduced oil production and nearly brought the country to a halt, whereupon the Abacha regime arrested and disbanded its leadership.

The Nigerian labor movement has been vulnerable to reprisals by the state and private employers. The government has always been the biggest single employer of labor in Nigeria, as well as the recognized arbiter of industrial relations between employers and employees. Efforts by military regimes to centralize and co-opt the unions caused their militancy and impact to wane. Moreover, ethnic, regional, and religious divisions have often hampered labor solidarity, and these differences have been periodically manipulated by the state.

General Abubakar removed government-appointed union administrators in 1998 and allowed the unions once again to elect their own leaders. Within a year, labor had regained its footing. Several waves of national strikes forced the Obasanjo government to forgo plans to raise the price of fuel, and additional strikes prompted significant wage increases. At moments during these campaigns, the Nigerian Labour Congress appeared to play a more commanding role as the political opposition to government than did any of the parties nominally in opposition.

Labor still claims an estimated 2 million members across Nigeria and remains one of the most potent forces in civil society. The unions have a great stake in the consolidation of constitutional rule in the Fourth Republic and the protections that allow them to organize and act freely on behalf of their members. Given the strength of the NLC, the PDP has sought to break it into its constituent unions to dilute its impact, but has so far been unsuccessful.

The Business Community

Nigeria has a long history of entrepreneurialism and business development. This spirit is compromised by tendencies toward rent-seeking and the appropriation of state resources. Members of the Nigerian business class have been characterized as "pirate capitalists" because of the high level of corrupt practices and collusion with state officials.[30] Many wealthy individuals have served in the military or civilian governments, while others protect their access to state resources by sponsoring politicians or entering into business arrangements with bureaucrats. Nevertheless, as economic and political conditions in Nigeria have deteriorated, the state has afforded fewer avenues for businesspeople, as well as a declining capacity to provide the necessary infrastructure for business development.

Nonetheless, private interests have proven surprisingly resilient, as organized groups have emerged to represent the interests of the business class and to promote general economic development. There are numerous associations throughout Nigeria representing a broad variety of business activities and sectoral interests. Many local or regional groups are also members of national organizations. National business associations, such as the Nigerian Association of Chambers of Commerce, Industry, Mines, and Agriculture (NACCIMA), the largest in the country, have taken an increasingly political stance. Business groups pressed the military leadership to resolve the June 12 crisis in 1993, and they have had a strong voice in advocating better governance. In their bid to reduce uncertainty, halt economic decline, and protect their economic interests, business associations increasingly perform what are clearly political roles. The continuing influence of the Economic Summit and other business associations in shaping government policies underscores this trend.

Other Social Groups

Student activism continues to be an important feature of Nigerian political life. University and other student groups play an important political role. Along with their teachers, students have suffered countless closings of the universities during the Babangida and Abacha regimes in addition to direct government harassment, banning, and attempts to engineer divisions in their unions and associations. Many professional associations of doctors and lawyers have also become champions of democracy and human rights, often supporting campaigns conducted by human rights organizations.

The activities of these organizations increased significantly with the introduction of the structural adjustment program (SAP) in the 1980s. Politically marginal groups, including women, youth, the urban poor, and people in rural areas, perceived an imbalance in the distribution of the benefits and burdens generated by the economic reform program. Not surprisingly, flagrant displays of wealth by senior members of the military alienated these groups and encouraged a "culture of rage" among many disenfranchised segments of urban society. Growing restiveness over economic hardship and military oppression led to a sharp increase in the number of human rights groups and other nongovernmental organizations (NGOs) in the 1990s.[31] Greater funding for NGOs from foreign governments and private foundations assisted the growth of this sector, most notably in the south but gradually in the north as well. They have generally focused on such issues as civil protection, gender law, health care, media access, and public housing. Most are urban based, although efforts to develop rural networks are underway.

Personality conflicts, ethnic divisions, and scarce resources hampered the efforts of civil society to resist military dictatorship.[32] Prodemocracy efforts by NGOs peaked in the 1993–1994 struggle over June 12, when they managed to stage numerous successful stay-home strikes in Lagos and other southern cities. The Campaign for Democracy in 1993 and then the National Democratic Coalition (NADECO) in 1994 built an antimilitary front that also included students, academics, some labor unions, and women's and professional groups. As Abacha moved forward with his self-succession campaign in 1997–1998, this sector attempted to counter the regime's machinations, although it faced very restrictive political conditions.

The return of political freedoms under the Fourth Republic has allowed organizations in civil society to proliferate and become influential. The end of military government has also left many of the prodemocracy and human rights groups without the strong central focus they had in the 1990s, and specialized groups are gradually supplanting the older, broader organizations that were active in preceding decades.

Civil society groups are making a substantial contribution to consolidating democracy in Nigeria. Their relationships with the political parties, however, remain distant, although many are engaged in advocacy, and some leaders of the prodemocracy struggles of the 1990s ran for office in the 2003 elections. Nigeria's prospects for building a sustainable democracy during the Fourth Republic will depend, in part, on the willingness of many of these advocacy groups to increase their collaboration with the political parties, while maintaining a high level of vigilance and activism.

Section ❺ Nigerian Politics in Transition

Despite the slow progress of the Fourth Republic, Nigerians overwhelmingly favor democratic government over military rule. About 70 percent of respondents in a recent survey said that they still prefer democracy to any other alternative, although popular frustration is growing with the slow pace of reform and continued corruption in politics.[33] Will democracy in Nigeria be consolidated sufficiently to meet minimal levels of public satisfaction, or will the nation again succumb to destructive authoritarian rule?

Nigerian politics must change in fundamental ways for democracy to become more stable and legitimate. First and foremost, the nation must turn from a system of politics dominated by "big men"—for all intents and purposes, a semi-competitive oligarchy—to a more representative mode of politics that addresses the fundamental interests of the public. Second, Nigerians must conclusively settle the national question and commit to political arrangements that accommodate the nation's diversity. In short, Nigeria's Fourth Republic must find ways of moving beyond prebendal politics and develop a truly national political process in which mobilization and conflicts along ethnic, regional, and religious lines gradually diminish.

Political Challenges and Changing Agendas

Nigeria's fitful transition to democratic rule between 1985 and 1999 was inconclusive, largely because it was planned and directed from above. This approach contrasts sharply with the popular-based movements that unseated autocracies in Central and Eastern Europe. The military periodically made promises for democratic transition as a ploy to stabilize and legitimate their governments. General Abubakar dutifully handed power to the civilians in 1999, but only after ensuring that the military's interests would be protected under civilian rule and creating an overly powerful executive that reinforces **patrimonialism,** a system of power in which authority is maintained through patronage. The military's rapid transition program produced a tenuous, conflicted democratic government that faces daunting tasks of restoring key institutions, securing social stability, and reforming the economy. The continuing strength and influence of collective identities, defined on the basis of religion or ethnicity, are often more binding than national allegiances. The parasitic nature of the Nigerian economy is a further source of instability. Rent-seeking and other unproductive, often corrupt, business activities remain accepted norms of wealth accumulation.

Nonetheless, Nigerians are sowing seeds of change in all of these areas. Attitudes toward the military in government have shifted dramatically. The decline in the appeal of military rule can be attributed to the abysmal performances of the Babangida and Abacha regimes in economic oversight and governance. Many now recognize that the military, apart from its contributions to national security, is incapable of promoting economic and social progress in Nigeria. With the armed forces discredited for the moment, the nature of the struggles among civilian political elites will decide the direction of political and economic change. Thus, democratic development may be advanced in the long run if stable coalitions appear over time in a manner that balances the power among contending groups, and if these key elites adapt to essential norms and "rules of the game.

Initially, members of the new political class confined their struggles within the constraints of the democratic system: using the courts, media, legislatives struggles, and even legal expediencies such as impeachment. Political actors largely worked through formal institutions, contending openly and offsetting the power of a single group or faction. Disturbingly, the 2003 elections reflected a growing willingness of the political elite to use extra-systemic measures to forward their interests through election rigging, corruption, and militia-led violence. Many of these tendencies have persisted.

The next critical step down the long road of democratic development for Nigeria is the creation of a viable, multiethnic opposition party that is also loyal, meaning that it plays by the rules of the system. Opposition parties help to reduce corruption in the system because they have an interest in exposing the misconduct of the ruling party, which in turn pressures them to restrain their own behavior. Furthermore, in order to unseat the ruling party and win elections, opposition parties need to engage the public to win their votes. In this manner, issues of interest to the public are engaged by the parties.

The introduction of so many new parties in 2002 has yet to facilitate the development of a viable, loyal opposition, but it could provide some of the groundwork if the PDP continues to exhibit strong internal divisions. It is also possible that the new parties may further dilute the opposition and allow the PDP to govern largely unchecked. If some minor parties manage to win only narrow ethnic constituencies, and the electoral commission does not rigorously apply the multiethnic rules of contestation, Nigeria may return to the ruinous ethnic politics of the past.

The project of building a coherent nation-state out of competing nationalities remains unfinished. Ironically, because the parties of the Fourth Republic generally do not represent any particular ethnic interest—indeed, they do not represent anyone's interests except those of the leaders and their clients—ethnic associations and militias have risen to articulate ethnic-based grievances. Ethnic consciousness cannot be eliminated from society, but ethnicity cannot be the main basis for political competition. If the current ethnic mobilization can be contained within ethnic associations arguing over the agenda of the parties, then it can be managed. If any of the ethnic associations captures one of the political parties or joins with the militias to foment separatism, instability will result.

Democratic development also requires further decentralization of power structures in Nigeria. The struggle on the part of the National Assembly and the state governors to wrest power from the presidency has advanced this process. The administration's efforts to privatize government para-statals could also reduce the power of the presidency over time, since it will no longer control all the productive sectors of the economy. A more decentralized system allows local problems to be solved within communities rather than involving national institutions and the accompanying interethnic competition. Decentralization also lowers the stakes for holding national offices, thereby reducing the destructive pressures on political competition and political office. The devolution of power and resources to smaller units, closer to their constituents, can substantially enhance the accountability of leaders and the transparency of government operations.

Civil society groups are the final link in democratic consolidation in Nigeria. These groups are critical players in connecting the Nigerian state to the Nigerian people. They aggregate and articulate popular interests into the policy realm, and they provide advocacy on behalf of their members. If the political parties are to reflect anything more than elite interests and clientelist rule, the parties must reach out and build alliances with the institutions of civil society. For opposition parties to become a viable opposition movement capable of checking the power of the PDP, they will have to build alliances with civil society groups in order to mobilize large portions of the population. Foreign pressure also plays an important role in maintaining the quest for democracy and sustainable development. In recent years, major external forces have been more forthright in supporting civil society and democratization in Nigeria. The United States, Britain, and some member states of the European Union quite visibly exerted pressure on Babangida to leave and applied modest sanctions in support of democracy. This has been made possible, in part, by a changing international environment, especially the willingness of the major industrial countries and the international financial institutions to support democracy around the world. Nigeria's weak economy and heavy debt, now estimated at $33 billion, have made it susceptible to this kind of pressure.

Western commitment to development and democracy in Africa is not guaranteed. Much of the initiative for Africa's growth therefore needs to emerge from within. In Nigeria, such initiatives will depend on substantial changes in the way Nigerians do business. It will be necessary to develop a more sophisticated and far less corrupt form of capitalist enterprise and the development of entrepreneurial interests within Nigeria who will see their interests tied to the principles of democratic politics and economic initiative. The middle class is beginning to grow under democratic rule, but it remains small and vulnerable to economic and political instability.

Nigerian politics has been characterized by turmoil and periodic crises ever since the British relinquished colonial power. Over forty years later, the country is still trying to piece together a fragile democracy, while per capita incomes are scarcely higher than at independence. Despite a number of positive trends, the nation continues to wrestle with slow growth in major productive sectors, enfeebled infrastructure and institutions, heightened sociopolitical tensions, an irresponsible elite, and an expanding mass culture of despondency and rage. Only responsible government combined with sustained civil society action can reverse this decline and restore the nation to what President Obasanjo has called "the path to greatness."

Nigerian Politics in Comparative Perspective

The study of Nigeria has important implications for the study of African politics and, more broadly, of comparative politics. The Nigerian case embodies a number of key themes and issues that can be generalized. We can learn much about how democratic regimes are established and consolidated by understanding Nigeria's pitfalls and travails. Analysis of the historical dynamics of Nigeria's ethnic conflict helps to identify institutional mechanisms that may be effective in reducing ethnic conflict in other states. We can also learn much about the necessary and sufficient conditions for economic development, and the particular liabilities of oil-dependent states. Each of these issues offers comparative lessons for the major themes explored in this book: the world of states, governing the economy, the democratic idea, and the politics of collective identities.

A World of States

Nigeria exists in two "worlds" of states: one in the global political economy and the other within Africa. We have addressed at length Nigeria's position in the world. Economically, Nigeria was thrust into the world economy in a position of weakness, first as a British colony and later as an independent nation. Despite its resources and the potential of oil to provide the investment capital needed to build a modern economy, Nigeria has grown weaker. It has lost much of its international clout, and in place of the international respect it once enjoyed as a developing giant within Africa, the country became notorious throughout the 1990s for corruption, human rights abuses, and failed governance. The return of democracy has restored some of Nigeria's former stature, but its economic vulnerability and persistent corruption keep it a secondary player in the world of states.

This chapter has remarked, "As Nigeria goes, so goes the rest of sub-Saharan Africa." The future of democracy, political stability, and economic renewal in other parts of Africa, and certainly in West Africa, will be greatly influenced for good or ill by unfolding events in Nigeria. Beyond the obvious demonstration effects, the economy of the West African subregion could be revitalized by substantial growth of the Nigerian economy. In addition, President Obasanjo has conducted very active public diplomacy across Africa, seeking to resolve major conflicts, promote democracy, and improve trade. Thus far, international political and business attention has shifted elsewhere on the continent, focusing on such countries as South Africa, Botswana, and Ghana. This portends a danger of greater marginalization, reflecting the expanding patchwork of Africa among areas of stability and growth, contrasted with areas of turmoil and decay.

Governing the Economy

Nigeria provides important insights into the political economy of underdevelopment. At independence in 1960, Nigeria was stronger economically than its Southeast Asian counterparts Indonesia and Malaysia. Independent Nigeria appeared poised for growth, with a wealth of natural resources, a large population, and the presence of highly entrepreneurial groups in many regions of the country. Today, Nigeria is among the poorest countries in the world in terms of per capita income, while many of its Asian counterparts have joined the ranks of the newly industrializing countries. One critical lesson Nigeria teaches is that a rich endowment of resources is not enough to ensure economic development. In fact, it may encourage rent-seeking behavior that undermines more productive activities.[34] Sound political and institutional development must come first.

Other variables are critically important, notably democratic stability and a capable developmental state. A developmentalist ethic, and an institutional structure to enforce it, can set limits to corrupt behavior and constrain the pursuit of short-term personal gain at the expense of national economic growth. Institutions vital to the pursuit of these objectives include a professional civil service, an independent judiciary, and a free press. Nigeria has had each of these, but they were gradually undermined and corrupted under military rule. The public "ethic" that has come to dominate Nigerian political economy has been prebendalism. Where corruption is unchecked, as in Nigeria, the Philippines under

Ferdinand Marcos, or Latin American countries such as Ecuador and Venezuela, economic development suffers accordingly.

Nigeria also demonstrates that sustainable economic development requires sound economic policy. Without export diversification, commodity-exporting countries are buffeted by the price fluctuations of one or two main products. This situation can be traced back to overreliance on primary commodity export-oriented policies bequeathed by the British colonial regime. Yet other former colonies, such as Malaysia and Indonesia, have managed to diversify their initial export base. Nigeria, by contrast, has substituted one form of commodity dependence for another, and it has allowed its petroleum industry to overwhelm all other sectors of the economy. Nigeria even became a net importer of products (for example, of palm oil and palm nuts) for which it was once a leading world producer. In comparative perspective, we can see that natural resource endowments can be tremendously beneficial. The United States, for example, has parlayed its endowments of agricultural, mineral, and energy resources into one of the world's most diversified modern economies. Meanwhile Japan, which is by comparison poorly endowed with natural resources, has one of the strongest economies in the world, achieved in large part through its unique developmental strategies. Each of these examples illustrates the primacy of sound economic policies implemented through consolidated political systems.

The Democratic Idea

Many African countries have experienced transitions from authoritarian rule.[35] With the end of superpower competition in Africa and the withdrawal of external support for Africa's despots, many African societies experienced a resurgence of popular pressures for greater participation in political life and more open forms of governance. Decades of authoritarian, single-party, and military rule in Africa have left a dismal record of political repression, human rights abuses, inequality, deteriorating governance, and failed economies. A handful of elites have acquired large fortunes through wanton corruption. Consider Nigeria's "missing" $12.2 billion windfall in oil revenues after the Gulf War in 1991 or the fact that former Zairian president Mobutu Sese Seko's personal wealth was estimated to be several billion dollars—perhaps as much as the country's entire external debt. Kenya's former president Daniel arap Moi is considered among the richest men in Africa, a group to which Ibrahim Babangida and the late Sani Abacha of Nigeria have belonged. The exercise of postcolonial authoritarian rule in Africa has contributed to economic stagnation and decline. The difficulties of such countries as Cameroon, Togo, and Zimbabwe in achieving political transitions reflects, in large part, the ruling elites' unwillingness to cede control of the political instruments that made possible their self-enrichment.

Nigeria exemplifies the harsh reality of authoritarian and unaccountable governance. Nigerians have endured six military regimes, countless attempted coups, and a bloody civil war that claimed over 1 million lives. They have also seen a once-prospering economy reduced to a near shambles. Today, democracy has become a greater imperative because only such a system provides the mechanisms to limit abuses of power and render governments accountable.

Collective Identities

Nigeria presents an important case in which to study the dangers of communal competition in a society with deep cultural divisions. How can multiethnic countries manage diversity? What institutional mechanisms can be employed to avert tragedies such as the 1967–1970 civil war or the continuing conflicts that have brought great suffering to Rwanda and the former Yugoslavia? This chapter has suggested institutional reforms such as multiethnic political parties, decentralization, and a strengthened federal system that can contribute to reducing tensions and minimizing conflict.

Insights from the Nigerian experience may explain why some federations persist, while identifying factors that can undermine them. Nigeria's complex social map, and its varied attempts to create a nation out of its highly diverse population, enhances our understanding of the politics of cultural pluralism and the difficulties of accommodating sectional interests under conditions of political and economic insecurity. Federal character in Nigeria has become a form of ethnic and regional favoritism and a tool for dispensing patronage. Yet the country has benefited in some ways from the attention devoted to creating state and local governments, and from giving people in different regions a sense of being stakeholders in the entity called Nigeria.

Nigeria's challenges reflect the frustrated hopes of its people for a better life, stable government, and a democratic political order, while suggesting the potential contributions that this country could make to the African continent and the wider international arena. The quest for responsive and capable democratic governance leads in one direction, while another direction presents the specter of military entrepreneurs, or ethnic and religious extremists, plunging Nigeria into another cycle of coups, decline, and possibly collapse.

Key Terms

authoritarian
legitimacy
accountability
unfinished state
jihad
acephalous societies
emirs
indirect rule
warrant chiefs
interventionist
clientelism
autocracy
rents
rent-seeking
structural adjustment
program (SAP)

international financial
institutions (IFIs)
balance of payments
privatization
self-determination
Economic Community
of West African
States (ECOWAS)
para-statals
shari'a
prebendalism
civil society
state corporatism
patrimonialism

Suggested Readings

Aborisade, Oladimeji, and Mundt, Robert J. *Politics in Nigeria,* 2nd ed. New York: Longman, 2002.

Achike, Okay. *Public Administration: A Nigerian and Comparative Perspective.* London: Longman, 1978.

Adamolekun, L. *Politics and Administration in Nigeria.* London: Hutchinson, 1986.

Agbaje, Adigun. *The Nigerian Press: Hegemony and the Social Construction of Legitimacy, 1960–1983.* Lewiston, N.Y.: Edwin Mellen Press, 1992.

———. "Twilight of Democracy in Nigeria." *Africa Demos* 3, no. 3:5. Atlanta: The Carter Center of Emory University, 1994.

Beckett, Paul A., and Young, Crawford, eds. *Dilemmas of Democracy in Nigeria.* Rochester, N.Y.: University of Rochester Press, 1997.

Bienen, Henry. *Political Conflict and Economic Change in Nigeria.* London: Frank Cass, 1988.

Diamond, Larry. *Class, Ethnicity and Democracy in Nigeria: The Failure of the First Republic.* London: Macmillan, 1988.

———. "Nigeria: The Uncivic Society and the Descent into Praetorianism." In Larry Diamond, J. Linz, and S. M. Lipset, eds. *Politics in Developing Countries: Comparing Experiences With Democracy,* 2nd ed. Boulder, Colo.: Lynne Rienner Publishers, 1995, 417–491.

Decalo, Samuel. *Coups and Army Rule in Africa,* 2nd ed. New Haven, Conn.: Yale University Press, 1990.

Dudley, Billy. *An Introduction to Nigerian Government and Politics.* Bloomington: Indiana University Press, 1982.

Ekeh, Peter P., and Osaghae, Eghosa E., eds. *Federal Character and Federalism in Nigeria.* Ibadan: Heinemann, 1989.

Falola, Toyin. *Violence in Nigeria: The Crisis of Religious Politics and Secular Ideologies.* Rochester, N.Y.: University of Rochester Press, 1999.

Forrest, Tom. *Politics and Economic Development in Nigeria.* Boulder, Colo.: Westview Press, 1993.

Horowitz, Donald L. *Ethnic Groups in Conflict.* Berkeley: University of California Press, 1985.

Joseph, Richard A. *Democracy and Prebendal Politics in Nigeria: The Rise and Fall of the Second Republic.* Cambridge: Cambridge University Press, 1987.

Kew, Darren. "Political Islam in Nigeria's Transition Crisis," *Muslim Politics Report* (Council on Foreign Relations: New York), May–June, 1996.

Kirk-Greene, Anthony, and Rimmer, Douglas. *Nigeria Since 1970: A Political and Economic Outline.* London: Hodder and Stoughton, 1981.

Lewis, Peter M. "Endgame in Nigeria? The Politics of a Failed Democratic Transition." *African Affairs* 93 (1994): 323–340.

Lewis, Peter M., Rubin, Barnett R., and Robinson, Pearl T. *Stabilizing Nigeria: Pressures, Incentives, and Support for Civil Society.* New York: Century Foundation, for the Council on Foreign Relations, 1998.

Lubeck, Paul. *Islam and Urban Labor in Northern Nigeria.* Cambridge: Cambridge University Press, 1987.

Luckham, Robin. *The Nigerian Military: A Sociological Analysis of Authority and Revolt, 1960–67.* Cambridge: Cambridge University Press, 1971.

Melson, Robert, and Wolpe, Howard, eds. *Nigeria: Modernization and the Politics of Communalism,* East Lansing: Michigan State University Press, 1971.

Nyang'oro, Julius, and Shaw, Tim, eds. *Corporatism in Africa: Comparative Analysis and Practice.* Boulder, Colo.: Westview Press, 1989.

Olukoshi, Adebayo, ed. *The Politics of Structural Adjustment in Nigeria.* London: James Currey Publishers, 1993.

Osaghae, Eghosa. *Crippled Giant: Nigeria Since Independence.* Bloomington: Indiana University Press, 1998.

Oyediran, Oyeleye, ed. *Nigerian Government and Politics Under Military Rule.* London: Macmillan, 1979.

Reno, William. *Warlord Politics and African States.* Boulder, Colo.: Lynne Rienner Publishers, 1998.

Sklar, Richard L. *Nigerian Political Parties: Power in an Emergent African Nation.* New York: NOK Publishers, 1983.

Soyinka, Wole. *Open Sore of a Continent.* Oxford: Oxford University Press, 1996.

Suberu, Rotimi. *Federalism and Ethnic Conflict in Nigeria.* Washington, D.C.: U.S. Institute of Peace, 2001.

Watts, Michael, ed. *State, Oil, and Agriculture in Nigeria.* Berkeley: University of California Press, 1987.

Wunsch, James S., and Olowu, Dele, eds. *The Failure of the Centralized State: Institutions and Self-Governance in Africa.* Boulder, Colo.: Westview Press, 1990.

Young, Crawford. *The Rising Tide of Cultural Pluralism: The Nation-State at Bay?* Madison: University of Wisconsin Press, 1993.

Suggested Websites

British Broadcasting Corporation: A 2002 interview with President Obasanjo
news.bbc.co.uk/2/hi/talking_point/1800826.stm
Gamji: A collection of news stories from Nigerian newspapers, as well as opinion pieces and other news links
www.gamji.com
The Guardian, Nigeria's leading daily newspaper
www.ngrguardiannews.com
Human Rights Watch reports
hrw.org/doc/?t=africa&c=nigeri
International Institute for Democracy and Electoral Assistance
archive.idea.int/frontpage_nigeria.htm
Stanford University's Center for African Studies
www.stanford.edu/dept/AFR/

Endnotes

[1]Much of this context is recounted in James S. Coleman, *Nigeria: Background to Nationalism* (Berkeley: University of California Press, 1958).

[2]Obafemi Awolowo, *Path to Nigerian Freedom* (London: Faber and Faber, 1947), 47–48.

[3]Billy Dudley, *An Introduction to Nigerian Government and Politics* (Bloomington: Indiana University Press, 1982), 71.

[4]Robin Luckham, The Nigerian Military: A Sociological Analysis of Authority and Revolt 1960–67 (Cambridge: Cambridge University Press, 1971).

[5]Peter Ekeh, "Colonialism and the Two Publics in Africa: A Theoretical Statement," *Comparative Studies in Society and History* 17, no. 1 (January 1975).

[6]Richard A. Joseph, *Democracy and Prebendal Politics in Nigeria: The Rise and Fall of the Second Republic* (Cambridge: Cambridge University Press), 55–58.

[7]Gavin Williams and Terisa Turner, "Nigeria," in John Dunn, ed., *West African States: Failure and Promise* (Cambridge: Cambridge University Press, 1978), 156–157.

[8]Michael J. Watts, *State, Oil and Agriculture in Nigeria* (Berkeley: University of California Press, 1987), 71.

[9]Watts, *State Oil and Agriculture in Nigeria,* 67.

[10]See Peter M. Lewis, "From Prebendalism to Predation: The Political Economy of Decline in Nigeria," *Journal of Modern African Studies* 34, no. 1 (1996), 79–103.

[11]Tom Forrest, *Politics and Economic Development in Nigeria,* 2nd ed. (Boulder, Colo.: Westview Press, 1995), 207–212.

[12]Dele Olowu, "Centralization, Self-Governance, and Development in Nigeria," in James S. Wunsch and Dele Olowu, eds., *The Failure of the Centralized State: Institutions and Self-Governance in Africa,* (Boulder, Colo.: Westview Press, 1991), 211.

[13]Robert Melson and Howard Wolpe, *Nigeria: Modernization and the Politics of Communalism* (East Lansing: Michigan State University Press, 1971).

[14]Toyin Falola, Violence in Nigeria: The Crisis of Religious Politics and Secular Ideologies (Rochester, N.Y.: University of Rochester Press, 1998).

[15]Billy J. Dudley, *Instability and Political Order: Politics and Crisis in Nigeria* (Ibadan: Ibadan University Press, 1973), 35.

[16]Pat A. Williams, "Women and the Dilemma of Politics in Nigeria," in Crawford Young and Paul Beckett, eds., *Dilemmas of Democracy in Nigeria* (Rochester, N.Y.: University of Rochester Press, 1997), 219–241.

[17]Anthony Kirk-Greene and Douglas Rimmer, *Nigeria Since 1970: A Political and Economic Outline* (London: Hodder and Stoughton 1981), 49.

[18]Rotimi Suberu, *Federalism and Ethnic Conflict in Nigeria* (Washington, D.C.: U.S. Institute of Peace, 2001).

[19]Henry Bienen, *Armies and Parties in Africa* (New York: Africana Publishing, 1978), 193–211.

[20]Human Rights Watch, *The Destruction of Odi and Rape in Choba* (New York: Human Rights Watch, December 22, 1999).

[21]Suberu, *Federalism and Ethnic Conflict in Nigeria,* 119–120.

[22]Samuel DeCalo, *Coups and Army Rule in Africa* (New Haven, Conn.: Yale University Press, 1976), 18.

[23]Larry Diamond, "Nigeria: The Uncivic Society and the Descent into Praetorianism," in Larry Diamond, J. Linz, and S.M. Lipset, eds., *Politics in Developing Countries: Comparing Experiences With Democracy,* 2nd ed. (Boulder, Colo.: Lynne Rienner Publishers, 1995).

[24]Joseph, *Democracy and Prebendal Politics in Nigeria,* 52–53.

[25]Richard Sklar, *Nigerian Political Parties* (Princeton: Princeton University Press, 1963).

[26]Babafemi Badejo, "Party Formation and Party Competitition" in Larry Diamond, Anthony Kirk-Greene, and Oyeleye Oyediran, eds., *Transition Without End: Nigerian Politics and Civil Society Under Babangida* (Boulder, Colo.: Lynne Rienner Publishers, 1997), 179.

[27]Eghosa Osaghae, *Crippled Giant: Nigeria Since Independence* (Bloomington: Indiana University Press 1999), 233–239.

[28]Peter M. Lewis, Barnett Rubin, and Pearl Robinson, *Stabilizing Nigeria: Pressures, Incentives and Support for Civil Society* (New York: Council on Foreign Relations, 1998), 87.

[29]Rotimi Suberu, *Public Policies and National Unity in Nigeria,* Research Report No. 19 (Ibadan: Development Policy Centre, 199), 9–10.

[30]Sayre Schatz, "'Pirate Capitalism' and the Inert Economy of Nigeria," *Journal of Modern African Studies* 22, no. 1 (March 1984), 45–57.

[31]Adebayo Olukoshi, "Associational Life" in Diamond, Kirk-Greene, and Oyediran, *Transition Without End,* 385–86.

[32]Osaghae, *Crippled Giant,* 301.

[33]Peter Lewis, Etannibi Alemika, and Michael Bratton, *Down to Earth: Changes in Attitudes to Democracy and Markets in Nigeria,* Afrobarometer Working Paper No. 20, Michigan State University, August 2002.

[34]See Terry Lynn Karl, *The Paradox of Plenty* (Berkeley: University of California Press, 1997); and Michael Ross, "The Political Economy of the Resource Curse," *World Politics* 51 (January 1999), 297–322.

[35]Michael Bratton and Nicolas van de Walle, *Democratic Experiments in Africa* (Cambridge: Cambridge University Press, 1997).

CHAPTER 7

Iran

Ervand Abrahamian

Islamic Republic of Iran

Land and People

Capital	Tehran	
Total area (square miles)	634,562 (slightly larger than Alaska)	
Population	68,017,860	
Annual population growth rate (%)	1975–2000	3.0
	2005–2015 (projected)	0.7
Urban population (%)	67.0	
Ethnic composition (% of total population)	Persian	51
	Azeri	24
	Gilaki and Mazandarani	8
	Kurd	7
	Arab	3
	Turkman	2
	Baluchi	2
	Other	3
Major language(s) (%)	Persian (Farsi)	58
	Turkic	26
	Kurdish	9
	Other	7
Religious affiliation (%)	Shi'a Muslim	89
	Sunni Muslim	9
	Zoroastrian, Jewish, Christian, and Baha'I	2

Economy

Domestic currency	Rial (IRR)	
	US$1: 8,614 IRR (2004 av.)	
Total GNI (US$)	133.2 billion	
GNI per capita (US$)	2010	
Total GNI at purchasing power parity (US$)	465.00 billion	
GNI per capita at purchasing power parity (US$)	$7,000	
GDP annual growth rate (%)	1983–1993	2.2
	1993–2003	3.7
	2003	6.6
	2004	6.3
GDP per capita average annual growth rate (%)	1983–1993	–0.5
	1993–2003	2.2
	2003	5.2
Inequality in income or consumption (1996–1997)	Data Not Available for Iran	

Structure of production (% of GDP)	Agriculture	11.2
	Industry	40.9
	Services	48.7
Labor force distribution (% of total)	Agriculture	30
	Industry	25
	Services	45
Exports as % of GDP	25.3	
Imports as % of GDP	22.9	

Society

Life expectancy at birth	71	
Infant mortality per 1,000 live births	30	
Adult literacy (% over age 15)	Male	83.2
	Female	70
Access to information and communications (per 1,000 population)	Telephone lines	169
	Mobile phones	32
	Radios	281
	Televisions	163
	Personal computers	69.7

Women in Government and the Economy

Women in the national legislature		
Lower house or single house (%)		4.1
Women at ministerial level (%)		9.4
Female economic activity rate (age 15 and above) (%)		30
Female labor force (% of total)		27
Female legislators, senior officials, and managers (% of total)		13
Female professional and technical workers (% of total)		33
Estimated earned income (PPP US$)	Female	2,835
	Male	9,946

Composite Ratings and Rankings

Human Development Index (HDI) ranking (value) out of 177 countries	101 (.732)
Gender-Related Development Index (GDI) ranking (value) out of 144 countries	82 (.713)
Gender Empowerment Measure (GEM) ranking (value) out of 78 countries	72 (.313)
Corruption Perception Index (CPI) ranking (value) out of 145 countries	87 (2.9)
Environmental Sustainability (ESI) Index ranking (value) out of 146 countries	132 (39.8)
Freedom in World Rating	6.0 (Not Free)

Political Organization

Political System A mixture of democracy and theocracy (rule of the clergy) headed by a cleric with the title of the Leader.

Regime History Islamic Republic since the 1979 Islamic Revolution.

Administrative Structure Centralized administration with 30 provinces. The interior minister appoints the provincial governor-generals.

Executive President and his cabinet. The president is elected by the general electorate every four years. The president chooses his cabinet ministers, but they need to obtain the approval of the *Majles* (parliament).

Legislature Unicameral. The *Majles*, formed of 270 seats, is elected every four years. It has multiple member districts with the top runners in the elections taking the seats. Bills passed by the *Majles* do not become law unless they have the approval of the clerically dominated Council of Guardians.

Judiciary A Chief Judge and a Supreme Court independent of the executive and legislature but appointed by the Leader.

Party System The ruling clergy restricts most party and organizational activities.

Section ❶   The Making of the Modern Iranian State

Politics in Action

Iran shook the world, not to mention its own establishment, first in 1997 by electing Muhammad Khatami, a relatively unknown moderate cleric, as president of the Islamic Republic in a landslide victory, and then again in 2001 by reelecting him with even a larger majority. Khatami, a former director of the National Library, was a mild-mannered middle-ranking cleric, a hojjat al-Islam ("Proof of Islam"), not a high-ranking **ayatollah** or grand ayatollah ("Sign of God"). In the elections, he vigorously campaigned on the theme of creating "civil society" and improving the "sick economy." He stressed the importance of an open society that would protect individual liberties, freedom of expression, women's rights, political pluralism, and, most essential, the rule of law. He had even authored books applauding Western thinkers such as Locke, Voltaire, and Rousseau. His electoral campaigns also stressed the need for a "dialogue between civilizations." This was a far cry from the early days of the 1979 Iranian Revolution, when its leader, Grand Ayatollah Ruhollah Khomeini, had denounced the United States as the "Great Satan" and incited students to seize the U.S. embassy. This takeover and the resulting hostage crisis lasted 444 days and prompted a break in U.S.-Iranian diplomatic relations that lasts to this day.

Khatami's initial electoral success was especially surprising since much of the religious establishment had openly endorsed his rival. Most commentators, both inside and outside the country, had considered the election a shoo-in for this conservative candidate. After all, he had been endorsed by an impressive array of newspapers, radio stations, television programs, state institutions, quasi-state foundations, clerical organizations, and local **mosques** (Muslim houses of worship). They had warned that any opening up of the system could endanger the whole regime and that Khatami could become another Mikhail Gorbachev, the reformist leader who had inadvertently presided over the demise of the Soviet Union. Even Ayatollah Ali Khamenei, the Leader who is often mistitled in the West as Iran's Supreme Leader, had implicitly endorsed the conservative candidate. In the upset election, Khatami took 70 percent of the vote in a campaign that attracted 80 percent of the electorate. Much of Khatami's vote came from women, university students, and young adults throughout the country—even from those serving in the armed forces. He followed up his victory by trying to liberalize the press, establishing political parties, and initiating a dialogue with the United States. He even bolstered the case for liberalization by citing *Democracy in America,* the classic book by nineteenth-century French writer Alexis de Tocqueville. Khatami also assured the West that Iran had no intention of implementing the *fatwa* (religious decree) that the late Ayatollah Khomeini had placed on the Muslim-born British writer Salman Rushdie in 1989. Khomeini had condemned Rushdie to death on the grounds that his book, *Satanic Verses,* blasphemed Islam and thus proved that its author was an apostate from Islam, which is a capital offense according to a narrow interpretation of Islamic law. The 2001 presidential elections, as well as the 2000 parliamentary elections, further strengthened Khatami's mandate. In 2005, former president Clinton observed that Iran was the only country in the world where "liberals" and "progressives" had, in recent years, won a series of resounding electoral victories.

These elections vividly illustrated the main dilemmas confronting the Islamic Republic that had been established by Ayatollah Khomeini in the aftermath of the 1979 revolution. The Islamic Republic of Iran today is a mixture of **theocracy** and democracy: it is a political system based on clerical authority as well as popular sovereignty, based on the divine right of the clergy as well as the rights of the people, based on concepts derived from early Islam as well as from modern democratic principles such as the separation of powers. The country has regular elections for the presidency and the *Majles* (Parliament), but a clerically dominated **Guardian Council** determines who can and cannot run in these elections. The president is the formal head of the executive branch of government, but he can be overruled, even dismissed, by the chief cleric known as the **Leader.** The president appoints the minister of justice, but the whole judiciary is under the supervision of the chief judge, who is appointed directly by the Leader. The *Majles* is the legislative branch of government, but its bills do not become law unless the Guardian Council deems them compatible with Islam and the Islamic constitution. In short, contemporary Iranian politics resonates with both *vox dei* (the voice of God) and *vox populi* (the voice of the people).

Geographic Setting

Iran—three times the size of France, slightly larger than Alaska, and much larger than its immediate neighbors—is notable for two geographic features. The first is that most of its territory is inhospitable to agriculture. A vast arid zone known as the Great Salt

Desert covers much of the central plateau from the capital city, Tehran, to the borders with Afghanistan and Pakistan. The Zagros mountain range takes up the western third of the country. Another range, the Elborz, stretches across the north. Rain-fed agriculture is confined mostly to the northwest and the provinces along the Caspian Sea. In the rest of the country, population settlements are located mostly on oases, on the few rare rivers, and on constructed irrigation networks. Only pastoral nomads can survive in the semiarid zones and in the high mountain valleys. Thus, 67 percent of the total population of 68 million is concentrated on 27 percent of the land—mostly in the Caspian region, in the northwest provinces, and in the cities of Tehran, Qom, Isfahan, Shiraz, and Ahwaz.

In the past, Iran's inhospitable environment was a major obstacle to economic development. In recent decades, this obstacle has been partly overcome by oil revenues that totaled $28 billion in 2004. Iran is the second largest oil producer in the Middle East and the fourth largest in the world, and oil revenues account for the fact that Iran is now an urbanized and partly industrialized country. Nearly 67 percent of the population lives in urban centers; 70 percent of the labor force is employed in industry and services; 77 percent of adults are literate; life expectancy has reached seventy years; and the majority of Iranians enjoy a standard of living well above that found in most of Asia and Africa.

Iran's second notable geographic feature is that it lies on the strategic crossroads between Central Asia and Turkey, between the Indian subcontinent and the Middle East, and between the Arabian Peninsula and the Caucasus Mountains, which is often considered a boundary between Europe and Asia. This has made the region vulnerable to invaders: Indo-Europeans in the distant past (they gave the country the name of Iran, Land of the Aryans), Islamic Arab tribes in the seventh century, and a series of Turkic incursions in the Middle Ages.

The population today reflects these historic invasions. Some 51 percent of the country speaks Persian **(Farsi),** an Indo-European language, as their first language; 26 percent speak various dialects of Turkic, mainly Azeri and Turkman; 8 percent speak Gilaki or Mazandarani, distant Persian dialects; 7 percent speak Kurdish, another Indo-European language; and

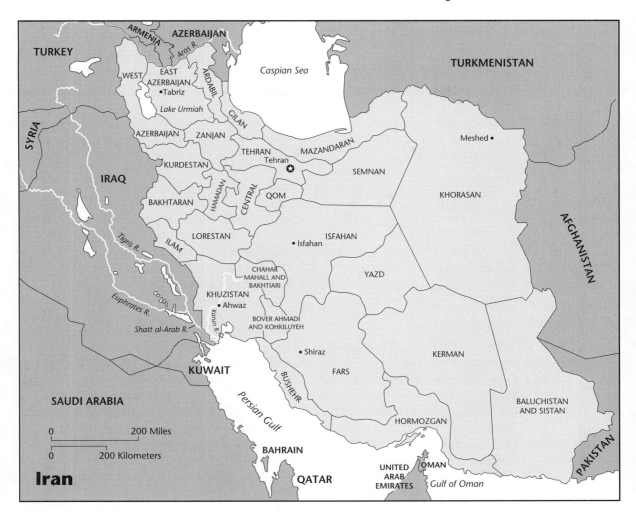

Iran

3 percent speak Arabic. Europeans long referred to the country as Persia, but since the third century Iranians have called their country Iran and their main language Farsi, after the central province (Fars), the original home of the languages. In 1935, Iran formally asked the international community to cease calling the country Persia.

Critical Junctures

Although modern Iran traces its roots to an ancient empire of the sixth century B.C. and its Islamic religion to the Arab invasions of the seventh century, its current national identity, geographic boundaries, particular

interpretation of Islam—**Shi'ism**—and political system were formed by four more recent critical junctures: the Safavid (1501–1722), Qajar (1794–1925), and Pahlavi (1925–1979) dynasties, and the Revolution of 1979, which led to establishment of the current Islamic Republic.

The Safavids (1501–1722)

Modern Iran, with its Shi'i Islamic identity and its present-day boundaries, can be traced to the sixteenth century, when the Safavid family conquered the territory with the help of fellow Turkic-speaking tribes. They revived the ancient Iranian titles of shah-in-shah

Critical Junctures in Modern Iran's Political Development

1921	Colonel Reza Khan's military coup
1925	Establishment of the Pahlavi dynasty
1941–1945	Allied occupation of Iran
1951	Nationalization of the oil industry
1953	Coup against Mosaddeq
1963	White Revolution
1975	Establishment of the Resurgence Party
1979	Islamic Revolution
1979–1981	U.S. hostage crisis
December 1979	Referendum on the constitution
January 1980	Bani-Sadr elected president
March 1980	Elections for the First Islamic *Majles*
1980–1988	War with Iraq
June 1981	President Bani-Sadr ousted
October 1981	Khamenei elected president
1984	Elections for the Second Islamic *Majles*
1988	Elections for the Third Islamic *Majles*
1989	Khomeini dies; Khamenei appointed Leader; Rafsanjani elected president
1992	Elections for the Fourth Islamic *Majles*
1996	Elections for the Fifth Islamic *Majles*
1997	Khatami elected president on reform platform
2000	Reformers win elections for the Sixth Islamic *Majles*
2000	Khatami reelected president for the Sixth Islamic *Majles*
2004	Elections for the Seventh Islamic *Majles*

(King of Kings) and Shadow of God on Earth, and proceeded to forcibly convert their subjects to Shi'ism. Although small Shi'i communities had existed in this area since the beginning of Islam, the vast majority had adhered to the majority Sunni branch

(see "Background: Islam and Shi'ism"). The Safavid motivation for this drastic conversion was to give their kingdom and population a distinct identity separate from the surrounding Sunni powers: the Ottomans in the west, the Uzbeks in the north, and the Afghans in the east.

By the mid-seventeenth century, the Safavid dynasty had succeeded in converting nearly 90 percent of their subjects to Shi'ism. Sunnism survived only among the tribal groups at the periphery: Kurds in the northwest, Turkmans in the northeast, Baluchis in the southeast, and Arabs in the southwest. It should be noted that the Safavids failed to capture from the Ottomans Shi'i's two most holy sites (both located in modern Iraq): Karbala, where Imam Husayn, one of their most important martyrs, had been killed in 680 A.D.; and Najaf, the nearby theological center.

In addition to the Sunni minority, Safavid Iran contained small communities of Jews, Zoroastrians, and Christians (Armenians and Assyrians). These small minorities lived mostly in Isfahan, Shiraz, Kerman, Yazd, and Azerbaijan. Jews had lived in Iran since ancient times, predating the great diaspora prompted by the Roman destruction of Jerusalem. Zoroastrians were descendants of Iranians who retained their old religion after the Arab invasions. The Christians had lived in the northwest long before the advent of Islam. To strengthen their foothold in central Iran, the Safavids transported there some 100,000 Armenians, encouraging them to become craftsmen and merchants, especially in the lucrative silk trade. The Safavids, like most other Muslim rulers, but unlike medieval Christian kings, tolerated religious minorities as long as they paid special taxes and accepted royal authority. According to Islam, Christians, Jews, and Zoroastrians were to be tolerated as legitimate **People of the Book.** They were respected both because they were mentioned in the Holy **Qur'an** and because they had their own sacred texts: the Bible, the Torah, and the Avesta.

The Safavids established their capital in Isfahan, a Persian-speaking city, and recruited Persian scribes into their court administration. Such families had helped administer the ancient Iranian empires. They proceeded to govern not only through these Persian scribes and Shi'i clerics but also through tribal chiefs, large landowners, religious notables, city merchants, guild elders, and urban ward leaders.

Background: Islam and Shi'ism

Islam, with some 1 billion adherents, is the second largest religion in the world. Islam means literally "submission to God," and a Muslim is someone who has submitted to God—the same God that Jews and Christians worship. Islam has one central tenet: "There is only one God, and Muhammad is His Prophet." Muslims, in order to consider themselves faithful, need to perform the following four duties to the best of their ability: give to charity; pray every day facing Mecca, where Abraham is believed to have built the first place of worship; make a pilgrimage at least once in a lifetime to Mecca, which is located in modern Saudi Arabia; and fast during the daytime hours in the month of Ramadan to commemorate God's revelation of the Qur'an (Koran, or Holy Book) to the Prophet Muhammad. These four duties, together with the central tenet, are known as the Five Pillars of Islam.

From its earliest days, Islam has been divided into two major branches: Sunni, meaning literally "followers of tradition," and Shi'i, literally "partisans of Ali." Sunnis are by far in the majority worldwide. Shi'is constitute less than 10 percent of Muslims worldwide and are concentrated in Iran, southern Iraq, Bahrain, eastern Turkey, Azerbaijan, and southern Lebanon.

Although both branches accept the Five Pillars, they differ mostly over who should have succeeded the Prophet Muhammad (d. 632). The Sunnis recognized the early dynasties that ruled the Islamic empire with the exalted title of caliph ("Prophet's Deputy"). The Shi'is, however, argued that as soon as the Prophet died, his authority should have been passed on to Imam Ali, the Prophet's close companion, disciple, and son-in-law. They further argue that Imam Ali passed his authority to his direct male heirs, the third of whom, Imam Husayn, had been martyred fighting the Sunnis in 680, and the twelfth of whom had supposedly gone into hiding in 941.

The Shi'is are also known as Twelvers, since they follow the Twelve Imams. They refer to the Twelfth Imam as the *Mahdi*, the Hidden Imam, and believe him to be the Messiah who will herald the end of the world. Furthermore, they argue that in his absence, the authority to interpret the *shari'a* (religious law) should be in the hands of the senior clerical scholars—the ayatollahs. Thus, from the beginning, the Shi'is harbored ambivalent attitudes toward the state, especially if the rulers were Sunnis or lacked genealogical links to the Twelve Imams. For Sunnis, the *shari'a* is based mostly on the Qur'an and the teachings of the Prophet. For Shi'is, it is based also on the teachings of the Twelve Imams.

The Safavid army was formed mostly of tribal cavalry led by tribal chieftains. Financial constraints prevented the Safavids from creating a large bureaucracy or an extensive standing army. Their revenues came mostly from land taxes levied on the peasantry. In theory, the Safavids claimed absolute power; in reality, their power was limited since they lacked a central state and had no choice but to work along with many semi-independent local leaders. The central government was linked to the general population not so much through coercive institutions as through provincial and hereditary notables. It survived for the most part because the society below was sharply fragmented by geographic barriers (especially mountains) as well as by

tribal, communal, and ethnic differences. Moreover, many senior clerics who might have opposed the dynasty resided in Najaf, Iraq, at a safe distance from the seat of power of Iran. The Safavid shah did not control Iranian society. Rather, he hovered over it, systematically orchestrating its many existing rivalries.

The Qajars (1794–1925)

The Safavid dynasty collapsed in 1722 when Afghan tribesmen invaded the capital. The invasion was followed by a half-century of civil war until the Qajars, another Turkic tribe, reconquered much of Iran. The Qajars moved the capital to Tehran and recreated the

Safavid system of central manipulation and court administration, including the Persian scribes. They also declared Shi'ism to be the state religion even though they, unlike the Safavids, did not boast of genealogical links to the Twelve Imams. This was to have far-reaching repercussions. Since these new shahs did not pretend to wear the imam's mantle, the Shi'i clerical leaders could claim to be the main interpreters of Islam. In addition, many of them safeguarded their independence from the state by continuing to reside in Iraq and collecting religious contributions directly from the faithful in Iran. These contributions came mainly from wealthy merchants.

Qajar rule coincided with the peak of European imperialism in the nineteenth century. The Russians seized parts of Central Asia and the Caucasus region from Iran and extracted a series of major economic concessions, including a monopoly to fish for sturgeon (the source of the delicacy, caviar) in the Caspian Sea and exemption from import duties, internal tariffs, and the jurisdiction of local courts. The British Imperial Bank won the monopoly to issue paper money. The Indo-European Telegraph Company got a contract to extend communication lines through the country. Exclusive rights to drill for oil in the southwest were sold to a British citizen. The later Qajars also borrowed heavily from European banks to meet lavish court expenses. By the end of the century, these loans had become so heavy that the Qajars were obliged to guarantee repayments by placing the country's entire customs service under European supervision. Iranians felt that their whole country had been auctioned off and that the shah had given away far too many concessions, or capitulations, as they called them.

These resentments culminated in the constitutional revolution of 1905–1909. The revolution began with shopkeepers and moneylenders demonstrating against the handing over of customs collections to Europeans. They suspected that the shah would renege on local debts in favor of repaying his foreign loans. They also protested that the government was not doing enough to protect native merchants and industries. The protests intensified when the government, faced with soaring sugar prices due to political turmoil in Russia (Iran's major source of the commodity) publicly whipped two major sugar merchants.

The revolutionary movement peaked in 1906, when some 14,000 protesters took sanctuary inside the gardens of the British legation in Tehran and demanded a written constitution. After weeks of haggling, the shah conceded because the British diplomats advised compromise and because his army, led by Russians and called the Cossack Brigade, threatened to join the protesters. A British diplomat commented, "The shah with his unarmed, unpaid, ragged, starving soldiers, what can he do in face of the menace of a general strike and riots?"[1]

The 1906 constitution introduced essential features of modern government into Iran: elections, separation of powers, laws made by a legislative assembly, and the concepts of popular sovereignty and the nation (*mellat*). It also generated a heated debate, with some arguing that democracy was inherently incompatible with Islam and others countering that true Islam could not be practiced unless the government was based on popular support. Some even argued in favor of secularism—complete separation of religion from politics, church from state, and clergy from government authority. The new constitution retained the monarchy, but centered political power in a national assembly called the *Majles*. It hailed this assembly as "the representative of the whole people" and guaranteed seats to the recognized religious minorities: Jews, Zoroastrians, and Christians. Significantly, no seats were given to the Baha'is, a nineteenth-century offshoot of Shi'ism. The clerical leaders deemed the Baha'is to be apostates from Islam and "sinister heretics linked to the imperial powers."

The constitution endowed the *Majles* with extensive authority over all laws, budgets, treaties, loans, concessions, and the composition of the cabinet. The ministers were accountable to the *Majles,* not to the shah. "Sovereignty," declared the constitution, "is a trust confided (as a divine gift) by the people to the person of the shah." The constitution also included a bill of rights guaranteeing equality before the law, protection of life and property, safeguards from arbitrary arrest, and freedom of expression and association.

Although the constitution was modeled on the European liberal secular system of government, it made some concessions to Shi'ism. Shi'ism was declared Iran's official religion. Only Shi'is could hold cabinet posts. Clerical courts retained the right to implement the *shari'a* (religious law), especially in family matters. A Guardian Council formed of senior clerics elected by the *Majles* was given veto power over parliamentary bills deemed un-Islamic. In short, popular sovereignty was to be restricted by clerical veto power. In actual fact, this Guardian Council was not convened until the 1979 Islamic Revolution because of divisions within the clerical establishment and opposition from parliament.

The initial euphoria that greeted the 1905 constitutional revolution gave way to deep disillusionment in the subsequent decade. Pressures from the European powers continued, and a devastating famine after World War I took some 1 million lives, almost 10 percent of the total population. Internal conflicts polarized the *Majles* into warring liberal and conservative factions. The former, mostly members of the intelligentsia, championed social reforms, especially the replacement of the *shari'a* with a modern legal code. The latter, led by landlords, tribal chiefs, and senior clerics, vehemently opposed such reforms, particularly land reform, women's rights, and the granting of full equality to religious minorities.

Meanwhile, the central government, lacking any real army, bureaucracy, or tax-collecting machinery, was unable to administer the provinces, especially the regions inhabited by the Kurds, Turkmans, and Baluchis. Some tribes, equipped with modern European rifles, had more firepower than the central government. Moreover, during World War I, Russia and Britain formally carved up Iran into three zones. Russia occupied the north and Britain the south. Iran was left with a small "neutral zone" in the middle.

By 1921, Iran was in complete disarray. The shah was gathering his crown jewels to flee south. The British, in their own words, were hoping to "salvage" some "healthy limbs" of the fractured country in their southern zone. Left-wing rebels, helped by the new communist regime in Russia, had taken over Gilan province and were threatening nearby Azerbaijan, Mazandaran, and Khorasan. According to a British diplomat, the propertied classes, fearful of communism, were anxiously seeking "a savior on horseback."[2]

The Pahlavis (1925–1979)

That savior appeared in February 1921 in the person of Colonel Reza Khan, the recently appointed commander of the elite 3,000-strong Cossack Brigade. Carrying out a typical military **coup d'état**, he replaced the cabinet and, while paying lip service to the monarch, consolidated power in his own hands, especially the post of commander in chief of the armed forces. Four years later, he emerged from behind the throne; deposed the Qajars; crowned himself shah-in-shah in the style of his hero, the French emperor Napoleon; and established the Pahlavi dynasty, adopting a name associated with the glories of ancient Iran. This was the first nontribal dynasty to rule the whole of Iran. To forestall opposition from Britain and the Soviet Union, he assured both countries that Iran would remain strictly nonaligned. A compliant *Majles* endorsed this transfer of power from the Qajars to the Pahlavis.

Reza Shah ruled with an iron fist until 1941, when the British and the Soviets invaded Iran to stop Nazi Germany from establishing a foothold there. Reza Shah promptly abdicated in favor of his son, Muhammad Reza Shah, and went into exile, where he soon died. In the first twelve years of his reign, the young shah retained control over the armed forces but had to live with a free press, an independent judiciary, competitive elections, assertive cabinet ministers, and boisterous parliaments. He also had to confront two vigorous political movements: the communist Tudeh (Masses) Party and the National Front, led by the charismatic Dr. Muhammad Mosaddeq (1882–1967).

The Tudeh drew its support mostly from working-class trade unions. The National Front drew its support mainly from the salaried middle classes and campaigned to nationalize the British company that controlled the whole of the petroleum industry in Iran. Mosaddeq also wanted to sever the shah's links with the armed forces. He argued that according to the constitution, the monarch should reign, not rule, and that the armed forces should be supervised by cabinet ministers responsible to parliament. In 1951, Mosaddeq was elected prime minister and promptly nationalized the oil industry. The period of relative freedom, however, ended abruptly in 1953, when royalist army officers overthrew Mosaddeq and installed the shah with absolute power. The coup was financed by the U.S. Central Intelligence Agency (CIA) and the British, which intensified anti-British sentiment and created a deep distrust of the United States. It also made the shah appear to be a puppet of foreign powers. Muhammad Reza Shah ruled much in the style of his autocratic father until he was overthrown by the 1979 Islamic Revolution.

During its fifty-four-year rule, the Pahlavi dynasty built the first highly centralized state in Iran's history. This state rested on three pillars: the armed forces, the bureaucracy, and the royal patronage system. The armed forces grew from fewer than 40,000 in 1925 to 124,000 in 1941, and to over 410,000 in 1979, by which time Iran had the fifth largest army in the world, the largest navy in the Persian Gulf, the largest air force in western Asia, and one of the best-equipped tank brigades in the Third World. The armed forces were supplemented by a pervasive secret police known as SAVAK—the Persian acronym for the Organization to Protect and Gather Information for the State.

Iran's bureaucracy expanded from a haphazard collection of hereditary scribes, some without fixed offices, to twenty-one ministries employing over 300,000 civil servants in 1979. The Education Ministry grew twentyfold, administering 26,000 primary schools with some 4 million children and 1,850 secondary schools with 740,000 pupils. Meanwhile, the Ministry of Higher Education supervised 750 vocational schools with 227,000 students and thirteen universities with 154,000 students. The powerful Interior Ministry appointed provincial governors, town mayors, district superintendents, and village headmen. Since it also appointed electoral supervisors, it could rig *Majles* elections and provide the shah with rubber-stamp parliaments.

The Justice Ministry supplanted the *shari'a* with a European-style civil code and the clerical courts with a modern judicial system culminating in a Supreme Court. Lawyers and judges had to pass government-administered exams based on European jurisprudence. The legal system was further secularized in the 1960s, when the shah decreed a controversial Family Protection Law that contradicted the traditional interpretation of the *shar'ia* on a number of points, including raising the marriage age to twenty for men and eighteen for women. It also allowed women to override spousal objections and work outside the home if they got court permission and restricted polygamy by stipulating that husbands could marry more than one wife only if they first obtained permission from previous wives and the courts.

Other ministries experienced similar expansion. For example, the Transport Ministry built an impressive array of bridges, ports, highways, and railroads known as the Trans-Iranian Railway. The Ministry of Industries financed the construction of numerous factories specializing in consumer goods. The Agricultural Ministry attained prominence in 1962 when the shah made land reform the centerpiece of his much-heralded "White Revolution," which was designed partly to forestall the possibility of a communist-led "red revolution." The government bought land from large absentee owners and sold it to small farmers through low-interest, long-term mortgages. It also undertook the task of transforming small farmers into modern commercial entrepreneurs by providing them with fertilizers, cooperatives, distribution centers, irrigation canals, dams, and tractor repair shops. The White Revolution included the extension of the vote to women and a Literacy Corps to eradicate illiteracy in the countryside. Thus, by the late 1970s, the state had set up a modern system of communications, initiated a minor industrial revolution, and extended its reach into even the most outlying villages.

The state also controlled a number of major institutions: the National and the Central Banks; the Industrial and Mining Development Bank, which channeled money to private entrepreneurs; the Plan Organization in charge of economic policy; the national radio-television network, which monopolized the airwaves; and most important, the National Iranian Oil Company, which grew from a leasing firm in the 1950s to become a large exploring, drilling, refining, and exporting corporation.

The Pahlavi state was further bolstered by court patronage. The dynasty's founder, Reza Shah, the son of a small landowner, used coercion, confiscations, and diversion of irrigation water to make himself one of the largest landowners in the Middle East. As a British diplomat put it, Reza Shah had an "unholy interest in property," especially other people's property.[3] This wealth transformed the shah's court into a large military-landed complex, providing work for thousands in its numerous palaces, hotels, casinos, charities, companies, and beach resorts. This patronage system grew under his son, Muhammad Reza Shah, particularly after he established his tax-exempt Pahlavi Foundation, which by the 1970s, controlled 207 large companies active in tourism, insurance, banking, agribusiness, mining, construction, and manufacturing.

The Pahlavi drive for secularization, centralization, industrialization, and social development won some favor from the urban properties classes. But arbitrary rule, the 1953 coup that overthrew a popular prime minister, the disregard for constitutional liberties, and the stifling of independent newspapers, political parties, and professional associations produced widespread resentment, particularly among the clergy, the intelligentsia, and the urban masses. In short, this state was strong in the sense that it controlled the modern instruments of coercion and administration. But its roots were very shallow because of its failure to link the new state institutions to the country's social structure. The Pahlavi state, like the Safavids and the Qajars, hovered over, rather than embedding itself into, Iranian society. Furthermore, much of the civil society that had existed in traditional Iran had now been suffocated by the modern state.

In 1975, the shah announced the formation of the Resurgence Party. He declared Iran to be a one-party state and threatened imprisonment and exile to those refusing to join the party. In heralding the new order, the shah replaced the traditional Islamic calendar with a new royalist one, jumping from the Muslim year 1355 to the royalist year 2535; 2,500 years were allocated to the monarchy in general and 35 years for the shah's own reign. The King of Kings and the Shadow of God also accrued two new titles: Leader to the New Great Civilization and Light of the Aryans (Aryamehr).

The Resurgence Party was designed to create yet another organizational link with the population, especially with the **bazaars** (traditional marketplaces), which, unlike the rest of society, had managed to retain their guilds and thus escape direct government control. The Resurgence Party promptly established its own bazaar guilds as well as newspapers, women's organizations, professional associations, and labor unions. It also prepared to create a Religious Corps, modeled on the Literacy Corps, to go into the countryside to teach the peasants "true Islam." The Resurgence Party promised to establish an "organic relationship between rulers and ruled," "synthesize the best of capitalism and socialism," and chart the way toward the New Great Civilization. It also praised the shah for curbing the "medieval clergy," eradicating "class warfare," and

becoming a "spiritual guide" as well as a world-renowned statesman. For his part, the shah told an English-language newspaper that the party's philosophy was "based on the dialectical principles of the White Revolution" and that nowhere else in the world was there such a close relationship between a ruler and his people. "No other nation has given its commander such a *carte-blanche* [blank check]."[4] The Western terminology, as well as the boast, revealed much about the shah at the height of his power—or, as some suspected, his megalomania.

The Islamic Revolution (1979–2001)

On the eve of the 1979 Islamic Revolution, a newspaper published by Iranian exiles denounced the Pahlavis in an issue entitled "Fifty Indictments of Treason During Fifty Years of Treason."[5] It charged the shah and his family with establishing a military dictatorship, collaborating with the CIA, trampling on the constitution, creating SAVAK, rigging parliamentary elections, organizing a fascistic one-party state, taking over the religious establishment, and undermining national identity by disseminating Western culture. It also accused the regime of inducing millions of landless peasants to migrate into urban shantytowns, widening the gap between rich and poor, funneling money away from the small bourgeoisie into the pockets of the wealthy comprador bourgeoisie (the entrepreneurs linked to foreign companies and multinational corporations), wasting resources on bloated military budgets, and granting new capitulations to the West—the most controversial being the extension of diplomatic immunity to U.S. military advisers in Iran.

These grievances were given greater articulation when a leading anti-shah cleric, Ayatollah Ruhollah Khomeini—from his exile in Iraq—began to formulate a new version of Shi'ism (see "Leaders: Ayatollah Ruhollah Khomeini"). His version has often been labeled Islamic **fundamentalism;** it would better be described as Shi'i populism or political Islam. The term *fundamentalism,* derived from American Protestantism, implies religious dogmatism, intellectual inflexibility and purity, political traditionalism, social conservatism, rejection of the modern world, and the literal interpretation of scriptural texts. Khomeini, however, was less concerned about literal interpretations of the Qur'an

Leaders: Ayatollah Ruhollah Khomeini

Ruhollah Khomeini was born in 1902 into a landed clerical family well known in central Iran. During the 1920s, he studied in the famous Fayzieh Seminary in Qom with the leading theologians of the day, most of whom were scrupulously apolitical. He taught at the seminary from the 1930s through the 1950s, avoiding politics even during the mass campaign to nationalize the British-owned oil company. His entry into politics did not come until 1962, when he, along with most other clerical leaders, denounced Muhammad Reza Shah's White Revolution. Forced into exile, Khomeini taught at the Shi'i center of Najaf in Iraq from 1964 until 1978.

During these years, Khomeini developed his own version of Shi'i populism by incorporating socioeconomic grievances into his sermons and denouncing not just the shah but the whole ruling class. Returning home triumphant in the midst of the Iranian Revolution after the Shah was forced from power in 1979, he was declared the Imam and Leader of the new Islamic Republic. In the past, Iranian Shi'is, unlike the Arab Sunnis, had reserved the special term *imam* only for Imam Ali and his twelve direct heirs, whom they deemed to be semidivine and thereby infallible. For many Iranians in 1979, Khomeini was charismatic in the true sense of the word: a man with a special gift from God. Khomeini ruled as Imam and Leader of the Islamic Republic until his death in 1989.

than about articulating resentments against the elite and the United States. He was more of a political revolutionary than a social conservative.

Khomeini denounced monarchies in general and the Pahlavis in particular as part and parcel of the corrupt elite exploiting the oppressed masses. For him, the oppressors consisted of courtiers, large landowners, high-ranking military officers, wealthy foreign-connected capitalists, and millionaire palace dwellers. The oppressed consisted of the masses, especially landless peasants, wage earners, bazaar shopkeepers, and shantytown dwellers. His proclamations often cited the Qur'anic term *mostazafin* (dispossessed) and the biblical promise that "the poor (meek) shall inherit the earth."

In calling for the overthrow of the Pahlavi monarchy, Khomeini injected a radically new meaning into the old Shi'i term *velayat-e faqih* (**jurist's guardianship**). He argued that jurist's guardianship gave the senior clergy—namely, the grand ayatollahs such as himself—all-encompassing authority over the whole community, not just over widows, minors, and the mentally disabled, as had been the interpretation previously. He insisted that only the senior clerics had the sole competence to understand the *shari'a;* that the divine authority given to the Prophet and the imams had been passed on to their spiritual heirs, the clergy; and that throughout history, the clergy had championed the rights of the people against bad government and foreign powers. He further insisted that the clergy were the people's true representatives since they lived among them, listened to their problems, and shared their everyday joys and pains. He claimed that the shah secretly planned to confiscate all religious endowment funds and replace Islamic values with "cultural imperialism." These pronouncements added fuel to an already explosive situation.

By 1977, Iran needed a few sparks to ignite the revolution. These sparks came in the form of minor economic difficulties and international pressures to curb human rights violations. In 1977–1978, the shah tried to deal with a 20 percent rise in consumer prices and a 10 percent decline in oil revenues by cutting construction projects and declaring war against "profiteers," "hoarders," and "price gougers." Not surprisingly, shopkeepers felt that the shah was diverting attention from court corruption and planning to replace them with government-run department stores and that he was intending to destroy the bazaar, which some felt was the real pillar of Iranian society.

The pressure for human rights came from Amnesty International, the United Nations, and the Western press, as well as from the recently elected Carter administration in the United States. In 1977, after meeting with the International Commission of Jurists, the shah permitted Red Cross officials to visit prisons and allowed defense attorneys to attend political trials. This international pressure had allowed the opposition to breathe again after decades of suffocation.[6]

This slight loosening of the reins, coming in the midst of the economic recession, sealed the fate of the shah. Political parties, labor organizations, and professional associations—especially lawyers, writers, and university professors—regrouped after years of being banned. Bazaar guilds regained their independence from the government party. College, high school, and seminary students, especially in the religious center of Qom, took to the streets to protest the quarter-century of repression. On September 8, 1978, known as Bloody Friday, troops in Tehran fired into a crowded square, killing hundreds of unarmed demonstrators. By late 1978, a general strike had brought the whole economy to a halt, paralyzing not only the oil industry, the factories, the banks, and the transport system but also the civil service, the media, the bazaars, and the whole educational establishment. Oil workers vowed that they would not produce any petroleum for export until they had exported the "shah and his forty thieves."[7]

Meanwhile, in the urban centers, local committees attached to the mosques and financed by the bazaars were distributing food to the needy, supplanting the police with militias known as *pasdaran* (Revolutionary Guards), and replacing the judicial system with ad hoc courts applying the *shari'a*. Equally significant, antiregime rallies were now attracting as many as 2 million protesters. The largest rally was held in Tehran in December 1978 on the day commemorating the martyrdom of Imam Husayn in the seventh century. Protesters demanded the abolition of the monarchy, the return from exile of Khomeini, and the establishment of a republic to preserve national independence and provide the masses with social justice in the form of decent wages, land, and a proper standard of living.

Although these rallies were led by pro-Khomeini clerics, they drew support from a broad variety of organizations: the National Front; the Lawyer's, Doctor's, and Women's associations; the communist Tudeh Party; the Fedayin, a Marxist guerrilla group; and the Mojahedin, a Muslim guerrilla group formed of nonclerical intellectuals. The rallies also attracted students, from high schools and colleges, as well as shopkeepers and craftsmen from the bazaars. A secret Revolutionary Committee in Tehran coordinated protests throughout the country, kept in telephone contact with Khomeini in Paris, and circulated recordings of his messages within Iran. This was a revolution made in the streets and propelled forward by audiotapes. It was also one of the first revolutions to be televised worldwide. Later on, many felt that these demonstrations inspired the revolutions that swept through Eastern Europe in the 1980s.

After a series of such mass rallies in late 1978, the *Washington Post* concluded that "disciplined and well-organized marches lent considerable weight to the opposition's claim of being an alternative government."[8] Similarly, the *Christian Science Monitor* stated that the "giant wave of humanity sweeping through the capital declared louder than any bullet or bomb could the clear message, 'The shah must go.' "[9] Confronted by this opposition and aware that increasing numbers of soldiers were deserting to the opposition, the shah decided to leave Iran. A year later, when he was in exile and dying of cancer, there was much speculation, especially in the United States, that he might have mastered the upheavals if he had been healthier, possessed a stronger personality, and received full support from the United States. But even a man with an iron will and full foreign backing would not have been able to deal with millions of demonstrators, massive general strikes, and debilitating desertions from his own pampered military.

On February 11, 1979—three weeks after the shah's departure from Iran and ten days after Khomeini's return—armed groups, especially Fedayin and Mojahedin guerrillas, supported by air force cadets, broke into the main army barracks in Tehran, distributed arms, and then assaulted the main police stations, the jails, and eventually the national radio-television station. That same evening, the radio station made the historic announcement: "This is the voice of Iran, the voice of true Iran, the voice of the Islamic Revolution." A few hours of street fighting had completed the destruction of the fifty-four-year-old dynasty that claimed a 2,500-year-old heritage.

The Islamic Republic (1979–2001)

Seven weeks after the February revolution, a nationwide referendum replaced the monarchy with an Islamic Republic. Of the 21 million eligible voters, over 20 million—97 percent—endorsed the change. Liberal and lay supporters of Khomeini, including Mehdi Bazargan, his first prime minister, had hoped to offer the electorate a third choice: that of a democratic Islamic Republic. But Khomeini overruled them on the grounds that the term *democratic* was redundant because Islam itself was democratic. The structure of this new republic was to be determined later. Khomeini was now hailed as the Leader of the Revolution, Founder of the Islamic Republic, Guide of the Oppressed Masses, Commander of the Armed Forces, and most potent of all, Imam of the Muslim World.

A new constitution was drawn up in late 1979 by a body named the Assembly of Religious Experts (*Majles-e Khebregan*). Although this 73-man assembly—later increased to 85—was elected by the general public, almost all secular organizations as well as clerics opposed to Khomeini boycotted the elections on the grounds that the state media were controlled, independent papers had been banned, and voters were being intimidated by club-wielding vigilantes known as the **Hezbollahis** ("Partisans of God"). The vast majority of those elected, including forty **hojjat al-Islams** and fifteen ayatollahs, were pro-Khomeini clerics. They proceeded to draft a highly theocratic constitution vesting much authority in the hands of Khomeini in particular and the clergy in general—all this over the strong objections of Prime Minister Bazargan, who wanted a French-style presidential republic that would be Islamic in name but democratic in structure.

When Bazargan threatened to submit his own secular constitution to the public, the state television network, controlled by the clerics, showed him shaking hands with U.S. policymakers. Meanwhile, Khomeini declared that the U.S embassy had been a "den of spies" plotting a repeat performance of the 1953 coup. This led to mass demonstrations, a break-in at

The Shah's statue on the ground, February 1979.
Source: © Abbas/ Magnum Photos.

the embassy, and the seizure of dozens of American hostages, and the resignation of Bazargan. Some suspect that the hostage crisis was engineered to undercut Bazargan.

A month after the embassy break-in, Khomeini submitted the theocratic constitution to the public and declared that all citizens had a divine duty to vote. Although 99 percent of the electorate endorsed it, voter participation was down to 75 percent despite full mobilizations by the mass media, the mosques, and the Revolutionary Guards. Some 5 million voters abstained. The clerics had won their constitution but at the cost of eroding some of their broad support.

In the first decade after the revolution, a number of factors helped the clerics consolidate power. First, few people could challenge Khomeini's overwhelming charisma and popularity. Second, the Iraqi invasion of Iran in 1980—prompted by Saddam Hussein's ambition to gain control over vital borders—rallied the Iranian population behind their endangered homeland. Third, international petroleum prices shot up, sustaining Iran's oil revenues. The price of a barrel of oil, which had hovered around $30 in 1979, jumped to over $50 by 1981, which enabled the new regime, despite war and revolution, to continue to finance existing development programs. In fact, in the 1980s, modern amenities, especially electricity, indoor plumbing, televisions, telephones, refrigerators, motorcycles, and medical clinics, made their first significant appearance in the countryside.

The second decade after the revolution brought the clerics serious problems. Khomeini's death in June 1989 removed his decisive presence. His successor, Ali Khamenei, lacked not only his charisma but also his scholastic credentials and seminary disciples. Khamenei had been considered a mere hojjat al-Islam until the government-controlled press elevated him to the rank of ayatollah and Leader. Few grand ayatollahs deemed him their equal. The 1988 UN-brokered cease-fire in the Iran-Iraq War ended the foreign danger. A drastic fall in world oil prices, which plunged to less than $10 a barrel by 1998, placed a sharp brake on economic development. Even more serious, by the late 1990s, the regime was facing a major ideological crisis, with many of Khomeini's followers, including some of his closest disciples, now stressing the importance of public participation over clerical hegemony,

of political pluralism over theological conformity, of populism over fundamentalism, and of civil society over state authority—in other words, of democracy over theocracy. The regime was grappling with the difficult problem of how to permit mass participation without undermining the entrenched conservative clergy.

Iran after September 11th (2001 to the Present)

The terrorist attacks of September 11, 2001, and the subsequent American invasions of Afghanistan in October 2001 and Iraq in March 2002, had profound consequences on Iran—probably more profound than on any other country with the exception of these three directly involved in the so-called War on Terror. The effect became even more pronounced in January 2002, when President Bush, in his famous "Axis of Evil" speech, specifically mentioned Iran, accusing it of secretly building nuclear weapons and aiding "international terrorists." He also urged the "people" of Iran to "liberate themselves" from their "unelected leaders."

The United States and Iran have entered a new cold war with one another in which both enjoy some advantages. On one hand, Iran is no match to the U.S. military—especially since it is now surrounded by American bases in Iraq, Afghanistan, Turkey, the Persian Gulf, and Central Asia. What is more, the United States could always further tighten the economic sanctions it has imposed on Iran ever since the 1979 hostage crisis. On the other hand, Iran, unlike Iraq and Afghanistan, is far too big a country to occupy—especially since the U.S. military is already overextended. Ironically, the United States, by invading these two countries, had eliminated Iran's two main regional enemies—Saddam Hussein in Iraq and the Taliban in Afghanistan. In addition, the Shi'i in Iraq and the anti-Taliban forces in Afghanistan are long-standing allies of Iran who could make the difficult American task in those occupied countries even more difficult if they chose to do so. Ironically, the United States, by invading these two countries, had eliminated Iran's two main local enemies—Saddam Hussein and the Taliban. And by occupying these two countries, it had also made itself more vulnerable to Iranian pressures since the Shi'i in Iraq and the anti-Taliban forces in Afghanistan had long-standing ties with Iran. The United States and Iran have entered a new cold war—one that is likely to last a long time.

Themes and Implications

Historical Junctures and Political Themes

The critical historical junctures discussed above have shaped contemporary Iran, especially the way it deals with the democratic idea, its role in the world of states, its attempts to govern the economy and meet the rising expectations of its citizens, and its need to overcome internal ethnic divisions.

In internal affairs, by far the most important challenge facing the republic is the task of reconciling Islam with democracy. Iran has been a Muslim country since the seventh century and Shi'i Muslim since the sixteenth century. It has also aspired to attain democracy, mass participation, and popular sovereignty since the 1905 constitutional revolution. The dual aspirations for Islam and for democracy culminated in the 1979 Islamic Revolution. Khomeini argued that Islam and democracy were compatible since the vast majority supported the clerics, had faith in them, respected them as the true interpreters of the *shari'a,* and wanted them to oversee the activities of state officials. Islam and democracy, however, appear less reconcilable now that the public has lost its enthusiasm for clerical rule. Some Khomeini followers have continued to give priority to his concept of theocracy, but others have begun to emphasize the need for democracy. In other words, Khomeinism has divided into two divergent branches in Iran: political liberalism and clerical conservatism.

The fate of democracy in Iran is bounded by the very nature of the *shari'a.* Democracy is based partly on the two principles that all individuals are equal, especially before the law, and that all people have inalienable natural rights, including the right to choose their own religion. The *shari'a,* at least in its traditional and conventional interpretations, rejects both of these democratic principles. Formulated in the seventh century, the *shari'a* is based on the principle of inequality, especially between men and women, between Muslims and non-Muslims, between legitimate minorities, known as the People of the Book, and illegitimate ones, known as unbelievers. In addition, the

shari'a, like all other religious law, not only considers rights to emanate from God rather than nature, but also deems the individual to be subordinate to the larger religious community. This is of special concern for Muslims who lose their faith or join another religion since the *shari'a* can condemn them to death as apostates. This is no mere technicality; over 250 Baha'is and over 400 leftist prisoners who professed atheism have been executed in Iran on just such grounds. But there are many moderate clerics in Iran who want to reform the *shari'a* to make it compatible with the modern concepts of individual freedom and human rights. They also favor treating those who do not believe in religion in the traditional manner of "don't ask, don't tell."

In international affairs, the Islamic Republic is determined to remain the dominant power in the Persian Gulf, even though it attained this position under the shah thanks mainly to the support of the United States. In his last years, the shah had become known as the American policeman in the Gulf region. By denouncing the United States as an "arrogant imperialist," canceling military agreements with the West, and condoning the taking of U.S. diplomats as hostages, Khomeini asserted Iranian autonomy in the region, but he also inadvertently prompted Saddam Hussein to launch the Iraq-Iran War. When Khomeini's government ministers suggested that the Persian Gulf be renamed the Muslim Gulf to improve relations with Arab countries, he responded that it should remain what it had always been: the Persian Gulf. Khomeini was as much an Iranian nationalist as a Muslim revolutionary.

Before he died, Khomeini initiated policies that have made it difficult for his successors to improve relations with the West, especially the United States. He called for revolutions throughout the Muslim world, denouncing Arab rulers in the region, particularly in Saudi Arabia, as the "corrupt puppets of American imperialism." He strengthened Iran's navy, and bought nuclear submarines from Russia. He launched a research program to build medium-range missiles and nuclear installations—possibly even nuclear weapons. He denounced the proposals for Arab-Israeli negotiations over Palestine. He sent money as well as arms to Muslim dissidents abroad, particularly Shi'i groups in Lebanon, Iraq, and Afghanistan. He permitted the intelligence services to assassinate some one hundred exiled opposition leaders living in Western Europe, and he issued the *fatwa* death decree against the British writer Salman Rushdie. These policies helped isolate Iran not only from the United States but also from the European Community, human rights organizations, and the United Nations. Khomeini's successors have had to grapple with this heritage, especially since these acts have direct bearing on economic development and prospects for obtaining foreign investment.

The Islamic Republic began with the conviction that it could rapidly develop the economy if it relied less on oil exports and more on agriculture and manufacturing. It blamed the shah for the single-export economy, the migration of peasants into the towns, the increasing gap in incomes, the continued high illiteracy rate, the lack of medical and educational facilities, and, in general, the low standard of living.

The new regime soon discovered that the country's underlying economic problems were formidable. Peasants continue to migrate to the cities because of the lack of both agricultural land and irrigation. Industry in Iran remains limited because of the lack of investment capital. Inflation and unemployment are high. Meanwhile, the population has steadily increased, and real per capita income has fallen due to forces outside the control of the state, particularly the price fluctuations of the international petroleum market. To deal with this economic crisis, some leaders have favored conventional state-interventionist strategies: price controls, five-year plans, and further redistribution of wealth through high taxation and social investment. Others have advocated equally conventional **laissez-faire** strategies: open markets, removal of state controls, more business incentives, and the wooing of foreign capital. Some clerics now openly admit that religion does not have answers to such problems as inflation, unemployment, and the volatility of world oil prices. This is a sharp contrast to the early days of the revolution, when Khomeini had confidently declared that Islam had all the solutions and that economics was a subject best left to "donkeys."

Finally, the Islamic Republic began with a strong and widely shared collective identity since 99 percent of Iran's population is Muslim. But this major asset was squandered in the two decades after the revolution. The stress on Shi'ism naturally alienated the 10 percent of Iranians who are Sunnis. In addition, the regime's insistence on a theocratic constitution on Khomeini's antagonized other top clerics as well as lay secular Muslims, who lead most of the political parties. Similarly, the inadvertent association of Shi'ism with the central Persian-speaking regions of Iran carries with it the potential danger of eventually alienating the important Turkic minority in Azerbaijan province. Thus, the Iranian regime, like most other developing states, has to solve the problem of how to allocate scarce resources without exacerbating ethnic, regional, and sectarian differences.

Implications for Comparative Politics

The Iranian Revolution, the emergence of religion as a force in Middle Eastern politics, and the collapse of the Soviet Union convinced many Americans that a new specter was haunting the West: that of Islamic fundamentalism. Some scholars predicted that a "clash of civilizations" would replace the cold war, arguing that the fault lines in world politics would no longer be over political ideology but over religion and culture. One of the main clashes would be between the West and the Muslim world, headed by the Islamic Republic of Iran.[10] Islam was seen as a major threat not only because of its size but also because it was deemed "inherently bellicose," "militant," and antagonistic to the West.

Such dire predictions have turned out to be gross exaggerations. It is true that the early Islamic Republic began denouncing the United States, arming militants in other parts of the Middle East, and calling for a struggle, sometimes termed a *jihad* (crusade), against the West. But these rhetorical denunciations have become muted, as reflected in the election of the reformist Muhammad Khatami as president. The call for Muslim unity has fallen on deaf ears, especially in Sunni countries, such as Saudi Arabia, which remains a very close ally of the United States. Iranian assistance to Shi'i Muslims is limited to Iraq, Lebanon, and Afghanistan. In Afghanistan, Iran even pressured its Shi'i allies to help the United States overthrow the Taliban after 9/11. In Iraq, it urged the Shi'i population not to resist the American invasion and to channel their activities into the electoral arena. What is more, Iranians themselves, including the clerics, have divided sharply into ultraconservative, conservative, liberal, and radical political camps. They even use the Western terms *left, right,* and *center* to describe themselves. Contemporary Iran shows that Muslim politics comes in many forms and, that as a blanket category, it has as little meaning as that of Christian politics. In the same way that one does not study the Bible to understand modern Europe, one does not need the Qur'an to analyze Middle Eastern politics.

Iran is a major power in the Middle East. It has one of the region's biggest armies and the largest navy in the Persian Gulf, a large land mass, considerable human resources, a respectable gross domestic product (GDP), and vast oil production. Iran also has plans, predating the Islamic Revolution, to become a nuclear power, which remains a major issue of tension in U.S.-Iranian relations.

But Iran is also, in many ways, a much weakened power. Its GDP is only about that of New Jersey, and its armed forces are a mere shadow of their former selves. The brutal eight-year conflict with Iraq (1980–1988) made the military war-weary. The officer ranks have been decimated by constant purges. The country's military hardware has been depleted by war, age, and lack of spare parts. In the last years of the shah, military purchases accounted for 17 percent of the GDP; they now account for 2 percent. Plans to build nuclear plants have been delayed, largely because the U.S. has successfully persuaded Europe not to transfer potentially dangerous technology to Iran.

Iran is unlikely to obtain nuclear weapons in the immediate future. Moreover, the United States, after 9/11 and the occupation of Iraq in March 2003, surrounded Iran with a string of military bases in the Gulf, Turkey, Azerbaijan, Georgia, Afghanistan, and Central Asia.

It is true that Iran has viewed itself as the vanguard of the Islamic world. But that world turns out to be as illusory for its champions as for its detractors. Just as there never was a communist monolith seeking global domination, the Muslim world is formed not of one unitary bloc but of many rival states, each with its own national self-interest. In theory, their rulers stress the importance of Islamic solidarity. In reality, they pursue conventional national interests, even allying with non-Muslims against Muslims, if necessary. For example, at the height of the American hostage crisis, Iran obtained military equipment from Israel and the United States to pursue the war against Iraq. Similarly, in recent years, Iran has sided with Hindu India against Muslim Pakistan, with Christian Armenia against Muslim Azerbaijan, and with Russia against Muslim Chechnya. Those who see the future as a clash of civilizations and a replay of the medieval Crusades forget that during those wars, both Muslims and Christians were often divided and sometimes sided against their own coreligionists. The Muslim world is no more united now than it was then. Iran, like its neighbors, formulates policies based on state and national interests, not on cultural, religious, and so-called civilizational sentiments.

Section ❷ Political Economy and Development

State and Economy

In 2002, Iran drafted a dramatically new investment law permitting foreigners to own as much as 100 percent of any firm in the country, to repatriate profits, to be free of state meddling, and to have assurances against both arbitrary confiscations and high taxation. Its intention was to attract foreign investments, especially from the European Union, and pave the way for joining the World Trade Organization (WTO). In the past, Iran's application to join the WTO had failed in

part because of its legal impediments against foreign investments and in part because of U.S. opposition. The new investment law was a far cry from the early days of the revolution when Khomeinists had vociferously denounced foreign investors as imperialist exploiters, waxed eloquent about economic self-sufficiency, and criticized the 1965 investment law, which limited foreign capital to less than 49 percent of any firm, as another example of the shah selling the country to Western corporations. Although some leaders continued to warn against Western consumerism and cultural imperialism, the regime as a whole was now eager to attract foreign investment and to rejoin the world economy.

The Economy in the Nineteenth Century

The integration of Iran into the world system began in a modest way in the latter half of the nineteenth century. Before then, commercial contact with the outside world had been limited to a few luxury goods and the famous medieval silk route to China. A number of factors account for this nineteenth-century integration: the economic concessions granted to the European powers; the opening up of the Suez Canal and the building of the Trans-Caspian and the Batum-Baku railways; the laying of telegraph lines across Iran to link India with Britain; the outflow of capital from Europe after 1870; and, most important, the Industrial Revolution in Europe and the subsequent export of European manufactured goods to the rest of the world.

In the course of the nineteenth century, Iran's foreign trade increased tenfold. Over 83 percent of this trade was with Russia and Britain; 10 percent with Germany, France, Italy, and Belgium; and less than 7 percent with countries in the Middle East. Exports were confined to carpets and agricultural products, including silk, raw cotton, opium, dried fruits, rice, and tobacco. Imports were mostly tea, sugar, kerosene, and such industrial products as textiles, glassware, and guns. Modest foreign investment also flowed into banking, fishing, carpet weaving, transport, and telegraph communications within Iran.

Contact with the West had far-reaching repercussions. It produced economic dependency, a situation common to much of the Third World, in which less developed countries become too reliant on developed countries; poorer nations are vulnerable to sudden fluctuations in richer economies and dependent on the export of raw materials, the prices of which often stagnate or decline, while the prices of the manufactured products they import invariably increase. Some scholars argue that this type of dependency lies at the root of the present-day economic problems in much of Africa, Latin America, and Asia, including the Middle East.

The nineteenth-century influx of mass-manufactured goods into Iran devastated some traditional handicrafts, especially cotton textiles. The import of cheap, colorful cotton goods undercut not only the local weavers, dyers, and carders but also the thousands of women who in the past had supplemented their family incomes with cottage industries and home spindles.[11] They naturally blamed foreign imports for their plight. Carpet manufacturers, however, benefited, since they found a ready market in Europe and North America.

The introduction of cash crops to be sold on the market, especially cotton, tobacco, and opium, reduced the acreage available for wheat and other edible grains. Many landowners ceased growing food and turned to commercial export crops. This paved the way for a series of disastrous famines in 1860, 1869–1872, 1880, and 1918–1920. Opium cultivation in Iran was particularly encouraged by British merchants eager to meet the rising demands of the Chinese market brought about by the notorious Opium Wars between China and Britain in the mid-nineteenth century.

Furthermore, the foreign competition, together with the introduction of the telegraph and the postal systems, brought many local merchants, shopkeepers, and workshop owners in the bazaars together into a national propertied middle class aware for the first time of their common interests against both the central government and the foreign powers. This new class awareness played an important role in Iran's constitutional revolution of 1905.

The Oil Economy

Deeper integration of Iran into the world system came in the twentieth century. Its main engine was oil. British prospectors struck oil in Khuzistan province in 1908, and the British government in 1912 decided to fuel its navy with petroleum rather than coal. It also decided to buy most of its fuel from the Anglo-Iranian Oil Company, in which it was a major shareholder. Iran's oil revenues increased modestly in the next four decades, reaching $16 million in 1951. After the nationalization of the oil industry in 1951 and the agreement with a consortium of U.S. and British companies in 1955, oil revenues rose steadily, from $34 million in 1955 to $5 billion in 1973 and, after the quadrupling of oil prices in 1974, to over $23 billion in 1976.

Between 1953 and 1978, Iran's cumulative oil income came to over $100 billion.

Oil became known as Iran's black gold. It financed over 90 percent of imports and 80 percent of the annual budget and far surpassed total tax revenues. Oil also enabled Iran not to worry about feeding its population, a problem that confronts many developing countries. Instead, it could undertake ambitious development programs that other states implemented only if they could squeeze scarce resources from their populations. In fact, oil revenues created in Iran what is known as a **rentier state,** a country that obtains a lucrative income by exporting raw materials or leasing out natural resources to foreign companies. Iran as well as Iraq, Algeria, and the Gulf states received enough money from their oil wells to be able to disregard their internal tax bases. The Iranian state thus became relatively independent of society. Society, in turn, had few inputs into the state. Little taxation meant little representation. It also meant that the state was totally reliant on one commodity, oil, whose worth was dependent on the vagaries of the world market.

Muhammad Reza Shah tried to reduce Iran's dependency on oil by encouraging other exports and attracting foreign investment into non-oil ventures. Neither policy succeeded. Despite some increase in carpet and pistachio exports, oil continued to dominate: on the eve of the 1979 Islamic revolution, it still provided 97 percent of the country's foreign exchange. Even after the oil boom, foreign firms, mostly U.S., European, and Japanese, invested no more than $1 billion in Iran, and much of this was not in industry but in banking, trade, and insurance. In Iran, as in the rest of the Middle East, foreign investors were put off by government corruption, labor costs, small internal markets, potential instability, and fear of confiscations. Apparently Western companies did not share their own government's confidence that Iran was an "island of stability" under the shah.

Society and Economy

Some oil revenue was squandered by Muhammad Reza Shah's regime on palaces, bureaucratic waste, outright corruption, ambitious nuclear projects, and ultrasophisticated weapons too expensive even for many NATO countries. But significant sums were also channeled into socioeconomic development. GNP grew at the average rate of 9.6 percent every year from 1960 to 1977, making Iran one of the fastest developing countries in the Third World at that time. The land reform project, the linchpin of the White Revolution, created over 644,000 moderately prosperous farms (see Table 1). The number of modern factories tripled from fewer than 320 to over 980 (see Table 2). Enrollment in primary schools grew from fewer than 750,000 to over 4 million; in secondary schools, from 121,000 to nearly 740,000; in vocational schools, from 2,500 to nearly 230,000; and in universities, from under 14,000 to more than 154,000. The Trans-Iranian Railway was completed, linking Tehran with Tabriz, Meshed, Isfahan, and the Gulf. Roads were built connecting most villages with the provincial cities.

Table 1

Land Ownership in 1977

Size (hectares)	Number of Owners
200+	1,300
51–200	44,000
11–50	600,000
3–10	1,200,000
Landless	700,000

Note: One hectare is equal to approximately 2.47 acres.
Source: E. Abrahamian, "Structural Causes of the Iranian Revolution," *Middle East Research and Information Project,* no. 87 (May 1980).

Table 2

Number of Factories

Size	1953	1977
Small (10–49 workers)	Fewer than 1,000	More than 7,000
Medium (50–500 workers)	300	830
Large (over 500 workers)	19	159

Source: E. Abrahamian, "Structural Causes of the Iranian Revolution," *Middle East Research and Information Project,* no. 87 (May 1980).

The expansion in health services was equally impressive. Between 1963 and 1977, the number of hospital beds increased from 24,126 to 48,000; medical clinics, from 700 to 2,800; nurses, from 1,969 to 4,105; and doctors, from 4,500 to 12,750. These improvements, together with the elimination of epidemics and famines, mainly due to food imports, lowered infant mortality and led to a population explosion. In the two decades prior to the 1979 revolution, the overall population doubled from 18 million to nearly 36 million. This explosion gave the country a predominantly youthful age structure. By the mid-1970s, half the population was under sixteen years of age. This was to have far-reaching repercussions in the street politics of 1977–1979 when young people were one of the driving forces leading up to the Islamic Revolution.

Socioeconomic development did not necessarily make the shah popular. On the contrary, his approach to development tended to increase his unpopularity with many sectors of Iranian society. The Industrial and Mining Development Bank channeled over $50 billion of low-interest loans to court-connected entrepreneurs, industrialists, and agribusinessmen. The shah believed that if economic growth benefited those who were already better off, some of the wealth that was produced would gradually trickle down to the lower levels of society. But in Iran, as elsewhere, the benefits of this development strategy got stuck at the top of society and never trickled down. By the mid-1970s, Iran was one of most unequal countries in the world in terms of income distribution.[12] Similarly, land reform, despite high expectations, created a small stratum of prosperous farmers but left the vast majority of peasants landless or nearly landless; over 1.2 million received less than 10 hectares (approximately 24.7 acres), not enough to survive as independent farmers given the productivity of agricultural land in Iran (see Table 1). Not surprisingly, many of the rural poor flocked to the urban shantytowns in search of work.

The factories spawned by the shah's modernization program drew criticism on the grounds that they were mere assembly plants and poor substitutes for real industrial development (see Table 3). His medical programs still left Iran with one of the worst doctor-patient ratios and child mortality rates in the Middle East. Educational expansion created only one place for

Table 3

Industrial Production

Product	1953	1977
Coal (tons)	200,000	900,000
Iron ore (tons)	5,000	930,000
Steel (tons)	—	275,000
Cement (tons)	53,000	4,300,000
Sugar (tons)	70,000	527,000
Tractors (no.)	—	7,700
Motor vehicles (no.)	—	109,000

Source: E. Abrahamian, "Structural Causes of the Iranian Revolution," Middle East Research and Information Project, no. 87 (May 1980), 22.

every five university applicants, failed to provide primary schools for 60 percent of children, and had no impact on the rate of illiteracy, which was 68 percent. In fact, the population explosion increased the absolute number of illiterates in Iran. The priority given to the development of Tehran increased disparities between the capital and the provinces. By the mid-1970s, Tehran contained half the country's doctors and manufacturing plants. According to one study, the per capita income in the richest provinces was ten times more than in the poorest ones. By the end of the shah's rule, Iran had the second highest (after Brazil) regional income disparity in the developing world.[13] According to another study, the ratio of urban to rural incomes was 5 to 1, making it one of the worst in the world.[14]

These inequalities created a **dual society** in Iran. On one side was the modern sector, headed by the elites with close ties to the oil state. On the other side was the traditional sector comprising the clergy, the bazaar middle class, and the rural masses. Each sector, in turn, was sharply stratified into unequal classes. Thus, Iranian society was divided vertically into the modern and the traditional, and horizontally into a number of urban as well as rural classes (see Figure 1).

The upper class—the Pahlavi family, the court-connected entrepreneurs, the military officers, and the senior civil servants—constituted less than 0.01 percent of the population. In the modern sector, the middle class—professionals, civil servants, salaried personnel, and college students—formed about 10

Iranian society was divided sharply not only into horizontal classes, but also into vertical sectors—the modern and the transitional, the urban and the rural. This is known as a dual society.

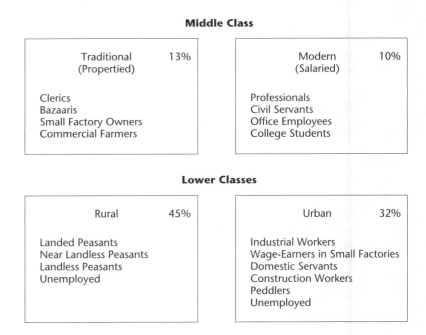

Figure 1

Iran's Class Structure in the Mid-1970s

Upper Class

Pahlavi Family; Court-Connected Entrepreneurs; Senior Civil Servants and Military Officers	0.1%

Middle Class

Traditional (Propertied)	13%	Modern (Salaried)	10%
Clerics Bazaaris Small Factory Owners Commercial Farmers		Professionals Civil Servants Office Employees College Students	

Lower Classes

Rural	45%	Urban	32%
Landed Peasants Near Landless Peasants Landless Peasants Unemployed		Industrial Workers Wage-Earners in Small Factories Domestic Servants Construction Workers Peddlers Unemployed	

percent of the population. The bottom of the modern sector—the urban working class, which included factory workers, construction laborers, peddlers, and unemployed—constituted over 32 percent. In the traditional sector, the middle class—bazaar merchants, small retailers, shopkeepers, workshop owners, and well-to-do family farmers—made up 13 percent. The rural masses—landless and near-landless peasants, nomads, and village construction workers—made up about 45 percent of the population.

The government's own statistics reveal the widening inequality. In 1972, the richest 20 percent of urban households accounted for 47.1 percent of total urban family expenditures; by 1977, it accounted for 55.5 percent. In 1972, the poorest 40 percent accounted for 16.7 percent of urban family expenditures; by 1977, it accounted for 11.7 percent (see Table 4).

These inequalities fueled resentments against the ruling elite, which were expressed more in cultural and

Table 4

Measures of Inequality of Urban Household Consumption Expenditures

Year	Percentage Share in Total Expenditures		
	Poorest 40%	Middle 40%	Richest 20%
1972	16.7	36.2	47.1
1977	11.7	32.8	55.5

Source: V. Nowshirvani and P. Clawson, "The State and Social Equity in Postrevolutionary Iran," in M. Weiner and A. Banuazizi (eds.), *The Politics of Social Transformation in Afghanistan, Iran, and Pakistan* (Syracuse, N.Y.: Syracuse University Press, 1994), 248.

religious terms than in economic and class terms. Among those who articulated these resentments was a gadfly writer named Jalal Al-e-Ahmad (1923–1969). A former communist who had rediscovered his Shi'i roots in the 1960s, Al-e-Ahmad shook his contemporaries by publishing a polemical pamphlet entitled *Gharbzadegi* (*The Plague from the West*). He argued that the ruling class was destroying Iran by mindlessly imitating the West; neglecting the peasantry; showing contempt for popular religion; worshipping mechanization, regimentation, and industrialization; and flooding the country with foreign ideas, tastes, luxury items, and mass-consumption goods. He stressed that developing countries such as Iran could survive this "plague" of Western imperialism only by returning to their cultural roots and developing a self-reliant society, especially a fully independent economy. Al-e-Ahmad inspired the long search for cultural authenticity and economic self-sufficiency that would culminate in the Islamic Revolution of 1979.

These themes were developed further by another young intellectual, Ali Shariati (1933–1977). Studying in Paris during the turbulent 1960s, Shariati was influenced by Marxist sociology, Catholic liberation theology, the Algerian revolution, and, most important, Frantz Fanon's theory of violent Third World revolutions against colonial oppression as laid out in his book, *Wretched of the Earth.* Shariati returned home with what can be called a fresh and revolutionary interpretation of Shi'ism, echoes of which would later appear in Khomeini's writings.

Shariati argued that history was a continuous struggle between oppressors and oppressed. Each class had its own interests, its own interpretations of religion, and its own sense of right and wrong, justice and injustice, morality and immorality. To help the oppressed, Shariati believed, God periodically sent down prophets, such as Abraham, Moses, Jesus, and Muhammad. Muhammad had been sent to launch a dynamic community in "permanent revolution" toward the ultimate utopia: a perfectly classless society.

Although Muhammad's goal had been betrayed by his illegitimate successors, the caliphs, his radical message had been preserved for posterity by the Shi'i imams, especially by Imam Husayn, who had been martyred to show future generations that human beings had the moral duty to fight oppression in all places at all times. Shariati equated Imam Husayn with

Che Guevara, the Latin American guerrilla fighter who helped lead the Cuban Revolution and was killed in Bolivia in 1967. According to Shariati, the contemporary oppressors were the imperialists, the modern-day feudalists, the corrupt capitalists, and their hangers-on, especially the "tie-wearers" and "the palace dwellers," the carriers of the "Western plague." He criticized the conservative clerics who had tried to transform revolutionary religion into an apolitical public opiate. Shariati died on the eve of the 1979 revolution, but his prolific works were so widely read and so influential that many felt that he, rather than Khomeini, was the true theorist of the Islamic Revolution.

Iran in the Global Economy

Under the Shah

The oil boom in the 1970s gave the shah the opportunity to play a significant role in international politics. As the second most important member (after Saudi Arabia) of the **Organization of Petroleum Exporting Countries (OPEC),** Iran could cast decisive votes for raising or moderating oil prices. At times, the shah curried Western favor by moderating prices. At other times, he pushed for higher prices to finance his ambitious projects and military purchases. These purchases rapidly escalated once President Richard Nixon began to encourage U.S. allies, such as the shah, to take a greater role in policing their regions. Moreover, Nixon's secretary of state, Henry Kissinger, openly argued that the United States should finance its ever-increasing oil imports, most of them from the Persian Gulf, by exporting more military hardware to the region. The shah was now able to buy from the United States almost any weapon he desired. Arms dealers began to jest that the shah read their technical manuals in the same way that some men read *Playboy*. The shah's arms buying from the United States jumped from $135 million in 1970 to a peak of $5.7 billion in 1977. Between 1955 and 1978, Iran spent more than $20.7 billion on U.S. arms alone.

This military might gave the shah a reach well beyond his immediate boundaries. He occupied three small but strategically located Arab islands in the Strait of Hormuz, thus controlling the oil lifeline through the Persian Gulf but also creating distrust among his Arab neighbors. He talked of establishing a presence well beyond the Gulf on the grounds that Iran's national interests reached into the Indian Ocean. "Iran's military expenditures," according to a 1979 U.S. congressional report, "surpassed those of the most powerful Indian Ocean states, including Australia, Indonesia, Pakistan, South Africa, and India."[15]

In the mid-1970s, the shah dispatched troops to Oman to help the local sultan fight rebels. He offered Afghanistan $2 billion to break its ties with the Soviet Union, a move that probably prompted the Soviets to intervene militarily in that country. The shah, after supporting Kurdish rebels in Iraq, forced Baghdad to concede to Iran vital territory on the Shatt al Arab estuary. This had been a bone of contention between the two countries ever since Iraq had come into existence after World War I. A U.S. congressional report summed up Iran's overall strategic position: "Iran in the 1970s was widely regarded as a significant regional, if not global, power. The United States relied on it, implicitly if not explicitly, to ensure the security and stability of the Persian Gulf sector and the flow of oil from the region to the industrialized Western world of Japan, Europe, and the United States, as well as to lesser powers elsewhere."[16]

These vast military expenditures, as well as the oil exports, tied Iran closely to the industrial countries of the West and to Japan. Iran was now importing millions of dollars' worth of rice, wheat, industrial tools, construction equipment, pharmaceuticals, tractors, pumps, and spare parts, the bulk of which came from the United States. Trade with neighboring and other developing countries was insignificant. In the words of the U.S. Department of Commerce, "Iran's rapid economic growth [provided America with] excellent business opportunities."[17]

The oil revenues thus had major consequences for Iran's political economy, all of which paved the way for the Islamic Revolution. They allowed the shah to pursue ambitious programs that inadvertently widened class and regional divisions within the dual society. They drastically raised public expectations without necessarily meeting them. They made the rentier state independent of society. They also made Iran an oil-addicted rentier state highly dependent on oil prices and imported products and vulnerable to the world market. Economic slowdowns in the industrial countries could lead to a decline in their oil demands,

which could diminish Iran's ability to buy such essential goods as food, medicine, and industrial spare parts. One of the major promises made by the Islamic Revolution was to end this economic dependency on oil and the West.

Iran's Economy Under The Islamic Republic

The Islamic Republic began with high hopes of rapidly developing the economy and becoming fully independent of oil and the West. The results have been mixed.

The main economic problem plaguing the Islamic Republic has been instability in the world oil market despite OPEC's attempts to preserve prices by limiting production and setting quotas for its members. The price of a barrel of oil, which had quadrupled from $5 to $20 in 1974, peaked at $52 in late 1980 but plunged sharply thereafter, reaching $18 in 1985, hovering around $12 to $14 in the late 1980s and 1990s, and descending to a new low of $10 in 1999. This meant that Iran's oil revenues, which continued to provide the state with 80 percent of its hard currency and 75 percent of its total revenues, fell from $20 billion in 1978 to less than $10 billion in 1998. They did not improve until the early 2000s when oil prices began to edge upwards again. Still a rentier state, Iran remains vulnerable to the vagaries of the international petroleum market.

The decline in oil prices during the 1980–1990s was due to a number of factors outside Iran's control: the slackening of the demand in the industrialized countries (especially with the recession in the late 1990s); the glutting of the international market by the entry of non-OPEC producers, such as Britain and Mexico; and the tendency of some OPEC members to preserve their revenues by cheating on their production quotas. Iran's oil revenues were also affected by the war with Iraq and its own failure to raise production. In some years, Iran was not able to meet even its OPEC quotas. To raise oil production, Iran needs an influx of capital and new deep-drilling technology, both of which can be found only in the West. This explains why the Islamic Republic has so dramatically changed its policy towards foreign investment.

Iran's economic problems have been compounded by the population explosion, the Iran-Iraqi war, and the emigration of some 3 million Iranians. The annual population growth rate, which had hit 2.5 percent in the late 1970s, jumped to nearly 4 percent by the late 1980s, mainly because the new regime encouraged large families. This was the highest rate in the world, causing a major strain on government resources, especially social services and food imports. The Iraqi war not only hurt the oil industry but also wrought as much as $600 billion in property damage—whole border cities were flattened. It also led to half a million Iranian casualties. The Islamic Revolution itself frightened many professionals and highly skilled technicians, as well as wealthy entrepreneurs, and industrialists into fleeing to the West. Of course, they carried their portable assets with them.

The overall result was a twenty-year economic crisis that lasted into the late 1990s. GNP fell 50 percent, per capita income declined 45 percent, and inflation hovered around 20 to 30 percent every year. The value of real incomes, including salaries and pensions, dropped by as much as 60 percent. Unemployment hit 20 percent; over two-thirds of entrants into the labor force could not find jobs. The absolute number of illiterates increased. Peasants continued to flock to urban shantytowns. Tehran grew from 4.5 million to 12 million people. The total number of families living below the poverty level increased. By the late 1990s, over 9 million urban dwellers lived below the official poverty line.[18] Shortages in foreign exchange curtailed vital imports, even of essential manufactured goods. The value of the currency plummeted. Before the revolution, the U.S. dollar had been worth 70 Iranian rials; by 1998, it was worth as much as 1,750 rials on the official exchange rate, and more than 9,000 rials on the black market. What is more, the regime that came to power advocating self-sufficiency now owed foreign banks and governments over $30 billion, forcing it to renegotiate foreign loans constantly.

Despite this ongoing economic crisis, the Islamic Republic has scored some notable successes. The Reconstruction Ministry, established mainly for the rural population, built 30,000 miles of paved roads, 40,000 schools, and 7,000 libraries. It brought electricity and running water to more than half of the country's 50,000 villages. The number of registered vehicles on the roads increased from 27,000 in 1990 to over 2.9 million in 1996. More dams and irrigation canals were built, and the Agricultural Ministry distributed some

630,000 hectares of confiscated arable land to peasants and gave farmers more favorable prices, especially for wheat. By the late 1990s, most independent farmers had such consumer goods as radios, televisions, refrigerators, and pickup trucks. The extension of social services narrowed the gap between town and country and between the urban poor and the middle classes. The adult literacy rate grew from 50 percent to 76 percent, and by 2000 the literacy rate among those in the six to twenty-nine age range hit 97 percent. The infant mortality rate fell from 104 per 1,000 in the mid-1970s to 30 per 1,000 in 2003. Life expectancy climbed from fifty-five years in 1979 to sixty-eight in 1993 and further to seventy in 2004—one of the best in the Middle East. The UN estimates that by 2000, 94 percent of the population had access to health services and 95 percent to safe water. On the whole, the poor in Iran are better off now than their parents had been before the Islamic Revolution. Moreover, the country, despite initial setbacks, was able to become more self-sufficient in food production. By the mid-1990s, it was importing no more than 5 percent of its wheat, rice, sugar, and meat requirements. The regime has also been able to diversify foreign trade and become less dependent on the West. By 2000, Iran's main trade partners were Japan, South Korea, and Russia.

The Islamic Republic also made major strides toward population control. At first, it closed down birth control clinics, claiming that Islam approved of large families and that Iran needed workers. But it reversed direction once the ministries responsible for social services felt the full impact of this growth. The regime also realized that only food imports could meet the rising demands. In 1989, the government declared that Islam favored healthy rather than large families and that one literate citizen was better than ten illiterate ones. It reopened birth control clinics, cut subsidies to large families, and announced that the ideal family should consist of no more than two children. It even took away social benefits from those having more than two children. By 2003, the regime could boast that it had reduced the annual population growth to 1.2 percent. This is an impressive accomplishment. It is also a sign that the regime is highly pragmatic when it comes to economic issues.

The 2000–2005 rise in petroleum prices—from $19 per barrel in 1999 to $53 per barrel in 2005—further helped the situation. Oil revenues jumped from less than $10 billion in 1998 to over $28 billion in 2001 and $30 billion in 2004. Foreign reserves increased to $4.8 billion, wiping out the external debt, stabilizing the currency, and improving the country's creditworthiness. Iran became one of the few developing countries to be free of foreign debt and was even able set aside some oil revenues as a hedge against leaner times. The GDP grew 7.4 percent in 2002 and 6.6 percent in 2003. Both the official unemployment and inflation rates, while still high, have fallen, and the currency has stabilized. The

government has floated its first international bond and, despite U.S. opposition, foreign investments—to the tune of $12 billion—have been contracted to flow into oil and gas ventures, petrochemicals, minerals, and car factories. The World Bank lent Iran $232 million for medical services and sewage lines, again despite American opposition. Oil revenues have allowed the government to channel additional funds into the infrastructure, especially power stations, hydroelectric dams, and education. The earlier oil bust had brought Iran economic stagnation; the new boom has brought it some hope.

Section ❸ Governance and Policy-Making

Iran's political system is unique in the contemporary world. It is a theocracy with important democratic features. It is a theocracy (which means, from the Greek, "God's power") for the simple reason that the clergy—in other words, the theologians—control the most powerful political positions. The system nevertheless contains elements of democracy with some high officials, including the president, elected directly by the general public.

Organization of the State

The Iranian state rests on the Islamic constitution designed by the Assembly of Religious Experts immediately after the 1979 revolution. It was amended between April and June 1989 during the last months of Khomeini's life by the Council for the Revision of the Constitution, which was handpicked by Khomeini himself. The final document, with 175 clauses and some 40 amendments (ratified by a nationwide referendum in July 1989) is a highly complex mixture of theocracy and democracy.

The constitution's preamble affirms faith in God, Divine Justice, the Qur'an, the Day of Judgment, the Prophet Muhammad, the Twelve Imams, the eventual return of the Hidden Imam (the Mahdi), and, of course, Khomeini's doctrine of jurist's guardianship that give supreme power to senior clergy. All laws, institutions, and state organizations have to conform to these "divine principles."

The Leader

The constitution named Khomeini to be the Leader for life on the grounds that the public overwhelmingly recognized him as the "most just, pious, informed, brave, and enterprising" of the senior clerics—the grand ayatollahs. It further described him as the Leader of the Revolution, the Founder of the Islamic Republic, and, most important, the imam of the whole community. It stipulated that if no single Leader emerged after his death, then all his authority would be passed on to a leadership council of senior clerics. After Khomeini's death, however, his followers so distrusted the other senior clerics that they did not set up such a council. Instead, they elected one of their own, Ali Khamenei, a middle-ranking cleric, to be the new Leader. Most of Khomeini's titles, with the exception of imam, were bestowed on Khamenei. The Islamic Republic has often been described as a regime of the ayatollahs (high-ranking clerics). It could be more aptly called a regime of the hojjat al-Islams (middle-ranking clerics), since few senior clerics want to be associated with it. None of the grand ayatollahs and few of the ordinary ayatollahs subscribed to Khomeini's notion of jurist's guardianship. On the contrary, most disliked his radical populism and political activism.

The constitution gives wide-ranging powers to the Leader. Enshrined as the vital link between the three branches of government, he can mediate between the legislature, the executive, and the judiciary. He can

The shah turning into Khomeini, from an émigré newspaper. *Source:* Courtesy Nashriyeh.

"determine the interests of Islam," "supervise the implementation of general policy," and "set political guidelines for the Islamic Republic." He can eliminate presidential candidates as well as dismiss the duly elected president. He can grant amnesty. As commander in chief, he can mobilize the armed forces, declare war and peace, and convene the Supreme Military Council. He can appoint and dismiss the commanders of Revolutionary Guards as well as those of the regular army, navy, and air force.

The Leader has extensive power over the judicial system. He can nominate and remove the chief judge, the chief prosecutor, and the revolutionary tribunals. He can dismiss lower court judges. He also nominates six clerics to the powerful twelve-man Guardian Council, which can veto parliamentary bills. It has also obtained (through separate legislation) the right to review all candidates for elected office, including the presidency and the national legislature, the *Majles.* The other six members of the Guardian Council are jurists nominated by the chief judge and approved by the *Majles.* Furthermore, the Leader appoints the powerful **Expediency Council,** which has the authority to resolve differences between the Guardian Council and the *Majles* (the legislature) and to initiate laws on its own.

The Leader is also authorized to fill a number of important nongovernment posts: the preachers (**Imam Jum'ehs**) at the main city mosques, the director of the national radio-television network, and the heads of the main religious endowments, especially the **Foundation of the Oppressed** (see below). By 2001, the Office of the Leader employed over six hundred in Tehran and had representatives placed in the most sensitive institutions throughout the country. The Leader has obtained more constitutional powers than dreamed of by the shah.

The later constitutional amendments expanded and transformed the Assembly of Religious Experts into an eighty-six-man house elected every four years. Packed with clerics, the assembly not only elected Khamenei as Khomeini's successor but also reserved the right to dismiss him if it found him "mentally incapable of fulfilling his arduous duties." In effect, the Assembly of Religious Experts has become an upper chamber to the *Majles.* Its members are required to have a seminary degree equivalent to a master's degree. Figure 2 illustrates the hierarchy established by the constitution of the Islamic Republic of Iran.

The general public elects the *Majles,* the president, and the Assembly of Religious Experts. But the Leader and the Guardian Council decide who can compete in these elections.

The general public elects the *Majles,* the president, and the Assembly of Religious Experts. But the Supreme Leader and the cleric-dominated Guardian Council decide who can compete in these elections.

Figure 2

The Islamic Constitution

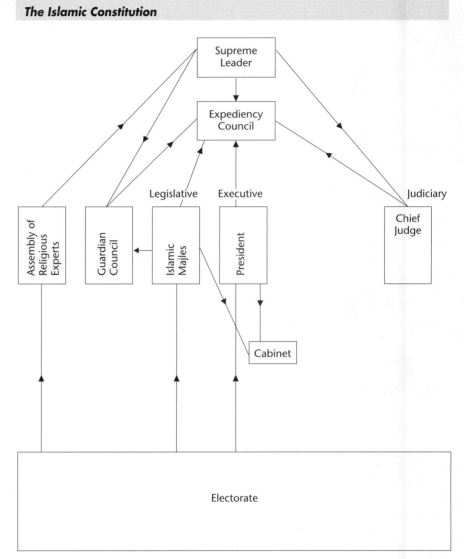

Because the constitution is based on Khomeini's theory of jurist's guardianship, it gives wide-ranging judicial powers to the Leader in particular and to the clerical strata in general. Laws are supposed to conform to the religious law, and the clergy are regarded as the ultimate interpreters of the *shari'a.* In fact, the constitution makes the judicial system the central pillar of the state, overshadowing the executive and the legislature. Bills passed by the Islamic *Majles* are reviewed by the Guardian Council to ensure that they conform to the *shari'a.* All twelve members of this Guardian Council are either clerics or lay jurists knowledgeable in the *shari'a.* The minister of justice is chosen by the president but needs the approval of both the *Majles* and the chief judge. The judicial system itself has been Islamized all the way down to the district courts, with seminary-trained jurists replacing university-educated judges. The Pahlavis purged the clergy from the judicial system; the Islamic Republic purged the university-educated.

The Executive

The President and the Cabinet

The constitution, particularly after the amendments, reserves some power for the president. He is described as chief executive and the highest state official after the Leader. He is chosen every four years through a national election. He must be a pious Shi'i faithful to the principles of the Islamic Republic. He cannot be elected to more than two terms. He draws up the annual budget, supervises economic matters, and chairs the plan and budget organization. He can propose legislation to the *Majles*. He conducts the country's internal and external policies. He signs all international treaties, laws, and agreements. He chairs the National Security Council responsible for defense matters. The president has the power to select the vice presidents and cabinet ministers. A separate parliamentary law, however, stipulates that he has to choose his minister of intelligence from the ranks of the clergy.

The president appoints most senior officials, including provincial governors, town mayors, and am-

bassadors. Furthermore, he names the directors of some of the large public organizations, such as the National Iranian Oil Company, the National Electricity Board, and the National Bank.

Khomeini often promised that trained officials would run the executive branch in the Islamic Republic, but clerics—also called mullahs have, in fact, dominated the presidency. Of the five presidents since the revolution, three have been mullahs: Khamenei, Rafsanjani, and Khatami. The main exception, Abol-Hasan Bani-Sadr, was ousted in 1981 precisely because he denounced the regime as "a dictatorship of the mullahtariat," comparing it to a communist-led "dictatorship of the proletariat." The fifth was assassinated.

The Bureaucracy

The president, as the chief of the executive branch, heads a huge bureaucracy. In fact, this bureaucracy continued to proliferate after the revolution, even though Khomeini had often taken the shah to task for having a bloated government. It expanded, for the most part, to provide jobs for the many college and high school graduates. On the eve of the revolution, the ministries had 300,000 civil servants and 1 million employees. By the early 1990s, they had over 600,000 civil servants and 1.5 million employees. The Iranian Revolution, like many others, ended up creating a bigger bureaucracy.

Leaders: *Ayatollah Ali Khamenei*

Ali Khamenei succeeded Khomeini as Leader in 1989. He was born in 1939 in Meshed into a minor clerical family originally from Azerbaijan. He studied theology under Khomeini in Qom and was briefly imprisoned in 1962. Active in the anti-shah opposition movement in 1978, he was given a series of influential positions immediately after the revolution, even though he held only the middle-level clerical rank of hojjat al-Islam. He became Friday prayer leader of Tehran, head of the Revolutionary Guards, and, in the last years of Khomeini's life, president of the republic. After Khomeini's death, he was elevated to the rank of Leader even though he was neither a grand ayatollah nor a recognized senior expert on Islamic law. He had not even published a theological treatise. The government-controlled media, however, began to refer to him as an ayatollah. Some ardent followers even referred to him as a grand ayatollah qualified to guide the world's whole Shi'i community. After his elevation, he built a constituency among the regime's more diehard elements: traditionalist judges, conservative war veterans, and antiliberal ideologues. Before 1989, he often sported in public a pipe, a mark of an intellectual, but gave up the habit upon becoming Leader.

Among the most important ministries of the Islamic Republic are Culture and Islamic Guidance, which has responsibility for controlling the media and enforcing "proper conduct" in public life; Intelligence, which has replaced the shah's dreaded SAVAK as the main security organization; Heavy Industries, which manages the nationalized factories; and Reconstruction, which has the dual task of expanding social services and taking "true Islam" into the countryside. Its mission is to build bridges, roads, schools, libraries, and mosques in the villages so that the peasantry will learn the basic principles of Islam. "The peasants," declared one cleric, "are so ignorant of true Islam that they even sleep next to their unclean sheep."[19]

The clergy dominate the bureaucracy as they do the presidency. They have monopolized the most sensitive ministries—Intelligence, Interior, Justice, and Culture and Islamic Guidance—and have given posts in other ministries to their relatives and protégés. These ministers appear to be highly trained technocrats, sometimes with advanced degrees from the West, but in fact are powerless individuals chosen by, trusted by, and related to the ruling clergy.

Semipublic Institutions

The Islamic Republic has set up a number of semipublic institutions. They include the Foundation of the Oppressed, the Alavi Foundation (named after Imam Ali), the Martyrs Foundation, the Pilgrimage Foundation, the Housing Foundation, the Foundation for the Publication of Imam Khomeini's Works, and the Fifteenth of Khordad Foundation, which commemorates the date (according to the Islamic calendar) of Khomeini's 1963 denunciation of the shah's White Revolution. Although supposedly autonomous, these foundations are directed by clerics appointed personally by the Leader. According to some estimates, their annual income may be as much as half that of the government.[20] They are exempt from paying state taxes and are allocated foreign currencies, especially U.S. dollars, at highly favorable exchange rates subsidized by the oil revenues. Most of their assets are property confiscated from the old elite.

The largest of these institutions, the Foundation for the Oppressed, administers over 140 factories, 120 mines, 470 agribusinesses, and 100 construction companies. It also owns the country's two leading newspapers, *Ettela'at* and *Kayhan.* The Martyrs Foundation, in charge of helping war veterans, controls confiscated property that was not handed over to the Foundation for the Oppressed. It also receives an annual subsidy from the government. These foundations together control $12 billion in assets and employ over 400,000 people. They can be described as states within a state—or rather, as clerical fiefdoms favored by the Leader.

Leaders: *Sayyid Muhammad Khatami*

Muhammad Khatami was elected president of the Islamic Republic in 1997 and reelected in 2000. He was born in 1944 into a prominent clerical family in central Iran. His father, an ayatollah, was a close friend of Khomeini. His mother came from a prosperous landed family. He studied theology in Qom and philosophy at Isfahan University. At the outbreak of the revolution, he was in charge of a Shi'i mosque in Germany. After the revolution, he first headed a state publishing house, was a member of the *Majles,* and then served as minister of culture and Islamic guidance. Arousing the wrath of the conservatives, he resigned from the last post in 1992 and took up the teaching of philosophy at Tehran University. He uses the title *sayyid* and wears a black turban to indicate that he is a male descendant of the Prophet. Although a cleric by appearance and training, he seems to many more like a university professor interested in liberal political philosophy.

Other State Institutions

The Military

The clergy have taken special measures to control Iran's armed forces—both the regular military of 370,000, including 220,000 conscripts, and the irregular forces formed of 120,000 Revolutionary Guards established immediately after 1979, and 200,000 volunteers of the Mobilization of the Oppressed (*Basej-e Mostazafin*) created during the war against Iraq. The Leader, as commander in chief, appoints the chiefs of staff as well as the top commanders. He also fills the post of defense minister with his own confidant, who reports directly to him, bypassing the president and the cabinet. Moreover, he places chaplains in military units to watch over regular officers.

After the revolution, the new regime purged the top ranks of the military, placed officers promoted from the ranks of the Revolutionary Guards in command positions over the regular divisions, and built up the Revolutionary Guards as a parallel force with its own uniforms, budgets, munitions factories, recruitment centers, and even small air force and navy. According to the constitution, the regular army defends the borders, while the Revolutionary Guards protect the republic from internal enemies. Despite these measures, political sentiments within the regular military about the Islamic Republic remain unknown, if not ambivalent, especially among the 18,000 professionals in the navy, 45,000 in the air force, and 150,000 in the regular army.

The Judiciary

The Islamic Republic regime Islamized the judiciary by enacting a penal code, the Retribution Law, based on a reading of the *shari'a* that was so narrow that it prompted many modern-educated lawyers to resign in disgust, charging that it contradicted the United Nations Charter on Human Rights. It permitted injured families to demand blood money on the biblical and Qur'anic principle of "an eye for an eye, a tooth for a tooth, a life for a life." It mandated the death penalty for a long list of "moral transgressions," including adultery, homosexuality, apostasy, drug trafficking, and habitual drinking. It sanctioned stoning, live burials, and finger amputations. It divided the population into male and female and Muslims and non-Muslims, and treated them unequally. For example, in court, the evidence of one male Muslim is equal to that of two female Muslims. The regime also passed a "law on banking without usury" to implement the *shari'a* ban on all forms of interest taking and interest giving.

Although the law was Islamized, the modern centralized judicial system was not dismantled. For years, Khomeini argued that in a truly Islamic society, the local *shari'a* judges would pronounce final verdicts without the intervention of the central authorities. Their verdicts would be swift and decisive. This, he insisted, was the true spirit of the *shari'a*. After the revolution, however, he discovered that the central state needed to retain ultimate control over the justice system, especially over life and death issues. Thus, the revolutionary regime retained the appeals system, the hierarchy of state courts, and the power to appoint and dismiss all judges. State interests took priority over the spirit of the *shari'a*.

Practical experience led the regime to gradually broaden the narrow interpretation of the *shari'a*. To permit the giving and taking of interest, without which modern economies would not function, the regime allowed banks to offer attractive rates as long as they avoided the taboo term *usury*. To meet public sensitivities as well as international objections, the courts rarely implemented the harsh penalties stipulated by the *shari'a*. They adopted the modern method of punishment, imprisonment, rather than the traditional one of corporal public punishment. By the early 1990s, those found guilty of breaking the law were treated much as they would be in the West: fined or imprisoned rather than flogged in the public square.

Subnational Government

Although Iran is a highly centralized state, it is divided administratively into provinces, districts, subdistricts, townships, and villages. Provinces are headed by governors-general, districts by governors, subdistricts by lieutenant governors, towns by mayors, and villages by headmen.

The constitution declares that the management of local affairs in every village, town, subdistrict, district, and province will be under the supervision of councils whose members would be elected directly by

Leaders: Hojjat al-Islam Ali-Akbar Hashemi Rafsanjani Ali-Akbar

Rafsanjani was born in 1934 into a fairly prosperous business and farming family in the heartland of the Shi'i and Persian-speaking provinces. He studied in Qom under Khomeini; found himself in prison four times during the 1960s; set up a number of commercial companies, including one that exported pistachios; and wrote a book praising a nineteenth-century prime minister who had made an abortive attempt to industrialize the country. Nevertheless, Rafsanjani remained active enough in clerical circles to be considered a hojjat al-Islam. After the revolution, he became a close confidant of Khomeini and attained a number of cabinet posts, culminating with the presidency in 1989. After serving two four-year terms, the maximum allowed by the constitution, he was given the chairmanship of the powerful Expediency Council. In some ways, his institutional power rivals that of President Khatami, but not, of course, that of Leader Khamenei.

the local population. It also declares that governors-general, governors, mayors, and other regional officials appointed by the Interior Ministry have to consult local councils. These clauses creating local councils had been incorporated into the constitution mainly because of mass demonstrations organized in 1980 by the left—notably the Mojahedin and the Fedayin. The **Assembly of Experts** would have preferred to have remained silent on the issue.

Because of conservative opposition, no steps were actually taken to hold council elections until 1999 when Khatami, the new president, insisted on holding the country's very first nationwide local elections. Over 300,000 candidates, including 5,000 women, competed for 11,000 council seats—3,900 in towns and 34,000 in villages. Khatami's supporters won a landslide victory, taking 75 percent of the seats, including twelve of the fifteen in Tehran. The top vote getter in Tehran was Khatami's former interior minister, who had been impeached by the conservative *Majles* for issuing too many publishing licenses to reform-minded journals and newspapers. These elections showed that the vitality of participatory democracy on the grassroots. But in February 2003, in a second round of local elections, conservatives won fourteen of the fifteen council seats in Tehran. This political swing was due largely to widespread voter abstention. Following appeals by reformers for their supporters to boycott the elections, only about 10 percent of the electorate in Tehran cast ballots.

The Policy-Making Process

Policy-making in Iran is highly complex in part because of the cumbersome constitution and in part because factionalism within the ruling clergy has resulted in more amendments, which have made the original constitution even more complicated. Laws can originate in diverse places, and they can be modified by pressures coming from numerous directions. They can also be blocked by a wide variety of state institutions. In short, the policy-making process is highly fluid and diffuse, often reflecting the regime's factional divisions.

The clerics who destroyed Iran's old order remained united while building the new one. They formed a distinct social stratum as well as a cohesive political group. They were convinced that they alone had the divine mandate to govern. They followed the same leader, admired the same texts, cited the same potent symbols, remembered the same real and imaginary indignations under the shah, and, most important, shared the same vested interest in preserving the Islamic Republic. Moreover, most had studied at the same seminaries and came from the same lower-middle-class backgrounds. Some were even related to each other through marriage and blood ties.

But once the constitution was in place, the same clerics drifted into two loose but identifiable blocs: the Society (*Majmu'eh*) of the Militant Clergy, and the Association (*Jam'eh*) of the Militant Clergy. The former can be described as statist reformers or populists, and the latter as laissez-faire (free-market) conservatives. The radicals hoped to consolidate lower-class support by using state power for redistributing wealth, eradicating unemployment, nationalizing enterprises, confiscating large estates, financing social programs, rationing and subsidizing essential goods, and placing price ceilings on essential consumer goods. In short, they espoused the creation of a comprehensive welfare state. The conservatives hoped to retain middle-class support, especially in the bazaars, by removing price controls, lowering business taxes, cutting red tape, encouraging private entrepreneurs, and balancing the budget, even at the cost of sacrificing subsidies and social programs. In recent years, the statist reformers have begun to emphasize the democratic over the theocratic features of the constitution, stressing the importance of individual rights, the rule of law, and government accountability to the electorate. In many ways, they have become like social democrats the world over.

The conservatives were originally labeled middle-of-the-roaders and traditionalists. The statists were labeled progressives, seekers of new ideas, and followers of the imam's line. The former liked to denounce the latter as extremists, leftists, and pro-Soviet Muslims. The latter returned the insult by denouncing the free-marketers as medievalists, rightists, capitalists, mafia bazaaris, and pro-American Muslims. Both could bolster their arguments with apt quotes from Khomeini.

This polarization created a major constitutional gridlock since the early Islamic *Majles* was dominated by the reformers, whereas the Guardian Council was controlled by the conservatives who had been appointed by Khomeini. Between 1981 and 1987, over one hundred bills passed by the reformer-dominated *Majles* were vetoed by the Guardian Council on the grounds that they violated the *shari'a,* especially the sanctity of private property. The vetoed legislation included a labor law, land reform, nationalization of foreign trade, a progressive income tax, control over urban real estate transactions, and confiscation of the property of émigrés whom the courts had not yet found guilty of counterrevolutionary activities. Introduced by individual deputies or cabinet ministers, these bills had received quick passage because the

The clerical regime and its two stilts: the sword and the oil wells. *Source:* Courtesy *Mojahed* (in exile).

radical statists controlled the crucial *Majles* committees and held a comfortable majority on the *Majles* floor. Some ultraconservatives had countered by encouraging the faithful not to pay taxes and instead to contribute to the grand ayatollahs of their choice. After all, they argued, one could find no mention of income tax anywhere in the *shari'a.*

Both sides cited the Islamic constitution to support their positions. The conservative free-marketers referred to the long list of clauses protecting private property, promising balanced budgets, and placing agriculture, small industry, and retail trade in the private sector. The reformers referred to an even longer list promising education, medicine, jobs, low-income housing, unemployment benefits, disability pay, interest-free loans, and the predominance of the public sector in the economy.

To break the constitutional gridlock, Khomeini boldly introduced into Shi'ism the Sunni Islamic concept of *maslahat*—that is, "public interest" and "reasons of state." Over the centuries, Shi'i clerics had denounced this as a Sunni notion designed to bolster illegitimate rulers. Khomeini now claimed that a truly Islamic state could safeguard the public interest by suspending important religious rulings, even over prayer, fasting, and the pilgrimage to Mecca. He declared public interest to be a primary ruling and the others mere secondary rulings. In other words, the state could overrule the views of the highest-ranking clerics. In the name of public interest, it could destroy mosques, confiscate private property, and cancel religious obligations. Khomeini added that the Islamic state had absolute authority, since the Prophet Muhammad had exercised absolute (*motalaq*) power, which he had passed on to the imams and thus eventually to the Islamic Republic. Never before had a Shi'i religious leader claimed such powers for the state, especially at the expense of fellow clerics.

As a follow-up, Khomeini set up a new institution named the Expediency Council for Determining the Public Interest of the Islamic Order—known for short as the Expediency Council. He entrusted it with the task of resolving conflicts between the Islamic *Majles* and the Guardian Council. He packed it with thirteen clerics, including the president, the chief judge, the Speaker of the *Majles,* and six jurists from the Guardian Council. The Expediency Council eventually passed some of the more moderate bills favored by the reformers. These included a new income tax, banking legislation, and a much-disputed labor law providing workers in large factories with a minimum wage and some semblance of job security.

The constitutional amendments introduced after Khomeini's death institutionalized the Expediency Council. The new Leader could now not only name its members but also determine its tenure and jurisdiction. Not surprisingly, Khamenei packed it with his supporters—none of them prominent grand ayatollahs. He also made its meetings secret and allowed it to promulgate new laws rather than restrict itself to resolving legislative differences between the Guardian Council and the *Majles*. In effect, the Expediency Council is now a secretive supraconstitutional body accountable only to the Leader. In this sense, it has become a powerful body rivaling the Islamic *Majles* even though it did not exist in the original constitution. By 2002, the Expediency Council contained thirty-two members. These included the president; chief judge; speaker of the *Majles;* ministers of intelligence, oil, culture, and foreign affairs; chief of the General Staff; commander of the Revolutionary Guards; jurists from the Guardian Council; directors of radio and television as well as of the Central Bank, Atomic Energy Organization, and National Oil Company; heads of the main religious foundations; chairman of the Chamber of Commerce; and editors of the main conservative newspapers. Seventeen were clerics. These thirty-two can be considered the inner circle of the ruling elite.

Section 4 Representation and Participation

Although the Islamic Republic is predominantly a theocracy, some claim that it is also a democracy. According to the constitution, the general electorate chooses the president as well as the Assembly of Experts, which in turn chooses the Leader. What is more, the elected legislature, the *Majles,* exercises considerable power, and according to one of the founders of the regime, it is the centerpiece of the Islamic constitution.[21] Another architect of the constitution has argued that the people, by carrying out the Islamic Revolution, implicitly favored a type of democracy confined within the boundaries of Islam and the guardianship of the jurist.[22] But another declared that if he had to choose between the democracy and power of the clergy as specified in the concept of jurist's guardianship, he would not hesitate to choose the latter since it came directly from God.[23] On the eve of the initial referendum, Khomeini himself declared: "This constitution, which the people will ratify, in no way contradicts democracy. Since the people love the clergy, have faith in the clergy, want to be guided by the clergy, it is only right that the supreme religious authority oversee the work of the [government] ministers to ensure that they don't make mistakes or go against the Qur'an."[24]

The Legislature

According to Iran's constitution, the *Majles* "represents the nation" and is granted many powers, including enacting or changing ordinary laws (with the approval of the Guardian Council), investigating and supervising all affairs of state, and approving or ousting the cabinet ministers. In describing this branch of government, the constitution uses the term *qanun* (statutes) rather than *shari'a* (divine law) so as to gloss over the fundamental question of whether legislation passed by the *Majles* is derived from God or the people. It accepts the rationale that God formulates divine law (*shari'a*) but elected representatives can draw up worldly statutes (*qanuns*).

The *Majles* has 290 members and is elected by citizens over the age of sixteen. It can pass *qanun* as long as the Guardian Council deems them compatible with the *shari'a* and the constitution. It can choose, from a list drawn up by the chief judge, six of the twelve-man Guardian Council. It can investigate at will cabinet ministers, affairs of state, and public complaints against the executive and the judiciary. It can remove cabinet members—with the exception of the president—through a parliamentary vote of no confidence. It can withhold approval for government budgets, foreign loans, international treaties, and cabinet appointments. It can hold closed debates, provide members with immunity from arrest, and regulate its own internal workings, especially the committee system.

The *Majles* plays an important role in everyday politics in Iran. On occasion, it has changed government budgets, criticized cabinet policies, modified development plans, and forced the president to replace some of his ministers. In 1992, 217 deputies circulated an open letter that explicitly emphasized the prerogatives of the *Majles* and thereby implicitly downplayed those of the Leader. Likewise, the speaker of the House in 2002 threatened to close down the whole *Majles* if the judiciary violated parliamentary immunity and arrest one of the liberal deputies.

Political Parties and the Party System

Iran's constitution guarantees citizens the right to organize, and a law passed in 1980 permits the Interior Ministry to issue licenses to political parties. But political parties were not encouraged until Khatami's 1997 election as president. Since then, three parties have been active: the Islamic Iran Participation Front and the Islamic Labor Party, both formed by Khatami reformist supporters, and the conservative Servants of Reconstruction created by Hojjat al-Islam Ali-Akbar Hashemi Rafsanjani, the former president and now chairman of the Expediency Council. According to the Interior Ministry, licenses have been granted to some seven hundred political, social, and cultural organizations, but all are led by people deemed politically acceptable by the regime. Real political opposition has been forced into exile, mostly in Europe. The most important opposition groups are

- **The Liberation Movement.** Established in 1961 by Mehdi Bazargan, the Islamic Republic's first prime minister. Bazargan had been appointed premier in February 1979 by Khomeini himself, but had resigned in disgust ten months later when the Revolutionary Guards had permitted students to take over the U.S. embassy. The Liberation Movement is a moderate Islamic party, which despite its religious orientation is secular and favors the strict separation of mosque from state.
- **The National Front.** Originating in the campaign to nationalize the country's oil resources in the early 1950s, the National Front remains committed to Mossadeq's twin political ideals of nationalism and secularism. Because the conservative clergy feel threatened by the National Front's potential appeal, they have banned the organization.
- **The Mojahedin.** Formed in 1971 as a guerrilla organization to fight the shah's regime, the Mojahedin tried to synthesize Marxism and Islam. It interpreted Shi'i Islam to be a radical religion favoring equality, social justice, martyrdom, and redistribution of wealth. Immediately after the

revolution, the Mojahedin opposed the clerical regime and attracted a large following among students. The regime retaliated with mass executions, forcing the Mojahedin to move their base of operations to Iraq. Not unexpectedly, the Mojahedin became associated with a national enemy and thereby lost much of its appeal.

- **The Fedayin.** Also formed in 1971, the Fedayin modeled itself after the Marxist guerrilla movements of the 1960s in Latin America, especially those inspired by Che Guevara and the Cuban revolution. Losing more fighters than any other organization in the struggle against the shah, the Fedayin came out of the revolution with great mystique and popular urban support. But it soon lost much of its strength because of massive government repression and a series of internal splits.
- **The Tudeh (Party of the Masses).** Established in 1941, the Tudeh is a mainstream, formerly pro-Soviet communist party. Although the Tudeh initially supported the Islamic Republic as a "popular anti-imperialist state," it was banned, and most of its organizers were executed during the 1980s.

Elections

Iran's constitution promises free elections. In practice, however, *Majles* elections have varied from relatively free but disorderly in the early days of the republic, to controlled and highly unfair in the middle years, and back again to relatively free—and now orderly—in the last decade. The main obstacle to fair elections has been the Guardian Council with its powers to approve all candidates. For example, in 1996, this Council excluded over 44 percent of some 5,000 parliamentary candidates by questioning their loyalty to the concept of jurist's guardianship. Electoral freedom is also restricted by the government-controlled radio-television network, the main source of information for the vast majority. The Interior Ministry can ban dissident organizations, especially their newspapers on the grounds that they are anti-Islamic. In some years, especially in the 1980s, ballot boxes were placed in mosques with Revolutionary Guards supervising the voting. Neighborhood clerics were on hand to help illiterates complete their ballots. Club-wielding gangs, the pro-regime Hezbollahis, assaulted their opponents.

Moreover, the electoral law, based on a winner-take-all majority system rather than on proportional representation, was designed to minimize the voice of the opposition. There have been seven elections since the founding of the Islamic Republic in 1979. The course and the outcomes of those elections reveal a lot about the evolution of representation and participation in Iran.

The First Majles (1980)

In the election in 1980 for the First *Majles* after the revolution, there were over 4,400 candidates, over 40 parties, over 200 dailies and weeklies, and thousands of political organizations in the bazaars, campuses, high schools, factories, and offices. The parties represented the whole range of the ideological spectrum from the far right to the extreme left. By shattering the old state structures, the revolution had unleashed a wide variety of political, social, and ethnic groups. It was as if, after years of silence, every professional and occupational association, every political party and ideological viewpoint, and every interest and pressure group rushed into the open to air its views, print its newspapers and broadsheets, and field its parliamentary candidates.

On the political right was the Islamic Republican Party (IRP), established immediately after the revolution by Khomeini's closest disciples. It had the support of the Islamic Chamber of Commerce, Islamic Association of Bazaar Guilds, Islamic Association of Teachers, Islamic Association of University Students, Association of Qom Seminary Teachers, and, most important of all, Association of Militant Clergy. Not surprisingly, it championed Khomeini's notion of jurist's guardianship.

At the center was Bazargan's Liberation Movement, which favored free markets, limited government, cordial relations with the United States, and a pluralistic political system. It also advocated a liberal interpretation of Islam, arguing that the clergy should advise rather than rule. Bazargan was a veteran of the nationalist movement against the British, but also liked to couch his politics with quotations from Islamic scriptures.

Closely allied with the Liberation Movement was the National Front, which was led by Western-educated, middle-aged professionals and technocrats. Unlike the Liberation Movement, they avoided making political use of Islam and separated politics from religion and treated the latter as a private matter.

The political left in the 1980 elections was fragmented into religious and nonreligious groups. The religious left included Islamic yet anticlerical groups such as the Mojahedin, Movement of Militant Muslims, and Movement for the Liberation of the Iranian People. The nonreligious groups included Marxist and ethnic parties: the Tudeh, the Fedayin, the Kurdish Democratic Party, and at least a dozen smaller Marxist-Leninist organizations. To complicate matters further, Abul-Hassan Bani-Sadr, a left-leaning French-educated intellectual supporter of Khomeini who had been elected president of Iran in January 1980, fielded his own candidates. Many of these parties had their own student, labor, professional, and women's organizations. Tehran alone had over a dozen women's organizations.

Not surprisingly, the elections for this First *Majles* were extremely lively, even though the IRP manipulated the state machinery to favor its candidates. On the eve of the voting, the minister of the interior declared that all were free to run, but only "true Muslims" would be permitted to sit in parliament.[25] Some 80 percent of the electorate participated in the first round.

The competition in the 1980 election was so intense in some constituencies that the Interior Ministry stepped in, impounded the ballot boxes, harassed candidates, and indefinitely postponed the second round of run-off elections. By the time the second round was held, the regime had cracked down on the opposition, forcing Bani-Sadr into exile, banning many leftist parties, and executing hundreds of Mojahedin.

Of the 216 deputies elected in 1980, 120 were supporters of the IRP, 33 of Bani-Sadr (who were later purged), and 20 of the Liberation Movement. Thirty-three described themselves as independents. Some of these had their parliamentary credentials promptly rejected on the grounds that documents found in the recently occupied U.S. embassy "proved" them to be U.S. spies. The IRP had won only 35 percent of the popular vote but had collected over 60 percent of the seats in the *Majles*. The Mojahedin, on the other hand, got 25 percent of the popular vote but did not obtain a single seat. In the end, the conservative IRP wound up with a solid majority in the Islamic Republic's first "elected" legislature.

The Second Majles (1984)

The elections for the Second *Majles* were carried out under very different circumstances. The spring of the Iranian Revolution was over. The opposition was now either banned outright or else highly restricted in its activities. The IRP monopolized the political scene, manipulating state institutions and controlling a vast array of organizations, including large foundations, local mosques, Revolutionary Guards, and thousands of town preachers. Not surprisingly, it won a landslide victory, leaving a few seats to independent-minded clerics with their own local followings. Also not surprisingly, voter participation fell sharply, to less than 60 percent, even though Khomeini declared that abstaining was tantamount to betraying Islam. Over 54 percent of the 270 deputies were clerics, almost all middle ranking.

The Third (1988), Fourth (1992), and Fifth (1996) Majleses

In 1987, Khomeini abruptly dissolved the IRP. No official reason was given, but the decision was prompted by the intense conflict within the party between statists demanding economic reforms and conservative free marketers favoring the bazaars. One radical deputy claimed that "the party had been infiltrated by opportunistic time-servers pretending to be devout followers of the Imam's Line."[26]

In dissolving the IRP, Khomeini declared that the clergy were free to establish two competing organizations as long as both opposed imperialism, communism, and capitalism, but supported Islam, the Islamic Republic, and the jurist's guardianship. "Political differences," he commented, "are natural. Throughout history our religious authorities have differed among themselves. . . . Besides Iranians should be free to express themselves."[27] He could have added, "within reason and within the context of Islam as defined by myself."

In preparation for the 1988 elections, the reformers left the Association of Militant Clergy and formed their own Society of Militant Clergy. From then on, there were two rival clerical organizations: on one side, the statist reformers with their Society and at least five major newspapers; on the other side, the conservative free marketers with their Association and a major newspaper called *Resalat* (*Message*). The conservatives became known as the Resalat group. Both groups had adherents in the seminaries and among the local preachers (Imam Jum'ehs).

The reformers won the lackluster elections for the Third *Majles.* The new parliament had eighty-six clerics, a 23 percent decline from the previous assembly. This, however, did not signify the demise of clerical power. Some clerics had gone on to higher positions, especially to the Assembly of Religious Experts. Moreover, many of the new lay deputies were young protégés of the clerics recruited into their fold from the students who had taken over the U.S. embassy.

Although the reformist clerics began the Third *Majles* with a clear majority, their influence soon ebbed because of Khomeini's death in June 1989, and because the new Leader Khamenei and President Rafsanjani began to adopt free-market policies once the war with Iraq ended. During the war, both men had been vocal advocates of price controls, rationing, high taxes, nationalization, and large government budgets. Now, with peace, they argued that the best way to jump-start the economy was to encourage private enterprise and cut state expenditures. In his eulogy for the late founder of the Islamic Republic, Rafsanjani downplayed Khomeini as the revolutionary leader of the downtrodden and instead praised him as a world-famous statesman who had restored Iran's national sovereignty.

In the following months, Rafsanjani, and to a lesser extent Khamenei, asked their followers to put away "childish slogans" and acknowledge the fact that the revolution had been "guilty of excesses." They talked increasingly of realism, stability, efficiency, managerial skills, work discipline, expertise, individual self-reliance, modern technology, entrepreneurship, and business incentives. They warned that the worst mistake a state could make was to spend more than its revenue. Rafsanjani declared, "Some people claim that God will provide. They forget that God provides only for those willing to work." Khamenei sermonized on how Imam Ali, the founder of Shi'i Islam, had taken great pride nourishing his plantations. Khomeini had often depicted Imam Ali as a humble

water carrier; Khamenei now depicted him as an entrepreneurial plantation owner.

To ensure a smooth change of course, Khamenei handed over control of the two main newspapers, *Kayhan* and *Ettela'at,* to the conservatives and authorized the Guardian Council to monitor the 1992 *Majles* elections. The Guardian Council announced that all candidates had to prove their "practical commitment to the Leader and the Islamic Republic." The Council further restricted the campaign to one week, permitting candidates to speak in mosques and run newspaper advertisements but not to debate each other in open forums. The head of the Guardian Council announced that he would use pesticides to cleanse parliament of anyone with "difficult attitudes." Seventy-five radical candidates withdrew. Forty were disqualified by the Guardian Council. Only a handful of reformers were allowed to be elected. Voter participation dropped to a new low. In Tehran, less than 55 percent of the eligible voters bothered to cast ballots despite Khamenei's proclamation that every true Muslim had the "religious obligation to vote."

Ayatollah Khalkhali, a prominent judge, was barred from running on the grounds that he did not have appropriate theological training. He retorted that conservatives who had sat out the revolution were now weaseling their way into the Guardian Council. Another disqualified candidate, who had earlier dismissed human rights as a "foreign conspiracy," now complained that the Guardian Council had violated his rights by failing to inform him of why he had been barred. The Guardian Council replied that its reasons had been kept out of the mass media in order to protect both state secrets and the public reputations of those deemed unqualified. Those who had been purged were expected to be grateful for this sensitivity. It also argued that it had followed precedent, reminding reformers that they themselves had used similar procedures to keep out "undesirables" from the previous three parliaments.

The conservative purge of the *Majles* was relatively easy to carry out. For one thing, the extensive constitutional powers entrusted to the Leader left the reformers vulnerable. As Hojjat al-Islam Mohtashami, a leading reformer, complained, the institution of jurist's guardianship was now being used to clobber revolutionary heads. When reformers complained that they were being slandered as traitors for merely questioning the turn to free-market economic policies, their opponents countered that disobedience to the Leader was tantamount to disobedience to God. They argued that only proponents of "American Islam" would dare question the decisions of the Leader. They also reminded them that the new oath of office required parliamentary deputies to obey the Leader as "the Vice Regent of the Hidden Twelfth Imam." Khamenei may not have inherited Khomeini's title of imam, but he had obtained the new exalted position of the Hidden Imam's Vice Regent.

The conservatives also threw populist rhetoric at the reformers. They described them as the "newly moneyed class" and as "Mercedes-Benz clerics." They accused them of misusing official positions to line their own pockets, give lucrative contracts to their friends, and deceive the masses with unrealistic promises. "They," exclaimed one conservative, "act like a giant octopus, giving with one tentacle but taking away with the others." They also placed the responsibility for the country's economic malaise squarely on the shoulders of the radicals. They argued that a decade of the kind of statist policies favored by the reformers had increased poverty, illiteracy, inflation, unemployment, and slum housing. Before the revolution, these problems were blamed on the shah and his family. Now they were blamed on the "pseudo-clerical radicals."

The purge was so decisive that immediately after the Fourth *Majles* elections the reformers temporarily suspended the activities of their Society of Militant Clergy. Some reformers went to head foundations, seminaries, and libraries. Others began to write for newspapers, arguing that the public should choose the Leader and that the Guardian Council should stay out of the electoral process. Yet others remained in the political arena, mildly criticizing the regime and quietly awaiting a better day.

This expectation was not far-fetched. The conservative majority began to splinter once President Rafsanjani implemented probusiness policies. He relaxed price controls, liberalized imports, ended rationing, disbanded courts that penalized price gougers, returned some confiscated property, and ended all talk of land reform, nationalization, and income distribution. He also set up a stock exchange in Tehran and

free-trade zones in the Persian Gulf. Some 170 deputies associated with Khamenei supported these measures but continued to favor highly conservative policies in the cultural realm. They demanded strict control over the media, silencing of liberal intellectuals, and rigid implementation of the dress code for women. They were also reluctant to challenge the financial privileges of the large foundations or open up the economy to international and émigré capital; they saw foreign competition as a threat to the bazaar. Meanwhile, some forty deputies, associated more with President Rafsanjani, favored cultural liberalization and the attraction of foreign capital as well as the probusiness policies. They also favored balancing the budget by downsizing the clerical foundations and cutting state subsidies. The remaining sixty deputies were independent, voting sometimes with the cultural conservatives, sometimes with the cultural liberals.

To get a working majority, President Rafsanjani had to water down his programs. He took only limited measures to privatize large enterprises, trim the foreign exchange privileges of the huge clerical foundations, and cut subsidies that absorbed much of the oil revenue. Moreover, he was unable to increase business taxes: all the taxes raised by the bazaar guilds together still constituted less than 9 percent of the government's annual tax income. Moreover, he had to shelve his daring bill designed to attract foreign investment. This bill would have raised the share that foreign interests could own in Iranian enterprises from 49 percent to 100 percent. It would have been a total policy reversal since the Islamic revolutionaries had relished accusing the shah of selling the country to foreign capitalists. Rafsanjani now argued that he could not revive the ailing economy without an injection of massive foreign capital.

Frustrated by these setbacks, Rafsanjani created a new political organization, Servants of Reconstruction, to run candidates for the Fifth *Majles*. Although supported by many cabinet ministers and the popular mayor of Tehran, who had made the city livable by building highways, libraries, and parks, Rafsanjani's party won only eighty seats. Over 140 seats went to the conservatives, who were able to prevent the implementation of economic and cultural changes favored by Rafsanjani. The conservative judiciary also imprisoned the mayor of Tehran on trumped-up embezzlement charges and closed down the newspaper, *Zanan* (*Women*), edited by Rafsanjani's daughter, on the grounds that it had offended religious sensibilities. Furthermore, term limits inevitably turned Rafsanjani into a lame duck president.

The Sixth Majles (2000)

The upset victory of the reform-minded Khatami in Iran's 1997 presidential election paved the way for the Sixth *Majles* elections in 2000, the first to be both orderly and competitive since the founding of the Islamic Republic. The reformers—labeling themselves the Khordad Front after the month (in the Iranian calendar) when Khatami had won the presidency—ran a highly successful campaign in 2000. The Khordad Front brought together the Islamic Iran Participation Front (headed by Khatami's brother); the Society of Militant Clergy; the Islamic Labor Party and the Workers House, a quasi-union; the Mojahedin Organization of the Islamic Revolution (a twenty-year-old group of reformist technocrats not to be confused with the guerrilla Mojahedin); a new campus organization called the Office for Strengthening Solidarity; a number of recently established and highly popular newspapers; and a host of liberal Muslim organizations, including the Islamic Association of Women. The Front was even supported, at least initially, by former president Rafsanjai's Servants of Reconstruction.

The associations that backed the Kordad Front had previously been proregime but had started to speak out in favor of a free press, government accountability, and fewer privileges for the clergy. Their views were articulated by a number of prominent intellectuals and journalists who had started their careers as staunch regime supporters—some had even participated in the takeover of the U.S. embassy in 1979–1980—but who had come to the conclusion that the democratic features of the constitution should take priority over the theocratic ones.

The best known of these intellectuals was Abdol-Karim Soroush who had been a follower of the Islamist ideologue Shariati. But Soroush now argued that Islam had become an "overbloated ideology" transgressing its true role in the realm of personal ethics and individual morality. He and his fellow reformers often denounced intolerant conservatives as "religious fascists." If the works of Shariati and Khomeini had been replete with concepts like revolution, imperialism, cultural roots, martyrdom, the dispossessed, and the Western plague, those of Soroush and the new reformers were full of concepts such as pluralism, democracy, freedom, equality, modernity, citizenship, dialogue, civil society, human rights, rule of law, and political participation. These reformers not only championed democratic concepts but also tried to make them compatible with Islam.

The reformers won the Sixth *Majles* elections in 2000 in a landslide, winning 80 percent of the vote in a campaign that drew over 70 percent of the electorate. In elections held for the Assembly of Experts a few months earlier, the reformers had abstained, and consequently voter participation had dropped to 46 percent. Over 6,800 candidates competed for the 290 seats in the Sixth *Majles*. Although the Guardian Council barred some prominent reformers from the election, it permitted most to participate, probably because of pressure from the Leader. Many supporters of secular parties—all banned from the campaign—voted for the reformers, who won over 195 seats. Candidates endorsed by the most prominent conservative organizations won fewer than forty seats, while the total number of "turbaned deputies" (clerics) fell to a new low of thirty-seven. President Khatami's brother, who had created the reformist Islamic Iran Participation Party, topped the winners in Tehran. Many prominent conservatives with long experience in high positions failed to get elected. Even the country's religious capital, Qom, voted overwhelmingly for the reformers. Former president Rafsanjani, who in the last days had openly courted the conservatives, was humiliated. He came in thirtieth in the first round of the Tehran election and quietly withdrew instead of continuing in the runoffs. After the elections, the London *Economist* magazine commented: "Iran, although an Islamic state, imbued with religion and religious symbolism, is an increasingly anti-clerical country. In a sense, Iran resembles some Roman Catholic countries where religion is taken for granted, without public display, and with ambiguous feeling towards the clergy. Iranians tend to mock their mullahs, making mild little jokes about them; they certainly want them out of their bedrooms. In particular, they dislike their political clergy."[28]

In the next two years, the reformist majority in the *Majles* drew up over one hundred bills, some of which implicitly challenged the conventional interpretations of the *shari'a*. The measures supported by the reformers eliminated the distinction between men and women, Muslims and non-Muslims, in weighing court evidence and awarding compensation. They raised the marriageable age for girls from nine to fifteen; gave scholarships to women to study abroad; ruled that divorce courts should divide property on an equal basis between husbands and wives; allowed women deputies to wear the *hejab* (headscarf) rather than the *chadour* (full covering); permitted school girls to wear colorful clothing; and ratified the UN Declaration on the Elimination of Discrimination against Women—a declaration too egalitarian even for the U.S. Congress. They permitted private banking, denationalized some enterprises, unified the exchange rate, diminished the privileges enjoyed by the clerical foundations, and liberalized the foreign investment law, thereby attracting some capital from Europe and Japan. The reformers purged the Intelligence Ministry of "rogue elements" who had carried out a series of political assassinations. They set up committees to investigate prison conditions and hosted a visit from the European Union's Commission on Human Rights. They proposed a special press court—outside the authority of the conservative judiciary—to handle libel and censorship cases. They nourished a "thousand flowers to bloom" by channeling subsidies into cultural activities and encouraging the publication as well as translation of thousands of works. They stipulated that trials were to be held before juries; that the function of the prosecutor was separate from that of the judge; that judges in serious cases had to have at least ten years' experience; that defendants had the right to counsel and access to their families; and that prisoners under no circumstances were to be blindfolded, deprived of sleep, or placed in solitary confinement. Equally contentious, they passed a bill (which was later vetoed) transferring the authority to approve parliamentary candidates and supervise elections from the Guardian Council to the Interior Ministry.

The conservative Guardian Council as well as the judiciary—often supported by the Leader—retaliated against the reformers. They vetoed much of their legislation on the grounds that they violated the *shari'a*

and the constitution. They closed down over fifty papers in what became known as the "great newspaper massacre," and hauled reformist journalists before the courts, accusing them of libel, slander, and blasphemy. They even tried unsuccessfully to strip deputies of parliamentary immunity.

Far more serious, the Guardian Council—this time even against the advice of the Leader—barred some 3,533 candidates including 87 reform deputies—among them Khatami's brother—from running in the Seventh *Majles* elections in 2004. Another 40 deputies resigned in protest. Ironically this drastic purge was greatly facilitated by the United States—both by President Bush's Axis of Evil speech and by the military occupation of Afghanistan and Iraq. Reluctant to rock the boat at a time of apparent and imminent national danger, most reformers restrained themselves and withdrew from active politics. Not surprisingly, the conservatives won a hollow victory in the 2004 elections. They received a clear majority, but the voter turnout was less than 51 percent, and in Tehran only 28 percent. This was the worst showing since 1979. For a regime that liked to boast about mass participation, this was seen as a major setback—even as a crisis of legitimacy.

The 2005 Presidential Elections

These elections were a mirror image of the 1997 presidential elections—except in reverse. Mahmoud Ahmadinezhad, a little known forty-nine-year-old university lecturer who had been appointed mayor of Tehran by the conservatives, won not only a surprise but a landslide surprise victory over Rafsanjani, the well-known seventy-year old ex-president now running on a broad reform platform that included the hope to improve relations with the United States. Ahmadinezhad received 17.2 million votes (62 percent); Rafsanjani, 10 million (36 percent). The turnout, however, was considerably less than in 1997. The following four reasons explain the reversal of fortunes.

First, the reformers were sharply divided. Some encouraged their followers to boycott the election as a protest against the Leader and the Guardian Council. Others had to split their votes among two reform candidates in addition to Rafsanjani.

Second, Ahmadinezhad skillfully tapped into class resentments. He campaigned on the theme that he was a hard-working "man of the people" who could speak on their behalf against "nepotism," "cronyism," "elitism," "corruption," "profiteering," and "luxury living." While keeping the language of reform and development, he revived Khomeini's populist rhetoric about the "mostazafin," "social justice," and "palace dwellers." He argued that the "real problem" confronting the nation had little to do with "what people wore," but much to do with jobs, decent wages, work conditions, housing, pensions, health coverage, and unemployment insurance. He opposed privatization, favored interest-free loans for small farmers, and advocated more state expenditures for welfare programs and the underdeveloped provinces. He implied that his main rival had siphoned off oil revenues to his family. These themes resonated well among the poor; for, although their actual standard of living had improved since the revolution, their relative standard of living compared to the upper middle class had not. What is more, the regime has so far failed to meet their rising expectations. These themes also resonated since he himself came from a poor family and had achieved success by doing well in university examinations and by volunteering to fight in the Iraqi war. His own father had been a blacksmith—an occupation potent with symbolic meaning since the Robin Hood of Iranian mythology had been a blacksmith. On the eve of the elections, Ahmadinez had invited television crews into his home where the public could see that he lived in a modest working class apartment—in sharp contrast to his competitor.

Third, Ahmadinez had received military support. On the eve of the elections, the heads of the revolutionary guards, the basij militia, and veteran organizations encouraged their members to rally votes for him. It is estimated these forces, together with their families, could muster some six million votes. This helped expand the conservative "base," which in the previous elections had been no more than 20 percent of the electorate.

Finally, the Bush administration inadvertently helped the conservatives. The administration's vocal calls for "regime change," together with the invasions of Afghanistan and Iraq, the courting of such unpopular exiles as the Mojahedin, the establishment of military bases around the country, and the insistence that the nuclear program should be dismantled, created within Iran the fear that the country was in "mortal danger." Such a mood inevitably undermined the reformers whom the public associated with the West. Some reformers blamed the Bush administration for undermining their position. Conversely, some conservatives thanked the administration.

Political Culture, Citizenship, and Identity

In theory, the Islamic Republic of Iran should be a highly viable state. After all, Shi'ism is the religion of both the state and the vast majority of the population. Shi'ism can also be described as the central component of Iranian popular culture. Moreover, the constitution guarantees basic rights to religious minorities as well as to individual citizens. All citizens, regardless of race, color, language, or religion, are promised the rights of free expression, worship, and organization. They are guaranteed freedom from arbitrary arrest, torture, and police surveillance.

The constitution extends additional rights to the recognized religious minorities: Christians, Jews, and Zoroastrians. Although Christians (Armenians and Assyrians), Jews, and Zoroastrians form just 1 percent of the total population, they are allocated five *Majles* seats. They are permitted their own community organizations, including schools, their own places of worship, and their family laws. The constitution, however, is ominously silent about Baha'is and Sunnis. The former are deemed heretics from Islam; the latter are treated in theory as full citizens but their actual status is not spelled out.

The constitution also gives guarantees to non-Persian speakers. Although 83 percent of the population understands Persian, thanks to the educational system, over 50 percent continue to speak non-Persian languages at home—languages such as Azeri, Kurdish, Turkic, Gilaki, Mazandarani, Arabic, and Baluchi. The constitution promises them rights unprecedented in Iranian history. It states that "local and native languages can be used in the press, media, and schools." It also states that local populations have the right to elect provincial, town, and village councils. These councils can watch over the governors-general and the town mayors, as well as their educational, cultural, and social programs.

These generous promises have often been honored more in theory than in reality. The local councils—the chief institutional safeguard for the provincial minorities—were not convened until twenty years after the revolution. Subsidies to non-Persian publications and radio stations remain meager. Jews have been so harassed as "pro-Israeli Zionists" that more than half—40,000 out of 80,000—have left the country since the revolution. Armenian Christians have had to end coeducational classes, adopt the government curriculum, and abide by Muslim dress codes, including the veil. The Christian population has declined from over 300,000 to fewer than 200,000.

The Baha'is, however, have borne the brunt of religious persecution. Their leaders have been executed as "apostates" and "imperialist spies." Adherents have been fired from their jobs, had their property confiscated, and been imprisoned and tortured to pressure them to convert to Islam. Their schools have been closed, their community property expropriated, and their shrines and cemeteries bulldozed. It is estimated that since the revolution, one-third of the 300,000 Baha'is have left Iran. The Baha'is, like the Jews and Armenians, have migrated mostly to Canada and the United States. This persecution did not ease until the election of President Khatami in 1997.

The Sunni population, which forms as much as 10 percent of the total, has its own reasons for being alienated. The state religion is Shi'ism, and high officials have to be Shi'i. Citizens must abide by Khomeini's concept of jurists' guardianship, a notion derived from Shi'ism. Few institutions cater to Sunni needs. There is not a single Sunni mosque in the whole of Tehran. Iran's Kurds, Turkmans, Arabs, and Baluchis are also Sunnis, and it is no accident that in the immediate aftermath of the 1979 revolution, the newborn regime faced its most serious challenges in precisely the areas of the country where these linguistic minorities lived. It crushed these revolts by rushing in Revolutionary Guards from the Persian Shi'i heartland of Isfahan, Shiraz, and Qom.

The regime's base among the Azeris, who are Shi'i but not Persian speakers, remains to be tested. In the past, the Azeris, who form 24 percent of the population and dwarf the other minorities, have not posed a serious problem to the state. They are part of the Shi'i community and have prominent figures in the Shi'i hierarchy—most notably the current Leader, Khamenei. What is more, many Azeri merchants, professionals, and workers live and work throughout Iran. In short, Azeris can be considered well integrated into Iran.

But the 1991 creation of the Republic of Azerbaijan on Iran's northeastern border following the disintegration of the Soviet Union has raised new concern since some Azeris on both sides of the border have begun to talk of establishing a larger unified Azerbaijan. It is no accident that in the war between Azerbaijan and Armenia in the early 1990s, Iran favored the latter. So far, the concept of a unified Azerbaijan has little appeal among Iranian Azeris.

Interests, Social Movements, and Protest

In the first two decades after its founding, the government of the Islamic Republic often violated its own constitution. It closed down newspapers, professional associations, labor unions, and political parties. It banned demonstrations and public meetings. It incarcerated tens of thousands without due process. It systematically tortured prisoners to extract false confessions and public recantations. And it executed some 25,000 political prisoners, most of them without due process of law. The United Nations, Amnesty International, and Human Rights Watch all took Iran to task for violating the UN Human Rights Charter as well its own Islamic constitution. Most victims were Kurds, military officers from the old regime, and leftists, especially members of the Mojahedin and Fedayin.

Although the violation of individual liberties affected the whole population, it aroused special resentment among three social groups: the modern middle class, educated women, and organized labor. The modern middle class, especially the intelligentsia, has been secular and even anticlerical ever since the 1905 revolution. Little love is lost between it and the Islamic Republic. Not surprisingly, the vast majority of those executed in the 1980s were teachers, engineers, professionals, and college students. Youth, especially college students, are a force to be reckoned with: over half the current population was born after 1979 and as many as 1.15 million are enrolled in higher education. In 1999, eighteen different campuses, including Tehran University, erupted into mass demonstrations against the chief judge, who had closed down a reformist newspaper. Revolutionary Guards promptly occupied the campuses, killing and seriously injuring an unknown number of students. Again in late 2002, thousands of students protested the death sentence handed down to a reformist academic accused of insulting Islam. But in 2004, when the Guardian Council barred thousands of reformers from the elections, the campuses remained quiet—partly out of fear, partly out of disenchantment with the reformers for failing to deliver on their promises, and partly because of the concern about the looming danger from the United States military presence in Iraq.

Educated women in Iran also harbor numerous grievances against the conservative clerics in the regime, especially in the judiciary. Although the Western press often dwells on the veil, Iranian women consider the veil one of their less important problems. Given a choice, most would probably continue to wear it out of personal habit and national tradition. More important are work-related grievances: job security, pay scales, promotions, maternity leave, and access to prestigious professions. Despite patriarchal attitudes held by the conservative clergy, educated women have become a major factor in Iranian society. They now form 54 percent of college students, 45 percent of doctors, 25 percent of government employees, and 13 percent of the general labor force, up from 8 percent in the 1980s. They have established their own organizations and journals, reinterpreting Islam to conform with modern notions of gender equality. Women do serve in the Majles and on local councils, but one grand ayatollah has even argued that they should be able to hold any job, including president, Leader, and court judge, positions from which women have been barred since 1979.

Factory workers in Iran are another significant social group with serious grievances. Their concerns deal mostly with high unemployment, low wages, declining incomes, lack of decent housing, and an unsatisfactory labor law, which, while giving them mandatory holidays and some semblance of job security, denies them the right to call strikes and organize independent unions. Since 1979, wage earners have had a Workers' House—a government-influenced organization—and its affiliated newspaper, *Kar va Kargar* (*Work and Worker*), and, since 1999, the Islamic Labor Party to represent their interests. In most years, the Workers' House flexes its political muscle by holding a May Day rally. In 1999, the rally began peacefully with a greeting from a woman reform deputy who had received the second-most votes in the 1996 Tehran municipal elections. But the rally turned into a protest when workers began to march to parliament denouncing conservatives who had spoken in favor of further watering down of the Labor Law. Bus drivers spontaneously joined the protest, shutting down most of central Tehran.

President Khatami's reform movement drew much of its core support precisely from these three social groups: college youth, women, and workers. In the 1997 and 2001 presidential campaigns, as well as in the elections for municipal councils and the Sixth *Majles,* crucial roles were played by the Islamic Student Associations, the Office of Student Solidarity, the Islamic Women's Association, and the Workers' House. The reformers were also supported by a number of newspapers, which have quickly gained a mass circulation, even though they initially catered mainly to the intelligentsia. For example, the reformist *Hayat-e No,* launched in late 2000, had a circulation of over 235,000 by April 2001, almost double that of the long-established conservative newspaper *Ettela'at.*

Section ⑤   Iranian Politics in Transition

Political Challenges and Changing Agendas

Contemporary Iran faces two major challenges—one internal, the other external. Internally, the Islamic Republic continues to grapple with the vexing question of how to synthesize theocracy with democracy, and clerical authority with mass participation. The conservative clerics, who already controlled the judiciary, took over the *Majles* in 2004 and the presidency in June 2005. Even though the conservatives appear to control the political heights, they have lost much of their support in the general public. The conservatives thus, face the challenge of how to maintain some semblance of mass participation while not actually sharing power with the reformers.

This challenge is particularly vexing since the country has in recent decades gone through a profound cultural revolution embracing such key concepts as political pluralism, mass participation, civil society, human rights, and individual liberties. Even the conservatives have begun to incorporate such terms into their language and openly describe themselves as "neoconservatives" and "pragmatic" in order to broaden their appeal.

Meanwhile, those in the general public who feel excluded from national politics remain active in vibrant nongovernmental organizations. The most visible of these is a human rights group headed by Shirin Ebadi, the winner of the Nobel Peace in 2003. If completely excluded from the political arena, activists such as Ebadi may well conclude that reform is not possible within the system and that the whole regime has to be changed either through constitutional or other, perhaps less peaceful, means.

The external challenge to the Islamic Republic comes from the United States. The Bush administration, by naming Iran as a member of the Axis of Evil and openly calling for "regime change," dramatically increased pressures on Iran—pressures that already existed because of economic sanctions, lack of diplomatic relations, and successful barring of Iran from the World Trade Organization. In the past, the United States has accused Iran of sabotaging the Arab-Israeli peace process; helping terrorist organizations, especially Hamas in Palestine and Hezbollah in Lebanon; and "grossly violating" democratic and human rights of its own citizens. More recently, it has highlighted the danger of weapons of mass destruction in Iran and accused the country of intending to transform its nuclear energy program into a nuclear weapons program. Of course, the external challenge to Iran drastically increased once the United States occupied Iran's neighbors, Afghanistan and Iraq.

The conservative clerics, however, have been able to inadvertently transform this external threat into an asset. They intimidated many reformers into toning down their demands, even silencing them, by declaring that the country was in danger, that the enemy was at the gates, and that any opposition to the government in such times would play into the hands of foreigners. Few were willing to appear unpatriotic at a time when the nation was perceived as facing imminent invasion.

Iranian Politics in Comparative Perspective

Iran is unlike most developing countries in that it is an old state with institutions that go back to ancient times. It is also not a country that only relatively recently achieved independence since it was never formally

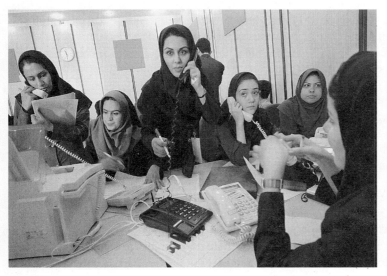

Electoral campaigners
Source: Lynsey
Adderio/New York Times

colonized by the European imperial powers. Unlike many other Third World states that have a weak connection with their societies, Iran has a religion that links the elite with the masses, the cities with the villages, the government with the citizenry. Shi'ism, as well as Iranian national identity, serves as a social and cultural cement, giving the population a strong collective identity. Iran also has the advantage of rich oil resources that give it the potential for rapid economic growth that would be the envy of most developing countries. Finally, Iran produced two popular upheavals in the twentieth century: the constitutional (1905) and the Islamic (1979) revolutions in which the citizenry actively intervened in politics, overthrew the old regime, and shaped the new. Both of these revolutions were the result of authentic homegrown political movements, not foreign imports.

Yet Iran shares some problems with other Third World countries. It has failed to establish a full-fledged democracy. Its economy remains underdeveloped, highly dependent on one commodity, and unable to meet the rising expectations of its population. Iran's collective identity, although strong in religious terms, is strained by other internal fault lines, especially those of class, ethnicity, gender, and interclerical political conflicts. And its ambition to enter the world of states as an important player has been thwarted by international as well as domestic and regional realities, which have combined to keep the country pretty much on the global sidelines. Democracy in Iran has been constricted by theocracy. Some argue that Islam has made this inevitable. But Islam, like Christianity and the other major religions, can be interpreted in ways that either support or oppose the democratic idea. Some interpretations of Islam stress the importance of justice, equality, and consultation as political principles. Islam also has a tradition of tolerating other religions, and the *shari'a* explicitly protects life, property, and honor. In practice, Islam has often separated politics from religion, government legal statutes from holy laws, spiritual affairs from worldly matters, and the state from the clerical establishment.

Moreover, theocracy in Iran originates not in Islam itself but in the concept of the jurist's guardianship as developed by Khomeini. On the whole, Sunni Islam considers clerics to be theological scholars, not a special political stratum, which helps explain why the Iranian regime has found it difficult to export the revolution to other parts of the Muslim world. The failure of democracy in Iran should be attributed less to anything intrinsic in Islam than to the confluence of crises between 1979 and 1981 that allowed a particular group of clerics to seize power. Whether they remain in power depends not so much on Islam but on how they handle economic problems and the demands for public participation—in other words, how they deal with the challenges of governing the economy and synthesizing theocracy with the democratic idea.

Politics in the Islamic Republic of Iran remains sharply divided over the question of how to manage an economy beset by rising demands, wildly fluctuating petroleum revenues, and the nightmarish prospect that in the next two generations, the oil wells will run dry. Most clerics favor a rather conventional capitalist road to development, hoping to liberalize the market, privatize industry, attract foreign capital, and encourage the propertied classes to invest. Others envisage an equally conventional statist road to development, favoring central planning, government industries, price controls, high taxes, state subsidies, national self-reliance, and ambitious programs to eliminate poverty, illiteracy, slums, and unemployment. President Khatami charted a third way, combining elements of state intervention with free enterprise that is strikingly similar to the social democracy favored in some other parts of the world such as the Labour Party in Britain

As the clock of history ticks, Iran's population grows, oil revenues fluctuate, and the per capita national income could fall again. Economic problems like those that undermined the monarchy could well undermine the Islamic Republic. The country's collective identity has also come under great strain in recent years. The emphasis on Shi'ism has antagonized Iran's Sunnis as well as its non-Muslim citizens. The emphasis on clerical Shi'ism has further alienated all secularists, including lay liberals, radical leftists, and moderate nationalists. Furthermore, the official emphasis on Khomeini's brand of Shi'ism has alienated those Shi'is who reject the whole notion of jurist's guardianship. The elevation of Khamenei as the Leader has also antagonized many early proponents of jurist's guardianship on the grounds that he lacks the scholarly qualifications to hold the position that embodies the sacred and secular power of the Islamic Republic.

In sum, Iran's ruling regime has gradually reduced the social base that brought it to power. Only time will tell whether growing discontent will be expressed through apolitical channels, such as drug addiction, emigration, and quietist religion, or whether those seeking change will look to reformist movements or turn to more radical insurrectionary organizations or ethnic-based movements.

Finally, the Islamic Republic's initial attempt to enter the international arena as a militant force for the spread of its theocratic version of Islam proved counterproductive. This effort diverted scarce resources to the military. It frightened Saudi Arabia and the Gulf sheikdoms into the arms of the United States. It prompted the United States to isolate Iran, discouraging investment and preventing international organizations from extending economic assistance. Iran's militancy also alarmed nearby secular Islamic states such as Turkey, Tadzhikistan, and Azerbaijan. In recent years, the regime has managed to overcome many of these problems. It has won over the Arab states and has established cordial relations with its neighbors. Most important, it has managed to repair bridges to the European Community. Only time will show how its tortuous relations with the United States will work out and how this will affect the future of politics in Iran.

Key Terms

ayatollah
mosques
fatwa
theocracy
Majles
Guardian Council
Leader
Farsi
Shi'ism
People of the Book
Qur'an
shari'a
coup d'état
bazaars
fundamentalism
jurist's guardianship
pasdaran
Hezbollahis
hojjat al-Islam
laissez-faire
jihad
rentier state
dual society
Organization of Petroleum Exporting Countries (OPEC)
Expediency Council
Imam Jum'ehs
Foundation of the Oppressed
Assembly of Experts
Maslahat

Suggested Readings

Abrahamian, E. *Iran Between Two Revolutions.* Princeton, N.J.: Princeton University Press, 1982.

———. *Khomeinism.* Berkeley: University of California Press, 1993.

Akhavi, S. *Religion and Politics in Contemporary Iran.* Albany: State University of New York Press, 1980.

Bakhash, S. *Reign of the Ayatollahs.* New York: Basic Books, 1984.

Baktiari, B. *Parliamentary Politics in Revolutionary Iran.* Gainesville: University Press of Florida, 1966.

Bill, J. *The Eagle and the Lion.* New Haven, Conn.: Yale University Press, 1988.

Brumberg, D. *Reinventing Khomeini: The Struggle for Reform in Iran.* Chicago: University of Chicago Press, 2001.

Buchta, W. *Who Rules Iran?* Washington, D.C.: Washington Institute for Near East Policy, 2000.

Chehabi, H. *Iranian Politics and Religious Modernism.* Ithaca, N.Y.: Cornell University Press, 1990.

Dabashi, H. *Theology of Discontent: The Ideological Foundation of the Islamic Revolution in Iran.* New York: New York University Press, 1993.

Fischer, M. *Iran: From Religious Dispute to Revolution.* Cambridge: Harvard University Press, 1980.

Garthwaite, F. *The Persians.* Oxford: Blackwell, 2005.

Hooglund, E. *Twenty Years of Islamic Revolution.* Syracuse, N.Y.: Syracuse University Press, 2002.

Kazemi, F. "Civil Society and Iranian Politics." In A. Norton (ed.), *Civil Society in the Middle East.* Leiden: Brill, 1996.

Keddie, N. *Modern Iran: Roots and Results of Revolution.* New Haven, Conn.: Yale University Press, 2004.

Kurzman, C. *The Unthinkable Revolution in Iran.* Cambridge: Harvard University Press, 2004.

Milani, M. *The Making of Iran's Islamic Revolution.* Boulder, Colo.: Westview Press, 1994.

Mir-Hosseini, Z. *Islam and Gender.* Princeton, N.J.: Princeton University Press, 1999.

Moin, B. *Khomeini: Life of the Ayatollah.* London: Tauris, 1999.

Mottahedeh, R. *The Mantle of the Prophet.* New York: Simon & Schuster, 1985.

Schirazi, A. *The Constitution of Iran.* London: Tauris, 1997.

Suggested Websites

The Story of the Revolution, British Broadcasting Corporation
www.bbc.co.uk/persian/revolution
Iranian Mission to the United Nations
www.un.int/iran

Islamic Republic News Agency
www.irna.ir/en
Iran Report, Radio Free Europe
www.rferl.org/reports/iran-report
News Related to Iran
www.farsinews.net

Endnotes

[1]Quoted in E. Browne, *The Persian Revolution* (New York: Barnes and Noble, 1966), 137.

[2]British Financial Adviser to the Foreign Office in Tehran, *Documents on British Foreign Policy, 1919–39* (London: Her Majesty's Stationery Office, 1963), First Series, XIII, 720, 735.

[3]British Minister to the Foreign Office, *Report on the Seizure of Lands,* Foreign Office 371/Persia 1932/File 34–16007.

[4]*Kayhan International,* November 10, 1976.

[5]"Fifty Indictments of Treason During Fifty Years of Treason," *Khabarnameh,* no. 46 (April 1976).

[6]M. Bazargan, "Letter to the Editor," *Ettela'at,* February 7, 1980.

[7]*Iran Times,* January 12, 1979.

[8]*Washington Post,* December 12, 1978.

[9]*Christian Science Monitor,* December 12, 1978.

[10]Samuel P. Huntington, *The Clash of Civilizations and the Remaking of World Order* (New York: Simon & Schuster, 1996).

[11]Mirza Hosayn Khan Tahvildar-e Isfahan, *Jukhrafiha-ye Isfahan* [The Geography of Isfahan] (Tehran: Tehran University Press, 1963), 100–101.

[12]International Labor Organization, "Employment and Income Policies for Iran" (Unpublished report, Geneva, 1972), Appendix C, 6.

[13]A. Sharbatoghilie, *Urbanization and Regional Disparity in Post-Revolutionary Iran* (Boulder, Colo.: Westview Press, 1991), 4.

[14]*Wall Street Journal,* November 4, 1977.

[15]U.S. Congress, *Economic Consequences of the Revolution in Iran* (Washington, D.C.: U.S. Government Printing Office, 1979), 184.

[16]U.S. Congress, *Economic Consequences of the Revolution in Iran,* 5.

[17]U.S. Department of Commerce, *Iran: A Survey of U.S. Business Opportunities* (Washington, D.C.: U.S. Government Printing Office, 1977), 1–2.

[18]Cited in H. Amirahmadi, *Revolution and Economic Transition* (Albany: State University of New York Press, 1960), p. 201.

[19]Cited in *Iran Times,* July 9, 1993.

[20]J. Amuzegar, *Iran's Economy Under the Islamic Republic* (London: Taurus Press, 1994), 100.

[21]A. Rafsanjani, "The Islamic Consultative Assembly," *Kayhan,* May 23, 1987.

[22]S. Saffari, "The Legitimation of the Clergy's Right to Rule in the Iranian Constitution of 1979," *British Journal of Middle Eastern Studies* 20, no. 1 (1993): 64–81.

[23]Ayatollah Montazeri, *Ettela'at,* October 8, 1979.

[24]O. Fallaci, "Interview with Khomeini," *New York Times Magazine,* October 7, 1979.

[25]*Kayhan,* March 6, 1980.

[26]*Kayhan,* April 21, 1987.

[27]*Kayhan-e Hava'i,* November 16, 1988.

[28]*Economist,* February 9, 2000.

Glossary

abertura (Portuguese for "opening"; *apertura* in Spanish) In Brazil, refers to the period of authoritarian liberalization begun in 1974 when the military allowed civilian politicians to compete for political office in the context of a more open political society. See also **glasnost.**

accommodation an informal agreement or settlement between the government and important interest groups in response to the interest groups' concerns for policy or program benefits.

accountability a government's responsibility to its population, usually by periodic popular elections and by parliament's having the power to dismiss the government by passing a motion of no confidence. In a political system characterized by accountability, the major actions taken by government must be known and understood by the citizenry.

acephalous societies literally "headless" societies. A number of traditional Nigerian societies, such as the Igbo in the precolonial period, lacked executive rulership as we have come to conceive of it. Instead, the villages and clans were governed by committee or consensus.

Amerindians original peoples of North and South America; indigenous people.

anticlericalism opposition to the power of churches or clergy in politics. In some countries, for example, France and Mexico, this opposition has focused on the role of the Catholic Church in politics.

Anti-Rightist Campaign was launched by Chinese Communist Party (CCP) Chairman Mao Zedong in 1957 in the aftermath of the **Hundred Flowers Movement.** The Campaign was aimed at critics of the CCP who were labeled as "rightists," that is, counterrevolutionaries. Millions of people were affected and hundreds of thousands sent to labor reform camps, many were not released until after Mao's death in 1976.

Assembly of Experts nominates the and can replace him. The assembly is elected by the general electorate but almost all its members are clerics.

authoritarianism a system of rule in which power depends not on popular legitimacy but on the coercive force of the political authorities. Hence, there are few personal and group freedoms. It is also characterized by near absolute power in the executive branch and few, if any, legislative and judicial controls. See also **autocracy; partrimonialism.**

autocracy a government in which one or a few rulers has absolute power, thus, a **dictatorship.** Similar to **authoritarianism.**

autonomous region in the People's Republic of China, a territorial unit equivalent to a province that contains a large concentration of ethnic minorities. These regions have some autonomy in the cultural sphere but in most policy matters are strictly subordinate to the central government.

ayatollah literally, "sign of God." High-ranking clerics in Iran. The most senior ones—often no more than half a dozen—are known as grand ayatollahs.

balance of payments an indicator of international flow of funds that shows the excess or deficit in total payments of all kinds between or among countries. Included in the calculation are exports and imports, grants, and international debt payments.

bazaar an urban marketplace where shops, workshops, small businesses, and export-importers are located.

Brahmin highest caste in the Hindu caste system.

bureaucratic authoritarianism a term developed by Argentine sociologist Guillermo O'Donnell to interpret the common characteristics of military-led authoritarianism regimes in Brazil, Argentina, Chile, and Uruguay in the 1960s and 1970s. According to O'Donnell, bureaucratic authoritarian regimes led by the armed forces and key civilian allies emerged in these countries in response to severe economic crises.

bureaucratic rings a term developed by the Brazilian sociologist and president Fernando Henrique Cardoso that refers to the highly permeable and fragmented structure of the state bureaucracy that allows private interests to make alliances with midlevel bureaucratic officers. By shaping public policy to benefit these interests, bureaucrats gain the promise of future employment in the private sector. While

---

*Note: Boldface terms *within* a definition can be found as separate entries in the Glossary.

in positions of responsibility, bureaucratic rings are ardent defenders of their own interests.

cadre   a person who occupies a position of authority in a **communist party-state;** cadres may or may not be Communist Party members.

caste system   India's Hindu society is divided into castes. According to the Hindu religion, membership in a caste is determined at birth. Castes form a rough social and economic hierarchy. See also **Brahmin; untouchables.**

civil society   refers to the space occupied by voluntary associations outside the state, for example, professional associations (lawyers, doctors, teachers), trade unions, student and women's groups, religious bodies, and other voluntary association groups. The term is similar to *society*, although *civil society* implies a degree of organization absent from the more inclusive term *society*.

clientelism (or **patron-client networks**)   an informal aspect of policymaking in which a powerful patron (for example, a traditional local boss, government agency, or dominant party) offers resources such as land, contracts, protection, or jobs in return for the support and services (such as labor or votes) of lower-status and less powerful clients; corruption, preferential treatment, and inequality are characteristic of clientelist politics. See also **patrimonialism; prebendalism.**

collectivization   a process undertaken in the Soviet Union under Stalin in the late 1920s and early 1930s and in China under Mao in the 1950s, by which agricultural land was removed from private ownership and organized into large state and collective farms.

command economy   a form of **socialist** economic organization in which government decisions ("commands") rather than market mechanisms (such as supply and demand) are the major influences in determining the nation's economic direction; also called central planning.

communism   a system of social organization based on the common ownership and coordination of production. According to Marxism (the theory of German philosopher Karl Marx, 1818–1883), communism is a culminating stage of history, following capitalism and **socialism.** In historical practice, leaders of China, the Soviet Union, and other states that have proclaimed themselves seeking to achieve communism have ruled through a single party, the Communist Party, which has controlled the state and society in an authoritarian manner, and have applied **Marxism-Leninism** to justify their rule.

communist party-state   a type of nation-state in which the Communist Party attempts to exercise a complete monopoly on political power and controls all important state institutions. See also **communism.**

co-optation   incorporating activists into the system while accommodating some of their concerns.

corporatist state   a state in which **interest groups** become an institutionalized part of the structure. See also **corporatism; democratic corporatism; state corporatism.**

coup d'état   a forceful, extra-constitutional action resulting in the removal of an existing government.

danwei   a Chinese term that means "unit" and is the basic level of social organization and a major means of political control in China's **communist party-state.** A person's *danwei* is most often his or her workplace, such as a factory or an office.

decentralization   policies that aim to transfer some decision-making power from higher to lower levels of government, typically from the central government to subnational governments.

developmental state   a **nation-state** in which the government carries out policies that effectively promote national economic growth.

developmentalism   an ideology and practice in Latin America during the 1950s in which the state played a leading role in seeking to foster economic development through sponsoring vigorous **industrial policy.** See also **import substitution industrialization.**

dual society   a society and economy that are sharply divided into a traditional, usually poorer, and a modern, usually richer, sector.

Economic Community of West African Studies (ECOWAS)   the organization established in 1975 among the sixteen governments in West Africa. Its goals are to strengthen and broaden the economies in the region through the removal of trade barriers among its members (such as import quotas and domestic content laws), freedom of movement for citizens, and monetary cooperation.

economic liberalization   the dismantling of government controls on the economy.

ejidatario   recipient of *ejido* land grant in Mexico.

ejido   land granted by Mexican government to an organized group of peasants.

Emergency (1975–1977)   the period when Indian Prime Minister Indira Gandhi suspended many formal democratic rights and ruled in an **authoritarian** manner.

emir   traditional Islamic ruler. The emir presides over an "emirate," or kingdom, in northern Nigeria.

Expediency Council   a committee set up in Iran to resolve differences between the *Majles* and the **Guardian Council.**

export-led growth   economic growth generated by the export of a country's commodities. Export-led growth can occur at an early stage of economic development, in which case it involves primary products, such as the country's mineral resources, timber, and agricultural products; or at a later stage, when industrial goods and services are exported.

Farsi   Persian word for the Persian language. Fars is a province in Central Iran.

fatwa   a pronouncement issued by a high-ranking Islamic cleric.

favelas   in Brazil, huge shantytowns of homes made out of cardboard, wood from dumps, and blocks of mortar and brick. These shantytowns create rings of extreme poverty around cities like Rio de Janeiro and São Paulo. Similar shantytowns can be found in other Latin American cities, although terms to describe them vary by country. In Peru, for example, these shantytowns are called *barriadas.*

Foundation of the Oppressed   a clerically controlled foundation in Iran set up after the revolution there.

Four Cardinal Principles   ideas first enunciated by Chinese leader Deng Xiaoping in 1979 asserting that all policies should be judged by whether they uphold the socialist road, the dictatorship of the proletariat, the leadership of the Communist Party, and Marxism-Leninism–Mao Zedong Thought. The main purpose of the Four Cardinal Principles was to proscribe any challenge to the ultimate authority of the Chinese Communist Party, even during a time of farreaching economic reform. The Principles have been reaffirmed by Deng's successors and continue to define the boundaries of what is politically permissible in China.

fundamentalism   a term recently popularized to describe radical religious movements throughout the world.

Great Leap Forward   a movement launched by Mao Zedong in 1958 to industrialize China very rapidly and thereby propel it toward **communism.** The Leap ended in economic disaster in 1960, causing one of the worst famines in human history.

Great Proletarian Cultural Revolution   the political campaign launched in 1966 by Chairman Mao Zedong to stop what he saw as China's drift away from socialism and toward capitalism. The campaign led to massive purges in the Chinese Communist Party, the widespread persecution of China's intellectuals, extensive political violence, and the destruction of invaluable cultural objects. The Cultural Revolution officially ended in 1976 after Mao's death and the arrest of some of his most radical followers.

green revolution   a strategy for increasing agricultural (especially food) production, involving improved seeds, irrigation, and abundant use of fertilizers.

guanxi   a Chinese term that means "connections" or "relationships," and describes personal ties between individuals based on such things as common birthplace or mutual acquaintances. *Guanxi* are an important factor in China's political and economic life.

Guardian Council   a committee created in the Iranian constitution to oversee the *Majles* (the parliament).

guerrilla warfare   a military strategy based on small, highly mobile bands of soldiers (the guerrillas, from the Spanish word for war, "guerra") who use hit-and-run tactics like ambushes to attack a better-armed enemy.

hezbollahis   literally "partisans of God." In Iran, the term is used to describe religious vigilantes. In Lebanon, it is used to describe the Shi'i militia.

hojjat al-Islam   literally, "the proof of Islam." In Iran, it means a medium-ranking cleric.

household responsibility system   the system put into practice in China beginning in the early 1980s in which the major decisions about agricultural production are made by individual farm families based on the profit motive rather than by a **people's commune** or the government.

Hundred Flowers Movement   refers to a period in 1956–57 when Chinese Communist Party Chairman Mao Zedong encouraged citizens, particularly intellectuals, to speak out ("Let a hundred flowers bloom, let a hundred schools of thought contend!") and give their views on how to improve China's government. Mao was shocked by the depth of the criticism of communist rule and cracked down by silencing and punishing the critics by launching the **Anti-Rightist Campaign** of 1957.

Imam Jum'ehs   prayer leaders in Iran's main urban mosques. Appointed by the **Supreme Leader,** they have considerable authority in the provinces.

import substituting industrialization (ISI)   strategy for industrialization based on domestic manufacture of previously imported goods to satisfy domestic market demands. See also **developmentalism.**

Indian Administrative Service (IAS)   India's civil service, a highly professional and talented group of administrators who run the Indian government on a day-to-day basis.

indigenous groups   population of **Amerindian** heritage in Mexico.

indirect rule   a term used to describe the British style of colonialism in Nigeria and India in which local traditional rulers and political structures were used to help support the colonial governing structure.

informal sector (economy)   that portion of the economy largely outside government control in which employees work without contracts or benefits. Examples include casual employees in restaurants and hotels, street vendors, and day laborers in construction or agriculture.

international financial institutions (IFIs)   generally refers to the International Bank for Reconstruction and Development (the World Bank) and the International Monetary Fund (IMF), but can also include other international lending institutions. See also **structural adjustment program (SAP).**

interventionist   an interventionist state acts vigorously to shape the performance of major sectors of the economy.

interventionist   an interventionist state acts vigorously to shape the performance of major sectors of the economy.

interventores   in Brazil, allies of Getúlio Vargas (1930–1945, 1950–1952) picked by the dictator during his first period of rulership to replace opposition governors in all the Brazilian states except Minas Gerais. The *interventores* represented a shift of power from subnational government to the central state. See also **politics of the governors.**

iron rice bowl   a feature of China's socialist economy during the Maoist era (1949–76) that provided guarantees of lifetime employment, income, and basic cradle-to-grave benefits to most urban and rural workers. Economic reforms beginning in the 1980s that aimed at improving efficiency and work motivation sought to smash the iron rice bowl and link employment and income more directly to individual effort.

jihad   literally "struggle." Although often used to mean armed struggle against unbelievers, it can also mean spiritual struggle for more self-improvement.

jurist's guardianship   Khomeini's concept that the Iranian clergy should rule on the grounds that they are the divinely appointed guardians of both the law and the people. He developed this concept in the 1970s.

legitimacy   a belief by powerful groups and the broad citizenry that a state exercises rightful authority. In the contemporary world, a state is said to possess legitimacy when it enjoys consent of the governed, which usually involves democratic procedures and the attempt to achieve a satisfactory level of development and equitable distribution of resources.

Lok Sabha   the lower house of parliament in India where all major legislation must pass before becoming law.

maharajas   India's traditional rulers—monarchs—who retained their positions during the colonial period but were removed from power when the Indian republic was established.

majles   Arabic term for "assembly"; used in Iran to describe the parliament.

maquiladoras   factories that produce goods for export, often located along the U.S.-Mexican border.

Marxism-Leninism   the theoretical foundation of communism based on the ideas of the German philosopher, Karl Marx (1818–1883), and the leader of the Russian Revolution, V. I. Lenin (1870–1924). Marxism is, in essence, a theory of historical development that emphasizes the struggle between exploiting and exploited classes, particularly the struggle between the bourgeoisie (capitalists) and the proletariat (the industrial working class). Leninism emphasizes the strategy and organization to be used by the communist party to overthrow capitalism and seize power as a first step on the road to communism.

maslahat   Arabic term for "expediency," "prudence," or "advisability." It is now used in Iran to refer to reasons of state or what is best for the Islamic Republic.

mestizo   a person of mixed white, indigenous (Amerindian), and sometimes African descent.

moderating power (*poder moderador*)   a term used in Brazilian politics to refer to the situation following the 1824 constitution in which the monarchy was supposed to act as a moderating power, among the executive, legislative, and judicial branches of government, arbitrating party conflicts, and fulfilling governmental responsibilities when nonroyal agents failed.

mosque   **Muslim** place of worship, equivalent to a church, temple, or synagogue.

nationalism   an ideology seeking to create a **nation-state** for a particular community; a group identity associated with membership is such a political community. Nationalists often proclaim that their state and nation are superior to others.

New State (*Estado Novo*)   in Brazil, an authoritarian government led by Getúlio Vargas in 1937 that legitimized its rule through state corporatism, massive public sector investment through *para-statals*, and paternalistic social policies.

newly industrializing countries (NICs)   a term used to describe a group of countries that achieved rapid **economic development** beginning in the 1960s, largely stimulated by robust international trade (particularly exports) and guided by government policies. The core

NICs are usually considered to be Taiwan, South Korea, Hong Kong, and Singapore, but other countries, including Argentina, Brazil, Malaysia, Mexico, and Thailand, are often included in this category.

nomenklatura a system of personnel selection under which the Communist Party maintained control over the appointment of important officials in all spheres of social, economic, and political life. The term is also used to describe individuals chosen through this system and thus refers more broadly to the privileged circles in the Soviet Union and China.

nonaligned bloc countries that refused to ally with either the United States or the USSR during the **cold war** years.

nongovernmental organizations (NGO) a private group that seeks to influence public policy and deal with certain problems that it believes are not being adequately addressed by governments, such as Amnesty International (human rights), Oxfam (famine relief), and Greenpeace (the environment).

North American Free Trade Agreement (NAFTA) a treaty among the United States, Mexico, and Canada implemented on January 1, 1994, that largely eliminates trade barriers among the three nations and establishes procedures to resolve trade disputes. NAFTA serves as a model for an eventual Free Trade Area of the Americas zone that could include most Western Hemisphere nations.

oligarchy narrowly based, undemocratic government, often by traditional elites. See also **autocracy; authoritarianism.**

OPEC Organization of Petroleum Exporting Countries. Founded in 1960 by Iran, Venezuela, and Saudi Arabia, it now includes most oil-exporting states with the notable exceptions of Mexico and former members of the Soviet Union. It tries to regulate prices by regulating production.

other backward classes the middle or intermediary castes in India that have been accorded reserved seats in public education and employment since the early 1990s.

panchayats in India, elected bodies at the village, district, and state levels that have development and administrative responsibilities.

para-statals state-owned, or at least state-controlled, corporations, created to undertake a broad range of activities, from control and marketing of agricultural production to provision of banking services, operation of airlines, and other transportation facilities and public utilities. See also **interventionist.**

pasdaran Persian term for guards, used to refer to the army of Revolutionary Guards formed during Iran's Islamic Revolution.

patrimonialism (or **neopatrimonialism**) a system of governance in which a single ruler treats the state as personal property (patrimony). Appointments to public office are made on the basis of unswerving loyalty to the ruler. In turn, state officials exercise wide authority in other domains, such as the economy, often for their personal benefit and that of the ruler, to the detriment of the general population. See also **authoritarianism; autocracy; prebendalism.**

People of the Book the Muslim term for recognized religious minorities, such as Christians, Jews, and Zoroastrians.

people's communes large-scale rural communities first implemented during the **Great Leap Forward** that were in charge of nearly all aspects of political, social, and economic life in the Chinese countryside from the late 1950s until the early 1980s, when they were disbanded and replaced by a system of household and village-based agricultural production.

personalist politicians demagogic political leaders who use their personal charisma to mobilize their constituency.

politics of the governors in Brazil, refers to periods of history in which state governors acquire extraordinary powers over domains of policy that were previously claimed by the federal government. The term refers most commonly to the Old Republic and the current state of Brazilian federalism. See also **federalism.**

populism gaining the support of popular sectors. When used in Latin American politics, this support is often achieved by manipulation and demagogic appeals.

prebendalism patterns of political behavior that rest on the justification that official state offices should be utilized for the personal benefit of officeholders as well as of their support group or clients. Thus, prebendal politics is sustained by the existence of **patron-client networks.** See also **patrimonialism; clientelism.**

privatization the sale of state-owned enterprises to private companies or investors. Those who support the policy claim that private ownership is superior to government ownership because for-profit entities promote greater efficiency. Privatization is a common central component of **structural adjustment programs** to curtail the losses associated with these enterprises and generate state revenue when they are sold. For Russia, see **spontaneous privatization.**

proportional representation (PR) a system of political representation in which seats are allocated to parties within multimember constituencies, roughly in proportion to the votes each party receives. PR usually encourages the election to parliament of more political parties than single-member-district winner-take-all systems.

Qur'an   the Muslim Bible.

Rajya Sabha   India's upper house of parliament; considerably less significant politically than the ***Lok Sabha.***

rentier state   a country that obtains much of its revenue from the export of oil or other natural resources.

rents   above-market returns to a factor of production. Pursuit of economic rents (or "rent-seeking") is profit seeking that takes the form of nonproductive economic activity.

reservations   jobs or admissions to colleges reserved by the government of India for specific social groups, particularly underprivileged groups.

revisionism   a label used by the Chinese Communist Party (CCP) during the late Maoist era (1965–1976) to refer to the ideology of those political parties (particularly the Communist Party of the Soviet Union) or individuals (including members of the CCP) judged to have betrayed what they believed to be the true meaning of the theory and practice of **Marxism-Leninism** as interpreted by Mao Zedong.

scheduled castes   the lowest caste groups in India; also known as the **untouchables.**

self-determination   the right of a sovereign state or an ethnic or other group that shares cultural and historical ties to live together in a given territory and in a manner they desire. It is often the basis of the claim by a state or group for political independence and cultural autonomy.

sexenio   the six-year administration of Mexican presidents.

shari'a   Islamic law derived mostly from the **Qur'an** and the examples set by the Prophet Muhammad.

Shi'ism   a branch of Islam. It literally means the followers or partisans of Ali. The other branch is known as Sunni, or the followers of tradition.

Sikhs   an important religious minority in India.

socialism   in a socialist regime, the state plays a leading role in organizing the economy, and most business firms are publicly owned. A socialist regime, unlike a **communist party-state,** may allow the private sector to play an important role in the economy and be committed to political pluralism. In **Marxism-Leninism,** socialism refers to an early stage in development of communism. Socialist regimes can be organized in a democratic manner, in that those who control the state may be chosen according to democratic procedures. They may also be governed in an undemocratic manner when a single party, not chosen in free competitive elections, controls the state and society.

socialist democracy   the term used by the Chinese Communist Party to describe the political system of the People's Republic of China. Also called the *people's democratic dictatorship*. The official view is that this type of system, under the leadership of the Communist Party, provides democracy for the overwhelming majority of people and suppresses (or exercises dictatorship over) only the enemies of the people. Socialist democracy is contrasted to bourgeois (or capitalist) democracy, which puts power in the hands of the rich and oppresses the poor.

socialist market economy   the term used by the government of China to refer to the country's current economic system. It is meant to convey the mix of state control (socialism) and market forces (capitalism) that China is now following in its quest for economic development. The implication is that socialism will promote equality, while the market (especially the profit motive) will encourage people to work hard and foreign companies to invest.

state corporatism   a political system in which the state requires all members of a particular economic sector to join an officially designated **interest group.** Such interest groups thus attain public status, and they participate in national policymaking. The result is that the state has great control over the groups, and groups have great control over their members. See also **corporatism; corporatist state.**

state technocrats   career-minded bureaucrats who administer public policy according to a technical rather than a political rationale. In Mexico and Brazil, these are known as the *técnicos*. For contrasting concepts, see **clientelism; patrimonial state; prebendalism.**

state-led development   the process of promoting economic development using governmental machinery.

state-led economic development   the process of promoting economic development using governmental machinery.

structural adjustment program (SAP)   medium-term (generally three to five years) programs (which include both action plans and disbursement of funds) established by the World Bank intended to alter and reform the economic structures of highly indebted Third World countries as a condition for receiving international loans. SAPs often involve the necessity for **privatization,** trade liberalization, and fiscal restraint. See also **international financial institutions (IFIs).**

technocrats   career-minded bureaucrats who administer public policy according to a technical rather than a political rationale. In Mexico and Brazil, these are known as the *técnicos.* For contrasting concepts, see **clientelism; patrimonial state; prebendalism.**

theocracy   a state dominated by the clergy, who rule on the grounds that they are the only interpreters of God's will and law.

totalitarianism   a political system in which the state attempts to exercise total control over all aspects of public and private life, including the economy, culture, education, and social organizations, through an integrated system of ideological, economic, and political control. Totalitarian states are said to rely largely on terror as a means to exercise power. The term has been applied to both **communist party-states** including Stalinist Russia and Maoist China and fascist regimes such as Nazi Germany.

township and village enterprises (TVEs)   nonagricultural businesses and factories owned and run by local governments and private entrepreneurs in China's rural areas. TVEs operate largely according to market forces and outside the state plan.

unfinished state   a state characterized by instabilities and uncertainties that may render it susceptible to collapse as a coherent entity.

untouchables   the lowest caste in India's **caste system,** whose members are among the poorest and most disadvantaged Indians.

warrant chiefs   employed by the British colonial regime in Nigeria. A system in which "chiefs" were selected by the British to oversee certain legal matters and assist the colonial enterprise in governance and law enforcement in local areas.

zamindars   landlords who served as tax collectors under the British colonial government. The *zamindari* system was abolished after independence.

About the Editors and Contributors

Ervand Abrahamian is Distinguished Professor of History at Baruch College and the Graduate Center of the City University of New York. His recent publications include *Khomeinism: Essays on the Islamic Republic* (University of California Press, 1993) and *Tortured Confessions: Prisons and Public Recantations in Modern Iran* (University of California Press, 1999).

Amrita Basu is Paino Professor of Political Science and Women's and Gender Studies at Amherst College. Her main areas of interest are social movements, religious nationalism, and gender politics in South Asia. She is the author of *Two Faces of Protest: Contrasting Modes of Women's Activism in India* (University of California Press, 1992) and several edited books, including *Localizing Knowledge in a Globalizing World, Community Conflicts and the State in India* (with Atul Kohli) (Syracuse University Press, 2002), and *Appropriating Gender: Women's Activism and Politicized Religion in South Asia* (Routledge, 1998).

Merilee S. Grindle is Edward S. Mason Professor of International Development at the John F. Kennedy School of Government, Harvard University. She is a specialist on the comparative analysis of policy-making, implementation, and public management in developing countries and has written extensively on Mexico. Her most recent book is *Audacious Reforms: Institutional Innovation and Democracy in Latin America* (The Johns Hopkins University Press, 2000).

William A. Joseph is Professor of Political Science at Wellesley College and an Associate of the Fairbank Center for East Asian Research at Harvard University. His research focuses on contemporary Chinese politics and ideology. He is the editor of *China Briefing: The Contradictions of Change* (M.E. Sharpe, 1997), co-editor of *New Perspectives on the Cultural Revolution* (Harvard University Press, 1991), and contributing editor of *The Oxford Companion to Politics of the World* (Oxford University Press, 2nd ed., 2001).

Mark Kesselman is Professor of Political Science at Columbia University. A specialist on the French and European political economy, his recent publications include contributions to *The Mitterrand Era: Policy Alternatives and Political Mobilization in France* (Macmillan, 1995), *Mitterrand's Legacy, Chirac's Challenge* (St. Martin's Press, 1996), and *Diminishing Welfare: A Cross-National Study of Social Provision* (Greenwood, 2002). He is the coauthor of *A Century of Organized Labor in France* (St. Martin's Press, 1997) and *The Politics of Power: A Critical Introduction to American Politics* (Wadsworth, 2005), coeditor of *Readings in Comparative Politics* (Houghton Mifflin, 2006), and editor of *Politics of Globalization: A Reader* (Houghton Mifflin, 2007).

Darren Kew is Assistant Professor in the Graduate Program in Dispute Resolution at the University of Massachusetts, Boston. He studies the role of civil society in democratic development and conflict prevention in Africa. Professor Kew has written on elections, civil society, and conflict prevention in Nigeria. He has worked with the Council on Foreign Relations' Center for Preventive Action to provide analysis and blueprints for preventing conflicts in numerous areas around the world, including Nigeria, Central Africa, and Kosovo, and he has also observed elections in Nigeria.

Atul Kohli is Professor of Politics and International Affairs at Princeton University. His principal research interest is the comparative political economy of developing countries, especially India. He is the author of *Democracy and Discontent: India's Growing Crisis of Governability* (Cambridge University Press, 1990) and *State-Directed Development: Political Power and Industrialization in the Global Periphery* (Cambridge University Press, 2004).

Joel Krieger is Norma Wilentz Hess Professor of Political Science at Wellesley College. His publications include *Globalization and State Power* (Pearson Longman, 2005), *Blair's War*, coauthored with David Coates (Polity Press, 2004), *British Politics in the Global Age: Can Social Democracy Survive?* (Polity Press, 1999), and *Reagan, Thatcher, and the Politics of Decline* (Oxford University Press, 1986). He is also editor-in-chief of *The Oxford Companion to Politics of the World* (Oxford University Press, 1993; 2nd ed., 2001).

Peter Lewis is Associate Professor at the School of International Service, American University. He has written extensively on Nigerian political economy, as well as on broader regional issues of participation, democratic transition, and economic adjustment in Africa. He is currently working on a study of the comparative political economies of Indonesia and Nigeria.

Alfred P. Montero is Associate Professor of Political Science at Carleton College. His research focuses on the political economy of decentralization and comparative federalism in Latin American and European countries. He is the author of *Shifting States in Global Markets: Subnational Industrial Policy in Contemporary Brazil and Spain* (Penn State University Press, 2002) and coeditor of *Decentralization and Democracy in Latin America* (University of Notre Dame Press, 2004). He has also published his work in several edited volumes and journals such as *Latin American Politics and Society, Comparative Politics, Studies in Comparative International Development, Publius: The Journal of Federalism,* and the *Journal of Interamerican Studies and World Affairs.*

Index

Abacha, Sani, 258, 268, 271, 274, 275, 278, 279, 280, 281, 282, 286, 291–294

Abertura (opening), **201**, 231, 235, 236

Abiola, Moshood, 258, 289

Abubakar, Abdulsalami, 258–259, 293, 291–292, 295

Accommodation, **180**

Accountability, **250**

Acephalous societies, **253**

Action Group (AG, Nigeria), 255, 289

Activism, globalization and, 4–5

Advani, L. K., 126

Afghanistan, 319–320, 321, India and, 105

African Union (AU), 275

Afro-Brazilians, 194

Ahmadinezhad, Mahmoud, 345–346

Al-e-Ahmad, Jalal, 327

All-China Federation of Trade Unions (ACFTU), 81

Alliance for Change (Mexico), 178

Alliance for Mexico, 178

All Peoples Party (APP, Nigeria), 291, 292

American Political Science Association, 4

Amerindians, **146**, 149

Amnesty International, 235

Amorim, Celso, 240

Amparo (Mexico), 168

Anticlericalism, **150**

Anti-Rightist Campaign, **42**

Apartheid, 2

Argentina, financial crisis in, 202

Asia, "economic miracle" in, 24

Assembly of Experts (Iran), **336**, 338, 344

Assembly of Religious Experts (Iran), 318, 331, 332

Association of Militant Clergy, 336–337, 341–342

Authoritarian, **3**

Authoritarian governance, **250**

Authoritarianism, 18–19, 20 in East Asia, 24

Authority, 22–23

Autocracy, **262**

Autonomous regions, **39**

Awolowo, Obafemi, 255, 289

Ayatollah, **307**

Azerbaijan, 347

Azikiwe, Nnamdi, 289

Aztecs, 149

Babangida, Ibrahim, 257–258, 274, 275, 279, 280, 281, 282, 289, 294

Baha'is, 347

Balance of payments, **264**

Balewa, Tafawa, 256

Bangladesh, 103

Bani-Sadr, 341

Bazaars, **315**

Bazargan, Mehdi, 318, 339

Beijing, 37

Berlin Wall, 2, 3

Better Life Program (Nigeria), 272

Bharatiya Janata Party (BJP), 95, 104, 116, 121, 128–130, 132–133

Bhopal, 134

Biafra, 256–257, 263

Bloody Friday (Iran), 317

Bracero program, 184

Brahmin caste (India), **114**

Branco, Castelo, 199

Brasilia, 199, 200, 208

Bräuer, Walter Werner, 220

Brazil, 15
  agrarian reform in, 212–213
  bureaucracy in, 218–220
  bureaucratic authoritarianism in, 199–201

citizenship in, 232–235

collective identity in, 203–204, 232, 240

comparative politics and, 204, 240–242

democracy and, 195, 199, 200, 201–202, 203, 217, 234, 242

economy in, 192, 196, 200–202, 203, 205–216, 238–239

education in, 233

elections in, 201, 231–232

empire in, 194–195

environmental costs in, 207–208, 239

ethnicity and immigration in, 194, 212

executive in, 216, 217–218

financial crisis in, 202

fiscal system in, 208–210

geographic setting of, 194

governance in, 216–223

history of, 194–203

identity in, 232–235, 240

inflation in, 202, 209–210

interest groups in, 235–237

international political economy and, 203–204, 213–216, 241–242

judiciary in, 218, 221–222, 239

legislature in, 201, 217, 225–226

military and police in, 197–199, 200, 201–202, 207, 220–221, 222

1930 revolution in, 197–199

Old Republic in, 196–197, 222

policy-making in, 223–224

political culture in, 232–235

political economy and development in, 205–214, 239–240

political parties and party system in, 193, 199, 226–231

politics in transition in, 237–242

populist republic in, 199

protests in, 235–237

---

*Numbers in boldface indicate the page where a key term is defined.

racial identity in, 204
religion in, 204, 235
representation and participation in, 224–237, 241
after September 11, 2001, 202–203, 235, 241–242
social movements in, 235–237
society in, 192, 210–213
state in, 205–210, 216–217
subnational government in, 222–223
themes in, 203–204
United States and, 202–203, 240
welfare in, 211–212
women in, 192, 204, 210, 232–233, 236
Brazilian Communist Party (PCB), 229
Brazilian Democratic Movement (MDB, Brazil), 200, 201
Brazilian Labor Party (PTB), 199, 228
"Brazilian miracle," 200–201
Brazilian Progressive Party (PPB), 228
Brazilian Socialist Party (PSB), 229
Britain
    India and, 98, 107–108
    Nigeria and, 254–255
Buddhism, 96
Buhari, Muhammadu, 257, 295
Bureaucracy, **7**
Bureaucratic authoritarianism (BA, Brazil), **199**–201
Bureaucratic rings, **223**
Bush, George H. W., 215
Bush, George W., 21, 154, 351

Cabinet, **7**
Cabral, Pedro Alvares, 194
Cadres, **69**
Calles, Plutarco Elías, 150–151
Camarillas (Mexico), 218
Campaign for Democracy (Nigeria), 298
Canada, *see* North American Free Trade Agreement (NAFTA)
Cárdenas, Cuauhtémoc, 176–177, 178
Cárdenas, Lázaro, 151–152, 158
Cardoso, Fernando Henrique, 202, 203, 208, 209, 218, 223, 228, 231, 232, 234, 237, 238
Carranza, Venustiano, 150
Caste system, in India, **113–114,** 132
Caudillos (strongmen), 195
Causal analysis, 8–10

Central Committee (China), 63–66
Central Intelligence Agency (CIA), 313–314
Central Pollution Control Board (India), 134
Chamber of Deputies (Brazil), 225–226
Chamber of Deputies (Mexico), 154, 165, 171
Chen Shui-bian, 43–44
Chiang Ching-kuo, 43
Chiang Kai-shek, 41, 43
Child mortality rate, **13**
China, 13, 15, 19
    bureaucracy in, 67–69
    citizenship in, 78–81
    collective identity in, 49
    comparative politics in, 49–50, 88–90
    democracy and, 49, 73, 75, 76, 87–88
    economy in, 15, 36, 48–49, 50–61, 85–86, 90
    education in, 77–78
    elections in, 75–76
    ethnicity in, 49, 79–81
    executive in, 63–69
    geographic setting of, 38–39
    governance in, 37, 61–72, 86–87
    history of, 39–47
    Hong Kong and, 49, 60, 78
    identity in, 49, 78–81
    interest groups in, 81–84
    international political economy and, 46, 47–48, 58–61
    Internet access in, 77
    Japan and, 59
    judiciary in, 71
    labor in, 83
    legislature in, 73–74
    Mao in, 41, 42–45, 61–62, 64, 66, 72, 77
    military and police in, 45, 69–72
    party and state leaders in, 64
    policy-making and, 72–73
    political culture in, 76–78
    political economy and development in, 50–55
    political parties and party system in, 74–75
    politics in, 37–39
    politics in transition in, 84–90
    population of, 36, 39

protests in, 45, 47, 82–84
provinces in, 84–85
religion in, 78
representation and participation in, 73–84
revolutionary leaders to technocrats in, 45–47
September 11, 2001, and, 48, 79–81
social control in, 82
social movements in, 82–84
society in, 36, 55–58, 85–87
state in, 50–55, 61–63
subnational government in, 71–72
Taiwan and, 43–44, 87
themes in, 47–50
Tibet and, 79
United States and, 48
warlords, nationalists, and communists in, 40–42
women in, 36, 57–58, 75
China Democratic League, 75
Chinese Communist Party (CCP), 38, 41, 42, 63–66, 68, 72–73, 74–75
Chinese Party for the Public Interest, 75
Chinese People's Political Consultative Conference (CPPCC), 75
Chipko movement, 134
Choice, 9
Choice theory, *see* Rational choice theory
Cientificos, 148–149
Citizenship
    in Brazil, 232–235
    in China, 78–81
    in India, 132
    in Iran, 348–349
    in Mexico, 178–180
    in Nigeria, 292–295
Civil society, **155, 287,** 298
Class, *see* Social class
Clientelism, **152,** 179, 180, **197,** 238, **261**–262, 279
Cold war, **2**
Collective identities, **5,** 16, 25–27
Collectivization, **42**
Collor de Mello, Fernando, 202, 209, 214, 218, 219, 220, 222, 231, 235
Colosio, Luis Donaldo, 153, 165–166
Command economy, **50**–51
Communism, **42**
    failure of, 3

Communist Party (China), *see* Chinese Communist Party (CCP)

Communist Party of Brazil (PC do B), 229

Communist Party of India, Marxist (CPM), 95, 130–131

Communist party-states, **2**, 11, **37**

Comparative politics, **6**–10
  Brazil and, 204, 240–242
  causal analysis of, 8–10
  China and, 49–50, 88–90
  India and, 106–107, 139–141
  Iran and, 321–322, 349–351
  levels of analysis, 7–8
  Mexico and, 156, 187–188
  Nigeria and, 262, 298–300
  themes for, 17–27

Comparativists, **6**–7

Confederation of Mexican Workers (CTM), 159, 172

Conference of Nigerian Political Parties (CNPP), 292

Confucius, 40

Congress (Mexico), 165, 170–171, 172

Congress Party (India), 95, 102, 103, 117, 126–128

Consolidated democracies, 19

Convergence for Democracy (Convergencia, Mexico), 178

Co-optation, **181**

Coronelismo (Brazil), 197

Corporatist state, **155**

Corruption Perceptions Index (CPI), **29**

Cortés, Hernán, 149

Costa e Silva, Artur, 199

Council for the Revision of the Constitution (Iran), 330

Countries, **7**

Coup d'état, **17, 150, 315**

Courts, *see* Judiciary

CPI (ML)—People's War Group (India), 121

Cultural imperialism, 164

Cultural Revolution (China), 44–45, 62, 72, 74

Culture, political, 9

Dalai Lama, 37, 80

Danwei system, **82**

Decentralization, **55**

De la Madrid, Miguel, 152, 165, 171

Democracy, 7, 10, 11, 17–21

Democratic Labor Party (PDT, Brazil), 229

Democratic Revolutionary Party (PRD, Mexico), 176–177, 179

Democratic Social Party (PDS, Brazil), 201

Democratic transitions, **10**

Democratization, 2, 3

Deng Xiaoping, 42, 45, 48, 49, 51, 54, 55, 58, 62, 63, 64, 66, 76–77

Dependencistas, 206

Dependency school, 206

Descamisados (Brazil), 202

Developing world, 2
  diversity in, 12, 13
  globalization and, 3–5
  use of term, 11–12
  in world of transition, 11–17

Development
  gap in, 12–15
  measures of, 14

Developmentalism, **206**

Developmental state, **89**

Díaz, Porfirio, 148–150

Dictatorships, **10**
  democracies and, 2

Distributional politics, **26**

Dual society, **325**

East Asia, 24

Ebadi, Shirin, 349

Echeverría, Luis, 181

Ecology, economy and, 24

Economic and Financial Crimes Commission (EFCC, Nigeria), 267

Economic Community of West African States (ECOWAS), **273**

Economic liberalization, **24, 109**–110

Economy, 8–9, 23–25
  in Brazil, 192, 196, 200–202, 203, 205–216, 238–239
  in China, 15, 36, 48–49, 50–61, 85–86, 90
  growth of, 11
  in India, 94, 105–106, 107–112, 139
  in Iran, 308, 324–332
  in Mexico, 144, 151, 152–153, 156
  in Nigeria, 248, 260–261, 263–275, 301–302

ECOWAS Monitoring Group (ECOMOG), 273

Ejidatorios, **151,** 163, 173

Ejidos, **151,** 157

Elections, 30
  in Brazil, 201, 231–232
  in China, 75–76
  in India, 95–96, 131
  in Iran, 342–348
  in Mexico, 175, 178
  in Nigeria, 290–292

Electoral Supreme Tribunal (Brazil), 221

Emergency (India), **103,** 107, 116, 119, 140

Emirs, **254**

"End of History, The?" (Fukuyama), 3

England (Britain), *see* Britain

Enterprise for the Americas Initiative, 215

Environmental Sustainability Index (ESI), **29**

Equality, democracy and, 19

Ethnicity and immigration, 26
  in Brazil, 194, 212, 226
  in China, 49, 79–81
  in India, 138–139
  in Iran, 308–309, 310, 328, 346–347
  in Mexico, 183–185
  in Nigeria, 250–251, 255, 256, 261–262, 270–272, 273, 300

European Union (EU), **4,** 215

Exchange rates, 14

Executive, **7**

Expediency Council (Iran), **331,** 338

Export-led growth, **205**

Failed states, 22

Falae, Olu, 293

Falun Gong (FLG), 83

Family Support Program (Nigeria), 272

Farsi, **308**

Fatwa death decree, **307**–308, 321

Favelas, **212**

Fedayin, 317, 340

Federalism, 276, 277

Federation of São Paolo Industries, 224

Figueiredo, João, 199, 201

Financial crisis, in Mexico, 161, 163, 181

First World, 11

Ford, Gerald, 273

Foundation of the Oppressed, **331,** 334

Four Cardinal Principles, **77**

Fourth World, 12

Fox Quesada, Vicente, 145, 153, 154–155, 171, 176, 179, 185
Franco, Itamar, 202, 209, 219, 229
Freedom in the World Rating, **29**
Free Trade Area of the Americas (FTAA), 214, 215, 240
Freyre, Gilberto, 232
Fukuyama, Francis, 3, 4
Fulani people, 253, 254
Fundamentalism, **315**

Gandhi, Mohandas (Mahatma), 99, 100, 101
Gandhi family (India). *See also* Nehru, Jawaharlal
    Indira, 102–105, 107, 116, 117
    Rajiv, 104, 117–118
    Sonia, 95, 117
Geisel, Ernesto, 199, 201
Gender Empowerment Measure (GEM), **28–29**
Gender-Related Development Index (GDI), **28**
General Agreement on Tariffs and Trade (GATT), 164
Germany, 19
Gerschenkron, Alexander, 23
Global era, use of term, 4
"Global Inequalities," use of term, 4
Globalization, **3–5**
Gomes, Ciro, 229
Goulart, João, 206
Governance, 29–30
Gowon, Yakubu, 256, 257
Great Leap Forward, **42**, 48, 53
Great Nigeria Peoples Party (GNPP), 289
Great Proletarian Cultural Revolution, **44**
Green Ecologist Party of Mexico (PVEM), 177–178
Greenpeace, 235–236
Green revolution (India), **108**
Gross Domestic Product (GDP), **14**
Gross National Income (GNI), **12, 14**
Gross National Product (GNP), **14**
Group of 8, 15
Guanxi, **57,** 63, 73
Guardian Council (Iran), **308,** 313, 331, 332, 337, 338, 345
Guerrilla warfare, **41–42**
Guevara, Che, 340

Hall, Peter A., 24
Han Chinese, 79
Hausa-Fulani, 271, 284
"Haves" and "have-nots," 4
Hezbollahis, **318**
Hidalgo, Miguel, 147
Hindus, 99, 113, **130,** 132–133
History, end of, 3
Hobbes, Thomas, 22
Hojjat al-Islams, **318**
Hong Kong, 49, 60, 78
Household responsibility system, **53**
Hua Guofeng, 64
Hui people, 79
Hu Jintao, 46–47, 49, 64, 66, 67, 74, 79
Human Development Index (HDI), **14, 28**
Hundred Flowers Movement, **42**

Ibrahim, Waziri, 289
Igbo people, 255, 256, 271, 272, 284
Ijaw people, 271
Illiteracy, **13**
Imam Jum'ehs, **331**
Immigration, *see* Ethnicity and immigration
Import substitution industrialization (ISI), **157, 205,** 206
Income, 12
Independent National Electoral Commission (INEC, Nigeria), 292
India, 13, 15, 19, 22
    Britain and, 98
    bureaucracy in, 118
    cabinet in, 117–118
    caste system in, 113–114, 132
    citizenship in, 132
    civil liberties in, 121
    coalition governments and growth of BJP, 104–105
    collective identity in, 106
    colonial legacy in, 97–101, 107–108
    comparative politics and, 106–107, 139–141
    democracy and, 106, 121, 139–141
    economy in, 94, 105–106, 107–112, 139
    education in, 112–113, 140
    elections in, 95–96, 131
    ethnic groups in, 138–139
    executive in, 116–118, 120
    Gandhi, Indira, era in, 102–105

geographic setting of, 96–97
    global position of, 105
    governance of, 116–123
    history of, 97–105
    identity in, 131–133
    interest groups in, 133–135
    international political economy and, 114–115
    international role of, 105
    judiciary in, 119–121
    legislature in, 116, 124–126
    military and police in, 118–119
    nationalist movement in, 98–101
    Nehru era in, 101–102
    as nuclear power, 138
    partition of, 99
    policy-making in, 123–124
    political culture in, 131–133
    political economy and development in, 107–115
    political parties and party system in, 95–96, 126–131
    politics in transition in, 136–141
    prime ministers of, 104
    privatization in, 109–110
    protest in, 134–136
    reforms in agriculture, 110–111
    representation and participation in, 124–136
    social movements in, 133–136
    social welfare policy in, 111–112
    society in, 94, 112–114
    state organization in, 116
    states in, 111, 121–122
    subnational government in, 121–123
    terrorism and, 105, 121
    themes in, 105–107
    United States and, 105
    women in, 94, 123, 125
Indian Administrative Service (IAS), **118**
Indian National Congress (INC), 99, 100
Indians, *see* Amerindians; Indigenous groups
"India shining," 136
Indigenous groups, **146**
    in Brazil, 235–236
    in Mexico, 146, 149
Indirect rule, **254**
Industrial democracies, 11
Informal economy, **208**
Informal sector, **159**

Information technology, 4
Institutional Revolutionary Party (PRI, Mexico), 145, 151, 152, 153–154, 156, 164, 171, 172–174
Inter-American Development Bank, 214
Interest groups
    in Brazil, 235–237
    in China, 81–84
    in India, 133–136
    in Iran, 349–350
    in Mexico, 180–183
    in Nigeria, 294–296
International financial institutions (IFIs), **264,** 266
International Monetary Fund (IMF), **21,** 109, 160, 164, 210, 213, 242, 260, 266
International political economy
    Brazil in, 203–204, 213–216, 241–242
    China in, 46, 47–48, 58–61
    India in, 114–115
    Iran in, 329–332
    Mexico in, 155–156
    Nigeria in, 260–262, 273–275
Interventionist, **205, 260**
Interventores, **197**
Iran, 22
    bureaucracy in, 333–334
    cabinet in, 333
    citizenship in, 346–347
    class structure in, 325–327
    collective identity in, 321
    comparative politics in, 321–322, 349–351
    democracy and theocracy in, 308, 321
    economy in, 306, 322–330
    education in, 348
    elections in, 340–346
    ethnicity and immigration in, 308–309, 310, 328, 346–347
    executive in, 333–334
    geographic setting of, 308–309
    governance in, 307, 330–336
    history of, 309–320
    human rights in, 316–317
    identity in, 346–347
    interest groups in, 347–348
    international affairs of, 349–351
    international political economy and, 327–330

Islamic Republic in, 318–319, 328–330
Islamic Revolution in (1979-2001), 315–318
judiciary in, 332–333, 335
legislature in, 308, 331, 339
military in, 327–328, 335, 346
oil in, 323–324, 327, 328, 329–330
Pahlavi dynasty in, 309, 313–315
policy-making in, 336–338
political culture in, 346–347
political economy and development in, 322–330
political parties in, 339–340
politics in transition in, 348–351
president in, 333
protests in, 312, 347–348
Qajar dynasty in, 309, 311–313
religion in, 309, 321, 346
representation and participation in, 338–348
revolution of 1905-1909, 312–313
Revolution of 1979, 309, 313
Safavid dynasty in, 309–311
semipublic institutions in, 334
after September 11, 2001, 319–320
social movements in, 347–348
society in, 306, 324–327
state in, 322–324, 330–333
subnational government in, 335–336
themes in, 320–322
United States and, 313–314, 318–320, 341, 349
West and, 320–321, 323
White Revolution in, 314–315, 324
women in, 306, 345, 348, 349
Iran-Iraq War, 319, 320, 328
Iran Participation Party, 344
Iraq war, 154–155
Iron rice bowl, **55**
Ironsi, Aguiyi, 256
Islamic Republic (Iran), 318–319, 328–330, 348–351
Islamic Republican Party (IRP, Iran), 340, 341
Islamic Revolution (Iran, 1979-2001), 315–318

Jains, 96
Jamaat-e-Islami Party, 121
Janata Party (India), 128

Jiang Qing, 64
Jiang Zemin, 45–46, 49, 55, 62, 63, 64, 66, 67, 69, 77
Jihad, **253, 321**
João VII (Portugal), 195
John Paul II (Pope), 176
Juárez, Benito, 148
Judiciary
    in Brazil, 218, 221–222, 239
    in China, 71
    in India, 119–121
    in Iran, 334–335, 337
    in Mexico, 165, 168–169
    in Nigeria, 281–282
Jurist's guardianship, **316**

Kaduna Mafia (Nigeria), 286
Kano, Mallam Aminu, 289
Karzai, Hamid, 105
Kashmir, 118, 136–138
Kerala, 107, 140
Khalkhali (Ayatollah), 342
Khamenei, Ali (Ayatollah), 307, 330, 333–334, 342, 350
Khatami, Muhammad, 333, 334, 336, 344, 347
Khomeini, Ruhollah (Ayatollah), 307, 308, 315–319, 320–321, 330, 331, 338–339, 341
Khordad Front (Iran), 343
Kissinger, Henry, 327
Kubitschek, Juscelino, 199, 232
Kurds, 8
Kyoto, Japan, 208

Labor and labor unions
    in Brazil, 197, 210, 224
    in China, 55–57, 83
    in Mexico, 151–152, 158–159
    in Nigeria, 294–295
Labor Party (PT, Mexico), 178
Laissez-faire, **23, 321**
Land
    in Brazil, 194, 212
    in China, 36
    in Iran, 306, 324
    in Mexico, 144
    in Nigeria, 248
Landless Workers' Movement (Brazil), 212
Latin America, 2

Law of Fiscal Responsibility (Brazil), 210
Leader (Iran), **310**, 330–333, 338, 345, 351
Lee Teng-hui, 43
Legislature, 30
    in Brazil, 201, 217, 225–226
    in China, 73–74
    in India, 116, 124–126
    in Iran, 310, 314, 333, 341
    in Mexico, 165, 170–171
    in Nigeria, 249, 287
Legitimacy, **8, 196, 250**
Less developed countries, 11
Leviathan (Hobbes), 22
Lhoba people, 79
Liberal Party (PL, Brazil), 228
Liberation Movement (Iran), 341, 342
Life expectancy, **13,** 15
Li Hongzhi, 83
Lin Biao, 64
Li Peng, 69
Literacy, 13
Liu Shaoqi, 42, 64
Lok Sabha (House of the People, India), **116,** 124–126
Long March, 41
López Obrador, Andrés Manuel, 177, 179
López Portillo, José, 159, 165, 171
Lost Decade (Brazil), 213
Lula da Silva, Luis Inácio, 202–203, 211–212, 214, 223, 224, 226, 228, 229–231, 232, 234, 237–238, 240, 241–242

Macao, 78
Madero, Francisco I., 150
Madrazo, Roberto, 174
Maharajas, **98**
Mainwaring, Scott, 226
Majles (Iran Parliament), **308,** 312, 313, 331, 332, 336, 337, 338, 339, 340–345, 348
Manchu dynasty, 40
Maoist Communist Center (India), 121
Mao Zedong, 41, 42–45, 61–62, 64, 66, 72, 77
Maquiladoras, **146**
Market economies, 3
    socialist, 53
Market reform, 57
Marxism-Leninism, **37,** 77, 121

Maslahat, **338**
Material demands, 27
Maximilian (Mexico), 148
Mbeki, Thabo, 274, 275
Médici, Emilio, 199
MERCOSUL, 215–216, 242
Mercosur, 215
Mestizo, **146**
Mexico, 15
    agriculture and industrialization in, 157–160
    bureaucracy in, 167
    citizenship in, 178–180
    communication with comic books in, 179
    comparative politics and, 156, 187–188
    congressional representation by party, 175
    democracy and, 145, 187
    economy in, 144, 152–153, 156–162
    education in, 187
    elections in, 175, 178
    executive in, 165–167
    financial crisis in, 161, 163, 181
    geographic setting of, 146
    governance in, 144–145, 164–169
    history of, 146–155
    human rights in, 185–187
    identity in, 149, 178–180
    independence and instability in, 147–148
    interest groups in, 180–183
    international political economy and, 155–156, 163–164
    judiciary in, 165, 168–169
    legislature in, 165, 170–171
    migration to U.S. from, 184–185
    military in, 167–168
    NAFTA and, 161–162
    oil in, 160–161, 167, 183
    para-statal sector in, 167
    policy-making in, 169–170
    political culture in, 178–180
    political economy and development in, 156–164
    political parties and party system in, 171–178
    politics in, 145–146
    politics in transition in, 183–188
    Porfiriato in, 148–149, 156

    president in, 165–167
    protests in, 180–183
    rebellion in Chiapas, 153, 183
    religion in, 148, 150, 151, 176
    representation and participation in, 170–183
    Revolution of 1910 in, 146–147, 149–151, 183
    after September 11, 2001, 154–155
    social movements in, 180–183
    society in, 144, 162–163
    Sonoran dynasty in, 150–151
    state in, 145–146, 156–162
    subnational government in, 169
    themes in, 155–156
    United States and, 153, 164, 171
    women in, 144, 171, 181–182
Middle East, religion in, 323
Middle-level theory, **10**
Migration, Mexican, 183, 184–185
Military
    in Brazil, 197–199, 201–202, 207, 220–221
    in China, 45, 69–71
    in India, 118
    in Iran, 337
    in Mexico, 167–168
    in Nigeria, 256–257, 278, 285–286, 287
Minorities, 26
Moderating power, **195**
Mohtashami, Hojjat al-Islam, 342
Mojahedin, 317, 339–340, 341, 344, 346
Mongols, 40
Mortality, 12
Mosaddeq, Muhammad, 313–314, 339
Mosques, **307**
Movement for the Survival of the Ogoni People (MOSOP, Nigeria), 271
Muhammad, Murtala, 257, 278
Mullahs, 333
Muslims
    in India, 96, 99, 121, 133–134
    in Iran, 309

Narmada Bachao Andolan (NBA), 134
National Action Party (PAN, Mexico), 145, 166, 174–176, 178
National Assembly (Nigeria), 249, 259, 279, 287–288
National Bank for Economic and Social Development (Brazil), 219

National Confederation of Popular Organizations (CNOP, Mexico), 172
National Conference of Brazilian Bishops (CNBB), 235
National Convention of Nigerian Citizens (NCNC), 255
National Democratic Coalition (NADECO, Nigeria), 296
National Democratic Union (UDN, Brazil), 199
National Destatization Program (Brazil), 219
National Economic Empowerment and Development Strategy (NEEDS, Nigeria), 267, 268
National Environmental Council (CONAMA), 207–208
National Front (Iran), 315, 341, 342–343
National identity
    in Brazil, 232–235, 240
    in China, 78–81
    in India, 131–133
    in Iran, 346–347
    in Mexico, 149, 178–180
    in Nigeria, 292–294
Nationalism, 26, **199**
    in Brazil, 199
    in India, 98–101, 102
    in Mexico, 151
Nationalists (China), 41, 43, 44
National Party of Nigeria (NPN), 257, 289
National peasant association (CNC, Mexico), 182
National People's Congress (China), 67, 74
National Petroleum Employees Union (NUPENG, Nigeria), 294
National Political Reform Conference (Nigeria), 259–260, 275, 277, 282, 285
National Renovation Alliance (ARENA, Brazil), 200, 201
National Republican Convention (NRC, Nigeria), 289
Nation-building, 21
Nation-state, **8**
Natural sciences, 9
Nehru, Jawaharlal, 99, 100, 101–102, 108, 117
Nehru-Gandhi family (India), 117. *See also* Gandhi family (India); Nehru, Jawaharlal

Neo-imperialism, **24**
New Federalism (Mexico), 162
Newly industrialized countries, 155
Newly industrializing countries (NICs), **58**–59
New Partnership for Africa's Development (NEPAD), 275
New State (Brazil), **197**, 205, 226
Niger Delta Development Commission (NDDC, Nigeria), 279
Nigeria, 13, 15
    bureaucracy in, 280–281
    business in, 295
    citizenship in, 292–295
    civil war and military rule in, 256–257
    collective identities in, 255, 261–262, 301
    colonialism and, 254–255, 261
    comparative politics and, 262, 298–300
    democracy and, 261, 271, 286–287, 294, 296–298, 299, 300
    economic crisis in, 264–270
    economy in, 248, 260–261, 263–275, 299–300
    education in, 270
    elections in, 290–292
    ethnicity in, 250–251, 255, 256, 261–262, 270–272, 273, 284–285, 300
    executive in, 276–281
    federalism in, 276, 277, 282
    First Republic in, 255–256
    Fourth Republic in, 259–260, 287, 293–294, 295, 296
    gender differences in, 272–273
    geographic setting of, 250–251
    governance in, 248–249, 275–286
    history of, 251–260
    identity in, 292–294
    interest groups in, 294–296
    international political economy and, 260–262, 273–275
    judiciary in, 281–282
    labor in, 296–297
    legislation in, 282
    legislature in, 287–289
    military in, 278, 285–286, 287
    modernity vs. traditionalism in, 295
    Obasanjo administration in, 249–250, 252, 257, 259–260, 267–270, 272, 273, 274–275, 277, 278–280, 285

    oil in, 263, 264, 265, 271–272, 273
    para-statals in, 281
    party system in, 289–294
    policy-making in, 286–287
    political challenges in, 296–298
    political culture in, 292–294
    political divisions in, 283
    political economy and development in, 262–275
    political economy of West and, 273–275
    political parties in, 289–294
    politics in, 249–250
    politics in transition in, 296–300
    precolonial period in, 253–254
    press in, 294
    protests in, 272, 291
    regional political economy and, 282–286
    religion in, 250–251, 253–254, 270–272, 280, 282, 293
    representation and participation in, 287–289
    Second Republic in, 257–259, 276–278
    social movements in, 294–296
    social welfare in, 269–270
    society in, 248
    state in, 262–270, 275–276, 282–286
    structural adjustment in, 264–267
    themes in, 260–262
    Third Republic in, 257–259, 287
    women in, 248, 272–273
    in world of states, 299
Nigerian Association of Chambers of Commerce, Industry, Mines, and Agriculture (NACCIMA), 295
Nigerian Labour Congress (NLC), 294
Nigerian National Petroleum Corporation (NNPC), 281
Nigerian Peoples Party (NPP), 289
Nixon, Richard, 327
Nomenklatura system, **73**
Nonaligned bloc, **114**
Noncooperation movement (India), 100
Nongovernmental organizations (NGOs), 81, 208, 235–236, 296
Non-material demands, 27
North (global), 12
North American Free Trade Agreement (NAFTA), **152**, 162, 164, 214, 215

North Atlantic Treaty Organization (NATO), **2**

Northern People's Congress (NPC, Nigeria), 255, 289

North-South split, 4

Obasanjo, Olusegun, 249–250, **252**, 257, 259–260, 267–269, 272, 273, 274–275, 277, 278–280, 285

Official international currency exchange rates, **14**

Ogoni people, 271, 282

Oligarchy, **195**

Olympic Games, 37, 49, 78

One-Child Policy (China), 55, 56

100 Women Groups (Nigeria), 273

One-party states, 10

Open-list proportional representation, 227

Opium War, 40, 49

Organization of Petroleum Exporting Countries (OEPC), 274, **327**, 328

"Other Backward Classes" (India), **128**

Pahlavi dynasty, 309, 313–315, 316, 325, 327–328

Pahlavi Foundation, 314–315

Pakistan, 99, 102–103, 107, 121. *See also* India

authoritarian system in, 107

India and, 136–138, 141

Panchayats, **122**–123

Para-statals, **167, 206**–207, **281**

Parliament. *See also* Legislature

in India, 116, 124–126

Parliamentary systems, 217

Participation, 30

Party of Brazilian Social Democracy (PSDB), 228

Party of National Reconstruction (PRN, Brazil), 202

Party of the Brazilian Democratic Movement (PMDB), 228, 229–230

Party of the Liberal Front (PFL, Brazil), 228, 231

Party system, *see* Political parties

Pasdaran (Revolutionary Guards), **319**

Patrimonialism, **197, 297**

Patron-client politics, **17**

Peace and Reconciliation Commission (Nigeria), 279

PEMEX, 167

Pentagon, attack on, 4

People of the Book, **312**

People's communes, **53**

People's Democratic Party (PDP, Nigeria), 259, 288, 297

People's Liberation Army (PLA, China), 45, 69–70

Peoples Redemption Party (PRP, Nigeria), 289

People's Republic of China (PRC), *see* China

Per capita income, 15

Personalist politicians, **203**

Plan de Ayala, 150

Police

in Brazil, 220–221, 222

in India, 118–119

Policy-making process, 29–30

in Brazil, 223–224

in China, 72–73

in India, 123–124

in Iran, 336–338

in Mexico, 169–170

in Nigeria, 286–287

Politburo (China), 66

Political culture, **9**

in Brazil, 232–235

in China, 76–78

in India, 131–133

in Iran, 346–347

in Mexico, 178–180

in Nigeria, 292–294

Political economy, **23**, 27–29

Political entrepreneurship, 26

Political parties, 324

in Brazil, 193, 226–231

in China, 74–75

in India, 126–131

in Iran, 338–340, 341–347

in Mexico, 171–178

in Nigeria, 289–294

Political science, scientific nature of, 9

Political systems, 15–16

Politics

globalization and, 5

real world vs. scholarship on, 9

in transition, 11–17, 30

Politics of the governors, **197**

Popular Socialist Party (PPS, Brazil), 229

Population

of Brazil, 192, 194, 211

of China, 36, 39

of India, 94, 96–97

of Iran, 306, 308–309, 328, 350

of Mexico, 144

of Nigeria, 248

Populism, **199**

Portugal, Brazil and, 194–195

Powell, Colin, 48

Prebendalism, 280, **286**

Premier (prime minister), in China, 67

President

in Brazil, 216, 217–218

in India, 116–117

in Iran, 332, 333

in Mexico, 165–167

Prevention of Terrorism Ordinance (POTO, India), 121

Privatization, **193**, 218–220, **264**–265

Proportional representation, **165, 226,** 227

Purchasing power parity (PPP), **14**

Qajar dynasty, 309, 311–313

Qing dynasty, 40

Qur'an, **310**

Race and racism, *see* Ethnicity and immigration

Rafsanjani Ali-Akbar, Hojjat al-Islam Ali-Akbar Hashemi, 336, 339, 342, 343, 344

Rajya Sabha (upper house, India), **116,** 124–126

Rao, Narasimha, 104, 107, 117

Rashtriya Swayam Sevak Sangh (RSS), 101, **128**

Rational choice theory, **9**–10

Real Plan (Brazil), 202, 209–210, 238

Red Guards (China), 44–45

Regimes, **2,** 22

Regulations, **7**

Religion, 26

Rentier state, **324**

Rents, **263**

Rent-seeking, **263**

Representation, 26, 30

in Brazil, 224–237, 241

in China, 73–84

in India, 124–136

in Iran, 340–350

in Mexico, 170–183

in Nigeria, 287–289

Republic of China, *see* Taiwan
Reservations, in India, 113
Resurgence Party (Iran), 317
Revisionism, **44**
Revolution
  in Brazil, 197–199
  in Iran, 309, 312–313
  Islamic (Iran, 1979-2001), 315–318
  in Mexico, 146–147
Reza Shah (Iran), 313, 314
Reza Shah, Muhammad, 313–315, 318,
  324, 327–328
Rice, Condoleezza, 48
Rio de Janeiro, Brazil, 207, 208, 212, 221
Rio Grande do Sul, Brazil, 207
Rotberg, Robert, 22
Rumsfeld, Donald, 48
Rushdie, Salman, 308, 321
Russia, Iran and, 314

Saddam Hussein, 319, 320
Safavid dynasty, 319–311
Salinas, Carlos, 152, 153, 161–162, 165,
  182
Sarney, José, 201, 209, 213–214, 220,
  224
Saro-Wiwa, Ken, 271, 282
SAVAK (Persia), 314
Scarcity, 26–27
Scheduled castes (India), **114**
Seattle, WTO meeting in, 4–5
Second World, 11
Secularism, 96
Security Council (UN), 154
Self-determination, **271**
Sen, Amartya, 17
Senate
  in Brazil, 225–226
  in Mexico, 165, 170–171
September 11, 2001, attacks, 3–4
  Brazil after, 202–203, 235, 241–242
  China after, 48, 79–81
  India after, 105
  Iran after, 319–320
  Mexico after, 154–155
Servants of Reconstruction (Iran), 343,
  344
Sexenio, **152**
Shagari, Shehu, 278
Shari'a, **282**, 293, **313**, 314, 320, 332,
  335, 337, 339

Shariati, Ali, 327
Shastri, Lal Bahadur, 102
Shekhar, Chandra, 117
Shi'ism, **309**, 310, 311, 312–313, 321,
  338, 347, 350
Shonekan, Ernest, 258, 268
Sikhs, **96**, 104
Singh, Manmohan, 95, 104, 121
Singh, V. P., 117, 132
Sino-American relations, 48
Social class, **25**
Social Democratic Party (PSD, Brazil), 199
Social Democratic Party (SDP, Nigeria),
  289
Socialism, **42**
Socialist democracy, **73**
Socialist market economy, **53**
Social movements, **20**
  in Brazil, 235–237
  in China, 82–84
  in India, 133–136
  in Iran, 347–348
  in Mexico, 180–183
  in Nigeria, 294–296
Social sciences, 9
Society
  in Brazil, 192
  in China, 36, 55–58
  in India, 94, 112–114
  in Iran, 326–329
  in Mexico, 144, 162–163
  in Nigeria, 248, 270–273
Society of Militant Clergy, 336–337,
  341–342, 343
Sokoto Caliphate, 253
Soros, George, 193
Soroush, Abdol-Karim, 344
Soskice, David, 24
South (global), 12
Soviet bloc, 11
Soviet Union, *see* Russia
Standing Committee (China), 66
State, **7**, 8, 22
  in Brazil, 205–210, 216–217
  in China, 61–63
  in India, 95–96, 107–112, 116
  in Iran, 322–324, 330–333
  in Mexico, 145–146
  modern, 27
  in Nigeria, 275–276
  weak legitimacy of, 16–17

State capitalism, **157**
State corporatism, **197, 294**
State Council (China), 67, 69
State formation, **8**
State-led development, **200**
State-led economic development (India),
  108–109
State-owned enterprises (SOEs), 52
State technocrats, **205**
Structural adjustment programs (SAP),
  264, 266
Student Islamic Movement (SIMI), 121
Subnational government
  in Brazil, 222–223
  in China, 71–72
  in India, 121–123
  in Iran, 335–336
  in Mexico, 169
Sub-Saharan Africa, 15
Suez Canal, 325
Summit of the Americas (1994), 214
Sunni Islam, 309, 311, 347
Sun Yat-sen, 40–41, 49
Supreme Federal Tribunal (Brazil), 217,
  221
Supreme Leader (Iran), 332
Sustainable development, **24**

Taiwan, 43–44, 87
Taliban, 105, 319–320, 321
Taping Rebellion, 40
Technocrats, **166**
Tenochtitlán, 149
Terrorism, 4
  Brazil and, 202–203
  China and, 79–80
  India and, 105, 121
Texas, 148
Theocracy, **308,** 321
Third World, **2,** 11, 13, 19–20, 50, 89,
  205
  Fukuyama's thesis and, 3
  globalization in, 4
  political systems in, 15–17
  use of term, 11–12
"Three Represents" (China), 77, 78
Tiananmen Square, 37, 45, 47, 49, 83, 88
Tibet, 16, 79
Totalitarianism, **88**
Township and village enterprises (TVEs),
  53–54

Transitional democracies, 19–20
Transitions from Authoritarian Rule: Tentative Conclusions about Uncertain Democracies, 20
Truth and Reconciliation Commission (South Africa), 279
Tudeh (Masses) Party (Iran), 313, 340

UN, *see* United Nations (UN)
Unfinished state, **250**
Union Carbide disaster, 134
United Nations (UN)
 Conference on the Environment (Rio), 208
 Conference on the Human Environment, 207
United Nations Economic Commission for Latin America (ECLA), 205–206
United States, 21
 India and, 105
 Mexican migration to, 184–185
 Nigerian oil and, 273–274
 September 11, 2001, attacks and, 3–4
Unity Party of Nigeria (UPN), 289
Untouchables (outcastes), **114**
Usury, 335
Uthman dan Fodio, 253
Uyghur people, 79

Vajpayee, Atal Behari, 104, 117, 118
Vale (Brazil), 193–194
Vargas, Getúlio, 197–199, 205, 219, 234
Villa, Pancho, 151
Vision 2010 (Nigeria), 268
Voting, *see* Elections

Warrant chiefs, **254**
Welfare programs
 in Brazil, 211–212
 in India, 111–112
 in Nigeria, 269–270
Wen Jiabao, 67
West Bengal, 140
Western world, 2, 40
White Revolution (Iran, 1962), 314, 324
Women
 in Brazil, 192, 204, 210, 232–233, 236
 in China, 36, 57–58, 75
 in India, 94, 123, 125, 134–135
 in Iran, 306, 345, 348, 349
 in Mexico, 144, 171, 181–182
 in Nigeria, 248, 272–273
Women's Federation (China), 81
Workers' Party (PT, Brazil), 202, 203, 229, 230, 237
World Bank, **12,** 13, 86–87, 213, 242, 266

World Economic Forum, 237–238
World-of-states theme, 21–23. *See also* International political economy; State
World order, 2–3
World Social Forum, 214
World Trade Center, 4
World Trade Organization (WTO), **4,** 46, 111, 115, 240, 322, 349
Wu Yi, 75

Xiaokang (China), 57
Xu Wenli, 82

Yoruba people, 255, 259, 271, 272, 284

Zamindars, **98**
Zapata, Emiliano, 150, 151
Zapatista Army of National Liberation (EZLN), 153
Zedillo, Ernesto, 145, 153, 162, 166–167, 168, 171, 174
"Zero Hunger" program (Brazil), 212, 214
"Zero Illiteracy" program (Brazil), 212
Zhao Ziyang, 45
Zhou Enlai, 64
Zhuang people, 79